Mariner's Notebook

A guide to boating fundamentals

By Captain William P. Crawford

Master Mariner

Fifth Edition / Published by the Book Division / Miller Freeman Publications, Inc. / San Francisco, California

This book is dedicated to Jane. . .

a gentle lady who taught our children and me

a priceless lesson not found on the pages of

this or, perhaps, of any other book. . .how

to live and, then, to die in grace.

W.P.C.

Library of Congress Catalog Card Number 70-160444

© Copyright 1960, 1962, 1964, 1966, 1968 and 1971 by William P. Crawford.

Published by MILLER FREEMAN PUBLICATIONS, INC., 500 Howard Street, San Francisco, California 94105. Printed in the United States of America by Kingsport Press, Kingsport, Tennessee.

Introduction
From the author

Seafaring has been our family affair for generations . . . an affair that began long ago on the Irish Coast and on the restless waters of the Western Ocean. By comparison, our tradition of training seafarers seems young. Yet it has passed its forty-eighth year.

In 1923 my late uncle, Captain John T. Sullivan, founded his school for shipmasters and officers in New Orleans. Twenty years later my father, Captain Lorcan F. Crawford, came ashore to carry on that service, to be joined in time by me. MARINER'S NOTEBOOK must, of course, reflect those decades of experience . . . a background I proudly acknowledge.

All seafaring is essentially the same, for the sea gives quarter to no one. Neither purpose nor size earns amnesty. The challenge remains undiminished. Our family affair has filled a treasure house of knowledge and of proved techniques to meet the challenge. MARINER'S NOTEBOOK is the key by which that treasure house opens for your use.

□ □ □

The Sailing Orders issued this book are to bring a full cargo of practical knowledge to the reader. Before Departure, though, it is only seamanlike to scan the ship's plans to learn a why or two.

For most days of the year's twelve months my schedule includes classroom lectures on navigation, ship operation and related subjects. So it is understandable that the ways of the schoolmaster show through on these pages. Presenting a subject to a class is a very solitary pursuit. What is said and done is almost entirely up to the teacher. When things come off well, he can smugly stroke his lapel. But should the picture be murky, he is the lone cause. MARINER'S NOTEBOOK is no different. It is not a committee report nor a result of statistical survey. It is one person's best effort to present what is worth knowing about boating fundamentals. My lapel, then, stands ready to buff. . .and my handkerchief to wipe off the egg.

A classroom tone is probably to be recognized throughout the book. The conversational air, the teacher's quips . . . all are here with no effort at conceal-ment. I've been told that a controlled measure of humor is considered relevant to the learning process. Any show of fun on these pages, though, is not nearly so deliberate. The fact is, I just happen to enjoy it.

□ □ □

Here, then, is the course plotted for MARINER'S NOTEBOOK. In delivering its cargo, it follows a route similar to a curriculum of study. Subjects are pre-sented a bit at a time . . . just as by an academic class schedule. There are no massive doses to overwhelm the attention span but enough to maintain interest for about the length of an actual lecture.

Specifically, the text is divided into eleven Sections and they, in turn, into Chapters. As you progress through the book, section by section, you are intro-duced to various subjects; and then you meet them again in succeeding sections until they are thoroughly familiar to you. For example, Section I presents Rules of the Road, Charts, Piloting, Weather and Safety Afloat. In the chapters of Section II, the same material is carried along further. New subjects are taken up as others are completed . . . until the full spectrum of fundamentals has sailed across the pages.

And you'll find that spectrum quite varied. Attention to the essentials of Rules of the Road, Piloting, Weather and Safety is as indispensable as a keel. But there is much more to the story than that. Charts and publications, buoys and aids, seamanship, magnetism, signaling, basics of ship stability . . . they are all found aboard MARINER'S NOTEBOOK. And today's world of seafaring has encoun-tered the electron. The scope of radio and electronic aids ready to assist the mariner is reviewed with an eye to realistic use.

There has been a conscious effort throughout to keep realism in mind. Part of the appeal of boating is a return to uncluttered, simple patterns of operation. Yet this all takes place well into the second half of our century. We seek a balance between the Old, which still has usefulness, and the New which has practical application to small vessels.

The log of a voyage is punctuated by Position Reports to show progress and to prompt course corrections back to the track. You'll find a locker full of them here. At the end of each text section . . . like a weekly reckoning in class . . . there is a quiz. As for your mark, no cause to fret. Only you and the Mariner need ever know for sure!

You have another advantage over the student in class. You can put the book down, start over, skip ahead or make adjustments in speed as you will. Unavoidable, though, is a cumulative note . . . a page in Section V might depend on one in Section II. So to start at the beginning and then to read through is recommended.

But MARINER'S NOTEBOOK is more than a text. It is intended also to be a reference. The index pages are your key to focus on particular points. Section XII, Ready Reference, goes much further. It not only recaps highlights of the text, but also presents tables, facts, procedures and signal displays important to operation. In effect, it is a book within a book, in which material selected from some other books is digested for your use aboard.

One further comment on approach. Seafaring covers a wide scope, and no one book will capture every detail. That is not the mission of MARINER'S NOTE-BOOK. Rather, in it are selections from oceans of materials to build a framework for safe operation. From that base, individual experience and aptitude can do the rest.

□ □ □

The aim is an enjoyable passage through the bays, backwaters and open oceans of the seafarer's world. So, being in all respects ready for sea, take an early departure . . . and Good Sailing!

W. P. C.
San Pedro, California
May, 1971

Contents/sequential

Contents/by subject

Acknowledgements

Each of us is so influenced by his world that to segregate what might be his from what is a reflection of others can be arduous. MARINER'S NOTEBOOK and I, though, find the task greatly minimized, for there have been two persons without whom I would have no occasion to write these words.

To Jack West, my gratitude for counsel and for singular forbearance. His expert knowledge of marine electronics, acquired by decades of boating, was the critical screen through which this book's chapters on that topic were passed. No text could have been more fortunate. And as an author of international recognition, Jack so exercised restraint as to capture my great admiration. For a veteran writer to view another's work and not kibitz is rare, indeed. My further thanks to Jack for such objectivity.

The assistance of the late Les Michaelis I find difficult to recount. His enthusiastic labors on the original MARINER'S NOTEBOOK did much to lay the base for this present volume. Like the greater part of the iceberg, his work lies submerged . . . but nonetheless, very real.

□   □   □

Credit is acknowledged to the following organizations and agencies for charts, tables and photographs reprinted herein, as well as for assistance in verifying the accuracy of content . . .

American Red Cross
Federal Aviation Administration
Federal Communications Commission
National Aeronautics and Space Administration
National Ocean Survey
National Oceanic and Atmospheric Administration
National Weather Service
Port of Long Beach Harbor Department
Port of Los Angeles Harbor Commission
U.S. Coast Guard
U.S. Coast Guard Auxiliary
U.S. Navy Oceanographic Office
U.S. Power Squadrons

And finally my thanks to the many contributors of information, photographs, and other materials needed to make the book more helpful and informative, and to my publisher and his very fine crew—all the good people I do not have the space to list here.

section 1
contents

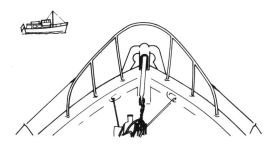

1/Rules of the Road
Introduction

Today's mariner has dozens of handy aids to Rules of the Road. Placards, pamphlets, photobooks . . . they come in all shapes and sizes. And all aim to recall basic signals and maneuvers. Not so numerous, though, are general discussions of the rules . . . more of the **whys** and not so much of the **wherefores**. So that's a good point of departure for our study.

To read a book calls for more than just knowing the alphabet. Words formed by the letters must have meanings. Knowing Rules of the Road is the same. To operate sensibly a few of the **whys** behind the alphabet of signals and lights must be understood.

Yet this need not be a bone-dry subject. No one expects a book on the rules ever to become a bestseller. But on the other hand, it doesn't have to read like a study of the depopulation of the buffalo. For there is romance to it. A busy harbor entrance is like the lobby of the UN. The big freighter to starboard is Japanese. And during World War II the man on the bridge was on a DD slipping reinforcements into Rabaul. Standing aft on the ship ahead is a Spaniard. Above his head fly the stripes and single star of Liberia. The owners are Greeks living on the Riviera. Dead astern is a trim West German heading back to Hamburg. Her master first saw the American coast through a U-Boat periscope. Often on a single ship there are nationals from a score of countries.

This is the polyglot world that pleasure mariners enter as they cruise toward the sea buoy. The Rules of the Road are the passwords to bridge the gap from one to the other. If you were to ask the man on the ship ahead for the time of day he probably wouldn't understand the question. But blow some whistle signal under these rules and he knows your meaning without falter. Let's spend a few moments on the development of such an unusual system.

The year is 1889 . . . the Victorian age and the twilight of the day of sail. Representatives of seafaring nations meet in Washington to draft a set of laws for ships on the High Seas. They speak for 10,000 ships from dhows to the wrought-iron monsters of the Western Ocean. Twenty languages and ways of life come together at a Tower of Babel. But from potential confusion emerge the International Rules. These were very remarkable regulations to direct all those ships and all those tongues when they should meet on the High Seas. There were, of course, concessions to local circumstance. So on Turkish ships it was allowed that a drum could be used instead of a bell. But the product of the discussions was a workable code.

Congress made them apply to US vessels in 1897. And ever since they have stood with surprisingly little change . . . a unique example of what can be done when there is a common problem and a single axe to grind. Some key words, like the terms in an insurance policy, have acquired esoteric meaning. But in general the rules survive as guides used by seamen the world over without serious confusion on the High Seas.

But these International Rules are intended to apply only on the No-Man's Land of the High Seas. Local authority was left to make its own regulations in territorial waters. However, if none such were made, then the International Rules apply there as well. Canadian waters are an example.

In our country Congress has passed special laws—the Inland Rules—to cover much of our territorial waters. The boundary line between the two codes is not the same as the territorial limits; that is much too argumentative a subject for clarity. The frontier by Rules of the Road is called the **line of demarcation**. Often it is specified in detail. In the absence of such definition, it is a line which follows the general trend of the shore and passes through the sea buoy or outermost navigation aid at a particular place. An example of a specified line is Los Angeles-Long Beach harbors. There it is drawn along the breakwaters from the LA Entrance Lighthouse and on to the Seal Beach Naval Depot at Anaheim Bay. Outside that line the International Rules apply; inshore, the Inland Rules control. If no such limit were defined, the line would probably be taken as that from Point Fermin to the sea buoy and then on a line skirting the Huntington Beach shoreline.

Congress knew that no single code could possibly cover all regions of US waters. So special rules were made for the Great Lakes, the rivers emptying into the Gulf of Mexico and for the Red River of the North. Incidentally, most salt-water sailors haven't the vaguest idea where that river is. But the name rolls smoothly off the tongue; and with scant urging they sing out this exception to the Inland Rules as if they had made a landfall there only last trip. That's not likely: it flows north through eastern North Dakota to Lake Winnipeg in Manitoba.

Yet even in areas where Inland Rules apply, it was never intended they be so detailed as to answer all local needs. They were to be a framework; but a proper government agency would fill out the details for local conditions. The US Coast Guard has done so in the Pilot Rules.

And in each port speed limits and similar laws can be made by State, County or Municipal government.

So the mariner is subject to a series of telescoping regulations. On the High Seas he serves the International Rules. In territorial waters he can serve more than one master: Inland and Special Rules made by Congress, Pilot Rules made by the US Coast Guard, local rules made by harbor authorities. And the astonishing fact is the system works.

Ships also come in different shapes and sizes. One might stop dead in the water within a hundred feet; another may need two miles. One's propeller is the size of a table fan; another weighs hers by the ton. One skipper has a clear view all round his ship; another peers through a forest of masts and cargo booms over a high bow 200 feet ahead of him. Yet each can progress safely past the other because—and only because—he **respects** the Rules of the Road. Not only does he follow them, he respects them as rules to prevent collision. He can expect the other fellow to be predictable and to do what the rules require.

A refreshing change from the freeway free-for-all, isn't it? What makes it even more remarkable is that no policemen are around to enforce the rules at all times and to keep people in line. But actually it should not be surprising at all. Unless the rules are followed, they cannot work. And without them seafaring would be impossible. Ships are man's largest mobile creations. The force of a 10,000-tonner moving at 10 knots is that of a jet slamming into a mountain. It isn't a case of high morality; it is a matter of survival.

Of course there are exceptions. Some masters step over the edge of the rules while hurrying to make a tide or to cut down the standby charges for waiting longshoremen. But these are really exceptions. For seamen are very conscious of the enormous destruction collision can bring.

The rules are often described as assigning "privilege" and "burden." One ship is said to have a privilege of action while the other has a burden of avoidance. But the privilege is not a right or a vested interest. It can't be waived or enforced at will like a property right. **Both** ships are burdened. It is just as necessary for the privileged one to do what she is privileged to do as it is for the burdened vessel to abstain. There would be chaos if the ship with the "right of way" (a most misleading phrase) could take it or leave it. She is burdened to take it; otherwise, her action is unpredictable. And the essence of the rules is predictability. Everyone is uncertain if anyone is free to do as he wishes. There can be no zigging when you should zag. The rules would be more harm than good without this common sense requirement.

In this introduction we have only touched on the high points of background and purpose. But underscored is the marvelous character of probably the world's most unusual, and successful, attempt at international harmony. For more than 70 years ships have operated on them day after day from the Farallones to the Hooghly River. Compared to volume of shipping, the percentage of sinkings and collisions—and even near-misses—is microscopic. Men who would be stopped by a language barrier from making small talk in a tavern can meet at sea and maneuver large ships at close quarters without confusion. The reason? Good rules followed with diligence and respect.

Foredeck of modern cargo liner.

Photo by American President Lines

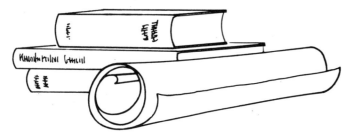

2/Charts and Publications
How the chart is made

Remember the story of the blind men from India who had their first encounter with an elephant? Each gained a different impression because he touched a different part of the beast. Our purpose is to avoid such misconceptions of the nautical chart. Pleasure mariners need not be expert in the subject . . . but when they find occasion to use a chart they should certainly use it intelligently. And a little attention to background now is bound to pay dividends later.

Marine charts are representations of portions of the surface of the Earth preserving as much as possible the relative proportions of the locality. Have you ever tried to peel an orange without splitting the skin? That is a sample of the cartographer's problem. He tries to peel Mother Earth and then lay the skin out on a flat surface with no splits and with a minimum of stretch. Actually his job is an impossibility. The surface of spherical Earth cannot be depicted on a plane surface without distortion. And the greater the area shown, the more aggravated are the errors. On Harbor and other large scale charts the loss is relatively minor; but on small scale charts, as of an ocean area, the errors become very significant.

The ideal chart preserves true shape, direction and proportion . . . and has a constant scale for measurements. Sometimes, in order to achieve these aims, one distortion is deliberately introduced to neutralize another. This is true of the most common chart, the **Mercator projection**. The idea was developed 400 years ago by a Flemish geographer, and the end of its usefulness is still not in sight.

By it the sphere is projected on the surface of a cylinder which touches Earth at the Equator. It is as if the meridians of longitude (which actually converge to meet at the Poles) were unhooked and straightened out to run vertically on the cylinder; and as if the parallels of latitude (which are actually circles on Earth paralleling the Equator) were in turn straightened out to run horizontally on the cylinder as parallel lines of equal length. When the cylinder is flattened out the result is a Mercator chart. **Figure 1** is an illustration of how it works.

But there is a great difference between the picture on the chart and that on Earth. Let's say you are on an ice floe and three feet from the North Pole. Walk in a circle around the Pole. You've just gone around the world. You've covered 360° of longitude, just as if you had traveled around the Equator. The only difference is the distance covered. On the ice floe, your journey is about 19 feet. Every foot

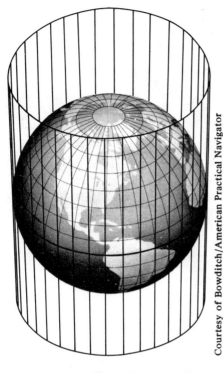

Courtesy of Bowditch/American Practical Navigator

Figure 1

covers about 19°, or 1140', of longitude. On the Equator, though, you would travel 21,600 miles. For there every mile is 1' of longitude. On Earth the east-west circles, or **parallels of latitude**, become smaller from the Equator to the Poles. One that is 21,600 miles long (the Equator itself) has no more longitude in it (360°) than the overgrown hula hoop which parallels it at the top of the world. Measured in arc, they are equal; measured in units of distance their ratio is 7 million-to-1. Now, how would they look on a Mercator chart? They're all horizontal, or east-west lines . . . which are projections of the parallels of latitude and are the same length. They are all as long as the Equator. So the 19-foot trip would appear as long as that of 21,600 miles.

On Earth, all meridians are the same length. If you left Los Angeles, and traveled due North over the Pole and then South over the South Pole and back to Los Angeles, you would have gone around the world north-to-south. And you would have traveled 21,600 miles. Each mile would cover 1' of latitude. A similar trip would be the same length from any other point on the Earth . . . New York, Paris or Timbuktu. But notice that only at the Equator does an east-west circle equal a north-south one in length. There, both are 21,600 miles long. As you go farther north or south, the ratio between north-south circles, or **meridians of longitude**, and the east-west circles, or **parallels of latitude**, gets more and more. It is 2-to-1 at 60°N and 60°S; about 4-to-1 at 75°; about 10-to-1 at 85°; and then it skyrockets towards our 21,600 miles-to-19 feet ratio on the ice floe.

Since on the chart the east-west lines are not getting any shorter from Equator to the Poles, but remain the same length, we must take in the slack another way. This is done by progressively stretching the meridians from Equator to the Poles. On the chart's Equator, 1' north or south (1' of latitude) is the same length as 1' east or west (1' of longitude). At 60°, 1' in a north-south direction (latitude) equals 2' east-west (longitude). At 75°, 1' north-south equals about 4' east-west.

To appreciate this point fully look at Greenland on the world chart shown as **Figure** 2. It seems to dominate the North Atlantic area between our East Coast and Europe. Yet it is, in fact, really not much bigger than Mexico, and is less than one-fourth the size of the United States.

Look at the horizontal lines, or parallels of latitude. The middle one is the Equator. Each successive one above and below it represents a change of 20° of latitude. But the space between the Equator and 20°N (the next horizontal line

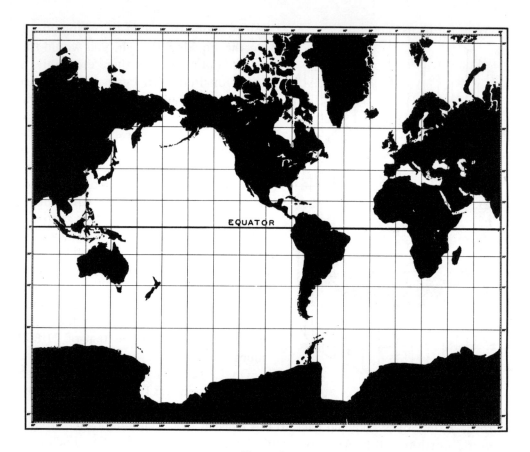

Figure 2

above it) is much less than the space between 60°N (the line at the lower tip of Greenland) and 80°N (the line just below the top margin of the chart). Yet on Earth they are the same distance apart: 1200 miles. Notice also that the vertical lines (meridians) are equidistant from top to bottom. On this particular chart, they are spaced 20° of longitude apart. So this chart shows 20° of longitude to be the same distance in Greenland as at the Equator. Not so. On Earth that much longitude is 1200 miles at the Equator, while at the lower tip of Greenland, it is only 600 miles. What has happened should now be clear by reference again to **Figure 1.** When Earth's skin is projected on the cylinder, the east-west lines all become equal in length. The length from 20°W to 40°W is the same at any latitude. To offset this the north-south lines are gradually stretched so that the spacing on the chart between 60°N and 80°N is much greater than between 0° and 20°N. In this way the correct proportions are maintained throughout the chart. Greenland is in correct proportion to Northern Canada, to Spitzbergen and to Northern Norway. But they are all shown in larger scale than New Guinea and Brazil. The north-south scale is constantly changing throughout the chart.

There are other ways of showing the Earth as a flat surface: Conic, Polyconic, Gnomonic, Stereographic, Orthographic, Polar. But in everyday work the navigator uses Mercator.

The rules for its use are simple.

To find the latitude of a position:
Use the vertical margins, left or right. They are marked in units of arc—degrees (°) and minutes (′) and, sometimes, seconds (″).

To find the longitude of a position:
Use the horizontal margins, top or bottom. They are also marked in units of arc.

To measure a direction:
Find the angle that the course line or line of bearing makes with a vertical line on the chart. Circles of direction, or **compass roses**, marked clockwise from 0° at the top (North) around to 360° are printed on the chart for the purpose.

To measure distance in nautical miles:
Use the vertical margins only . . . do not use the top or the bottom margins. One nautical mile equals 1′ on the vertical margin.
And
Measure on the vertical margin at the same level as the points in question. Remember Greenland!

A few more notes on charts:

Chart scale is the ratio between the dimensions of something on the chart and of the same thing on Earth. It can be presented three ways:

1. **Natural scale** states how many units on Earth are represented by one of the same units on the chart. It is a simple ratio, as in this example—1:80,000. The meaning: one unit (for example, an inch) represents 80,000 (inches in this case) on the surface of the Earth.
2. **Numerical scale** states the relationship between a convenient chart unit (as, one inch) and a convenient Earth unit (as, one mile). Example: one inch to the mile.
3. **Graphic scale** uses an actual measuring stick on the chart. The vertical margins are such on Mercator charts. And a line drawn to scale and calibrated in miles and yards is often found.

Classified by natural scale, nautical charts fall into these four groups:

1. **Sailing charts,** for open ocean . . . . 1:600,000 or smaller
2. **General charts,** for coastwise . . . . .1:100,000 to 1:600,000
3. **Coast charts,** for inshore work . . . . .1:50,000 to 1:100,000
4. **Harbor charts** . . . . 1:50,000 and larger scales

Two government agencies have the burden of preparing these nautical charts for US mariners. The **Oceanographic Office** of the US Navy takes care of those for foreign areas. This agency was known for many years as the Hydrographic Office, and the initials **HO** are still used by seamen to designate its work. The **National Ocean Survey** prepares and distributes nautical charts for American coastal waters, for the Great Lakes, and for navigable waters of the New York State Barge Canal System, Lake Champlain and the Minnesota-Ontario Border Lakes. It is a new agency stemming from **NOAA,** the National Oceanic and Atmospheric Administration. **NOAA,** in turn, was created within the Department of Commerce in October 1970, as a government conglomerate to cluster, among other things, the functions of the Weather Bureau, the Coast and Geodetic Survey, and elements of the US Lake Survey of the Army Corps of Engineers. Generations of mariners have identified coastal charts by the abbreviation **C&GS.** Perhaps the future holds a change to **NOS,** or **NOAA** . . . or maybe an impertinent "Ark Chart." In any case, we'll stick with **C&GS** as an identification while awaiting the inevitable acronym advisory.

Chart catalogues are issued by each agency. And distribution is through direct government sales offices such as Branch HO offices, and also through authorized dealers in nautical books and supplies. Every port usually has at least one.

Of course, making the chart is only part of the problem. To some extent it is yesterday's news as soon as it leaves the press. For changes occur constantly in buoys, in wrecks and obstructions, in data on soundings and depths. Essential is a means to keep the chart up to date. This is done by *Notice to Mariners,* a weekly HO service that publishes changes to be made on all charts issued by US government agencies. Each chart has a number, as, *HO 1208* or *C&GS 5102.* It is catalogued by number, it is ordered by number, and it is corrected by number as well.

Next time we will take a long look at a typical Coast chart, *C&GS 5142.* This one covers the Southern California coast from Dana Point to Point Vicente and seaward to Santa Catalina. Even if you are not in Southern California, a study of this chart will be quite helpful. For charts are standard in format, markings and symbols. If you have a copy available, break it out and start looking it over. If you don't have one, but would like to, contact a government chart agent. The cost is $1.50. It isn't necessary, however, that you have the chart to follow our discussion, because we include reproductions of the areas on the chart that we'll talk about.

3/Piloting
Compass course corrections

Navigation can be boiled down to the art of telling the answer to two basic questions: "Which way?" and "How far?"

Adam undoubtedly knew directions, or "which way," in the Garden of Eden. He knew when something was in front of him, behind him, on one side and on the other. His reference point was himself. Perhaps he even used the apple tree. In either case the "which ways" were front, back, left and right.

Aboard ship, even before the compass, the bow was used as the reference point. Hence, the terms "ahead," "astern," "on the port beam" and "on the starboard beam." Today the circle is employed as the measuring stick and directions relative to the ship's head, **relative bearings**, are expressed from 000° at the bow, clockwise around a full circle back to 360°.

The discovery of the magnetic properties of lodestone, an iron oxide, brought with it a new concept for navigators: a means to use North as the reference point in all weathers. For the lodestone always seemed to point northerly. An early compass was simply a circular card attached to a sliver of the stone, and fitted to swing in a horizontal plane on a central pivot. Since North on the card always remained in line with the needle, the direction of the ship's head could easily be

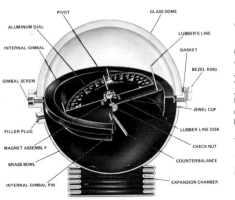

Modern magnetic compass with cross section.

found. Modern magnetic compasses are precision instruments when compared with the originals; but they are no different in concept.

Every device is subject to instrument error, including a compass. It is designed to point to the Magnetic North Pole. But because of other magnetic influences it can be deviated from its aim. The error so caused is called **Deviation**: the difference between north as indicated by Compass and the actual direction of Magnetic North. **Figures** 3 and 4 each show two concentric circles. The outer ones represent directions as they should be magnetic; the inner, as they appear by compass. Take an extra moment to study these two sketches. For they are essential to a clear understanding of compass error.

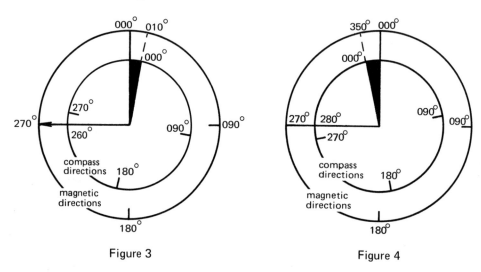

Figure 3   Figure 4

In **Figure** 3 note that North by compass is 10° to the right, or East of Magnetic North. So the angle measured clockwise from Compass North (the inner circle) to the Ship's Head (the arrow on the left) will be 10° less than that from Magnetic North (the outer circle). The compass, then, will under-read by 10°. Deviation is named, in this case, as 10°East. In **Figure** 4 Compass North is 10° to the left or West of Magnetic North. So the compass will over-read by 10°, and Deviation is named 10°West.

Correcting the compass course for Deviation requires, then, that the amount **be added to Compass if Deviation is East**, and **be subtracted from Compass if Deviation is West**. The amount of Deviation is found by comparing compass directions with known magnetic directions. To **swing ship** is to check the compass bearing of a fixed object as the ship is turned through a full circle. When Deviation is minimized or reduced by compensating magnets, the procedure is called **Compass Compensation**.

But we've not finished! For Magnetic North is not at the top of the Earth. It is not the same as the geographic or True North Pole. The Magnetic North Pole is on Bathurst Island in Northern Canada . . . about 850 miles south of the True Pole. An efficient magnetic compass doing its job need not point to True North at all. Whether it does or not depends on point of view. **Figure** 5 shows Point **T** as the top of a ball, and **M** just below it. Viewed from **A**, **M** is to the right of **T**.

Viewed from **B**, **M** is to the left of **T**. But from **C**, **M** and **T** are on the same line of bearing.

The picture is no different on Earth. In **Figure 6** **T** is True North and **M** is Magnetic North. **A** is a compass located at Anchorage, Alaska. **B** is one in Ireland and **C** is one in Miami. Each is pointing to the Magnetic North Pole. But only one of them, Miami, is also pointing to True North. The two others vary from True. At Anchorage, Magnetic North bears **east** of True North. In Ireland, it bears **west**. That difference in bearing is **Variation**. Like Deviation it will cause a compass to under-read if it is East, and to over-read if it is West.

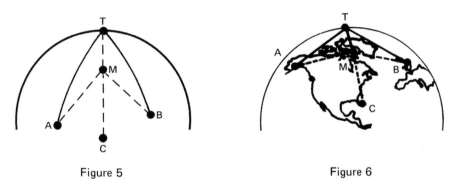

Figure 5   Figure 6

There are, then, two inherent errors in every magnetic compass: **Deviation** of Compass North from Magnetic North, and **Variation** of Magnetic North from True. Deviation results from magnetic influences in and about the compass. It differs from one ship to another; and on the same ship it can change from heading to heading. Variation depends on location. It changes as the ship changes position on Earth. But it is constant on all headings, and is the same for all ships in the same area. Variation is marked on most charts either by curves called **isogonic lines,** or in the center of the Compass Rose.

Figure 7 shows three circles to represent Compass, Magnetic and True direction. True North is at the top of the outer circle. The Variation is taken as 15°East, so Magnetic North is marked on the middle circle as 15° to the right of True. Deviation is 10°East, so Compass North is marked on the inner circle as 10° to the right of Magnetic. As a result of Deviation and Variation, the Compass North is 25° to the right, or East, of True. And that total difference between Compass North and True North is called **Compass Error.** When the Compass shows the ship is on a heading of 245°, the True direction is 25° more, or 270°. And the Magnetic direction is 10° more than Compass, or 255°.

Figure 8 is another combination. There, Deviation is 15°West while Variation is 15°East. So the Compass Error is 0° . . . Compass and True are identical. The amount that Magnetic North is East of True North is exactly offset by the amount Compass North is West of Magnetic. The True direction of 270° will be 255° Magnetic; but on the compass it will be back to 270° again.

It is said that Compass Error is the algebraic sum of Variation and Deviation. This means that if both are the same name (East or West) you add them together to find Compass Error; but if one is East and the other is West, then you subtract the smaller from the greater and name the Compass Error after the greater. Note

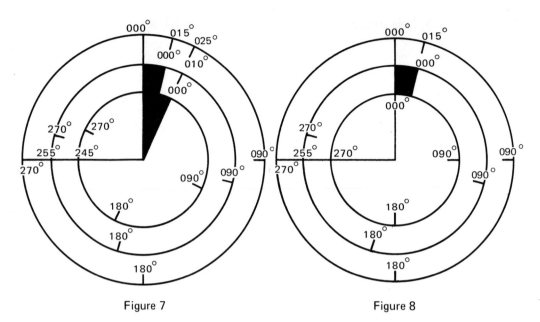

Figure 7   Figure 8

the following examples, and try to picture them as drawn in the manner of
Figures 7 and 8.

Variation ....10°E	Variation .... 10°W
Deviation ....+15°E	Deviation .... +15°W
Compass Error ....25°E	**Compass Error** .... 25°W

Variation ....10°E	Variation ....20°E
Deviation ....- 5°W	Deviation ....-20°W
Compass Error .... 5°E	**Compass Error** .... 0°

Deviation .... 15°W	Deviation ....10°E
Variation ....-10°E	Variation ....- 8°W
Compass Error .... 5°W	**Compass Error** .... 2°E

Seamen use all sorts of pithy rhymes to help their work. In meteorology there
are gems such as

> *Rainbow in the morning, Sailor take warning;*
> *Rainbow at night, Sailor's delight.*

And Rules of the Road have produced

> *If colored lights are seen ahead,*
> *Port your helm and show your red.*

or, the wag's version

> *If ahead are red and green,*
> *Steady your helm and go between!*

The magnetic compass has not been a barren field. As a matter of fact, it has probably spawned more jingles than any of the others. For example, there is

Compass least, Error east;
Compass best, Error west.

Even Kipling has been pressed into jingle service by a variation of his rhyme—the obvious

Least is East and Best is West

The grammar might be open to criticism, but the principle is sound. For when Compass is less than Magnetic or True, the error is East; and when Compass is more the error is West.

Two more memory aids are used for the sequence to apply errors in progressing from a Compass Course to True, or in backtracking from True to Compass. The sequence from Compass to True

Compass . . Deviation . . Magnetic . . Variation . . True

The memory aid is

Can . . Dead . . Men . . Vote . . Twice

Conversely, if you wish the Compass equivalent of a known True course, use **T-V-M-D-C**. And remember to reverse the rules for East and West errors. This time you are uncorrecting a True course, so subtract East Deviation and Variation and add West. The memory aid, designed for those few sailors who find politics not their dish of tea:

Timid . . Virgins . . Make . . Dull . . Companions

Now for two examples of how to use these aids. What is the True course equivalent to 205° by compass when Deviation is 7°W and Variation is 15°E?

C	D	M	V	T
205°	7°W	198°	15°E	213°

And in reverse . . . what is the Compass course to steer to make a True course of 080° when the Deviation is 4°E and the Variation is 15°E?

T	V	M	D	C
080°	15°E	065°	4°E	061°

The rules for compass correction have a habit of slipping out of focus. Even the 50-year veteran of the bridge is not immune. But remember the "whys." Then, should you forget the jingles, just draw three circles for the compass cards as was done in **Figures 5** and **6, 7** and **8**. Put dots to represent your compass Norths (True, Magnetic and Compass). Draw a line to represent the known course . . . at the proper angle from Compass North if Compass Course is known, or from Magnetic North if Magnetic Course is known, or from True North if True Course is known. Then note where the line crosses the other two circles. By that time your head will be ringing with jingles and the answer will be loud and clear.

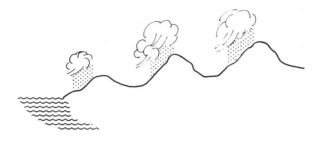

4/Weather
Introduction and instruments

The Royal Astronomer of Ireland, according to a very old quote, said that the most difficult problem in his field was less complicated than an everyday weather phenomenon. Even after generous allowance for blarney, the remark holds a lot of truth. For weather and forecasting weave a very complex fabric. Actually the general principles of meteorology are not so intricate. It is their application to constantly changing factors which creates the difficulties.

We'll start with fundamentals and work out a general picture of the elements causing weather. Then, perhaps, personal observations underway, as well as official predictions, will make more sense.

Our atmosphere is a layer of gases about 300 miles thick covering every point on Earth. Many vapors mix together to form the air. Greatest is nitrogen (78%). Oxygen makes up 21%; and a minor, but important part, is water vapor. The remaining ingredients read like the recipe of a medieval alchemist. Even Superman has representation . . . air is seasoned with 0.0001% krypton. The weight of air on the surface varies with time and place; but its average value is 14.7 pounds per square inch.

It is the function of the **barometer** to measure this pressure. If the air bears down on a dish of mercury in which a glass tube is placed open end down, it will force mercury up the tube. The height to which a standard atmosphere will raise the metal is 29.92 inches. Measured in metric units, the reading is just less than 760 millimeters. Another and uniquely meteorological unit is the **millibar** . . . a measure, not of length, but of force. Standard atmosphere will produce a reading of 1013.2 millibars.

So atmospheric, or barometric, pressure can be expressed in inches, millimeters or millibars. Since a mercurial barometer is unwieldy aboard ship, another type, the **aneroid barometer,** is used. The word "aneroid" describes the instrument well, for it means "without liquid." A partial vacuum is created inside a thin metal envelope which air pressure, pushing in from all sides, tends to collapse. Spring action works against the pressure. And changes in tension are transmitted by levers and links to a pointer, usually painted black. In turn, the pointer moves over an indicator card calibrated in inches, millimeters or millibars. Nearly all American instruments use inches and millibars. Many are also fitted with a second, brass, pointer to serve as a memory aid. This one is not connected to the envelope, but is pivoted at the center of the dial so it can be moved over the black one. Later on, the black hand can be read again. The brass pointer "remembers" the previous reading. And changes in pressure can be detected by noting which way and by how much the black pointer moves from the brass. To read an aneroid barometer: tap the face of the glass lightly with the eraser end of a lead pencil. This frees the linkage from any friction restrictions. Incidentally, some indication of the barometric tendency—whether it is rising or falling—can be found by noting which way the pointer jumps when you tap the glass. Friction would tend to stick it at a previous reading. If it jumps towards a higher number, the "glass" would seem to be rising; if the jump is the other way, it probably is falling. **Figure 9** is a barometer.

Another important weather tool is a thermometer . . . or rather, two thermometers. The first one is the familiar slim glass column filled with a fluid, usually mercury. It measures air temperature by expansion and contraction of the fluid metal. The other, called the **wet and dry bulb thermometer** or **hygrometer** or **psychrometer**, measures water content of the air. Two regular thermometers are mounted side by side. Around the bulb of one is wrapped a strip of muslin, kept moistened with water. As the water evaporates into the atmosphere, it takes up heat from the bulb, and so cools that thermometer. The drier the surrounding air, the more the evaporation . . . and so the lower will be the reading on that "wet bulb." In soggy air there will be little or no evaporation, and so little or no difference in reading between the wet and dry thermometers. By comparing the two readings, a navigator can determine relative humidity. He refers to a graph or chart to find the percentage of capacity that water vapor in his air contains at the time of observation. In **READY REFERENCE** you will find such a humidity table. And **Figure 9a** is a picture of the instrument used.

But when we know the pressure, temperature and the humidity and how they are changing . . . so what? So we are better able to judge how the atmosphere might be changing. For it is movement and change of the belt of air around Earth that is weather.

Figure 9

Photo by Science Associates, Inc.

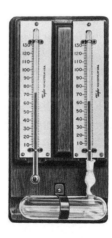

Figure 9a

Photo by Taylor Instrument Div., Sybron Corp.

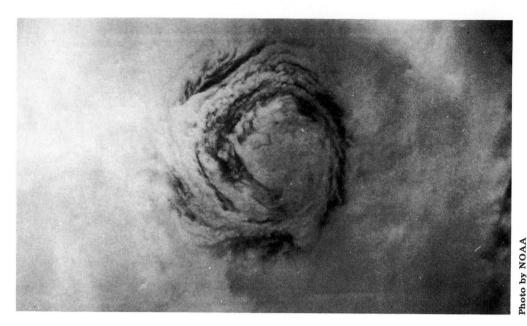

Aerial view of tropical cyclone.

To understand this movement, let's suppose an Earth that is totally covered with water. The Sun's heat is greatest in the Tropics, so in that area air will be warmer than in higher latitudes. And when a gas is heated, it will expand and rise. The tropical atmosphere moves upward from the surface and produces less pressure on the surface. A low pressure area is formed. The colder air to the north and south then begins to flow in on the surface to replace the rising warm air. In turn, the warmer air cools as it rises and flows north and south over the top to descend and join the Ferris wheel cycle of "up-over-down-under." At the surface, the motion of the air caused by this convection process would be expected to be from north in the Northern hemisphere and from south in the Southern, and towards the Equator.

So it would be, if another factor didn't come to bear. All this time the Earth is turning from west to east. The speed: at the Equator it is 900 knots, or more than 1000 statute miles per hour. This gradually diminishes to a theoretical 0 at the Poles. Miami Beach is a fast-moving area . . . 810 knots. Los Angeles zooms by at 748 knots. More conservative, San Francisco does 711. Point Barrow, Alaska, is quite moderate at 289 knots. Little America in Antarctica finds it tough sledding to make 180 knots. This spin of Earth deflects the movement of air to the right in the Northern Hemisphere and to the left in the Southern. As a result, the northern winds moving to the Equator seem to come from the northeast; and the southern winds seem to come from southeast. These are the **Trade Winds**. And the deflecting process is called **Coriolis Force**. Incidentally, winds are always described by the direction from which they blow, and not that towards which they blow. So a northeast wind is one that is moving southwest.

We assumed an Earth covered with water because then the surface would have a uniform cover and a uniform rate of heating and cooling. But now let's be realistic and put land masses back on the surface. Dry land has a different rate of cooling and heating than ocean areas. It will heat up faster and cool faster. So the air over land can be expected to get warmer in daytime than over adjacent water . . . and, of course, cooler at night. This causes a daily cycle of winds that is familiar to people living in coastal regions. During the day the Sun, beating on the land, warms it up more than the sea. By afternoon the temperature difference is enough to create a difference in air pressure over the land and water; it is lower over the warmer land. So the heavier sea air moves towards the land, producing the on-shore breeze felt in the afternoon. After sunset the air and surface begin to cool. But the land cools more than the sea. By early morning the land air is colder than that over the sea and is of higher pressure. So it begins to move towards the sea. This is the daily offshore breeze.

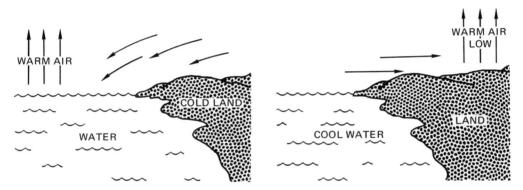

Early morning offshore breeze.   Typical afternoon onshore breeze.

Not only does land change temperature faster than water, but different land covers will create different rates. This lack of uniformity in rates of temperature change with differences in makeup of ground cover will, of course, produce a corresponding lack of uniformity in air pressure over land areas. The shape and contour of land also influence wind and weather. A mountain ridge can dam up the air; a pass can funnel it from one region to another.

The **Santa Ana** of California's southern coast is created by such a circumstance. High pressure over Nevada and northern Arizona with relatively low pressure on the Coast sets up the combination. The air moves quickly into the low area, and the land contours then conduct it like pipes until it emerges with a violent blast from the Santa Ana Canyon and rushes out to sea.

The vicious winds of Mexico's Gulf of Tehuantepec are typical of the mountain ridge case. The Northeast Trades pile up against the eastern side of the spine of mountains stretching through Mexico and Central America. Finally they spill over the top. At Tehuantepec, the land narrows to a thin isthmus. When the winds pour over the ridge they roar down on the Gulf of Tehuantepec with very great violence.

Description of air masses as "warm" or "cold," "high" pressure or "low" is relative. More important is that one is warmer or colder, higher or lower than an adjacent one. Generally speaking, warm air exerts lower pressure than cold air. For in warming, it expands and so has less weight per unit of volume. And high pressure will move towards an area of lower pressure, as if it were water flowing into a depression.

We can picture air as grouped into individual masses. When two such meet they don't mix together like gin and vermouth . . . rather they tend to maintain individuality and to push each other around. These contests or collisions of air masses cause "weather." When a warm mass moves towards a cold, the result is called a warm front; when a cold moves towards warm, the result is a cold front. And the front line is marked by a change in temperature, pressure, humidity and wind direction.

One job of the meteorologist is to track and to predict the migration of these air masses. The mariner observes the changes in temperature, pressure, humidity and wind direction in his area. Then he applies the data of the meteorologist to his situation and gains a better idea of what might be in the wind for him.

Scientific meteorology is relatively new. But skill in observing the weather is as old as seafaring. To the pleasure mariner, the development of a faculty to make shrewd predictions from observations is much more practical than a deep study of the fine points of the science. But the seaman's eye, when it is reliable, is unconsciously accurate in the light of science. So there is value to a general appreciation of "why."

Later on we will go over some of the signs to look for when judging local weather. But first there are some more basic factors to discuss. Next time, a look at the place of water vapor in the atmospheric scheme of things.

And to recap the points of importance in what we've already said:

Warm air tends to be of lower pressure than cold.

High pressure air will want to blow towards low.

The spin of Earth diverts such movement . . .

To the Right, in the Northern Hemisphere;

To the Left, in the Southern Hemisphere.

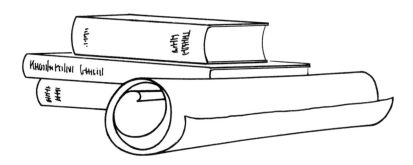

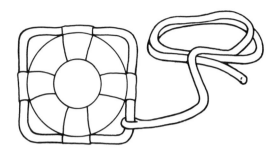

5/Safety Afloat
Fire

Fire aboard is an ugly companion . . . so ugly that all precautions should be taken to avoid its appearance. And every mariner should know how to fight it. There are no fire alarm boxes to call the shiny red trucks . . . there are no shiny red trucks. And there are no sidewalks to run to when the ship begins to burn. One tongue of flame can make you a fire department—in fact, the only fire department for your boat. So there is little need to emphasize the importance of this subject.

A fire requires three basic elements: **heat, oxygen** and **fuel**. All three must be present, and continue to be present, before there can be fire. And the cornerstone of all firefighting is the elimination of at least one of those essential ingredients.

Obviously an effective means to control a fire is to remove the fuel. But that is not always possible aboard ship. Yet one of the first steps should be to clear away from heat and flames as much combustible material as possible.

Fire is a chemical reaction by which a substance is vaporized in combination with oxygen. All materials are burnable . . . they will vaporize at some temperature. But the cause of the process and the temperature at which it starts will vary. So a fireproof material is not necessarily one that will never burn; rather it won't take fire within specified temperature ranges.

A fire will start without outside "help" when a substance reaches its **ignition temperature**. At that point the material will begin to vaporize, and when its gases mix with oxygen, a fire will start. The fire, in turn, will keep the material at the ignition temperature and so prolong the cycle of vaporizing and mixing until there is nothing left. Of course some influence must raise the temperature to that ignition point. If the material can do so itself—generate heat within itself faster than it is cast off—the process is called **spontaneous combustion**. But the heat can and usually does come from outside. So another reason to move material away from a fire: it otherwise might not only "catch" fire from the flames, it might "take" fire independently by being heated to its ignition temperature.

Heat can be transferred in three ways:

1. **Convection** . . . by the circulation of a gas or liquid.
   Example: heat rising to the top of the cabin.

2. **Conduction** . . . by passing through a substance: solid, liquid or gas.
   Example: outside of a stove gets hot by heat passing through the metal.

3. **Radiation** . . . by emission of rays.
   Example: the heat from the Sun.

A substance need not be at the ignition temperature before fire can exist. Another level, **fire point**, is the temperature at which it will give off vapors which can be ignited and will then continue to burn.
So to recap . . .

> A fire can be ignited when the fire point is reached; but it needs no lighting to start at the ignition temperature. It can get the heat to reach those points from other objects, or it can manufacture its own and produce spontaneous combustion.

> When the heat comes from an outside source it can be transferred by convection, conduction or radiation.

The aim of the firefighter is, again, to knock out one or more of the basic ingredients: heat, oxygen, fuel. The attack on fuel is obvious . . . throw it overboard, shut the valve, open the switch. It is also easier said than done. Carry it to the extreme and you'll be swimming; for usually most of the vessel is fuel of some sort.

The control of oxygen, though, is not so self-defeating. A fire cannot "breathe" without oxygen. It must mix with the material's vapors before there can be combustion. The whole purpose of throwing sand on a fire is to snuff out the air. And a foam-type fire extinguisher has the same purpose. CO_2 extinguishers are designed to dilute the air with a non-combustible vapor (carbon dioxide) so that the atmosphere at the fire does not hold enough oxygen to burn. But to seal off all the air from a burning area is almost impossible. So the practical aim is temporary and local isolation of oxygen from the fire.

The attack on the third ingredient, heat, is one with which all are familiar. "Wet down well and keep it wet" is a fireman's maxim. It is also the source of much complaint against his "needless" damage. But by this "needless" damage he keeps burnable material below the ignition temperature and the fire point. He knocks heat out and so controls the fire.

It is no different aboard ship. So long as heat can be kept below the critical levels, there can be no fire. The water hose is still high on the list of effective measures . . . on some fires it is the most effective.

And fires do come in types or classes. The standard ranking is this:

Class A: wood, paper, canvas, mattresses, etc.
The primary method of control: lowering of heat by water.

Class B: petroleum products.
The primary method of control: cutting off oxygen by a blanket of foam, CO_2 or water vapor. Liquid water is not effective because petroleum is lighter and will float.

Class C: electrical.

The primary method of control: cutting off air. **But** water is an electrical conductor and so can cause electrical shock. This type should never be fought with water.

The common portable fire extinguishers, and the fires on which they are used, are:

Water   By hose or bucket.

OK for Class A fires.
No good on Class B fires.
Dangerous on Class C fires.

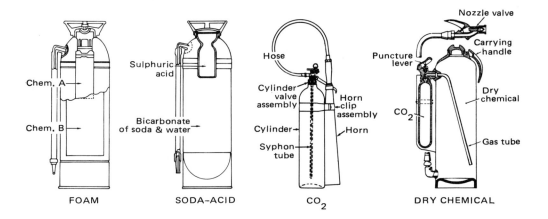

Soda-Acid   The container is a cylinder filled with a mixture of water and bicarbonate of soda, and fitted with a vial of sulphuric acid. When turned upside down, the ingredients mix and produce carbon dioxide (CO_2) to force the liquid out a small hose.

OK on Class A fires.
No good on Class B fires.
Dangerous on Class C fires.

Foam   A generator of a foaming mixture of water and CO_2.

OK on Class B fires.
Could be dangerous on Class C fires.

**Vaporizing
Liquid**   A container of a liquid chemical and fitted with pump for ejection. The liquid vaporizes in the heat of the fire and displaces oxygen with its non-combustible vapor.

Not suitable for Classes A and B fires.

Good for Class C fire.

But . . . the chemical, carbon tetrachloride, produces phosgene, a poisonous gas. This is very **dangerous** in enclosed spaces. So do not carry a "carbon tet" extinguisher!

CO_2

A pressure bottle filled with carbon dioxide which expands and vaporizes when released from a small orifice.

OK to hold Class A fires until water can be brought to bear.

Good for Classes B and C fires.

Dry Chemical

A container of powdered chemicals fitted with a CO_2 cartridge to expel the powder. When the dry chemicals are heated, they produce carbon dioxide gas.

OK to hold Class A fires.

Good for Classes B and C fires.

The best extinguishers for pleasure craft would seem to be some water buckets, a hose and pump, and dry chemical hand units.

Some final notes: it is better, of course, to prevent fire than to fight it. So keep an eye on oily rags, bilges, electric insulation, open flames, and concentrations of heat and gases. But if a fire starts, fight it and fight it fast. Usually the battle is decided in the first round, so be familiar with how to operate your extinguishers. And let the weather work for you. If the fire is in the stern, go head to windward. If it is in the bow, go stern to windward.

But above all . . . Use, not lose, your head.

Questions

Now to see how you're doing. Here are 25 questions, 5 of them from each of the study topics in Section I.

They are multiple-choice questions, and you are to select the answer you believe is most correct. You'll find no curves, no tricks. We've tried to set out only one correct answer. So don't read in more than the words normally mean.

Go to it . . . and Good Sailing!

Rules of the road

1. International Rules of the Road apply
   a)   only on the High Seas.
   b)   on the High Seas and in all harbors.
   c)   on the High Seas and in harbors where no national rules have been made applicable.

2. Lines of demarcation between International and Inland
   a)   are always specified in detail.
   b)   are never specified in detail.
   c)   neither of above.

3. Pilot Rules
   a)   do not apply on the High Seas.
   b)   do not apply on waters covered by Inland Rules.

4. The ship with the "right of way" is
   a)   free to do as she wishes.
   b)   always the slower ship.
   c)   required, normally, to hold course and speed.

5. Inland Rules
   a)   do not apply to foreign vessels in US waters.
   b)   do not apply to naval vessels in US waters.
   c)   apply to all vessels in US waters.

Charts and Publications

1. On Earth's surface, parallels of latitude run
   a)   east and west.
   b)   parallel to the Equator.
   c)   both of above.
   d)   none of above.

2. On Earth's surface, meridians
   a)   remain a constant distance apart.

b) converge at the North Pole only.

c) converge at both North and South Poles.

3. On a Mercator chart
   a) all parallels are the same length.
   b) the parallel at Latitude 75°N is shorter than the parallel at Latitude 10°N.
   c) all parallels are shorter than the Equator.

4. On a Mercator chart the space between Latitude 60°N and Latitude 75°N is
   a) the same as that between 10°N and 25°N.
   b) more than that space.
   c) less than that space.

5. On a Mercator chart distance should be measured
   a) on a vertical margin at the latitude of the points in question.
   b) on a horizontal margin at the longitude of the points in question.
   c) on any margin at any place.
   d) on no margin.

Piloting

1. With reference to the magnetic compass
   a) Deviation is the difference between Compass North and Magnetic North.
   b) Variation is the difference between Magnetic North and True North.
   c) both of above.
   d) none of above.

2. If Variation is 15°E and Deviation is 5°E, Compass Error is
   a) 10°E.
   b) 20°W.
   c) 10°W.
   d) 20°E.

3. With Compass Course of 100°, Deviation of 5°W and Variation of 15°E, the True Course is
   a) 110°.
   b) 090°.
   c) 120°.
   d) 080°.

4. With True Course of 300°, Deviation of 10°E and Variation of 10°W, the Compass Course is
   a) 290°.
   b) 320°.
   c) 280°.
   d) 300°.

5. With True Course of 050°, Compass Course of 060° and Variation of 5°W, the Deviation is
   a) 5°E.
   b) 10°W.
   c) 0°.
   d) 5°W.

Weather

1. The type barometer usually found aboard ship is
   a) a mercurial barometer.
   b) an aneroid barometer.
   c) neither of above.

2. In coastal regions a breeze from sea is usually felt
   a) in mid-afternoon.
   b) in early morning.

3. Generally, the daily onshore coastal breeze is caused by
   a) lower pressure over the land.
   b) lower pressure over the sea.

4. Wind deflection due to the Earth's rotation is
   a) to the right in the Northern Hemisphere.
   b) to the left in the Northern Hemisphere.
   c) called cyclonic drift component.
   d) none of above.

5. A wet-and-dry bulb thermometer
   a) measures relative humidity.
   b) measures by using two thermometers.
   c) is also called hygrometer.
   d) all of above.
   e) none of above.

Safety Afloat

1. The essential ingredients of a fire
   a) are heat, fuel and oxygen.
   b) are as yet undetermined.
   c) have little influence on firefighting techniques.

2. A foam-type extinguisher
   a) is safe to use on any type fire.
   b) is dangerous on a Class B fire.
   c) can be dangerous on an electrical fire.
   d) does not contain water.

3. A CO_2 fire extinguisher
   a)   can be safely used on any type fire.
   b)   can only be used on oil fires.
   c)   cannot be used on electrical fires.

4. Carbon tetrachloride
   a)   is a vaporizing liquid used in fire extinguishers.
   b)   is recommended for Class A fires.
   c)   is safe to use in enclosed spaces.
   d)   all of above.

5. A dry chemical extinguisher
   a)   contains water.
   b)   is a type of foam extinguisher.
   c)   is dangerous on electrical fires.
   d)   produces CO_2 gas by heating of the powder.

...and answers

Time for a fitness report . . . and score 4 points for each correct answer. Here are the standards:
   92 - 100:   Passed with Great Distinction.
   84 - 90:   Passed with Distinction.
   76 - 82:   Passed.
   Below 76:   Turn the TV off and take another look.

Rules of the Road

1. (c)   2. (c)   3. (a)   4. (c)   5. (c)

Charts and Publications

1. (c)   2. (c)   3. (a)   4. (b)   5. (a)

Piloting

1. (c)   2. (d)   3. (a)   4. (d)   5. (d)

Weather

1. (b)   2. (a)   3. (a)   4. (a)   5. (d)

Safety Afloat

1. (a)   2. (c)   3. (a)   4. (a)   5. (d)

section 2
contents

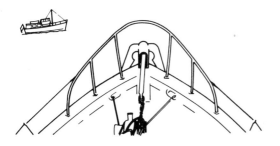

6/Rules of the Road
The meeting situation

The Steering and Sailing Rules are those sections of the International and Inland Rules of the Road defining how vessels maneuver when they approach each other close enough to risk collision.

The rules are supposed to be practically foolproof. Followed absolutely, they make collision almost impossible. But it is not for lack of foolproof rules ashore that each year more than 40,000 people meet death on the highways. The difficulty is not to understand the simple requirements, but to know how to use them in situations created by human conduct.

At the outset, let's limit our discussion to power-driven vessels, and talk about sailing ships later on. And the power-driven rules we'll look at from three points of view:

1. What are the simple requirements?
2. What mechanical factors of ship operation color them?
3. What added problems can humans be expected to create?

First, to the simple requirements. We live in a right-handed world. Except for United Kingdom countries and some of continental Europe, motor traffic follows the right-hand side of the road. The British custom of directing the flow to the left may have stemmed from a medieval precaution for self-defense; for horsemen brushing right arms as they passed were instantly alert to combat without leaning over the horse's neck. Our custom of shaking right hands in greeting is a carry-over from an ancient peace gesture . . . presentation of sword hands.

But aboard ship everywhere the right-hand rule persists. The traffic follows the right-hand side of a waterway. And all the conceivable patterns of two ships coming together can be reduced to three:

1. They are on the same track but opposite courses . . . they are **meeting** end on.
2. They are on the same track and the same course . . . one is **overtaking** the other.
3. The track of one intersects the track of the other . . . their courses are **crossing**.

So the lawmakers have divided the Steering and Sailing Rules accordingly: **Meeting**, **Overtaking** and **Crossing** situations.

To the Meeting Case. Vessels are said to meet when they approach end on, or nearly so. Each must alter course to the right and pass clear of the other. The rule: neither is privileged. Each is burdened to go right and then to pass clear on a "port-to-port" basis. Two pedestrians do this instinctively on a sidewalk. The same is required afloat. When meeting each goes right and they pass port-to-port.

What practical factors color this situation? First off, in this case the speed of approach is greater than in the other converging situations. The time interval from danger to deliverance, or to disaster, is the least. And the impact in any collision will be greatest. But there is usually greater awareness of the peril. A ship coming head on is pretty obvious.

Yet how nimble is that oncoming ship? A pleasure craft can dart from course to course with the agility of a jackrabbit. But the fellow ahead might be a hare of a different hue. Every operator, no matter how handy his ship, should appreciate the basic mechanics of maneuvering a large vessel.

In normal operation the bridge of a merchant vessel is manned by a watch officer and a helmsman. Orders to change speed are transmitted from bridge to engine room by electromechanical means. Down below, an engine watch officer then manipulates valves and controls to carry out the orders. If the Engineer has been alerted by a "Stand By" order, he will be at the throttles; otherwise, he may be making his rounds in another part of the engine room when an urgent order is given. So delay between the order and the beginning of execution should be anticipated.

Even if the Engineer is at the controls, there are physical limitations to the speed with which a procedure will take effect. If a middle-size tanker (16,000 tons displacement) is moving ahead at full speed and stops her engine, she will not stop her forward motion for two miles. A supertanker (40,000 tons and up) requires five miles! Should the ship suddenly reverse her engine so the propeller turns full astern, she will, of course, stop faster. But she has no air brakes like a truck. How long it will take varies from ship to ship, and even from time to time. For the Engineer must first get to the controls. Don't overestimate the ability of a large ship to come to a crash stop. It can be several minutes and thousands of feet of ocean.

Of course she can change course; and rudder action takes effect faster than propeller change. But remember, she's neither on tracks nor held to the road by the friction of rubber tires. When a ship begins to turn, she is still traveling in her original direction. Her old forward motion becomes a sideways one until she settles down to the new course. For instance, suppose a ship traveling due North suddenly changes course 90° to the right. Before she steadies on East, she may move from 500 yards to half a mile north of the point of first rudder action.

And a final thought: the man on the large ship might not see you. This seems strange, but often it is true. Standing on a high bridge, perhaps 60 feet above the water, he must often peer through a screen of masts and cargo booms. Although his ship will be quite apparent to you, your vessel can be hidden by sea or swell.

Being very practical, don't expect a big ship to behave like a power cruiser.

Liner's wake shows continuation of forward motion while ship turns right.

Understand her problems. Give her a fair chance . . . and a wide berth.

The human problems in this situation stem from the interpretation of when ships are really meeting. What is end on or nearly so?

Obviously two vessels following the same track but on exactly opposite courses are meeting end on. Each would see the other with stem and masts nicely lined up. At night both sidelights would be visible.

But is that the only case when vessels meet? The rules say . . . end on, or "nearly so." What is meant by "nearly so"? By International and Inland the phrase does not apply when only one sidelight, red or green, is seen on the other vessel, or when the alignment of masts is so broken that the ships are obviously not opposite.

Yet when vessels are moving around or bobbing up and down, it is hard to judge when they are really end on. The court-tested guides are these:

1. If dead ahead is seen only one sidelight, red or green, the ship is crossing and not meeting.
2. If any place **BUT** dead ahead are seen both sidelights, the ship is crossing and not meeting.

Even so, there is room for confusion. For example, look at **Figure 10**. To **A**, it is a meeting situation; but **B** thinks they are passing clear starboard-to-starboard. If **A** should turn right and **B** does not, a collision is in the making.

Exchanging proper whistle signals will help to uncover the disagreement. But both **A** and **B** must know how to nip that potential disagreement in the bud. The best treatment for any ill is taken early. So keep a sharp and continuous watch on ships ahead which might be meeting you. If the bearing from you doesn't change much, consider him dangerous. If he seems to be within a point or two (about

20°) of opposite to your course, he may be dangerous ... he may be meeting you.

And if you decide to alter course, do it with a substantial rudder change. Don't inch to the right a little at a time. Give **him** a chance to notice your movement. One 30° course change to the right when there is still a comfortable distance between you is much more apparent than a sideling over in 2° or 3° dribs and drabs.

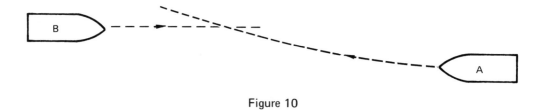

Figure 10

Naturally, every time you see another vessel you are not required to begin maneuvering. The rules only demand action when "risk of collision" exists. But this does not mean "immediate danger." The meaning is much broader. Whenever ships so approach that by misunderstanding, carelessness, mistake or accident, a collision is possible, then there is risk of collision. You won't be gored by a bull if you stay out of his pasture. But once you enter that pasture, the chance of injury arises, no matter how well-behaved he might be.

But when the state of risk of collision is unavoidable, follow the rules:

1. You are meeting if the approach is end on or nearly so;
2. Go right and gain sufficient room to pass clear.

What whistle signals are to be exchanged in this case? Under International, passing signals are only given when the course is actually changed or engines are going astern. **Rule 28** requires a power vessel when in sight of another ship and maneuvering under the rules to indicate his actions thus:

1. **One Short Blast** when he turns to starboard;
2. **Two Short Blasts** when he turns to port;
3. **Three Short Blasts** when his engines are going astern.

When he changes course in a meeting situation he must announce the fact by the proper whistle signal. But unless he changes course he makes no signal.

The weakness here is no announcement of intention. But the Inland Rules seem to cure this by **Article 18-1**, and also by the Pilot Rules **Section 80.4**. The signals are the same as International; but they are exchanged in advance of rudder action. They are, in effect, a proposal and an acceptance of a maneuver. Whichever ship initiates the signal, the other must reply. If the first ship wants to pass port-to-port, he blows one short blast to show his intention. The other ship must then answer. If he wants to pass port-to-port and no rudder action is necessary, he must still blow the one blast, and the other must answer. If he wants to pass starboard-to-starboard, he proposes it by two blasts. The signals are not of rudder action; they are of proposed passing.

Notice again the big difference in the rules. Under International, the one and two blast signals are given **only if the course is changed**. And there is no reply. So . . . if **A** and **B** are meeting as in **Figure 10**, **A** blows no signal until he begins to turn right. And **B** blows no signal unless he alters course. If **B** keeps silent, **A** may be confused as to his intentions.

Under Inland Rules, though, as soon as **A** decides to go right, **but before he does so**, he blows one blast. By that signal he proposes a passing maneuver. If **B** agrees, he answers with one blast. Then they maneuver to pass port-to-port. However, **until B** replies, **A** does not go right. If **B** disagrees, he objects by blowing not less than four short rapid blasts, the **danger signal**. Then they settle down to "negotiate" by whistle signals to an agreeable maneuver. But the important fact is that they have spotlighted the misunderstanding.

Incidentally, **B** would **never** answer **A**'s one blast signal with two. He cannot "cross-signal" his disagreement. The proper way is to use the danger signal. Then having alerted **A** to the impasse, he can if he wishes propose a starboard-to-starboard passing.

Note also that the three blast signal under either set of rules is given whenever engines are going astern in sight of another vessel. The International Rules say

Engines are going astern.

Inland says

Engines are going at full speed astern.

But by court decision both are to be read the same way: engines going astern at any speed. More than that: the courts have stretched the three blast signal to apply when the propeller is stopped, but the ship is still moving astern through the water; and even to the case where the propeller is actually turning ahead, if

Photos by Morgan Yacht Corp.   From left: port tack, running free, starboard tack.

the ship is still moving astern. So "engines astern" and the three blast signal seem to apply:

1. Whenever the propeller is turning at any speed astern, no matter which way the ship is actually moving.
2. Whenever the ship is actually moving astern, no matter which way the propeller is turning . . . or whether it is turning at all.

A word more about whistles. It is sometimes hard to know if the other ship **has** blown a signal. The sound may be whisked away by the wind. If she is a steamer, look for the plume of steam from the whistle. But if she doesn't have a steam-type whistle, sound might be your only notice. **Rule 28(c)** International allows a white light to be synchronized with the whistle. To avoid missing a signal . . . eyes and ears open.

Everything so far was intended to apply only to power vessels. That category includes any mechanical propulsion: inboard, outboard, full-powered or auxiliary. A steamer being towed is not covered here, although the tug is. And an auxiliary ketch under sail only is not included . . . not until the propeller goes to work. But then she is covered even though the sails are still set.

Sailing craft are treated separately. The power vessel stays out of the way when they meet. There are very few exceptions to this rule. When two sailing vessels meet, their rights and duties are set out in **Rule 17(a)** this way:

1. The vessel with the wind blowing on the port side keeps clear of the one with the wind on starboard.
2. If both have the wind on the same side: the vessel to windward keeps clear of the one to leeward.

Notice there are **no** whistle signals ever given by sailing craft in the meeting situation. Nor are whistle signals given by sail vessels in any maneuvering situation. The only time a sail vessel sounds off under the rules is in fog or in distress.

But **Rule 21** International and **Article 21** Inland require every vessel, including sail, to hold course and speed when privileged if the circumstances allow. Even though a power vessel be burdened to sail, the sail craft is obliged, within the limitations of circumstances and the ship, to keep course and speed . . . she must try to remain predictable until danger is past. The rules, as well as common sense and ordinary courtesy, direct a sail vessel not to change tack in front of a power vessel, unless the maneuver is necessary.

In summary . . . the requirements of the rules in the meeting situation are not difficult to state. But like most things maritime, the art is in the execution. And there the key is early appreciation of the risk, and then discreet avoidance. The fearless seaman is a bum shipmate. He just doesn't know any better.

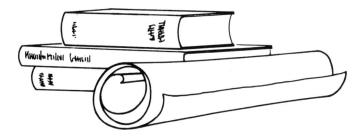

7/Charts and Publications
Use of a chart

Now to begin our close look at *C&GS 5142,* a typical nautical chart. Reproductions are included here for your convenience. They are not, of course, to be used for navigation purposes; only for guidance in this discussion. **Plate A** is a reduced view of the entire chart. **Plate B** is a reproduction of the upper right-hand corner.

No. 5142 is titled *San Pedro Channel.* The land areas are the mainland of Southern California from Dana Point to Palos Verdes, and Santa Catalina Island. It is prepared by National Ocean Survey, a NOAA agency.

Water depths are given in fathoms and at the level of Mean Lower Low Water (**MLLW**); land heights are in feet and measured from Mean High Water (**MHW**). Translated, this means:

1. Depths presume the state of tide when the water level is the average of the lower low waters. This **chart datum,** or plane of reference, is used because, on the West Coast of the US, tides are mixed and unequal. Successive tides can be of quite different heights. To assure the navigator a greater degree of safety, a lower-than-average plane of reference is used. By contrast, charts of Atlantic and Gulf Coasts, where tides are more equal, use Mean Low Water, average level of all low waters, as chart datum.
2. Heights are measured from the average water level at High Tide, a more general reference plane, because the elevation of landmarks is less important. Another reason: clearance indicated under bridges would then be on the lesser side and so preserve a measure of safety.

Land and water areas are shown with contour lines. On land they are drawn at 100-foot intervals. Water contour lines, or **fathom curves**, are given for depths of 1, 2, 3, 6, 10, 20 and 50 fathoms; thereafter appear at 50-fathom intervals.

Now look at **Plate A** for some general but important data on the chart. On the top margin, just to the left of the title, is found:

MERCATOR PROJECTION
Scale 1:80,000 at Lat 33° 31'

By this we know it was prepared on the Mercator principle and that the scale was

NOTE B
Recommended Traffic Lanes from Pt. Conception to Santa Monica Bay, north of latitude 33°41'43" and west of longitude 118°36'17", are not shown on this chart. See charts 5101 and 5202.

RACING BUOYS
Racing buoys within the limits of this chart are not shown hereon. For location and description see the Coast Guard Local Notices to Mariners and Light List.

LIGHT VISIBILITY
The charter of either the nominal or the geographic range is charted. See U.S. Coast Guard Light List for additional information.

Mercator Projection
Scale 1:80,000 at Lat. 33°31'
SOUNDINGS IN FATHOMS
AT MEAN LOWER LOW WATER
HEIGHTS
Heights in feet above Mean High Water.
AUTHORITIES
Hydrography and topography by the Coast and Geodetic Survey with additions and revisions from the Corps of Engineers, Geological Survey and Department of the Navy.
ABBREVIATIONS
For list of Symbols and Abbreviations see C. & G. S. Chart No. 1

UNITED

SAN PE

Nautical Miles

Yards

(CONTINUED ON CHART 5144)

WILMINGTON

PALOS VERDES HILLS

LOS ANGELES

TERMINAL ISLAND

YOK

SAN PEDRO

SAN PEDRO BA

TRAFFIC LANES
(see note B)

PROHIBITED DUMPING GROUND

VAR 1950'E (1968)
ANNUAL DECREASE 1'

SAN PEDRO CHANNEL

Catalina Canyon

Long Point

OUTER SANTA BARBARA PASSAGE

118°30'

8th Ed., Apr. 18/70 (corr. thru N.M. 16/70)
5142
PRICE $1.50

CAUTION
This chart has been corrected only to the print date shown in the lower left-hand corner. Corrections subsequent to this date should be made from the weekly Notice to Mariners.

Published
U.S. DEPART
ENVIRONMENTAL SCIE
COAST AND

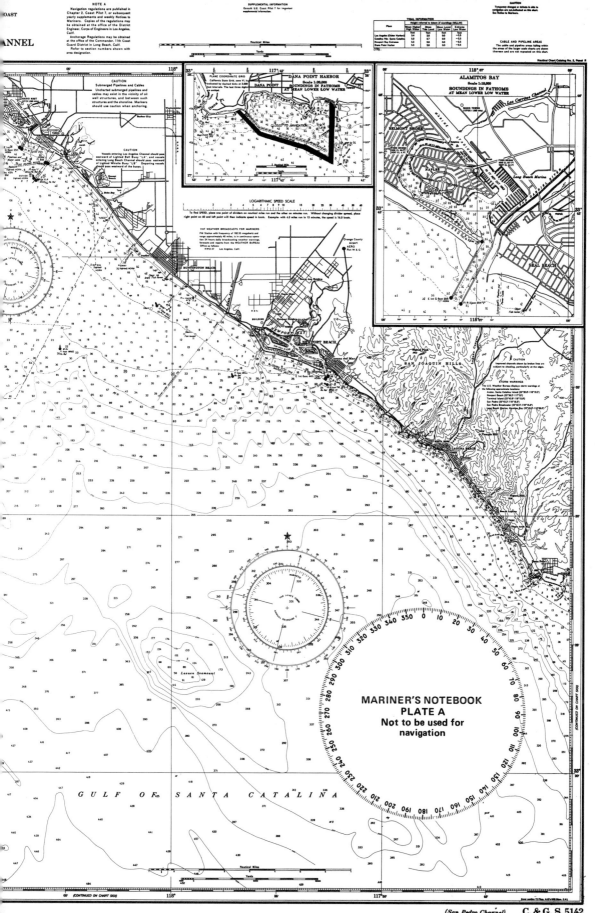

MARINER'S NOTEBOOK
PLATE A
Not to be used for
navigation

determined for Latitude 33°31′N, the middle latitude of the chart. The ratio between chart and Earth is 1:80,000 . . . one inch on this chart is the same as 80,000 inches on Earth. As explained already, this is the **natural scale**; and since it falls between 1:50,000 and 1:100,000, *No. 5142* is a Coast Chart.

Simple arithmetic produces the **numerical scale** as "one inch equals 1.097 nautical miles." For 80,000 inches is 6,666.67 feet; and that divided by 6076.1 is 1.097 nautical miles.

Also on the top margin (as well as on the lower part of the chart and in the upper right corner inset chartlet) are **graphic scales** for nautical miles and yards. And the left and right margins, as meridians are graphic scales on all Mercator charts. Here, each 5′ of latitude is numbered, and then subdivided into 1′ blocks. Each 1′ is divided into 10 sub-parts, equal to 0.1′ or 6″. So the meridian scale is cut to tenths of a minute. It can also be read as tenths of a nautical mile.

Printed in the lower left corner is:

8th Ed., Apr. 18/70 (corr. thru N.M. 16/70)

Printed on the top margin, just below the title, is:

1st Ed., Mar. 1951 G-1953-818

Printed to the right in the bottom margin is:

> *This Chart has been corrected only to the print date shown in the lower left-hand corner. Corrections subsequent to this date should be made from the Weekly Notice to Mariners.*

These notations tell the history of this copy of the chart. The first edition was released in March 1951. Through the years other editions were prepared; by 1970, changes had reached the point where still another was necessary. An eighth edition, of which this is a print, was prepared for April 18, 1970.

The user buys this copy as accurate as of April 18, 1970, and is so cautioned. To keep it up-to-date (rather up-to-week), he must check the weekly issues of *Notice to Mariners (NM)* after that date. On merchant ships, chart correction is a task of the navigating officer. His ship may have charts for all parts of the world; and to make weekly changes is quite an undertaking. A periodic call at the nearest Oceanographic Office (HO) to check a *NM* index should be adequate for the pleasure mariner.

Plate B is a closer view of part of the chart, with inset chartlets of Alamitos Bay and Dana Point Harbor. All charts use symbols and abbreviations . . . and *5142* is no exception. But not all charts have a summary of their meanings printed someplace on their faces . . . and *5142* is one that does not. The complete index to chart markings is published as *Chart No. 1* by C&GS and also by HO. It is in booklet form and is sold at authorized chart agencies for 50 cents. Such a guide is worthwhile . . . and more so when you encounter a chart without a key to the code of markings used. In **READY REFERENCE** is a summary of some of the

View from Apollo
of San Pedro Channel.
Photo by NASA

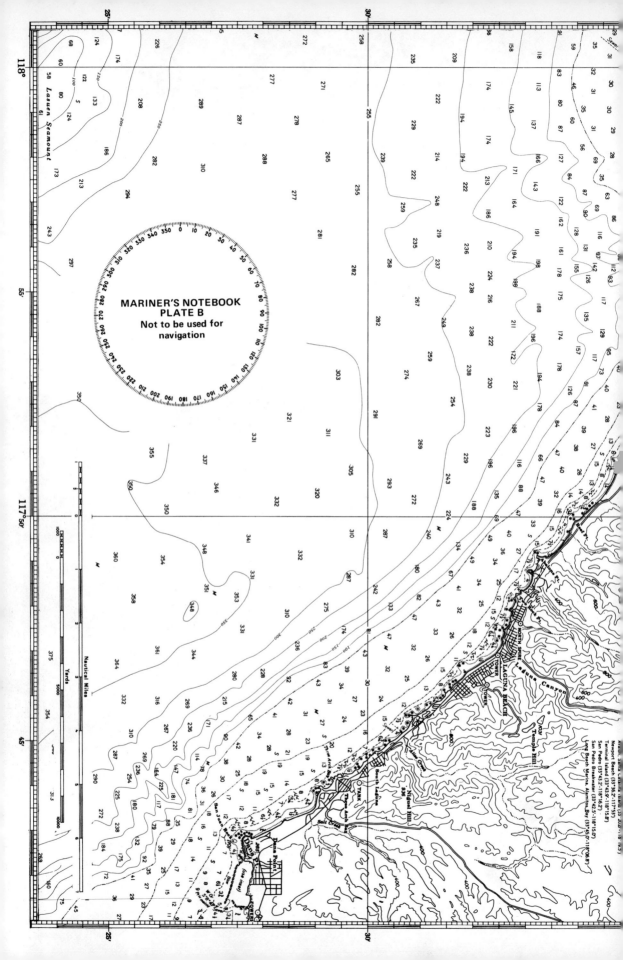

MARINER'S NOTEBOOK
PLATE B
Not to be used for
navigation

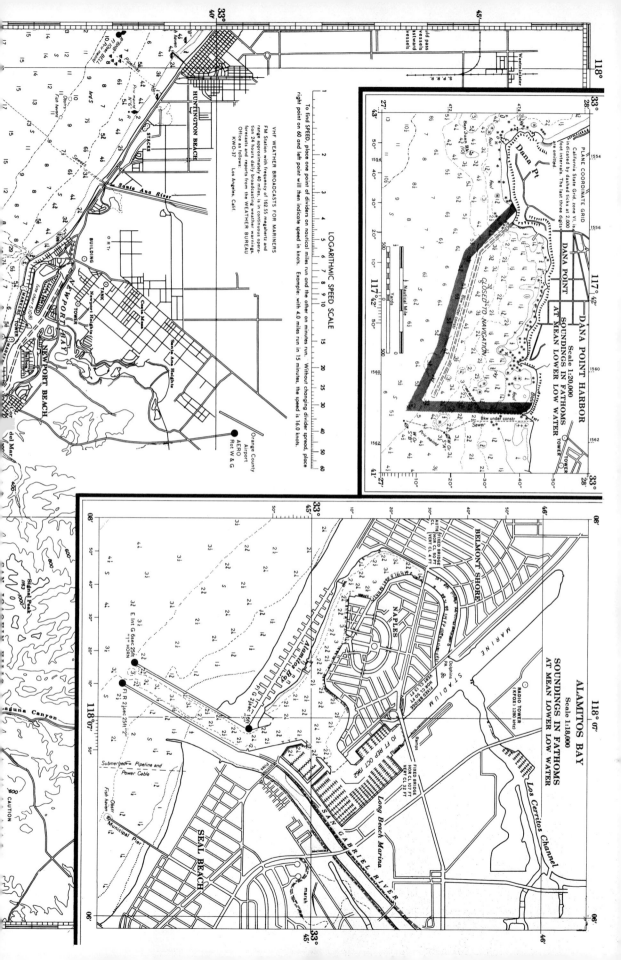

most frequently encountered abbreviations. But complete coverage will only be found in *Chart No. 1*.

Now to examine a few of the chart symbols on **Plate B** and to see how they are read. At the entrance to Newport Bay, you find a light on each jetty and a buoy between the 10- and 20-fathom curves. The meaning of the chart notation for each is this:

> **The Buoy**: its location is the black dot at the end of the diamond. The shaded circle around the dot shows it is lighted. The diamond is solid black because it is a port-hand mark entering from sea. The abbreviations shown are:
>
> *Fl G 4 sec "1" RaRef BELL*
>
> The *"1"* means it has the numeral 1 painted on its structure, and is Buoy No. 1 in the area. *BELL* means it is equipped with a bell. *RaRef* means it is also equipped with a radar reflector, a special metal collar to return strong and reciprocal radar echoes. *Fl G 4 sec* says its light is green . . . with one flash every four seconds.
>
> **East Jetty**: its light is *Fl R 4 sec* . . . a red flash every four seconds. The *"4"* below indicates it is channel marker No. 4 in the Newport Beach area buoyage pattern.
>
> **West Jetty**: this is the important aid in this location. The abbreviations shown are:
>
> *E. Int. 6 sec 44 ft 12 M "3"*
> *Horn*
>
> From these we know that the light is white, for there is no abbreviation *G* or *R*. The characteristic is three seconds of light followed by three seconds of darkness (equal intervals), repeating every six seconds. The light source is placed 44 feet above Mean High Water, and has a geographic range of 12 miles. In Piloting we'll have more to say about the range of lights. For now, let's accept that West Jetty Light should be seen at 12 miles by an observer 15 feet above sea level. Also at West Jetty is a horn fog signal. On the tip of land at the base of West Jetty is a small circle with a larger one around it. To the left is *R Bn 285 kHz*. This indicates a radiobeacon transmitting on 285 kiloHertz.

Now look at the contour lines on the land. **Signal Peak**, inland from the coast about midway between Corona del Mar and Laguna Beach, is the high point at 1163 feet. Behind Laguna you find **Temple Hill** at 1031 feet. The contour lines here are at 200-foot intervals, and show how the land plunges down into Laguna Canyon, then rises on the west side of the canyon to 800-foot heights.

Between Newport Beach and Santa Ana, you'll notice **Aero**, at the Orange County Airport. The abbreviation is quite obvious: aeronautical beacon with a rotating white and green light.

Along the shore at Corona del Mar, the beach line shows as short, comb-like lines. These are **hachures**, drawn at right angles to a contour line to indicate a steep bluff or cliff. In the water nearby you see these symbols:

* for rocks
⊱€ for kelp and seaweed

Note the 10-, 20- and 50-fathom curves:

    10 fathoms is *one dot between dashes* (-··-)
    20 fathoms is *two dots between dashes* (-···-)
    50 fathoms is *five dots between dashes* (-······-)

The 6- and 3-fathom curves:

    6 fathoms is *a series of three dash groups* (--- ---)
    3 fathoms is *a chain of dots* (........)

Knowing the code is not important; the soundings around the curve are an easy guide to the value. But there is a definite code. Depth contour lines are not haphazardly marked.

About a mile and a half offshore from the Newport Peninsula you'll see the symbol

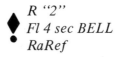

R "2"
Fl 4 sec BELL
RaRef

On the chart itself, the diamond is colored as magenta to indicate red; for this is a red buoy, No. 2. The red color and the even number denote a starboard buoy. This buoy has a light, flashing white every four seconds, and is equipped with a bell sound signal and a radar reflector collar.

To the northeast of this buoy is a measured nautical mile between markers on the beach. The course shown, *111° 37′ True,* (or its reciprocal *291°37′*) is proper for the run.

Printed inside the harbor near Lido Isle is (*Use Chart 5108*). This indicates that the large scale chart for Newport Bay, including the entrance, is *C&GS 5108.* On that chart, harbor aids and installations will appear in much greater detail.

Now to measure some distances. We'll use the right-hand margin as the scale. Remember that each subdivision is 0.1 nautical mile. The distance from West Jetty Light to No. 1 Buoy is one-fourth mile. West Jetty itself is just less than 0.4 mile long. From West Jetty Light to East Jetty Light is about 300 yards. In making these measurements on the meridian scale, we use that part of the margin at the same level as the measurement . . . Remember Greenland!

The Aero Beacon at Orange County Airport is 5.1 miles from West Jetty Light. Signal Peak is 2.4 miles inland from the shoreline at the closest point. And that point is found 0.7 mile to the northwest of Reef Point.

The most convenient way to measure distances is with a pair of chart dividers.

A satisfactory pair is relatively inexpensive at any instrument shop, and should be owned by anyone intending to use nautical charts.

Look closely at the chartlet of Alamitos Bay, in the upper right corner of **Plate B.** Note the scale indicated . . . 1:18,000. It is more than four times larger than the rest of the chart. And notice that the meridian scale on the right vertical margin is interrupted by the insert . . . as is the parallel of latitude at the top right margin. So, to determine the longitude of Laguna Beach, you would measure it on the **bottom** margin longitude scale. To find the latitude of Huntington Beach, you go to the **left-hand** margin. Otherwise you would run afoul of the switch in scale at the chartlet.

The other chartlet depicts Dana Point Harbor. Note the two buoys in the lower right portion. The diamond symbols show a vertical center line in each case and the abbreviations alongside are:

W Or S "A" and *W Or S "B"*

Between them is printed *Priv Maintd.* This all adds up to two special purpose buoys placed and maintained by private interests after receiving Coast Guard permission. They are painted white and orange. The vertical center line on the buoy diamond symbol shows vertical stripes. They are unlighted, for no light data are set out. Each is of the spar shape.

There is really no profit in itemizing further the things to be found on **Plates A** and **B.** You can do better by rummaging around on your own. Time spent looking at a nautical chart is never wasted. But more of that when the subject of charts next comes into range. Then we'll concentrate on other portions of *5142,* and finish up with a bathymetric saunter.

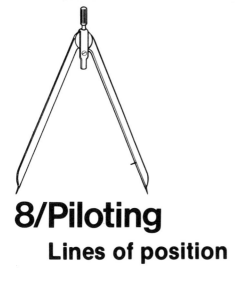

8/Piloting
Lines of position

Which way? and How far? . . . in discussing compass error we mentioned these as the fundamental questions for the navigator to answer. And the compass is his key to "which way."

But direction from a known position is just part of the story. Actually, instead of telling him where he is, direction tells him where he **isn't**. If he knows he is south of a lighthouse, one thing is certain: he is not anywhere but south of the lighthouse. But he doesn't know how far south.

What he learns from direction is the line on which his position can be found. He has a **line of position**, or **LOP**. In **Figure 11** the observer is south of Lighthouse **A**. The line of bearing drawn south from **A** is the line of position (LOP).

He may be anyplace on it, from just below **A** to as far away as the South Pole. All he knows from the LOP is that he is someplace on the line and not in any other direction.

Perhaps this might seem silly. Anyone knows that if he's south of a place he isn't west or east, or even a wee bit west or east. He's south. What is obvious on land, though, is not immediately so at sea. Ashore we seldom bother to analyze how we find our way. The process is automatic and second nature. But the ocean is not our natural habitat. So we must define the steps in the procedure, give them names and be sure we understand their meaning. Even if you still think this discussion overcomplicates a simple notion, bear with us . . . taking time now to think about it will really be worthwhile.

The line of position, then, is the identification of the track on which you are located. But it takes more to pinpoint **where** you are located on that line. In **Figure 12** the observer is south of Lighthouse **A** and west of Buoy **B**. The lines **OA** and **OB** are lines of position. Obviously the only place he can be is at their intersection. For only at **O** is he south of **A** and west of **B**. Only there will the lighthouse bear 000° and the buoy bear 090°. He has fixed his position by cross-bearings. The intersection of two simultaneous lines of position tells him exactly where he is.

However, any observation can be in error. Perhaps **A** does bear 000°. But suppose the bearing of **B** is not so accurate. **Figure 13** shows how an error in one bearing can change his position. **B₁** is the line of position when the bearing of

Buoy **B** is 095°. **B₂** is the LOP when the bearing is 090°. **B₃** is the LOP when the bearing is 085°.

A third LOP taken at the same time as the other two will, fortunately, erase the doubt. **Figure 14** brings in another reference point, Lighthouse **C**. **O** finds himself south of **A**, west of **B** and northeast of **C**. The bearings from him are 000° to **A**, 090° to **B** and 225° to **C**. Now, there is no question. He **is** at **O**. It is customary whenever possible to take three simultaneous bearings: two to fix position and the third to prove.

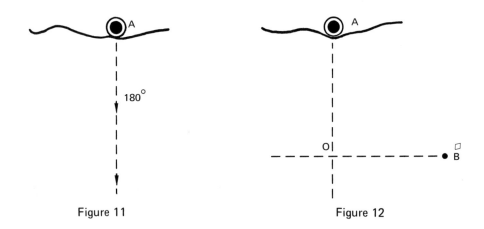

Figure 11   Figure 12

What happens if the three lines do not cross at a pinpoint? In **Figure 15**, **A** bore 000°, **B** bore 095° and **C** bore 225°. In this case there are **three** intersections: 1, 2 and 3. The observer made an error. He has isolated himself to a triangle of position . . . but which corner should he pick?

Normally he would pick none of the corners; instead, he would use the middle of the triangle as his position. That point, **O**, is a place he probably **isn't**. But it is the closest point to 1, 2 and 3. He minimizes the possible error by taking a neutral or mean position. The triangle is called the **cocked hat**. And experienced navigators encounter it so often they suspect a little self-delusion when it doesn't appear. There is an exception to choosing the center of the hat. If one of the three corners places the ship close to a danger, then the navigator selects it as his position. By presuming the worst, his error is on the side of caution.

The ideal fix has two lines of position 90° apart and a third midway between them, as in **Figures 14 and 15**. But not always will you be so fortunate. Often the reference objects are on bearings that are close together . . . and the fix is less reliable. An error in one bearing can make a large error in position. In **Figure 16** an error of a few degrees in the bearing of **C** can make a very large "cocked hat." So use care in selecting the objects observed. It is, in fact, better to have only two objects at right angles than three that are close together.

But much of piloting uses only one object, such as **A** in **Figure 11**, and finds position by successive, not simultaneous, bearings of it. The basis is in plane geometry and trigonometry. But no need to fret . . . throughout navigation, no knowledge of any kind of higher mathematics is necessary. The procedures are

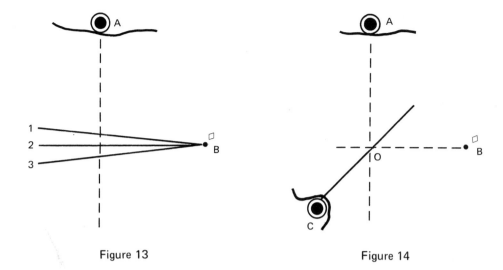

Figure 13

Figure 14

very simple to use and simple to remember. The next Piloting chapter will cover it in detail.

A word now on how these bearings are taken. The **pelorus** is the instrument made specially for the job. Its other name is **dummy compass** because in many respects it looks like a compass, but has no magnetized needles or other means of directive force. It is, essentially, a circle graduated into 360° and fitted with sight vanes attached to an arm pivoted at the center of the circle. When the 000°-180° line on its face is parallel to the keel of the ship, every bearing will be from the ship's head. **Figure 17** is a photo of one. Now refer back to **Figure 12** for an example of its use. If **A** bears 090° when using the pelorus, it is 90° to the right of the bow . . . on the starboard beam. And if at the moment of bearing, the boat is headed 270°True, then **A** bears 90° to the right of 270°, or 360°. This, of course,

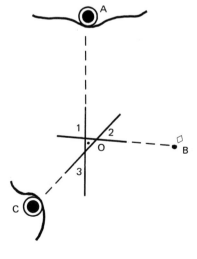

Figure 15

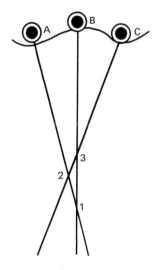

Figure 16

is the same as 000°, Due North. If **B** bears 180° by pelorus, it is 180° from the bow, or dead astern. With a ship's head of 270°True, **B** bears the opposite of 270° or 090°. . . Due East.

The **hand bearing compass** featured for small craft is like a pelorus; but it gives compass bearings directly without reference to the ship's bow. For the hand bearing compass is actually a magnetic compass. The bearings it measures are from North on the compass, and not from the bow of the ship. They would, of course, require correction for Variation and also for the Deviation on the hand bearing compass, in order to be converted to the true bearings.

But the boat itself can also be used as a pelorus. Look again at **Figures 14** and **15**. All that **O** need do is . . . steer directly at **A**, then at **B** and then at **C**. When each point is in line with his bow he reads the compass. He has then taken three compass bearings in the length of time and space it takes to change course and to aim at each point in succession.

Or he can use a little ingenuity. Years ago an active trade on the Pacific Coast was the operation of "steam schooners," little lumber ships plying from the timberlands of the Northwest. They were all very functional: all available space was for cargo and the bridge was cramped and bare of all but minimum equip-

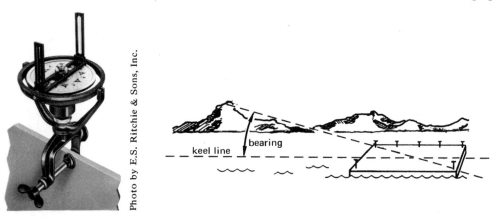

Photo by E.S. Ritchie & Sons, Inc.

keel line   bearing

Figure 17   Figure 18

ment. On them developed a bearing device nicknamed the "steam schooner cribbage board." It was a piece of wood about one foot square . . . today it could be scrap plywood. One straight edge was lined up parallel to the keel. The lines were drawn on the board to make desired angles with the edge. **Figure 18** is a sketch of how it worked. Pegs, or even nails, were tapped in at the corner of the board and at the ends of the lines. The pegs then became sight vanes, and the board was a serviceable pelorus.

A plastic drafting triangle can also be used. For example, suppose you have a 30°-60° right angle triangle. With a short side placed on the windshield or other part of the boat that is at right angles to the keel, the hypotenuse becomes a line of sight. Using first the 30° angle and then, by reversing the triangle, the larger 60° angle, two consecutive 30°-60° bearings can be taken.

Another do-it-yourself thought: acquire a large plastic protractor, a heated ice pick and a handful of matchsticks. Prick holes in the circumference of the protractor at desired angles from the mid-line . . . for example, 22½°, 26½°, 30°, 45°, and 60°. Then by placing a matchstick in the center hole and one at the desired angle, you have "sight vanes" and a pelorus.

These thoughts are not impractical. They do not give precise answers, of course. But don't think navigation requires a lot of expensive equipment and a roomy bridge. Naturally, the better the tools the better the work. But you can do adequate work with any device that measures a reasonably accurate angle. Many an experienced shipmaster has built his reputation for "uncanny" coastal navigation on bearings taken over a turnbuckle on the foremast shroud and along the edge of the bridge rail.

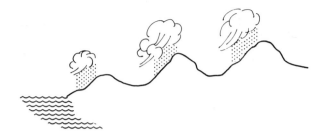

9/Weather
Water vapor in the air

Of all the gases that make up our atmosphere, water vapor is only a tiny part. We can't see it or taste it or smell it. But from it come clouds, fog, rain, snow and ice.

Matter can have three states: liquid, solid or gas. Obviously, water vapor is a gas; and it must change to a liquid or a solid before we can sense it. This discussion is of how and when it does change state, and what is the result.

If you take a given volume of atmosphere—for example, a cube that is 10 feet long, high and wide—there is a limit to how much water vapor it can hold. As soon as that capacity is reached, the vapor will change state. If the air is warm it can hold more water vapor than if cold. Capacity varies with temperature. And when the cube has all the water vapor it can hold, the atmosphere is said to be "saturated." Add still more and something's bound to happen.

A given volume of atmosphere can reach its water capacity two ways: either by having more added or by cooling the air. In the first case, the allowable quota of vapor is filled; in the second, no vapor is added, but because of the cooling, that allowable quota is decreased. In either case, though, the atmosphere will become saturated.

The temperature at which capacity is reached is called **dew point** . . . below that mark, condensation takes place.

The entire atmosphere around Earth gains its heat from Earth. It's true, the surface gets the heat from the Sun in the first place; but the Sun's rays passing through the atmosphere to strike the surface do not heat the air enroute. It is the warmth radiated back up by the surface that heats the air. So air is warmer close to the surface than at high altitudes. The atmosphere gets colder as altitude increases. One way, then, for a volume of atmosphere to be cooled is for it to rise.

There is another, even more obvious way: it can come in contact with something cold. Warm air passing over a cold surface will be cooled.

Another means is "diluting" it with a colder mass of air. One mass at 80° which swirls around with air at 40° is going to end up at less than 80°.

But cold or hot, much or little, the measure of the water vapor in a volume of atmosphere is **humidity**. The actual amount of vapor in a unit of air is called **absolute humidity**. When we compare that amount with what the air can hold, the term is **relative humidity**. An example of absolute humidity is "five grains of water vapor per cubic foot." A relative humidity expression would be "68%." The first states that in each cubic foot of air there are five grains of water vapor. It doesn't at all indicate closeness to saturation. The second, relative humidity, is the one we usually encounter. It means, in our example, that the air has 68% of all the water vapor it can hold.

Suppose, though, a volume of air reaches capacity, not by being cooled, but by having more water vapor added . . . where does the extra water vapor come from? From a source outside the atmosphere itself: by evaporation of surface water on Earth. This starts a natural endless chain. Water on Earth evaporates into the air. There it eventually reaches capacity and, condensing back to liquid or perhaps a solid, falls to the surface ready to begin the cycle all over again.

But a link in the chain is still missing. For saturation is not condensation. Just

Earth's cloud cover as seen from space.

Photo by NOAA

because air is full of water vapor does not mean it's going to rain. The saturated air needs something else . . . something for the water vapor to condense on. This link is supplied by solids. If the saturated air contacts the cool Earth, then water vapor can condense on the surface, to appear as dew or frost. But if the saturated air doesn't touch Earth, it must find these indispensable solids someplace else . . . and it does: within itself.

These are microscopic bits of matter . . . such as salt crystals from the ocean, carried up into the atmosphere during evaporation. Should the air get saturated, water vapor can condense around the little particles. But without particles, no saturated air can condense . . . not even if more water vapor is added. Air with that extra overload of water vapor that can't condense is **supersaturated**.

Now we have the necessary links in the chain: the atmosphere has in it bits of matter; the water vapor in the air reaches capacity; the water then condenses on the particles and becomes liquid or solid.

Next step . . . when condensation occurs, will the change be to a liquid or a solid? That depends on the temperature at the time of the change. Water condensing above freezing will change from a gas to liquid. But if the temperature is below freezing, it will skip over the liquid state and go directly from gas to solid.

Let's see how this actually works out. First of all, when atmosphere is moist and near capacity, not much change is necessary for saturation. When that kind of air hovers over a cold surface, it will suddenly be cooled. At the dew point, the thin layer near the cold surface will become saturated. And then water vapor will condense on the solid surface as **dew**. If the dew point, though, is below freezing, then the change is directly to a solid . . . **frost**.

What about a cloud? Well, what it is we can now pretty well guess: a mass of atmosphere in which water vapor has condensed. But the water droplets are so small they "float" in the air currents and don't fall to the ground. If some of them begin to fall, they tend to warm up, re-evaporate into a gas, and then, to go back up to become part of the cloud again.

When you see a flat-based cloud, or a sheet stretching across the sky, you can assume a series of events like this. A mass of air began to rise from the surface. In it was water vapor, evaporated from surface water. As the air went up, it dropped in temperature and the relative humidity rose steadily. Finally, at the dew point temperature, it reached 100% capacity. There were solids in the air on which the saturated vapor condensed into water droplets. All this took place at the same altitude. When rising air reached that height it flipped en masse from gas to liquid and all at once became visible. Then currents and drafts of air molded it, shredded it and packed it into shapes and forms.

Often you notice wisps of extremely high clouds. They were formed by moist air rising to tremendous altitude before reaching the dew point. By that time the temperature was below freezing. So the water vapor changed directly to solid, to ice crystals. What you've seen were frozen clouds.

When the water droplets within a cloud reach sufficient size, they overcome the buoyant effect of air currents and begin dropping. On the way down they warm up and decrease in size. The drops that do arrive we call **rain**. When there is only a small loss in size, they are large drops, as in a cloudburst or a tropical rain. But

Sea fog blanketing channel at Brunswick, Georgia.   Photo by NOAA

often they never survive the trip; they just hang as streamers from the bottom of a cloud. These ragged whiskers hanging from the cloud are actually streaks of rain that fall until they evaporate again into water vapor.

When condensation in the cloud takes place at below-freezing, and in super-saturated air, the vapors change to **snow flakes**. They, in turn, start the trip to the surface and arrive as large or small flakes, depending on the loss enroute.

Often the vapor changes to liquid at above freezing; but then on the way down the drops pass through freezing air. Then we have **sleet**. Or perhaps the drops may be swept up by a violent air current and meet freezing temperature. Then they will freeze and arrive down on Earth as **hail**.

So rain is water that passed from vapor to liquid and then fell as drops. Snow is water that passed from vapor directly to solid and fell in flakes. Sleet is vapor that became liquid and then froze on the way down. And hail is water that passed from vapor to liquid, but by an updraft reached a freezing temperature. There the liquid froze, and started to fall as ice. It might then partly melt, only to be thrown up again and refrozen. Finally, though, it plunged to Earth as a hailstone.

Now let's consider **fog**. It, like a cloud, is the product of condensed water vapor. In fact a fog is a cloud, one that is at the surface. And, as in a cloud, the water vapor must be at the saturation point. This is done either by cooling or by addition of more water vapor.

One type is called **radiation fog**. Moist air hovers over a cold surface. It cools to saturation and vapor condenses to small water droplets that don't drop, but float just above the surface as fog. The term "radiation" is used because the surface cools by radiating its heat after the Sun goes down. When the Sun rises again the fog evaporates or "burns up" as invisible water vapor.

Another, and frequent, type is **advection fog**. Here, moist air moves horizontally along the surface of Earth. When the surface temperature differs from that of the air, a change takes place. If the air is cold and moves across a warmer surface of the ocean, water vapor rising from the sea will strike the cold air and immediately condense into a steamy fog. This, an arctic phenomenon, is called **sea smoke.** But the process can happen the other way around, and often does. Warm, moist air can move over a cold surface. The resulting drop in temperature causes condensation and a fog. California's rolling banks of fog from seaward are examples. Warm sea air moves over a cold surface current near the shore. It reaches the saturation point and condenses. The onshore afternoon breeze does the rest. Thick weather off Newfoundland's Grand Banks is another example. There the Labrador Current supplies the cold surface. And fogs on the Great Lakes often develop in a similar way.

We mentioned that air becomes saturated either by cooling or by having more water vapor added. So far we've talked of fog caused by cooling. But let's imagine a situation where warm air is saturated and water droplets begin to fall. On the way down they evaporate back to water vapor. But in this case they enter into a new mass of air underneath . . . one that is already near saturation. They add water vapor to the lower layer and bring it to capacity to form **frontal fog.**

These are the forms in which the atmosphere's water vapor becomes visible. They all involve the same elements. How they form and what they look like differ with the circumstances. And the circumstances vary with all sorts of things: temperature, pressure, form and texture of the Earth's surface. That is why, for example, some areas on Earth are notorious for heavy fogs while others nearby are quite free. Your goal is to gain a general understanding of these atmosphere changes. But, frankly, don't be too concerned about terms. Much more valuable is a "more or less" idea of the physical cycles within the air.

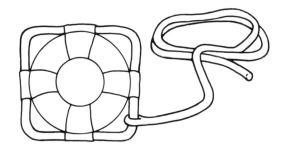

10/Safety Afloat
Explosion

Think of the cavemen living among the dangers of fierce monsters and you wonder how they ever survived to carry on the race. The dinosaurs and dragons are gone. But today in our carefree atmosphere of do-it-yourself, we manufacture our own monsters to do us in.

Boating is for fun, a haven from the tensions of everyday life. But it is an **intelligent** recreation where common sense makes a good shipmate. Without being crepe-hangers and shouting "Sailor, Beware!" from the masthead, let's take a look at gases and explosions . . . "instant beasts" that can spoil our sport.

A boat can, under some conditions, supply the basic elements of a bomb: explosive material, a container and a detonator. The hull itself is the container; for one of the aims of design is to produce a tight, staunch, leakproof vessel. Small wonder, then, that in her are formed many spaces where gases can pocket.

An explosion is a special type of combustion. We should know it very well because we meet it constantly. An automobile on the highway has hundreds of thousands of them each hour. For the principle of the spark ignition engine involves the harnessing of controlled explosions of gaseous vapors.

What then is an explosion of gases? It is a chemical reaction of air and vapor mixed in certain percentages to generate sudden heat and pressure. But the proper mixture is essential. With too much air the mixture is lean; with too much vapor it is rich. To explode best, the mixture cannot be too lean, or too rich, but just right.

Here is a table of the limits of percentage by volume for explosive mixtures of air and some particular vapors. Obviously the wider the range, the greater the chance of forming an explosive mixture. These are the ranges for vapors commonly found aboard:

Table of Percentages

Gasoline	1.4% to 6.0%
Carbon Monoxide	12.5% to 74.0%
Butane	1.7% to 5.7%
Hydrogen	4.1% to 71.0%
Propane	2.2% to 7.4%

Of course you first have to get the vapors. Come aboard as we smell around for some of those named above. The gasoline vapor we get from fuel, and the carbon monoxide from exhaust. Butane and propane arrive already packaged for the job. And a bank of batteries can give the hydrogen.

But what else do we need for an explosion? We need combustion. The vapor mixture must be made to burn. So we are interested in the temperature at which substances will evaporate into inflammable vapors. This varies with the substance. Carbon monoxide and hydrogen are already inflammable vapors; no evaporation is needed. For butane and propane, just crack the valve on the pressure storage cylinder. Gasoline produces those vapors at temperatures down to -45°F.

Now we have the vapors and the air. What else is needed? We've mentioned the container . . . the boat supplies that only too well. All that is left is the detonator. That is heat. It can be self-induced if the temperature gets high enough. But usually the mixture flashes on meeting flame or a spark. A match, a cigarette, a candle, burning oil, an electric switch or a static discharge . . . any of them could serve.

And there is the Bomb.

Let's go back and see how we might prevent these elements from teaming up on board.

First of all, can we keep the vapors from forming? Again, that depends on the vapors. Fluids are going to evaporate to some extent when they stand in air. Gasoline will do it even at temperatures below 0°! So we risk the formation of vapors whenever we let a fluid stand open. The answer? Air-tight containers. An empty gasoline can is often much more dangerous than one nearly full. For the empty is full of vapor. If you don't want to dispose of it, by all means make it gas-free. The Navy way: fill it with water to force out the gases. A volume of

The result of explosion and fire.

Photo by Proceedings of the Merchant Marine Council

liquid gasoline the size of a cube of butter will produce the explosive mixture when evaporated into a space the size of a home refrigerator. A quart of gasoline will do the same in an empty space eight feet square and eight feet high.

An enclosed fire with not enough oxygen to make full combustion will produce carbon monoxide. This happens in the cylinders of an engine. Many smog-control devices use an afterburner to complete the combustion of carbon monoxide. Left to accumulate in an enclosed space, it not only can be asphyxiating, it can form an explosive mixture. But you can't keep the vapor from forming aboard a power-boat; the engine creates it as a leftover.

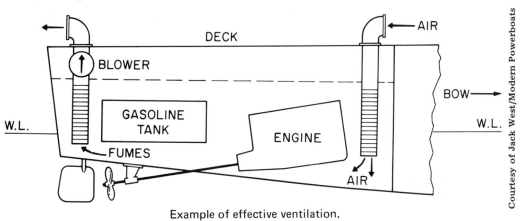

Example of effective ventilation.

Butane and propane vapors are released whenever the valve on their pressure cylinder is opened . . . or they leak out unexpectedly from the line or fittings. No matter how the substance gets out of the gas bottle, it will vaporize on the spot.

Hydrogen vapors are a necessary chemical by-product in the wet battery process. If you have the batteries you have the gas.

But if you can't prevent the vapors, how do you get rid of them? Butane and propane are easy: don't bring them aboard. Yet they are handy. As with any liquified petroleum gas (**LPG**) they own the advantages of easy handling and economy. But don't overlook the dangers. The gas is heavier than air, so it'll settle to the lowest pocket it can find. If you must carry it, use some cautions:

1. Be sure you buy **odorized** LPG so you can detect a leak.
2. Take special care that lines and fittings are tight, and stay tight.
3. Stow the containers out in the weather when possible, so any leaks will carry clear of the cabin.

Carbon monoxide? Have an effective and adequate exhaust system and keep it in good condition.

As for hydrogen: if you carry the batteries that produce the gas, be sure they are so placed that vapors will not pocket but will be vented clear and overboard. This gas is lighter than air. The pockets will be near the overhead. There is the place for the vent.

Gasoline? Here we are back to another heavier-than-air vapor. Be very careful with ventilation. Vent pipes should always lead to the open air, should be fitted with flame screens and should be away from below-deck hatches and openings. Don't give the vapors a chance to get underdeck. As a matter of fact, cultivate a healthy respect for these vapors. Never tolerate any gasoline in an open container underdeck. Better yet, never carry it in any underdeck container—open or closed—except a permanently fitted fuel tank.

How do we eliminate the detonator? It's a hard job to counter all possible sources of heat and sparks. Matches, cigarettes, lighters, stoves . . . they are going to be used on board. Switches are going to be thrown; metallic objects will be struck together; static electricity will develop. But practice the Confucian philosophy of all things in moderation. Don't do these things when there is any reasonable chance of igniting an explosive mixture.

Treat the fueling operation as if you were loading a 250,000-barrel tankship . . . No Smoking, No Open Lights, Use Non-Sparking Tools. Keep the hose nozzle firmly in contact with the fillpipe. Close off openings into the cabin. Afterwards, air out and ventilate well before you use any electrical equipment and before you start the engine.

Be an "old woman" on this subject. Be a Captain Bligh. Be a Bully Mate. No matter how the metaphors are mixed, be aware of a much more murderous mixture . . . gas vapors and the air you breathe.

Questions

Here is another chance for a fitness report. These 25 multiple-choice questions are arranged in groups of 5 for each of the topics covered.

Rules of the Road

1. When two ships meet in Inland Waters and one rejects a two-blast signal from the other, he blows
   a)   one short blast.
   b)   no signal but does as he wishes.
   c)   cross signals.
   d)   the danger signal.

2. At night a red sidelight dead ahead means a vessel
   a)   is crossing your course.
   b)   is meeting you.
   c)   is being overtaken by you.

3. In Inland Waters two short whistle blasts mean
   a)   you are turning to the right.
   b)   you intend to turn to the left.
   c)   you are turning to the left.
   d)   you intend to turn to the right.

4. In International Waters three short blasts mean
   a)   your engines are going astern.
   b)   your ship is moving stern first.
   c)   the same as in Inland Waters.
   d)   all of above.

5. When two vessels under sail meet bow-on, the one with the wind from the port side
   a)   has neither privilege nor burden respecting the other.
   b)   is privileged over the other.
   c)   keeps out of the way of the other.

Charts and Publications

1. The abbreviation "MLLW" on a nautical chart
   a)   stands for Mean Lower Low Water.
   b)   is the reference plane for charts of US Atlantic Coast.
   c)   is the reference plane for charts of US Pacific Coast.
   d)   (a) and (c) above.
   e)   (b) and (c) above.

2. A contour line in a water area is also called a
   a) fathom curve.
   b) hachure.
   c) graphic scale.

3. The ratio 1:80,000 on a chart means
   a) one inch on the chart is 80,000 feet on Earth.
   b) one mile on the chart is 80,000 feet on Earth.
   c) one inch on the chart is 80,000 inches on Earth.
   d) one unit on the chart is 80,000 of the same units on Earth.
   e) none of above.
   f) (c) and (d) above.

4. When you buy a chart you can assume
   a) it is correct to the day you buy it.
   b) it is correct only to the date of the edition printed on the chart.
   c) it is correct subject to the rubber-stamped data in the lower margin.

5. The abbreviation "Gp Fl R (4) 20 sec" means
   a) a red light flashing in groups of 4 every 20 seconds.
   b) 4 red lights grouped together and flashing once every 20 seconds.
   c) a group of red lights flashing 20 seconds and dark 4 seconds.
   d) a red light group-flashing once every 20 seconds and visible 4 miles.

Piloting
1. A line of position
   a) fixes your position.
   b) represents the line on which you are located.
   c) can only be gained from a visual bearing.
   d) all of above.
   e) none of above.

2. When 3 lines of bearing do not cross exactly, you should pick as your position
   a) any intersection of two of the lines.
   b) the intersection showing least danger to navigation.
   c) the intersection showing greatest danger to navigation.

3. When selecting points for cross-bearings it is better to use
   a) 3 points close together than 2 at right angles.
   b) 2 that are $40°$ apart on the port side than 2 that are $60°$ apart on the starboard side.
   c) a buoy than a lighthouse.
   d) 2 points at right angles than one dead ahead and one dead astern.

4. If your True Course is $137°$ and a lighthouse bears $137°$ from your bow, the True bearing of the lighthouse is
   a) $000°$.

b) 137°.
c) 356°.
d) 358°.
e) 223°.
f) 274°.

5. If your True Course is 002° and a lighthouse bears 358° from your bow, the True bearing of the lighthouse is
   a) 004°.
   b) 000°.
   c) 356°.
   d) 358°.
   e) 223°.
   f) 274°.

Weather

1. Compared to cold, warm air can hold
   a) more water vapor.
   b) less water vapor.
   c) the same amount of water vapor.

2. Air can become saturated by
   a) raising the temperature.
   b) lowering the temperature.
   c) adding more water vapor.
   d) (b) and (c) above.
   e) (a) and (c) above.

3. The water in clouds at extremely high altitudes is usually
   a) liquid.
   b) vapor.
   c) frozen.

4. Fog formed by the horizontal movement of an air mass over a surface of different temperature is called
   a) advection fog.
   b) radiation fog.
   c) frontal fog.

5. A snow flake is
   a) a raindrop that froze.
   b) water vapor that condensed at freezing temperature directly into the solid state.
   c) water vapor that condensed to liquid and then was lifted by air currents to a freezing temperature.

Safety Afloat

1. Gasoline will vaporize at temperatures above
   a) 45°F.
   b) -45°F.
   c) 32°F.
   d) 0°F.
   e) all of above.

2. The vapors of gasoline are
   a) heavier than air.
   b) lighter than air.
   c) lighter than hydrogen gas.

3. Butane gas is
   a) heavier than air.
   b) lighter than air.
   c) lighter than hydrogen gas.

4. When a compartment is only 3% filled with gasoline vapors
   a) there is little danger of explosion.
   b) an explosive mixture can form.

5. When loading gasoline into fuel tanks through fillpipes on the open deck
   a) be sure to keep all cabin hatches and underdeck openings open during the process.
   b) be sure to keep all cabin hatches and underdeck openings closed during the process.
   c) it doesn't matter whether such openings are kept open or are closed.

...and answers

Score 4 again for each correct response; and rank yourself as follows:
92 - 100:   Well Done!
84 - 90:   Medium.
76 - 82:   Medium Rare.
Below 76:   Raw Recruit.

Rules of the Road

1. (d)   2. (a)   3. (b)   4. (d)   5. (c)

Charts and Publications

1. (d)   2. (a)   3. (f)   4. (c)   5. (a)

Piloting

1. (b)   2. (c)   3. (d)   4. (f)   5. (b)

Weather

1. (a)   2. (d)   3. (c)   4. (a)   5. (b)

Safety Afloat

1. (e)   2. (a)   3. (a)   4. (b)   5. (b)

section 3
contents

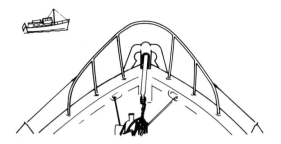

11/Rules of the Road
The crossing situation

When two power-driven vessels are crossing, a most dangerous scene is being set. The rules are stated in just a few words. **Rule 19** (International), **Article 19** (Inland) and **Section 80. 7** (Pilot) boil down to this:

> When two power-driven vessels are crossing so as to involve risk of collision, the one which has the other on her own starboard side shall keep out of the way of the other.

The Pilot Rule also requires the privileged vessel to hold course and speed. But then **Rule 21** and **Article 21** in the other regulations demand that of every privileged vessel.

Figure 19 illustrates a crossing situation. **B** is the burdened vessel and **P** is privileged. **P** holds his course and speed. And **B** turns to avoid him, or slows down, or stops, or goes astern . . . but he doesn't cross ahead.

The rule should be as simple to practice as it is to state. But unfortunately this is often not the case. We've stated the rule . . . but what about the mechanics of operation? Do they color the manner it all works out? The limitations of maneuvering discussed before apply here; but they do at all times. The important factor in the crossing situation is the human element.

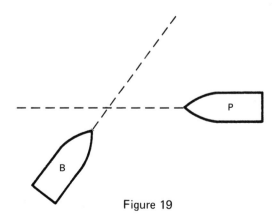

Figure 19

Seamen tend to keep an extra keen eye on their "arc of burden," the starboard side. The next time you're in the harbor, notice the radar antennas on large ships. Whenever possible the radar mast will be in line with the keel. But if offset, you'll see that most of the time it will be on the starboard side. When radar blind spots must result from masts and cargo booms, they are better on the port bow. It is almost intuitive for the seaman to take special pains in observing traffic to starboard. He tries to look everyplace, but he knows that as to traffic to starboard, he must do the avoiding.

Even so, problems arise. A tug, for example, tied up on the port side of a high barge may have difficulty in observation. She should allow for it by posting a lookout in a clear spot on the tug or barge. But that might not be done. And the watch officer standing on the port wing of a freighter's bridge may have his starboard bow blocked by masts and booms. He should be alert to both bows, particularly to the starboard; but he does walk across the bridge from starboard to port while on watch. And he might be over there at the wrong time. For the pleasure mariner, it's another case of knowing what can interfere, and then making allowances.

The contrast between International and Inland requirements when crossing should be noted. Look again at **Figure 19**. Under International, **P** must hold his course and speed; but he makes no whistle signal to indicate it to **B**. For under International, he will not signal unless he actually changes course or goes astern, or is in doubt whether **B** is doing enough to avoid collision. But until he changes course, or until he goes astern, or until he doubts, he just keeps coming silently.

B, on the other hand, keeps clear by any means that will not cross **P**'s course. He can go left, go right, slow down, stop or reverse. He just doesn't cross ahead. If he slows down, he gives no signal. If he goes left, he sounds two blasts **when** he begins to turn. If he goes right, he sounds one blast **when** he begins to turn. If he goes astern on his engines, he sounds three blasts when he does so. But if he doubts the situation, he cannot give the five-blast **danger signal**, for that is limited to **P**.

Under Inland Rules, though, the picture is quite different. **P** holds course and speed, but he announces his intention by blowing one blast. And **B** must answer. The Pilot Rules require **B** to avoid **P** by turning right and passing behind him, or else by slowing down, stopping or going astern. But **B** cannot go left. If either **P** or **B** has a doubt, he can blow the danger signal of at least four short blasts.

So far, the obvious differences are these:
1. International . . . **B** can turn left or right.
   Inland . . . . **B** can only turn right.

2. International . . . **P** gives no signal until he changes course.
   or goes astern or doubts **B**'s action.
   Inland . . . . **P** signals intention to hold course and speed.

3. International . . . only **P** can signal doubt.
   Inland . . . . either **P** or **B** can blow the danger signal.

What happens when **B** decides to cross ahead? Under International, **P** can blow the doubt signal and then maneuver under **Rule 27**, meeting any of the special circumstances that arise. Inland, **B** would first have blown two blasts. This puts **P** on the spot. If he agrees by answering with two, what has developed is an agreement to change the rules. **B** does not then become privileged. It is he who suggested the new conduct; **P** has only deferred to his judgment. **P** need not accept, however . . . and, until he does, **B** must not start his unusual maneuver.

This discussion might sound somewhat unnecessary. But think a moment how easily the situation could arise. Look at **Figure 20**. **P** is a tug with a string of barges stretched out hundreds of feet behind. The speed of this long procession is five knots. **B** is a powerboat moving at 10 knots. They are each one-half mile from the intersection of their course lines. **P** will be there in six minutes; **B** can get there in three minutes. The temptation arises for **B** to cross ahead. He had better make it, because in the attempt he will probably be betting on success. Even if **P** assents to the maneuver, he doesn't become an accomplice. He is relieved of the burden of holding course and speed, and then adopts a "wait and see" attitude. The next move is up to **B**. **P** can slow down; he probably should slow down. But he **need not** slow down. It was **B** who said he could make it, based, presumably, on an observation of **P**'s course and speed.

Actually, both **B** and **P** are foolish. If there is a risk of collision as they approach, they should not improvise. **P** should keep going and **B** should stay clear. Then the problems will nearly always evaporate.

What happens if **P**, a Good Samaritan, offers to let **B** pass ahead? This is just as foolish. Until **B** agrees, **P** must keep going as before. And by the time **B** does agree, **P** might be so close he wants to change his mind. Then everyone will have

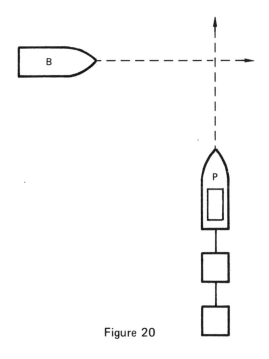

Figure 20

to straighten out the tangle caused by misguided courtesy. If **B** agrees in time, they must operate under the special circumstances as they emerge. The confusion that can arise is a high price to pay. The rules are based on predictability; special circumstance is "playing it by ear," and dangerous.

Everyone has seen two pedestrians meet at a street corner and, like Alphonse and Gaston, give way together and lock elbows. Vessels don't just lock elbows; they break open gaping holes to let tons of water crash aboard. The rules are products of painful experience, and should be followed to the letter.

In every crossing situation on the High Seas, **P**'s hair tends to get a little bit grayer. He must hold course and speed, but he cannot signal. **B** will not signal until he does something. So **P** keeps a wary eye to port, as they come closer together. How long must he wait for **B** to show avoiding action? It is his job to remain reasonably predictable and to give **B** every chance to avoid him. But for how long? The answer in words is . . . until it is apparent that no action by **B** alone can avert a collision. But how different the words work out in practice! **P** can't be too doubtful and take action too early; he might move just when **B** moves and actually cause a collision. But he can't be too trusting either. For he has a paramount duty to keep out of collisions.

This much is clear: the privileged vessel is very definitely burdened. He **must** hold course and speed. There is no "may" or "might" or "if he wants to" about it. And he must do it for so long as, in his seamanlike judgment, **B** can still avoid him. However, as soon as that point is reached, then **P** must act. The whistle signals are certainly attractive in the light of this discussion. Under International Rules, **P** can give the five blasts when doubt sets in . . . and should do so. If that doesn't wake **B** up, then **P** can prepare to break off. Under Inland, **P** should at the outset give the one-blast signal for holding course and speed. If there's going to be confusion, he can expose it early in the game.

When two sailing vessels are crossing, their general maneuvering rules found in **Rule** 17 and in **Article 17** apply. And they nearly always are privileged over the power vessels they meet. **Rule 20** and **Article 20** give them this edge. But **Rule 20(b)** expresses a limitation which good seamanship has always implied: there is no right to hamper, in a narrow channel, the safe passage of a power vessel which can only navigate inside such channel.

To summarize:

1. When meeting, you are burdened to the vessel on your starboard.
2. The burdened vessel keeps clear.
3. The privileged vessel remains predictable by holding course and speed.

When these things are done, there are no collisions. When not done, everyone begins to worry.

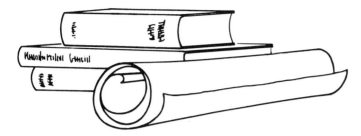

12/Charts and Publications
Use of a chart, continued

There is still more to learn from a close study of *C&GS No. 5142.* So in this section we will again examine reproductions of parts of that chart.

First, to **Plate C**, which shows the area around Santa Catalina Island. The water contour lines, or fathom curves, emphasize the character of the island as a large undersea mountain rising from ocean valleys off the continent. Its coast is particularly steep-to on the northeast side. But on the southwest and south the 100-fathom curve fans outward almost four miles. On this irregular shelf where depths of less than 100 fathoms are shown, the chart indicates several types of bottom. The abbreviations used are found summarized in **READY REFERENCE** . . . and completely discussed in *C&GS Chart No. 1,* as already mentioned.

Let's start at Avalon Bay and go clockwise around the island, noting the chart symbols for bottom characteristic. Off Pebbly Beach, it is *shells (Sh).* Near Jewfish Point, it is *sand (S).* Close to East End Light and Church Rock, it continues sand; but farther offshore to the southeast, it is *rocky (rky).*

In the open bight between Church Rock and Salta Verde Point, the showing is mixed: sand, rocky, *sand and mud (SM)* and *sand and shells (SSh).* Around China Point to Little Harbor, it is sand and rocky. Midway between there and Catalina Harbor, a patch of *mud (M)* is found. From there on, the coastal shelf is a mixture of the types already found: rocky, sand, shells, mud, and combinations of them.

Little Harbor on the west side is at the head of a submarine valley, Catalina Canyon. This crease in the Earth plunges from sea level to a depth of more than 3000 feet in less than seven miles.

There are few offshore rocks that bear names. Church Rock off East End is marked as:

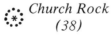 *Church Rock*
(38)

The symbol * indicates a rock. The dotted circle around it can be taken as a fathom curve . . . Church Rock rises from a pedestal less than three fathoms deep. The bracketed numerals *(38)* show that the rock is always uncovered and its height is 38 feet above Mean High Water.

Eagle Rock, near West End, is shown with this symbol: 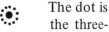 The dot is also indicative of a rock. And the dotted circle could be the three-

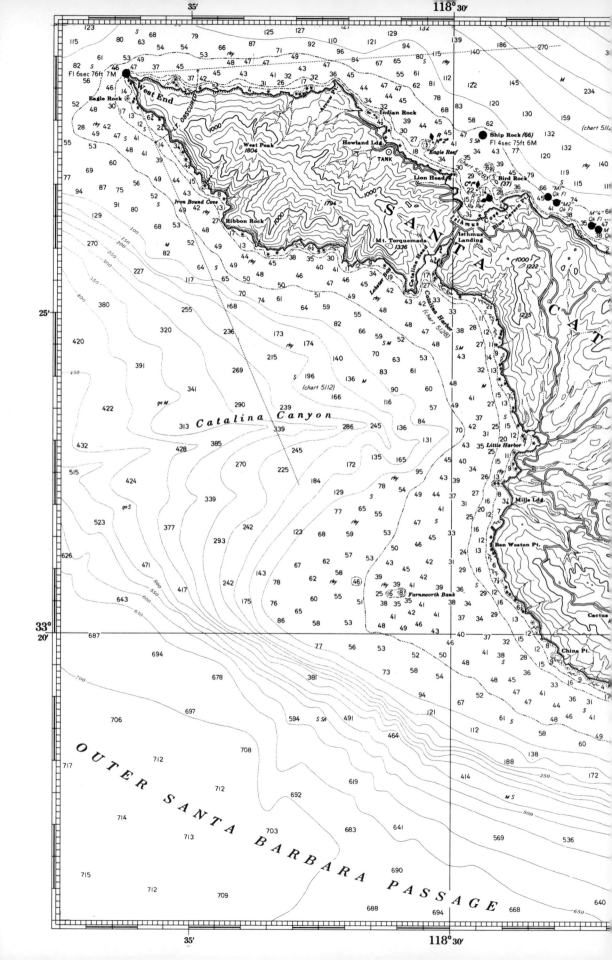

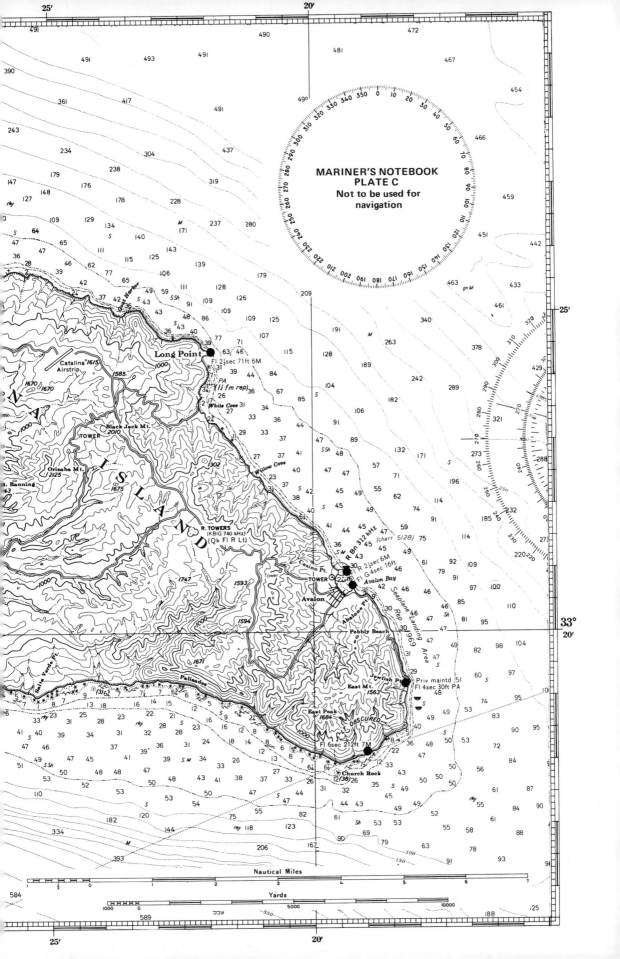

MARINER'S NOTEBOOK
PLATE C
Not to be used for
navigation

fathom curve. However, an alternative meaning for the rock symbol circled by dots is "dangerous to navigation." Note that no height of Eagle Rock above sea level is shown. In fact, Eagle Rock rises well above the sea at all times. Farther down the west coast, almost to Iron Bound Cove, is a very similar symbol near the 10-fathom curve. Without local knowledge, how can we tell which one is always above and which might be awash? To be on the safe side, read that symbol as a rock, sunken or otherwise, which in any case is at no more than three fathoms and should be considered a danger to navigation.

Moving down the northeast coast, we note Ship Rock and Bird Rock as obvious above-water objects, with the elevations in feet given in brackets.

Now let's start again at Avalon and go clockwise around the island noting some other symbols and abbreviations. At the north end of Avalon Bay, the symbol ⬛ is a mooring buoy. Also note the marking for a radiobeacon (*RBn*), with a frequency of *312 kHz*.

Two more mooring buoys are seen south of Jewfish Point. At East End Light note two long dotted lines radiating outward. An arc is drawn between the lines on the north side and marked *Lt. Obscured*. This indicates that the steep cliffs on the shore block off the light to the north, or above, the dotted lines.

Close to the shore, notice the markings for many sunken rocks: dangerous (marked ∴+∴), and otherwise (marked +). Also, note the kelp beds (marked ⫞⫞).

On the southern coast, between the Palisades and Salta Verde Point, is a dangerous rock jutting three feet above Mean High Water. The symbol is ⦿ (*3*).

The inshore markings follow the same general pattern all the way around to West End. There, another obscured light sector is shown.

Eagle Reef, just north of Isthmus Cove, is marked with a symbol for a buoy:

◆ *R*
• *N "2"*

The meaning: it is unlighted, is painted red, is nun or conical in shape, and it is numbered as 2.

Between Long Point and White's Cove we see this:

 (1½ fm rep)

This is unscrambled to show a sunken wreck. The position is approximate. The wreck is always submerged, and a depth of 1½ fathoms over it has been reported.

Just above Casino Point, a Restricted Area is shown. The reference, *207.620,* is to a Navigation Regulation of the Army Corps of Engineers, found reprinted in the *Coast Pilot 7.* In this case the restriction is:

§ 207.620   **Pacific Ocean in vicinity of Santa Catalina Island, Calif.; seaplane restricted area near Avalon.** (a) The area. Beginning at White Rock; thence 55° true, 5,000 feet; thence 325° true, 5,000 feet; thence 235° true, 5,400

feet; thence southeasterly along the shoreline to the point
of beginning.

(b) The regulations. This area is reserved for the use
of seaplane landings and take-offs. Floats or buoys are prohibited, except those authorized by the Department of the
Army. Anchoring of vessels is prohibited. Vessels are not
prohibited from passing through this area provided they
proceed as expeditiously as practicable by the most direct
route, and give seaplanes the right-of-way at all times.

Now a look at the land. Along the coastline, the comb-like short lines, **hachures**, show steep cliffs. The roads are easily found: as, for example, leading
from Avalon past the KBIG radio towers and then looping around in several
directions.

At many spots—for instance, near China Point at the southwest corner of the
island—notice the beaded broken lines leading from the shore inland. These are
intermittent streams. It is hard to find anything but such occasional streams on
Santa Catalina. Perhaps the only exceptions are those very short lines (but solid
and so indicating constant stream) found running down to the shore at Jewfish
Point and on either side of East End Light.

Not much detail is given for each of the island's harbors . . . Avalon Bay, Isthmus Cove and Catalina Harbor. Data given here are not adequate for entering any
of them. But the notation (*Chart 5128*) found at each refers to a larger scale chart
which depicts the three in close-up views.

The landbased lights maintained by the Coast Guard around the island are at
East End, West End, Ship Rock, Long Point, and one on each side of the entrance
to **Avalon Bay.** Privately maintained is one at **Jewfish Point.** The particulars are
shown by:

1. **The signal:** flashing in each case.
2. **The period:** every six seconds for East End and West End; four seconds
   at Ship Rock, the south side of Avalon entrance and the private light at
   Jewfish Point; 2½ seconds at Long Point and on the north side of
   Avalon entrance.
3. **The height of the light above Mean High Water:** 212 feet at East End, 76
   feet at West End, 75 feet at Ship Rock, 71 feet at Long Point, 16 feet
   for each of the Avalon entrance lights, and 30 feet for the private light.
4. **The range:** seven miles for East End and West End, six miles for Ship
   Rock, Long Point and the Avalon entrance lights, and none indicated for
   the private light at Jewfish Point.

The Avalon lights are colored: red on the right side entering and green on the left.
All the others are white, for no color abbreviation is shown. The private light is
also marked as *PA;* its position is to be considered as approximate. The importance of that notation to a navigator using the light as a reference for bearings is
quite evident.

The period of each light has importance. Timing the interval between flashes is

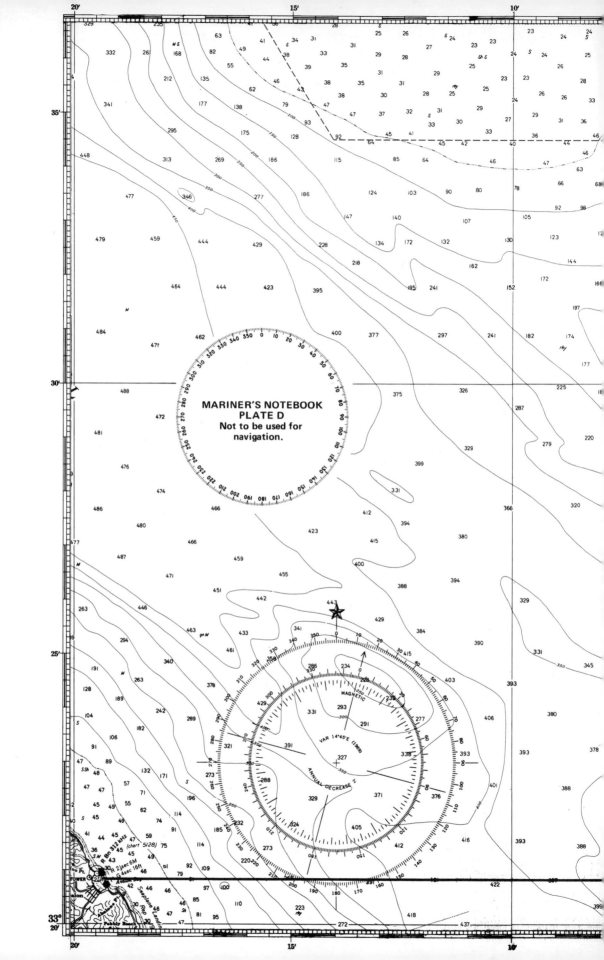

MARINER'S NOTEBOOK
PLATE D
Not to be used for
navigation.

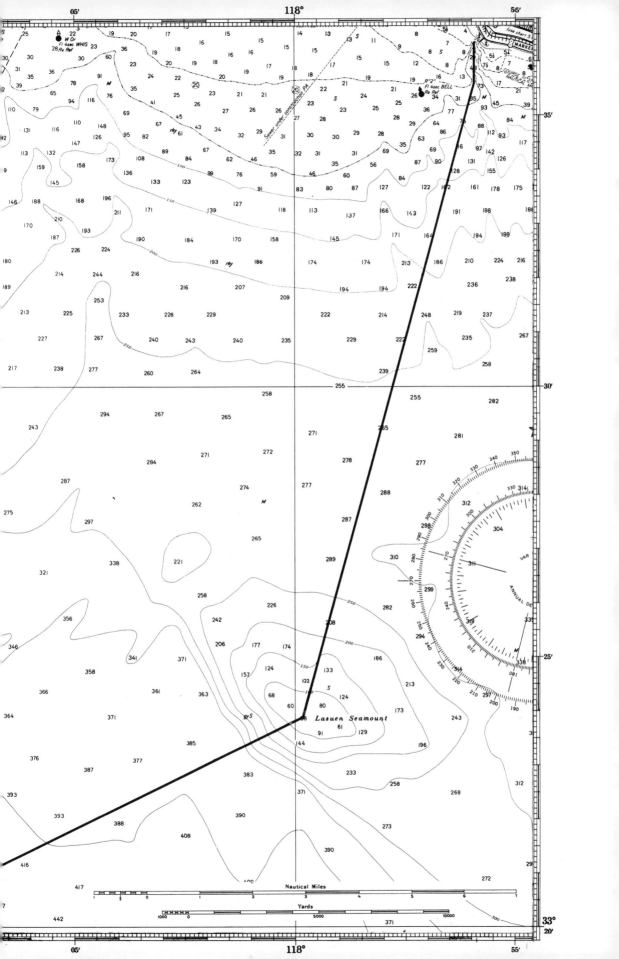

a key to identity. And the chances for confusion are not very great. East End and West End have the same period; but they are at opposite ends of the island and miles apart. The same is true of Ship Rock and Jewfish Point. And the Avalon entrance lights are unique by color.

Note also the relationship between height and range. More of this will be found in later chapters. But enough here to spotlight these examples. West End, Ship Rock and Long Point are all about the same height, 71 to 76 feet. And by the geometry of the earth's curves, the range for each to the sea level horizon is, rounded off, 10 miles. An observer at an arbitrary standard height of 15 feet could be about 4½ miles farther back and still pick up these lights. So the **geographic range** of each to such an observer is 14 miles. East End, at 212 feet high, is three times the height of any of them. Based on geography, its range to that 15-foot observer should be 21 miles. The two lights at Avalon Bay should reach out to our observer at nine miles. But all this doesn't square with the ranges listed on the chart. Instead of being 21 miles, East End shows up as visible only seven . . . the same as West End. Ship Rock, Long Point, and the Avalon lights appear as six miles. The private aid at Jewfish Point bears no estimate of range. How come? Each light on Santa Catalina is described on the chart by **nominal range** . . . based on its strength and presuming a clear atmosphere. None of them has sufficient power to reach out to our standard observer; and it's basic that range depends on power as well as height. A penny match on East End's 212-foot point of vantage would not have the range of a three-cell flashlight on Church Rock, 175 feet lower. Another chapter will explore all this in greater detail. Enough for now to say it is often, but not always, true that the high light is the first seen.

Near each peak on the land you'll find its elevation marked in feet. **Orizaba** is the high point at 2125 feet. **Black Jack** is next at 2010. And **West Peak**, near the western tip, is third highest at 1804. Near each elevation number is a dot; this marks the peak. An example: just inland from **China Point** on the southwest shore you find:

Cactus Peak
1560

The use that a careful navigator can make of all this disconnected information is surprising. The more knowledge available, the better prepared he is for the unexpected. But even in normal operation, he will find it useful to know the exact location of **Cactus Peak** . . . maybe it's his only reference for a bearing. Or if he is near **Ben Weston Point**, a sudden finding of eight fathoms by hand lead or echo sounder would be explained by **Farnsworth Bank**. Knowing that **East End Light** is invisible for more than three miles south of **Salta Verde Point** would save him from worry when it didn't show up as he coasted down the southwest shore. The value of knowing there are offshore mooring buoys near **Jewfish Point** is obvious. And being aware of the wreck near **Long Point** might be worth the price of a new anchor. But, in addition, there is more pleasure to boating when you know more of the surroundings. The chart is an encyclopedia of such knowledge.

But now for another dimension. Some people find it strangely reassuring that, no matter where they travel at sea, they will never be more than half a dozen miles from land . . . straight down. But those of us with less imagination seldom think of the ocean floor. Until recently it was the rare seafarer who had an interest in what lay beneath his keel. The limit of inquiry was usually: "Is there water enough?" or "Will the bottom hold an anchor?" Lately though, we've all begun to realize that, after centuries of exploration on the rim of this planet, the greater part of its surface is still unknown. But modern Magellans are changing all that. And to mariners the sea has a new character.

Plate D is a reproduction of another part of *5142.* This time the water area to the south of Newport Bay is shown. Our aim is to look at it from an oceanographer's viewpoint. But first we must get rid of the water. So . . . out comes the plug and Catalina Channel is drained dry.

Now a very strange world suddenly appears. Peaks, valleys and deep canyons are uncovered between the mainland and the enormous mountain that is Santa Catalina. Let's take a quick trip along the bottom. And perhaps, by studying the fathom curves and soundings on the chart, we can picture the scene.

Our departure point is a small pier off Newport Peninsula. Close to shore is a ledge of hard sand, shelving to the northwest to several miles wide. But at the pier, it narrows to the brink of a steep gorge.

Within 100 yards is the brim of a green chasm and our path leads south down its center. After a short half mile of slipping down its walls, we are on a ledge 400 feet below the rim. And the next five miles are spent sliding over tilting shelves of gray-green mud until we reach the floor of a long wide plain which slopes gently down to a low pit far ahead. Behind us now the mainland stands more than 1500 feet up to the sky.

On we go southward along the easy slope of the floor. Ahead looms **Lasuen Seamount,** heaped on the rim of another slope. From its 20-square-mile base, the eastern face grades up a thousand feet to an almost level lid and then tumbles down twice as far in less than a mile. We trudge up its northern side, then skid along the steps and folds slanting towards the true sea bed, far to the west.

Now our steps turn west towards the peaks of a gigantic Santa Catalina, which towers almost 5000 feet. We plod along a canted waste of mud and sand almost half a mile below Newport Beach. At last . . . the hard climb up the east wall of the island. The first mile brings us up 300 feet. But from then on, as we scramble over the terraced ridges, we climb 1800 feet in barely four miles to emerge in the bowl of Avalon Bay.

The dog-leg track has led us some 30 miles from Newport Beach . . . first south and then a long westerly reach. The lowest point is about 2500 feet below the buoy. For nearly the whole trek, the bottom is more than 1200 feet down. And **Lasuen's** cap comes within 350 feet of the surface level some 13 miles from where we left.

It's fascinating to ponder on this unseen world of mountains and plains. In fact, on stormy days when Warning Flags are up, why not become an armchair Captain Nemo? All it takes is a chart and some imagination. And, in the process, you will begin to think in terms of the nautical chart . . . which was why on **Plate D** we took the long, hard way to reach Casino Point.

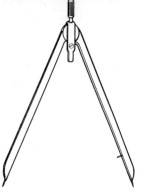

13/Piloting
The five special cases

Position finding by bearings of the same landmark is a large part of piloting. Let's start with an example and see what we are going to discuss. In **Figure 21** a ship travels north at six knots. At 0800 Lighthouse **A** bears 45° on the starboard bow. At 0900 it bears 90°, or is abeam. In the hour between bearings the ship moves six miles. By applying the elements of geometry, the navigator learns he is six miles off the light when it is abeam.

In this chapter we'll see how he finds distance off by two successive bearings when he knows the distance run on course between them. And particularly we'll investigate five special bearing combinations which yield quick mental solutions to the problem.

All practical navigation is usually done with no higher mathematical application beyond division. But since the bases of piloting are found in higher mathematics, all condensed into suitable tables or rules of thumb for immediate use, a restatement of some "common knowledge" facts is in order.

1. A **circle** has 360°

A **straight line** has 180°

2. A **right angle** has 90°   An **acute angle** has less

An **obtuse angle** has more

3. The three angles in a plane triangle always total 180° . . .
   In each case, $A + B + C = 180°$

4. When two angles in a triangle are equal, the sides opposite them are equal . . . this is an **Isosceles Triangle**:
   if Angle A = Angle B, then
       Side a = Side b

Now let's take another look at the six-knot ship off Lighthouse **A**. **Figure** 22 is a right triangle. **BC** is a straight line which at **C** is divided into two 90° angles by the line **AC**. Angle **C** in the triangle is, then, 90°. Angle **B** is known to be 45°. So it follows, that angle **A** is also 45° . . . for **A+B+C=180°**. Since angles **A** and **B** are equal, side **AC** must equal side **BC**.

To the navigator, **A** is the lighthouse and **BC** is his course line. At **B** he took a 45° bearing; at **C** he took a 90° or beam bearing. **BC** is the distance run between the bearings. **AC** is the distance off the lighthouse when it is abeam. If he runs six miles from **B** to **C**, then at **C** he is six miles off the lighthouse . . . the distance off abeam equals the distance run between bearings.

This is the well-known **45° . . . 90°** or **Bow & Beam** Rule, and is a basic tool in piloting. We'll call it **Case 1** and describe it this way:

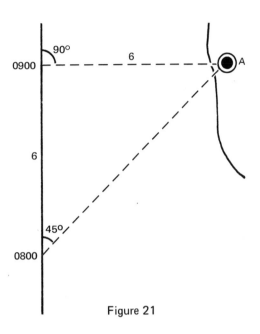

Figure 21

Case I, Bow & Beam
When the First Bearing is 45°; and the Second Bearing is 90°; then
Distance Off Abeam = Distance Run Between Bearings.

Another combination is **Figure 23**. Here, the second φ (meet the symbol for bearing) is twice the first. We've made them 36° and 72°; but they can be other values, so long as the second value is twice the first. Angle **C** in the sketch must be 108°, for a straight line has 180°, and **C** is 180°-72°. Angle **A** must be 36°, for the three angles of a triangle total 180°; and since **B+C= 144°**, then **A** is 180°-144°, or 36°. No matter the values, if the second is twice the first, **A** will always equal **B** . . . and side **AC**, in turn, will always equal side **BC**. The distance off at the second bearing equals the distance run between bearings.

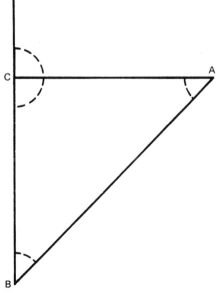

Figure 22

And this is . . .

Case II, Doubling the Angle on the Bow:
   When the 2nd ϕ = Twice the 1st ϕ; then
Distance Off at 2nd ϕ = Distance Run Between ϕs

Note that Case I is also one of Doubling, for 90° is twice 45°. The difference . . . in Case I, the second ϕ is abeam, so the distance off at second ϕ is also the distance off abeam. But in Case II, the second ϕ is not abeam, and the distance off there is not the distance off abeam. Other combinations are needed for that.

One of these is **Case III.** Here the first ϕ is 30° and the second ϕ is 60°. Since this is Doubling, we know side **AC=BC** . . . Distance Off at 60° = Distance Run Between Bearings. But, look at **Figure 24.** When the angle combination is 30° . . . 60°, we can also find **AD**, the distance off abeam. It is 7/8 or 0.87 times the distance run. If **BC** is 10 miles, we are 10 miles off at **C**, and will be 10 x 0.87, or 8.7 miles off at **D**, abeam of that lighthouse.

This is **Case III, 7/8 Rule:**
   When 1st ϕ = 30°; and
      2nd ϕ = 60°; then
Distance Off at 60° = Distance Run;
Distance Off Abeam = 7/8 Distance Run.

On to the next special case, **IV.** This is the 22½° . . . 45° combination. Look at **Figure 25.** Since 45° is double 22½°, we know by Case II that the distance off at 45° equals **BC**, the distance run from 22½° to 45°. What makes this a special rule is that the distance off abeam (**DA**) is 0.7 of the distance run.

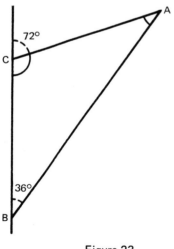

Figure 23

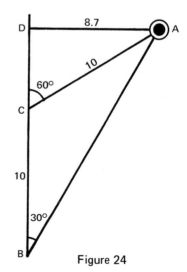

Figure 24

The rule is stated this way:

Case IV, 22½° . . . 45° or 0.7 Rule:
When the 1st ϕ = 22½°; and
the 2nd ϕ = 45°; then
Distance Off at 45° = Distance Run;
Distance Off Abeam = 0.7 Distance Run.

Another thing about Case IV: the distance off abeam is the side **AD**. It is equal to **CD** . . . the distance to run from the 45° ϕ to abeam. So we can predict not only the distance off abeam, but also the distance from 45° to abeam . . . and so, the time abeam. Take this example: A ship traveling at 10 knots takes a 22½° ϕ at 0800 and a 45° ϕ at 0900. The distance run is one hour at 10 knots, or 10 miles. And the distance off the lighthouse at C is 10 miles. The distance off abeam, at **D**, will be 10 x 0.7, or seven miles. So the distance to run from **C** to **D** must also be seven miles. At 10 knots this will take 0.7 of an hour, or 42 minutes. So the lighthouse will be abeam at 0942. ,

This brings us to **Case V**, the 26½° . . . 45° combination. Here, we do not have doubling the angle, for 45° is not twice 26½°. It is a special rule for other reasons. In **Figure 26** the distance run, **BC**, equals the distance off abeam, **AD**. And the distance off at 45° (at **C**) is 1.4 times the distance run. As soon as we know **AD**, the distance off abeam, we also know **CD**, the distance to run from 45° to abeam . . . they are equal. So we can state this rule in these words:

Case V, 26½° . . . 45 or Prediction Bearings:
When the 1st ϕ = 26½°; and
the 2nd ϕ = 45°; then
Distance Off Abeam = Distance Run
Distance off at 45° = 1.4 x Distance Run
Distance from 45° to Abeam = Distance Run

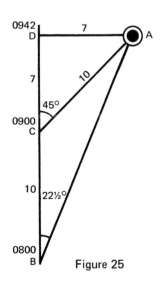

Figure 25

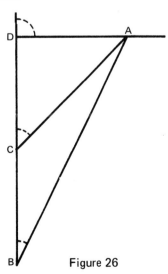

Figure 26

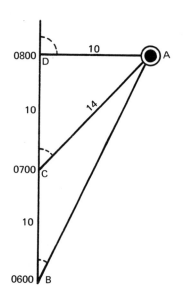

Figure 27

An example is shown in **Figure 27**. A 10-knot vessel takes a 26½° φ at 0600 and a 45° φ at 0700. The run between the two bearings is one hour, or 10 miles. So, at **C**, the second φ, she is 1.4 x 10 or 14 miles off the lighthouse. When the light is abeam, at **D**, the ship will be 10 miles off. Also . . . the distance to run from **C** to **D** will be 10 miles. This will take one hour at her speed, so she will be abeam of the lighthouse at 0800.

Since the distance off abeam and the time are predicted by this rule, it is called the **Prediction Bearing Case**.

In **READY REFERENCE** you'll find a chart restating these five special cases. Look at it now, and then keep it handy for use when underway.

14/Weather
Air masses and fronts

Beneath an aircraft flying at 36,000 feet lies the troposphere, a layer of air containing 75% of our atmosphere. Above for hundreds of miles stretch other layers with less and less air until finally space itself is reached. We say the pilot flies above the weather, and that is true. For in the belt of air from the surface to a height of about seven miles occur the changes which produce our ordinary weather.

What about the air beneath his wings? Chemically, it is a mixture of many gases; and the chemical makeup varies little. Like sugar, air is air. But it certainly isn't true that in every respect air is the same the world over. For air masses acquire distinct personalities. They vary in temperature, in pressure, in the amount of water vapor they contain.

If the pilot could see these characteristics, he would know immediately how different one column above the surface was from those alongside. It might be colder, or perhaps more moist. Maybe it would press more on the surface. He would also see one column undercutting another, or rising above it. He would see these masses flowing along the surface, being first over one spot and then moving on to cover another. In effect, he would see what we can only detect by measurements of pressure, heat and other factors. He would see surface weather in the making.

Try to picture, then, these differing columns of air resting on the surface. And let's talk a little about how they got to be different, how they change their form and substance, and how they move about.

The basic cause of personality traits in an air mass is the nature of the surface beneath it. When a column rests on a warm ocean, it will not only be heated by the surface; it will also receive quite a bit of water vapor. The mass will tend to become warm and moist. But one rising above the steppes of Russia will be colder and drier. The one stopping over a tropical rain forest will differ from that over a high plateau. Surface material, texture, shape and location have tremendous control over the nature of the air mass above.

We've already noted that warmer air rises, that as it rises it expands and cools, that as it cools it reaches saturation, and that, when saturated, it releases water back to the surface. Nature has built in a remarkable cycle to maintain a balance

A B-57 airplane from NOAA's Research Flight Facility gathers weather data.

of heat and water throughout the atmosphere. The warmer air, since it is rising, will exert less pressure on the surface; it is partly pushing up against gravity and offsetting some of the burden of its weight. Colder air, more dense, exerts higher pressure. A warm air mass goes together with low pressure and a cold air mass suggests high pressure. Notice again, "warm" and "cold", and "high" and "low" are relative terms. "Warm" is warmer than something else; "low" has less pressure than another area.

When you are on the surface beneath a cold mass, you have one kind of weather. But should that mass move away and be replaced by a warm sector, the weather will change. The temperature will rise and the barometer will fall. Moreover, since warm air can hold more water vapor than cold, the new air can be more moist. Not only that . . . while the substitution is being made, you have a different sequence of weather.

For remember, air masses do not tend to mix and dilute each other. Rather, they collide along a battle line called a "front" and push each other around until one has nudged the other along either by undermining or by overriding. If a warm mass is replacing a cold, the fracas is a **warm front.** If the cold is shouldering out the warm, it is a **cold front.** And the weather caused by each situation is quite predictable.

Warm air supplants cold by overlapping the cold mass along a gentle incline. **Figure 28** shows the disposition of the two, along a warm front. Notice that the warm flows up over the cold far in advance of the main body of the warm sector. As the warm mass slides up the incline, it cools and produces clouds. First they are very high; then they form at lower and lower altitudes as, progressively, more and more warm air is overhead. Finally the cold is nudged on and the surface is beneath warm air. The weather to be expected while this is all taking place? No better description than the following sentences found on Page 802, 1962 Edition, of *American Practical Navigator (HO No. 9),* the famous "Bowditch" published by the Navy Oceanographic Office:

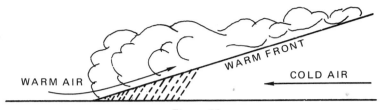

Figure 28

"The approach of a well-developed warm front is usually heralded not only by falling pressure, but also by a more-or-less regular sequence of clouds. First, cirrus appear. These give way successively to cirrostratus, altostratus, altocumulus and nimbostratus. Brief showers may precede the steady rain accompanying the nimbostratus.

"As the warm front passes, the temperature rises, the wind shifts to the right (in the northern hemisphere) and the steady rain stops. Drizzle may fall from low-lying stratus clouds, or there may be fog for some time after the wind shift. During passage of the **warm sector** between the warm front and the cold front, there is little change in temperature or pressure. However, if the wave is still growing and the low deepening, the pressure might slowly decrease. In the warm sector the skies are generally clear or partly cloudy, with cumulus or stratocumulus clouds most frequent. The warm air is usually moist, and haze or fog may often be present."

But when cold air is on the move to invade a warm sector, the picture is quite different. The denser cold mass won't ride over the top of the warm; it will undermine it. **Figure 29** shows how the forces are deployed along this battle line, along a **cold front**. And the abrupt push upwards of the warm air by the cold produces more violent weather. The sequence of that weather, as described on the same Page 802 of Bowditch, is this:

"As the faster-moving, steeper cold front passes, the wind shifts abruptly to the right (in the northern hemisphere), the temperature falls rapidly, and there are often brief and sometimes violent showers, frequently accompanied by thunder and

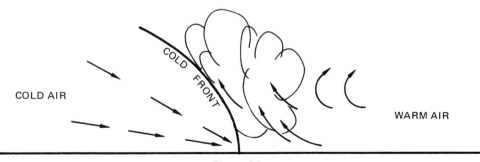

Figure 29

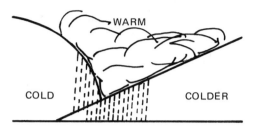

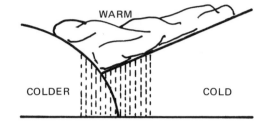

Figure 30   Figure 31

lightning. Clouds are usually of the convective type. A cold
front usually coincides with a well-defined **wind-shift line**, (a
line along which the wind shifts abruptly from southerly or
southwesterly to northerly or northwesterly in the northern
hemisphere and from northerly or northwesterly to southerly
or southwesterly in the southern hemisphere). At sea a series
of brief showers accompanied by strong, shifting winds may
occur along or some distance (up to 200 miles) ahead of a cold
front. These are called **squalls,** and the line along which they
occur is called a **squall line.** Because of its greater speed and
steeper slope, which may approach or even exceed the vertical
near the earth's surface (due to friction), a cold front and its
associated weather passes more quickly than a warm front.
After a cold front passes, the pressure rises, often quite rapidly,
the visibility usually improves, and the clouds tend to diminish.''

In close pursuit of a warm mass that is overtaking a cold will come still another
cold. And the complete sequence of weather from departure of the first cold mass
through passage of the warm sector to arrival of the second cold would be a
combination of **Figures** 28 and **29.** Sooner or later, though, the pursuing cold is
going to catch up with the point where the warm front line touches the surface of
the earth. The warm will then be pinched out or occluded from surface contact.
This is an **occluded front.** How the two cold masses will meet depends on which is
the colder. In **Figure 30** you'll see the chase of a warm sector after a cold, (to the
right), with a not-so-cold catching up from the left. The cool air to the left
undercuts the warm; but when it meets the cold air, it begins to ride up over the
top. In **Figure 31**, the reverse happens. There, the warm is still chasing after a cold
(to the right). But charging in from the left is still colder air. When it meets the
cold air, it will begin to undercut the cold as well as the warm, and push both of
them aloft.

The warm sector we've discussed is a low pressure area, or a **Low.** The cold
sector is a **High.** When the Low is surrounded by High, the colder air will undercut
from every side, seeking to flow into the Low from all directions at once. But,
remember back in the first chapter on Weather we mentioned the diversion of
wind movement caused by the spin of the Earth . . . the **Coriolis Force?** Well, it
swings the wind movement at the front lines to the right in the northern hemisphere and to the left in the southern. In the northern hemisphere, the air from the

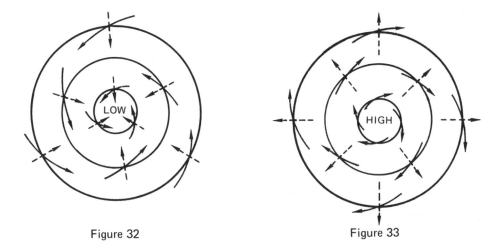

| Figure 32 | Figure 33 |

High moves, not directly to the Low, but turns to the right. What develops is a circular wind motion around the Low . . . clockwise in the southern hemisphere, where the wind deflection is to the left, but counterclockwise in the northern hemisphere. **Figure** 32 is a sketch of such a northern hemisphere condition. Notice that the air from the High is slanted to the right as it flows inward, and so ends up as a counterclockwise swirl. This is a **cyclone**. The name itself suggests a violent, twisting monster of a wind. But actually a cyclone is any movement of wind around a low pressure center. Should the warm air mass be large and the increase in pressure throughout the high area be gentle and gradual, there will be no shattering force to the wind. This is the usual middle latitude cyclonic disturbance, or the extratropical cyclone. But if the Low is small and the pressure difference abrupt, the circumstances are those of a tropical cyclone . . . and that is a real danger. Whether it is called hurricane or typhoon is only geographical; all are vicious, tropical-born disturbances caused by severe Lows surrounded by Highs.

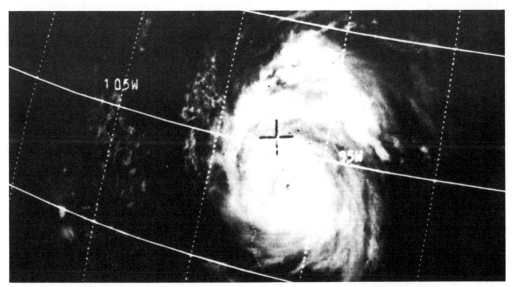

Satellite view of Hurricane Beulah southwest of New Orleans.

Photo by NOAA

Water spout reaching from low clouds to sea.

A whirlwind of dust skimming across an empty lot is a miniature cyclone . . . and the twist should be counterclockwise in the northern hemisphere. Fill your washbasin with water and then pull the plug. Notice the dry core at the drain? That is a Low and the water rushing into the drain around it is in the High. The flood is not directly into the center . . . it is diverted into a circular motion around the center. All things being equal, the swirl should be counterclockwise in the northern hemisphere. We have many daily examples of the action that, on an enormous scale, produces cyclonic storms. And there was at least one knowing sailorman who injected this bit of weather lore into his "line" for the girl in every port . . . he could always tell an Australian girl by the clockwise curl to her hair.

When a high pressure pocket is ringed by a low, a different situation develops. The High will again seek to flow to the Low. And in the northern hemisphere it will again be diverted to the right. But here a whirling funnel does not form around the center; for there is plenty of room for the High to spin clear, like the sparks from a Fourth of July pinwheel. **Figure 33** is a sketch of this high pressure pocket, the anticyclone, as found in the northern hemisphere. Note that the winds from the center turn to the right, causing a clockwise swirl. South of the Equator, they would turn left. Southern California has particular interest in the anticyclone because of its place in the development of the local **Santa Ana** wind. When a High develops over the mountain states of the Far West so there is an appreciable difference in pressure between its center and the Coast, winds will blow out from the center and start towards the Coast. Dust is picked up by the dry air as it passes over Nevada and southern Arizona; and it arrives at the Coast as a cloudless, dusty gale.

Next time a closer look at some examples of local weather, tying it in to the generalities already discussed . . . and also a chance to see how some of the choice weather rhymes of seamen stand up to the test of science.

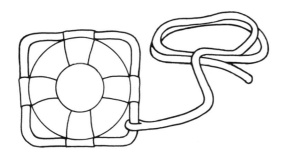

15/Safety Afloat
Precautions and drills

Suppose a friend suggests you invest $500 in his new business. When you ask about his experience and about the equipment needed, and about the details of operation, he replies:

> "Well, frankly, I've never done this before. As a matter of fact, I've never even tried out the equipment. Actually, I haven't given much thought to how I'd really go about all this.
>
> "But after all, any level-headed, fairly bright person should be able to handle this business.
>
> "Don't be a pessimist! I'm sure it will all work out perfectly the first time."

You'd think he was pretty stupid. Worse, you'd suspect he thought you were pretty stupid.

Now what about the boat owner who never bothers to think about an emergency? He has the equipment, but he's never used it. He's never visualized what he'd do if trouble comes. But he's sure he can handle it. Without a qualm he invests absolutely everything—his present and his future—in an untried, unplanned skill to do the right thing the very first time.

The fun of pleasure boating far, far outweighs any risk. But there are risks. Actually you can gain a lot of pleasure from the satisfaction of being prepared. There can be all kinds of emergencies, and we won't try to catalogue them. But let's discuss a few categories so the thought processes can start. It's surprising how much latent information each of us has, ready to be called out to meet the unexpected. We all have different skills to draw upon. But give them a break. Let them enjoy a little advance warning.

First of all, the medical emergency. Every boat should have a First Aid Kit and a First Aid Manual. There are several excellent marine kits on the market. Ask your physician for his recommendations. All bookstores offer good manuals.

Particularly, though, you should be familiar with a few basic procedures: artificial respiration, burns and bleeding, shock, heat stroke and heat exhaustion. **READY REFERENCE** sets out the instructions for these emergencies as found in official publications.

The next category is firefighting. We've already said much on this score. Here are a few additional suggestions. How about actually trying out a portable extinguisher? Have you ever done it? Maybe there isn't much to learn, but you will feel better by doing it. Take a bucket, aim the stream in it, and let fly. Use common sense, of course; don't do it unless you have another extinguisher for replacement; don't do it in an enclosed space; and be sure to recharge the extinguisher afterwards.

Take the trouble to find and to remember the location of important valves and pipes aboard. And trace out the wiring circuits so you know which goes to what. Run an occasional eye over connections and insulation. The ship isn't a fixed structure on dry land; she's always working in a pliable sea and in a moist atmosphere. Things can twist, break and also weather away.

How about a tool kit? Why not set aside a box for keeping a few basic emergency tools: screwdriver with insulated handle, hatchet, hammer, friction tape, pliers, crescent wrench, some assorted nuts and bolts, a piece of canvas and some twine, a small can of white lead, perhaps one of the new "strong as iron" patching compounds. The list can be long or short, and the items we've mentioned need not all be on it. But a kit is a good idea; select the tools your judgment suggests as good sense.

Have you ever worn a life preserver . . . in the water? If not, put one on and go over the side. Seriously, try it out. It's a little late to be fumbling with unfamiliar straps when the water is lapping over the rail.

Where do you keep the life preservers? They're no good to you in a locker overstowed with boxes of spare parts. In fact, they're really not a lot of protection if they are in the cabin at all. Should you need them, you want them ready at hand, not in a clothes locker with the door jammed. Stow them in a protected place in the cockpit, free of grease and oil, but ready to grab when and where you need them.

And the life ring buoy . . . how would you use it? How should it be thrown? Usual practice says throw it to windward of the person in the water. It'll drift towards him, and he can help out by swimming up to it instead of having to chase it. But don't hit him with it! Incidentally, in our air age there seems to be a confusion of the terms "windward" and "leeward." "Windward" is the same as "upwind" . . . into the wind. "Leeward" is "downwind" . . . away from the wind.

Suppose a man fell overboard, what would you do? The intuitive thing is to be sure he clears the propeller. Spin the wheel towards the side he fell over, and stop the propeller. But you haven't much time! If someone falls over the bow of a 30-foot boat going six knots, he'll be at the stern in three seconds! And don't forget to throw him a ring buoy, or some flotation gear. If a life ring is not at hand, don't orbit off to spend valuable minutes looking for it. First throw him something that will float. Whenever possible, the cushions, pillows and similar gear you put aboard should be buoyant.

Now you want to pick that person out of the water. How do you approach? The recommended procedure, if there is a standard, is to nose up to him from leeward, from downwind. Then grab hold, stop the propeller, work him along the hull to the stern, and drag him aboard. But have you ever tried it? Why not practice with a box or some kind of float? Throw it overboard; circle around to approach from leeward. See how close you can get without touching the box. Remember, it simulates a man's head.

Why not try to haul someone aboard from the water? Experiment a little in still water and under no pressure. You could hardly invest ten minutes of time more profitably. If you put another person into the water to help, be sure he wears a life preserver and has a line tied around his waist . . . one, and only one crisis at a time, please.

What would you do if the hull began to leak? There are two obvious steps: stop water from coming in, and get rid of the water that's already aboard. If the leak is above the waterline, plug it as best you can and head for help. If it is below water, maybe you can raise it by transferring weights to the other side . . . at least you'll lessen the pressure of the inflowing water. To plug a hole from inside when water is pouring through is almost impossible. A hole one foot below the surface and one inch in diameter will admit nearly half a gallon of sea water per second. Picture that hole a more realistic foot square and four feet below the surface. Then the inflow would be a murderous 120 gallons per second!

But what about a collision mat? A big piece of canvas or a few large blankets might do. Take two long ropes up to the bow and, holding the ends, pass the bights under the stem. Then walk aft so the ropes pass from one side under the keel and up on the other. Attach one end of each line to the bottom corners of the mat. Then secure the other two ends to the top corners. Now you have two ropes leading from the bottom of the mat under the keel and up on the other side, and two more ropes leading from the top of the mat to the deck. Center the mat on deck above the hole. Work it overboard carefully by hauling on the two bottom ropes and slacking off on the top ones. Then, the mat should slide over

Photo by U. S. Coast Guard/Recreational Boating Guide

Vest type life preserver.

the hole to be kept in place by water pressure. This should stop the inflow long enough for you to get inside and fix a temporary patch.

Remember that accidents seldom occur when conditions favor an easy remedy. In fact, their very cause might be a condition which greatly impedes the cure. They happen on dark and dirty nights, or when you're short-handed, or when some gear aboard has carried away . . . or when all of these dire things have come to pass. So each situation tends to be individual, with no fixed pattern to follow. If there is one "first of all" thing to do in any emergency, it is to take a realistic and long look at the problem. If you see a real danger to the boat or to anyone aboard, start making a call for assistance. Don't bet on the success of your remedy and find afterwards there isn't time enough to get help. Use discretion . . . but don't confuse pride with ability.

And now, consider one final suggestion. Anyone who has had military experience knows the device of assigning a task, no matter how small, to each person. This encourages teamwork, and allows no time for idle kibitzing. Nothing will erode confidence more than the seeds of doubt cast by an idle straw boss. On large ships a **Station Bill**, or duty roster, is made up. Each crew member has a job to do in an emergency. Would it be ludicrous on a small craft to do the same? Not at all!

A typewritten sheet framed under glass in the cabin is all that's needed. Assign basic and simple duties for say, three people. If more are aboard, they can "subdivide"; if less, they can double up. Perhaps you could separate the duties into **Fire, Man Overboard** and **Abandon Ship**. The tasks could be major or slight, as you prefer. But even if your preference would be to meet the problem single-handed, the duty roster might keep your shipmates occupied and out from under-foot.

Maybe this isn't practical. Maybe people would be getting in each other's way . . . but if you achieve nothing else, you'll set the mood for conduct aboard at all times. Explain, if you wish, that you're a throwback to an ancestor who was a cold-eyed sailorman out of Portsmouth. But no matter how casual and easy-going your cruise, **you** are in command. A device such as a Station Bill can diplomatically announce that you intend to be in command when trouble brews.

Questions

Another 25 questions to check your course. The channel might get a bit treacherous, so go at a moderate speed.

Rules of the Road

1. Under International Rules the Privileged Vessel in a Crossing Situation
   a) blows one blast to signify holding course and speed.
   b) always blows five or more blasts on the whistle.
   c) only blows one blast when he actually changes course to the right.
   d) both (a) and (b) above.

2. Under Inland Rules the Privileged Vessel in a Crossing Situation
   a) blows one blast to signify holding course and speed.
   b) only blows one blast when he actually changes course to the right.
   c) blows no whistle signals at all.

3. Under International Rules the Burdened Vessel in a Crossing Situation
   a) cannot blow five or more blasts if he has doubt as to the other's actions.
   b) will not blow any signal until he actually changes course or goes astern.
   c) both (a) and (b) above.

4. The Danger Signal in Inland Waters
   a) can be used by either Privileged or Burdened Vessel.
   b) can be used only by the Privileged Vessel.
   c) can be used only by the Burdened Vessel.

5. In a crossing situation the Privileged Vessel
   a) must hold course and speed until clearly the action of the Burdened Vessel alone cannot avoid collision.
   b) is free to change course and speed so long as he passes in front of the Burdened Vessel.
   c) has no restrictions at all on course or speed.

Charts and Publications

1. East End Light on Santa Catalina Island
   a) is visible from sea in a 360° arc.
   b) has an arc of obscurity to the northward.
   c) has an arc of obscurity to the southward.

2. East End Light on Santa Catalina Island
   a) is higher than West End Light.
   b) has the same distance of visibility as West End Light.
   c) both (a) and (b) above.

3. The abbreviation "SSh" in a water area on a chart means
   a)   seals and sharks.
   b)   soft shore.
   c)   sand and shells.

4. Catalina Canyon
   a)   is a submarine valley off the west coast of Santa Catalina Island.
   b)   is a mountain valley inland from Avalon.
   c)   is a shallow underwater basin off Long Point.

5. The numerals (38) under "Church Rock" off East End, Santa Catalina Island as shown on *No. 5142* indicate
   a)   38 feet above Mean High Water.
   b)   38 feet below Mean Lower Low Water.
   c)   38 fathoms above the bottom.

Piloting

You'll find here 10 problems combining bearings and compass correction. On the answer pages they are worked out for your convenience. Don your thinking cap and go to it!

1. A lighthouse bears 45° on the starboard bow at 0800. At 0830 it is abeam to starboard. Your speed is 10 knots. Your distance off at 0830 is
   a)   10 miles.
   b)   5 miles.
   c)   7 miles.
   d)   8.7 miles.

2. A lighthouse bears 22½° on the port bow at 1000. At 1100 it bears 45° on the port bow. Your speed is 10 knots.
   a)   at 1100 the distance off is 10 miles.
   b)   the distance off abeam will be 7 miles.
   c)   the distance to run from 1100 to abeam is 7 miles.
   d)   the time abeam will be 1142.
   e)   all of above.

Given these facts: Your course by compass is 078°. Variation is 15°E. Deviation is 3°W. At 0900 a lighthouse bears 120° True. At 1000 it bears 150°True. Your speed is 10 knots.

3. The distance off at 1000 is
   a)   10 miles.
   b)   7 miles.
   c)   5 miles.

4. The distance off abeam is
   a)   5 miles.
   b)   10 miles.
   c)   8.7 miles.

5. The vessel's True Course is
   a)   096°.
   b)   066°.
   c)   090°.

Given these facts: A vessel is on course 125° by compass. Deviation is 5°W. A lighthouse bears 085° Magnetic at 1100. At 1212 it bears 050° Magnetic. The vessel's speed is 6 knots.

6. The distance off at 1212 is
   a)   6 miles.
   b)   9 miles.
   c)   7.2 miles.

7. The vessel's magnetic course is
   a)   130°.
   b)   120°.
   c)   125°.

Given these facts: At 1415 a lighthouse bears 000.5° by compass. At 1445 it bears 019° by compass. The vessel's course is 334° by compass. Her speed is 8 knots.
8. The distance off at 1445 is
   a)   5.6 miles.
   b)   4 miles.
   c)   2.8 miles.

9. The distance off abeam is
   a)   5.6 miles.
   b)   4 miles.
   c)   8 miles.

10. The time abeam will be
   a)   1500 hours.
   b)   1530 hours.
   c)   1515 hours.

Weather

1. When a warm air mass is displacing a cold air mass
   a)   the line between them is a warm front.
   b)   the line between them is a cold front.

2. As a warm front approaches
   a) the barometer will fall.
   b) the temperature will rise.
   c) both of above.
   d) none of above.

3. A cyclone is formed by
   a) a low pressure area surrounding a high.
   b) a high pressure area surrounding a low.

4. An extratropical cyclone is
   a) a cyclone forming in other than tropical latitudes.
   b) a cyclone forming in the Tropics out of season.
   c) much more severe than a tropical cyclone.

5. A warm air mass moving in to a cold air sector
   a) will override the cold air.
   b) will undercut the cold air.
   c) will usually give signs of its approach hundreds of miles in advance.
   d) will abruptly begin to replace the cold air with little advance warning.
   e) (a) and (c) above.
   f) (b) and (d) above.

Safety Afloat

No Quiz this time; the subject matter asks more action than words. And anyway, we've already had 25 questions. Don't count these in your scoring, but at your first opportunity, why not carry out these 5 simple exercises?

1. Put on a life preserver.
   Then get into the water and try it out. (But don't jump in!)

2. Throw a box overboard. Then circle around and touch it lightly with your bow.

3. Throw another box overboard. Then practice throwing a life ring buoy near it.

4. Personally check the location and operation (if practical) of your fire extinguishers.

5. Twice and slowly read over an approved method of artificial respiration. Then write it out in your own choice of words. (See **READY REFERENCE** for the description of the mouth-to-mouth technique, as given in CG-175.)

...and answers

This time value each correct reply as 5 points, and base your score on the first 20 questions only. The standards? Here they are:

    90 - 100:   First Class Pilot.
    80 - 85:   Promising Apprentice.
    70 - 75:   Proceed with Caution.
    Below 70:   Drop Anchor and Take Some Bearings.

Rules of the Road

1. (c)   2. (a)   3. (c)   4. (a)   5. (a)

Charts and Publications

1. (b)   2. (c)   3. (c)   4. (a)   5. (a)

Piloting

1. A special Case I problem: $45° \ldots 90°$.
   Distance Off Abeam = Distance Run Between Bearings.
   Distance Run = 30 minutes at 10 knots = 5 miles.
   Therefore, answer selected is (b) 5 miles.

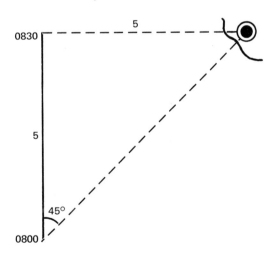

2. A Special Case IV problem: $22\frac{1}{2}° \ldots 45°$.
   Distance Off at $45°$ = Distance Run Between Bearings.
   Distance Off Abeam = 0.7 x Distance Run.
   Distance to Run from $45°$ to Abeam = Distance Off Abeam.
   Distance Run = 1 hour at 10 knots = 10 miles.

Therefore, answer selected is (e) all of above
for:
a) Distance Off at 45° ϕ is 10 miles.
b) Distance Off Abeam is 0.7 x 10 or 7 miles.
c) Distance to Run from 1100 to Abeam is same as Distance Off Abeam, or 7 miles.
d) 7 miles at 10 knots is 0.7 of 60 minutes or 42 minutes; 1100 + 42 minutes = 1142.

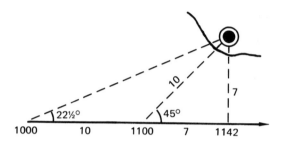

3. | C | D | M | V |
    | --- | --- | --- | --- |
    | 078° | - 3°W = 075° | + 15°E = 90° | |

    True Course = 090°

0900 ϕ: 120°True
    -090°True Course
    30° on starboard bow

1000 ϕ: 150°True
    -090°True Course
    60° on starboard bow

This is Special Case III: 30° . . . 60°.
Distance Off at 60° = Distance Run Between Bearings.
Distance Off Abeam = 0.87 x Distance Run.
Distance Run = 1 hour at 10 knots = 10 miles.
Therefore, Distance off at 1000 = (a) 10 miles.

4. Distance Off Abeam = 0.87 x 10 = (c) 8.7 miles.

5. Vessel's True Course = (c) 090°.

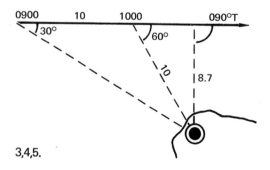

3,4,5.

6.　C　　D　　M

125° - 5°W = 120°, Magnetic Course

Magnetic Course: 120°	
1100 ϕ	: -085°
1st ϕ	: 35° on port bow

Magnetic Course: 120°	
1212 ϕ	: -050°
2nd ϕ	: 70° on port bow

This is Special Case II: doubling the angle, 35° . . . 70°.
Distance Off at 2nd ϕ = Distance Run.
Distance Run = 1 hr. 12 min. at 6 knots, or 1.2 x 6 or 7.2 miles.
Therefore, Distance Off at 1212 is (c) 7.2 miles.

7.　Magnetic Course is (b) 120°.

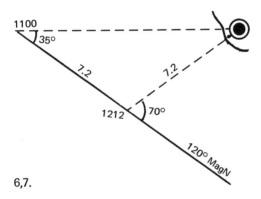

6,7.

8.　1415 ϕ: 000.5° by Compass
Course: 334.0° by Compass

1st ϕ : 26.5° on starboard bow

1445 ϕ: 019.0° by Compass
Course: 334.0° by Compass

2nd ϕ : 45.0° on starboard bow

This is Special Case V: 26½° . . . 45°, or Prediction Bearings.
Distance Off at 2nd ϕ (45°) = Distance Run x 1.4.
Distance Off Abeam = Distance Run.
Distance to Run from 2nd ϕ to Abeam = Distance Off Abeam.
Distance Run = 30 minutes at 8 knots = 4 miles.
Therefore, Distance Off at 1445 = (a) 5.6 miles.

9.　Distance Off Abeam = (b) 4 miles.

10. Time abeam is 30 minutes after 2nd ϕ . . . the interval to cover 4 miles at 8 knots.
Time Abeam = (c) 1515 hours.

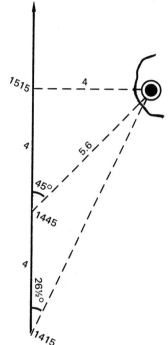

8,9,10.

Weather

1. (a)   2. (c)   3. (b)   4. (a)   5. (e)

section 4
contents

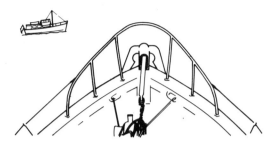

16/Rules of the Road
The overtaking situation

The third situation of vessels maneuvering close to each other is the overtaking case. It has been described as the simplest of all to state, and so it is. The overtaking craft must keep clear of the vessel being overtaken. Some powerboat men relish this opportunity to "even the score" with the sailing fraternity . . . for whether the overtaker is sailing, towing or in any other category of normal privilege, she must carry the burden and keep clear of the vessel ahead.

The familiar distinctions between International and Inland sound signals apply here as well as in cases of meeting and crossing. Under the High Seas rules, neither vessel will signal unless she actually changes course. The only exception: if the overtaken vessel becomes alarmed by the other's action, she can blow the five-or-more danger signal. Under Inland, however, the procedure of Proposal and Acceptance is to be followed. The overtaking craft suggests by whistle signal which side she desires to pass. One short blast offers passing up the other's starboard side, and two propose the port. The overtaken ship, then, must declare her consent or disapproval. Should the maneuver be acceptable, she will answer with the same signal. But if for any reason she disapproves, she sounds the danger signal. From then on the overtaker is forbidden to pass until satisfactory to the ship ahead.

Both sets of rules expressly state the limits of arc for overtaking: whenever one vessel comes up with another from any direction more than 22½° (two points) abaft the beam of the other, she is overtaking. In **Figure 34**, a craft coming up on Ship **P** from any direction between Line **A** and Line **B** is an overtaker. **P** will then be privileged and the other must keep clear. Two cautions are also stated in the rules. First, the overtaker remains the overtaker until she at last passes clear . . . she will be just as obliged to keep clear when she is off **P**'s bow as when she was dead astern. Second, if the ship astern cannot clearly decide whether she is in the arc of overtaking, she must assume she is and keep out of the way.

There are, then, four ingredients of the situation:

1. The vessels must be in sight of each other.
2. They must be traveling more or less in the same direction.
3. The ship astern must be traveling at a greater speed.

4. The ship astern must be in the arc of overtaking, actually or by assumption.

Unlike the meeting case, more maneuvering time is given here. For the speed at which the vessels come together is the difference in their individual speeds. A seven-knot ship **meeting** a five-knot ship a mile away will have five minutes before they pass. But when she is **overtaking** the five-knot ship a mile ahead, she must wait a half hour. And the force of any impact will, of course, be less.

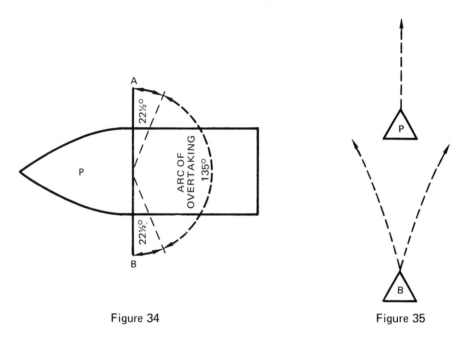

Figure 34   Figure 35

The entire maneuver seems simple enough. But what problems we humans create when we start carrying it out! First of all, let's consider the case from the lead ship's point of view. In **Figure 35** we are on Ship **P** being overtaken by **B**. Although the privilege is ours, it is still qualified. Under International we are obliged to maintain our course and speed . . . to continue predictable as **B** passes by. If she's going twice our speed, the burden is relatively slight. But suppose she is just a trifle faster than we are . . . so little difference that it takes 30 minutes for her to pass us by. For that entire time we have surrendered our freedom of choice . . . we must keep course and speed. The inclination to help her by slowing down is overpowering. But should we do so and should there somehow be a collision, we have, by changing speed, become involved. We have little to say about how **B** passes. We may signal only when her maneuver creates a doubt as to safety. And we will not know which side she chooses to pass until she begins to do so.

By Inland Rules we are, perhaps, better off. **B** can't pass until we let her. It is our waterway first. Of course, there must be a valid reason for our veto. But mutual agreement is essential. And we are free to juggle course and speed until **B**, the overtaker, makes her proposal. In effect, we have no obligation or involve-

Large motor yacht seen in overtaking sector.

ment until **B** offers a signal. Then we are obliged to agree to her terms or to disapprove.

What happens when we do agree to **B**'s proposal? Suppose **B** suggests she go left and pass up our port side, and we signal two blasts in assent. Do we then lose any privilege? Not at all. The overtaken vessel is privileged until the other is finally past and clear. By agreeing to the maneuver we don't take responsibility for its success. But from the moment of agreement we do incur some burden . . . the same one borne all along in International Waters. We must from that instant do everything reasonable to keep the status quo. We should hold our course and speed. Of course, if we see a danger ahead which, perhaps, is unknown to **B** and which makes her proposal risky, then we cannot consent. If we do so and something happens, we must bear some responsibility.

Suppose **B** offers two blasts and, after sounding the danger signal, we exchange one-blast signals for passage starboard-to-starboard. Have we now changed the situation? No. So long as our offer was based on good common sense and reasonable facts, we assume no extra responsibility for her passing. Just because we made the suggestion doesn't burden us with insuring she does it correctly. She still has to do the passing and the keeping clear.

From **B**'s point of view, the case is one of paramount burden. But the maneuvers are fairly clear cut. **B** can pass on either side. In narrow waters, **P** will probably be close to the right side of the channel, so **B** will probably overtake to port. But normally she can go either way. For **B** the problem is quite basic . . . stay out of **P**'s way.

When the maneuver is over, the privileges and burdens are discharged. But should **P** then put on a burst of speed and catch up with **B**, the shoe is on the other foot.

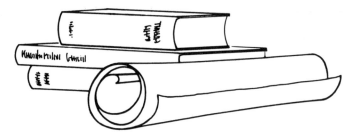

17/Charts and Publications
Coast Pilots and Sailing Directions

One of the basic, and the most used, freedoms we enjoy is the right to complain about how the country is being run. And each year at tax time we have a field day making comments on what we get for our money.

But in one area, there is no room for criticism: that of governmental nautical publications. Three examples of excellence are *Coast Pilots, Great Lakes Pilot* and *Sailing Directions.*

An important tool for any navigator is a reference guide that will tell him what he can expect to encounter on the coast ahead. The ideal would be a shipmate who knew intimately the important maritime features in every strange area on Earth. But that's not practical. A very adequate substitute, however, is a book written by experts in local knowledge and presenting the key facts in a simple, correct and reliable fashion. That, in essence, is the function of *Coast Pilots, Great Lakes Pilot* and *Sailing Directions.* The story of their evolution has some interest.

When astronauts return from a mission, they are subjected to a debriefing process. Their observations and impressions of the space voyage are carefully elicited and recorded in order to aid future trips. The information noted might be of the twentieth century but the procedure is very ancient. Polynesians returning from a venture into unknown seas were questioned closely about their trip. Arabs pushing down the east coast of Africa were given similar quizzing. But this should not be surprising, for seeking guidance in the experiences of others is good sense.

Early in the game, though, these records were often unwritten; and much error appeared over generations of raconteurs. Imagine how immense would be "the fish that got away" when, sixty years later, the great-grandson of the fisherman recounted his father's version of the patriarch's tale. But in many cultures all this was a most important and serious matter, with little tolerance for editorial comment and embellishment. Such data gained the status of state secrets to be jealously guarded and passed down.

About twenty-five centuries ago, the records began to appear in written form. A name given to such guide books was *periplus,* a Greek word derived from *sailing around* or circumnavigation. The best known ancient periplus preparer was Skylax, a Macedonian pilot for Darius, king of Persia. The book attributed to him was a detailed account of coasting along both shores of the Mediterranean from Gibraltar to the Middle East.

To a merchant, knowledge of the shortest and most efficient routes, coupled with hints on availability of cargoes, stores and water, could mean competitive advantage. So, the records of travelers often became trade secrets as well. A joint venture of two merchants brought the sharing of information . . . and the next thing they knew the records were becoming international. The result today is a world-wide pattern of such guides prepared by maritime nations and in many languages. Few veils of secrecy are left. For little more than $5.00, one can buy a publication which specifies courses and ranges for transiting Russia's Divinskiy Farvater waterway in the Barents Sea. And for less than the change left out of a ten dollar bill, he can buy another book to give courses and ranges entering Florida's Port Canaveral.

So, then, to particulars on such remarkable books. A *Coast Pilot* is a publication of the **National Ocean Survey**. In describing its own content, *Coast Pilot 4* speaks for all such books. On Page 1, it refers to itself as follows:

> **UNITED STATES COAST PILOTS.**—The C&GS Coast Pilots are a series of eight nautical books that cover a wide variety of information important to navigators of United States coastal and intracoastal waters. Most of this book information cannot be shown graphically on the standard nautical charts and is not readily available elsewhere. Coast Pilot subjects include navigation regulations, outstanding landmarks, channel and anchorage peculiarities, dangers, weather, ice, freshets, routes, pilotage, and port facilities.

There are eight *Coast Pilots* . . . each covering a different portion of US coastlines. The Atlantic Coast from Eastport, Maine, to Key West is detailed in *Volumes 1* through *4*. The Gulf Coast, Puerto Rico and the Virgin Islands are covered by *No. 5*. California, Oregon, Washington and Hawaii are found in *Coast Pilot 7*. Alaskan waters are treated in *8* and *9*. The cost is $2.50 for a hard-cover

volume and $2.00 for the one available in paperback. Customary for years has been to update the volumes by periodic supplements. Now being introduced is publication of a new edition each year. Continuing, though, will be the updating procedure by weekly *Notice to Mariners.*

Great Lakes Pilot is the companion piece. It details Lakes Ontario, Erie, Huron, Michigan and Superior, with their connecting rivers and waterways. Also included are the Hudson River, New York State Canals and Lake Champlain. The agency doing the job is, again, National Ocean Survey.

Coming from the US Navy Oceanographic Office are *Sailing Directions,* and they are in the same class of book. There are about 70 volumes altogether, detailing important data for foreign areas of the globe. An official definition of a *Sailing Directions* says it contains:

> description of coast lines, harbors, dangers, aids, winds, currents, tides, directions for navigating narrow waters and for approaching and entering harbors, port facilities, signal systems, pilotage service, and other data that cannot be conveniently shown on the charts.

Notice again the emphasis on information not readily shown on a chart. These volumes are intended to supplement charts; and between them the navigator has a complete reference library on local maritime conditions throughout the world.

The West Coast of Mexico and Central America, from Los Coronados to the Republic of Colombia, is found in *Sailing Directions, HO 26.* British Columbia, from Strait of Juan de Fuca to Cape Caution, is covered in *HO 10.* The publications are in a two-digit numbering sequence. The first digit refers to the area; the second, to the volume within the area. So, Nova Scotia is *HO 12,* the St. Lawrence appears in *HO 13* and Newfoundland in *HO 14.* The general territory of Area 1 is Canada, Greenland and Iceland. Area 2 is Latin America and Antarctica. *HO 20* handles the East Coast of Central America and Mexico. *HO 21* and *HO 22* take care of the West Indies . . . Bermuda, Bahamas, Greater Antilles, Lesser Antilles and the coast of Venezuela. The *HO 30's* focus on the British Isles and Northwestern Europe. The *40's* have the Baltic, Scandinavia and Northern USSR. In the *50's* are the Mediterranean and Western Africa. East Africa, Southern Asia and the Middle East are in the *HO 60's.* The *70's* take care of Australia and the Southwest Pacific. The *80's* have the rest of Polynesia, Melanesia and Mirconesia. And the *90's* finish up the Pacific with the Philippines, China, Japan, Korea and Siberia. The content is staggering, and the accuracy is astounding. For all these books are not just to entertain or to supply fodder for book reports. They are intended to be relied on by keel, deck and rudderpost. The form is loose-leaf; the price is $5.50 per volume.

Now, of what use is all this encyclopedic information to a pleasure mariner? Not much, perhaps, if he's content to dodge outside the entrance, feel a little spray and then skip back for a cocktail. But information has a sneaky way of becoming crucial at the most unexpected times. And knowing where to find the accurate and important—and up-to-date—information has obvious value.

Take, for instance, *Coast Pilot 7,* with California, Oregon, Washington and Hawaii. Its Chapter 1 contains general information. This includes a review of functions and operations of National Ocean Survey and of the signals displayed by its survey vessels; it includes important data on US Coast Guard activities, and its Search and Rescue procedures; it includes data on the National Weather Service, on the US Public Health and on radio services available. Chapter 2 details the local navigation regulations for ports along the coastlines. Chapter 3 gives general information on suggested courses and routes, on tides and currents and on weather to be expected. An example would be a comprehensive discussion of the **Santa Ana,** Southern California's troublesome desert wind. Beginning with Chapter 4, particular sections of the coast are treated in detail. And the appendix is an assortment of useful tables, interesting weather statistics and reference data.

Each volume is studded with pithy data ranging from pertinent cautions to a few little-known facts hardly worth knowing. An example of the worthwhile is the admonition in *Coast Pilot 7* that radiobeacon bearings within 0.5 miles of Golden Gate Bridge are not reliable. Another is this warning regarding Moore Haven Lock where Florida's Okeechobee Waterway enters the Caloosahatchee River:

> During periods of discharge through the lock, the currents and turbulence are extremely hazardous to all craft. Under no circumstances shall any craft approach nearer to the lock than the standby areas until discharge has been stopped and the water pool stablized.

Of, perhaps, less navigational value is the *Coast Pilot 7* mention that Pearl and Hermes Reef in the Hawaiian Archipelago was accidentally discovered on the dark night of April 26, 1822, by two British whaling ships whose names are as evident as the date their voyages terminated.

Chapter 12 of *Coast Pilot 4,* on three dozen fully packed pages, offers some 36,000 words on the Atlantic Intracoastal Waterway from Norwalk to Key West.

There is only one way to find out if a *Coast Pilot* or *Great Lakes Pilot* is for you: go to a nautical bookstore and take a look. Certainly, for any coastal voyaging you should have it aboard. But even if your trips are restricted to local waters, you will find things of interest and of potential value. And should you not even own a boat . . . who can say what might flower from such a conversational gambit as the true facts surrounding Pearl and Hermes Reef?

All this applies equally to *Sailing Directions.* On a trip along a foreign coast, the proper volume of *Sailing Directions* is as essential as your compass. Frankly, though, unless you do plan such a voyage, the books have little practical value. Nonetheless you should know they exist, who prints them, what they're for. So while you are at the bookstore looking over the *Coast Pilot* or inquiring about *Great Lakes Pilot,* ask to see a copy of *Sailing Directions.* Be prepared to exercise a measure of self-restraint. There is a hazardous facet to these books . . . they can be habit forming. Hours of enjoyable vicarious voyages might well lie ahead.

18/Piloting
More on bearings

In this chapter we'll complete the discussion of bearings. The five special cases studied last time are the "old reliables" that require no tables, no charts, no tools . . . only common sense, a simple bearing circle and a knowledge of course, speed and time. But obviously they are limited to the special combinations required by each rule.

Tables have been prepared which list multiplying factors for many other combinations. When the distance run between the bearings is multiplied by a factor, the distance off at the second bearing or the distance off abeam can be found.

One is Table 7 in *American Practical Navigator (HO No. 9)*. To use it the navigator enters with the difference between his course and the first bearing and the difference between his course and the second bearing. In the proper columns for those values will be found two factors. The left-hand one is the multiplier of the Distance Run to find Distance Off at the second bearing; the right-hand one is the multiplier for Distance Off Abeam.

Page 124 reproduces a page of that table . . . with first bearing values of 20° to 32° and second bearing values from 30° to 160°. Notice that the bearings are in even numbers and at 2° intervals. Rapid use of the table requires that no odd-number bearings, such as 23°, be taken. In such cases interpolation between listed factors would have to be done. But in nearly all cases it will be convenient to take even-number bearings.

Let's contrast Table 7 with one of the special cases. By Case III we know that when the difference between the course and the first bearing is 30° and the difference between the course and the second bearing is 60°, then the Distance Off at the second bearing (60°) is equal to the Distance Run Between Bearings. We also know that the Distance Off Abeam will be 0.87 times that Distance Run.

Look at Page 124 and you will get the same data. Find 30° at the top of the page. Go down the columns beneath it to the level of 60° as found in the left margin. The two factors listed are 1.00 and 0.87. Distance Run x 1.00 = Distance Off at Second Bearing. Distance Run x 0.87 = Distance Off Abeam.

The value of Table 7 is that it gives many combinations of first and second bearings. If the first is 26°, for example, and the second is 78°, the factors shown are

0.56 and 0.54. Distance Run x 0.56 = Distance Off at Second Bearing. Distance Run x 0.54 = Distance Off Abeam.

Notice also that bearings can be taken when the landmark falls behind you . . . abaft the beam. **Figure 36** is a sketch of such a situation. There, a first ϕ is taken when Lighthouse **A** bears 24° on the starboard bow. But because of fog the next ϕ is not taken until **A** bears 138° on the starboard bow. The ship travels 10 miles between the two bearings. From Table 7 we find that under 24° in the top margin, and opposite 138° in the left margin, the factors indicate 0.45 and 0.30. Since the ship moves 10 miles, we know she is 10 x 0.45 or 4.5 miles off at the time of the 138° ϕ. And we also learn that she is 10 x 0.30 or three miles off when abeam at **C**. What good is it to know where you **were** when abeam? This seems a fair question. Well, knowing your position at any time is valuable at sea. And key locations are those abeam of prominent landmarks. There is a continuity to coastal piloting when progress is reckoned from landmark abeam to landmark abeam. Also, since that position is the closest on the course line to the object, it more clearly defines the margin of safety.

Each of the special cases can also be worked in reverse, so to speak. If you miss all the bearings while the object is forward of the beam, then take a beam bearing as the first. Next, take one when the object is 45° abaft your beam . . . a "quarter-and-beam" case. The distance run between the two bearings is the distance you were off when abeam. And if you take one at 30° abaft the beam and another at 60° abaft the beam, then the distance you were off at the first ϕ, (30° abaft the beam) is the distance run. And the distance you were off when abeam is 0.87 times the distance run. Everything works in reverse.

Figure 37 illustrates a "backwards" case. There, a ship was unable to take any

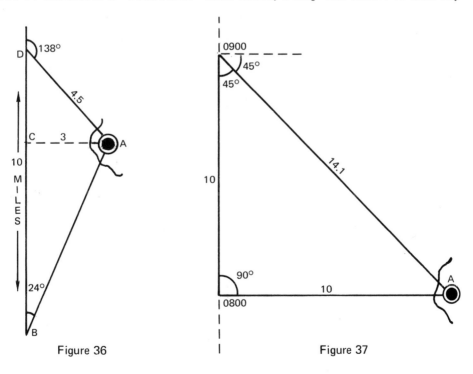

Figure 36

Figure 37

TABLE 7

Distance of an Object by Two Bearings

Difference between the course and second bearing	20°		22°		24°		26°		28°		30°		32°	
30	1.97	0.98												
32	1.64	0.87	2.16	1.14										
34	1.41	0.79	1.80	1.01	2.34	1.31								
36	1.24	0.73	1.55	0.91	1.96	1.15	2.52	1.48						
38	1.11	0.68	1.36	0.84	1.68	1.04	2.11	1.30	2.70	1.66				
40	1.00	0.64	1.21	0.78	1.48	0.95	1.81	1.16	2.26	1.45	2.88	1.85		
42	0.91	0.61	1.10	0.73	1.32	0.88	1.59	1.06	1.94	1.30	2.40	1.61	3.05	2.04
44	0.84	0.58	1.00	0.69	1.19	0.83	1.42	0.98	1.70	1.18	2.07	1.44	2.55	1.77
46	0.78	0.56	0.92	0.66	1.09	0.78	1.28	0.92	1.52	1.09	1.81	1.30	2.19	1.58
48	0.73	0.54	0.85	0.64	1.00	0.74	1.17	0.87	1.37	1.02	1.62	1.20	1.92	1.43
50	0.68	0.52	0.80	0.61	0.93	0.71	1.08	0.83	1.25	0.96	1.46	1.12	1.71	1.31
52	0.65	0.51	0.75	0.59	0.87	0.68	1.00	0.79	1.15	0.91	1.33	1.05	1.55	1.22
54	0.61	0.49	0.71	0.57	0.81	0.66	0.93	0.76	1.07	0.87	1.23	0.99	1.41	1.14
56	0.58	0.48	0.67	0.56	0.77	0.64	0.88	0.73	1.00	0.83	1.14	0.95	1.30	1.08
58	0.56	0.47	0.64	0.54	0.73	0.62	0.83	0.70	0.94	0.80	1.07	0.90	1.21	1.03
60	0.53	0.46	0.61	0.53	0.69	0.60	0.78	0.68	0.89	0.77	1.00	0.87	1.13	0.98
62	0.51	0.45	0.58	0.51	0.66	0.58	0.75	0.66	0.84	0.74	0.94	0.83	1.06	0.94
64	0.49	0.44	0.56	0.50	0.63	0.57	0.71	0.64	0.80	0.72	0.89	0.80	1.00	0.90
66	0.48	0.43	0.54	0.49	0.61	0.56	0.68	0.62	0.76	0.70	0.85	0.78	0.95	0.87
68	0.46	0.43	0.52	0.48	0.59	0.54	0.66	0.61	0.73	0.68	0.81	0.75	0.90	0.84
70	0.45	0.42	0.50	0.47	0.57	0.53	0.63	0.59	0.70	0.66	0.78	0.73	0.86	0.81
72	0.43	0.41	0.49	0.47	0.55	0.52	0.61	0.58	0.68	0.64	0.75	0.71	0.82	0.78
74	0.42	0.41	0.48	0.46	0.53	0.51	0.59	0.57	0.65	0.63	0.72	0.69	0.79	0.76
76	0.41	0.40	0.46	0.45	0.52	0.50	0.57	0.56	0.63	0.61	0.70	0.67	0.76	0.74
78	0.40	0.39	0.45	0.44	0.50	0.49	0.56	0.54	0.61	0.60	0.67	0.66	0.74	0.72
80	0.39	0.39	0.44	0.44	0.49	0.48	0.54	0.53	0.60	0.59	0.65	0.64	0.71	0.70
82	0.39	0.38	0.43	0.43	0.48	0.47	0.53	0.52	0.58	0.57	0.63	0.63	0.69	0.69
84	0.38	0.38	0.42	0.42	0.47	0.47	0.52	0.51	0.57	0.56	0.62	0.61	0.67	0.67
86	0.37	0.37	0.42	0.42	0.46	0.46	0.51	0.51	0.55	0.55	0.60	0.60	0.66	0.65
88	0.37	0.37	0.41	0.41	0.45	0.45	0.50	0.50	0.54	0.54	0.59	0.59	0.64	0.64
90	0.36	0.36	0.40	0.40	0.45	0.45	0.49	0.49	0.53	0.53	0.58	0.58	0.62	0.62
92	0.36	0.36	0.40	0.40	0.44	0.44	0.48	0.48	0.52	0.52	0.57	0.57	0.61	0.61
94	0.36	0.35	0.39	0.39	0.43	0.43	0.47	0.47	0.51	0.51	0.56	0.55	0.60	0.60
96	0.35	0.35	0.39	0.39	0.43	0.43	0.47	0.46	0.51	0.50	0.55	0.54	0.59	0.59
98	0.35	0.35	0.39	0.38	0.42	0.42	0.46	0.46	0.50	0.50	0.54	0.53	0.58	0.57
100	0.35	0.34	0.38	0.38	0.42	0.41	0.46	0.45	0.49	0.49	0.53	0.52	0.57	0.56
102	0.35	0.34	0.38	0.37	0.42	0.41	0.45	0.44	0.49	0.48	0.53	0.51	0.56	0.55
104	0.34	0.33	0.38	0.37	0.41	0.40	0.45	0.43	0.48	0.47	0.52	0.50	0.56	0.54
106	0.34	0.33	0.38	0.36	0.41	0.39	0.45	0.43	0.48	0.46	0.52	0.50	0.55	0.53
108	0.34	0.32	0.38	0.36	0.41	0.39	0.44	0.42	0.48	0.45	0.51	0.49	0.55	0.52
110	0.34	0.32	0.37	0.35	0.41	0.38	0.44	0.41	0.47	0.44	0.51	0.48	0.54	0.51
112	0.34	0.32	0.37	0.35	0.41	0.38	0.44	0.41	0.47	0.44	0.50	0.47	0.54	0.50
114	0.34	0.31	0.37	0.34	0.41	0.37	0.44	0.40	0.47	0.43	0.50	0.46	0.54	0.49
116	0.34	0.31	0.38	0.34	0.41	0.37	0.44	0.39	0.47	0.42	0.50	0.45	0.53	0.48
118	0.35	0.31	0.38	0.33	0.41	0.36	0.44	0.39	0.47	0.41	0.50	0.44	0.53	0.47
120	0.35	0.30	0.38	0.33	0.41	0.36	0.44	0.38	0.47	0.41	0.50	0.43	0.53	0.46
122	0.35	0.30	0.38	0.32	0.41	0.35	0.44	0.37	0.47	0.40	0.50	0.42	0.53	0.45
124	0.35	0.29	0.38	0.32	0.41	0.34	0.44	0.37	0.47	0.39	0.50	0.42	0.53	0.44
126	0.36	0.29	0.39	0.31	0.42	0.34	0.45	0.36	0.47	0.38	0.50	0.41	0.53	0.43
128	0.36	0.28	0.39	0.31	0.42	0.33	0.45	0.35	0.48	0.38	0.50	0.40	0.53	0.42
130	0.36	0.28	0.39	0.30	0.42	0.32	0.45	0.35	0.48	0.37	0.51	0.39	0.54	0.41
132	0.37	0.27	0.40	0.30	0.43	0.32	0.46	0.34	0.48	0.36	0.51	0.38	0.54	0.40
134	0.37	0.27	0.40	0.29	0.43	0.31	0.46	0.33	0.49	0.35	0.52	0.37	0.54	0.39
136	0.38	0.26	0.41	0.28	0.44	0.30	0.47	0.32	0.49	0.34	0.52	0.36	0.55	0.38
138	0.39	0.26	0.42	0.28	0.45	0.30	0.47	0.32	0.50	0.33	0.53	0.35	0.55	0.37
140	0.39	0.25	0.42	0.27	0.45	0.29	0.48	0.31	0.51	0.33	0.53	0.34	0.56	0.36
142	0.40	0.25	0.43	0.27	0.46	0.28	0.49	0.30	0.51	0.32	0.54	0.33	0.56	0.35
144	0.41	0.24	0.44	0.26	0.47	0.28	0.50	0.29	0.52	0.31	0.55	0.32	0.57	0.34
146	0.42	0.24	0.45	0.25	0.48	0.27	0.51	0.28	0.53	0.30	0.56	0.31	0.58	0.32
148	0.43	0.23	0.46	0.25	0.49	0.26	0.52	0.27	0.54	0.29	0.57	0.30	0.59	0.31
150	0.45	0.22	0.48	0.24	0.50	0.25	0.53	0.26	0.55	0.28	0.58	0.29	0.60	0.30
152	0.46	0.22	0.49	0.23	0.52	0.24	0.54	0.25	0.57	0.27	0.59	0.28	0.61	0.29
154	0.48	0.21	0.50	0.22	0.53	0.23	0.56	0.24	0.58	0.25	0.60	0.26	0.62	0.27
156	0.49	0.20	0.52	0.21	0.55	0.22	0.57	0.23	0.60	0.24	0.62	0.25	0.64	0.26
158	0.51	0.19	0.54	0.20	0.57	0.21	0.59	0.22	0.61	0.23	0.63	0.24	0.66	0.25
160	0.53	0.18	0.56	0.19	0.59	0.20	0.61	0.21	0.63	0.22	0.65	0.22	0.67	0.23

Difference between the course and first bearing

bearings of Lighthouse **A** until it was abeam. But the beam bearing was taken at 0800. She ran for one hour at 10 knots and then, at 0900, the lighthouse bore 45° abaft the beam. So the navigator then knew his distance off abeam was the distance he ran between the bearings, or 10 miles. Incidentally, should he recall a little more math, he'd know his distance off at 0900 to be 1.41 times 10 miles, or 14.1 miles. In the 45°-90° combination, the distance run is the distance off at 90°; but also, distance run times 1.41 is the distance off at the 45° ϕ. There are numerous practical applications useful to the navigator . . . all variations of more common and convenient rules of thumb.

For example, there are other combinations than our basic five which could also be called "special cases." We list a few below; but others which may strike an individual fancy can be found from Table 7 of *HO No. 9,* or by applying a little trigonometry. Frankly, though, the point of diminishing returns is almost upon us. A population explosion of "special cases" has dubious value. We could soon end up all "rules of thumb." In any case, here is a schedule of some auxiliary combinations:

First Bearing	Second Bearing	Distance Abeam
34°	64°	Equals Distance Run
38°	74°	Equals Distance Run
44°	88°	Equals Distance Run
60°	113°	Equals Distance Run
38°	52°	Equals Twice Distance Run
52°	74°	Equals Twice Distance Run
63½°	90°	Equals Twice Distance Run

A final handy piloting formula . . . the **Rule of Sixty.** In **Figure** 38 a ship at **B** is 15 miles from Lighthouse **A.** And the bearing of **A** is 20° on the port bow. How far will she pass off the lighthouse when abeam? There is only one ϕ, and so none of the special cases will apply. But by the Rule of Sixty:

$$\text{Distance Abeam} = \frac{\text{Range x } \phi}{60}$$

The Distance Abeam is 15 miles times 20° divided by 60 . . . or five miles. This rule works well when the angle does not exceed 45°. Over that, it becomes inaccurate. Actually, the rule can be expressed three different ways, as shown on the following page.

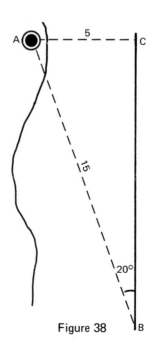

Figure 38

1. Distance Abeam $= \dfrac{\text{Range x Bearing}}{60}$

2. Bearing $= \dfrac{\text{Distance Abeam x 60}}{\text{Range}}$

3. Range $= \dfrac{\text{Distance Abeam x 60}}{\text{Bearing}}$

A practical example is shown in **Figure 39.** Lighthouse **A** is 15 miles due north of the ship. A rock lies 10 miles west of the lighthouse. What course must you steer to pass midway between the lighthouse and the rock? Here, we know the range as 15 miles. We know the distance to pass abeam, for we want to pass midway between two objects 10 miles apart, and so are to pass five miles from each. We want to find the angle. So the variation of the rule used is (2), and it works out this way:

$\text{Bearing} = \dfrac{\text{Distance Abeam x 60}}{\text{Range}}$

$\text{Bearing} = \dfrac{5 \text{ x } 60}{15}$

$\text{Bearing} = 20°$

The difference between the course and the bearing of the lighthouse must be 20°. Now the lighthouse bears Due North (000°). Since the ship is to pass to the left, or west, of the lighthouse, the course to steer is 20° to the left of 000°. This is 340°. And that course will place the ship five miles west of the lighthouse when abeam.

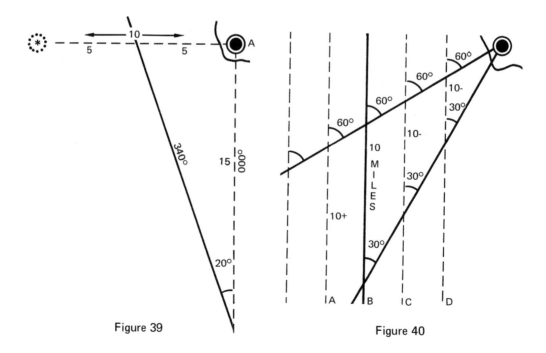

Figure 39

Figure 40

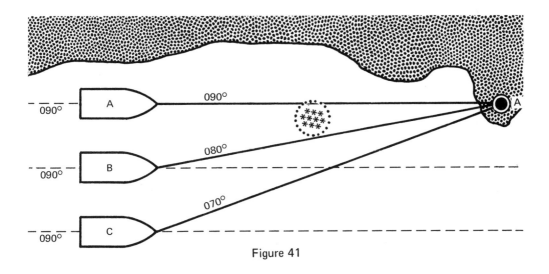

Figure 41

Now to relate all this to the discussion we've had on Line of Position. Each of the successive bearings taken is a **line of position**. And location on the LOP is determined by the course and distance run between the lines. In **Figure 40** the first and second bearings are 30° and 60°. The course is Due North, and the distance between bearings is 10 miles. The course lines **A, B, C** and **D** are all Due North. But only on course line **B** is the distance between the two LOP's equal to 10 miles. So the ship is on line **B**. All this could be plotted on the chart, without the use of any Special Bearing Rules. But it would have to be done on a chart, away from the wheel and not on the job.

By contrast, the special rules do not take you away from the primary duty of handling the vessel. Now we see why the "steam schooner cribbage board" and all the other simple bearing aids developed. Almost literally, with a block of wood and a handful of spikes a ship can be piloted down many a coast.

A handy tool for safety is the danger bearing. In **Figure 41** an offshore rock is situated near Lighthouse **A**. The problem: a means to check whether you will clear a hidden danger. From a prominent object, such as a lighthouse, draw a line of bearing to a circle of safe radius from the danger . . . in this case, a nest of submerged rocks. The direction of that line is noted. Here it is 080°True . . . the **danger bearing**. When the danger is to be on the starboard side, the object must bear **more** than the danger bearing for safe passage. And when, as in **Figure 41**, the passage is with the danger to port, the bearing must remain **less** than the danger bearing . . . in this case, 080°. Each of the three vessels shown is on the same course, 090°. The danger bearing tells **A** he is standing into danger. **B** sees he has a margin of safety. **C** is obviously in the clear.

We'll close this discussion with the Case of the Barking Dog. Old-timers along the coast made good use of every shred of data coming their way. According to some fo'c'sle yarns, even the noisy pup on a coastal farm was used to warn of danger ahead. We don't recommend you navigate that close in. But sound does have a place in the navigator's tool box.

Sound's speed in air is approximately 1100 feet per second. It varies with atmospheric conditions, but we use an average constant of 0.18 nautical miles per second.

Now, suppose you are making a night passage of a narrow channel with a steep cliff to starboard. Blow your whistle and time the seconds until you hear an echo. If it comes in 10 seconds, then the sound has traveled 10 x 0.18 or 1.8 miles. Since it passed from you to the cliff and back again, your distance off the cliff is one-half the total, or 0.9 miles. The rule, then, for Distance Off by Sound when you make the signal:

Half the Time in Seconds x 0.18 = Distance in Miles

Try this one near a harbor entrance. When you see the white plume of steam from a freighter's whistle, start counting the seconds until you hear the sound. 0.18 x Time is your distance to the ship. Here, the sound only made a one-way trip so don't divide the time in half. Should you happen to notice a ship make a whistle signal at the entrance, you have a handy way to estimate your distance yet to go.

A variation on these is the old Alaska Pilot trick, used in the Inside Passage. Suppose a vessel is passing in a channel between two steep cliffs. The problem is to stay in mid-channel. So whistle blasts are made. When the ship is in mid-channel between the cliffs, the echoes will return simultaneously; but should she move closer to one side, the echo from the near cliff will arrive before the other.

It would seem that sound offers many possibilities for navigational aids . . . synchronizing a sound signal with a light, or a radio wave, or some other impulse. And this has been done. Later on we'll take some time on Distance Finding Radio Stations. They use a radio signal synchronized with a sound signal in air. But sound can be disappointing. The vagaries of the atmosphere cause it to follow devious paths and to do strange things. In an age when the alternatives were few, sound had its day. But now, with electronic aids aplenty, this type position-finding is on the wane.

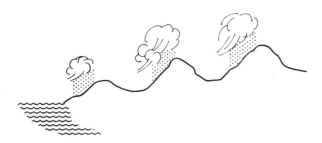

19/Weather
Highs, lows and weather

Weather forecasters own a special brand of courage. Their successes are diluted by the home seer with a football knee that "always aches before rain." And no one can bury a miscue affecting everyone in the area. But considering the many factors making up a weather prediction, the skill exhibited is astonishing. Meteorology has traveled far beyond the old seaman's rhymes.

The pleasure mariner should regularly avail himself of the wonderful services offered by the National Weather Service. Check with your local Weather office for details . . . it will be an inquiry well received and very worthwhile.

In this chapter we'll explore some of the elements of West Coast weather and tie them in with our previous discussions. With these examples perhaps we can work out a few general guides to become weather-wise while underway.

The Far West gets its climate from the breeding grounds of the Pacific Ocean. For the most part, the Cascades and Sierra Nevadas seal the area from polar continental air which sweeps the Middle West. Maritime air masses from various parts of the North Pacific are much in control.

All year round a gigantic battle is waged far out to sea west of the coast. An area of high pressure maritime air prowls the ocean, centered from about Latitude 20°N to about 40°N. It bears the character of the subtropical ocean surface beneath . . . warm and moist. An area of low pressure, the **Aleutian Low**, patrols to the north. During winter months the High is driven south until it is little more than a belt squeezed between the oncoming Low and the low pressure areas near the Equator. But during summer it advances north to control much more territory. So the battle front seesaws north and south during the year. In summer, the center of the High is in the latitude of San Francisco. The Low retreats so far north as almost to disappear. But in early fall the Low goes on the attack. By November the High is driven far south. Then in spring the High gains strength and begins its march north.

The result is that during summer months the High guards most of the Pacific Coast from the effects of low pressure. But as winter comes, this defense line weakens and contracts so that in greater frequency low pressure systems can move south and east to strike the coast. Southern California gains most protection

From observations made by ships, weather data are prepared
on charts at shore facilities and transmitted to ships at sea.

because the High usually retains enough front to blunt invading Lows and to shunt them eastward farther up the coast.

Three general rules are very helpful in predicting the effects of all this rivalry. First of all, air tends to move from high pressure areas towards low. Second, in the northern hemisphere, such movement is not directly from High to Low, but is diverted to the right. And third, air masses and weather disturbances in the middle latitudes drift from west towards the east.

Since this High we speak of is out to sea, westward of the coast, winds should blow from the west towards the coast. And that is true. The prevailing winds on the Pacific Coast are from the western half of the compass. Now, a west wind that is diverted to the right will blow from the northwest. Again, this is true for much of the coast. Since the center of the High is seldom farther north than 40°N Latitude, coastal regions from 40°N and down have a summer prevailing northwest wind. North of 40°N, the High is situated southwestward of coastal areas. So the southwest wind, diverted to the right, prevails as a westerly wind.

What happens when a Low breaks through the ramparts and begins to move towards the coast? Then the coastal area will have a higher pressure than that in the oncoming Low and wind will begin to blow from the land out towards the Low. It will blow from the eastern half of the compass. However, because of the diversion to the right, it will usually be a southeast wind. As the Low migrates towards the east (Rule Three says weather disturbances in the middle latitudes drift from west to east), it crosses the coastline . . . and the wind will change accordingly. Should it pass to the north of a location, the wind moving towards the Low will shift from southeasterly to south, then southwest, and so forth. This windshift is clockwise, and is called **veering**.

When the track of the Low is south of a position, the wind moving towards the Low will first be more or less from northeast. Then as the Low crosses the coastline, the wind will shift to north, then northwest, and so forth. Here, the windshift is counterclockwise, and is called **backing**.

When the track passes directly over an area, the winds would first be easterly to southeast and then as the Low passes over, move to westerly or northwesterly. **Figure 42** should clarify the general idea. A Low is sketched in **Figure 42a** as just westward of three places. It will pass north of **X**, south of **Y** and over **Z**. **Figure 42b** shows the Low as it passes over **Z**, north of **X** and south of **Y**. In **Figure**

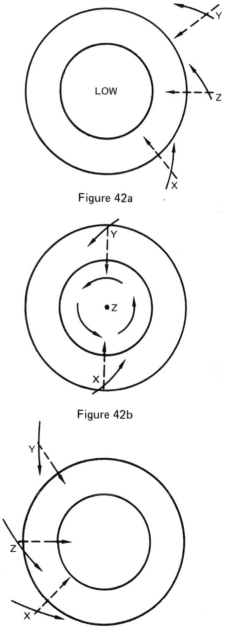

Figure 42a

Figure 42b

Figure 42c

42c the Low has moved eastward of all three of them. We emphasize that this is the **general** idea. At least a page would be filled with the special influences obscuring the generalities.

How does the mariner know the Low is on the move? Best of all is attention to weather reports. But even without them he gains some advance notice if he knows what to look for. The warnings are found by barometer . . . by windshifts . . . by clouds . . . by waves and swells.

A Low obviously has lower pressure than air not in the Low. So, as the Low approaches, the barometer is going to fall. As it passes, the barometer is going to rise.

And we've seen how the wind will shift during the invasion. Moreover, since a Low causes an atmospheric disturbance during its sortie, the clouds are going to move and to change by its influence.

"On-the-spot" weather prediction is founded on such observations. And the catchy rhymes of the Clipper Ships are still in point. We'll mention a few of them as we examine some of the telltale signs.

A very helpful guide for this work is the following table, prepared by the National Weather Service.

Wind—Barometer Table

Wind Direction	Barometer Reduced to Sea Level	Character of Weather
SW to NW	30.10 to 30.20 and steady	Fair, with slight temperature changes for 1 or 2 days.
SW to NW	30.10 to 30.20 and rising rapidly	Fair followed within 2 days by rain.
SW to NW	30.20 and above and stationary	Continued fair with no decided temperature change.
SW to NW	30.20 and above and falling slowly	Slowly rising temperature and fair for 2 days.
S to SE	30.10 to 30.20 and falling slowly	Rain within 24 hours.
S to SE	30.10 to 30.20 and falling rapidly	Wind increasing in force, with rain within 12 to 24 hours.
SE to NE	30.10 to 30.20 and falling slowly	Rain in 12 to 18 hours.
SE to NE	30.10 to 30.20 and falling rapidly	Increasing wind and rain within 12 hours.
E to NE	30.10 and above and falling slowly	In summer, with light winds, rain may not fall for several days. In winter, rain in 24 hours.
E to NE	30.10 and above and falling fast	In summer, rain probably in 12 hours. In winter, rain or snow with increasing winds will often set in when the barometer begins to fall and the wind set in NE.
SE to NE	30.00 or below and falling slowly	Rain will continue 1 or 2 days.
SE to NE	30.00 or below and falling rapidly	Rain with high wind, followed within 36 hours by clearing and, in winter, colder.
S to SW	30.00 or below and rising slowly	Clearing in a few hours and fair for several days.
S to E	29.80 or below and falling rapidly	Severe storm imminent, followed in 24 hours by clearing and, in winter, colder.
E to N	29.80 or below and falling rapidly	Severe NE gale and heavy rain; winter, heavy snow and cold wave.
Going to W	29.80 or below and rising rapidly	Clearing and colder.

Look at a few of the indications to see how our general ideas apply. Wind from the SW to NW, as shown in the top four categories, would suggest that a High is to the westward. The next eight lines show winds from S towards NE and tell that a Low is around, somewhere west or northwest. It will bring, in most cases, rain and

"Mare's Tail" Cirrus clouds.

wind and weather. Line 13 is a case of a Low that is moving eastward. It has brought its bad weather already. Lines 14 and 15 are signs of bad weather in store; for the barometer is low and going lower. The low pressure area is very close. The last one is the fair wind after a storm. The barometer has been low, but is rising and the wind is moving round towards west. We know then that the Low must be in the east and going away from us.

We can also see how readings of the barometer are so helpful. We are interested here in three things . . . what the barometer now reads, whether it is rising or falling, and how fast it is changing. A steady barometer means no invasion of air from a different source. A rising barometer says there is a High coming. And a falling barometer tells that a Low is on the way. The rate of change informs us much of what to expect. A fast rate means that the dividing line between Low and High is quite abrupt: there is a steep grade between the two, so the wind will whistle for a time. A slow rate shows the incline is much more gradual, and the movement will not be so vigorous.

Clouds tell a story all their own. They are formed by the condensation of water vapor in the air. And a major cause of this cooling is rapid ascension of warm air from a low altitude. When high pressure tumbles in towards a Low, it undercuts the warmer air and flings it upward. Result . . . squalls and thunderheads and the clouds that go with them. But a Low on the move tends to override the air masses ahead of it. The warmer air is forced gradually upward and makes a telltale trail of clouds ranging from the highest far in front to those of less altitude as the Low approaches.

Some authorities express disappointment in clouds as harbingers of weather. Since the litany of names and symbols given cloud forms often chills any enthusiastic study by the average seafarer, the argument remains strictly for experts.

But actually there are only two basic kinds of clouds: those caused by the vertical lifting of air . . . and those produced horizontally. The uplift type is **cumulus**; the stretched-out kind is **stratus**. Other names are only modifiers. **Nimbus** is rain; **fracto** is broken up; **alto** is middle altitude; **cirrus** is feathery and high altitude. The combinations seem endless . . . but they are really only variations on the basic two themes.

A moment's thought will tie this in with our previous discussion of warm fronts and cold. Since the warm front stretches out far ahead of the warm air mass, it causes that air to move gradually over the cold air being overtaken. The movement is as much horizontal as vertical . . . and so stratus-type clouds are formed. But the cold front digs under the overtaken warm air and gives it a hard push upward. The movement is vertical, and cumulus clouds form.

Generally speaking a cold front brings cumulus clouds. You would see heaps and piles of cumulus clouds on the western horizon as the front approached.

Generally speaking a warm front has stratus clouds. You would see cirrus and then cirrostratus and then altostratus and so forth.

Let's see how the fo'c'sle bards have met the challenge. From them have come many colorful weather rhymes. One is:

> *Mackerel sky and mares' tails*
> *Make tall ships take in small sails.*

Where did this come from? Well, a mackerel sky is a form of cirrocumulus cloud . . . a dappling of tufted clouds at extremely high altitude. And mares' tails are the wisps and streaks of cirrus clouds that seem to stream from a definite point on the horizon. These are the high clouds first formed when a warm front or Low approaches.

How about this one:

> *Rainbow at morning,*
> *Sailor take warning;*
> *Rainbow at night,*
> *Sailor's delight.*

To have a rainbow in the morning, the rain will be in the west. For what causes a rainbow is this: the sunlight enters the rain drops and then is reflected back out again. The sunlight from the east—in the morning—enters the rain drops in the west and then is reflected back out again. The rainbow will be in the west in the morning, proving that the rain is to the west . . . and coming towards you. But a rainbow at night, when the sun is west of you, must mean the rain is to the east of you. And then you know it has already gone by.

Another interesting one:

> *When the rain's before the wind,*
> *Topsail halyards you must mind;*
> *But when the wind's before the rain,*
> *Hoist the topsails up again.*

This developed from the observation that if rain comes first, a Low is approaching and the heavy winds are still to come. But, if the wind comes first, the bad weather is gone before the rain sets in.

One more and then the poetry recital is over:

Cumulonimbus type of cloud with great vertical development.

Photo by NOAA

Rain from the East,
Twelve hours at least.

This seems to contradict the . . . "rainbow at night" and so forth lines. For there, although the rain is also in the East, the jingle foretells good weather and the delight of the sailor. The difference . . . "rain from the East." Here, an easterly wind is involved. It would blow towards a Low which would be somewhere in the west. The Low has still to move past, and so unsettled weather will persist for some time.

Veering away from jingles . . . one last observation. The true direction of the wind is not immediately obvious from a moving vessel. So, a practical hint: Look at the water surface. Waves will be an excellent guide to wind direction. Take a bearing along the crests . . . see the direction of the lines of waves. Then add or subtract 90°.

For example, suppose the line of waves runs north-south. Then you know the wind to make them must be either from the east or from the west. Selecting which should be little problem . . . the waves will crest away from the wind. So if they curl to the west, you know the wind is from the east.

No rules of thumb or jolly jingles will make a meteorologist. Nor will they produce a competent marine weather observer. But then they were never intended to. Rely on expert data and expert interpretation when available. But still keep your eyes open. This is a complicated business, but it is also commonplace. A little reading, a rule of thumb and a dash of imagination can introduce a fascinating and new world of knowledge.

20/Signaling
Distress and emergency

One of the most important subjects we'll cover is Distress Signaling. Every mariner should have fingertip knowledge of the recognized signals for distress, not only to use them himself but also to recognize when given by another. Disaster at sea is bad enough . . . but a disaster that shouldn't have happened is really unforgivable.

The signals can be grouped in several categories:

1. Those established by the Rules of the Road.
2. Those transmitted by radiotelephone and radiotelegraph.
3. Those prescribed by the US Coast Guard as Beach Signals.
4. Those given by aircraft.
5. Those given by submarines.

Rule 31 of the International Rules and **Article 31** of Inland specify means to summon aid from another vessel or from the shore. On Page 139 you'll find them reproduced from *CG-169,* the Coast Guard publication of the Rules of the Road. Notice that the International Rule is much more comprehensive. If you're in Inland Waters and observe a signal that is listed under International but not Inland, still treat it as a distress signal. Trouble knows no line of demarcation.

Notice also that the age-old signal of the national ensign flying upside down is not found. For some time this was a recognized distress signal . . . but no more. And this is for a very good reason. Invert the French flag and it looks the same. So also with the Flags of Eire, Japan, Belgium and Italy. In fact many of the world's flags will be the same either way. When Poland is capsized the nationality is Indonesian. In other countries, as our United States, an ensign whipping bottom up from a jackstaff was often only the mark of a careless quartermaster. The signal was so indefinite it became meaningless. **But** should you see it, investigate. Someone out of fashion might really be in trouble. If not, you can at least teach him better manners.

Page 139 tells also of a signal specified by the Pilot Rules. It was developed especially for small craft, and is officially known as a *Manual Distress Signal for Daytime Use.* And the Coast Guard has said of it:

"This signal is simple. A boatman needs no special equipment. The visibility can be improved by holding in each hand a handkerchief, towel, shirt, bathing suit, etc."

Common sense tells you when to use it, and when not to use it. If this signal should be warped to suit every purpose from asking the time of day to scrounging ice cubes, it will end up like the inverted ensign . . . no signal.

But that, of course, should be said of all of them, for distress signals are reserved for distress. Misuse is prohibited. Seafaring people are usually easygoing. Life is too short and the ocean too large for them to get riled up over little things. But here is an exception. The man who trifles with distress signals trifles with everyone. All mariners have a legal obligation to interrupt their normal course and to give immediate aid. So they have little patience with the smart aleck who cries "Wolf."

Next: the radio procedures for emergency messages by radiotelegraph and radiotelephone. Our interest is in the telephone. But first, a few comments about wireless telegraphy.

The frequency for radiotelegraph distress messages is *500 kiloHertz* . . . within the reach of most marine radio direction finders. If you should have a receiver tuned to that frequency and hear an *SOS* (· · · - - - · · ·) you've heard a distress call. Probably many other receivers have also heard it, including people with the equipment to reply. But never disregard such a call as not your business. If your receiver is a radio direction finder, take a bearing right away. Try to contact the Coast Guard by the quickest means . . . radiotelephone, or via another vessel, or even by going ashore and phoning them. Give the facts as you know them . . . time of receipt, your location, and the bearing if you took one. But never pass over a distress call as "not in your field." Everyone's a general practitioner in marine safety.

As for radiotelephone: the frequency for distress, urgency and safety messages is *2182 kiloHertz.* This is the international Distress and Calling Frequency . . . and is also that used to initiate communication with the Coast Guard. After that contact the call is switched to *2670,* a frequency *only to be used* for communication with the Coast Guard.

There are three kinds of emergency messages sent on *2182.* Let's take them one by one and see what they are.

A **Distress** call is one regarding immediate assistance to the station in distress, and is sent only on the authority of the master or person responsible for the vessel in distress: It indicates the sender is threatened by grave and imminent danger and requests immediate assistance. When sent by radiotelephone, the call is a general one, to all stations, and the procedure is this:

First: *Mayday Mayday Mayday* spoken three times.
Then: *This is* (identification of station in distress) spoken three times.
Then: The position, nature of the distress, kind of help needed and other pertinent data.

Incidentally, *Mayday* is the phonetic spelling of *m'aider,* the French expression for *Help me!*

Distress calls have absolute priority over other messages. As soon as one is heard, other stations must stop any other call that might interfere and continue to listen on the frequency used for the distress call. All facets of this call are serious and grave. It marshals the combined efforts of all within hearing distance and holds them ready to come to the rescue. No one sins who sends it in good faith . . . even though hindsight proves it unnecessary. But there is no excuse, ever, for using it when you know it isn't needed. It is the holy of holies. On this subject there must be unqualified good faith.

When you receive a distress call from a station which, beyond any doubt, is in your vicinity, acknowledge it immediately. But wait until the complete distress message is received. If beyond any doubt the distressed station is not in your vicinity, wait a short interval before acknowledging. That will allow other stations closer than you to answer without interference.

In acknowledging a distress call tell the fellow in trouble your name, position, your speed of approach and any other data pertinent to the type distress.

Another emergency call is the **Urgency** message. It consists of the word *Pan* spoken three times and then the message. *Pan* is the phonetic spelling of *panne,* the French word meaning, generally, *breakdown.* This signal is sent on *2182 kHz* and given when you must transmit a very urgent message concerning the safety of a ship or aircraft, or of any person on board or close by. For example, it is given when a medical emergency occurs aboard. Its priority rank is junior only to distress . . . every other call must give way and not interfere. The urgency signal is usually directed to a particular station. Other stations may then go about their radio business, provided they don't interfere. But if the call is to all stations, then they must, as best they can, give the assistance requested.

The third type emergency call by radiotelephone is the **Safety** signal. It begins with *Saycuritay* spoken three times. This is the phonetic spelling of the French *sécurité,* meaning *safety.* Here, the sender has a message regarding safety of navigation or an important meteorological warning. The frequency is *2182 kHz* the same as distress and urgency. An example: you sight a derelict drifting in the channel. Vessels receiving such a call are to listen until they are certain it is of no interest to them. And they must not interfere with the message.

Government coastal stations monitoring *2182* for distress signals will rebroadcast any calls on *500 kHz* to invoke the aid of ships equipped with radiotelegraphy equipment. If desirable they will also do the reverse . . . rebroadcast a radiotelegraph distress call on *2182 kHz* for radiotelephone vessels.

The next category of signals is that of **Coast Guard Beach Signals.** They are employed in directing rescue operations by breeches buoy and for beach landings through a surf. The signals are fairly simple and easily learned. But should the need ever arise to use them, there will probably be little opportunity for a refresher. So it might be worthwhile to see their pattern.

On Page 140 you will see a recapitulation of the *Coast Guard Instructions for the Use of the Gun and Rocket Apparatus for Saving Life from Shipwreck.* The procedure is quite obvious and self-evident.

INTERNATIONAL RULES

RULE 31 (a) When a vessel or seaplane on the water is in distress and requires assistance from other vessels or from the shore, the following shall be the signals to be used or displayed by her, either together or separately, namely:—

(i) A gun or other explosive signal fired at intervals of about a minute.

(ii) A continuous sounding with any fog-signalling apparatus.

(iii) Rockets or shells, throwing red stars fired one at a time at short intervals.

(iv) A signal made by radio-telegraphy or by any other signalling method consisting of the group ... — — — ... in the Morse Code.

(v) A signal sent by radio-telephony consisting of the spoken word "Mayday".

(vi) The International Code Signal of distress indicated by N.C.

(vii) A signal consisting of a square flag having above or below it a ball or anything resembling a ball.

(viii) Flames on the vessel (as from a burning tar barrel, oil barrel, &c.).

(ix) A rocket parachute flare or a hand flare showing a red light.

(x) A smoke signal giving off a volume of orange-coloured smoke.

(xi) Slowly and repeatedly raising and lowering arms outstretched to each side.

NOTE: Vessels in distress may use the radiotelegraph alarm signal or the radiotelephone alarm signal to secure attention to distress calls and messages. The radiotelegraph alarm signal, which is designed to actuate the radio-telegraph auto alarms of vessels so fitted, consists of a series of twelve dashes, sent in 1 minute, the duration of each dash being 4 seconds, and the duration of the interval between 2 consecutive dashes being 1 second. The radiotelephone alarm signal consists of 2 tones transmitted alternately over periods of from 30 seconds to 1 minute.

(b) The use of any of the foregoing signals, except for the purpose of indicating that a vessel or seaplane is in distress, and the use of any signals which may be confused with any of the above signals, is prohibited.

INLAND RULES

ART. 31. *When a vessel is in distress and requires assistance from other vessels or from the shore the following shall be the signal to be used or displayed by her, either together or separately, namely:*

In the daytime—

A continuous sounding with any fog-signal apparatus, or firing a gun.

At night—

First. Flames on the vessel as from a burning tar barrel, oil barrel, and so forth.

Second. A continuous sounding with any fog-signal apparatus, or firing a gun.

PILOT RULES

80.37 Distress signals.

(a) *Daytime.* (1) Slowly and repeatedly raising and lowering arms outstretched to each side.

USE OF THE GUN AND ROCKET APPARATUS FOR SAVING LIFE FROM SHIPWRECK

If your vessel is stranded and a shot with a small line is fired over it, get hold of the line and haul on board until you get a tailblock with an endless line rove through it; make the tailblock fast to the lower mast, well up, or in the event the masts are gone, to the best place to be found; cast off small shot line, see that rope in block runs free, and make a signal to shore. (Figure 1.)

A hawser will be bent to the endless line on shore and hauled off to your ship by the lifesaving crew. Make hawser fast about 2 feet above the tailblock and unbend hawser from endless line. See that rope in block runs free and show signal to shore. (Figure 2.)

Lifesavers on shore will then set hawser taut and by means of the endless line haul off to your ship a breeches buoy. (Figure 3.)

Let one man get clear into breeches buoy, thrusting his legs through the breeches; make signal to shore, and he will be hauled ashore by the lifesavers and the empty buoy returned to the ship.

Figure 1

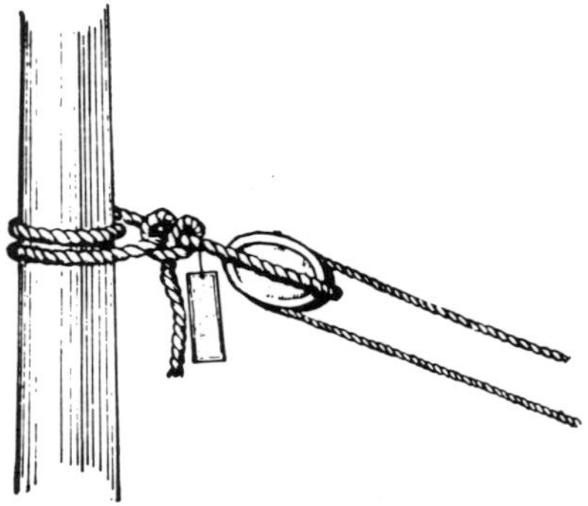

Figure 2

Figure 3

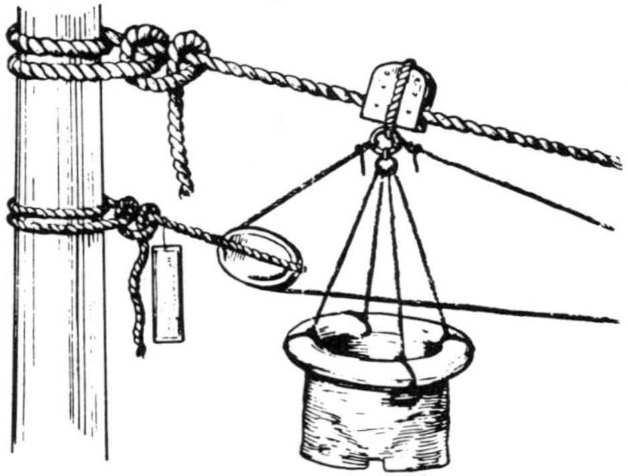

C. SIGNALS TO BE EMPLOYED IN CONNECTION WITH THE USE OF SHORE LIFESAVING APPARATUS

	DAY AND LIGHT SIGNALS	STAR SIGNALS	SIGNIFICATION
DAY	Vertical motion of a white flag or the arms.		In general: "Affirmative." Specifically: "Rocket line is held." "Tail block is made fast." "Hawser is made fast." "Man is in the breeches buoy." "Haul away."
NIGHT	Vertical motion of a white light or flare.	Firing of a green star signal.	
DAY	Horizontal motion of a white flag or arms extended horizontally.		In general: "Negative." Specifically: "Slack away." "Avast hauling."
NIGHT	Horizontal motion of a white light or flare.	Firing of a red star signal.	

RESCUE SIGNAL TABLE

The signals indicated in A, B, and C shall (1) be used by lifesaving stations and maritime rescue units when communicating with lifesaving stations and maritime rescue units when communicating with ships or persons in distress and (2) by ships or persons in distress.

A. REPLIES FROM LIFESAVING STATIONS OR MARITIME RESCUE UNITS TO DISTRESS SIGNALS MADE BY A SHIP OR PERSON

	SIGNAL	SIGNIFICATION
DAY	Orange smoke signal or combined light and sound signal consisting of 3 single signals which are fired at intervals of approximately one minute.	"You are seen—assistance will be given as soon as possible."
NIGHT	White star rocket consisting of 3 single signals which are fired at intervals of approximately one minute. If necessary the day signals may be given at night or the night signals by day.	(Repetition of such signals shall have the same meaning.)

B. LANDING SIGNALS FOR THE GUIDANCE OF SMALL BOATS WITH CREWS OR PERSONS IN DISTRESS

	DAY AND LIGHT SIGNALS	STAR SIGNALS	MORSE CODE SIGNALS	SIGNIFICATION
DAY	Vertical motion of a white flag or the arms.	Firing of a green star signal.	Code letter "K" (—.—) given by light or sound-signal apparatus.	"This is the best place to land."
NIGHT	Vertical motion of a white light or flare. A range (indication of direction) may be given by placing a steady white light or flare at a lower level and in line with the observer.			
DAY	Horizontal motion of a white flag or arms extended horizontally.	Firing of a red star signal.	Code letter "S" (...) given by light or sound-signal apparatus.	"Landing here highly dangerous."
NIGHT	Horizontal motion of a white light or flare.			
DAY	Horizontal motion of a white flag, followed by the placing of the white flag in the ground and the carrying of another white flag in the direction to be indicated.	Firing of a red star signal vertically and a white star signal in the direction towards the better landing place.	Code letter "S" (...) followed by either: Code letter "R" (.—.) if a better landing place for the craft in distress is located more to the right in the direction of approach, or Code letter "L" (.—..) if a better landing place for the craft in distress is located more to the left in the direction of approach.	"Landing here highly dangerous. A more favorable location for landing is in the direction indicated."
NIGHT	Horizontal motion of a white light or flare, followed by the placing of the white light or flare on the ground and the carrying of another white light or flare in the direction to be indicated.			

Pages 140 and 141 review the *Rescue Signal Table* prepared by the Coast Guard and presented in placard form on *CG-811* entitled *Lifesaving Signals and Breeches Buoy Instructions.*

Note that the signals are for day and night, appeal to the ear as well as the eye, and in some respects are multipurpose. Even so there is little basis for confusion. For a distressed crew will not be manipulating the rigging of a breeches buoy at the same time they're making a surf landing. The immediate meaning of the signal will always be clear in its context.

Spend a few moments on the table. You'll probably never have need for these signals. But now is the time to gain the general idea.

Suppose that as you are cruising offshore an aircraft suddenly "buzzes" you by circling your vessel, opening and closing his throttle. Then, flying off in a particular direction, he climbs, turns and does it again. What is his meaning? This is an **Aircraft Distress** call. The signals are very simple, and are stated in this way:

When precise instructions to direct a surface craft to a place where an aircraft or a surface craft is in distress cannot be given by an aircraft to the surface, then

1. to direct a surface craft towards that area the aircraft shall
   a) *circle the ship at least once.*
   b) *cross the ship's course close ahead at low altitude, opening and closing the throttle or changing the propeller pitch.*
   c) *head off in the direction to follow.*
2. to indicate that assistance no longer is needed, the aircraft shall
   a) *cross the ship's wake close astern at low altitude, opening and closing the throttle or changing the propeller pitch.*

To acknowledge receipt the surface craft shall (when equipped with International Code Signal flags) hoist the *Code Pennant* close up. Or she can flash a succession of *T*'s (-----) by signal lamp. Or she can change her heading. To indicate inability to comply, the ship (when equipped with flags) hoists *N*. Otherwise she can flash a succession of *N*'s (-·--·) by signal lamp.

Another important group of signals is that for **Submarines**. They are given by firing a submerged signal ejector to propel the device to a height of about 300 feet. The signal then floats downward suspended from a small parachute, giving illumination for about 30 seconds. And the signals are:

Green to indicate a torpedo has been fired. It will be used to simulate torpedo firing on special exercises.

Yellow to indicate that the submarine is about to come up to periscope depth. Surface craft should clear vicinity of the submarine *and not stop propellers!*

Red to indicate an emergency condition within the submarine and that she will surface immediately if possible. Surface vessels clear area, and stand by to give assistance after the submarine has surfaced. In case of repeated red signals, or if the submarine fails to surface within a reasonable time she may be assumed to be disabled. Buoy the location if possible. Look for a submarine marker buoy released by the submerged submarine. Advise the naval authorities.

Along with any other signals, submarines may employ a few other means to attract attention or to indicate presence and position. They might let out an oil slick, release a dye marker, release some air bubbles or start pounding on the hull. As to the messenger buoy they carry . . . it is two spheres three feet in diameter with a connecting structure and painted international orange. A wire cable leads from it to the submarine as a downhaul for a rescue chamber.

This messenger buoy is released by a submarine in trouble. Should you notice it, investigate and advise the naval authorities. By all means when you're under power and notice any of these signals, keep your propeller turning. If you are under sail, but have an auxiliary, start the engine. The propeller might be the submarine's only key to your position.

Now . . . the **Storm Warning Signals**. Little need be said about them. They will be flown at certain locations in each area . . . Coast Guard facilities, Pilot Stations, yacht clubs, marinas. The signals themselves are set out on Page 144. You will also find them repeated in **READY REFERENCE**. Look them over and keep the list at hand.

One more type signal that is in the urgent category . . . those given by minesweepers engaged in minesweeping operations. They are incorporated in **Rule 4** of International Rules of the Road and are found repeated in *Special Notice to Mariners* this way:

Minesweeper signals.—U.S. vessels engaged in minesweeping operations or exercises are hampered to a considerable extent in their maneuvering powers. With a view to indicating the nature of the work on which they are engaged, these vessels will show the signals hereinafter mentioned. For the public safety, all other vessels, whether steamers or sailing craft, must endeavor to keep out of the way of vessels displaying these signals and not approach them inside the distances mentioned herein, especially remembering that it is dangerous to pass between the vessels of a pair or group sweeping together.

All vessels towing sweeps are to show: **By day,** a black ball at the fore truck and a black ball at the fore yard on the side or sides on which it is dangerous to pass; there may be thus 2 or 3 black balls displayed; **By night,** all around green lights instead of the black balls, and in a similar manner.

Vessels or formations showing these signals are not to be approached nearer than 1,500 feet on either beam and vessels are not to cross astern closer than 3,000 feet. Under no circumstances is a vessel to pass through a formation of minesweepers. Minesweepers should be prepared to warn merchant vessels which persist in approaching too close by means of any of the appropriate signals from the International Code of Signals. In fog, mist, falling snow, heavy rainstorms, or any other condition similarily restricting visibility, whether by day or night, minesweepers while towing sweeps when in the vicinity of other vessels will sound whistle signals for a vessel towing (1 prolonged blast followed by 2 short blasts).

STORM WARNING SIGNALS

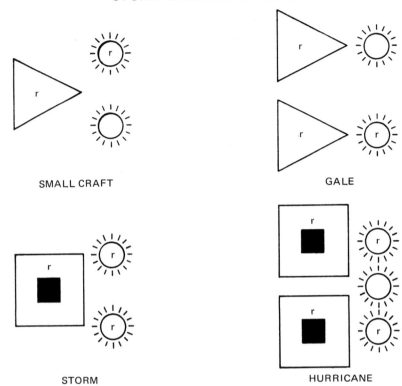

SMALL CRAFT

GALE

STORM

HURRICANE

SMALL CRAFT: one red pennant by day and **one red light over one white light** by night for winds and seas, or sea conditions alone, considered hazardous to small craft. Winds may range -as high as 33 knots (38 mph). 'Small Craft' means small boats, yachts, tugs, barges with little freeboard, and any other low-powered craft.

GALE: two red pennants by day and **one white light over one red light** by night for winds from 34 to 47 knots (39 to 54 mph).

STORM: one single square red flag with a **black center** by day and **two red lights** by night for winds to equal or exceed 48 knots (55 mph).

HURRICANE: two square red flags with black centers by day and **one white light between two red lights** by night for tropical cyclone with winds of 64 knots (73 mph) and above.

A memory aid for the Storm Signal lights . . . it relates them to Rules of the Road night signals . . .

STORM SIGNAL	RULES OF THE ROAD	COMMENT
Red over White (Small Craft)	Red over White, Fishing at Night.	You could fish while harbor-bound by some dirty weather.
White over Red (Gale)	White over Red, Pilot Ahead.	In a 40-knot wind . . . you might need one!
Red over Red (Storm)	Red over Red, Not under Command (International)	When it's blowing up a storm . . . who has control?
Red White Red (Hurricane)	Red White Red, Engaged in underwater operations (International)	Glug, Glug.

Heavy duty diesel cruiser.

Photo by Jones-Goodell Shipbuilding Corp.

Notice that the warning to give way is applied to sailing craft as well as power-driven. A triangle of three black balls by day and the wearing of three green lights by night is the signal for everyone to get out of the way. And in a fog, the hearing of one prolonged blast followed by two shorts can be a signal that over a square mile of ocean nearby is dangerous to enter.

You'll find emergency signals summarized in **READY REFERENCE**. There seems to be one for every circumstance. But if you meet trouble and must summon help, don't be satisfied with just one signal. Use as many as might help. Call on the emergency frequency, keep your whistle blowing, fire a gun, make smoke, fire a rocket, hoist a square cloth with a ball above or below, use a pocket mirror or a flashlight and send *SOS*. You don't care which one brings attention; but, more important, you don't know which one will! So use them all. These are signals to be made only in an emergency; but then they are to be used as vigorously as possible.

Questions

Time again to take five . . . questions, that is, on each of the five topics just covered. As for a time limit . . . no need to be carried away by all this. Take whatever time is necessary. Just watch for practice torpedoes . . . and Full Speed Ahead!

Rules of the Road

1. A sailing vessel overtaking a power-driven vessel
   a) has the right of way.
   b) is the burdened vessel.

2. While being overtaken a vessel
   a) is free to alter course and speed.
   b) can alter course but not speed.
   c) can alter speed but not course.
   d) must maintain course and speed.

3. Under International Rules the overtaking vessel
   a) always sounds a whistle signal.
   b) never sounds a whistle signal.
   c) when in doubt can sound 5 or more short blasts.
   d) does none of the above.

4. Under Inland Rules the overtaken vessel
   a) must first agree before the other can pass.
   b) loses her privilege if she agrees to the other's proposal.
   c) assumes full responsibility if she does not agree.

5. The arc of overtaking is from
   a) abeam on one side, around the stern to abeam on the other.
   b) 2 points (22½°) abaft the beam on one side, around the stern to 2 points abaft the beam on the other.
   c) a relative bearing of 112½°, clockwise from the bow, to a relative bearing of 247½°, clockwise from the bow.
   d) (b) and (c) above.
   e) none of above.

Charts and Publications

1. The *Coast Pilot* is published by
   a) the Hydrographic Office (HO) of the Navy.
   b) The National Ocean Survey.

2. Information on the *Gulf of California will be found in
   a) a *Coast Pilot.*
   b) a *Sailing Direction.*

*This location is part of Mexican waters.

3. Information on Jamaica will be found in
   a) a *Coast Pilot.*
   b) a *Great Lakes Pilot.*
   c) the same *Coast Pilot* as that for California.
   d) a *Sailing Directions.*
   e) (a) and (c) above.

4. Changes in a *Coast Pilot* are published in
   a) the weekly *Notice to Mariners.*
   b) a periodic supplement to the *Coast Pilot.*
   c) both of above.
   d) neither of above.

5. *Coast Pilot 7* contains
   a) general weather information for the Pacific Coast of California, Oregon and Washington.
   b) harbor regulations for Santa Barbara, California.
   c) harbor regulations for Ensenada, Mexico.
   d) all of above.
   e) (a) and (b) above.

Piloting

1. A vessel is on course 000°True. At 0900 a lighthouse bears 090°True. At 0930 it bears 135°True. The speed is 10 knots. At 0900 the distance off was
   a) 7 miles.
   b) 10 miles.
   c) 5 miles.

2. A vessel is on course 000°True. At 0900 a lighthouse is dead ahead and 10 miles away. Using the Rule of Sixty, the course to steer to pass 3 miles west of the lighthouse is
   a) 342°.
   b) 350°.
   c) 018°.
   d) 000°.

3. A vessel is on course 270° by compass. A lighthouse bears 250° by compass and is 6 miles away. Using the Rule of Sixty, the vessel will pass abeam of the lighthouse
   a) 4 miles off.
   b) 2 miles off.
   c) 6 miles off.

4. A vessel blows her whistle and 15 seconds later hears an echo from a steep cliff on shore. Her distance off the cliff is
   a) 15 miles.

b) 2.7 miles.
c) 0.9 mile.
d) 1.35 mile.

5. You observe the steam plume from a freighter's whistle. 10 seconds later you hear the sound. Your distance from the freighter is
   a) 0.9 mile.
   b) 5 miles.
   d) 1.8 miles.
   d) 1100 feet.

Weather

1. The prevailing winds on the Pacific Coast are
   a) westerly.
   b) easterly.

2. The approach of a cold front is usually heralded by
   a) layers of clouds (stratus).
   b) heaped and lumpy clouds (cumulus).

3. Rain before the wind usually indicates
   a) a High is approaching.
   b) a Low is approaching.

4. A rapidly falling barometer and wind from the southeast would indicate
   a) a Low is approaching from the westward.
   b) a High is approaching from the westward.

5. A rising barometer and strong northwest winds would indicate
   a) a Low is approaching from the westward.
   b) a High is to the westward.

Distress signals

1. The radiotelephone frequency for distress is
   a) 2182 kiloHertz.
   b) used for *Mayday* calls only.
   c) both of above.
   d) none of above.

2. When you observe that a gun is being fired from a vessel
   a) disregard the incident; it is probably target practice.
   b) consider it as a possible distress signal.
   c) assume it is a government or police vessel of some sort.
   d) set a course to get out of range with all speed.
   e) never construe it as a distress signal.

3. You observe an aircraft fly low across your bow, closing and opening his throttle, and then fly off to the north. He is
   a) being friendly.
   b) telling you the nearest port is north of you.
   c) signaling you to proceed north to a vessel or aircraft in distress.

4. At sea you observe a vessel flying a square flag with a round shape above it. This is
   a) a minesweeper on maneuvers.
   b) a tug with a tow over 600 feet long.
   c) a distress signal.
   d) none of above.

5. You observe an International Orange buoy about 3 feet in diameter floating in the sea; you
   a) may keep going by because it marks a lobster pot.
   b) must keep clear because it marks a quarantine area.
   c) should approach and investigate because it might be from a submerged submarine in trouble.
   d) must keep clear of the area and keep your propeller turning because it is the signal of a submarine on maneuvers and about to surface.

...and answers

This time allow the standard 4 for each correct answer ... and here's your score card:

92 - 100:	All Ahead Full.
84 - 90:	Proceed at Standard Speed.
76 - 82:	Watch Out for Storm Signals.
Below 76:	Dive! Dive! Dive!

Rules of the Road

1. (b)   2. (d)   3. (d)   4. (a)   5. (d)

Charts and Publications

1. (b)   2. (b)   3. (d)   4. (c)   5. (e)

Piloting

1. (c) 5 miles.

> 1st ϕ : 090° True
> Course: 000° True
> _____
> 1st ϕ :   90° on the starboard bow, or abeam to starboard

2nd ϕ : 135° True
Course: 000° True

2nd ϕ : 135° on the starboard bow, or 45° abaft the abeam

This is 90°-45° combination: Distance Run is equal to
Distance you were off at the 1st ϕ, 90°.
Distance Run = 30 minutes at 10 knots, or 5 miles.
Therefore, Distance Off at 1st ϕ at 0900 = 5 miles.

2. (a) 342°.

By Rule of Sixty: $\text{Angle} = \dfrac{\text{Distance Abeam x 60}}{\text{Range}}$

$$\text{Angle} = \dfrac{3 \times 60}{10}$$

$$\text{Angle} = 18°$$

18° to the left, or west, of 000° = 360° - 18° = 342°.

3. (b) 2 miles off.

By Rule of Sixty: $\text{Distance Abeam} = \dfrac{\text{Angle x Range}}{60}$

$$\text{Distance Abeam} = \dfrac{20° \times 6}{60}$$

$$\text{Distance Abeam} = 2 \text{ miles.}$$

4. (d) 1.35 miles.
When ship creates whistle signal:

$$\text{Distance Off} = \dfrac{\text{Time in Seconds x 0.18}}{2}$$

$$\text{Distance Off} = \dfrac{15 \times 0.18}{2}$$

$$\text{Distance Off} = 1.35 \text{ miles.}$$

5. (c) 1.8 miles.
When the signal is not an echo of the ship's own whistle:
Distance Off = Time in Seconds x 0.18
$$= 10 \times 0.18$$
Distance Off = 1.8 miles.

Weather

1. (a)   2. (b)   3. (b)   4. (a)   5. (b)

Distress Signals

1. (a)   2. (b)   3. (c)   4. (c)   5. (c)

section 5
contents

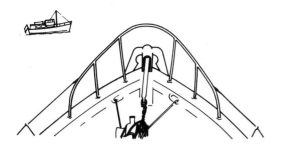

21/Rules of the Road
Lights

Reading the sections on lights in the Rules of the Road can be one of life's bewildering experiences. More than one person has felt like the student, overwhelmed by distinctions between a dredge and a vessel towing a submerged object, who exclaimed "They've got it so confused even lights must carry lights!"

Everyone will agree the scheme is complicated. But it shouldn't be called confused. For that's the whole point . . . to avoid confusion. The sad part is you really must know more than just the lights carried by your boat. Lights are carried for the benefit of the other ship. You must know how to interpret the signals shown by others. Perhaps we can find a general pattern to the scheme and then apply it to the lights for pleasure boats and to those vessels you're most likely to encounter. Lights can be placed in three categories:

1. **Running Lights . . .**
   those intended to show how a vessel is heading.
2. **Occupation Lights . . .**
   those intended to show the business or the type of craft.
3. **Condition Lights . . .**
   those intended to show present condition or plight.

This triumvirate is entirely arbitrary and unofficial. For all we know it's original with **Mariner's Notebook**. There is overlap from one group to another, and there certainly are exceptions, usually because of variance in size and construction. But as the start of a pattern, the division is quite helpful.

So . . . we'll begin with the first group, **running lights**. They show the direction of travel and are the red and green sidelights, the masthead and range lights and the stern light. No vessel shows them when she is anchored, moored, tied to a dock or aground. The reason: since she is not free to move, she has no direction to indicate. These lights are turned on when the craft is underway . . . that is, when her lines are cast off or the anchor ceases to hold, or she is free of the bottom. Until then the ship is made fast to Earth one way or another.

When free to follow her own head, the ship will show a running light combination that varies with her size and type. The basic ones are the sidelights: a red

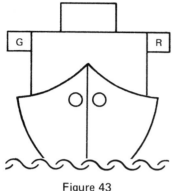

Figure 43

light to port and a green light to starboard. Each is shown from directly ahead through an unbroken arc of 10 points (112.5°) on the respective side. This means from dead ahead to two points (22½°) abaft each beam. Neither should be visible across the bow, but both should be visible to another vessel directly ahead. The result? When both lights are seen, the other will know this ship is approaching head on, with a course exactly opposite the bearing of the lights. In **Figure 43** the red and green lights are seen bearing due North. So the ship must be on a due South (180°) course.

When only the red light is seen, the course can be any one of many. But there are some limits. It can be any one from that almost opposite the bearing of the light, to that 112.5° more. In **Figure 44** the red light is seen bearing due North. The course of that ship, then, will be one that falls within these limits . . . from slightly more than South (opposite the bearing) to 112.5° more. Put another way, it will be one falling between 180° and 180°+112.5° . . . between 180° and 292.5°. If the bearing of the light had been East, then the course of the other vessel would be something from West to West+112.5° . . . between 270° and 022.5°. We've found a rule of thumb for narrowing down the possible courses for a vessel showing a red sidelight only: reverse the bearing and then add 112.5°. His course will be one of those in that arc.

When only the green light is seen, the course can be any one from almost opposite the bearing to 112.5° less. In **Figure 45** the green light is seen bearing

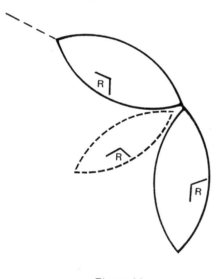

Figure 44

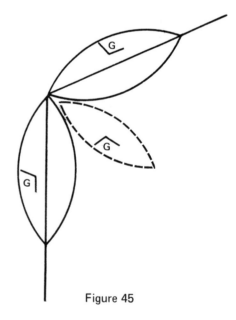

Figure 45

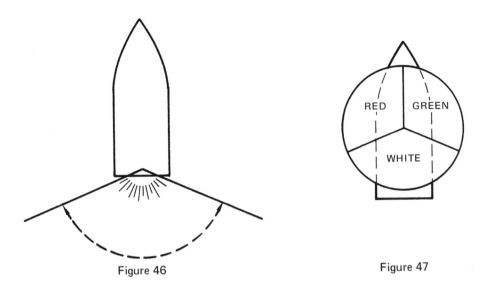

Figure 46

Figure 47

due North. The course of that other ship, then, can be anything from almost 180° to 067.5°. These two colored lights leave undesignated the arc astern of a ship. So a white stern light is fitted to show through 12 points (135°) from two points abaft the port beam around the stern to two points abaft the starboard beam. In **Figure 46** the stern of a vessel is shown, with the arc of the white stern light indicated.

Notice that each of these three lights has a different sector. And put together, they cover the full circle as shown in **Figure 47**.

The masthead and range lights are called **running lights**, but they are almost occupation lights. They are special running lights to mark power-driven vessels. And they are not carried by vessels under sail. The pattern is: a white masthead light on the foremast, or in the forward part of the ship, showing an arc of 20 points (225°) from the port limit of the red sidelight around the bow to the starboard limit of the green sidelight; and a white range light higher than the masthead and farther aft. In **Figure 48a** the arcs of these two lights are shown. **Figure 48b** combines them with the first three lights to offer the entire running light picture on a large power-driven vessel.

The function of the extra white light—the **range light**—is very important. By noting its position relative to the masthead light, an observer learns much more about the probable course of a ship. If the two are far apart, she must be seen from the side, or beam-on. But when in a vertical line the view is bow-on. **Figure 49** is the story told by all these lights when seen from different points of view. In **Figure 49a**, the ship is bow-on . . . for the two sidelights are visible as well as the masthead and the range. And they are in a vertical line. But **Figure 49b** is a different view . . . it is from the port beam. For there we see the port sidelight only; and the two white lights are opened quite wide. Moreover, even if we didn't see the port sidelight, we could tell that the ship was traveling to the left because the higher white light (the Range) is to the right. In **Figure 49c**, see the reverse: the green sidelight only is visible, with the two white lights opened wide and the higher one to the left. **Figure 49d** shows a more nearly meeting case, with the ship crossing from left to right but approaching. For there the starboard sidelight is visible with the two white lights much closer together. **Figure 49e** is the reverse . . . the ship is crossing from right to left and approaching. And **Figure 49f** is an overtaking case. Neither of the sidelights is visible . . . nor are the two white lights on the masts. All we see is the white stern light.

These are the basic running lights required by International Rules for power-driven vessels when 150 feet long, or more. Now let's see how the pattern will change for different vessels and also under different rules.

By the **Motorboat Act**, which applies to Inland Waters, power-driven boats are classed in this way:

Class A: Less than 16 feet long.
Class 1: 16 feet and less than 26 feet long.
Class 2: 26 feet and less than 40 feet long.
Class 3: 40 feet and not more than 65 feet long.

Classes A and 1 show a white light aft that has a 360° arc. In addition, they display a combined lantern forward and lower than the white light, showing red from dead ahead to 10 points on the port bow and green from dead ahead to 10 points on the starboard bow. So they carry the sidelights in one container, and substitute an all-around white light for the masthead and range light. But it is placed aft to serve a few other functions . . . because it is white, it marks the boat as power-driven; because it shows all-around, it serves as a stern light; and because it is aft, it can serve as a range with a sidelight to indicate heading.

Classes 2 and 3 have these lights: a white light forward that shows through 20 points . . . in other words, a masthead light; and another white light aft. This one is higher than the forward one, and is of 360° arc . . . all-around. It serves as a

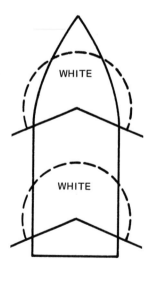

Figure 48a

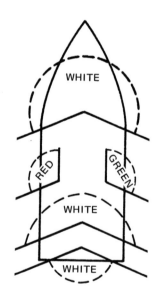

Figure 48b

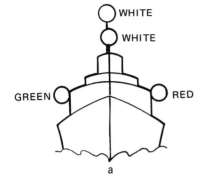

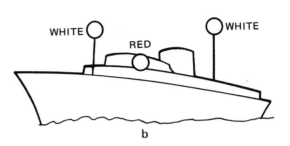

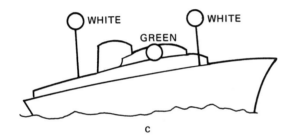

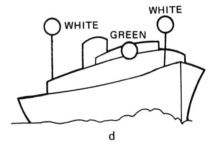

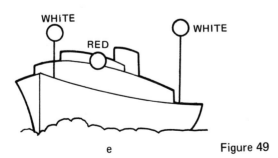

Figure 49

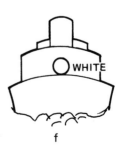

range light, and also as a stern light. And they carry separate sidelights, similar to the larger vessels. The Motorboat Act also says a few other things:

1. When Class A or Class 1 motorboats are propelled by sail alone, they carry the combined sidelight lantern, but not the white light aft.
   When Class 2 or Class 3 motorboats are under sail only, the sidelights are carried, but none of the white lights.
   But any class, when under sail only, shall carry a lantern or flashlight ready to show in time to prevent a collision. This seems to mean that under sail only, no class carries a stern light. But that isn't exactly so. An Interpretive Ruling, discussed on Page 159, clarifies the meaning.
2. Whenever a motorboat under sail also has its propeller turning, it will carry the lights for a motorboat, and not the lights for sail only.
3. Class A and Class 1 motorboats may carry the white light aft in a position off the centerline . . . to allow for an outboard installation.
4. The required white lights shall be strong enough to be seen two miles on a dark night with a clear atmosphere. The required colored sidelights shall be so visible for at least one mile.
5. Any Class motorboat may carry, in lieu of these lights, those required by the International Rules of the Road.

And so we come to the point of reconciling the lights specified under the Motorboat Act (for Inland Waters) with those required by International Rules on the High Seas. They dovetail very nicely . . . particularly since the 1960 International Rules speak of size by length rather than the older classification of tonnage.

By International **Rule 7**, a power vessel of less than 65 feet in length may carry the standard lights at standard heights but need not. If not, though, the requirements are these:

1. Forward, at a height above the gunwale of not less than nine feet, a white 20 point masthead light visible three miles.
2. Green and red sidelights either separately fixed, or in a combined lantern. The lights shall be visible at least one mile, and they shall be located below the white masthead light.
3. Required by **Rule 10**: a 12 point white stern light or, in bad weather, an electric torch kept at hand ready to show soon enough to prevent collision.

If less than 40 feet in length, she may lower the white masthead light below nine feet above the gunwale; but it must be kept at least three feet above the sidelights.

There are some differences, however, between the Motorboat Act and the International Rules. On the High Seas, the stern light is a stern light only . . . Inland, its purpose is served by an all-around white light aft. On the High Seas, the rule specifies that the white light for a powerboat, serving as its masthead light, shall be forward and be 20 points; the Motorboat Act allows Classes A and 1 to carry a white all-around light aft. It will take more than an Act of Congress to flatten out that divergence ... for the International Rules evolve from International conferences, and not just legislative action within our own walls.

Under Inland Rules, steam vessels (and the word "steam" means "power-driven") that are more than 150 feet long carry a range light ... but instead of being only 20 points, as at sea, the light is 32 points, or all-around. Since it is then also visible from astern, no separate stern light is necessary. And so, no separate stern light is specified. You will still see a white light when overtaking an Inland steamer; but since it is the range light up on a mast, it will be higher than a regular stern light.

Vessels under sail only will never carry the white lights on the masts ... they have no white masthead nor range light. But **Rule 5(b)** gives them a High Seas optional signal: two 20 point, two mile lights in a vertical line on the foremast ... red over green. This combination brings to sail vessels a welcome means to advertise their sails in the dark. And of course International requires they display the stern light. What about Inland? First off, there is no "red over green" option. The sail vessel turns off the white mast lights and makes no substitution. What about the stern light? Well the Motorboat Act says that the four classes, when under sail only, will turn off the white lights. This would seem to include the all-around light aft, and suggests they show no fixed stern light in Inland waters. But by interpretive ruling, the Commandant of the Coast Guard has determined that **Article 10** of the Inland Rules, which deals with the showing of a stern light

> ... *shall be applied to all vessels, including but not limited to, tugs, barges, sail vessels, motorboats when propelled by sail alone, etc.*
> **(Sections 86.05-5 of CG-169)**

The upshot is the same stern light requirement for sail vessels in either waters under either set of rules.

Vessels being towed have the same lights as a sailing vessel ... colored sidelights and a stern light. But they carry no lights on the masts.

We could fill many more pages with conversation about the many combinations of lights seen afloat. And every word could be justified by the argument that you may well encounter any of them on a summer night in the channel. But just over the horizon is the point of diminishing returns. We'll mention only a few more important classes, and then consider the ground sufficiently broken.

Under our arbitrary class of condition lights, we place those showing the temporary status of a vessel when she is in a condition part way between normal operation and tied to a dock. When she is at the dock no lights are specified. She is secured to Earth at a place where other ships can expect her to be. But when she's anchored, a signal must be given to warn others of her condition. The night signal is the anchor light.

If she is less than 150 feet long, the signal is a white, all-around light carried forward. If 150 feet or more, she will carry that light and also another white all-around light at her stern, and lower than the first one. **Rule 11** of International gives the smaller vessel the option to carry the second anchor light at the stern ... but she need not. **Article 11** gives the Inland vessel less than 150 feet long no such choice . . . one light only. **Figure 50** shows the two combinations for small and large vessels.

The anchor light is required, under International Rules, of all vessels. By Inland Rules, boats not more than 65 feet long need not carry it if they are anchored in an area designated officially as a *special anchorage area.* But if they drop the hook any other place, they must carry it. Even so, it sounds like good sense to show some light, no matter where you are, to warn others you are at anchor.

If you should see two red lights in a vertical line, you are looking at a vessel not under command. She is broken down: engine failure, or steering gear casualty, perhaps. She is not in full possession of her faculties to maneuver. If she is underway—meaning not in contact with the bottom—and also actually moving through the water, she'll also show the colored sidelights and the stern light. But, masthead and range lights will be out. If she is motionless in the water, only the two red lights in a vertical line will show. And if she is aground, the signal will be the two reds and the required anchor signal. But all this would only be seen on the High Seas . . . there is no combination for Not Under Command at night; and, presumably, you never go aground in Inland Waters. No matter how stuck you might think you are, Inland and Pilot Rules treat you as a vessel at anchor.

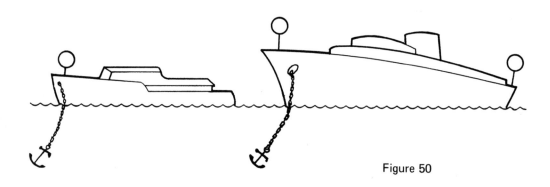

Figure 50

Note that the High Seas signal is not limited to the power vessel alone. **Rule 4** begins with the words "**A vessel** which is not under command . . . " And it is not spelled out that loss of control must be due to an accident; that expressed requirement was dropped from the rules over half a century ago. So it has been suggested that a sail vessel becalmed may carry it. From there it is only a short putt to the view that any vessel which encounters weather conditions seriously limiting her maneuverability can hoist the two red lights . . . even though she has suffered no casualty to herself, and is as sound from keel to truck as she was when she cleared port for sea. That is the stuff of which lawsuits and coffee-time arguments are made. There are, of course, guidelines set out by the courts to cover this as well as most other vague areas of the rules. But it is certainly not for us here to try to digest it all, chapter, verse and also the annotations.

Next time, we'll complete this discussion with mention of some of the occupation lights. Then we'll talk about daymarks and finish the kaleidoscope of visual signals under the Rules of the Road.

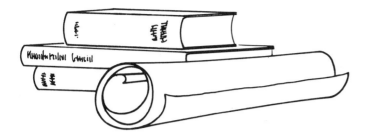

22/Charts and Publications
Books and tables

The list of published aids for the navigator is a fathom long. And each individual book is a model of completeness. But often the content is so complete it seems overwhelming. In one book you can find schedules for everything from the radiobeacon at Cape Kaliakra in Bulgaria to the time signal given at Sevastopol in the Black Sea. Another tells you the tidal set in the Pribilof Islands as well as the time of the next ebb at the Golden Gate Bridge. Even so, it's worthwhile to know that these books are, what they're for, and how they work. Here, we will talk about what they tell and how they tell it.

First off . . . there are *Tide Tables.* The publishing agency is the National Ocean Survey. There are four volumes which, put together, give world-wide coverage for more than 5000 ports. The Pacfic Coast area is found in *Tide Tables, West Coast North and South America, including Hawaiian Islands* . . . a book which has a scope from Cape Horn to St. Michael, Alaska. Our Eastern Seaboard and Gulf Coast are in *Tide Tables, East Coast of North and South America, including Greenland.* It tabulates tidal data for 2000 stations between the pole-side of Greenland and points south of Tierra del Fuego.

What each volume contains is a schedule of times and heights of High and Low Water for an entire year at selected places in a gigantic span. In the Pacific Coast book, 38 such **Reference Stations** have been chosen. For them the information is individually complete. Then more than 1100 **Subordinate Stations** are listed in a separate section. Each of them is "pegged" to a reference station and the differences in times and heights are listed. When these differences are applied to the data catalogued for the reference station, the times and heights at a given subordinate are found.

A tide table does not directly give you the **depth** of water at a certain time. You must use it in conjunction with a chart. The tables give the "more than" or "less than" factor applied to a charted depth to get the depth predicted for a certain time. Suppose, for example, the *Tide Tables* list High Water for Los Angeles Outer Harbor as 0800 with a height of two feet more than the charted depth. If that on the chart is 40 feet, then at 0800 the depth will be 42 feet. And if the height of Low Water is listed as -2 feet, then at Low Water the depth would be 38 feet.

The coverage in subordinate stations is very wide. In San Francisco Bay and environs, for example, there are 102 subordinates, all referred to the Golden Gate as the basic reference.

Tidal action is a vertical movement caused by the gravitational pull of the Moon and the Sun. Because the Moon is much closer, its influence is about two and a half times greater than that of the Sun. Every time the Moon is on our meridian—north or south of us—and every time it is over the side of Earth opposite to us, we would expect a High Tide. When it is 90° away, east or west, we should have a Low Tide. Since the Moon revolves around Earth about once a day, we would expect two High Tides and two Lows about every 24 hours. And that is the pattern, called **semidiurnal tides**, found on the Atlantic Coast of the US.

But sometimes other factors can slow down a tide or cancel it out entirely. The Sun, for example, can offset part of the Moon's pull. And topography or heavy river outflows can be of influence. On the Pacific Coast, we experience these variations. Some days we have four tides, but often we only have three. And successive tides will be unequal in height. So the cycle is called **mixed tides**.

The vertical rise and fall is only part of the story. For water always seeks a level. When lifted or lowered, it will flow horizontally from the highest point towards the low until equal level is reached. This horizontal motion is **tidal current**.

At first you would assume that, as soon as High Tide occurred, the water would begin to flow out towards Low, and as soon as Low happened, the inflow would begin. But this is most often not the case. Shapes and contours and a dozen other factors combine to make any synchrony between tide and tidal current seem coincidental. So a book is prepared to list tidal currents, *Tidal Current Tables.*

Its format is quite similar to the *Tide Tables,* with reference stations and subordinates. But instead of High and Low Waters, it lists flood and ebb tides and times of slack water, the period of no current flow.

The Pacific Coast area is found in *Tidal Current Tables Pacific Coast of North America and Asia.* The Atlantic and Gulf Coasts are covered by *Tidal Current Tables Atlantic Coast of North America.* In addition, *Tidal Current Charts* are published by the National Ocean Survey. *Coast Pilot* describes them as follows:

> "Tidal Current Charts . . . depict the direction and velocity of the current for each hour of the tidal cycle. They present a comprehensive view of the tidal current movement in the respective waterways as a whole and when used with the proper current tables or tide tables supply a means for readily determining for any time the direction and velocity of the current at various localities throughout the areas covered."

Nine such are presently available:

> Boston Harbor, Narragansett Bay to Nantucket Sound, Long Island Sound and Block Island Sound, New York Harbor, Delaware Bay and River, Tampa Bay, San Francisco Bay, Puget Sound Northern Part, and Puget Sound Southern Part.

Another book . . . the *Light List.* This is a US Coast Guard publication in several parts. The Pacific Coast is treated in *CG-162, Complete List of Lights and*

Other Marine Aids, Pacific Coast of the United States. The preface to that book describes it this way:

> "Lights and other marine aids to navigation maintained by or under authority of the United States Coast Guard on the Pacific Coast of the United States and Pacific Islands are listed in one volume. For the convenience of mariners, there are also included the lighted aids, fog signals and radiobeacons maintained by British Columbia which may be used by vessels proceeding directly from the United States to Alaska."

Companion volumes are printed for the Atlantic Coast and for the Great Lakes. It would be redundant to set out the "hows" of their use. Much is self-evident by inspection. What isn't, you'll find covered well in the introductions. Enough here to say that all CG-maintained aids within the areas are catalogued and described in detail. And a complete index leads you to the aid you seek.

One more book . . . or, rather, two . . . *Radio Navigational Aids.* These are US Navy Oceanographic volumes. *HO 117a* covers the Atlantic Ocean and Mediterranean areas; *HO 117b* handles the Pacific and Indian Ocean areas. In minute detail they list data on radio navigational aids the world over; but they are books for which a pleasure mariner might have little need. Should he carry radio equipment and be inclined in such directions, they will be informative aids . . . but he can operate without them. A lot of the content applicable to US waters is repeated on charts, in the *Light Lists* and in the *Coast Pilot.*

A browsing expedition to your nearest branch Oceanographic Office or authorized HO and NOS dealer can be very enlightening. The aficionado will react like an eight-year-old in a candy factory. For there are dozens of available publications, all of which make a good case for utility. At the other extreme are the self-sufficient who feel that no such aids are useful. Here, the old Bo'sun's saying is appropriate:

"Different ship, Different long splice."

Sample the field and buy what strikes your fancy.

23/Piloting
Current sailing and leeway

Somehow it seems profane to speak of seafaring as "motion over the ground and through two fluid media." That definition is colorless and much too scientific, but it is apt. For in traveling over the bottom, a vessel **does** move through water and air. Since our subject is wind and current, we can't avoid some cold analysis of their influence. But afterwards, let's restore the romance. Let's then forget fluid media and return to a world of scudding clouds and boiling sea.

Wind, the horizontal movement of air, and current, the horizontal movement of water, both affect the direction and advance of a vessel. But the outcome is different in each case. Waves will hammer at her . . . yet of themselves they cause no horizontal movement. Drop a match in a basin of water and then rough up the surface with waves. The match will ride up to the crest and slide down into the trough. But it won't travel horizontally. The wave will move by, but the match will stay put. To speak of wave motion, then, is not to speak of a current. For one is a disturbance of the surface while the other is an **en masse** horizontal flow of an entire layer of water.

Currents are started by prevailing winds and by differences in water temperature and pressure. Tremendous rivers flow in the deep oceans. A surface layer may flow westerly and then curve north or south while far below another stream moves just as steadily towards the east. The **Gulf Stream** is so distinct that the water it carries has different color, temperature and salinity from the gray Atlantic on either side.

Off the Pacific Coast we have a general southerly flow, called the **California Current**. It is part of a vast surface cycle in the North Pacific. Near the Equator, the Trade Winds start the ocean flowing westward as the **North Equatorial Current**. On nearing the Asiatic mainland, it curves to the north and scours past the Japanese islands as the **Kuroshio**, Japan's Black Current. Off the island of Hokkaido, it turns again to the right and starts east near the Aleutian chain. Then it reaches the North American continent to curve again to the right. And it travels down our coastline as the **California Current**. Off Central America it changes course to the southwest and completes the cycle. Note the constant changes to the right. This we've already met in discussing weather . . . the **Coriolis Force**. Because of Earth's rotation, things in motion on the surface turn right in the

PERU CURRENT

Depicted are the surface currents along the West Coast of South America. Published at regular intervals and prepared by US Navy Oceanographic Office and the National Weather Service of NOAA are *Pilot Charts* on which surface currents appear in detail.

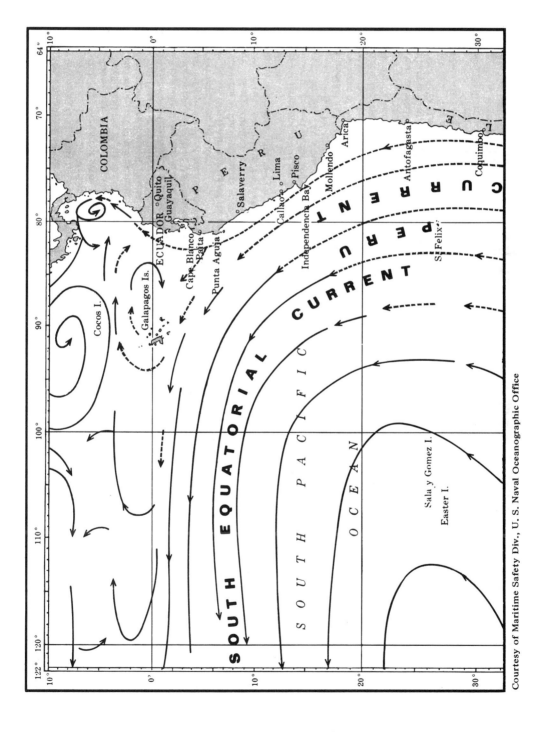

Courtesy of Maritime Safety Div., U. S. Naval Oceanographic Office

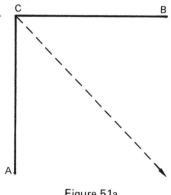

Figure 51a

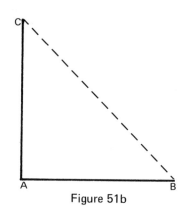

Figure 51b

Northern Hemisphere and to the left in the Southern. True to form, the North Atlantic has its clockwise, or right-turning cycle. And the South Pacific and South Atlantic have counterclockwise currents. These enormous ocean rivers are primarily wind-driven. The Trade Winds start the movement near the Equator. Coriolis takes it from there.

But local currents are those whose influence is most felt in coastal piloting. The Southern California coastline has the **Davidson Inshore Current,** flowing north and so counter to the main offshore stream. And other localities will feel the influence of tidal currents and runoffs from river deltas.

Information on current predictions is found in *Coast Pilot, Sailing Directions* and *Tidal Current Tables.* And a lot of data will be volunteered at the end of a dock by the Old-timer. But learning what to expect is only part of the job. How to use the data is the next step.

More romance is about to go. Now we must talk about vectors and vector analysis. These impersonal terms are old friends of mathematicians and engineers. Yet even the rest of us, though not realizing it, meet them often. Look at **Figure 51a.** There, **A** is pulling on a rope at the same time **B** is tugging in another direction. It's easy to see how **C** will move . . . along the dotted line. This is nothing but a slingshot. In **Figure 51b** we see a simple vector analysis of what happened. The line **CA** is drawn first to represent the direction and force of **A**'s pull. From the end, **A**, the line **AB** is drawn to show **B**'s pull. The dotted line **CB**, the resultant of the two pulls, shows how **C** will actually move. Draw it to scale and you determine both the direction and the force of **C**'s motion.

Now to apply this to a current problem. Suppose you sail due east at 10 knots while the current flows due south at three knots. What course and speed will you actually make good? **Figure 52a** pictures the two forces vying to move you from

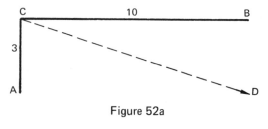

Figure 52a

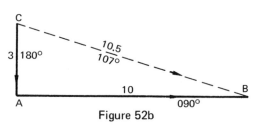

Figure 52b

Departure Point **C**. The current wants to move you three miles south in one hour to point **A**. In the same hour the ship's course and speed want to go 10 miles east to point **B**. Where will the ship actually go? Towards point **D**. A Current Diagram, or vector analysis, readily will give course and speed made good. **Figure 52b** is the sketch of the result. First, one hour of current action is drawn . . . CA, in the direction of 180° and, to scale, three miles long. From **A**, the end of the current line, the course and speed through the water are shown. AB is in a 090° direction and is 10 miles long. The resultant, **CB**, is the course and speed made good . . . 107° at 10.5 knots.

The Current Diagram, then, can be drawn as follows:

1. Draw the current for its **set** (direction) and **drift** (distance) in one hour.
2. From the end of the current line, draw the course through the water for a distance equal to your speed through the water . . . one hour's worth.
3. Connect the beginning and the end. The direction of this third line is your course made good over the bottom. Its length is your speed made good per hour.

However, this diagram is really "the horse out of the barn." You are finding out what the current did to you because you did not make allowance for it.

Figure 53 shows you a different situation. Here, you know the course you want to make good from departure point to destination . . . 200°True. You learn

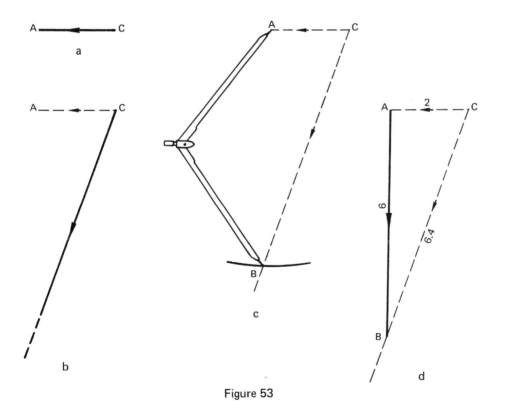

Figure 53

from a publication or from the Old-timer that the current will set 270° True at two knots. And the speed you can make through the water is six knots. What you want to find out is the course you should steer, and also the speed you'll actually make good over the bottom.

First, draw the current line, **CA**, for one hour (**Sketch a**). Then draw the "make good" course line of 200° (**Sketch b**). Since you don't know how long it should be, make the length indefinite. Next, set your dividers to the span for the ship's speed, six knots (**Sketch c**). Place one leg on **A**, the end of the current line. Draw an arc to cut the "make good" line, which it does at **B** (**Sketch c**). Last, connect points **A** and **B** (**Sketch d**). The direction is the course to steer . . . 181.5°. Its length you already know as six, the ship's speed. The speed you'll make good is the length, **CB** . . . 6.4 knots.

There are other ways to manipulate the basic diagram to find one or another missing factor, but this is as easy as any.

One more situation: how can bearings and fixes tell us what the current is?

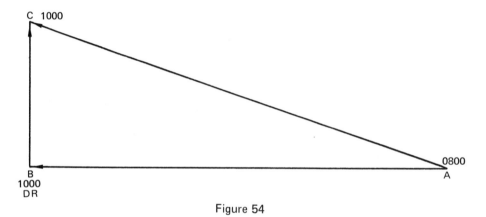

Figure 54

Figure 54 is an example. You leave **A** at 0800 on a course of 270° True at nine knots. Two hours later (1000) cross-bearings fix your position at Point **C**. Based on course and speed, you should have been at **B**, a point 18 miles and due West (270°) from **A**. What moved you from **B** to **C** is current. The **set** is the direction from the **Dead Reckoning (DR)** position at **B** to the position by **Fix** at **C** . . . 000° True. **Total drift** is six miles, the length of **BC**. Usually **drift** is expressed as a rate in knots. Divide six miles by two hours . . . the drift is three knots. The course and speed made good is found from **AC** . . . 289° True at 9.5 knots.

Now to **Figure 55**, another means to tell current. A ship left **A** at 0800 and steered 270° True at nine knots until 1000. She should then have been at **B**. Instead, she found herself at **C**. Because of current her course made good was not 270°; because of current her speed made good was not nine knots. What course and speed were made good? And what was the set and drift of the current? **Figure 55** shows a quick solution. Line **AB**, drawn from departure point **A** to DR position **B** (at 1000) represents the course and distance traveled through the water. Line **AC**, drawn from departure point **A** to Actual Fix **C** at 1000 is the course and

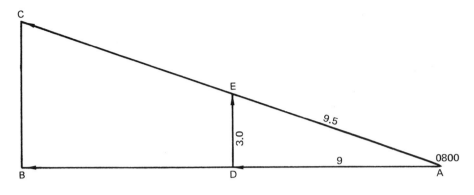

Figure 55

distance traveled over the ground. And **BC** is the set and total drift of the current. So far this is no different from **Figure 54**. Now to the difference. The ship's speed is nine knots. So measure out nine miles from **A**, along **AB**, to point **D**. **AD** represents one hour of course and speed through the water. With parallel rulers set to the direction of the current, **BC**, transfer that direction back to **D**. Now draw·a line from **D** to intersect the **AC** line. We've completed a smaller triangle, **ADE**. Since **AD** represents one hour's worth of course and speed through the water, we gain immediately two more rates per hour . . .

DE is the current drift; **AE** is the speed made good. So by transferring **BC**, the current line, back to **D**, we find:

The **direction** of **DE** is the set of the current .... .000°
The **length** of **DE** is the drift of the current .... .3 knots
The **direction** of **AE** is the course made good .... .289°
The **length** of **AE** is the speed made good .... 9.5 knots

In practice, current is a somewhat abused term. During a two-hour run you're bound to fall off course from human error, and you're bound to miss a bit on your estimate of speed. There are many little causes to vary a steady course and speed through still water. But at the end, when you compare where you are with where you should be . . . current is the scoundrel. There **are** currents, of course. And when in operation they are of much greater effect than any momentary drifting off course. But we should recognize that the difference between DR and Fix is not always just the current.

What about the other of the "fluid media" . . . what about air? Wind affects a ship's progress by causing **leeway**, a deflection downwind from the intended track. But it is not the result of a movement of the water; rather it is wind pressure on the exposed surfaces of the vessel. A deep keel resists the pressure; it stops the skid sideways. And, as would be expected, the force will increase as the hull area exposed becomes greater. There are formulas to reveal the total wind loading on the hull; but in practice the seaman's eye and educated guess are universal guides. The estimate is expressed in degrees of expected course deflection. Whatever the means to reach the estimate, it is allowed for when selecting a

Modern wind speed and wind direction indicators.

course. Should you expect the wind to divert you 2° to the right of the course, then by all means steer 2° to the left.

How do you determine wind direction and force aboard? First of all, some definitions of terms. **True Wind** means the direction and force of the actual movement of air. This is independent of any movement of the ship. **Apparent Wind** is the direction and force it appears to have as observed on a moving craft. Should you be in a dead calm and go north at 10 knots, the "wind" will seem to be from north at 10 knots. But there is really no breeze; you feel the current of air created by your own motion. On the other hand, if the true wind **was** from north at 10 knots, it would **apparently** be north at 20. Our friend the vector diagram will serve us here again. **Figure 56** shows a vessel moving east at 10 knots. The apparent wind is from north at 10 knots. What is the true wind? First, draw **CA** to represent the ship's course and speed for one hour . . . 090°, 10 miles. Next, draw **AB**, the apparent wind, for one hour . . . from 000° and 10 miles. Now connect **C** to **B**. This line is the true wind.

We should note another thing about wind. Unlike nearly everything else maritime, it is never described by the direction **towards** which it blows. Always the direction is that **from** which it blows. A North wind blows South. So, although our wind vector represents the apparent wind as blowing towards 180° (**AB**), remember it is named a **North** wind. And since **CB**, the true wind, is blowing Southeast (135°) at 14.1 knots, it is designated Northwest at 14.1 knots.

The difficulty with wind vectors is

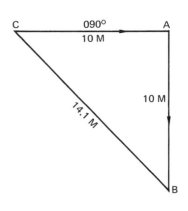

Figure 56

not in drawing the lines. The big problem is estimating the force of the apparent wind. Equipped with a wind vane and an anemometer, you can reach a fairly good estimate. But without them you are speaking in generalities. More helpful than wind vectors are seaman's hints to gain that general idea.

The best guide is not a moistened finger held aloft. It is observation of the water surface. Wind streaks and spray will give direction quite handily. As for force . . . it's a matter of acquired skill and judgment.

A useful fact: the true wind will always be striking the ship on the same side as the apparent, but farther aft. So, if the wind seems to be hitting your starboard beam, it is actually blowing someplace on the starboard quarter. Should it appear to be on the port bow, it is actually near the port beam, or, perhaps, even on the quarter.

In **READY REFERENCE** we've reprinted the **Beaufort Scale**. This is a numerical code used on shipboard to represent various wind strengths. Some mariners get quite expert at using it for estimates of the wind. Of course, without an anemometer and a vector diagram, there's no way to contradict them!

It is enough to know how wind is expressed, what it can do to the course, and how to offset its influence. It is handy to be able to learn the true wind from its apparent direction. It is "shipshape and Bristol fashion" to express it in nautical terms. But most of the time expect to be using a "guessometer."

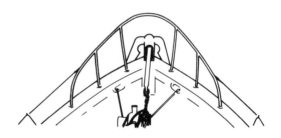

24/Sea Terms
A sampler of words and phrases

On voyages from Victorian England to India the most select cabins were those favored by prevailing winds. Outward bound the port side was choice; bound for England the preference was starboard. A mark of the VIP was the location of his stateroom. On the port side bound "out East," and on the starboard coming home, was posh. In fact, some etymologists say it was the prototype of posh . . . that the word itself came from Port Out Starboard Home.

Seafaring is rich with such words and phrases reflecting not only different cultures but also customs and eras long past. Always the terms are colorful and quaint, but nowadays some seem cryptic as well. There are several good maritime dictionaries available. On hundreds of pages are defined thousands of nautical words. There would be no purpose here in following a similar course. Of more value would be to shoot with a rifle and not a shotgun . . . to aim at patterns, at terms not elsewhere mentioned in **Mariner's Notebook,** or at those with exceptional saltiness and color. For knowledge of every discipline is heralded by authentic-sounding jargon. To have all words and little know-how is to invite ridicule. But too much scoffing at jargon is also faulty. The middle ground is a blend of appearances and understanding.

First off, then, to some general keys. The prefix **a-** can often mean **without** . . . as, in **aneroid** barometer (without liquid) and **agonic** line (without magnetic variation). But it can also suggest **towards** . . . as, **alee** (towards the lee or downwind); **aweather** (towards the wind and weather); **amidships** (towards the middle of the ship); **abaft** (towards the stern or rear of the ship); **astern** (to the rear of, or behind a vessel). **Astern** is used to describe a location not aboard the ship; **abaft** usually indicates where things aboard are relative to each other. So, a mariner looking through a porthole abaft the wheelhouse might see a coastline astern. **Ahead** is clearly to the head, or in front of. **Abeam** says to the beam, or at right angles.

Broad on the— denotes a direction differing by 45° from a stated reference point. So, **broad on the starboard bow** means a bearing or direction 45° to the right of directly ahead; **broad on the port bow** says 45° to the left of directly ahead. And **broad on the beam** is not a sailor's Tally Ho or mating call.

The suffix -**board** generally refers to the ship or ship's side. **Starboard** (which probably began as **steering side**) has evolved to mean the right side looking forward. **Larboard** (from **laden** or **loaded side**) now means the left side looking forward . . . the same as **port**. **Outboard** is towards the outside of the ship; **inboard** is in from the ship's sides. **Freeboard** refers to the part of the hull free of, or above, the waterline. It is the vertical distance from the waterline up to a specified horizontal level. **Garboard** speaks of planking or plating of the hull right next to the keel.

The suffix -**ward** more or less suggests **in the direction of** . . . homeward, landward, seaward. So it follows that **leeward** means in the direction of the lee, or away from the wind. The nautical pronunciation is distinctive. It is not **lee** as in **glee**, but **loo** as in **gloom**. **Windward** is in the direction of the wind. And its seagoing pronunciation drops the second **w** . . . **wind'ard**.

Yard is a tapered spar to spread the top of a sail. -**yard** probably derives from it but often connotes a line attached to something. So, **halyard** is literally a hauling yard, a line by which to raise or to lower something . . . signal halyard, flag halyard and topsail halyard. **Lanyard** is a strap from which something hangs, such as a bucket, or for which it serves as a flexible handle: the clapper of a bell or the pull on a whistle.

A **line** is a piece of rope with a specific use. By contrast, **rope** is the cord from which the line is formed. Even though slight, this distinction is carried out in some related terms. A **bowline** is a line used to keep the weather edge of a square sail taut. **Ratlines** are small lengths of rope attached horizontally to shrouds to form a ladder. A **gantline** is a line leading through a fixed block and used to hoist a weight aloft. A **dummy gantline** is one made of old rope and left in position leading through the block when the working gantline is not in use. Whenever needed, the real gantline is **bent on** (fastened) to the dummy gantline which then acts as a **messenger** to lead the working line through the block. And a final note: the pronunciation of bowlines and ratlines and gantlines is not to rhyme with **fine** as in **nice**, but with **fin** as on **fish** . . . bowlin', ratlin', gantlin'.

Sometimes, though, the distinction between rope and line seems waived. A **boltrope** is cordage sewed to the edge of a sail as a strengthening border. And, **manrope** is the general term for safety lines aboard . . . rope handrails on a ladder, knotted lines hanging over the side to assist in climbing aboard, lifelines rigged on deck during heavy weather.

The materials used in making rope vary. Wire rope is often of plow steel, stainless steel or bronze. It is usually measured by diameter and consists of wires wound into strands around fibrous cores. The strands are then twisted together to form the cord. A numerical pattern is used to describe the rope. So, **6 x 19** is unscrambled this way. The first number counts the strands and the second denotes the wires in each strand.

Synthetic fibers are relatively new to the scene. They bring greater strength and durability, and also some special problems of care in handling and stowage. Natural fibers used aboard for centuries are manila, sisal, hemp and jute. Among them, manila is the strongest and most durable. Sisal doesn't stand up too well under salt water. Hemp needs tarring to withstand the weather. Jute is of little use

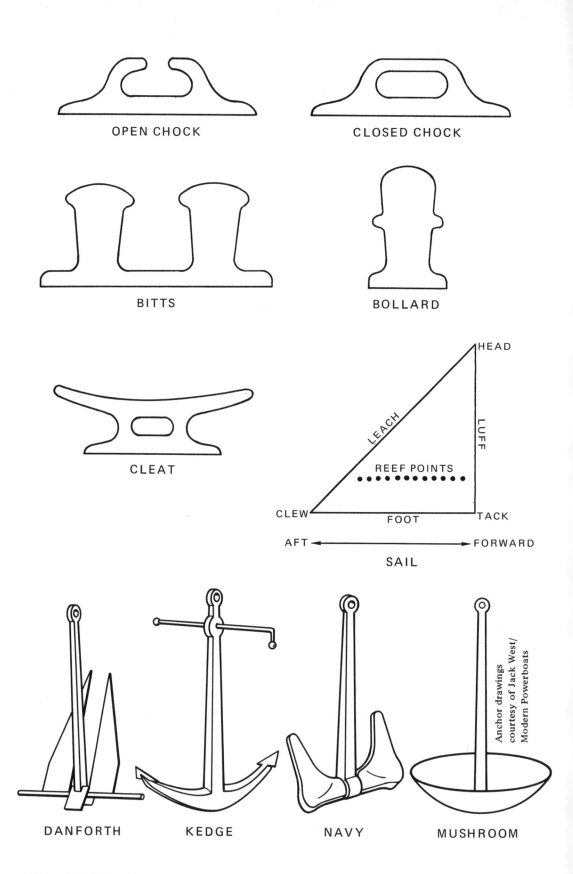

OPEN CHOCK

CLOSED CHOCK

BITTS

BOLLARD

CLEAT

HEAD

LEACH

LUFF

REEF POINTS

CLEW

FOOT

TACK

AFT

FORWARD

SAIL

DANFORTH

KEDGE

NAVY

MUSHROOM

Anchor drawings
courtesy of Jack West/
Modern Powerboats

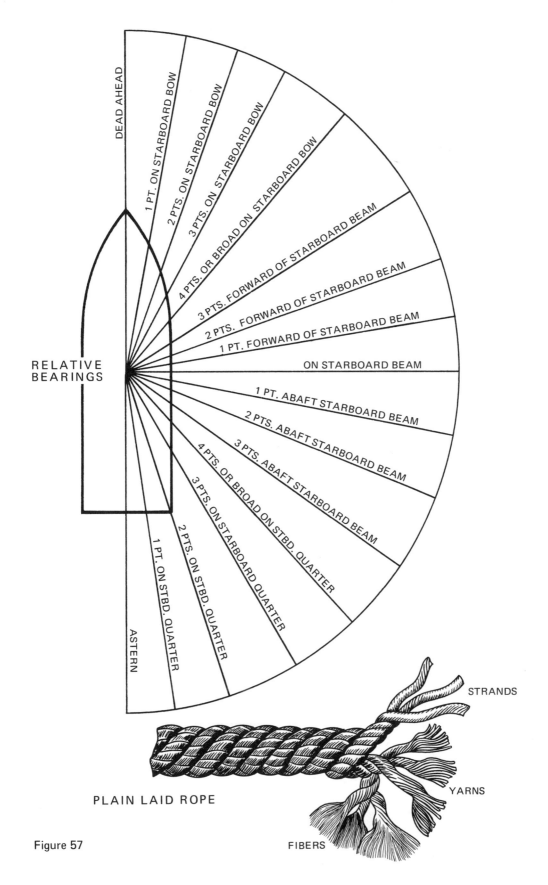

RELATIVE
BEARINGS

DEAD AHEAD

1 PT. ON STARBOARD BOW

2 PTS. ON STARBOARD BOW

3 PTS. ON STARBOARD BOW

4 PTS. OR BROAD ON STARBOARD BOW

3 PTS. FORWARD OF STARBOARD BEAM

2 PTS. FORWARD OF STARBOARD BEAM

1 PT. FORWARD OF STARBOARD BEAM

ON STARBOARD BEAM

1 PT. ABAFT STARBOARD BEAM

2 PTS. ABAFT STARBOARD BEAM

3 PTS. ABAFT STARBOARD BEAM

4 PTS. OR BROAD ON STBD. QUARTER

3 PTS. ON STARBOARD QUARTER

2 PTS. ON STBD. QUARTER

1 PT. ON STBD. QUARTER

ASTERN

STRANDS

YARNS

FIBERS

PLAIN LAID ROPE

Figure 57

by itself. It can shape the core of another rope or, by mixture with other fibers, form an inexpensive cord.

Fiber is made up of yarns or threads twisted into strands. Rope less than 1½-inch in circumference is usually called **small stuff**, and described by the number of its threads; **9-thread**, then, has nine yarns plaited into strands. Larger sizes are described by circumference.

The **lay** of the rope describes the twist of the strands. In essence it refers to the angle from the axis of the rope that the strands take as they intertwine. Turning the strands at a large angle produces a more compact rope than the loose or soft lay resulting from a smaller angle. **Figure 57** has a sketch of the general idea. Some of the terms used to describe the lay are **cable-laid, hawser-laid, plain-laid, soft-laid** and **hard-laid.**

Standing rigging refers to rope more or less fixed and permanent in position and used to support and strengthen other structures. **Running gear** or rigging consists generally of blocks and tackles and similar mechanical devices expected to move or to run in use.

A **stay** is considered part of the standing rigging. The **forestay** leads from the top or head of the structure it supports forward towards the bow and offsets strains tending to push the structure towards the stern. **Backstays** lead the other way and outboard. A **bobstay** leads from the bowsprit down and back to the stem to offset the tendency of the forestay to pull up on the bowsprit. A **jumper stay**, of its many meanings, can be said to describe an extra support used to meet unusual strains. Often one so used is called a **preventer stay**, or just a **preventer.**

Nautical measures also have to be different from those ashore. The **fathom**, a depth unit, is six feet long. It originated in the span between arms outstretched to the sides. **Cable length** refers to the standard length of a ship's anchor chain . . . and ends up not being standardized at all. In Europe it can be from the British one-tenth of a nautical mile (and so, 608 feet) via the French 200 meters (656 feet) to the Portuguese 846 feet. The American measure is still another: 120 fathoms or 720 feet. A **league** also varies. Usually the **marine league** is taken to be three nautical miles.

The nautical unit for speed is the **knot**, a nautical mile per hour. To speak of knots per hour is to suggest a change of rate and not the rate of speed itself, for that phrase literally means nautical miles per hour per hour. The idea of the knot stems from an old-time means to measure speed. A **log line** was streamed astern of the vessel, its end buoyed by a chip of wood. Knots were tied in the line at specified intervals. And a sand glass to measure time was the key to the length between knots. In the old US Navy the glass was good for 28 seconds, so the knots were tied 47 feet 3 inches apart. A good question about now would be "how come?" Because the ratio of 28 seconds to that distance is the same as the ratio of 3600 (the seconds in one hour) to 6080 (the then length of a nautical mile). If one of those knots passed over the **taffrail** (railing around the stern) every 28 seconds, the vessel was moving at one nautical mile per hour. By counting the knots going overboard in the length of time it took for sand to run out of the glass, the navigator knew the speed through the water. Hour glasses and chip logs have little place in the jet age, but the knot is still in common use.

The straight-forward procedure of making a vessel fast to land has spun off a bagful of terms. **Berth** generally describes the area or place where the ship is secured. That location could consist of a **wharf** or **pier** . . . the structure alongside which the ship lies. **Quay** might also be used, although it probably should be reserved for solid-wall construction rather than the open pilings of a pier. And **quay** is pronounced **key**, as in Key West. Not only are they pronounced alike, they mean the same.

The space between piers in which the vessel lies afloat is a **slip**. Often it is called a **dock**. But a purist would insist on **wet dock** to distinguish it from a **dry dock**. The one is a basin filled with water in which the vessel floats; in the other a vessel is propped up for repair work after the water has been pumped out. This brings us to further distinctions . . . between dry dock, floating dock, graving dock and marine railway. All support a vessel out of the water so underbody maintenance and repair can be done. How they do it makes the difference. The **marine railway**, for smaller vessels, has wide-set tracks on which a cradle moves. The boat floats over the outer, submerged end of the railway and is secured to the cradle assembly. Then cradle and vessel are hauled up over the tracks to dry land. A **floating dock** is a large pontoon with open ends and high sides. By flooding tanks, the dock is submerged so its flat bottom is deeper than the ship's keel. The ship then floats in over the sill of the pontoon bottom and between the sides. Landing blocks are strategically arranged on the bottom to take the ship's weight. Then the tanks are pumped out. Dock and ship rise out of the water together.

A true dry dock is often called a **graving dock**. There a set of watertight doors, acting the same as doors on canal locks, seal off the dock from the adjacent channel. With the doors open, the dock is flooded and a ship floated into position over landing blocks. Close the doors, pump out the water and the ship is in a **dry dock**. This arrangement can handle the largest of vessels.

Having placed the vessel in, or on, her dock, the next task is to secure her in position. The lines pass through chocks and are made fast to bollards and bitts or, perhaps, to cleats. So, to more definitions. A **chock** is a fitting on deck through which a mooring line leads over the side. If it has jaws and an uncovered top, it is called an **open chock**. Ease of placing the line in this fitting is obvious. If the top forms an enclosed eye it is a **closed chock**. The advantage is protection against the line jumping out of the chock. The disadvantage lies in the inconvenience of placing the line in the chock in the first place. **Bollard** and **bitt** are nearly synonymous. They describe heavy metal or wooden horns around which a mooring line is made fast. Bitts usually are in pairs and are found aboard ship. A single bollard can be encountered, although the usual pattern is paired. And bollards are found on piers . . . and wharves and quays and keys.

A **cleat** is a much lighter shipboard fitting with horns projecting out sideways. It is used to belay a rope or line. And **belay**? That names the act of making a line fast by winding it around a cleat in "figure-eight" turns. **Belay**, when used as an order, is a direction to cancel a previous instruction . . . a meaning getting close to **avast**, which is an order to cease or to stop doing something.

Fo'c'sle is a nowadays term for crew's quarters. It is an abbreviation of **forecastle**, the raised portion over the bows and used in ancient times as a fort for seagoing soldiers. And **fo'csle head** (no one will really become incensed if an apostrophe is dropped) is the foredeck of the vessel where the forward bitts and mooring and anchoring machinery are located. Unavoidable now is a mention of **head**, the seagoing latrine. Unfamiliar terms best given a fleeting glance are **ceiling**, which is the flooring of a hold, and **overhead**, which is the ceiling, and **floor**, which is neither top nor bottom but is a vertical plate placed between the inside and outside bottoms.

At the after end of the vessel we meet **fantail**, an overhanging stern. **Lazarette** tells us of a small 'tween deck storage space in the stern. **Poop** is an enclosed deckhouse on the stern. An unusual term is **jury**. On shipboard it describes something makeshift or improvised in an emergency. So, there is a **jury rudder** and a **jury mast**. The general term for something assembled in a hurry out of odds and ends is **jury rig**.

Too much more of this and we'll all seek haven in the **booby hatch**. What's that? A small entrance or hatchway from deck into a cabin area. And that's not to be confused with **scuttle** . . . a small opening through which fuel or stores can be passed. Deliberately to allow the sea to enter and so sink a vessel is **to scuttle** her. In days of sail the **scuttle butt** was a cask from which drinking water was dispensed. Inevitably, just as with the water hole, village pump and Koffee Klatch ashore, the scuttle butt became the focus for seagoing gossip and rumor . . . to which it has now given its name.

Strange and wondrous terms are hull down on the horizon . . . and probably should stay there. To speak of **saloon** and **mess**, of **Seattle Head** and **suji-muji** is to lead us further off course. Well, maybe we can stay out on this tack for just a few lines more. Those last two terms can't be left to lie mute on the page. A **Seattle Head** is a special type of **Charlie Noble** (galley smokestack) shaped like a "T" so that downdrafts of air will not extinguish the fire. And suji-muji? This gem, also called **soogee**, refers to a mixture of caustic soda and all sorts of pre-TSP ingredients for washing down decks and bulkheads. Which leads us to . . . AVAST DEFINING!

The point of diminishing returns has probably been passed. And without doubt we've failed to discuss terms much more deserving of mention than those defined. Perhaps, though, a purpose has been served . . . to whet an appetite for this exotic semantic world. And the menu is so bewildering, you might be able to con listeners into accepting word inventions of your own . . . distinguish that **con**, please, from **conn**, which refers to directing a ship's movements. But there's no occasion to indulge in such pioneering. What's already on the lists is rich with the flavor of the sea and ships and seafarers for thousands of years past.

25/Signaling
Flag, blinker and semaphore

It is the exceptional pleasure craft that carries a set of the International Code flags. And it is an exceptional circumstance when the pleasure mariner has use for them. But that is not to say he shouldn't know something about them.

The International Code of Signals is a remarkable "language" by which people of many tongues exchange detailed messages. The system is contained in the US Navy Oceanographic Office publication *International Code of Signals, HO 102.* Sold at nautical bookstores for $4.00, it contains the code sections and details of procedure and usage.

Although the pleasure mariner will never, perhaps, need *HO 102,* he should have an idea how the system works . . . and keep at hand the most important signals with their meanings. In **READY REFERENCE** are displayed each of the flags with capsuled single flag meanings; the full meanings are also given in that section. In the next few paragraphs we'll take a quick look at the general pattern of the code.

First off, the system now in use is very new. It became effective for US vessels on April 1, 1969. The new code book replaces *HO 103* and *104,* and is applicable to all means of communication . . . flags, flashing light, sound, radio, semaphore. Each signal is intended to have a complete meaning, and books are prepared in English, French, Italian, German, Japanese, Spanish, Norwegian, Russian and Greek.

Single-letter signals convey very urgent, important or common meanings. **Two-letter** signals express the General Signal Code. **Three-letter** signals which begin with **M** make up the Medical Code. When another letter leads off, the nationality of the ship or aircraft would be indicated: **A, K, N** and **W** prefix a US identity. Combining letters and numerals can indicate such things as position, time, speed and direction. When context requires amplification of a skimpy meaning, numeral pennants used as **complements** fill the bill.

The Medical section is a fascinating study. It aims to make feasible an understandable medical dialogue between a doctor and a seafaring layman . . . under the most desperate conditions. Sketched, labeled and coded are regions of the body; catalogued are common diseases; set out with coded references is a long list of

Photo by Harry Merrick

Nippon Maru standing out to sea as one of the last of world's training ships in sail.

medicaments . . . with Latin names included so a correct translation can be found in each language.

A doctor would send *MTD37* to prescribe seasick pills. If that wasn't comprehensible in Japanese, the medication would be identified as *Compressi Hyoscini Hydrobromidi.* Should you intercept *MQF77* you have eavesdropped on this: *My alternative diagnosis is Quinsy.* And *MGS38* would be the means for the seafarer to report that his patient suffers from a snake bite on the back of the neck.

Much of this is interesting, but not essential . . . that's quite evident. There is, however, practical value in the single flag hoists. But don't expect to recognize the flags exchanged by naval vessels. They use their own system for intraservice signals. Only in communicating with a commercial or private vessel would they employ the International Code of Signals.

Signaling by blinker and semaphore can sometimes be useful, but in most cases there will be no call for the knowledge. If you've ever done it, polish up your skill and add it to your reserve of available tools. But what if you don't know how . . . should you learn? The safe answer, of course, is "Yes." And the only way to learn is by memorizing the alphabet, and then some practice. With that knowledge you are better equipped to cope with an emergency. So if you're inclined to learn, do it by all means.

But it isn't knowledge you must have. It isn't an essential like the emergency signals. Nor is it as important as Rules of the Road. In a few words, place it in its proper rank, and learn if you feel so inclined. But first learn more important procedures.

Questions

The end of another section . . . and so time for an accounting. Watch out for the auditor, though. He's armed with a sharp red pencil, poised to pounce!

Rules of the Road

1. You are steering due North in International Waters at night. Directly ahead you observe 3 lights as follows:
   on the left is a white light;
   on the right but higher up is another white light;
   between them and lower than both is a red light.
   You see
   a)   a power-driven vessel more than 150 feet long and on a westerly course.
   b)   a power-driven vessel more than 150 feet long and on an easterly course.
   c)   3 vessels at anchor.

2. At night directly ahead of you is one white light. It can be
   a)   the stern light of a large vessel.
   b)   the stern light of a sailing vessel.
   c)   the stern light of a motorboat.
   d)   all of above.
   e)   none of above.

3. Under the Motorboat Act, a 35-foot auxiliary ketch under sail and power at night will show
   a)   only the colored sidelights.
   b)   only a white light forward and a white light aft.
   c)   the regular lights required of her when under power only.

4. In International Waters at night, you see the following lights:
   a green light; and near it,
   2 red lights in a vertical line.
   You are looking at
   a)   the port side of a vessel.
   b)   the starboard side of a vessel not under command but actually moving through the water.
   c)   the starboard side of a vessel not under command and not moving through the water.

5. A motorboat at anchor in Inland Waters
   a)   need show no anchor light.
   b)   must always show an anchor light.
   c)   must show an anchor light unless she is in a special anchorage area.

Charts and Publications

1. For a particular place at a particular time, a *Tide Table* will tell you directly
    a)   the depth of water.
    b)   the amount to apply to the charted depth to find the depth of water.

2. Tidal current is
    a)   a horizontal movement of water.
    b)   a vertical movement of water.

3. In order to find the time of ebb tide you use
    a)   a *Tide Table.*
    b)   a *Tidal Current Table.*
    c)   either a *Tide Table* or a *Tidal Current Table.*

4. On the Pacific Coast of the United States there are
    a)   always 4 tides each day.
    b)   never 4 tides each day.
    c)   mixed tides.

5. *Radio Navigational Aids* is published by
    a)   the US Coast Guard.
    b)   the National Ocean Survey.
    c)   the US Navy Oceanographic Office.

Piloting

1. The California Current flows along the Pacific Coast
    a)   in a northerly direction.
    b)   in a southerly direction.

2. You are steering due North at 10 knots. The current sets due South at 3 knots. Your speed over the bottom is
    a)   10 knots.
    b)   13 knots.
    c)   7 knots.

3. You want to travel due East at 8 knots. A current sets due East at 2 knots. Your speed through the water should be
    a)   8 knots.
    b)   6 knots.
    c)   10 knots.

4. At 0800 you depart from the sea buoy. At 1100 your position as found by cross-bearings is 9 miles in a direction of 045° from where you expected to be. The current set and drift is
    a)   North East at 3 knots.

b) 045° at 3 knots.

c) both of above.

d) none of above.

5. As you travel at 6 knots, the wind is apparently on your starboard bow. The true wind is on

a) your port beam.

b) your port bow.

c) your starboard side farther aft than the apparent wind.

Sea Terms

1. Larboard means the same as
   a) starboard.
   b) port.
   c) lee side of the ship.

2. Clew refers to
   a) the after lower corner or corners of a sail.
   b) a hint to an investigator.
   c) the men working on a Chinese ship.

3. A dummy gantline is
   a) an ornamental piece of bunting streamed from the gangway.
   b) the crosshair in the sight of a dummy compass.
   c) a gantline of old rope used as a messenger to heave the working gantline into the block when ready to be used.

4. A boltrope is
   a) a safety lanyard attached to a bolt or pin used in a shackle, block or other device located aloft.
   b) a rope sewed to the edge of a sail to give it strength.
   c) the rope used to secure a bolt of canvas.

5. A cowl is
   a) a hood-shaped top of a weather deck ventilator.
   b) a Canadian owl.
   c) another name for a calf.

6. A deadlight is
   a) a false light from an aid to navigation seen during a temperature inversion.
   b) a steel disc screwed or dogged down over a portlight.
   c) a burned-out running light.

7. Lazarette is
   a) a storeroom above the after peak.

    b)   the same as the forepeak locker.

    c)   a small sailing vessel used in the Eastern Mediterranean.

8. The term holiday refers to
    a)   time off for exceptional painting ability.
    b)   an unpainted or unscraped surface overlooked in the work.

9. Dodgers are
    a)   indeterminate pips on a radarscope.
    b)   members of a shipboard athletic team.
    c)   canvas weather screens fitted in an exposed area.

10. Tide rode means a vessel is
    a)   riding to the wind and not the tide.
    b)   riding to the wind and tide together.
    c)   riding to the tide and not the wind.

Signaling

1. A single-flag hoist flown by a nearby ship
    a)   will never be of importance to you.
    b)   might have an important meaning to you.
    c)   is part of the ship's call letters.

2. The two-flag hoist NC
    a)   is relatively unimportant.
    b)   is the call for a pilot.
    c)   is a distress signal.

3. A four-flag hoist beginning with K
    a)   tells the call letters of a Panamanian ship.
    b)   tells the call letters of a US ship.
    c)   is part of a signal of a geographical position.

4. The single-flag hoist O means
    a)   I have a Doctor aboard.
    b)   Man Overboard.

5. Two naval vessels exchanging Code flag signals
    a)   will always use the International Code of Signals.
    b)   will probably use a special Navy Code System.

...and answers

Take the standard deduction of 4 for each entry disallowed (except on Sea Terms, where the deduction is 2 for each entry disallowed). Find your bracket by consulting this table:

92 - 100: Accounts in Order.
84 - 90: Minor Discrepancies Only.
76 - 82: Entertainment Expense Too High.
Below 76: Now, really! After all . . .

Rules of the Road

1. (a)   2. (d)   3. (c)   4. (b)   5. (c)

Charts and Publications

1. (b)   2. (a)   3. (b)   4. (c)   5. (c)

Piloting   (See following sketches for problems 2,3,4,5.)

1. (b)   2. (c)   3. (b)   4. (c)   5. (c)

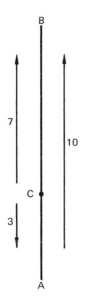

2.

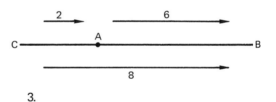

3.

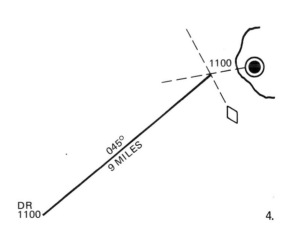

4.

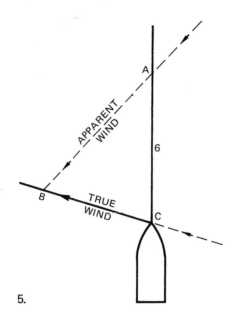

5.

Sea Terms

1. (b)   2. (a)   3. (c)   4. (b)   5. (a)   6. (b)   7. (a)   8. (b)   9. (c)   10. (c)

Signaling

1. (b)   2. (c)   3. (b)   4. (b)   5. (b)

section 6
contents

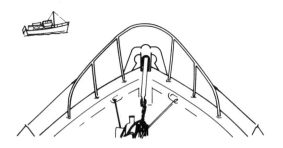

26/Rules of the Road
More on lights

Occupation lights and signals come in many combinations; and to talk of them all would take a long time. Of course, they're all important, and no one can foretell what ones you might see. But as a practical matter, we've selected those you're most likely to encounter.

Tows . . The towing vessel herself will show the normal colored sidelights and a light astern. But her occupation is signaled by white lights in a vertical line. When towing in International Waters, and the distance from the stern of the tug to the stern of the last tow is no more than 600 feet, she displays two white lights. But when that distance is more than 600 feet, she carries three such lights. In either case, they are 225° in arc like the masthead light. **Figure 58** indicates the combinations.

On Inland Waters, the setup is somewhat different. There, the difference is not based on the length of the tow . . . but on how they are being towed. When towing astern, no matter how long the tow might be, the signal for the tug is three white lights.

When towing alongside, the Inland signal is two such lights. When pushing ahead, the Inland tug shows two lights; but, in addition, she may show astern two amber lights in a vertical line.

The vessels being towed carry colored sidelights. On the High Seas, the last one in tow will carry a stern light. Those in between may substitute a small light for the followers to steer by. Inland, a stern light will also be shown by the tows. How, though, depends on the build of the vessel, and where she is being towed. From the Rio Grande around to Cape Sable, Pilot Rules order one setup on the Gulf Intracoastal Waterway and on Inland Waters connecting with it or with the Gulf of Mexico. Another display is ordered for the Hudson River and Lake Champlain. Still another stern view is dictated on other Inland Waters. Simply put (a fond but faint hope) there will be either one white stern light, or one such on each corner.

The rules are full of nice distinctions regarding tows. But be able to recognize the basic pattern. When you see a sidelight, or sidelights, and two or three white lights in a vertical line . . . you see a towboat. Its tow will be alongside, ahead or astern. Watch out for it. If you see three lights in the vertical line and are in Inland

Waters, the tow is definitely astern; if you see those three lights and are in International Waters, the tow is astern, but, in addition, is over 600 feet long. If you see two amber lights in a vertical line, you can be overtaking a tug that is pushing barges ahead on Inland Waters. Before you decide to pass him, be sure there will be plenty of room to pass the barges also.

When you see just a single colored sidelight and nothing more, it is probably a sailing vessel not using the optional colored mast lights. But it could be a vessel under tow, with the lights on her tug not yet visible . . . another reason to be cautious when all you see is a colored light.

One more caution on tows and then we promise to keep still. These lights—whether amber, white or blushing pink, whether ranged vertically or on the bias—need not be visible from every angle. They need not be 32 point, all-around lights. In fact, they probably won't be. From astern you may see no more than a stern

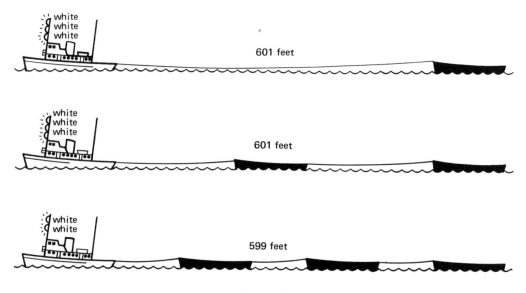

Figure 58

light or two. They may blend into a background of cabin and deck lights. But, Lo and Beware! They mask a complex of tug, barges and hawsers. Whenever you see lights on a moving object, be very alert to the less than obvious. Lurking under an innocuous lantern may be the largest "ship" afloat . . . a 90-foot tug and a 400-foot barge with a quarter-mile of cable between them.

Pilot Vessel . . A power-driven pilot vessel shows her job by a white light over red light . . . *White over Red, Pilot Ahead.* This is in addition to her colored sidelights and stern light when underway, and to her anchor lights when at anchor. This is the gist of the International Rule. Inland, the story is just a bit different: no anchor lights and silence on the stern light.

Fishing Vessels . . Under Inland Rules, they show a red light over a white . . . *Red over White, Fishing at Night.*

On the High Seas, the schemes are more complicated. If not engaged in fishing, they show regular lights. But as soon as they go to work, the light combination depends on the kind of fishing. If it is trawling—dragging a dredge net or other apparatus through the water—the signal is *Green over White.* In addition they may carry a white light, like the masthead light, below and abaft this combination. All other fishermen show *Red over White.* In either case, if the vessel is in motion through the water, sidelights and the stern light shall be shown. But if the fishing boat is not making way, then they will be dark. If a fisherman (other than a trawler) has outlying gear extending more than 500 feet horizontally, then he must display another white light in the direction of the gear. Finally, any fisherman may attract attention with a flare-up light, or beam a searchlight on a danger to safe passage.

Dredges and Vessels in Underwater Operations . . The International Rule here is quite simple: three lights in a vertical line. The top is red, the middle is white, the bottom is red.

But Inland, the pattern is very complicated. Under the Pilot Rules, there are different signals for different types of underwater operations: towing a submerged object, dredges, submarine construction, and several others. The signals range from two red lights in a vertical line to a four-light combination of whites and reds.

It is pointless to enumerate any more of them. They are shown, usually, in conjunction with basic running lights or anchor lights . . . and they indicate a state of maneuverability less than normal. Whenever you **don't** see the normal running light pattern, suspect the vessel has limited maneuverability and keep clear.

Daymarks . . Here the problem is much simpler. Anyone who sees a daytime shape should also see the ship underneath it. Then he knows a lot about direction of travel, aspect and occupation. What is usually missing is condition. So the daymarks seem primarily aimed at signaling any limitations on mobility a vessel might have.

A vessel at anchor on the High Seas displays a black ball forward. If she is Not Under Command, the signal is two black balls. If she is aground, the signal is three black balls. These shapes are to be visible all around the horizon and, when more than one, are to be hung in a vertical line.

By International Rules, a vessel under sail and power *shall* carry forward a black cone, point downwards. No chiseling in on the privilege of a sailing vessel when you are actually power-driven. In practice the signal is as rare as the mustache cup . . . nowadays, perhaps, even more so.

Fishermen? On the High Seas and 65 feet or more long, they show a black shape of two vertical cones, point to point. Less than 65 show the same as Inland fishermen: a basket. The High Seas fisherman with gear out more than 500 feet also shows a black cone, point upwards, in the direction of the gear. And at sea, when a tug-tow combination exceeds 600 feet, each sports a black diamond. Also in those waters, a craft engaged in underwater work will show a white diamond with a red ball above and a red ball below. Finally, a minesweeper at sea displays a black ball at the fore truck and another on the danger sides.

There they are . . . the daymarks under International Rules. The scheme is evident: marks to indicate impaired maneuverability or occupation, or both.

Now to exceptions and variations. The International Rules express no difference because of size. For example, **Rule 11c**, speaking of the anchor ball states:

(c) Between sunrise and sunset every vessel when at anchor shall carry in the forepart of the vessel, where it can best be seen, one black ball not less than 2 feet in diameter.

Rule 14, speaking of vessels under sail and power, says:

VESSEL UNDER SAIL AND POWER
BY DAY

RULE 14   A vessel proceeding under sail, when also being propelled by machinery, shall carry in the daytime forward, where it can best be seen, one black conical shape, point downwards, not less than 2 feet in diameter at its base.

There is no exemption to boats under 65 feet or under 40 feet or under two feet. Needless to say, these daymark regulations are often honored in the breach. But the requirement is clearly printed in the mother tongue. Ours not to say what is done; just to mention what should be done under the letter of the rules.

What about Inland and Pilot Rules? First of all, the anchor ball is not even mentioned under Inland Rules. **Section 80.25** of the Pilot Rules says this:

80.25 Vessels moored or at anchor

Vessels of more than 65 feet in length when moored or anchored in a fairway or channel shall display between sunrise and sunset on the forward part of the vessel where it can best be seen from other vessels one black ball not less than two feet in diameter.

Loaded container ship with restricted visibility.

Photo by Port of Los Angeles

This is one shape most pleasure mariners need not display; but they should know what it is.

Nothing in Inland or Pilot Rules mentions a day signal for an auxiliary under power and sail. The concern is not that a power-driven vessel might masquerade as a sailor; rather, it is that a sailor might be mistaken for power-driven. For **Article 14** of Inland Rules goes on the opposite tack:

STEAM VESSEL UNDER SAIL BY DAY

> ART. 14. *A steam vessel proceeding under sail only, but having her funnel up, may carry in daytime, forward, where it can best be seen, one black ball or shape two feet in diameter.*

This signal, which is not mandatory, allows a steamer to claim privilege as a sailing vessel when under sail only . . . to avoid the possibility that her overall appearance might mark her as driven by machinery.

Nor is there an Inland daymark for a vessel aground . . . no three black balls. And there is none for Not Under Command . . . no two black balls. The fishing vessel, though, will still show a basket.

The Inland marks for underwater work, though, are quite different. For example, a Coast Guard vessel servicing an aid to navigation **may** display, in a vertical line, two orange-and-white vertically striped balls. A submarine cable ship shall show a black-and-white vertically striped ball with a red ball below. A dredge moored in position will show two red balls; if dredging underway the balls will be black.

There is only one answer to all this . . . you should never approach another vessel closer than necessary. But when you see any type shape of **any** color, stay clear. Only one exception: when you see a square flag with a ball above or below it, that is a distress signal. Then you approach! In all other cases stay clear. Otherwise you're liable to run afoul of underwater wires or pipes or some paraphernalia . . . if you don't first get run down by a Not Under Command ship.

27/Piloting
Tools and techniques of plotting

Important in piloting is the laying out of courses and bearings and the measurement of distances on a chart. Unfortunately, a word description of the knack is inadequate. There is only one way to learn chart plotting . . . by doing it. Even so, we'll take a stab at a review of the tools and mention some wrinkles that will be second nature after a little practice.

The basic instruments are two: one to draw a straight line and to find its direction; and another to measure distance. A set of **parallel rulers** serves the first aim; a pair of **chart dividers** serves the second.

The most difficult problem with either instrument is grammatical. Is the name singular or plural? Somehow, "chart dividers is . . . " doesn't sound right. Say "a pair of dividers is" and you neatly dodge the issue. But surely the principle of them (or it) is not nearly so complicated. To look at both parallel rulers and dividers is to know how they work. **Figure 59** is a picture of typical instruments.

There are, though, a few hints worth noting. Parallel rulers have a bad habit of slipping. You "walk" a course all the way across a chart . . . and then the rulers slip. The answer? First of all, move them as little as possible. You shorten the "walk" by starting from the compass rose nearest your location on the chart. Try not to move too fast. Be sure to keep firm pressure on the stationary ruler while you pivot out the moving one. And don't take big steps. It is much easier to transfer them a little bit at a time than in a few giant strides.

As for a pair of dividers: be sure they (?) are tight. You want the legs to stay in the position you place them, and not flop together when you lift the points off the chart. When measuring a distance . . . don't just squeeze the legs to the span, lift them off and then place them on the scale. There is spring to the pivot. Stretch or squeeze the legs as necessary until the points cover the distance. But then release the pressure of your fingers and replace the points on the chart. More often than not, you'll see the legs have moved one way or the other. Nudge them a bit until the span is right, and then transfer to the scale.

The points are sharp . . . don't let them jab you. And don't let them spear the chart. The paper is heavy and tough, but it can still be damaged by the sharp legs.

Finally, don't spread the legs too far apart. They tend to slip as they widen out.

When measuring 20 miles, it is better to use two 10-mile spans than to stretch the points the full distance.

There are several other instruments to do the same job. One substitute for dividers is a mechanical device that looks like a pencil but has a little wheel at the tip. By rolling the wheel over a charted line, you read the distance off a scale on the body of the instrument. This can be handy, provided the scale set on the pencil is the same as the scale of the chart. "Almost the same" is not enough. If you have a chart scale of 1:18,000 the distance pencil must be set to 1:18,000. And as you change charts, you'll probably need a new scale. Not all such devices are adaptable to marine chart scales. If you buy one, be sure it will handle the chart scales you'll be using.

Two plastic triangles are a good substitute for parallel rulers. Line one edge of one triangle up with the direction to be transferred. Maintaining that direction, slide triangle along the edge of the other one to the proper chart location.

Some parallels have a 180° protractor on one side. This makes it unnecessary to "walk" them from a compass rose. Set the proper direction by using the protractor and a north-south line (a meridian) nearest the chart location. Then a very short movement will bring the rulers to the exact spot.

A substitute for both parallels and dividers is a plotter. This device combines a protractor and a straightedge, and has various distance scales printed on the face. But be sure to use the right scale.

Often there is a little problem when setting the parallels over a compass rose to get direction. You line up the center of the rose with the proper degree marking on the rim. But to do it right, your eye should be directly over the rose. On a large chart this sometimes seems to involve climbing on the chart table. A simple wrinkle: set one leg of the chart dividers in the center and the other at the exact degree mark on the rim. Then slide the parallels against the legs. This is precise and rapid, and much easier to do.

To check parallels for parallelism: move them from the left chart margin to the right and back several times. Each time, the straightedges should arrive in alignment with the margin. If not, look at the coupling arms for adjustment screws or knobs.

When working on a chart, draw light lines with a #2 pencil, and use a soft eraser. Don't score the paper into furrows and channels. You might want to pass that way again.

Figure 59

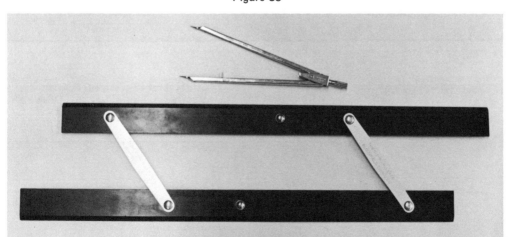

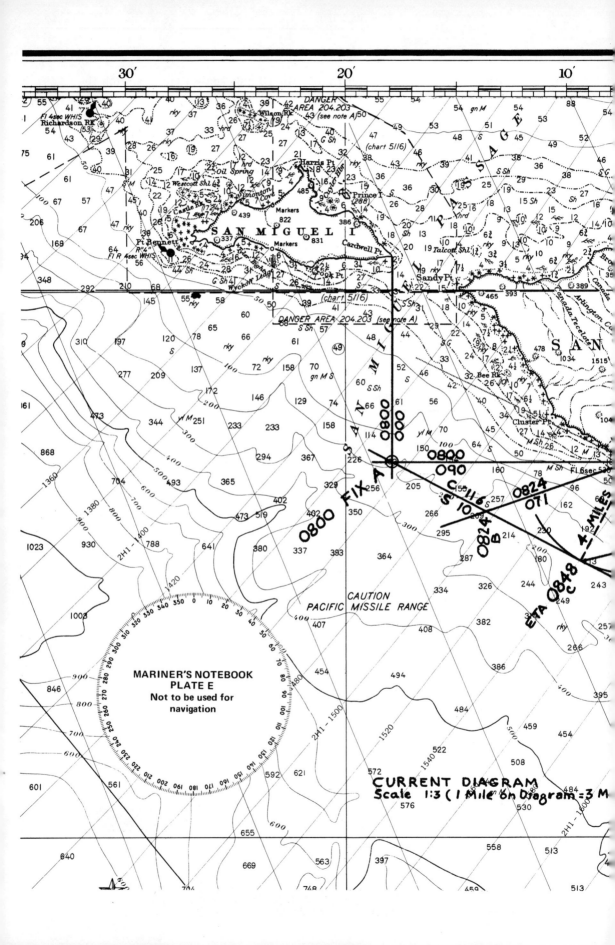

MARINER'S NOTEBOOK
PLATE E
Not to be used for
navigation

CURRENT DIAGRAM
Scale 1:3 (1 Mile on Diagram = 3 M

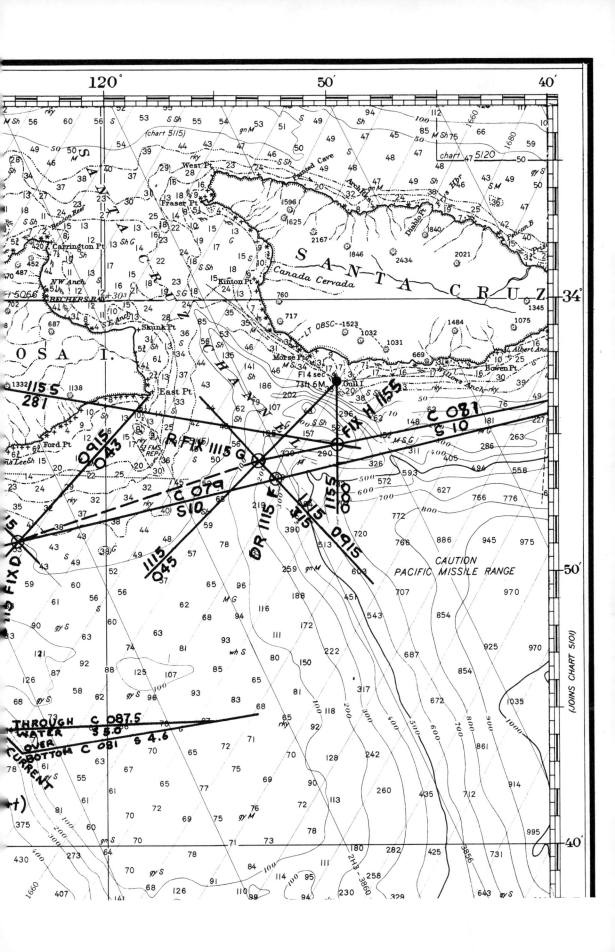

All right . . . we've seen the tools and we know the chart. Now: why do we plot, what do we plot, and how?

"Why" and "what" are quite evident. Modern nautical charts are faithful reproductions of an area. By drawing in course lines and bearings, we gain a very graphic picture of location and progress. But it was not always so. Generations of seamen struggled through reams of complicated mathematics to learn what we now find by a few pencil strokes. Incidentally, in the early days a shipmaster took practical advantage of the complications of his job. His work book, filled with cryptic sums and angles, was a protection. For the crew thought less of mutiny when those hieroglyphics were the passport back to shore. If position were readily seen by inspection of a chart, he would be much less indispensable.

Back to the subject! The "how" of plotting is best seen by following an example. **Plate E** is a reproduction of part of *C&GS 5202*. It shows the south coasts of Santa Rosa and San Miguel Islands. Sketched on it is a plot of part of a passage around these Channel Islands off Southern California. We've also added a compass rose and part of a vertical margin latitude scale for your convenience in following the discussion.

At 0800, position was fixed by two cross-bearings. **Cardwell Point** on San Miguel bore 000°True and **South Point Light** on Santa Rosa was 090°True. The two lines of position, when drawn on the chart, locate the vessel at **Position A**.

We wish to pass four miles off **South Point** abeam, so an arc is drawn from there as center and with four miles as radius. The parallel rulers are then laid down from **A**, tangent to the arc at **C**. Their direction is 116°True, our course on the first leg.

Next, the distance is measured from **A** to **C** . . . eight miles. How long should it take if our speed through the water is 10 knots? You'll find a nomograph and its explanation in **READY REFERENCE**; use it to figure Time, Speed and Distance. The expected time for eight miles is 48 minutes. Leaving **A** at 0800, we estimate the time of arrival (ETA) at **C** as 0848.

Let's add a few more facts. At 0824 **South Point** bears 45° on the port bow. So we draw in that line of bearing, 071°True. It intersects the course line at **B**. The distance from **A** to **B** on course is four miles. The running time was 24 minutes. So the speed is 10 knots. We've made good our estimated speed. And we should run another four miles to abeam; 24 minutes. Our ETA of 0848 seems confirmed.

Sure enough, at 0848 **South Point** is abeam to port. So we start the next leg of the passage. We are to pass three miles off **Anacapa Light**. Although not shown on **Plate E** that position would make our new course 079°True. As soon as **South Point** is abeam at 0848, we change course to 079°True for the run along the southern shore of Santa Rosa and Santa Cruz Islands.

Soon we observe that fog is setting in; so at 0915 we take cross-bearings of **South Point** (315°T) and **East Point** (043°T). This fixes us at **D** . . . on course and at speed. But immediately . . . thick fog. So at 0915 we reduce speed to five knots and start making fog signals.

Nothing further until, through a hole in the fog, we get a snap bearing of **Gull Island** at 1115 as 045°T. This line of bearing gives us only direction . . . we are somewhere on that line from Gull Island, but not fixed at any one point. If we are on course, our location is **E**. But two hours have passed since we left **D**. At five knots, we should be 10 miles beyond **D**; and **E** is not that far.

All the factors exist for a **Running Fix**. The time interval from **D** to the Gull Island line of position (LOP) is known as two hours. At our estimated speed this is 10 miles. We now measure 10 miles from **D** along the course line, to **F**. It is obvious we are **not** there, for it doesn't fall on the Gull Island LOP. But now advance the 0915 **South Point** LOP along the course and redraw it through **F**. It crosses the Gull Island LOP at **G** . . . our position by running fix at 1115.

What we've done is to combine a known LOP (Gull Island) with an earlier line (South Point) advanced for an estimated distance on an estimated course. The result is not a fixed position; for that requires two independent and simultaneous factors . . . two bearings, or a bearing and a sounding, or some other combination. But the running fix is a respectable estimate, and very worthwhile.

The course made good from **D** to **G** is 072°T. This is not the course we steered, but is 7° to the left. A current has set us north of the track. So the course from **G** to Anacapa is no longer our original 079°. Instead, it is 081°. **But**, we've just found out about a current. We'd better steer to offset it. And so, next, how to find the course to steer to make 081° good.

First, let's find out what current we **did** meet. The running fix placed us at **G**, but we had expected to be at **F**. So the current moved us from **F** to **G** . . . a direction or **Set** of 315°T and a distance or **Total Drift** of 1.4 miles. Since this happened in two hours, the rate of drift was 0.7 knot.

The short way to allow for current . . . if it set us 7° to the left, then steer 7° to the right. To make 081°, steer 088°. But since this is a "schoolbook" problem, let's use a current diagram . . . discussed in an earlier article. You'll find it in the lower left portion of **Plate E**, and it tells us to steer 087.5° to make 081°. It also tells us that at five knots through the water, we should make 4.6 knots good over the bottom.

The fog now lifts and we are able to confirm position by cross-bearings. At 1155, Gull Island bears 000°T and the highest peak on Santa Rosa Island bears 281°T. These two lines of position cross at **H**. This is right where we estimated . . . on the course made good of 081° from **G**, and at the expected speed of 4.6 knots. The fog sets in again, so we maintain 5 knots as we proceed towards our destination.

This example has combined practical piloting and practical plotting, and the chart gives a clear picture of the progress from **A** to **H**. Look closely and you'll note a few other piloting "friends" in the facts. Way back at **A**, the bearing of **South Point** was 090°T . . . this is 26° on the port bow relative to the then course of 116°. And at **B** the bearing was 45°; and at **C**, it was 90°, or abeam. This is a practical 26½°-45°-90° combination. The Special Case Rules could be used here instead of a chart.

All lumped together, these procedures may seem complicated and too involved. But each step is quite simple, when taken one-at-a-time. This all leads to safer navigation . . . for caught in a fog with the current setting towards shore can be risky. But far from being a chore, coastal piloting can be a lot of fun. Doing it right just adds to the enjoyment.

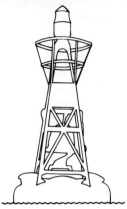

28/Aids to Navigation

Buoyage

If agreement on Rules of the Road is a bright example of international coopera-tion, discord in systems of buoys and channel markers dims the luster.

Despite several international conferences to arrive at some uniform standards, the maritime world now has quite a few different kinds of buoys and marker systems. What is a black buoy one place will be red in another; what looks like a can shape under one system will be spherical in another.

Fortunately our system is uniformly followed in US waters. So although there are Uniform Cardinal and Uniform Lateral and International Marine Conference systems, and in all shades and variations, and in all parts of the globe, we use our own variation consistently. It is, essentially, a method suggested by the Interna-tional Marine Conference of 1889, and is appropriately called the United States System. Reproduced in **READY REFERENCE** is a placard on buoys.

The general plan is fairly simple: buoys have distinctive shapes, colors, lights and numbers depending upon location as seen when entering from seaward . . .

    1. **Red** buoys are found on the right side of a channel, entering from sea.

    2. **Black** buoys are found on the left side of the channel.

This has brought on the sailor's jingle, *Red Right Returning.*

    3. Red channel buoys are given **even** numbers, beginning from sea.

    4. Black channel buoys are given **odd** numbers, beginning from sea.

A disciple of the School of Recollection by Association has suggested the word "Bore" . . . Black Odd Red Even.

    5. A **nun** shape (like an astronaut's space capsule) will be a **red** buoy.

    6. A **can** shape (cylindrical) will be **black**.

    7. A **spar** buoy (shaped like a boom or mast) can be on either side . . . **red or black**.

But if the marker is equipped with a sound device or a light, or both, shape will be of no significance. Then, its color and number and the color of the light will tell identity.

    8. **Red** buoys have **red or white lights**.

    9. **Black** buoys have **green or white lights**.

The characteristic of the light distinguishes further the type marker.

10. A **fixed** light intends no distinction by characteristic. It just marks something.
11. A **flashing** or **occulting** light is for buoys on channel edges.
12. A **quick flashing** light marks an important bend in the channel, or a wreck or an obstruction.

These red, or black, channel markers are like runway lights at an airport . . . they show the edge of the roadbed which runs between them. A flashing light blinks on and off, but its **period** or cycle is off more than on. An occulting light is one that is darkened at intervals; so during the cycle it is on for longer than it is off. The combinations of quick flashing, interrupted quick flashing, short-long flashing and slow flashing refer to the code or sequence of flashes. The display can be in other combinations . . . group flashing, group occulting and even more. It all depends on where the buoy is located and on what it is to tell.

13. An **interrupted quick flashing** marks a junction or a wreck which can be passed on either side.
14. A **short-long flashing** marks mid-channel.

We can see in this list of divisions a sort of pattern . . . shape, color and number of the buoy can be significant; color and characteristic of the light can be significant. Since buoys are used at channel edges, junctions, obstructions, in mid-channel, and at locations of special purpose (quarantine, anchorage, seadromes and the like) a workable code to identify the various markers is important.

Unless, though, you have occasion to engage in much night piloting, the full meaning of buoy lights and shapes and colors and numbers will not be "second nature." But to start a mental picture of the patterns, we set out here a series of tables to break down the various combinations. Schedule I deals only with shapes.

Schedule I . . Significance of Shape

1. The shape of a buoy only has significance if the marker is not equipped with a light or a sound device . . . all lighted or sound buoys can look the same regardless of meaning. The spar shape tells no story.
2. The shapes are . . .
   Nun: conical, used
      a) At right edge of channel; painted red and even numbered.
      b) At a wreck or obstruction which is to be passed on the starboard hand; painted red and unnumbered, but usually lettered **WR.**
      c) At a channel junction when the main channel is to the left; painted with red and black horizontal stripes, red on top; unnumbered but may be lettered.
      d) To mark the middle of the channel; painted with black and white vertical stripes; unnumbered but may be lettered.
      e) As a special purpose buoy or to mark a particular area; painted according to schedule of miscellaneous colors; unnumbered but may be lettered.

Can: cylindrical, used

    a) At left edge of channel; painted black, and odd numbered.

    b) At a wreck or obstruction which is to be passed on the port hand; painted black and unnumbered, but usually lettered **WR.**

    c) At a channel junction when the main channel is to the right; painted with black and red horizontal stripes, black on top; unnumbered but may be lettered.

    d) To mark the middle of the channel; painted with black and white vertical stripes; unnumbered but may be lettered.

    e) As a special purpose buoy or to mark a particular area; painted according to schedule of miscellaneous colors; unnumbered but may be lettered.

Spar: like a mast or a boom, used

    a) Any place a nun or a can may be placed . . . shape is really not significant; painted color and number or letter are used for identification.

The next schedule deals with the color of the paint job, and with number and letter. Since shape often has no significance, these marks are the major key to daytime identification.

Schedule II . . Significance of Paint, Number and Letter

1. The color, numbering and lettering of a buoy is followed on all buoys, whether unlighted, lighted or equipped for sound.

2. **Red:** used at

    a) Right edge of fairways and channels.

    b) Wreck or other obstruction which is to be passed on the starboard hand . . . this means the obstruction is kept on the right side of the ship as she passes.

Black: used at

    a) Left edge of fairways and channels.

    b) Wreck or other obstruction which is to be passed on the port hand . . . this means the obstruction is kept on the left side of the ship as she passes.

Black and Red Horizontal Bands: used at

    a) Channel junctions. When the main channel is to the

        1) **Left,** the red band is on top.

        2) **Right,** the black band is on top.

        3) **Left and right,** either color is on top.

Black and White Vertical Bands: used at the middle of the channel to indicate best depths, etc.

Yellow: used at a quarantine anchorage.

White: used at a general anchorage area.

Black and White Horizontal Bands: used to mark fish net limits.

White with Green Top: used to mark an area of dredging work or underwater survey.

A close look at No. 2 Red.

Yellow and Black Vertical Stripes: used at a seadrome area.

White and International Orange Bands, Horizontal or Vertical: used for a special purpose not otherwise provided for.

3. **Numbers**: only the Channel buoys will be numbered; only those on the edge of the channel.

    a) **Odd** will be on the left, entering from sea . . . on the **black** buoys . . . with numbers increasing from sea.

    b) **Even** will be on the right, entering from sea . . . on the **red** buoys . . . with numbers increasing from sea.

4. **Letters**: all may be lettered mid-channel, junction, wreck, quarantine, seadrome, fish net . . . and even channel markers can bear letters as well as their customary numbers. The scheme of lettering is not specified; but it will, of course, have some connection with the significance, as:

WR for Wreck

The last schedule deals with lights . . . their color and their characteristic. These marks are the major, almost the sole, keys to nighttime identification.

Schedule III . . Significance of Lights

1. **Red Lights**: only used on those buoys for which the color red is significant: red channel buoys; junction buoys with red band on top; wreck buoys which are painted red.

    Green Lights: only used on those buoys for which the color black is significant: black channel buoys; junction buoys with black band on top; wreck buoys which are painted black.

    White Lights:

    a) ONLY white lights will be found on mid-channel buoys, marking the middle of a channel or fairway.

    b) White lights may be on other buoys: red or black channel buoys, wreck buoys, junction, quarantine, seadrome, fish nets, etc. In other words, white is a neutral color often used instead of a red, green or other color light.

    c) Any other color except red or green may be found on a quarantine, seadrome, fish net, special purpose, etc.

2. **Light Characteristic:**
   a) A **fixed** light is one continuously on. It will be seen only on a miscellaneous or special purpose buoy.
   b) A **flashing** light is one which shows short periods of light . . . it is dark longer than lighted. It will be seen on channel, miscellaneous or special purpose buoys.
   c) An **occulting** light is one which shows short periods of darkness between the periods of light . . . it is lighted for a longer time than it is dark. It will be seen on channel, miscellaneous or special purpose buoys.
   d) A **slow flashing** light is a flashing light whose full period or cycle will contain a relatively few number of flashes . . . not more than 30 per minute. It will be seen on miscellaneous and special purpose buoys only.
   e) A **quick flashing** light is a flashing light whose full period or cycle will contain a relatively many number of flashes . . . at least 60 per minute. It will be seen on wreck and obstruction buoys and on channel buoys at important bends or turns in the channel.
   f) A **short-long flashing** light has a period of alternate short and long flashes. It will be on mid-channel buoys.
   g) An **interrupted quick flashing** light is a flashing light which isn't constantly flashing, but has a period broken or interrupted into a sequence of bursts of quick flashing. It will be found on junction buoys.
   h) An **equal interval**, or **isophase**, light is one with all durations of light and darkness equal. It is a new category to bridge between the flashing and the occulting lights.
   i) Morse Code light is one whose flashes produce a Morse character or characters; as, **K** (-.-) or **AR** (.- .-.). It is also a new category to fill the need for more precise identification in areas where buoys are very numerous. This type will appear in substitute for some mid-channel buoys. A potential example: the Los Angeles Sea Buoy is a mid-channel type, presently showing short-long flashes and carrying the painted mark **LA**. As a Morse Code light it would emit the Morse Characters for **LA** (.-.. .-).
   j) **Composite Group Flashing** and **Composite Group Occulting** lights are those whose flashes or eclipses, respectively, are combined in alternate groups of different numbers. More new categories; they will appear as needed and will be described this way:
   Gp. Fl. (2+3) . . . . a group of 2 flashes followed by a group of 3 flashes.
   Gp. Occ. (1+3) . . . 1 eclipse, followed by a group of 3 eclipses

There are other combinations of light displays; but these are the basic ones. Like nearly everything else maritime, the list seems endless. And we've already passed the point of practical recollection. But at least remember these points:

When coming in from sea . . .
RED means "keep me on your right."
GREEN means "keep me on your left."
Naturally, when going out the meanings are reversed.

At any place . . .
FIXED, FLASHING, EQUAL INTERVAL, OCCULTING or SLOW FLASHING:
"Notice me, but I am not of extra importance."
QUICK FLASHING, SHORT-LONG FLASHING, MORSE CODE LIGHT, or INTERRUPTED QUICK FLASHING:
"I am particularly important; check me closely."

Fortunately, buoys are not placed, removed and relocated as casually as highway flares. They will be changed occasionally; but once you know their pattern, the changes will immediately be apparent.

The best way to get the picture of buoys is to make it your business to locate and mentally tab the pattern in a particular region. Note them by day and then again at dusk when lights and location are both seen. Then do it again at night. Soon they will easily be identified and interpreted. If possible, select a main channel for your study. The chances are better that a variety of types will be found. Thereafter, when you see buoys in a strange US port, the system will be recognizable.

Now some cautions about buoys. Don't tinker with them. Not only is it against the law of the land; it violates good seamanship and common sense. And remember they are floating objects anchored to the bottom. They can break free and drift away. Or they can become damaged or out of repair. Whenever you note a discrepancy, report it to the nearest Coast Guard facility as soon as possible.

Finally, they are not small objects. The average buoy is a large structure . . . as much as 20 feet long and built in proportion. Should you hit one, expect to come off second best. Give them a wide berth . . . they are to be looked at but not handled.

Unrelated to their color or size, but handy in piloting and maneuvering is this hint on buoys . . . by watching the way the water moves past the buoy, by noting on which side is a wake, you can gain a good idea of the strength and direction of a current.

But no book or chart or picture will give a working knowledge of this subject. The only way is to observe them in action. Do that as a regular practice and they will soon be very old friends.

29/The Ship
Flotation

None of the material in this chapter is necessary. Sooner or later the pragmatist will ask, "Of what use is any of this in pleasure boating?" And the straight answer is—no more essential for the pleasure mariner than for a private flyer to know why his aircraft stays in the air. So long as everything goes well, he'll never use the knowledge. But he's a better flyer, and a safer one, when he understands the principles. We are going to talk about why a vessel floats and why it stays upright. Read along some more . . . at least, you might find it interesting.

A good starting point is the story of the very wise Sicilian who took a bath 22 centuries ago. The king of Syracuse ordered a crown of solid gold, but suspected the metalsmiths had cheated him by using part silver. So Archimedes was engaged to unmask the goings on.

At first the problem vexed the famous mathematician. Although gold was heavier than silver, weighing the crown proved nothing, for the rascals were shrewd enough to use the proper weight. But he did have one clue . . . a part-silver object, to be the same weight, would be bigger, would have more bulk, than one of gold. The real problem did not involve the **weight** of the crown . . . it was how to measure the precise **volume**. And even an Archimedes would hesitate at taking the exact dimensions of a filigree web of twists and curves.

Annoyed, he decided to relax in a soothing bath. He stretched out in the tub and idly watched water rise over his body. He sat upright and saw the water level fall. With a shout he bounded out and ran through the streets, stark naked, crying, "Eureka! I have found it."

What he found we now call **Archimedes' Principle . . . a body immersed in a liquid displaces a volume of the liquid equal to its own volume**. The crown was placed in a bowl brim-full of water and the overflow was caught. An equal weight of solid gold was put into another, and its overflow caught. If the crown actually was solid gold, the volume of water displaced would be the same as that by the gold weight. But if the crown contained lighter metals, more water would spill out. The fate of the crownmakers is not recorded. But even if they were gentle grafters, we owe them a vote of thanks. Because of them, Archimedes answered several marine problems . . . why vessels float, and how to weigh a floating ship.

The crown was heavier than water so it went to the bottom of the bowl. But suppose it had been made of wood? It would only partially submerge; in other words, it would float. Even so, there would still be some water spilled out of the bowl . . . an amount equal to the weight of the crown. If it were made of balsa, the weight of the water that overflowed would be less than if it were made of ironbark. But in each case the water spilled would be the weight of the crown. So a corollary to the first principle is this:

A floating body displaces a volume
of water equal to its own weight.

Why does a vessel float? Because the force of water pushing up on the bottom is exactly equal to the weight of the vessel. A 40-ton boat is supported by an upward water pressure of exactly 40 tons.

Now to the second question: how to weigh a floating ship. We can't put it on scales, nor can we float it in a bowl of water and catch the overflow. But because of King Hieron's crown, we don't have to. The water displaced has the same volume as the dimensions of the hull below the waterline. And the weight of that much water is exactly the same as the weight of the ship itself.

We can find the cubic measure of the underwater shape. Then all we have to know is how much that many cubic feet of water would weigh. The answer is the weight of the ship itself. Salt water weighs 64 pounds for each cubic foot, and it takes 35 cubic feet of it to make a ton. Fresh water is lighter . . . only 62.4 pounds per cubic foot. And it takes more fresh water to make a ton . . . about 36 feet.

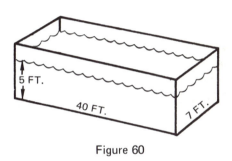

Figure 60

Let's suppose we have a boat built like a shoebox, as in **Figure 60**. It is 40 feet long and seven feet wide and is floating in salt water. The draft, or distance from the surface to the bottom of the box, is five feet. How heavy is the boat?

We know the underwater shape: a rectangular box that is 40 feet by 7 feet by 5 feet. This is 1400 cubic feet. Since 35 cubic feet of salt water make one ton, then 1400 cubic feet of salt water total 40 tons . . . the weight of the boat.

If the weight were only 20 tons, how deep would she float? This time we know the weight, and so we also know the weight of the salt water displaced . . . 20 tons. And we also know the volume of that salt water. It is 20 tons x 35 cubic feet, or a total of 700 cubic feet. The underwater shape must also have 700 cubic feet. We know the boat is 40 feet long and seven feet wide . . . it must, then, be 2½ feet deep. For, 40 x 7 x 2½ is 700 cubic feet. The draft is 2½ feet.

If the boat weighed 60 tons, how deep would she be? The volume of displaced water is 60 tons x 35 cubic feet, or 2100 cubic feet. The rest of the problem:

$$\text{Depth} = \frac{\text{Total cubic volume}}{\text{Length x Breadth}} \qquad \text{Depth} = \frac{2100}{40 \times 7} = 7\frac{1}{2} \text{ feet}$$

The draft will be 7½ feet.

Few boats, we must observe, are shaped like shoeboxes. The graceful curves of the hull trim off quite a bit from the rectangular block. **Block coefficient**, or **coefficient of fineness**, is the name given to the fractional part which the hull actually takes up. A blunt-nosed workboat might have a coefficient of 0.8. If you whittled her out of a block of wood, 80% of the block would make up the hull, and the balance would be shavings. Yachts are not nearly so full. Coefficients of less than 0.5 are frequent.

Back again to the gold crown and why things float. The crown sank because its weight was greater than the weight of an equal volume of water. Made of wood, it would float because the weight would be less than an equal volume of water. This ability to float is called **buoyancy**.

Buoyancy was not a great problem when vessels were made exclusively of wood. Perhaps it is better to say there was less need to understand it. Most people felt a wooden hull floated because wood was lighter than water. If a solid block would float, then hollowed out into a hull it would float even better. When metal was suggested, they firmly believed a metal hull could never float. Metal was heavier than water; and if a solid metal block would sink, then metal shaped like a hull would just sink more slowly.

A wooden hull does **not** float because it is lighter than water. The answer is not in the weight of the material at all. It is in the space enclosed between the sides from the bottom of the hull to the waterline. That space must be big enough so the weight of that much water equals the weight of the vessel. The gold crown could never float because it had no enclosed space. The material was heavier than water and it was solid. But hammered out into a bowl, it might have floated. The material would still be heavier than water, but there would be a space enclosed. If the space was big enough so the weight of that much water equalled the total weight of the bowl, then it would float.

A trio of giants...bulk carrier, passenger liner and aircraft carrier.

Photo by Port of Long Beach

Our 40-ton shoebox could only float if the sides were at least five feet high. For the space taken up by 40 tons of water would be 40 feet long by seven feet wide by five feet high. If the sides were only four feet high, the box would sink. If the same box weighed only 20 tons, the sides need only be 2½ feet high. If it weighed 60 tons, the sides would have to be 7½ feet high.

Suppose the sides were actually eight feet high. When the box weighs 40 tons, the sides will sink five feet into the water. But what about the remaining three feet? There is an extra enclosed space . . . a block which is 40 feet x 7 feet x 3 feet, or 840 cubic feet. This is extra space not being used to float the hull. But it is there, ready to go to work if the total weight should increase. This unemployed buoyancy is a factor of safety; is called **reserve buoyancy**. What makes a hull float is the enclosed space below the waterline, the **working buoyancy**. But, what makes it safe is the extra volume of enclosed space above the waterline . . . the reserve buoyancy.

Freeboard is the name for the height of this reserve. It is the distance from the waterline to the top of a predetermined part of the hull, for example, the main deck.

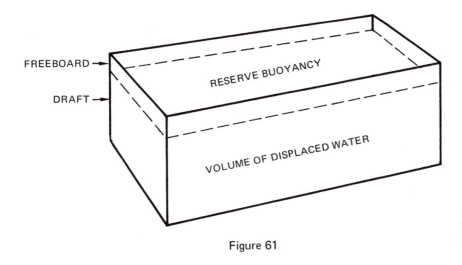

Figure 61

Figure 61 again shows the Case of the 40-Ton Shoebox, and indicates the factors discussed.

Now for the moral of the story . . . watch the reserve buoyancy. Be sure that the enclosed space not employed to float your boat and the weights you put aboard is enough to offset any extra weights that can come aboard from the sea. Be sure you have enough freeboard to handle water that might wash on board underway.

Next time we speak of the ship, we shall take a look at stability and find out how a hull stays right side up.

Questions

Racing over the horizon is another assault force, so be ready to run the gauntlet of a battery of questions.

Rules of the Road

1. At night in International Waters, you see dead ahead the following lights:
   2 white lights in a vertical line;
   below them and to the left, a green light;
   below them and to the right, a red light.
   You see
   a)   a pilot vessel.
   b)   a fishing vessel.
   c)   a tug towing one barge astern, with the stern of the barge 1000 feet behind the tug.
   d)   a tug towing one barge astern, with the stern of the barge 500 feet behind the tug.

2. If a tug was towing one barge astern at night in Inland Waters
   a)   you would see the same lights as in Question 1 above.
   b)   you would see one more white light in the vertical line, making three in all.
   c)   you would see the same lights as in Question 1 if the barge was less than 600 feet long.

3. Complete the following statement:
   White over Red, - - - - - Ahead

4. By day in International Waters you see two black balls in a vertical line. You see
   a)   a dredger at work.
   b)   a vessel at anchor.
   c)   a vessel not under command.

5. A 40-foot motor cruiser at anchor by day in Inland Waters
   a)   need not display one black ball.
   b)   shows the same day signal required by International Rules.

Chartwork

1. When measuring distance by chart dividers it is better to adjust them so the divider legs are
   a)   spread far apart.
   b)   not spread far apart.

2. Two triangles can be used in substitute for
   a)   parallel rulers.
   b)   chart dividers.
   c)   both of above.

3. In 29 minutes at a speed of 6 knots you will travel
   a)   4 miles.

b) 2 miles.

c) 2.9 miles.

4. From 0800 to 0909 you travel 8.9 miles. Your speed is
   a) 6 knots.
   b) 7.7 knots.
   c) 11.2 knots.

5. Of the following, the most accurate position is by
   a) cross-bearing fix.
   b) a running fix.
   c) one line of position.

Buoyage

1. Black and red horizontal bands on a buoy indicate
   a) a dredge.
   b) mid-channel.
   c) fish nets.
   d) a channel junction.

2. Black and white horizontal bands on a buoy indicate
   a) a wreck.
   b) mid-channel.
   c) fish nets.
   d) a channel junction.

3. Black and white vertical bands on a buoy indicate
   a) a wreck.
   b) mid-channel.
   c) fish nets.
   d) a channel junction.
   e) special purpose.

4. An even-numbered buoy when lighted may have
   a) a red light.
   b) a white light.
   c) a green light.
   d) (a) or (b) above.
   e) none of above.

5. The shape of a lighted buoy is
   a) nun.
   b) can.
   c) spar.
   d) none of above.

The Ship

1. Freeboard is
   a) the vertical distance from the water surface to the keel.

b) the vertical distance from the water surface to the top of a predetermined hull point, as, the main deck.
c) either of above.
d) none of above.

2. A boat is 30 feet long, 5 feet wide and draws 3 feet of water. Her block coefficient is 0.6. The displacement of the boat, in tons, when floating in salt water is
a) 7.7 tons.
b) 13 tons.
c) 2 tons.

3. Reserve buoyancy
a) always remains the same for the same boat.
b) increases as the draft of the boat increases.
c) decreases as the draft of the boat increases.

4. The coefficient of fineness of a square wooden box is
a) 0.5.
b) 0.8.
c) 0.7.
d) 1.0.
e) 1.5

5. Compared to a 60-ton wooden boat that is 40 feet long, 10 feet wide and with sides 7 feet high, a 40-ton steel boat of the same dimensions
a) has more reserve buoyancy.
b) has more freeboard.
c) has less reserve buoyancy.
d) has less freeboard.
e) (a) and (b) above.
f) (c) and (d) above.

...and answers

Only 20 salvos heading for you, so deduct 5 each time you are struck. Find your condition:
92 - 100:   Unscathed.
84 - 90:   Damage to Superstructure Only.
76 - 82:   A Few at the Waterline, but Under Control.
Below 76:   Abandon Ship!

Rules of the Road

1. (d)   2. (b)   3. Pilot   4. (c)   5. (a)

Chartwork

1. (b)   2. (a)   3. (c)   4. (b)   5. (a)

Buoyage

1. (d)   2. (c)   3. (b)   4. (d)   5. (d)

The Ship

1. (b)   2. (a)   3. (c)   4. (d)   5. (e)

section 7
contents

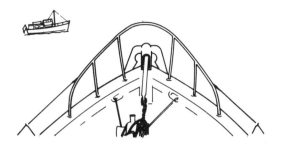

30/Rules of the Road
Sound signals

The acid test for the Rules of the Road—International, Inland or Pilot—is their performance in fog. They may work perfectly in clear weather by day or night, they may be most helpful in assisting identification or in organizing procedures to pass. But if they don't work in fog, they are no good.

For two ships in a fog are really quite helpless. It is necessary that they have some mutually predictable, mutually simple and mutually understood set of regulations.

On these pages we'll consider general requirements. But first, let's see what "fog" really means. Obviously, it includes the condition of soggy air, the cloud at the surface. But it also includes mist, falling snow, heavy rainstorm . . . any condition that similarly restricts visibility. It is "foggy" under the rules even though it might be clear as a bell nearly all around you. "Nearly" is the key word. If you are skirting a fog bank so you can't see objects within its area, then you know that it is foggy.

The rules are silent on a very crucial point . . . to what distance must visibility be cut before the condition is fog? Is it five miles, the measure used by lighthouses as the guide to starting fog signals? Or is it your hand fading out before your face? The courts are not much more definite than the rules themselves. One suggestion: when the distance is less than the range of the weakest running light, it is foggy.

The basic principle is to change speed in proportion to the visibility. Half the distance of visibility in a fog belongs to you. The other half is the property of the other ship. Suppose you are in fog when the visibility is cut to 1000 yards. Then the scope allowed you for stopping is only 500 yards. If each vessel stays to her half of the visible world, they can **never** collide. The principle, then . . . each must be able to stop in half the distance of visibility. Each must proceed at no greater speed than allows her to stop dead in the water within that half. The rules call this **moderate speed**. And it is obvious that speed in fog is no fixed amount. It will vary with the visibility, with the ship, and with the "existing circumstances and conditions." It could be quite fast under some conditions; it could be zero in many others.

What happens when a vessel hears the fog signal of another? If that signal seems to come from forward of the beam, the International Rules in **Rule 16b** say this:

> (b) A power-driven vessel hearing, apparently forward of her beam, the fog-signal of a vessel the position of which is not ascertained, shall, so far as the circumstances of the case admit, stop her engines, and then navigate with caution until danger of collision is over.

Inland Rules **Article 16** is identical.

Note that the command refers to power-driven craft only; a sailing vessel is not expected to stop her "engines" . . . lower the sails or come up into the wind.

And notice this . . . in a fog where vessels are **not** in sight of each other, there can be no meeting, crossing or overtaking situations. There is no privileged vessel; everyone is burdened to be cautious. So whenever a fog signal is heard, and it appears to come from a position forward of the beam, you stop your engines.

This doesn't mean stopping forward motion. The propeller no longer turns, but the ship can still be making headway. You will begin to slow down, but will not actually have to stop. An added factor to "stopping engines" . . . you can hear better. You have a better opportunity to determine from what direction the fog signal is coming when the steady grind of a working engine underfoot is not drowning it out.

Here another caution must be exercised. Sound in fog is very unreliable. It can be muffled, distorted and actually shunted this way and that. "Apparently forward of the beam" doesn't mean 089° and less. Don't try to gauge the bearing with a cross-hair sight. Any sound that might be from forward of the beam should be assumed to be there.

When you hear that other signal, consider yourself in an arena with a dangerous, unknown companion. Your only contact with him is by sound. You are both like blindmen, feeling your way with the foghorn as your cane tapping the route.

For sound **is** your only contact. None of the sound signals used to maneuver are given in fog, since the ships are not in sight of each other. No lights are specified for fog . . . they need only burn if coincidentally it also is between sunset and sunrise. The rules don't expect and so don't prescribe any other means of communication except sound signals expressly specified, in those rules, for fog.

Rule 16 says " . . . the fog signal of a vessel the position of which is not ascertained . . . " What does this mean? When the bearing and distance to the other is unknown, and you are ignorant of her course. This condition is met almost every time you hear a fog signal from an unseen ship forward of the beam . . . unless you have a radar.

So to the nub of a lively debate. Where does radar fit in the scheme of things? Can electrons and the oarlock coexist? Well, even though we might not own a radar, we live in a radar world. CRT's and PPI's and TPR's sift the fog on every side. Even the man with only a paddle must understand how electronic eyes fare under Rules of the Road.

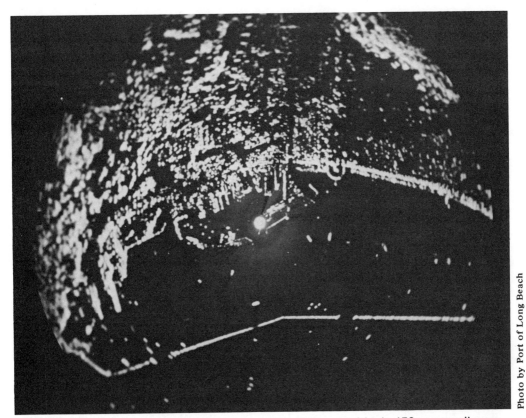

Radar view of ship movements, breakwaters, port facilities and cities in 150-square mile area surrounding Long Beach Harbor Pilot Station.

The radar devotee would like the word **visibility** to include electronic as well as natural observation. There can be no fog, says he, if you can "see" right through it. How can a ship be helpless if she knows what vessels are on the ocean for miles around? The Rules of the Road take no such optimistic view. **Rule 1(c) (ix)** short-circuits his outlook straight away by saying "Vessels shall be deemed to be in sight . . . only when one can be observed visually from the other." And now to the why.

First of all, radar is a complicated electromechanical device. It may see when the human eye cannot . . . but it can't see in the same way. To radar there are no distinctions based on color. By the usual marine installation an object doesn't even have a shape. It is just a reflector of radio energy. Either it sends back an echo or it doesn't. There is usually no difference between the bow or the stern, the smokestack or the poop. The typical set can't tell direction or speed . . . that can only be learned by radar plotting. On the other hand, a human sees the other vessel with much more discrimination. We see where the bow is relative to the superstructure, we see the alignment of the masts. We see things which, by intelligent deduction, cue us to direction. Radar only "sees" a bundle of reflected impulses. So, for close quarters navigation in fog, radar tells you something is hidden in the fog, and it tells you how far away it is and in what direction. But it can't tell you what. Nor can it say immediately how the thing might be moving.

So it really doesn't "ascertain" position as meant by **Rule 16**. Small wonder, then, that international regulations which for decades resisted the changes from a Turkish drum to a bell do not rush to embrace radar as the cure-all.

However, radar is accepted as a very great aid to piloting in fog, or in any weather. The critic will say it has caused many accidents. This is not true. Accidents involving radar ships have, occasionally, been whoppers . . . that's true. For by its nature, electronic eyesight is a temptation to speed. But used intelligently, it is the greatest anticollision device yet developed.

Where, then, does radar fit? As an aid but not a substitute. The data it produces must be used in determining "moderate speed"; its better-informed ship may well have greater responsibilities to take early and substantial action to avoid close quarters. Yet it gives no relief from the mandates of **Rule 16** to stop engines and navigate with caution when a fog signal is heard apparently forward of the beam. And knowing range and bearing of another by radar is not knowing her position.

Several times we've spoken of predictability under the rules. That is the keystone of the whole maneuvering system. When you see another vessel, you also assume that he sees you. You can predict what he will do under the rules, and he can predict what you will do. So far, radar cannot supply that element of predictability. Showing a pip of light on the scope is not enough. For you have no way of knowing whether the man on that "pip" sees you. And even if he does, he can't be sure you see him. Neither one of you is predictable to the other because neither can safely assume the other even knows he's around. A few of the so-called "radar accidents" have been tragic comedies of errors. Each ship assumed the other did **not** have radar, and so proceeded to navigate around her as if she were a slowly plodding blindman. They both zigged when they should have zagged . . . and steered into each other. And the solution is still not too clearly in view. For it must be a simple, foolproof and universal solution.

It's just common sense . . . Be realistic about the present state of radar. The dangerous facts are these. Radar detection is just as good as the radar target. What returns a good echo is a target of highly reflective material and in a shape best aligned to send back a reciprocal reflection. The radar beam strikes a target; if the material is reflective, the radar impulses will bounce off. If the shape is favorable, enough will bounce back to the radar antenna to give a good "pip" of light on the scope.

Pleasure craft, by and large, are poor targets on both scores . . . material and shape. Wood and canvas, fiberglass and plastics, are not so reflective as metal. And a low, smooth-lined silhouette is certainly not a good backboard. A squash court has a high vertical backboard to reflect the ball . . . not a low wall sloping away from the players.

Give serious thought to the fact that a radar ship might overlook you. For there are quite a few other factors making your detection difficult. In choppy seas, the wave crests reflect echoes . . . your image might get lost in the clutter. And you might be hidden in a swell or blocked by high waves.

The answer? A Radar Reflector. Carry one on board, and when fog sets in, hoist it aloft. There are several ready-made types available. Or you can fashion one yourself from two pieces of light sheet metal. Even a metal bucket is helpful. Give the radar beam a worthy target. You want to show up on the scope as a bright spot that can't be overlooked. Nowadays, this is as important as carrying a bilge pump.

One final word about fog in general. The rules intend that ships keep clear by reduced speed and by extreme caution. You are not expected to dodge or to sidestep. Until you see the other ship, it is good judgment to keep, not only slow speed, but also to keep your course. Predictability is the key, and you can't be predictable if you're weaving about while still unseen.

A double treatment of Rules of the Road this trip. For now we are to discuss sound signals in general, as specified by the rules.

One would hardly catalogue seafarers as strict conformists. We are world renowned as people who speak out whenever on whatever and however we please . . . with one exception. No Beep Beep on the ship's whistle to show good spirits; no saluting the girl friend with a flourish of trumpets. The Pilot Rules state flatly that unnecessary sounding of the whistle is forbidden within any US harbor limits. The International and Inland Rules say as much by specifying the only times a whistle can be blown.

This is proper. We've talked of the rules as being international. The whistle is their voice to speak in diverse tongues, but only to speak on business. The simple code of whistle blasts is the only specified mode of communication between ships; and the potential of destruction is too great to risk any confusion.

The schedule of signals is extremely simple. There are: short, long and prolonged blasts. A **short blast** is defined as about one second. A **prolonged blast** is

Nuclear ship Savannah being assisted stern-first into harbor under Coast Guard supervision.

Photo by Los Angeles Harbor Department

four to six seconds. Although the rules speak of a **long blast**, there is no definition given. The courts have filled the gap by suggesting it as eight to ten seconds. Notice that a long blast is longer than a prolonged. Obviously, a prolonged is a lengthened short blast and not a lengthened long one.

Before we get to the signals proper, a few more points: Whistle signals for maneuvering are only given when the vessels are in sight of each other. You don't blow passing signals unless you can actually see the other fellow.

Fog signals are the only signals given in fog . . . no maneuvering signals are blown when in fog and other ships are not in sight. International has no long blast.

Remember the distinction between signals under International and Inland. On the High Seas, the passing signals are given **only** when the course is changed. They are signals of execution. But under Inland and Pilot they are given as proposals, as signals of intention. And as we've seen, the result is quite different. On the High Seas, you don't answer the other ship's signal. All you announce is your course change, if any. Actually it is not a conversation . . . it is two monologues. But Inland and Pilot make it a conversation . . . even a negotiation.

Now to the whistles themselves. We've already discussed the "in sight" signals:

One Short Blast . . .
    International: "I am altering course to starboard."
    Inland-Pilot: "I intend to go to the right," or
                  "I am holding my course and speed."

Two Short Blasts . . .
    International: "I am altering course to port."
    Inland-Pilot: "I intend to go left."

Three Short Blasts . . .
    International: "My engines are going astern."
    Inland-Pilot: "My engines are going full speed astern."*
      *But, full speed astern really means astern at any speed.

The **Four-Blast Danger Signal** is peculiar to Inland and to Pilot Rules. It is given by either ship when doubt exists or when a proposed maneuver is objectionable. Although primarily an "in sight" signal, it has some court sanction for use in fog.

Under International Rules a **Doubt Signal** is specified by **Rule 28(b)**. It allows the Privileged Vessel to sound **at least five short and rapid blasts** to indicate doubt that the other is taking sufficient action to avoid collision. Notice that it is reserved to the vessel which keeps her course and speed . . . to the privileged one.

All these signals are for power-driven vessels **only**. Neither sailing vessels nor vessels towed can use them. So when in sight of another vessel, a sailing vessel makes **no** whistle signal whatever.

It is only in fog that a sailing ship can speak. The reason: other ships will know by the wind and by the set of the sails how she will go. She has a limited field of choice, restricted by the elements. So, she is predictable. Always, the aim of predictability crops up. In fog, though, the sails are invisible; consequently, tack signals are required:

One Short Blast on the fog horn . . .

when on the starboard tack; that is, the wind is coming over the starboard rail.

Two Short Blasts on the fog horn . . .

when on the port tack; that is, the wind is coming over the port rail.

Three Short Blasts on the fog horn . . .

when the wind is coming from abaft the beam.

These signals are not given on a whistle or siren, but on a fog horn . . . they are not only different signals, they also sound different.

Power-driven vessels also have fog signals . . . a prolonged blast. On the High Seas, it is given at least once every two minutes; Inland, it must be given more often . . . at least once each minute. And at sea the signal is two such blasts if the ship is underway (e.g. not at anchor) but not actually moving.

What about tugs and their tows? The tug has the same in-sight passing signals as any power-driven ship, and the tow has none. But in fog they give special signals:

The Tug . . .

One Prolonged followed by Two Shorts, at least once each minute. This is the International and the Inland Signal.

The Tow . . .

International: One Prolonged followed by Three Shorts, at least once each minute.

Inland: need not give any . . . but if so, then the same as the Tug: One Prolonged followed by Two Shorts.

The International fog signal for a tug (One Prolonged Blast followed by Two Shorts) is also given by a ship working on a submarine cable or navigation mark, by a vessel launching or landing aircraft, and by a vessel Not Under Command. A vessel which is fishing, either underway or at anchor, shall also give this signal . . . unless she is fishing with trolling lines. In that case, her signal is the same as any other of her propulsion: one or two prolonged blasts if she is under power and the tack signals if she is under sail.

Incidentally, what is the fog signal for a sailing vessel becalmed? None is specified in terms. Under International Rules, though, the Not Under Command signal of one prolonged followed by two shorts is applicable to all vessels and has been suggested for the sailing vessel in such a condition. Inland? Not even that signal is available. Perhaps the signal of the last tack.

How about at anchor signals for fog? There are two under International, depending on the size of vessel. When the ship is no more than 350 feet long, the signal is a five-second ringing of a bell in the forepart of the ship. For longer ships, this signal is followed by a gong or similar non-bell sound from the stern. Inland Waters have only one requirement, the bell at the bow.

There is no exemption by class or type as far as the anchor signal is concerned. Both sets of rules say:

" . . . a vessel . . . "

Nothing is said about sailing vessels, tugs, barges, motorboats, or otherwise. Everyone shall sound it.

When a ship is aground, International, she signals the same as at anchor, but adds—before and after the bell ringing—three extra strokes on a bell. Inland has no such requirement.

There is also a **whistle** signal for a vessel at anchor, International. To warn an approaching vessel she can sound the Morse Code sequence for **R**; that is ". - ." or, **one short, one prolonged, one short** to mean "The way is off my ship; you may feel your way past me."

And of course there is a catchall clause in each set of rules . . . **Rule 12** and **Article 12:**

SIGNALS TO ATTRACT ATTENTION

RULE 12 Every vessel or seaplane on the water may, if necessary in order to attract attention, in addition to the lights which she is by these Rules required to carry, show a flare-up light or use a detonating or other efficient sound signal that cannot be mistaken for any signal authorised elsewhere under these Rules.

SIGNALS TO ATTRACT ATTENTION

ART. 12. *Every vessel may, if necessary, in order to attract attention, in addition to the lights which she is by these rules required to carry, show a flare-up light or use any detonating signal that cannot be mistaken for a distress signal.*

This sounds like an open invitation to use any other signal, whether it's the National Anthem or Rock 'n Roll. But in practice, the section is used cautiously. For again, and always, we come back to predictability.

Getting complicated, isn't it? A case could be made for knowing all this perfectly. But who is going to take the time? Let's be practical and look for a pattern.

What **must** you know? The underway signals for power-driven and sail and for tugs and tows . . . plus the fact that bells or bells and gongs nearly always mean someone, big or small, is at anchor.

Remember a few of the hints:

1. Sound in fog is tricky; so if there's doubt, consider the source to be forward of your beam.
2. When you hear a sail foghorn, check the wind. It can give some idea how he's heading.
3. **Always** stop the propeller for a moment when you hear a signal ahead. During that interval, listen hard. Try to identify the signal and its direction.
4. When you hear one prolonged followed by two shorts, a tug may be nearby. Remember . . . **he has a tow and a towline!** Don't rely on maneuverability alone to take you around him. For the combination might be longer than an aircraft carrier. **And** . . . the tug and tow need not be in single file. As often as not, in heavy weather, the towed vessel will **not** be directly astern of its tug. It can be off to either side. It might even be abeam. In that case you would be meeting a very wide "ship," indeed!

5. International, there is a distinctive signal for a vessel in tow of another . . . one prolonged followed by three shorts, on the whistle or foghorn closely following the tug's signal.

But . . .

a) it is only required of a **manned** tow, and not every tow has a crew.

b) and when given, it is sounded by the last such vessel towed . . . not by every one of them. There may be a string of mute barges between that signal and the tug!

6. Inland, the towed vessel may (but need not) give the same signal as the tug, but on the foghorn only.

7. In short, be very wary of this signal: one prolonged and two or three shorts. It can be many things; it might cover a huge area; it is something or some things hard to maneuver. You can be certain of one thing, though . . . it is a danger to you. Let this unknown have its part of the sea while it moves well past and clear.

Most of all . . . try to visualize, or rather "auralize" these signals. Don't let them be just words on paper. They aren't complicated . . . but they must be real things in your mind.

31/Aids to Navigation
Lighthouses

The US Coast Guard is charged with the task of maintaining aids to navigation on all navigable waterways of the United States . . . a function discharged with a very high order of competence. This job includes the design, placement and maintaining of lighthouses and lightships, radiobeacons and loran stations, fog signals, buoys, markers and daybeacons.

The first lighthouses were erected on our coasts during colonial times. Today that handful of aids to navigation has grown to more than 40,000 of all kinds, shapes and purposes.

The lighthouse, of course, is the most elaborate of the aids to be found. Actually the modern lighthouse station is a complex of optical and electronic gear and the power devices to operate them.

There is no pattern, and so no identification significance, to the way a lighthouse is built. It might be a stone pylon, a tower on a caisson or a house on a spider web of steel. Principles of engineering and economy control. Nor is color of any particular significance. The paint job is used for contrast . . . to make the structure stand out from its background. Of course, the result is that each lighthouse **does** have a unique appearance. It would be difficult to confuse the cubistic structure at Los Angeles Breakwater with Point Loma at San Diego Entrance.

It is the light itself that is intended to be the distinguishing feature. By range, color and characteristic, one light differs from another. So let's consider these traits in more detail.

Most lighthouses exhibit a white light. The lens devices and timers allow a flashing signal which becomes the characteristic of the particular lighthouse. Colored glass may also be fitted so that the signal will appear as a different color in different sectors. So, a lighthouse emitting a group of five flashes every 20 seconds may show that signal as a white flashing light in one arc and as a red flashing light in another. Colored sectors are used to indicate danger areas, or perhaps a channel turn. Sometimes a narrow channel across a shoal will be indicated by a narrow colored beam. In every case the chart of the area would show any such unique usage.

A few cautions on colored sectors. Suppose, in examining the chart, you note a colored sector for a lighthouse, and that true bearings are given for the left and right limits of the sector. These bearings are given as directions **from the sea** towards the light, and not from the lighthouse looking to sea.

And when you are expecting a red sector, don't confuse red with the reddish hue sometimes given a white light. Atmospheric refraction may do the same thing to a lighthouse beam that it does to the setting sun . . . make it orange or even red.

And no matter how much care is used, there can be an overlap of sectors. The lenses, the timers or the glass itself might allow light of one color to "bleed" into an adjoining sector.

Perhaps for these and other reasons, colored sectors are the exception rather than the rule. But when one is employed, there is an overwhelmingly good reason. Red in particular will nearly always spell danger. With attention to the few cautions on the use of sectors, no serious problems should be expected.

To determine the characteristic of a light, use a stopwatch to time the flashes. The alternative of junior officers who can't afford a watch . . . a count "Mississippi One, Mississippi Two," and so on, is a close match to a count in seconds.

Now to the range of a light. Two factors control its range of visibility: the **intensity** of the lamp; and its **height** above sea level.

Visibility based on intensity is called **nominal** (formerly **luminous**) **range**. That based on height is called **geographic range**. Nearly all important lights have a greater nominal range than geographic; in other words, they are bright enough to reach beyond the horizon.

But geographic range is not a fixed value; it varies with the height of the observer. For example, a lighthouse 200 feet high will be visible 16.2 nautical miles. However, that is the distance to sea level at the horizon. If an observer's eye is 15 feet above the sea, the lighthouse will be visible 4.4 miles more, or a total of 20.6 miles. The lighthouse will not dip down below the horizon until he moves back the additional 4.4 miles.

Figure 62 is a sketch of the geographic range from that 200-foot lighthouse to

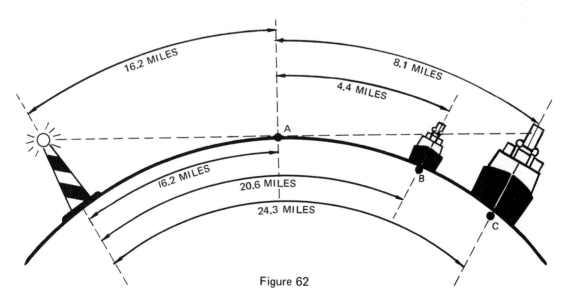

Figure 62

the observer at sea level (A), to another observer at 15 feet above the sea (B), and to a third observer at 50 feet (C). Tables are available to give distances of visibility based on various heights. In **READY REFERENCE** you'll find reproduced **Table 8** of *American Practical Navigator (HO 9)*.

To use it in finding the visibilities shown in **Figure 62**, do the following:

1. Enter with 200 feet as the height of the lighthouse and find the distance in nautical miles . . . 16.2 miles. This is the distance to **A**.
2. Enter with 15 feet as the height of observer **B** and find the distance in nautical miles . . . 4.4 miles. Add this to the 16.2 miles for 200 feet. The total, 20.6 miles, is distance to **B**.
3. Enter with 50 feet as the height of observer **C** and find the distance in nautical miles . . . 8.1 miles. Add this to the 16.2 miles for 200 feet. The total, 24.3 miles, is the distance to **C**.

Never—but never—add two heights together and then enter the table with their sum. 200+15 is 215 feet. The distance by table is 16.8 miles. This is **not** the distance to **B**. And 200+50 is 250 feet. The table gives the distance as 18.1 miles. This is **not** the distance to **C**. **Always** take from the table the distance based on the height of the light and the distance based on your height of eye. Then add the **distances** together . . . never the heights.

Should you not have a table handy (and we hope you'll always have **Mariner's Notebook** aboard!) there is a formula to give satisfactory results:

The Square Root of the Height in Feet x 1.15

This will give you the distance in nautical miles to the horizon. For example, your height is 16 feet. What is the distance to the horizon? The square root of 16 is 4; and 4x1.15 is 4.60 nautical miles. The table gives the distance as 4.6 miles. But use the table whenever you can . . . square root is frustrating.

Nautical charts and light lists will tell you the visibility of all lights. But what do they tell? Luminous range, geographic, or what?

A Coast Guard *Light List* shows four keys to visibility. One is **candlepower**, a somewhat archaic measure according to physicists and not too important to navigators. In the *Pacific Coast Light List* strengths on that base for fixed marine aids range from 100 candlepower for McDonald Point Light on Lake Coeur D'Alene, Idaho, to two million at the Molokai Lighthouse in Hawaii.

Another is **nominal range** defined in the *Light List* as ". . . the maximum distance at which a light may be seen in clear weather (meteorological visibility of 10 nautical miles . . . see International Visibility Code) expressed in nautical miles. Nominal range is listed only for lights having a computed nominal range of five nautical miles or more." McDonald Point Light in Idaho is given a nominal range of five miles; Molokai Light rates 28 miles.

The third is **luminous range**, defined as " . . . the maximum distance at which a light may be seen under the existing visibility conditions. By use of the diagram (Luminous Visibility Diagram contained in the *Light List*) luminous range may be determined from the known nominal range, or the intensity, and the existing visibility conditions." This suggests that under perfect conditions the Idaho light might reach out nearly 11 miles while in a light fog the Hawaiian aid could be invisible at no more than a mile.

And a fourth is **geographic range**, defined as " . . . the maximum distance at which a light may be seen under conditions of perfect visibility, limited only by the curvature of the earth; and is expressed in nautical miles for a height of observer's eye at 15 feet above sea level, without regard to the candlepower." McDonald Point here is listed as eight miles, while Molokai drops down to 21 miles.

Now to a closer look. **Candlepower** is neither precise nor consistent. McDonald Point is given 100 candlepower and a nominal range of five miles. Molokai Light, with 20,000 times the candlepower, is given only 28. Even so a navigator gleans some idea of distance from candlepower lists. **100** to **1000** seems to be five to nine miles range; **1000** to **100,000** takes it out to 20 miles. And from there to **two million** pushes it to 28 miles. About a dozen West Coast lights belong to the "million plus" club with 26 miles or more. But these are still only **nominal** ranges. Actual visibility involves the state of the atmosphere as well as the candlepower. So *Light Lists* include a **Luminous Visibility Diagram** to adjust tabulated nominal ranges to atmospheric conditions other than *Code 7 Clear* by the International Visibility Code. So, the McDonald Point Light might increase in range to eight miles when the atmosphere is *Code 9 Exceptionally Clear* and Molokai Light might drop to less than a mile when the prevailing condition is a *Code 3 Light Fog.* An old-timer calls all this "labeling for the sake of labels," and might ask how he measures other than by guess the *Code 3 Light Fog* and then distinguishes it from the *Code 4 Thin Fog* . . . not to mention a *Code 5 Hazel.*

And the chart will try his outrage even more, for there he will find noted the lesser of **nominal** range and **geographic**. This last is independent of candlepower and is concerned only with the height of the light and of the observer above the sea. An arbitrary observer's height of 15 feet is used as a base. For example, *Chart 5142* found on **Plate A** shows Los Angeles Breakwater Light to be 73 feet high and to have a visibility of 14 miles. Table 8 shows the distance to the horizon from 73 feet as 9.8 miles. For 15 feet it lists 4.4 miles. The sum is 14.2 miles . . . and the geographic range found on the chart is that amount rounded off to the nearest whole mile, or 14 miles. Charted visibility will always be in whole miles, and never a decimal. If the exact value is less than _.5, then only the whole miles are listed. If the exact is _.5 or more, then the next highest mile is shown. The *Light List,* however, shows the Los Angeles Entrance Light to have a nominal range of 19 miles. Here, the chart in showing the lesser of the two indicates **geographic** range. The other side of the coin is found in the charting of **Fourmile Rock Light** in Washington. It is 15 feet above the sea and charted at seven miles. Yet, Table 8 gives 4.4 miles for its height (15 feet); and adding another 4.4 miles for the standardized observer at 15 feet gives a total of 8.8 or nine miles. The *Light List* carries that as the geographic range. But the chart shows the lesser—in this case the **nominal range**—and so indicates seven miles. Let's spend the time for another example or two to see how this confusing scheme is supposed to work.

South Point Lighthouse on California's Santa Rosa Island is described as being located in a small white house on the southerly point of the island and at a height of 530 feet above the sea. The candlepower is 1000, the nominal range is nine miles. And the geographic range is listed as 31. It is a weak light, and under *Code 7 Clear* circumstances falls far short of its geographic range. By day an observer at 15 feet should pick up the small white house at a 31 mile distance. But at night, unless the atmosphere is *Code 9 Exceptionally Clear,* the maximum range of its little lamp would be much less.

Now to contrast **Point Arguello Lighthouse**. It is on California's southern coast and at a height of 124 feet. Candlepower is 1,300,000 and nominal range is 26 miles. But geographic range is only 17. By day a submarine at periscope depth would not see its tower until within 12.8 miles (Table 8 for 124 feet). A 15-foot observer could be 4.4 miles farther back, at a rounded off range of 17 miles. At night, though, when *Code 7* prevails, Arguello's beam reaches 26 miles . . . beyond the sub and beyond the standard observer. The submarine at 13 miles might not see it . . . unless he *up scope'd* quite a distance. Nor might the 15-footer were he beyond 17 miles. For in each case the beam would be far above. But if an observer had enough height—about 135 feet—he might detect it at the tabulated limit of nominal range, 26 miles. **Figure 63** tells the story.

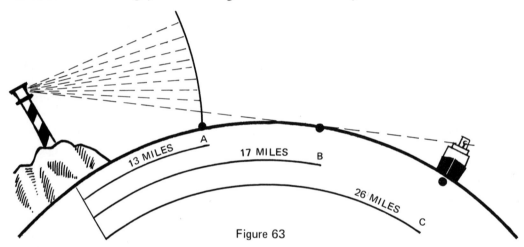

Figure 63

Why is all this important? Well, a weak light will not be seen as far as the lighthouse could be seen by day. It will fade before it will be cut off by the rim of the horizon. The importance of these distinctions is obvious when one considers the task of making a landfall at night. Expecting South Point at 30 miles would cause about 22 miles of fretting while it didn't appear. And a course change based, erroneously, on its failure to appear could be disastrous.

32/Seamanship
Rudder and propeller

According to some authorities, ships are graced with the feminine gender because they are individually so unpredictable and hard to master. Certainly it is true that wisdom in feminine ways is a rare achievement gained by few men. And no more contagious is complete expertness in the handling of a ship.

We attempt nothing like "Boat Handling Made Easy" or "Instant Seamanship." There is no effortless key to such an art of experience. What we can do is sketch a **general** framework of things to watch. Then, in practical application, the mariner may be more aware of what really happens when he does this or that.

First off . . . a boat is not a car. The steering gear of your automobile is connected to the **front** wheels. When you turn, the front end heads in a new direction and drags the rear end with it. But the steering device for a boat is at the stern. Move the tiller and the **stern** takes a new direction, pushing the bow ahead of it.

What turns the wheels of a car is your effort in turning the steering wheel. It might be easier to do when the wheels are rolling fast over the pavement; but the direction can be effectively changed regardless of speed. Not so afloat. What turns the boat is the rush of water against the canted rudder. You can turn the rudder as you wish . . . but the boat won't turn unless there is a wash of water at the stern. And the wash is a product of momentum. You must be moving in order to turn, and the faster you move, the more effective the turning. So rudder action gets sluggish as speed decreases. When maneuvering at slow speeds, expect to use more rudder.

With inboard power vessels, a major source of this rush of water on the rudder is the propeller . . .for it is usually set forward of the rudder. As the boat moves ahead, the currents flowing behind the screw exert a powerful force on the rudder. Obviously, this is not true under sail. Nor is it true for the power vessel going astern. For then the rudder is "ahead" of the propeller, and so influenced only by the flow of water caused by the movement of the vessel. The propeller wash has no effect. From this it follows that rudder action going astern should be quite different and not as effective as when going ahead.

But the propeller does more than propel. It has a very significant influence on steering. When you row a boat with balanced thrust on each oar, the force of the oar blades is directly opposite the direction of travel. A propeller that would do the same thing would be marvelous. Like jet thrust, all its push would be directed one way and so you would go the other. But the screw propeller is not so ideal. The force it generates can be viewed as two. Let's imagine a screw propeller turning to push a boat forward. The water is forced astern; but also there is a force to the left or to the right. The net result is that a screw not only pushes, it also "walks" sideways. **Figure 64** is an illustration.

Propellers are termed right-hand or left, depending on the way they turn. And that depends on point of view. A right-hand propeller turns clockwise as seen from astern. When the boat is out of the water, stand behind the stern and look forward. If the propeller turns clockwise going ahead, the screw is right-hand. Otherwise, it is left-hand.

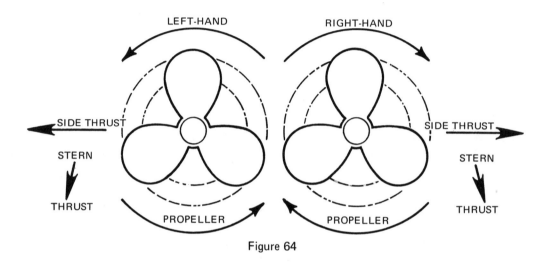

Figure 64

A right-hand propeller pushes the boat forward . . . but also "walks" the stern to the right. So when going ahead it will push the bow to port. Going astern, it will do the opposite . . . the stern moves to port and the bow to starboard. Hence, the saying: "She backs to Port."

A left-hand propeller is exactly contrary. Going ahead it tends to "walk to port" and so turn the bow to starboard. And in this case, "She backs to Starboard."

Most single screw powerboats have right-hand propellers. On twin screw craft the screws usually are counter-rotating. The port propeller turns outboard . . . is left-hand; and the starboard propeller also turns outboard . . . but that makes it right-hand. They tend to neutralize each other's side effects so there is no backing to port or bow canting to starboard.

So far, then, we've seen that, when the rudder is moved, the stern will change direction . . . and propeller action can either accentuate or offset that movement. But the force of the wind can also influence steering. It will act on the hull and superstructure either to enhance or to counteract rudder action.

Suppose you are steering north while a powerful force is pushing on the starboard side . . . you won't go north. That force is the wind. Normally it will push the ship bodily downwind. So a sailboat has a deep keel or centerboard to resist that skid. This power is changeable and hard to pin down; for it varies with the wind force and direction and with the hull and superstructure form and area.

The distribution of superstructure form and area is rarely uniform and balanced. The bow may be high and the stern low; or perhaps the stern cabin catches wind that goes over the bow. If the stern takes the greater force, then it will skid faster downwind than the bow . . . and so the boat will "steer into the wind." But if the bow takes the brunt, then she'll "fall off" from the wind. Draft also is a factor; for if the bow just planes over the surface with little water resistance, it may fall rapidly downwind. As you would expect . . . if the bow falls downwind going ahead, then it will do the same going astern. And since most powerboats do that, they will usually back into the wind.

The influence of the wind on the vessel's behavior is, of course, felt on the direction she takes through the water. An error in steering will result. For example, if she were heading 090° with the wind from North, the upshot would be an actual track of, say, 092°. This error is called **leeway**, and it is named East or West like other compass errors. If the result is a course to the right of that intended, the error is East; if it is to the left, the error is West. Put another way, wind pressure on the port side brings easterly leeway; wind on the starboard side brings westerly. It is a variable, of course, and is often difficult to predict. Offsetting it calls for steering into the wind the number of degrees your sea sense indicates. In our example, the leeway is 2°E; we would, then, steer 088° to make 090° good.

Judgment of leeway is usually by hindsight. When you don't get to the position sought, you must in our world of precision give an exact value and attribute it to someone or to something. Some people are Churchillian about the whole affair. It is said that in the 1950's, while Sir Winston was still Prime Minister, his opponents in Parliament were critical of the state of Britain's finances. To point up lax accounting, he was asked how much the war cost. After a hurried conference with his advisors, Churchill promised to give the answer in 24 hours. At that next session he grandly boomed a precise figure, as £9,562,491,507, 7s and 6d. Not only was the Opposition silenced, but his own advisors were dumbfounded . . . how did he arrive at the sum? His answer: "You said it would take years to compute; then it will take years to prove me wrong!"

And so with leeway. On a large ship, the navigator might blame the helmsmen. Or, if the Deck Department stands united, he might chide the Engineers for not maintaining proper RPM. On a happy ship, the culprit would be leeway. In fact, though, there are too many variables to yield an exact answer. Of course, there really is such an influence as leeway, but the possibility of human error in maintaining course and speed should also be considered.

You can go further dissecting the various influences on your boat underway. But eventually you reach the saturation point. Let's stop short of it and recap what's already been said. Then, the first chance you get, try your boat in a few situations to see how she reacts. It is essential to know how **your** vessel responds. Otherwise a flock of general principles and facts are only window dressing without the window.

Now to a review:

1. A single screw tends to cant the bow to port when going ahead and to pull the stern to port when going astern. Twin screws don't normally have the problem.
2. The rudder is least effective at slow speeds and increases in efficiency as the speed goes up. Going astern, it has less effect than going ahead, for then the "tail is wagging the dog."
3. Wind usually pushes the bow downwind and causes the stern to back into the wind.
4. These factors seldom are isolated . . . in most cases they will act simultaneously. So if the wind is on the port side, the tendency to back to port will be enhanced by "backing into the wind," and the stern may well swing faster to port then normally. On the other hand, if the wind strikes on the starboard side, the tendency to back to port may be neutralized or even overcome by the inclination to back into the wind.
5. The same enhancing, neutralizing or overcoming may apply when going ahead . . . the slight tendency for the bow to go to port being influenced by its fall off downwind.

All this is important when maneuvering in close quarters. The art of mooring and docking is the finished product; but the raw material is understanding how the boat behaves. Much is said of the smart maneuver to place the ship quickly in the desired position. But more should be said about the **satisfactory** maneuver . . . the one that puts the ship safely in position while always under control. There is an anecdote told of Admiral Cunningham when he commanded the British Mediterranean Fleet in WWII. His flagship was tied up to a dock and a bright destroyer captain was ordered to tie up astern. Full ahead came the destroyer. Then, with a swirl of foam and a shudder, Full Astern. The destroyer jerked to a stop neatly in position just feet astern of the flagship. From Cunningham came a one-word blinker signal, "Good." Before the destroyerman could fully enjoy the praise, he received another signal: "To last message, add God."

Admiral Cunningham's dismay at the spectacular is not unique. The right way is the careful way. Whenever possible, make a maneuver slowly and with plenty of reserve time to correct a miscue. And don't rely on the inanimate pistons and rods and gears of your engine to respond absolutely whenever called. They are by nature cold-blooded and have a nasty habit of balking at the most awkward times. It is only a step from being spectacular to being a spectacle.

33/The Ship
Stability

Our next question: what makes a vessel stay upright? This involves a discussion of the elements of stability.

All the weight of the vessel can be represented as concentrated in one point, the **center of gravity**. In **Figure 65** we see that, when the craft is on an even keel, the center of gravity (**G**) acts straight down through the keel.

But when the boat is listed, as in **Figure 66**, we see that **G**, although still acting vertically down, now aims to the side of the keel; and it follows that when **G** is located higher up, as at **G'** in **Figure 66**, its downward force will move farther out from the centerline.

The upward force of water can also be represented as at one point, the **center of buoyancy (B)**. It is the actual geometric center of the immersed part of the boat . . . the part of the hull from the waterline down. **Figure 67** shows it for a vessel on an even keel. In **Figure 68** the boat is listed. The form of the immersed part of the hull is now changed, so its center, **B'**, will shift. As the list increases, **B'** drifts out from the centerline towards the low side of the ship.

Take a few moments to look at these four sketches. They represent the basic influences on stability and show how they act in the two basic attitudes a ship takes: on an even keel and when subject to list.

Next, we'll combine these sketches and see what happens. In **Figure 69**

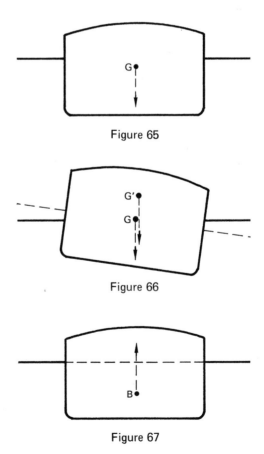

Figure 65

Figure 66

Figure 67

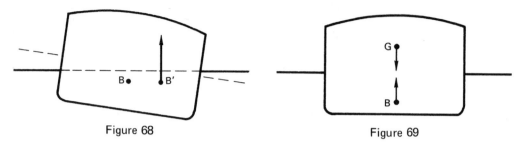

Figure 68   Figure 69

the boat is again on an even keel. Notice that **G** and **B** are in the same vertical line. They are exactly opposite. So they offset each other. Also they are exactly equal in force; otherwise the boat would either be sinking more or rising out of the water.

But not so in **Figure 70**, when the boat is listed again. Here, **G** acts straight down and **B'** acts straight up, as before. But they are acting in different lines of force. **G** is tending to capsize the boat while **B'** is trying to right her. This is **positive stability**. So long as **B'** can overcome the downward force of **G**, the boat will return to an even keel. The horizontal distance from **G** to the point **Z** is a measure of that stability, and is called the **righting arm**. As **GZ** gets longer, then greater force is exerted by **B'** to push the boat back to an even keel. **GZ** is like a crowbar, pivoted at **G**. The longer the crowbar, the more power is generated with the same upward force. Within limits this upward push gets bigger as the list increases. For **B'** will keep moving out towards the side and **GZ** will get longer and longer. Remember the cargo ship, the *Flying Enterprise*? Her Master tried to save her single-handed a decade or so ago. She floated on her side with water lapping in the smokestack because the upward force of **B'**, coupled with a very long righting arm, exerted a tremendous upward push.

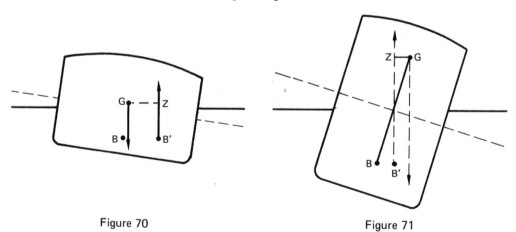

Figure 70   Figure 71

In **Figure 71**, though, things are different. Here, **G** is quite high. When the boat lists, **B'** can't move out far enough to get beyond the downward force through **G** . . . so the inevitable: **G** wants to topple her over, and **B'** lends a hand. They no longer will work against each other. Here, there is no stability, no power to overcome capsizing. Instead, the righting arm becomes actually an upsetting arm. The upward force will help the vessel turn over.

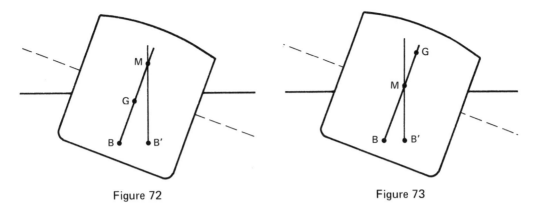

Figure 72   Figure 73

Two more sketches will illustrate another basic factor in stability: the **meta-center**. **Figure** 72 is a sketch of a ship with positive stability, and **Figure** 73 shows one with negative stability. Notice the straight line from **B** through **G** . . . it represents the vertical line in which the forces of gravity and buoyancy will oppose each other when the ship is on an even keel. Now look at the vertical line upward from **B'** . . . it is the force of buoyancy when she is listed. The two lines intersect at **M**. That is the **metacenter**.

In **Figure** 72 the intersection is above **G**; in **Figure** 73 it is below **G**. The distance **GM**, from **G** to **M**, is called the **metacentric height**. And in every case of positive stability, **M** will be above **G**; in every case of negative stability, it will be below.

What can be learned from these sketches? Most of it is already known, even though taken for granted. A high center of gravity can be dangerous, for the boat will be top-heavy. A low center of gravity is stable. But it is important to see how the forces are at work.

Actually, a very low center of gravity can be uncomfortable, and even damaging. When **G** is extremely low and the boat lists, the distance **GZ** gets long very quickly. And the force upward through **B'** just as quickly becomes very powerful.

Figure 74 shows this situation. The result: the upward force will snap her back to an even keel. The rolls will be short, jerky and quite uncomfortable. And severe strain will be placed on any gear aloft. The name given this condition is **stiffness**; and a stiff ship is not necessarily a staunch one.

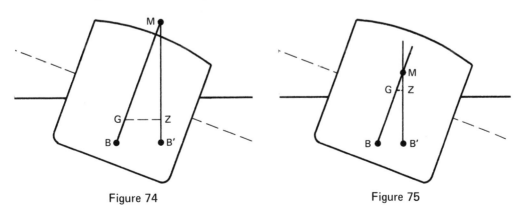

Figure 74   Figure 75

The opposite of stiffness is **tenderness**. When **G** is high, the ship is tender. Her rolls will be long, slow and agonizingly listless. She seems to pause, heeled over, as if gaining strength for the effort to swing back upright. **Figure 75** shows a tender ship. All that can be said for this condition is there is less strain on masts and gear aloft. But that is little compensation for the risks.

Everything discussed so far could be called **transverse stability**, the forces acting when a ship rolls or lists from side to side. But it is just as applicable to **longitudinal** stability. This refers to the action of pitching up and down from end to end. The difference . . . a matter of degree. Ships seldom turn end-over-end. If they capsize, it is by rolling over. When you stop to think about it, the reason is clear. They are longer than wide, so **B'** has plenty of room to move longitudinally. It will be rare that the upward force of **B'** cannot work against the forces of gravity to push the bow or stern back up again.

Most pleasure craft have good stability, with underdeck weights ample to assure a safely low **G**. They tend, if anything, to stiffness and snap quickly from side to side. But this is not necessarily a malady you want to cure. When next you step aboard and feel the deck slant under your weight, think of **B'** scurrying over to start pushing back up. He pushes so hard the deck slants the other way. So off he flies to the opposite side. Tirelessly and with complete reliability, **B'** shuttles from side to side, forcing the ship back to an even keel. The one thing he doesn't want is cooperation. So long as he and the force down through **G** are at odds, everything is safe. But let them work together and the jig's up. So just keep the center of gravity low.

One final facet before we close the book on this topic. Some inanimate weights aboard are fixed in position. The engine won't shift, nor will the keel. And so they cause no change in the location of the center of gravity (**G**). But liquids are a different story. Given freedom to move, they will redistribute weight . . . and a lot of it . . . in a flash. **G** will then certainly change position. And since liquids don't run uphill, they will shift **G** towards the low side. This makes extra trouble for poor **B'**. It shortens his lever and weakens his power to even things up.

The answer? Restrict the freedom of liquids to flow, limit their **free surface**. For this reason many tanks are fitted with swash plates, vertical dividers to interrupt the movement from side to side. And, of course, neither a full tank nor an empty one has any free surface. The caution is fairly obvious: operating with tanks half-filled can be dangerous to stability.

That's it . . . the basic elements to answer our two basic questions are on these pages. We still must say the review is not necessary. But let it start the thought processes. Whatever is the combination that spells Seamanship, it surely is made of many scattered and apparently unrelated facts and observations. And an analysis such as this can add to a rapid discovery of the secret.

Questions

Don't go away! Orders have been received for another condition survey, so we're off to meet the Inspector. Square up the decks and paint anything that doesn't move. Here he comes!

Rules of the Road

1. In a heavy rainstorm restricting visibility to 100 yards
   a) you will sound fog signals.
   b) you will not sound fog signals.

2. "Moderate Speed" in fog means that which
   a) allows a ship to stop within the range of visibility.
   b) allows a ship to stop within half the distance of visibility.
   c) is approximately half speed.

3. When, in fog, you hear the fog signal of another vessel apparently forward of your beam
   a) you must blow an answering signal immediately.
   b) you must stop your forward motion.
   c) both of above.
   d) none of above.

4. At noontime in a heavy fog
   a) you must burn sidelights.
   b) you must blow fog signals.
   c) both of above.
   d) none of above.

5. A radar reflector can
   a) strengthen the radar echo from a small vessel.
   b) reveal the presence of a small vessel in a choppy sea.
   c) both of above.
   d) none of above.

6. A prolonged blast is
   a) longer than a short blast.
   b) longer than a long blast.
   c) of no specified length.

7. Under both International and Inland Rules, three short whistle blasts can signify
   a) engines going full astern.
   b) engines going half astern.

c)   engines going slow astern.
d)   all of above.
e)   none of above.

8. A sailing vessel
   a)   always sounds passing signals when in sight of another vessel.
   b)   does not sound any whistle signal except in fog or distress.

9. In fog when meeting another vessel which is in sight
   a)   you sound only fog signals.
   b)   you sound passing signals.

10. In fog one prolonged blast followed by two short blasts
    a)   can mean a tug.
    b)   Inland, can mean a vessel being towed.
    c)   both of above.
    d)   none of above.

Aids to Navigation

1. Distance of visibility based on intensity of a light is called
   a)   geographic range.
   b)   nominal range.
   c)   optical range.

2. In using a table to find the geographic range of a light
   a)   you enter the table with the sum of the height of the light and the height of the observer above sea level and find the corresponding visibility in nautical miles.
   b)   you enter the table with the difference between the height of the light and the height of the observer.
   c)   you enter the table with the height of the light, and then separately with the height of the observer, and then add the mileages.

3. Geographic range when shown on a chart is computed to
   a)   an observer at 15 feet above the sea.
   b)   an observer at 10 feet above the sea.
   c)   an observer at 5 feet above the sea.
   d)   an observer at sea level.

4. The distance of visibility to the sea horizon from a height of 15 feet is
   a)   2.2 nautical miles.
   b)   3.3 nautical miles.
   c)   4.4 nautical miles.
   d)   5.5 nautical miles.

5. A light whose distance of visibility is 16.5 miles
   a) will be charted as 17 miles.
   b) will be charted as 16 miles.
   c) will be charted as 16.5 miles.

Seamanship

1. When looking forward at a right-hand propeller
   a) it will turn clockwise going ahead.
   b) it will turn clockwise going astern.
   c) it will be on the starboard side of the vessel.

2. Normally a right-hand propeller will
   a) back to port.
   b) back to starboard.

3. The steering action of a rudder
   a) decreases with increase in forward speed.
   b) increases with decrease in forward speed.
   c) increases with increase in forward speed.
   d) will not change with change in speed.

4. Twin screw propellers usually
   a) rotate in opposite directions.
   b) turn outboard.
   c) both of above.
   d) none of above.

5. Rudder action going astern
   a) is more effective than going ahead.
   b) is less effective than going ahead.

The Ship

1. The center of buoyancy is
   a) the same as the center of gravity.
   b) the point where all the weight of the vessel can be represented.
   c) the point where all the upward force of water can be represented.

2. Compared to a longer righting arm, a short one indicates that a vessel has
   a) greater force to return to an even keel.
   b) less force to return to an even keel.

3. A stiff ship has
   a) a lower center of gravity than a tender ship.
   b) a higher center of gravity than a tender ship.

4. A tank filled completely with liquid
   a)   has more free surface than one half empty.
   b)   has less free surface than one half empty.

5. An empty tank
   a)   has more free surface than a tank completely filled.
   b)   has less free surface than a tank completely filled.
   c)   has no free surface.

...and answers

Five points this time for each item found in good order. This schedule will tell what shape you're in:

90 - 100:   Seaworthy in All Respects.
80 - 85:   GM Could Be a Wee Bit Greater.
70 - 75:   Getting Too Tender!
Below 70:   Bottoms up!

Rules of the Road

1. (a)   2. (b)   3. (d)   4. (b)   5. (c)
6. (a)   7. (d)   8. (b)   9. (b)   10. (c)

Aids to Navigation

1. (b)   2. (c)   3. (a)   4. (c)   5. (a)

Seamanship

1. (a)   2. (a)   3. (c)   4. (c)   5. (b)

The Ship

1. (c)   2. (b)   3. (a)   4. (b)   5. (c)

section 8
contents

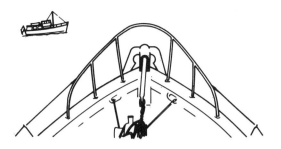

34/Rules of the Road
Prudence and precaution

There are two sections tucked away in the Rules of the Road which appear to be catchall generalities. Even their names are vague and innocuous: **general prudential** or **special circumstance precautionary** or **good seamanship**. But don't be misled. They are mortar poured between the blocks of cut and dried regulations . . . and just as essential. Here they are, reprinted from *CG-169:*

INTERNATIONAL RULES

GENERAL PRUDENTIAL RULE

RULE 27 In obeying and construing these Rules due regard shall be had to all dangers of navigation and collision, and to any special circumstances, including the limitations of the craft involved, which may render a departure from the above Rules necessary in order to avoid immediate danger.

RULE OF GOOD SEAMANSHIP

RULE 29 Nothing in these Rules shall exonerate any vessel, or the owner, master or crew thereof, from the consequences of any neglect to carry lights or signals, or of any neglect to keep a proper look-out, or of the neglect of any precaution which may be required by the ordinary practice of seamen, or by the special circumstances of the case.

INLAND RULES

GENERAL PRUDENTIAL RULE

ART. 27. *In obeying and construing these rules due regard shall be had to all dangers of navigation and collision, and to any special circumstances which may render a departure from the above rules necessary in order to avoid immediate danger.*

RULE OF GOOD SEAMANSHIP

ART. 29. *Nothing in these rules shall exonerate any vessel, or the owner or master or crew thereof, from the consequences of any neglect to carry lights or signals, or of any neglect to keep a proper lookout, or of the neglect of any precaution which may be required by the ordinary practice of seamen, or by the special circumstances of the case.*

Unless a mariner understands them—even though he has all the whistles and lights down pat—he doesn't know enough to operate safely. For in a few sentences they express the entire spirit of all the rules. Too often this spirit is skipped over. But we can do that no longer. With the "population explosion" on the water, obedience to the spirit of the rules is all that stands between us and just a bunch of wet freeways cluttered with people shrieking "right of way."

The whole point of the rules is safety. We're all out of our element on water, and with a common adversary. The rules organize and define our conduct up to a certain point. In doing so they seem to assign rights and duties. But this is really not true. For **Rules** 27 and 29 deny that any vested rights exist. Overriding everything is common sense and common interest. Ashore, we give lip service to these sentiments. But afloat, it must be different. They aren't just suggested; they are ordered.

Did you ever see a handy little sailboat dodging down the channel? She tacks back and forth in front of a lumbering supertanker that is plodding along, her keel just a scant few feet from the bottom. The sailboat too often thinks she has the right of way . . . and she uses it like a gnat buzzing at the head of a slow ox. Well, the sailboat couldn't be "wronger." She has no privilege at all. She may be violating both 27 and 29. No regard is shown for the limitations of the big ship, nor for the special circumstances. She not only neglects the ordinary practice of seamen . . . she doesn't even measure up to the standards of a child.

International **Rule 20(b)** has for years spelled out the burden of a sailboat towards the cumbersome ship. **Articles** 27 and 29 of Inland Rules have in substance said the same thing. And now **Article 20** erases all doubt in Inland Waters. After obliging steam vessels to stay out of the way of sailing vessels, it fixes the sailboat's burden in words almost identical to that of the International Rule by saying:

> "This rule shall not give to a sailing vessel the right to hamper, in a narrow channel, the safe passage of a steam vessel which can navigate only inside that channel. (Public Law 89-764.)"

International **Rule 25(c)** has also for years prohibited the powerboat of less than 65 feet from hampering a large ship transiting a narrow channel. And **Articles** 27 and 29 Inland have always done so in substance. Now, in order to drive that point home, **Article 25** Inland adds the same prohibition found in International 25(c) by these words:

> "In narrow channels a steam vessel of less than sixty-five feet in length shall not hamper the safe passage of a vessel which can navigate only inside that channel. (Public Law 89-764.)"

These changes involve nothing new in spirit. But in the past the mariner riding a balky monster was more aware of the danger and so more virtuous. Now the pattern is unequivocal. And **Mariner's Notebook** is just a bit "I told you so-ish," for all its earlier editions preached that spirit. There is no room for petulance. And the luxury of the slightest license "to do your own thing" is too expensive. Permissiveness afloat, at least, is a passport to disaster.

Every time you see a craft unreasonably demand her "rights" under the rules, think of **Rules** 27 and 29. Like a schoolboy, her operator should repeat one hundred times:

"There are no rights. There are no rights. There are no rights."

Ninety-nine percent of marine collisions are culpable . . . someone did not obey the rules. In 75 out of 100 accidents, the vessels were clearly in sight of each other. Common experience tells us they were not all one-sided. Many times one ship could act to cure the risk created by the other. And that is what, in essence, **Rules** **27** and **29** require.

You are to perform like an actor in a play. Follow the script as found in the rules, but with a watchful eye on unusual circumstances. When you sense immediate danger, then don't stick to the script if it means disaster. "Ad-lib" as best you can.

The parallel to the stage is quite apt. The actor follows the script until someone flubs or misses a cue. Then, if he can keep the scene moving, he'll improvise to cover up. You also meet the emergency caused by another vessel and do your impromptu best to maintain safe passage.

How untrue it is to speak of privilege and burden! The words don't even appear in the rules. Enforce your rights and you miss the point. There are no rights to enforce. You have a script to follow. One time you must portray a character called "Privileged," another time your part is "Burdened." But if "Burdened" blows a line, you must leave the script and help him cover up. There's not a permissive word in this paragraph. You are **obliged** to improvise.

Now for a close look at each of these general rules. **Rule 27** says we must be ready to depart from the rules when the special circumstances require. The only difference between the International and the Inland statement: on the High Seas there is an express statement to include, as a special circumstance, "the limitations of the craft involved." Inland, the inclusion is there . . . it is just not stated in terms. And the additions to **Articles 20** and **25** we've already discussed underscore the point.

However stated, **Number 27** means "contradict the rules, if necessary." If you

RMS Queen Mary arriving at Port of Long Beach with Rules 27 and 29 applicable.

are in a tight spot and going left will cure it when going right is normal . . . go left. **But** there is a very definite threshold to this independence. You can't throw over the specified procedures until immediate danger stares you in the face. And then you improvise only to the extent necessary. An example might be helpful. You leave the mooring and are proceeding down the channel when another vessel approaches on your port. It is a crossing situation. You blow one blast and hold course and speed. He answers with one. You continue on, watching for him to slow down or turn to pass behind you. But nothing happens. Your courses are now converging and yet he hasn't made a move. The danger signal doesn't rouse him. Then you reach the threshold. In your seamanlike judgment, immediate danger exists and there is grave doubt he can avoid it alone. So you must ad-lib to help cure his mistake. Up till then you were obliged to hold course and speed . . . you were burdened to be privileged. Now you're on your own. But that point of immediate danger first had to be reached. So long as it was reasonably possible for his tardy action to be effective, you follow the script and hold on. But when his action alone seems no longer enough for the job . . . then you do the best thing you can. **And** if you don't try to save the situation, you are not following the rules. While there is still a chance for the ships to miss if you act, you must act.

Of course, not the only case of special circumstance is this one . . . where one party had caused things by violating a rule. The classic and frequent case of no fault is the approach of more than two ships. Suppose you and two other craft become involved simultaneously in the approach. Perhaps you would otherwise be burdened to give way to a vessel on your right and to hold course and speed for the vessel on your left. This can't be done; so the normal rules are not able to meet these special conditions. The answer? Special Circumstances exist and **Rule 27** requires you to do your best. Slow down, blow signals, stop, back up . . . whatever is reasonably proper. Each of the three is burdened to act prudently under the facts.

Rule 29, by contrast, speaks of supplementing the rules, not disregarding them. You are required to do whatever **more** good sense would indicate under the special circumstances. An example is speed in clear weather. The rules make mention of moderate speed in fog, but don't discuss the clear weather case. But suppose you're passing near a vessel engaged in underwater work, let's say skin divers boarding. You must make sure your propeller wash and wake don't interfere. You do so, not because you are polite, not only because a harbor speed limit might be posted, but because you **must** do so under **Rule 29**. Good common sense tells you to slow down. And the rules require you to use good common sense under the special conditions.

We have completed a practical survey of the Rules of the Road. There are no shortcuts to learning the specifics, for that is memory work. Instead, we've found the framework and assembled the parts as we've gone along. Learn the particular requirements, of course. But also get the feel of the whole scheme. We began this series with the aim to find "whys" instead of "wherefores." To the extent that has been done, we can say "Mission Accomplished."

35/Aids to Navigation
Radiobeacons

A lighthouse nowadays possesses much more than just a light. For instance, it can emit audible fog signals, or have a radiobeacon, or be a Distance Finding Station, or be part of a Loran system . . . or be all those things.

Loran (**LO**ng **R**ange **A**id to **N**avigation) is an electronic system using the time interval between receipt of a radio signal broadcast by a "master" station and one simultaneously sent out by a "slave." This interval (determined electronically) places the receiver on a line of position (actually a **hyperbolic curve**) relative to the location of the transmitting pair. The Coast Guard maintains such stations throughout the world. We'll have more to say about Loran later on.

But the radiobeacon found at many lighthouse stations is certainly an aid available to nearly everyone. The Marine Electronics sections of **Mariner's Notebook** discuss radio direction finding aboard. Here, we'll limit comment to the installation at the lighthouse, and not aboard your vessel.

Marine radiobeacons vary by range, signal characteristic, time of transmission and transmission frequency. The signals are broadcast within the limits of 285 to 325 kiloHertz. Since about 200 US stations are maintained by the Coast Guard, there will, of course, be frequency overlap. So it follows that frequency is not a distinguishing characteristic of a radiobeacon.

What does specify a station is its signal characteristic: the arrangement of dots and dashes making up the transmission. In the same geographical area, at least, there will be no duplication of characteristic.

In mid-1963 the Coast Guard effected a major revision in the programming of RDF services. The old schedule of transmissions, familiar to more than a generation of mariners, has been supplanted by a New Look. The June 1963 issue of the *Proceedings of the Merchant Marine Council* of the US Coast Guard describes the changes this way:

> "Briefly, the revision is the time sharing of a frequency by six radiobeacons instead of three; the elimination of the 20-minute period of silence in clear weather; the adjustment of service ranges; the addition of a 10-second dash in the characteristic identifier and the superimposing of the characteristic on a continuous carrier."

Let's use that excerpt as a point of departure on our survey of radiobeacons.

First, to frequency. The present schedule groups up to six stations on the same frequency . . . and they, wherever possible, to be in the same geographical area. For example the four major beacons in Southern California's 11th Coast Guard District all transmit on 302 kHz. In a safely distant geographical area, another group can use the same frequency. So, in New England's First Coast Guard District, Nantucket, Pollock Rip and Boston Lightships share 302 kHz with Cape Cod radiobeacon.

The obvious next problem: how to keep the group members from jamming each other. The answer is in a round-robin kind of schedule. Each radiobeacon transmits for at least one minute out of every six minutes. In other words, its minimum schedule is one minute **on** and five minutes **off**. During its five minutes of silence the other five members of the group will each have a one-minute on. Group members, then, are assigned Roman numerals from I to VI identifying their place in the sequence. And if there are less than six stations in the group, then one or more of the stations may transmit for two one-minute intervals. The Southern California stations are scheduled this way:

Point Loma	 I	Point Arguello	 III
Los Angeles	 II	Point Loma	 IV
	Los Angeles	 V	

Point Loma transmits first for one minute, then Los Angeles sounds off, then Point Arguello, then Point Loma comes back again, and, finally, Los Angeles makes its second appearance. This doesn't take up a six-minute period because the membership of the "302 kHz Club" is not complete. There is space on the roster for one future member. Until then there is a one-minute silent interval between the last transmission from Los Angeles and the start of a new sequence from Point Loma.

Under the revision, radiobeacons transmit on the sequenced schedule around-the-clock. Before, only in poor visibility might they do so. For many stations the clear weather schedule was cut back to 10 minutes out of every 30. But now the service is constant. And there are some key beacons which transmit continuously. They don't even share a sequence with five or less partners.

As to the range: marine radio direction finding is, in any case, a short-range technique. The power of the transmitter can be such that the signal will travel great distances. But as the range increases, the precision of the bearing goes down. At 100 miles, the error in position goes above five miles. We must, then, make a distinction when the range values assigned by the Coast Guard to each station are discussed. For example, the range of one transmitter might be described as 150 miles, while another radiobeacon might be assigned a rating of just 70 miles. These figures refer to **service range**, based on the strength of the radiated signal . . . how powerful is the transmitter. When taking a bearing, we speak of **useful range** . . . the limit of distance for an accurate bearing.

The trend is now against long service ranges, and for many reasons. Not only is the navigational value in question, but the extra power of a long-range station

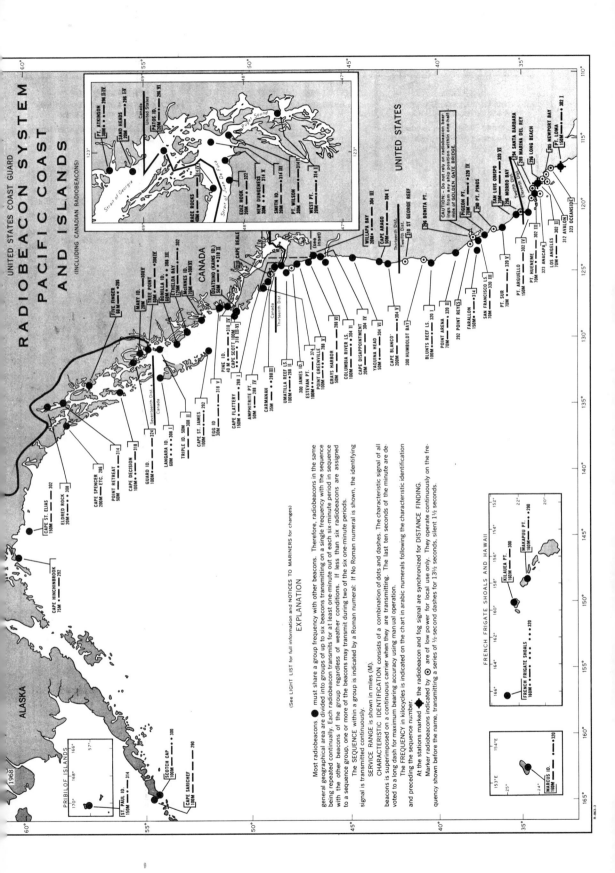

decreases the number of stations which can be scheduled for the same frequency at the same minute. Point Loma should not interfere with Cape Cod beacon, for they are a continent apart. But because the service range of each is 150 miles, they would have to be at least 655 miles apart to avoid interference. So, in planning for the population explosion in radio aids, the Coast Guard will probably reduce service ranges to approach more nearly the useful.

The characteristic signal of a radiobeacon is a series of dots and dashes. This call letter is kept simple so that no knowledge of Morse Code is necessary to use the aid. For example, Point Loma sends -.-., which is the Morse symbol for the letter C. But to avoid any inference that Morse know-how is required, the characteristic is described, not as C but as -.-. **(dah dit dah dit** or **dash dot dash dot)**. And now an additional assist is given the navigator so he can refine his bearing: a 10-second dash follows the sending of the characteristic. The result, for Point Loma: **dah dit dah dit dahhhhhhh** or -.-. ——————.

To keep up with our age of automation the New Look superimposes the characteristic on a continuous radio carrier wave which automatic direction finders can seek out efficiently. The navigator who is using his ears to determine the null is not aware of this "subliminal" signal.

There are special US radiobeacons for calibration of your radio direction finder. They transmit on a frequency differing from the radiobeacon band, and are of short service range. Prior to the revision, there was an additional way to use radiobeacons for calibration. During the 20-minute clear weather silent periods, radiobeacons would fire up on request for calibration purposes. Now, of course, when such beacons have an around-the-clock schedule, it cannot be done. This is, though, a minor price the navigator pays for constant radiobeacon service. If he doesn't use the special calibration station, he must work out his calibration on the working schedule of the beacon . . . waiting up to five minutes between bearings.

The special calibration stations are relatively scarce . . . only six, for example, to serve California, Oregon, Washington, Alaska and Hawaii. This is what the Coast Guard *Light Lists* have to say about them:

> "All stations transmit continuously during the time required for calibration with keyed tone modulated carrier . . . and have a reliable range of 10 miles. Their assigned characteristic is transmitted twice followed by a 20-second dash, the complete sequence being repeated twice per minute . . . In the event special calibration service interferes with the operation of regular radiobeacon transmission, the special calibration service will not be given."

And as to arranging for the service, the *Light List* says:

> "If it is not practicable to determine the time of calibration sufficiently in advance to contact the district commander, request may be made directly to the stations by means of telephone, telegraph, or a whistle signal consisting of **three long blasts followed by three short blasts,** this whistle signal to be repeated until it is acknowledged by

the station through the starting of the transmitter. The same group of signals should be sounded at the termination of calibration.

"If attention of station personnel is not attracted by the whistle signal, hoist the international code signal, **O over Q**, to indicate request for radio direction finder calibration.

"The work of station personnel is not confined to standing watch and there may be times when the whistle request for calibration is not immediately heard, due to the noise from operating station machinery, etc. Usually a repeated signal not too far from the station will attract attention."

Common sense, of course, says not to abuse this service. At best it is an accommodation. And the burden on a holiday weekend to take care of scores of boats circling around blowing horns would be overwhelming. Nonetheless, the service is offered: blow the signal, and the transmitter of the special calibration station will start up so you can check your receiver; then blow the whistle signal again to indicate that your test is concluded.

There is another type station . . . the **Marker Radiobeacon**. It is low power and is for local use only. Such an aid transmits a series of one-half second dashes for 13½ seconds, and then is silent for 1½ seconds. The full 15-second cycle is repeated continuously.

What about the fog signal at a lighthouse? It will be of distinctive tone and characteristic. There are diaphones, diaphragm horns, reed horns, whistles, sirens and bells. The sound can be of one pitch or two-tone. The familiar moaning and groaning heard on foggy nights in any harbor are examples of at least a few of the possible combinations.

The characteristic, other than tone, refers to the sequence of sounds and the time schedule of transmission . . . as, one blast of two-second duration made every 10 seconds; or a group of five strokes of a bell followed by 15 seconds of silence. The information on these distinctive signals will be found on charts and in the Coast Guard *Light List*.

Fog signals are, of course, made only during periods of low visibility. At manned stations, when visibility drops to five miles or less, the fog signal is begun. At automatic stations, there can be a delay in the beginning of the signal. Any fog signal, though, should be relied on with caution. Never expect its loudness to be a reliable indication of distance. Never think that, because no signal is heard, the station is not around. Fog has an unhappy way of muffling and distorting the sound. Moreover, it could be thick where you are but clear as a bell at the station! In a nutshell: a fog signal will tell you that the station is near, but it won't tell which way and how far.

What, never? Well, like the Captain of HMS *Pinafore,* we must say, "Hardly ever." For some installations couple a radiobeacon with a fog signal. This combination is a **Distance Finding Station (DFS** on a chart). As we've seen, the radiobeacon sends a 10-second dash after its characteristic. Normally this long dash immediately follows the characteristic . . . but not in the case of a DFS. It has a two-second silence between them, to serve as a standby warning. Then as soon as the 10-second dash begins, a five-second blast of the fog signal also begins. Aboard ship you receive the radio signal and then count the seconds until you hear the audible fog signal. We've mentioned sound in air before. But let's repeat it again. Sound travels in air at about 1100 feet per second, or 0.18 nautical miles per second. So, multiply the seconds by 0.18 to gain distance off. An alternative formula: divide the seconds by 5.5.

Here is an example. Suppose you hear the radiobeacon sending its normal characteristic signal of, say, .-- followed by ——————. This continues for 48 seconds of each minute. Then follows a two-second silence, during which time you go on the alert. Next you hear by radio the beginning of a 10-second dash. As soon as it begins (not ends) you start the countdown, timing the seconds while you listen for the fog signal. Soon you hear the beginning of a five-second blast through the air. The interval to the five-second air blast is, let's say, 28 seconds. Your distance off is 28x0.18 or 5.04 miles. The alternative: divide 28 by 5.5 for 5.09 miles.

As time goes on, new electronic devices will be installed to help coastal navigation. But seafarers should never get impatient because changes might not appear as fast as they expect. More important than convenience is reliability. A new system must be well-proved before it will replace an old-fashioned but old reliable device. For most vessels the services available are very adequate. Trouble usually comes, not from want of an aid ashore, but from misinterpretation afloat. No electronic device will ever be a total cure for that.

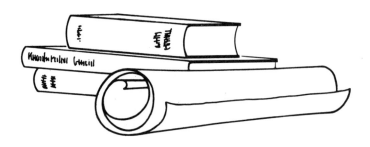

36/Seamanship
Common sense and sea sense

An afternoon of intelligent practice maneuvering your boat will teach more seamanship than a month reading manuals. What we best can do here is set the mood. For seamanship is an emotion as much as recollection of facts and what-to-do. No one, ever, has been truly a seaman by the process of intellect only. He must have the feeling . . . fear, love and also respect for the sea.

There's no reason to call this sentimental or adolescent. Perhaps even in other areas of our lives we'd do better to be more emotional participants, and less wary spectators. But at least in seafaring you can't be neutral. It is a dignified emotion, so never hesitate to let it grow. And it shows more as a gleam in the eye than by salty words or outfit.

A genuine liking for the ocean can't easily be analyzed; and perhaps it shouldn't be. Every pleasure mariner has it or he wouldn't own a boat. But the fear and respect are more rational. They can be catalogued with some precision. The ocean is a playful companion . . . but very, very powerful. The seaman never forgets this.

One cubic foot is not much space . . . a grocery box, a Christmas package or a small overnight bag. But one cubic foot of sea water weighs 64 pounds! To fill your bathtub a foot deep takes a quarter of a ton. How small seems a mere tubful compared to the tons of weight that lap against the hull! This is the power to rock you gently on a calm night. But let a wind drive it into legions of pile drivers and it can pulverize the strongest ship.

Respect, then, is born in the knowledge of the fantastic might the ocean can bring to bear. It's not really bright to drive headlong into a choppy sea. To watch this is to wince, as a horseman would when a colt is abused. Keel and forefoot were not built to slam against dead weight. Slow down, or ease the burden a few points on the bow. But don't challenge the sea to a butting contest . . . you'll lose eventually.

The stern on most boats is built to follow along . . . be very cautious whenever you present it to a sea. Anchoring stern to sea is very dangerous. Not only do you expose rudder, propeller and counter to unusual risk; but green water can easily come aboard. And underway, beware the following sea! There is treachery in the frightful way it towers up to swamp you with a crash.

The seaman doesn't challenge the ocean. There is no contest. His valor is always in discretion. In every case the task is to compromise; only when that is impossible does he stand and fight. Yet there is another side to the coin. He has a power the sea can never own . . . intelligence. Every move it makes can be anticipated. Sometimes there's plenty of time; occasionally, he has only a split second. But always there is an opportunity.

The reward for respect is ample time for decision. Actually, the true seaman is seldom caught off guard. He keeps alert to changes and accommodates them as they arise. But this doesn't mean you must stay on edge, concentrating to detect the vague overtones and nuances of the ocean's mood. That is to suggest the ocean is sophisticated, when in fact, it is not at all subtle. There are many obvious signs of its mood, wherever you look. What the seaman does is just never to take it for granted. He is aware of its nature and so attuned to the changes. There is no trick to it, nor even a lengthy apprenticeship. But the first step is to recognize the sea as a highway far different from a fixed, solid macadam roadbed.

From that point on, all sorts of respectful practices follow. Whenever possible, don't go boating alone. The Joshua Slocums who circumnavigate single-handed only prove the point. They are noteworthy, not for circling the globe, but for doing it solo. That is the unusual thing.

And when your shipmate is not in sight, sing out occasionally to check he's still aboard. We've all heard, and recently, of the Man Overboard cases discovered too late for help.

Coast Guard lifesaving unit fighting heavy sea and surf.   Photo by NOAA

Some will say these paragraphs just strain to recast common sense in a different guise . . . the same common sense every normal person uses to cross a crowded intersection. That's all we are doing. But strangely enough, common sense is often left ashore. Maybe this stems from being in a new environment. Or perhaps the cause is in motivation . . . flight from everyday restraints. Or is it the sudden freedom and independence of being on the Ocean Blue? Actually, though, seafaring is a most dependent activity. Few things on land can match it. The mariner is almost totally dependent on the mood and temperament of the sea.

A by-product of our exploding scientific age seems to be that the sea is developing a dangerous dependence on the intelligence of man. Since Adam disposed of the apple core, we've used the sea and its tributaries as our trash can. Long before then the natural flow of all Earth's waste products was an eventual return to the deep.

But we are not nearly so wise as nature. Our offal of synthetics is often alien to her cycles of disposal and regeneration. Nowadays we read much of such cycles, and of our need for biodegradable materials. We are being outfitted with machines and devices either to convert refuse to useful matter or, at least, to render it harmless. But the job of the mariner is much simpler and more direct. He need not decide whether a plastic bottle will or will not decompose; no grading of biodegradability is necessary. All he has to do is to substitute a smaller trash can for the sea.

Prohibitions against dumping refuse in US navigable waters are not new. Since 1899 it has been illegal for all craft to do so. Now, however, full national attention is being given to the problem; and with it come new regulations. The Water Quality Improvement Act of 1970 is a sample. Among many other regulatory features, it specifies the use of an approved marine sanitation device aboard to treat and dispose of sewage. The rules apply to every watercraft useful for transportation on our navigable waters. Enforcement on new vessels is specified as beginning in 1972; existing vessels are given until 1975. More controls will inevitably follow. The problem is dramatic when oil by the thousand tons spews out of a damaged tanker. But what about the litter generated by a weekend on a small craft? All by itself, the most one such vessel could produce would be of little consequence. Projected, however, to the crowded Fourth of July weekend, the pile of leftovers is monumental.

This is common sense again, of course. But bring that common sense aboard and it will lead you to what is all-important: respect for the sea in its power and in its vulnerability. Nothing is more refreshing than boating; there is no better way to recharge mental batteries. It is a new and different world. But recognize it as such. Then, common sense will acquire its other name: Seamanship.

37/Magnetism
Patterns of compass influence

To generations of seamen the subject of magnetism and the magnetic compass was wreathed in the clouds of mysteries of an occult art. The compass needle was a temperamental genie who could lead the ship to safe passage or, influenced by evil, could bring disaster without warning. As the years went by, mariners developed skill in anticipating whims and, by practical experience, shaped a pattern of compensation to keep the whims under control.

On large ships gyrocompasses and related electromechanical devices have taken over day-to-day direction. It is on the smaller vessel with fewer alternatives that the problem remains acute. We don't intend to get involved with deep theory. That would be to fall well off course. More misdirected would be to disregard theory as unnecessary and then base do-it-yourself compensation on murky principles and patterns. Within our scope is to survey fundamentals, both in theory and in practice, so that an idea of the basic problems and solutions can be formed.

We've already gone over some of this in Section I. There mention was made of the magnetic poles on Earth and of the characteristics of a compass needle to seek out their directions. Earth, like any magnet, gives out a magnetic field; and materials subject to magnetic influence will feel its effect. This Earth field has focal points or poles. They are not fixed positions, but change in time. The locations usually given are 74.9° North Latitude and 101.0° West Longitude for the Magnetic North Pole, with 67.1° South Latitude and 142.7° East Longitude for the Magnetic South Pole. Perhaps a more up-to-date set of values are those taken from *Magnetic Variation . . . Epoch 1970 (HO 1706),* a special world chart compiled jointly by the US Navy Oceanographic Office and National Ocean Survey. The Magnetic North Pole appears there to be at about 76° North and 101° West, on the northwest coast of Bathurst Island in Canada's Arctic Region; the Magnetic South Pole shows up at about 66° South and 139° East, on the coast of Wilkes Land in Antarctica.

It is customary in nautical discussions of magnetism to label these poles by colors. The North is **blue** and the South is **red**. Memory lets the color scheme sometimes switch around, so here's an aid for students of American history. During the Civil War, who wore the blue uniforms? The North. But, please, no gray magnetism; the analogy stops there.

A basic rule is that opposite poles attract and that likes repel. So the North-seeking end of the compass needle is red and the South-seeking end is blue. That is why a magnet used in compensating a compass often has one end painted red and the other blue . . . to denote polarity. But sometimes the North Pole is said to be really a south pole and the South, a north, and the pole that seeks the North Pole (which is really a south pole) is itself a north pole in disguise. Alice now arrives from Wonderland, and all is puzzlement. Then textbooks go to work, and heralding explanations by banners such as " . . . in order to clarify . . . ," encourage one to chuck the whole business and look for moss on a tree trunk.

Since, though, oak groves at sea are hard to find, we'll note the confusion and get back to colors. The North Pole (the one in Canada) is **blue**. The South Pole (the one in Antarctica) is **red**. The end of the compass needle pointing to the Canadian Pole is red; the other end is blue. Now, with that over, we'll stop jousting with jabberwocky and get back to worthwhile fundamentals.

The susceptibility of materials to magnetic influence varies widely. Many substances found aboard seem to be more or less immune: copper, wood, glass, lead and aluminum. Some mixed together become highly subject: **alnico**, an alloy of aluminum, nickel and cobalt, produces the strongest and most permanent of magnets. Generally, though, it is iron that is viewed as the common substance prone to magnetic influence. When such a substance is placed in a magnetic field, it receives a pattern of magnetism. Since we're aiming at a general idea of fundamentals, we can skim over technicalities, even though our version might cause a magnetician to wince. But his discomfort is small price for an extra measure of comprehension. What we'd like to suggest is a group of magnetic particles within that piece of metal. Some are blue and some are red, and there is the same number of each. When the substance is not subjected to magnetic influence, these particles are scattered helter-skelter in a random fashion. **Figure 76** shows that. We can also view the region around a magnet as giving off a pattern of lines of force. They seem to issue from one pole and then re-enter at the other. **Figure 77** is the idea. Now we put the two together in **Figure 78.** When an unmagnetized piece of iron is placed within the field of such lines of force, the blue and red particles within the iron are organized into a pattern. All the blue particles want to get as close as possible to the magnet's red pole; all the red particles rush to cluster close to the magnet's blue pole. The result is that, around the piece of iron, another magnetic field is set up with poles exactly opposite to the magnet to which it responds. This seems simple enough. Since opposites attract and likes repel, a magnet will create in a piece of unmagnetized iron, a red pole close to its

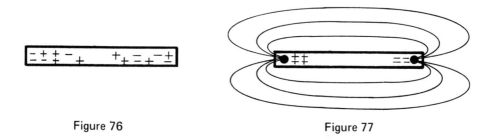

Figure 76   Figure 77

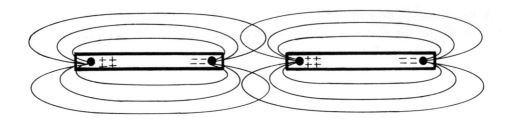

Figure 78

own blue or a blue pole close to its own red, and a pole of opposite polarity at the other end.

But not all magnetic metals react the same to magnetic influence. One type resists any attempt to change the status quo, but when a new pattern is enforced, wants to retain it. That quality of constancy is called **retentivity**, and the metal is termed magnetically **hard**. Another type is much more other-directed. It will be influenced by the field of the moment; but then, as soon as a new pattern comes along, it drops the first and adopts the new one. It is said to have high **permeability** and to be magnetically **soft**.

Before going too much farther, perhaps we should warn magneticians to join forces with oersteds and gammas and take cover behind a shield of parameters. Here comes a simplifying comparison designed to make Alice feel at home. This business of hard and soft metal can be likened to what happens in a piece of oak and in a sponge when placed into a bucket of water. The sponge is highly permeable and so picks up water quickly. But squeeze it and the water is gone. Now it's ready to accept milk, apple juice or all sorts of other liquids, for it has a low measure of retentivity. But the oak is different. When placed in the water, it will resist permeation. Sooner or later, though, water will soak in and things will change. Then the wood will want to retain the water, and it might take a kiln to dry it out. The sponge has high permeability and low retentivity; it is like soft metal. The oak has low permeability but high retentivity; it is like hard metal.

The magnetic needles in a compass are made of hard metal so they will retain their magnetic pattern regardless of disposition on Earth. But what complicates matters is that the compass with its magnets is placed aboard a most unsuitable platform: a magnet. For the vessel itself becomes magnetized and puts out a magnetic field which competes with that of Earth. Our task is to take a closer look at the personality of a magnetic field and then to see how the ship's influence can be neutralized.

Earth's magnetic pull is considerable, but not all of it acts on the compass. Lines of force seem to travel parallel to Earth's surface at the Magnetic Equator and enter Earth vertical to the surface at the magnetic poles. In between they run at an angle. And the value of that angle is called **magnetic dip** or **magnetic latitude**. At the Magnetic Equator there is no angle, for all Earth's magnetism parallels the surface. So the magnetic latitude is 0°. At the magnetic poles the Earth's force enters Earth at a right angle, and the magnetic latitude is said to be 90°. The dip angle is the magnetic latitude and **Figure 79** shows it in three situations.

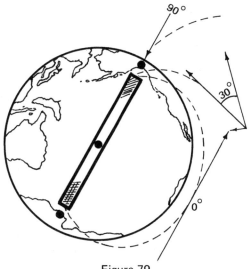

Figure 79

The nautical compass swings in a horizontal plane. It has no pivot to allow it to go up and down in response to Earth's magnetic influence. A magnet which can do that is called a **dip needle**. Set one at the Magnetic Equator and it will point parallel to the surface . . . horizontally. Set it at a magnetic pole and it will point vertically. For it is aligning itself with the magnetic lines of force of Earth's field. The compass, though, swings left and right to align itself with the magnetic meridian. It cannot stand on its nose at the magnetic pole, for it responds only to the horizontal component of Earth's magnetism. It then follows that a magnetic compass is most influenced by Earth at the Magnetic Equator . . . for there **all** Earth's pull is horizontal. And it loses effectiveness as it moves away from the Magnetic Equator. Finally, at each magnetic pole the magnetic compass is useless, for there is no horizontal component of Earth's magnetic influence to direct it.

What Earth's field does to metal around the compass involves such factors as latitude, ship's course and the type metal involved. Great masses of metal around the compass bring all sorts of problems to the large ship. Some of it is hard metal, some of it is soft. Some will create an influence in a horizontal plane; another will show up in the vertical; and a portion will not be a problem until the ship rolls. Each one of these sectors of interference has been closely studied and has its own compensating routine. There are permanent magnets in trays set in the compass binnacle fore-and-aft and athwartships. There are quadrantal spheres of soft iron placed on brackets jutting out from the binnacle. There are cylindrical segments of soft iron carefully stacked in a brass Flinders bar holder attached vertically to the binnacle. And there is a bundle of magnets suspended beneath the compass to neutralize heeling error. Part of the wartime protection of a ship against magnetic mines is to wrap her in an electric cable whose currents neutralize the magnetic field of the ship. Of course, as soon as this **degaussing** field is turned on, all the compass compensators have nothing left to neutralize. So the compensating devices can become deviators The cure can be a series of electric coils on the binnacle to put back something for the compensators to compensate.

All this is, of course, name dropping. But even name dropping, when done in context, can be tolerated. A dash of Flinders with a sprig of Degaussing need not be hard to take. A large binnacle is fitted to house the compass and its standard suit of correctors. The procedure for compensation involves a very careful pattern of checking for error, neutralizing, rechecking and then recording. The smaller vessel encounters less magnetic interference and so usually needs less complicated patterns of compensation. But many of the basic ideas and influences are still the same.

There is a distinction between knowing the deviation and doing something about it. One involves determination of error. Here the large and small craft have available similar tools. For error, simply put, is the difference between what a value should be and what it actually is. So the idea is to compare a direction indicated by compass with a known correct direction. When out of sight of landmarks, the procedures are part of celestial navigation and involve azimuth and amplitude. When reference points on Earth can be seen, it all really boils down to comparing a bearing taken by compass with what a chart or other reference publications state it should be.

But deviation is not constant . . . it changes as the vessel changes course. So the deviation on one heading is not necessarily the same as that on another. In fact, the chances are only one out of a hundred it will be. A schedule or record of deviations to be anticipated on different compass headings has obvious value. Made up in tabular form, it is called a **deviation table**. Prepared as a graph, it is called a **Napier's Diagram**.

How, then, to check for deviations? No sense running afoul of celestial azimuths and amplitudes. That whole field is loaded with interest, but not for now. Without involving anything alien to our planet, we have several ways to do the job. When your position is known and the magnetic bearing of a distant object is available from a nautical chart, the procedure goes this way: Keeping the boat in a small area, slowly turn through a full circle. When your craft is steadied on, say, 000° by compass, take the compass bearing of the distant object. Perhaps it is 310°. The chart might show it to be 312° from your location. The deviation on a heading of 000° is the difference between the compass bearing and the known magnetic bearing, or 2°E. Now follow the same procedure all the way around the compass circle. Perhaps you'll find that when the bow points 225° by compass, the distant object has a compass direction of 313°. Comparing it with the magnetic bearing of 312° indicates a deviation of 1° West. As the vessel goes around in the circle, the number of compass headings you stop and steady on is a matter of choice. No sense, though, in being carried away. Every 15° should be good enough.

The old-timer who didn't know the correct magnetic bearing would improvise. He'd take successive compass bearings of a distant object at, perhaps, 15° intervals. He wasn't concerned whether the object was a church steeple, a rock or a palm tree. All that was necessary was that it didn't move and that it gave him good bearings. Then he'd compute the average or **mean** bearing by adding them all up and dividing by their number. He'd now make use of the magnetic fact that deviations often follow a semicircular pattern. He'd assume that the deviations in one half of a full circle would cancel out those met in the other. So he'd accept the average bearing as equal to the correct magnetic bearing of that palm tree. Comparing each compass bearing with it gave him the deviation for each successive ship's heading.

A very satisfying means to determine deviation is by the use of a range. In most harbors there will be a location where two objects in line present a known correct direction. Often the structures are erected for the purpose of the range, and their location and direction listed in charts and publications. Sometimes, though, their utility as members of a range is quite accidental. In either case, though, the two objects when lined up have a known direction. A vessel can, then, use that range as the indication of correct bearing. And, following the same procedure as with one known reference object, she can swing in a full circle and compare compass bearings with the magnetic direction of the range in order to gain deviation.

Another method, available to those with a sense of community, is called **reciprocal bearings.** Find a friend whose magnetic compass has known error and whose compass bearings, then, can be corrected to a reliable value. Then you and he put to sea and stay separated by a good distance, but still within visual range. He takes bearings of you and applies his known deviation in order to yield correct magnetic bearings. Then you steam in a full circle and take successive bearings of him. The difference between your compass bearing of him and the reciprocal of his bearing of you is your deviation. Suppose his compass says you bear 270° from him. And further suppose his compass then has a known deviation of 4° East. The result is that you bear 274° Magnetic from him. Now you reverse the bearing, and say that he bears 094° Magnetic from you. The next step is to take a bearing of the other boat. Suppose she bears 091° by your compass. You've just found out she should bear 094°, so now you have the key to the deviation. It is 3° East.

Should you not be satisfied with just knowing the amount of an error, and want to correct it, you enter the realm of **compass compensation** or **compass adjustment.** Having learned the deviation on a particular heading, the navigator introduces an offsetting influence around the compass to reduce deviation to a minimum. How that is done, though, varies with the instrument and its installation. We've talked about large compasses with large binnacles. Smaller compasses might have some of the same devices, although most of the time the techniques used are quite different. Ideally it should be done by a professional, anyway. So we'll sheer off from that subject as one full of interest, perhaps, but not really worthwhile here. In fact, we've blocked out already large segments of the picture and are ready for touch-up.

The importance of knowing the amount of deviation and recording it for a series of headings, has been mentioned. What should be emphasized is that deviation is not constant. It is different for each vessel. It is different for each compass on each vessel. It is different for successive headings by each compass on each vessel. Changes can develop a pattern . . . semicircular is the usual design, with minimum deviation on two reciprocal compass headings, and maximum but opposite on reciprocal headings at right angles to the first ones. The deviation encountered at one time might well be different later on. This results from magnetic changes within the vessel, perhaps even within the compass, and maybe within

Earth. Of more importance is that deviation can change with location. A vessel on a 340° course in the Windward Islands might find that a deviating factor aboard causes only an insignificant error. But enroute to the Gulf of St. Lawrence, the horizontal strength of Earth's magnetic field declines with increase in magnetic latitude. And in passing through Belle Isle Straits, the navigator discovers that the insignificant deviating factor in the Barbados has assumed much larger proportions.

Technically, **deviation** refers to magnetic deflection resulting from interfering influences aboard the vessel. **Local attraction** is the term describing error caused by magnetic influences not aboard, but nearby. Often, however, what might be called local attraction by a purist is referred to by *Coast Pilot* or chart as Unusual Change in Variation. But the outcome in either case is an extraordinary change in the direction assumed by the compass needle. What is on Earth around you is often beyond your control. But you can certainly police the articles allowed aboard near the compass. *Handbook of Magnetic Compass Adjustment (HO 226),* prepared by the US Navy Oceanographic Office, has a helpful list of error-causing paraphernalia to avoid. Included are these: metal structural fittings such as doors, ports and drawers; signal pistols and projectile equipment; magnetic rudder mechanism; knives, ash trays, watches, eyeglass frames, belt buckles, metal pencils nearby; electric motors, controllers, conductors, indicators, circuits, switches; telephone headsets; windshield wipers; radar; radio transmitters and receivers. Sounds like the only proper navigator is one suffering from an iron deficiency and riding in a plastic tub. As usual, though, the answer is common sense. Know what can be an influence and take what precautions are practical. But we all can be forgetful. A good compass is a sensitive compass, eager to seek an opposite color. Carelessness in its surroundings will only bring confusion.

We've come to the end of a very general survey of the magnetic compass and its problems. No one instrument through the story of seafaring has met with less understanding, and needed it more. Our aim has not been to be detailed about anything. If, instead, we've isolated some of the features and made them more recognizable for further inquiry, then our job has been done.

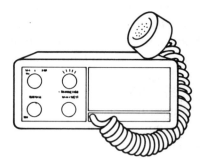

Questions

Time for another clean sweep fore and aft. Assemble the buckets, stir the soogee. And then, Sailors, Man Your Pencils!

Rules of the Road

1. A tug with a large lumber barge in tow is on your port side, and in a crossing situation. If you are on a highly maneuverable vessel
   a) you are always privileged.
   b) only if you are on the High Seas must you consider the limitations on his maneuverability.
   c) whether on Inland Waters or the High Seas, you must take into account the limitations of the other.

2. **Rule 27,** the General Prudential Rule, sanctions departure from the rules
   a) at any time.
   b) only by the privileged vessel.
   c) in order to avoid immediate danger.

3. **Rule 29,** the Precaution Rule, requires
   a) the exercise of good seamanship.
   b) the keeping of a proper lookout.
   c) the carrying of lights and signals.
   d) all of above.
   e) none of above.

4. The General Prudential and the Precaution rules apply
   a) only to power-driven vessels.
   b) only to commercial vessels.
   c) only to vessels over 65 feet long.
   d) to all vessels.

5. The General Prudential Rule is also known as
   a) the Special Circumstance Rule.
   b) the Good Seamanship Rule.
   c) **Rule 29.**
   d) **Article 29.**

Aids to Navigation

1. The frequency of one marine radiobeacon
   a) is different from that of any other.
   b) is the same as all others.
   c) may be the same as another.

2. US marine radiobeacons
    a)   transmit on a continuous around-the-clock schedule.
    b)   only transmit during poor visibility.

3. A marker radiobeacon
    a)   is intended for long range bearings.
    b)   operates continuously during periods of limited visibility but only during
         the first and fourth 10-minute intervals of the hour during other times.
    c)   neither of above.

4. A special calibration radiobeacon
    a)   is found at every USCG radiobeacon.
    b)   will operate whenever you signal it.
    c)   will operate only upon written request.
    d)   none of above.

5. In fog and near a Distance Finding Station, you hear the audible fog signal 7
   seconds after you receive the radio signal. Your distance off the station is
    a)   2.52 miles.
    b)   1.26 miles.
    c)   0.63 miles.

Seamanship

1. A cubic foot of sea water
    a)   weighs 6 pounds.
    b)   weighs 64 pounds.
    c)   weighs less than a cubic foot of fresh water.

2. Anchoring a small vessel stern-to-weather in a choppy sea
    a)   is to be recommended.
    b)   can be dangerous.
    c)   is usually no more dangerous than with bow-to weather.

3. A heavy sea is running with a strong North wind. Generally speaking, if you
   are going South, it is best
    a)   to run with the wind and sea dead astern.
    b)   to alter course so wind and sea are not dead astern.

4. A good seaman on a sound boat
    a)   can usually disregard wind and sea directions when selecting his course.
    b)   will always take the course of least strain to himself and to his craft, no
         matter how moderate the weather.

5. The most valuable aid to navigation is
    a)   a well-built vessel.

b) complete electronic equipment.
c) a full set of charts.
d) common sense.

Magnetism

1. A magnetic compass has more directive force
   a) when the magnetic dip is small.
   b) when the magnetic dip is large.
   c) when the magnetic latitude is 90°.

2. In order to determine deviation, a mariner takes bearings of a distant object. When his bow heads North, the bearing is 120° by compass. When his bow is East the bearing is 124°. When his bow is South the bearing is 120°. When his bow is West the bearing is 116°. The magnetic bearing could be assumed to be
   a) 117°.
   b) 124°.
   c) 116°.
   d) 120°.

3. Local attraction
   a) refers to the same influences as does deviation.
   b) would be the name given to an error caused by a nearby deposit of iron ore.
   c) is a passenger ship description of sunbathing by the swimming pool.

4. You take a bearing of a vessel and find it to be 100° by your compass. On that boat a bearing is taken of you and found to be 277°. Your compass has a known deviation of 2° West. The deviation of the compass on the other boat is
   a) 3° West.
   b) the same as on your boat.
   c) 1° West.
   d) 1° East.

5. The range is in line dead astern. Your heading by compass is 020°. The magnetic bearing of the range from your position is 199°. Your magnetic heading, after allowing for deviation, is
   a) 199°.
   b) 021°.
   c) 019°.
   d) 201°.

...and answers

Twenty more teasers to try the tars, with 5 points given for each proper reply. Here are the standards:

90 - 100:	Fly a Broom at the Masthead.
80 - 85:	Make it a Whisk Broom.
70 - 75:	Correction: a Toothbrush.
Below 70:	Report to the Quarterdeck!

Rules of the Road

1. (c)   2. (c)   3. (d)   4. (d)   5. (a)

Aids to Navigation

1. (c)   2. (a)   3. (c)   4. (d)   5. (b)

Seamanship

1. (b)   2. (b)   3. (b)   4. (b)   5. (d)

Magnetism

1. (a)   2. (d)   3. (b)   4. (d)   5. (c)

section 9 contents

38/Marine Electronics
Introduction

The advent of marine electronics exhilarates the modern, but often is actually frightening to the old salt. He was apprenticed to self-sufficiency as an ideal and fears the twilight of his breed.

There will be many more sunrises before that final twilight comes, for seafaring is not so easily adapted to the age of the free electron. So long as ships are islands of self-sufficiency, then the men who sail them must also be so. The routine practices can be automated; but when the power plant goes and the antenna carries away, the story is different. "Just a short-circuit away from the old-fashioned days" is the old-timer's warning. And to some extent he's right.

Electronics, though, are seafaring realities not to be ignored; and there is more myopia than manliness in reluctance to coexist. A better attitude is probably somewhere in mid-channel. These techniques and devices are valuable aids to navigation . . . yet they are still just aids. The ship has a new kind of fo'c'sle hand. The roster reads like the crew list of a Martian spaceship: Elektra, Sonne, Consol, Consolan, Gee, Decca, Shoran, Loran, Omega, Radar, Sonar, and quite a few more. But they're still crew members to be commanded and led. The wise mariner knows strengths and weaknesses of his vessel and crew. We'll look at Marine Electronics with such a view.

Since much of shipboard electronic gear involves wave energy and radio, a very general review of basic terms may be in order. But to keep things in perspective, no probing too deeply, lest we be overwhelmed by the flickers and zaps of cathodes bombarding anodes.

A rock thrown into a pond causes rings of ripples to spread out over the surface. They **radi**ate out from the center. More or less the same pattern of waves spreading out from a source is caused in electronics by the swift build-up and collapse of electric and magnetic fields. Hence the term **radio** from the radiating characteristic. Terminology used for radio is often related to that applicable to the ripples on the pond. There are crests and troughs . . . high points and lows. There are wave heights or amplitudes. A **wavelength** is the distance traveled by the radiating energy during one complete sequence of values. That sequence, in turn, is called a **cycle**. Count the number of cycles in a period of time (usually one second) and you have described the **frequency**. **Figure 80** sketches the idea.

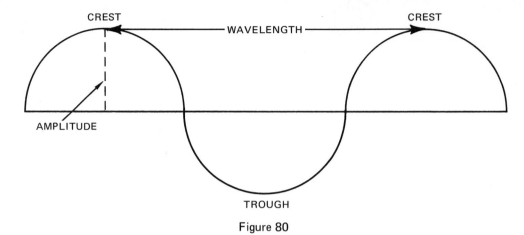

Figure 80

Cycles and wavelengths are usually expressed in the metric system. So one thousand repetitions per second is termed **kilocycle**, and one million is **megacycle**. Well, we should really say **was**, for a fairly recent change has been made. To honor Heinrich Hertz, nineteenth century German physicist who pioneered study of electromagnetic waves, the suffix **-cycle** has been supplanted by **-Hertz**. So today we have **kiloHertz (kHz)** and **megaHertz (mHz)** instead.

The speed of this radiated energy is about the speed of light: 186,000 miles per second. The mile is an unwieldy unit for this business, so the speed is converted to the metric system: 300,000,000 meters per second. If there were only one wave per second (a frequency of one), the wavelength from peak to peak would be 300,000,000 meters. Create 10 waves per second and the wavelength becomes 30,000,000. There is a relationship between frequency (waves per second), wavelength (in metric measure) and the 300,000,000:

$$\text{frequency x wavelength = speed}$$
$$\text{frequency x wavelength = 300,000,000.}$$

From this follows that:

$$\frac{300,000,000}{\text{frequency}} = \text{wavelength and } \frac{300,000,000}{\text{wavelength}} = \text{frequency.}$$

The higher the frequency, the shorter the wavelength. A frequency of one kilo-Hertz amounts to 100 waves per second. The wavelength, then, is:

$$\frac{300,000,000}{1000} \text{ or 300,000 meters.}$$

A frequency of one megaHertz is 1,000,000 waves per second. The wavelength is 300 meters. A table setting out the spectrum of this relationship is shown in **Figure 81**. In each case, if the magic number of 300,000,000 is divided by the frequency, out pops the wavelength. Divide that number by the wavelength and you have the frequency. Notice that, in turn, the types of transmission can be

Band	Abbreviation	Range of frequency	Range of wavelength
Audio frequency	AF	20 to 20,000 cps	15,000,000 to 15,000 m
Radio frequency	RF	10 kc to 300,000 mc	30,000 m to 0.1 cm
Very low frequency	VLF	10 to 30 kc	30,000 to 10,000 m
Low frequency	LF	30 to 300 kc	10,000 to 1,000 m
Medium frequency	MF	300 to 3,000 kc	1,000 to 100 m
High frequency	HF	3 to 30 mc	100 to 10 m
Very high frequency	VHF	30 to 300 mc	10 to 1 m
Ultra high frequency	UHF	300 to 3,000 mc	100 to 10 cm
Super high frequency	SHF	3,000 to 30,000 mc	10 to 1 cm
Extremely high frequency	EHF	30,000 to 300,000 mc	1 to 0.1 cm
Heat and infrared *		10^6 to 3.9×10^8 mc	0.03 to 7.6×10^{-5} cm
Visible spectrum *		3.9×10^8 to 7.9×10^8 mc	7.6×10^{-5} to 3.8×10^{-5} cm
Ultraviolet *		7.9×10^8 to 2.3×10^{10} mc	3.8×10^{-5} to 1.3×10^{-6} cm
X-rays *		2.0×10^9 to 3.0×10^{13} mc	1.5×10^{-5} to 1.0×10^{-9} cm
Gamma rays *		2.3×10^{12} to 3.0×10^{14} mc	1.3×10^{-8} to 1.0×10^{-10} cm
Cosmic rays *		$> 4.8 \times 10^{15}$ mc	$< 6.2 \times 10^{-12}$ cm

* Values approximate.

Figure 81

placed in categories or bands stretching from the audio frequency at the low level to cosmic rays at the high.

There's a point here, though, that we should look at closely. It involves the audio frequency shown on the table. There you see the range is 20 cps to 20,000 cps and the wavelength is from 15,000,000 to 15,000 meters. All is as it should be by manipulating the key number for the speed of the wave: 300,000,000 meters per second. But this, although described as audio frequency, is not talking about something we could hear. We'll have to tiptoe around theory and fact while trying to distinguish this type of wave energy from another. What we call sound also moves in waves. But there the action is a series of expansion and contractions . . . compressions and rarefications are the terms usually used. Vibrations are started and, accordion-like, spread out through a medium. And that is the distinction. Deigning to ignore theories like corpuscular and quantum, we'll say light and radio, and electrons in general, actually travel from point to point and need no medium to pass through. Hence, rays from the sun and stars and radio calls to space probes travel through emptiness. But sound is different. It must have a material to compress and rarefy. Sound has to pass through something, whether it is air, water or a clanging water pipe in the basement. The upshot is that radio and light travel at the enormous 300,000,000 meter speed, while sound travels much slower and at speeds differing with the medium. In air it is 1117 feet per second; in sea water it is 4945 feet per second; in the water pipe it might hit 17,000 feet per second. But we can still make use of the basic formula already mentioned, that speed = frequency x wavelength. Divide the speed by the frequency of vibrations and get the wavelength; divide the speed by the wavelength and learn the frequency. The difference is that the speed varies and we must use the correct speed for the medium and existing conditions. In any case, we start from the point of view that emanating from a source is energy in wave patterns. Sometimes it moves at the speed of light, sometimes it sets up vibrations in an intervening medium and moves through it at much slower frequencies. But in every case, energy is transferred from one place to another.

Man by nature is equipped with several sets of receivers to detect this energy. His ears are built to react to the vibrations of the medium. Some animals have audio ranges higher than ours . . . their eardrum detectors respond more sensitively. Hence the silent dog whistle. Possibly the tales of uncanny feats of communication among primitive people might be explained by the facility of natives living in the wild to hear frequencies not sensed by their city-bound brothers. But there's a limit to the niceties which any eardrum can detect. From supersonic vibrations such as those used in depth sounders up to the areas of medico-dental use for scanning and drilling the human ear is pretty much out of business. Unaided we remain unable to detect this wave energy until we get in the realm of the light-radio-electronic type and the frequency gets up to the heat range. Then another of man's natural receiving systems takes over. Beyond that, our eyes go to work and receive the visible spectrum with its fantastically high frequencies and short, short wave lengths. The color names we have fashioned to identify visible waves are language labels for the various frequency/wavelength combinations within the visible spectrum. What we term red is a signal of lower frequency and longer wavelength than what we call violet.

Now back to radio. Between the ear and the eye is the territory of the radio wave. There, man has to use special transmitters to create the signals and special receivers to detect them. Then he must modify the signal to make it recognizable by one of his natural receivers. The obvious choices are either to drop it to the audible range and have it set up vibrations so he can hear it through earphones or a speaker, or to push it up to the visible range so he can see it on a viewscope or screen. A car radio serves it to his ear; radar displays it to his eye; television does both.

The need for supervision of radio transmissions is understandable; the result of uncontrolled use of the spectrum would outdo biblical Babel. And there is such government direction, both within countries and on an international level. But a sort of natural selection also exists, for certain frequency/wavelength combinations are more appropriate to particular uses than are others. Some possess a good measure of ground-hugging proficiency. Others have more usable characteristics when bounced off Earth's ionosphere, layers of electrical energy high in the atmosphere. What electrons will do when they enter these ionized layers depends on their wave pattern, the height of the layer, the time of day, of the year and of the sunspot cycle. All this is not for us to sort through . . . enough to know that selection of a radio wave by its personality is directly tied to the task for which the wave is intended.

Figure 82 is another spectrum table. This one focuses on the marine applications of radio and shows which areas within the total radio range have been put to noteworthy use.

What we'll do is to group marine applications into categories by use and purpose, and then take a good look at each separate group. Our voyage through Marine Electronics will start with detection by sound wave and by radio wave . . . we'll start with the depth sounder and with radar. Then comes radiolocation, systems for determining position by radio. Last will be a survey of marine radio communications and supervision.

MARINE APPLICATION	BAND & ABBREVIATION	FREQUENCY RANGE
Omega	Very Low Frequency (VLF)	10-15 kHz
Decca and Loran-C	Low Frequency (LF)	70-130 kHz
Consol, Consolan and Marine Radiobeacons	Low Frequency (LF) Medium Frequency (MF)	190-400 kHz
Distress Signal by wireless telegraphy	Medium Frequency (MF)	500 kHz
Loran-A	Medium Frequency (MF)	1750-1950 kHz (or 1.75-1.95 mHz)
Voice communications (radiotelephone)	Medium Frequency (MF) High Frequency (HF) Very High Frequency (VHF)	1.6 mHz - 4.0 mHz 4.0 mHz - 23.0 mHz 156.0 mHz - 158.0 mHz
Omni/VOR	Very High Frequency (VHF)	108.0 mHz - 118.0 mHz
Radar, S-Band (10 centimeters)	Super High Frequency (SHF)	2900 mHz - 3100 mHz
Radar, X-Band (3 centimeters)	Super High Frequency (SHF)	9300 mHz - 9500 mHz

Figure 82

Electronic navigation opens a new world of precision and safety for seafaring. The mariner has means now to obtain data obscured for centuries in cloud cover and fog banks. The techniques involve new disciplines and make use of more sophisticated equipment. But there should never be dispute as to command. The navigator uses the tools and then makes use of his superior human sense to assess the situation. The old-timer's fear of these strangers coming aboard is foolishness. Just as foolhardy is he who assumes that the new makes obsolete all that went before. Since a vessel doesn't get its electrical power through a meter box "out by the water heater," it really is just a short-circuit away from the old-fashioned days. The modern mariner has not replaced any tools, he's gained some more. Common sense dictates he put them all in context and know where each one fits.

39/Marine Electronics
Depth sounders in principle

Almost as old as seafaring is the problem of measuring the depth of water. In this chapter we are to survey systems available to modern mariners. But an Overture before the curtain rises is first on the program.

Probably the first instrument used was no more sophisticated than a dip stick. The difficulty with that approach soon must have been apparent . . . for the stick could be bigger than the boat. So the next move was to concoct a flexible dip stick. It still persists under the name of **lead line**, a combination of braided cotton rope and a lead weight with a scooped-out bottom. A code of markings by color, material and shape was developed so selected depths could be identified day or night by sight and feel. Such a selected place on the lead line was termed a **mark**, and the stretch of unmarked line between two of them was called a **deep**. In **READY REFERENCE** is a depiction of the standard markings on a hand lead. As for the hollow part of weight's base . . . that is used to gain a sample of the ocean bottom for aid in fixing location and in selecting a good anchorage. Soap, tallow or a similar material sticky enough to pick up some of the bottom can be stuffed into the hollow before the weight is released. This is called **arming the lead**. And a reason for the great detail about nature of the bottom found on a nautical chart was, and still is, the value of these hand lead data.

But the lead line has an inherent fault: to measure depth it measures the length of the line from the ship to the lead weight. What the navigator wants is the **vertical** measure from ship to bottom; what the lead line might give him is a **diagonal** measure unless the line is straight up-and-down. And a diagonal measure is misleading. To meet this problem, there came aboard large ships a device called, among other things, the **mechanical**, **patent** or **Kelvin** sounding machine. It was mechanical, patented and developed by Lord Kelvin. It also was troublesome to use. Here in brief is how it worked. Attached vertically to the shank of a weight was a glass tube, open at the bottom. The weight in turn was connected to a length of thin wire rove through a block on the end of a short horizontal boom and then wound on a special reel on deck. As the weight descended, the increasing water pressure progressively compressed the air pocket caught in the closed top of the glass tube. The maximum height reached by water pressing up the tube was marked on the bore, either by chemical stain or by water film, and, when measured on a special scale, told the corresponding depth of water. This system minimized the problem of measurement on the bias, since pressure and **vertical** depth vary directly and the length of wire paid out was really not the measure. But few regretted the arrival aboard of the echo sounder which has now entirely supplanted wire and reel and thin glass tube.

Up, then, with the curtain and on with the idea of echo sounding. And the idea is very simple: make a sound on the ship and direct it towards the bottom of the sea. Then note the interval until an echo is received. With the speed of sound in water as a constant, figure out how far the sound traveled from the ship to the bottom and back again. Half that distance is the depth of water.

The earliest instruments used a hammer to bang on the hull and a microphone to detect the echo. But since no practical means was available to measure the tiny time interval, the angle of reception of the echo was measured. Trigonometry did the rest. Obviously the results were less than precise. Next came a device to measure the time interval. But an audible sound signal was still used, one within the range of the human ear. And so the system was called **sonic depth sounding**. The next advance was to use a supersonic signal. This "silent sound" has a frequency beyond the detection range of hearing and is free of interference from audible hull noises. The name given to this was **ultrasonic** or **supersonic depth sounding**.

Today we have quite a hierarchy of terms. **Sonar**—for Sound Navigation And Ranging—emerges as the generic name to cover all underwater navigating devices. Specifically, it refers to the measuring of horizontal ranges. **Sofar**, from **Sound Fixing And Ranging**, is a system of long distance fixing of sound origins. **Rafos**, which is **Sofar** backwards, comes out of the alphabet soup to signify the reverse process. But ordinary navigation, like Martha, deals only with simple, everyday things. So we'll use the term **echo sounding**.

The elements of an installation are these:

1. **A transducer** . . to send out and to receive vibrations at the proper frequency.
2. An **amplifier** . . to strengthen the received echo.
3. An **indicator** . . to measure and to display the depth.

The transducer is usually located at the keel, either inside or outside the hull. Its function is to convert electrical energy into sound vibrations in the water. After these sound waves travel through the incompressible water medium to the bottom and back, the transducer detects the echoed vibrations and converts them back to an electrical impulse. This is done hundreds of times a minute, and the interval between emission and return of the sound wave is measured to fractions of a second. Based on the speed of the vibration in water, the distance traveled by the wave—and, so, the depth—can be determined. **Figure 83** illustrates the general idea so far.

American echo sounders are calibrated on a constant of 4800 feet per second as the speed of sound in water. But this speed varies. Actually, the standard, based on an atmospheric pressure of 29.92 inches and a temperature of 60°F and a

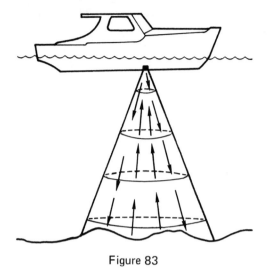

Figure 83

Photo by Benmar Div., Computer Equipment Corp.

Figure 84

salinity of 34.85 parts per thousand, is 4945 feet per second. The speed increases with increase in water pressure, temperature and salinity. So the American constant is a slow one, to be expected in cold, not-too-salty water. It is also a safe one, for a slower speed indicates less depth. Few should complain when an echo sounder is overcautious, and American devices tend to be so. When soundings, then, under-read known depths, charge part of it off to this speed variation.

Back to a rundown of the basic parts of the depth sounder. The job of the **amplifier** is fairly evident from the very name. It takes the echo impulse, which by now has been converted back from sound to electricity, and strengthens it so that effective measurement and display can be made by the next step in the process.

Now to consider the equipment for that next step. There are two principal types: **indicators** and **recorders**. We'll look at each in turn. But first, a glance back at some fundamentals. The sound signal, generated and dispatched at the ship, travels down to the bottom and then is reflected back. The time interval from dispatch to arrival back aboard is the time for a round trip . . . and we're really interested only in one-way. So the time interval involved in the measurement is **one-half** the time between transmission and reception. We've already mentioned that variations in speed of the vibrations influence the measurement. Suppose the time interval for a round trip were 0.2 second. The one-way passage, then, would be 0.1 second. An American instrument would say the depth was 0.1 of 4800 feet, or 480 feet. If, though, the speed of sound in water at the time was the standard rate of 4945 feet per second, then the depth would be a tenth of that, or 494.5 feet. And if this took place in the Red Sea with very high salinity, the depth would be over 500 feet. Of course, the error encountered is really not all that significant. With about 500 feet of water under the keel, the likelihood of grounding is much less than when the depth is about 15 feet. What might amount to a 20-foot depth error when 500 feet is involved, shrinks to less than a one-foot error in 15 feet. At that stage, factors such as tide, location of the transducer and trim of the vessel usually make the speed error pale a bit by comparison. But more of that later on. At least we've mentioned the potential of **speed error** and placed it in its proper niche. Now we can get back to discussion of how the measurement is made and displayed.

Indicators have a clock-like face with depths shown in fathoms or feet from **0** to maximum nominal range of the unit. The usual arrangement is this. Behind the face a motor-driven arm rotates at a fixed speed. Attached to the end of the arm is a neon bulb. The spin of the arm is synchronized with the transducer so that the bulb flashes at **0** when a signal departs from the transducer. Then when an echo comes back aboard, the bulb flashes again. By that time the arm has rotated so the flash appears at the appropriate depth indication. Relating the speed of the arm to the speed of sound in water, and then allowing for the one-way trip factor, causes the neon flashes to display the proper depth. By varying the speed of the arm, adjustment can be made to accommodate variations in the speed of sound in water, or to change the nominal range of the instrument, or to alter the unit of measure. In any case, the device is often called a **flasher sounder**. More correct, though, is **indicating depth sounder; Figure 84** pictures one.

What we've said so far about indicators is not of desperate urgency, but rather more for general guidance. Next, though, comes a quirk of these units which deserves closer attention. A typical sounder might have a scale range of 40 fathoms, or 240 feet. One of greater power can have a range up to 200 fathoms, or 1200 feet. It is the short-range unit whose quirk is now at issue . . . it has a tendency sometimes to show depths greater than its nominal range. A very hard bottom will reflect a stronger echo than will a soft mud bottom. So even on a machine with 240 feet as maximum nominal range, a readable echo might be detected from greater depth. Here's what can happen. Let's suppose an echo came back from a true depth of 360 feet. Since the indicator has a maximum range of only 240 feet, how might it react? The neon bulb will flash at the 120-foot mark. And the navigator . . . how might he react? Often with some confusion. Perhaps he'd conclude he was in 120 feet of water and doubt his dead reckoning which would say to expect greater depths. He could, of course, go the other way and brand the instrument as unreliable. Or, thinking big, he might pen a request to a government agency that his name be affixed to the seamount he had just discovered.

There are a couple of ways for him to avoid such problems. One involves the **gain control** on the depth sounder. Normally, when the depth indicated is near maximum nominal range of the unit, full gain or volume setting is required. The signal will have traveled a long distance from ship to bottom and return, so a greater measure of sensitivity and amplification will be in order. But when the depth is from mid-scale towards the shallow end, much less gain is needed to detect and display the echo. Best readings occur when the indicator displays a narrow, sharp flash. And how the gain control is set to produce such a flash is a way to judge whether the depth is what the dial is trying to say or whether, in fact, the depth is much greater. Here's how it would work out in our example. If our self-styled oceanographer was expecting a maximum depth, he would probably have set the gain at or near full. Were the indication of 120 feet really correct, the neon flash would be quite broad, for the increased sensitivity and amplification of high gain would produce a wide splash of light. If reducing the gain brought a narrow band, he could suspect the echo must have been from a shallow depth, and he might be on the threshold of fame. On the other hand, if the true depth were 360 feet, the flash would probably already be narrow with the high gain. That would indicate a weaker signal had been detected . . . a signal that had just completed a longer trip from ship to bottom and return. Another piece of evidence to help subdue ambiguity could be found in the dead reckoning position at the time. Plot it on the nautical chart and see what the chart has to say. If the sounding shown is 360 feet, our navigator can be fairly certain that his depth sounder is trying to agree . . . and that no seamount will receive his name that day.

Here are some more capricious habits of the depth sounder. When in water less than half the depth of the nominal range, the indicator might display "second bounce" flashes. What happens is that the bottom and the hull play Ping-Pong with the signal. It bounces back and forth, each time being detected but still having enough strength to make another round trip. Assume you are in 20-foot depths and the gain is set too high. The first flash will be quite wide, possibly spreading between the 20 and 30 markings on the dial. There will also be a weaker flash at 40 feet. Which is truthful? Adjusting the gain will bring the proof. Reduce gain to a point where there is a narrow, but still easily seen, flash. In the process the second bounce at the 40-foot mark will disappear and the 20-foot flash will be intelligible. The part of the flashing band to read is the trailing edge . . . the side near zero.

The echo you want is from the surface of the sea floor. But lots of other things can give echoes. Schools of fish are common reflectors . . . so much so that echo sounders have been adapted to fish-finding. Intermittant flashes between O and the proper depth will usually mean schools of fish, or a few great big ones. But when using an indicating depth sounder to find fish, be prepared to keep a sharp eye on the dial. You can cross over a school in a very short time.

Another source of misleading echoes is **aeration**. Air bubbles caused by propeller wash are troublesome. Often when the hull is skimming at shallow draft, the

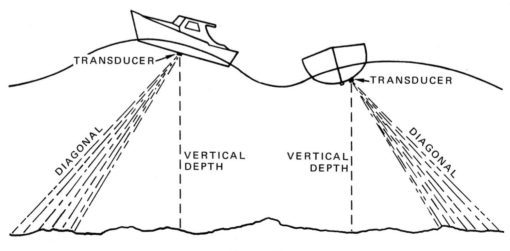

Figure 85

transducer is not deep enough to avoid surface froth and agitation. The result is a splash of weak echoes. Sometimes no bottom at all might show up. The signal is so weakened after a round trip through air bubbles that it hardly triggers an echo flash. Pretty evident is that going astern increases the hazard of aeration, for then the propeller wash is passing under the vessel towards the transducer.

Also worth noting is that the echo sounder can still have the lead line's problem of the diagonal measure. So long as the signal goes vertically down and the echo bounces straight up, the depth measured is in good style. But soundings taken while the vessel rolls and pitches can produce streams of sound waves leading not only down but also forward or towards the stern or out to either side. This can produce what is sometimes called the **Pythagorean error** . . . for the diagonal is really the hypotenuse of the right triangle, and that's Pythagoras' country. Obviously, since depth measure depends on the time interval, and since a longer time is involved to go up and down a hypotenuse than a vertical, the depth measured towards the bow, the stern or to either side will be greater than one measured straight down. (See **Figure 85.**) Since, though, the vessel in her bobbing will be mixing up verticals with hypotenuse of different lengths, the flashes will also bob around on the dial. The safest action at all times is to rely on the shallowest flash.

Recording depth sounders use paper on which a stylus scribes the depth as a continuing line while the paper moves underneath it. Horizontal lines are printed on the paper, usually one fathom apart; and at each five fathoms the line is heavy for easy reading. **Figure 86** pictures a recorder and an example of its graph. This

Figure 86. This recorder-type has 5 range scales and will show 300 feet.

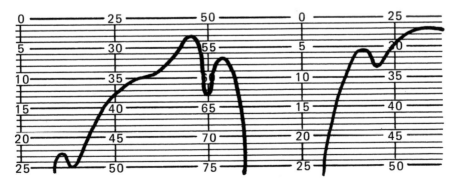

instrument has advantages over the indicator, but it is also subject to some of the same faults. It will display second bounces and suffers from Pythagoritis.

Both indicators and recorders give a clue to the type bottom under the boat. A soft, mushy bottom returns weak and broad flashes; and the scribed lines on the recorder will be broad and light. The old-time hand lead gives superior indications, for stuck to the soap or tallow in its wine-bottle-bottom is an actual sample. Even so, interpretation of flash or graph on an echo sounder, coupled with more continuous data on depth, can tell a very detailed story.

Choice between indicating and recording sounders, as well as selection of nominal ranges, can depend on where and why the boat will operate. Along the US South and Mid-Atlantic coasts, the waters are relatively shallow. You can be 50 miles at sea off Atlantic City and still be inside the 20-fathom curve. Off Florida and the coastline of the Gulf of Mexico, the story is more or less the same. So a unit of 50-fathom range might be entirely adequate. But things are different off New England, the Pacific Coast and Hawaii. In many of those regions, even a 200-fathom sounder runs out of range less than 10 miles offshore.

If range should suit the area, type should be governed by use. For those who do a lot of fishing, the recording type has several advantages. Not only is the operator relieved of standing watch at the unit for fish flashes to dart in sight . . . by inspection of the recorder paper, he learns not only the depth of a school but also can judge its size and spread.

In navigation the recorder has further advantages. Knowing that the paper moves at a certain speed can be a key to time intervals regarding depths. If, for example, the paper speed is one-half inch per minute, let's suppose that five inches of paper appear between the outline of a submarine valley and an underwater shelf. The time to pass from one to the other was, then, 10 minutes. If the vessel was doing six knots during those 10 minutes, the distance from valley to shelf can be computed as one mile. Combining all this with the course steered and a good look at the nautical chart, can tell the navigator a lot about his position.

But more of that later. Time now to surface for air before we get back to practical applications of echo sounding.

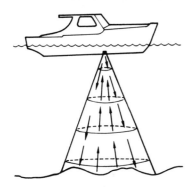

40/Marine Electronics
Depth sounders in practice

Time to get back again to the echo sounder, and particularly to further ins and outs of practical use. Like any piece of complicated equipment, it should only be operated after a careful reading of the manufacturer's manual. There would be no benefit here in a review of the operating particulars of "this" or "that" machine. The chances are your device would be "the other." In general it works out better to leave most adjustments up to the serviceman. Usually what is in your department will have an accessible knob or other unmistakable designation as operational.

But you can't delegate everything. Here are a few points to remember. A transducer unit mounted outside the hull requires special care at haul-out time. Be sure to tell the shipyard it's there . . . and where. Otherwise it might accidentally be crushed by a landing block or part of a cradle assembly. And when the vessel is out of the water, have the transducer face checked and cleaned. Carbon tetrachloride, alcohol or acetone are good cleaning agents. As for painting . . .the manufacturer usually specifies special paints to protect the transducer face. Be careful none of the regular hull paint is accidentally applied.

It's necessary every once in a while to check the accuracy of echo soundings by comparing them with known depths. The most accurate method is to use a hand lead. In still water with the vessel stopped, carefully lower a hand lead and measure the depth. Then turn on the echo sounder and read its indication. Allow for the depth of the transducer (more on that to come) and then compare the two soundings. Another alternative is to check the echo sounding by comparing it with a charted depth . . . a routine prickly with so many provisos and conditions that the accuracy of the check on accuracy gets mighty doubtful. But since the factors involved there are encountered in all navigation by echo sounder, we'll give them a close look.

First of all, no chart can tell you the depth of water "right now," for tidal action keeps changing it. All charts have to presume a particular stage of tide as prevailing at the time. This base is called a **chart datum**, and varies with the locality involved. **Mean Low Water (MLW)** is the level used on US Atlantic and Gulf Coast charts and for the Virgin Islands and Puerto Rico. These are areas having fairly regular and standard patterns of tidal change. **Mean Lower Low Water (MLLW)** is the base on the US Pacific Coast and Hawaii, where tidal patterns are

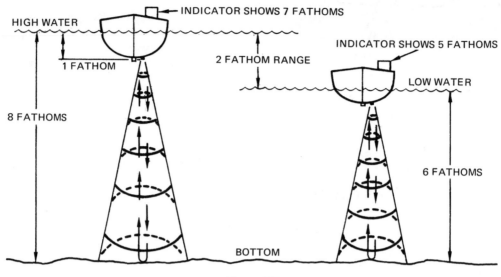

Figure 87

more irregular and unequal. Other areas use such esoteric labels as Indian Springs Low Water, Tropical Lower Low Water, and so on. But whatever the datum, depths shown by an echo sounder will differ from the chart unless the sounding is made when the tidal stage happens to be the same as that presumed. **Figure 87** shows a 12-foot or two-fathom tide. If the transducer were at the waterline and a sounding taken at high water, the sounding could be two fathoms more than that shown on the chart. If, though, you were on the spot when coincidentally the state of tide equalled that of the chart datum, then the echo sounding would be on the nose. And soundings between high water stage and the chart datum could be off by a pro rata of two fathoms.

The other factor is the depth of the transducer. It measures from its face to the bottom; and its soundings will differ from actual by the amount of its own depth. **Figure 87** shows the transducer at six feet or one fathom below the surface. That much, then, must be added to each indicated depth. A simple cure would be to adjust the indicator so it over-reads by the amount of the transducer depth. From then on, so long as the depth of the transducer remains the same, there should be no problem. For vessels such as cargo carriers whose draft changes much and often, this adjustment is impractical. But for others it solves the problem.

Let's get back to the tidal factor again. Knowing about it is one thing; knowing how important is another. Some cruising areas have very large tidal ranges: five fathoms-plus in Alaska and the Bay of Fundy. Obviously, soundings there require allowance for the tide. An indicator depth of 60 feet at high tide might be at a position where the charted depth is only 30 feet. In other areas, the changes are not so dramatic and the problem not so pronounced. But precise nagivation by echo sounder in any area requires that this tidal factor be considered. Having allowed for transducer depth, the navigator must account for the difference between chart datum and the state of the tide at the time of the sounding. It can be done by procedures of the *Tide Tables*. And here's a rule of thumb that can sometimes be helpful. By it you can, to an extent, prorate the range of tide for the time interval between High Water and your sounding. It presumes a six-hour duration from High to Low, and is practical for areas where the actual duration from High to Low amounts to about that much. Often such areas are ones whose charts are pegged to **Mean Low Water (MLW)**: the US Atlantic and Gulf Coasts and other areas of semidiurnal tidal cycle. But the rule is not realistic on the US Pacific Coast, or in Hawaii, or in areas where tidal patterns are mixed or diurnal and the interval between tides can be much longer or shorter. In any case . . . to the Six Hour Rule:

If the Time Interval from High Water to Your Sounding is

0 Hours		the total range of tide
1 Hour		7/8ths of the range
2 Hours		3/4ths of the range
3 Hours	deduct from sounder depth	One-half of the range
4 Hours		1/4th of the range
5 Hours		1/8th of the range
6 Hours		Nothing

The contour lines (or fathom curves) connecting equal depths on a chart, are somewhat like fingerprints. Every area has lines; and no two sets are exactly alike. Comparison of soundings with depths shown on a chart can give much information about position. Let's do some thought-nudging by a look at a few coastal navigation problems to see how the depth sounder aids solution.

First off, you are headed westward from Point **A** in poor visibility and want to pass Point **B** well off to avoid offshore rocks. At 1000 hours Point **A** is abeam and you are then on the five-fathom curve. A course of 280° is laid out to take you into deeper water. Within 15 minutes depths begin to increase. Looking at **Figure 88** let's see what takes place from then on.

Soundings at 1030 and 1100 exceed 10 fathoms. But a few minutes after 1100 they decrease to 10 fathoms. And by 1115 the showing is only five. Now there should be real concern, for the depth to be expected is more than 10 fathoms. Combining the depth sounder with plotting is in order.

With dividers set to the distance traveled from 1000 to 1115, place one end at the 1000 position off Point **A**. Draw an arc with the other end and see where it intersects the five-fathom curve. Right away it is evident you are not on course, but have been set inshore. To continue on a course of 280° would be to skirt dangerously close to the rocks off Point **B** a little before noon. A course change is immediately made to 290° for safe clearance. And around 1140 the sounder starts giving welcome reports of 10 fathoms as you progress towards deeper water.

In this problem the dividers were used to give a **line of position (LOP)** based on distance traveled, and the sounder was used to give another LOP, the contour curve of depth measured. Ordinary LOP'S seem to involve visual or radio bearings. But in this case distance and depth are "crossed" to give a fix. The distance traveled from Point **A** is one LOP, and the depth in fathoms at 1115 is the other.

Here's another problem. You are approaching land in fog and on a heading of

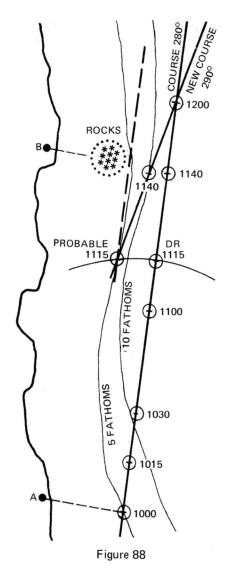

Figure 88

295°. Speed is five knots, or 12 minutes per mile. You don't know whether you are north or south of the harbor. **Figure 89** illustrates the problem. A study of the charted fathom curves shows a distinct pattern. To the north on Track **B** the bottom shoals gradually from 20 fathoms to 10, and then quickly comes up to five fathoms. Measuring the distances between fathom curves, you compute that from 20 fathoms to 10 is one mile, or 12 minutes; from 10 fathoms to five is a quarter of a mile, or three minutes.

The pattern on Track **A**, your intended course line, is different. There, from 20 to 10 fathoms is half a mile, or six minutes; from 10 to 5 fathoms is one mile, or 12 minutes. On Track **C** to the south, things figure out to six minutes between fathom curves. The idea, then, is to select the probable track by noting which set of time differences between fathom curves most closely matches those actually timed aboard. And once the matter of proper track is settled, a possible correction can be fashioned. Of course if you're on Track **A**, none is necessary. But should you find yourself to the north or south, you might select a fathom curve as a pathway and let the echo sounder ping-ping you along it back to the proper track. For example, if on Track **C**, watch the echo sounder for an indication of five fathoms. When you are crossing the five-fathom curve, turn right and follow that contour line northward to the sea buoy at the harbor entrance. If Track **B** was your location, turn left at the five-fathom curve and let the echo sounder guide you southward.

Always, though, the seaman's caution is to be exercised. In every case, judgment of course and speed must be carefully made. But here another element is injected. This sort of piloting places considerable reliance on the accuracy of the sounding and of the charted contour lines. Not to allow for the stage of tide could be disastrous. If the tidal range were 12 feet, or two fathoms, and your maneuver occurred at high tide, look what might happen: when the echo sounder said five fathoms, the chart would say three fathoms. Were you to assume the sounding placed you over the chart's five-fathom curve you would actually be making a course change to follow along a three-fathom line. That might lead you into danger.

What about the accuracy of the charted contour lines? How trustworthy they are depends, among other things, on the area covered, the scale of the chart, the age of the survey. Not to be overlooked is the possible change in bottom contour by shoaling, scouring or other submarine action . . . and the likelihood for such changes to take place at a harbor mouth.

Speed made good over the bottom can sometimes be as easily determined by sounder as by other means. If consecutive soundings are taken, the distance between corresponding depths shown on the chart might give a speed check. In **Figure 90** a boat is headed seaward with depths gradually increasing. But offshore is a shoal. The distance between point of departure and shoal, divided by the time in minutes or hours, gives speed: 15 miles in one hour and 30 minutes is 10 knots.

A depth sounder, onionskin paper and a pencil can work together. Lay a thin piece of paper over the chart, one edge squared up with a meridian or parallel. Then draw a penciled line on the paper in the direction of your course. On that line mark off half-mile intervals, using the same scale as the chart for measuring. If your speed is 10 knots, you know that every three minutes you cover half a mile. So every three minutes take a sounding and mark that depth on the tissue paper at the corresponding half-mile mark . . . remembering, though, first to correct it for state of tide and for depth of transducer. In 30 minutes you'll have taken 10 soundings and marked them in appropriate positions along the course line drawn on the paper. For greater accuracy you could continue the process for a full hour. What results in either case is a **line of soundings.**

Now lay the tissue sheet over the chart, properly orienting one edge to the chart meridian or parallel. By moving the tissue sheet until the chart soundings agree with the line of sounding on the paper,

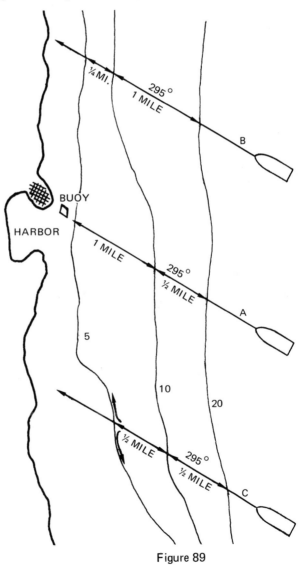

Figure 89

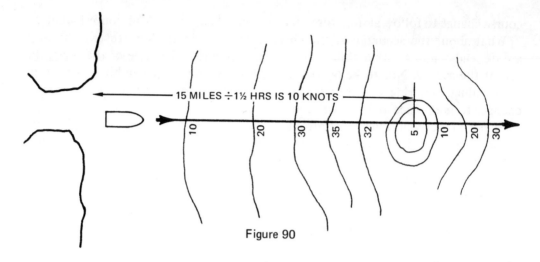

15 MILES ÷ 1½ HRS IS 10 KNOTS

Figure 90

you find the track made good. **Figure 91** illustrates the process. Changes in depth may not be very great between each half-mile interval; but in the course of 30 minutes (and, better, of a full hour), a distinct pattern of depth changes will develop. The interval of time and the distance between consecutive soundings can be any convenient factors. Cruising at 12 knots might suggest one mile as the distance interval and five minutes between soundings as the time. But here's a caution: it may be possible to match the line of soundings to several places on the chart. Another piece of information—perhaps a visual bearing—might settle the ambiguity.

A depth sounder and a radio direction finder (RDF) can also be teamed. Suppose you are homing on a radiobeacon at a harbor entrance and the line of bearing (LOP) is 040°, as shown in **Figure 92**. But you don't know how far out to sea on that line you really are. That's where the depth sounder can help. A sounding is taken and shows 50 fathoms. Locate the 50-fathom curve on the chart and you have a second line of position to use with the radio bearing. The intersection of that 040° bearing line with the 50-fathom curve is a position. As you continue on course, you can keep track of progress (and speed) towards the harbor by noting the depth changes and marking the times on the chart. Each

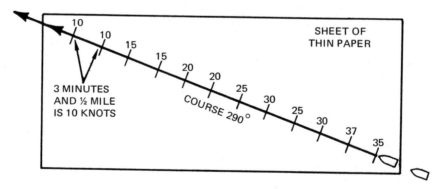

SHEET OF THIN PAPER

3 MINUTES AND ½ MILE IS 10 KNOTS

COURSE 290°

Figure 91

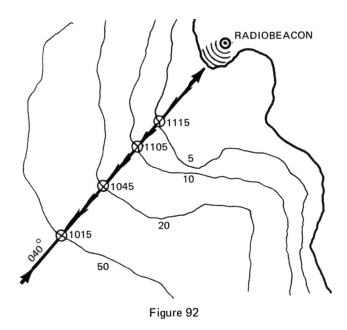

Figure 92

fathom curve serves as a check point as you travel up the 040° track towards the harbor.

The value of an echo sounder increases greatly with understanding of its principle, its strengths and its weaknesses. The virtues of this important device far, far outweigh its shortcomings. Make it a part of your operating routine to use the depth sounder as often as possible. Experiment with procedures in fair weather. Make a harbor approach along contour lines, develop a line of soundings on a piece of tissue paper and see what happens when you slide it over the chart. Cross an RDF bearing or a visual bearing with a fathom curve. Then, when the weather turns foul, you will know better what to expect. Keep in mind the few cautions to be exercised, and you will have a reliable shipmate and aid to safer piloting.

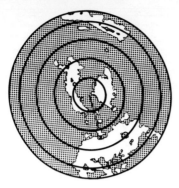

41/Marine Electronics
Radar in principle

So firmly entrenched is radar in all seafaring that it can now be accepted as a basic instrument. More and more, charts are acquiring features geared to the radar age. And development in manufacture has kept pace. Costs have been cut; operation has been simplified; power requirements are now minimal. Radar has joined RDF and the echo sounder as prime electronic tools of pleasure navigation. Without a general understanding of how radar works, there will be a large gap in the pleasure mariner's knowledge.

Let's start with the name. **Radar** is coined from the first letters of the words **Ra**dio **D**etection **A**nd **R**anging. The principle has been known for over 70 years; but necessity had to mother its development. At the opening of World War II, the Allies were junior to the enemy in materiel, so they needed a detection system to insure that what defenses they had would be in the right places at the right times. A crash program was begun and the radar principle was soon developed to a high degree of sophistication. Now the pioneer days are past and radar has come of age. It brings to seafaring all-weather eyesight, capable of presenting detailed facts about a surrounding area regardless of conditions which would restrict our eyesight. It also brings a different way to "see," a way more precise than our eyes in some ways and less precise in others. Our aim is to review the fundamentals of how this device works. More important, we'll concentrate on what it sees and how it sees. For this new lookout, on whom we might rely in rain and fog, does not see the way we do. And nothing could be more dangerous than to rely on reports which we can neither understand nor interpret.

What, then, is radar? Suppose you shout at a distant cliff and in one second hear the echo. Since sound moves through air at about 1100 feet per second, your voice traveled that distance . . . over and back. The cliff is half the distance, or 550 feet, away. Radar uses the same echo principle. A radio signal is beamed out from the ship. When it strikes a reflecting surface, the beam is rebounded towards the antenna. The interval is timed from transmission to reception. Using the speed of the radio wave as a base, the range of the object can be found.

There are startling differences, though, between echoing radio waves and sound waves. A radio signal travels, not at 1100 feet per second, but nearly 186,000 miles per second, the speed of light. Astronomers say it takes years for starlight to reach us, and that sunlight is enroute through space for more than eight minutes to get to Earth. Who ever saw light travel from a floor lamp to his newspaper? Yet there is an interval. We are just not able to measure it un-aided.

A radar set uses electronic timing devices to measure this fantastic speed. And the unit is not a second, but one-millionth of a second: a **microsecond**. In that time a radar impulse travels 328 yards. Applying the echo principle, we know that if one microsecond elapses from transmission to receipt of the echo, the impulses travel a total of 328 yards . . . 164 yards out and 164 yards back. The range of the reflecting object is 164 yards. Radar sends out, receives and times the interval thousands of times each second. The outgoing signal is projected in a beam rotating through the arc of a full circle. So not only is range measured, but direction also can be determined.

When the echo returns to the radar scanner, it is passed on to a receiver. There it is amplified and sent along to the display unit to be presented on a screen for observation. The components of the installation are: a **transmitter**, an antenna or **scanner**, a **receiver**, a display unit or **indicator**, and a system of regulating and **timing devices**. The signals used are in the Super High Frequency band. Marine radars employ either three-centimeter or 10-centimeter wavelengths, with corresponding frequencies of about 10,000 megaHertz and about 3,000 megaHertz.

That's the general idea of how things work. Now for a closer view. We're not going to spend a lot of time on the small print of radar equipment theory. But a certain amount of famil-

Slotted wave guide radar antenna.

Double-cheese radar antenna

Photos by Decca Radar

Tilted Parabolic Reflector
Figure 93

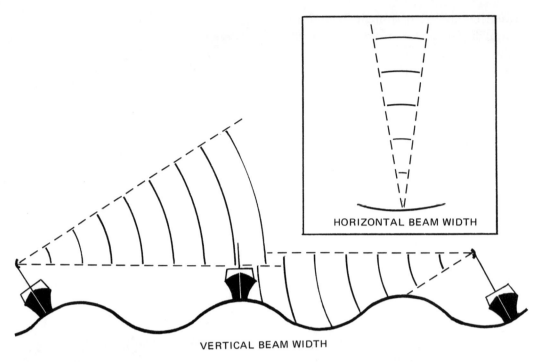

HORIZONTAL BEAM WIDTH

VERTICAL BEAM WIDTH

Figure 94

iarity is necessary to understand operation. So into the transceiver we go.

The term **transceiver** tells a lot about radar: a merger of **transmitter** and re-**ceiver**. It is the name given for the unit in which radar's two most important elements are housed. The transceiver is, on one side, an automatic transmitter of short, powerful bursts of radio energy streaming from a special radio tube called a **magnetron**. Then a particular kind of transmission line pipes the spurts of free electrons out towards the atmosphere. This line is in some cases **coaxial cable**, and in others, **wave guide**. In all cases the radio signal travels through it up to a focusing antenna or **scanner**. The names given to types of these over the years are valuable as ammunition for the devotee of one-upmanship. He might, with malevolent casualness, quiz the unwary on the wisdom of supplanting the **double-cheese** scanner with the **TPR**—which, (doesn't everyone know?) is Tilted Parabolic Reflector—particularly in view of the inevitable employment of the **slotted wave guide**. All this name-dropping involves different kinds of radar antennas to focus the transmitted signal into a directional beam, then to collect the reflected echo and send it down to the -**ceiver** part of the transceiver for detection and amplification prior to display. **Figure 93** shows the three scanner types.

The signal leaving the set has several dimensions. It streams over the side in a **vertical beam width** of 20° to 30°. This minimizes the chance of losing objects when the vessel is rolling and pitching. It also has a **horizontal beam width**, due in great part to the width and design of the scanner. **Figure 94** depicts what this is all about. Another dimension is **pulse length**. The burst of energy might be 0.08 microsecond long; it might be 0.5 microsecond long. A related factor is the **pulse repetition rate (PRR)** ... how many of these bursts leave the antenna during a

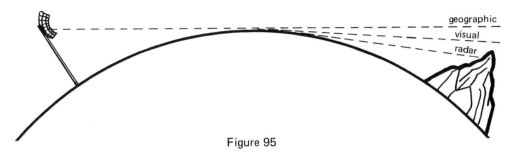

Figure 95

second: 2400 pulses per second with a pulse length of 0.12 microsecond might be a combination; 800 pulses per second with a pulse length of 0.4 microsecond might be another. Should your radar ever have the temerity to claim it is overworked, climb into the highest dudgeon and bring this mathematics to its attention: 2400 pulses, each 0.12 microsecond in length, amount to 288 microseconds of energy transmitted during each second of time; 800 pulses, each of 0.4 microsecond length, amount to 320 microseconds of energy during that second. But each second of time has 1,000,000 microseconds. That complaining radar transmits for a total of no more than 320 microseconds and listens for no less than 999,680 microseconds out of each 1,000,000 microseconds. It sends out a pulse, then listens for an eternity. Then it sends out another pulse and listens; then another and so on lazily during the enormity of one full second.

All these facts are fine cocktail-hour bonbons . . . but they really boil down to this. The radar creates a radio signal of a certain frequency wavelength personality. It beams this signal out from the ship in a series of controlled bursts, firing a given number of pulses per second, with each pulse having a particular length. This spray of electrons goes out in a circular pattern seeking objects in its path.

Next we have to see what happens to the signal after it leaves the ship. First off, these radio waves don't curve around Earth. They behave somewhat like light waves and want to follow straight lines. But they are subject to atmospheric refraction. In fact, they are bent down over the horizon even more than light rays. So radar range will exceed line of sight. **Figure 95** shows the contrast between three visibilities: **geographic**, which disregards any atmospheric refraction and assumes a perfectly straight line of sight; **visual**, which includes the extra range brought by atmospheric refraction of light rays; and **radar**, which brings into play the additional range due to greater atmospheric refraction of radio waves. As a general rule, the radar horizon can be taken to be distant about 15% more than its visual counterpart.

Of course, all such refraction varies with changes in the atmosphere. Under some conditions, the beam can bend down much more than normal and produce unusually long ranges. The name for that effect is **super-refraction**. Occasionally an atmospheric duct is caused, and the radar signal follows it for many extra miles to rebound off a far distant object. The reverse procedure can also come to pass. An unusual atmosphere might cause the radar energy to bend less than normal. In that case the radio wave will not travel as far around the curve of Earth, and radar range will be less than normal. The name for that effect is **sub-refraction**.

The distortions of light waves as they pass through different media are well known to all of us. We've seen reflections, mirages, inverted images and other optical aberrations inflicted on light as it courses around Earth. Radio waves encounter much the same. Radar "ghosts," false echoes and similar offbeat effects can often be attributed to the same sort of thing.

An influence on radar range which is self-evident is the height of the antenna. So also should be the height of the object detected. All this is in the same bin as distance of visibility of a lighthouse based on height of the observer and height of the lighthouse. But because of the extra 15% range of the radar signal, the visibility tables we mentioned in connection with the lighthouse are not directly applicable. Here is a workable one:

Height in ft.	Distance in n.m.	Height in ft.	Distance in n.m.	Height in ft.	Distance in n.m.
5	2½	55	9	110	13
10	4	60	9½	130	14
15	4½	65	10	150	15
20	5½	70	10	170	16
25	6	75	10½	190	17
30	6½	80	11	215	18
35	7	85	11	240	19
40	7½	90	11½	265	20
45	8	95	12	320	22
50	8½	100	12	380	24

Extreme elevation of a radar antenna is not necessarily desirable. At 10 feet it can see four miles; double the height to 20 feet and it only sees 40% more . . . 5½ miles. The most powerful radar on Earth, with its antenna at 20 feet above the sea, can only, on its own, see 5½ miles. Range also involves the height of the object detected. It could see a 40-foot object at 13 miles. The first 5½ miles would be based on antenna height; the remaining 7½ miles depends on the 40-foot height of the object. Related to all this is the problem of minimum range. We've mentioned vertical beam width: the angle from the top of the projected beam to the bottom. Place the antenna at deck level and the bottom edge of the beam will sweep the sea very close aboard. But as the antenna height increases, that bottom edge keeps hitting the sea farther and farther out. There is a point at which the greater range achieved by a higher antenna height is far outweighed by the bad minimum range it might cause. See **Figure 96.**

Another influence on radar range is **attenuation**: loss of strength of the transmitted signal. It's pretty reasonable for the radar pulse to get tired as it travels out and back, mile after mile. And occasionally it might return so weakened that it cannot be detected. Some atmospheric conditions cause more attenuation than do others. Through a vacuum the signal could go on indefinitely; through a very heavy atmosphere the story is different. So here is another factor to be reckoned with: decrease in range by abnormal loss of signal strength. All this ties in with the pulse length assigned to a transmitted signal. For short ranges, many short bursts are transmitted. One combination is 3000 pulses per second, each of 0.08

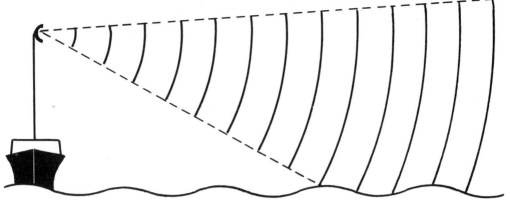

High antenna creates poor minimum range.

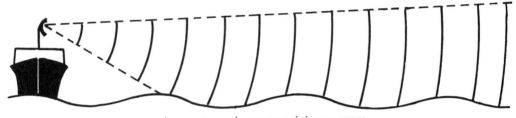

Low antenna improves minimum range.

Figure 96

microsecond length. But such a short pulse would not be strong enough to survive a 36-mile round trip. So for long ranges the set dispatches a longer pulse, but fires less of them. Such a combination could be 1500 pulses per second, each of 0.5 microsecond length.

A fair statement is that one can't listen well while he's shouting. An absolute statement about the normal marine radar is that it can't receive at all while it is transmitting. While the transmitter side of the transceiver is working, the receiving side does not function. While the transmitter is sending out a pulse of 0.08 microsecond length, the receiver cannot detect anything. We've already mentioned that a unit of radar ranging is 164 yards per microsecond. On that basis, a pulse of 0.08 microsecond length represents, rounded out, 14 yards. During the interval of one such pulse, 14 yards of range are blocked out. The receiver isn't receiving for the first 40-odd feet, which hardly presents any practical impediment. But a price is paid for this precision. The maximum range will decrease because the packet of energy fired from the antenna is not strong enough to make it out a long distance and back. So for long range, the radar installation would send a longer pulse . . . perhaps 0.5 microsecond. This amounts to over 80 yards of geography. The minimum range of the set has now been worsened by nearly six times as much . . . the price for putting a stronger pulse out in search of an object. Long ranges, then, require longer pulses; short ranges require short pulses. The minimum range on a long range scale is not as good as the minimum when the range scale is short.

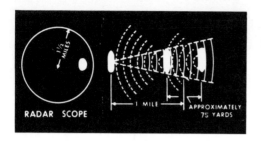
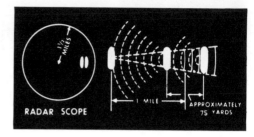

Figure 97

This characteristic is termed **resolution in range**, sketched in **Figure 97**. Notice something else. More than just minimum range is controlled by the pulse length. Also involved is the minimum distance two objects can be separated and show up on the radarscope as two objects. With the 0.08 pulse we've mentioned, objects on the same bearing could be only 14 yards apart and still appear as two objects; with the 0.5 pulse, they would appear as one reflection. For their minimum range separation with the long pulse is more than 80 yards.

This has a counterpart in bearing. We've mentioned that the beam has a horizontal width expressed in degrees of arc. But a description of a beam as, say, 3°, can be misleading. What it means is that the **effective** arc of the beam under normal conditions is 3° wide. And this effective area is the arc from half strength on one side through maximum strength at mid-beam to half strength on the other. A normally tuned set will detect objects within the half strength limits, but will not pick up those in the fringe areas. And here's a further rub. The spray of electrons issuing from the antenna is somewhat like a searchlight beam. Anything in the beam is illuminated at the same instant. Picture a strong beam of light cast on three deer in a forest. For an instant they are frozen in position. Our eyes are marvelous instruments . . . even if they might need the supplement of bifocals and tinted lenses. For our eyes can tell there are three deer in the spotlight. But radar might not. In fact, if all three deer were at the same distance, radar probably could not. The radar beam strikes three deer and rebounds to the antenna. The range of the deer is computed by the time interval for the signal to reach the deer and to rebound. But the echoes from all three deer come back at the same time, and from the same direction. On the scope that direction is not a fan or an arc . . . it is a single line representing the mid-point of the actual beam. The three deer appear as one blob of venison for they are bracketed by one beam width.

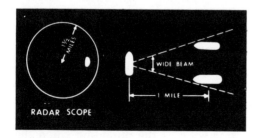
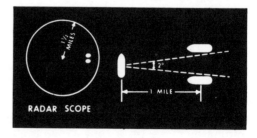

Figure 98

Radar has only two means of distinguishing objects: range and bearing. And no matter the number of objects at the same range appearing in the same beam width, radar will "see" them as one. What we're talking about is called **resolution in bearing,** and **Figure 98** sketches the idea.

Radar is not as precise as the human eye. It can see things when the eye cannot. But it has less discrimination. Seeing with the eyes involves much more than does seeing with radar. We have a wide angle of natural view, with an incredibly narrow beam width. We can distinguish by color, shape, size, range and bearing. Then we add in much unconscious judgment by our minds. We interpolate, allow for, accommodate, and in instinctive ways take many factors into account. Seeing by radar involves only the two basics of range and bearing. It is only realistic when the mind knows what judgments and allowances will have to be made. And we have no instinct to guide us. We must learn the limitations and capabilities of the system in order to use it safely.

Here, then, is the gist of the two resolutions. A shorter pulse means better resolution in range, better ability to separate objects on the same bearing but at different ranges. A narrower beam means better resolution in bearing, better ability to separate objects at the same range but on different bearings.

We've so far discussed things about transmission and about the trip to the detected object. Now what about the object itself? First off, there is one school of thought that doesn't like it described as a target . . . power of suggestion and all that. We probably should use a less aggressive term. Radar plotting sometimes uses "him" as the description . . . a practice festooned with perils no mariner should lightly encounter. So, in deference to psychic persuasion and to Women's Lib, we'll stick to **object.** When we speak of the appearance of the object on the radarscope, we can use **blip** or **pip.** Let's stay with **pip** as being a little more popular.

How the object will appear as a pip depends on such factors as the object's shape and material. The radar antenna will not recapture every impulse **de**flected off the object . . . it will only be able to stop those which **re**flect. And reflection depends on shape. The worst target shape is a sphere. Radio waves striking such an object as the ball-shaped buoy in **Figure 99** will bounce off in many directions, few of which will be straight back. Very reflective is a pocket or concave shape into which the radio signal enters to skitter around and then ricochet out. Radar reflectors fitted on important buoys (which are then marked on charts as **Ra Ref**) double the range of their detection. **Figure 100** shows the difference in reflective characteristics between one side of a headland and another. When the

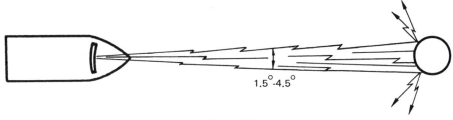

1.5°-4.5°

Figure 99

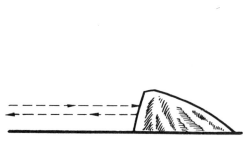

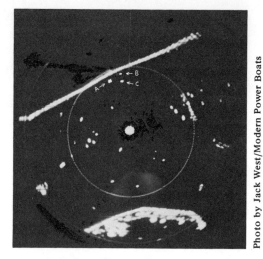

Photo by Jack West/Modern Power Boats

Figure 100

Figure 101

land mass presents a steep face, it is much more likely to show up well as a pip than if its face is sloping away.

Another factor is the material of which the object is composed. A rule of thumb is that good conductors of electricity are good reflectors and poor conductors are not. Iron, steel, water . . . they are good materials likely to deflect a workable echo. But wood, rubber, glass, canvas . . . they are not. Considerations of shape and material often make the pleasure craft a poor object for radar detection. First of all, the aim of much design is to present a sloping, streamlined profile with surfaces curving away from the viewer. Combined with wood and fiberglass materials, this causes poor radar visibility. What should be a must is the use of a radar reflector to enhance the electronic view. A corner-type reflector will rebound radio waves with little regard for the aspect of the boat carrying it. Three flat metallic surfaces, meeting to form right-angled corners, and displayed as high as possible, will make even an outboard runabout appear as large as a cruiser. In **Figure 101**, C, a dinghy with reflector, contrasts well with 50-foot A and far better than sailboat B. And in **READY REFERENCE** is sketched how to make a reflector.

Now to the aspect of the object. Viewing a fixed location, such as a bluff or point of land, minimizes the problem somewhat; for any change in the face it displays to your radar antenna is caused by a change in your position. But when

Figure 102

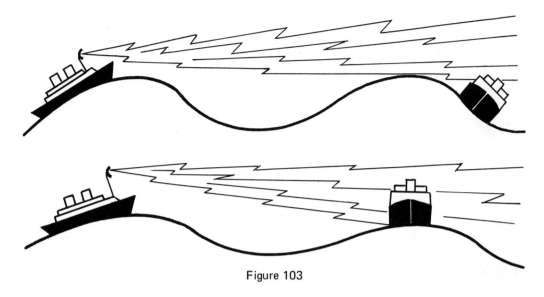

Figure 103

the object viewed is another vessel, free to move up and down in the seaway and to change course, the matter gets complicated. Sketched in **Figure 102** is the increase in radar echo to be expected when the object vessel changes course from bow-on to broadside. **Figure 103** tells the story of her movement in the sea. When in the trough or rolling away from your antenna, she will present much less of a reflective face than when she is on the crest of a wave or rolling towards you. Such influences as these can cause reflections to be intermittent and to vary in strength.

Next, the subject of shadows. One can hardly expect light to reflect off a mirror unless light shines on the mirror. Just as certain is that no radar reflection is possible unless the object has been hit by radar energy. And the beam can be blocked by intervening objects. The result is creation of a **blind sector**: an arc into which, because of some obstruction, no radar energy is transmitted, and so into which no radar visibility is possible. Avoidance of onboard obstructions is often as simple as mounting the antenna in the clear, where it has an unimpeded 360° arc of visibility. Off the ship, though, there can still be difficulty from such block-outs. If no pulses are allowed into the area, there will be no pips. Sometimes the obstructing is not total. The radar impulse enters, but is not strong enough to trigger detection. That produces a **shadow sector**. At normal settings of controls, the radarscope might show no more than a blind sector. But if gain or sensitivity is increased, some object might be discerned in the area. **Figure 104** repeats the radar view of Long Beach-Los Angeles Harbors from a radar installation at the Port of Long Beach Pilot Station. We've already seen this picture in Section VII's chapter on Rules of the Road. The bright spot in the center is the location of the radarscope. To the south of it (that is, below it in the photograph), is a line showing the middle breakwater section in the harbor. Between them is an ellipti-cal spot of light, an echo from a ship at anchor. Now let your eye move from the center out through that ship and then on to the breakwater. See the black hole? Well, it isn't really there. Neither Los Angeles nor Long Beach would long tolerate

Figure 104

a broken breakwater. That is an electronic hole caused by the ship at anchor. It is either a blind spot or a shadow area. In any case, no echo from that location was detected. If it is a blind spot, no stream of electrons ever entered that arc so no echo at all rebounded. If it is a shadow sector, weak energy might have struck the breakwater and bounced back . . . but the radar was not tuned to such high sensitivity as to detect it. If we were in the pilot station and increased the gain control, we might then find that the breakwater would be filled in as it should be.

Now we've gotten this far . . . the signal has been manufactured by the **trans** side of the transceiver, has traveled through the atmosphere, has rebounded from an object, has negotiated the return trip to the ship and has been netted by the antenna. Down the pipeline it goes to the **ceiver** part of the transceiver. There it is detected and amplified and sent along to the **indicator** for display. This is done by the unit called, variously, the **radarscope**, the **PPI** (for Plan Position Indicator), the **CRT** (for Cathode Ray Tube).

The usual picture seen is a radial sweep of light sweeping around a circular glass screen. A trailing sprinkle of brightness outlines objects which have reflected echoes. Every time the scanner swings in a full circle, the sweep on the screen does the same . . . perhaps 30 revolutions per minute. Range is measured from the center out, and direction is found by referring to a bearing circle fitted around the scope.

Range is indicated by superimposed fixed range circles. Typical are four different range scales, such as: ½, 1½, 5 and 15 miles. This means that from the center of the scope to the outer circumference, distances are to be taken alternatively as one-half mile, one and one-half miles, five-miles, and 15 miles. On each of those settings, fixed range circles will appear. On the 1½-mile range, for example, they might appear at one-half and at one mile. An object midway between the one-mile

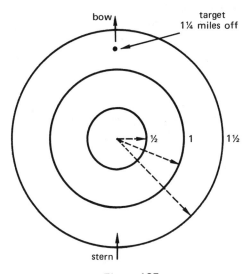

Figure 105

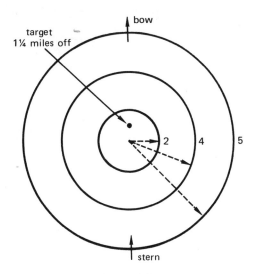

Figure 106

range ring and the outer circumference would be 1¼ miles away. By turning a knob, the navigator can change the pattern to the five-mile range. Now the fixed range circles might show up at two miles and at four miles. The same target whose range is 1¼ miles will now appear between the center and the first range circle. **Figures 105** and **106** show the story.

This pattern requires eyeball-estimation to determine the range. In our example, when viewing the object on the five-mile range setting, one observer might judge the range to be 1.1 miles and another might insist on 1.4 miles with equal certainty. A device called a **variable range marker**, (found on large sets), could settle the argument. It draws a special range circle through the pip and then shows on a meter the distance involved.

As for bearing, that can be measured by a rotatable **cursor** or pointer so that it passes through the pip of the object. Where the cursor intersects the bearing circle fitted around the radarscope gives the bearing. **Figure 107** shows a lighthouse four miles away. The **heading flasher** marks the ship's bow. Rotating the cursor so it lines up with the pip of the lighthouse, the navigator notes the angle on the rim as 20° to the right of the heading flasher. This tells him the bearing of the lighthouse is 20° to the right of his bow, or 020° Relative. If his compass course was then 050°, he would know the bearing of the lighthouse was 070°.

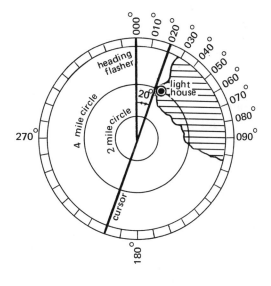

Figure 107

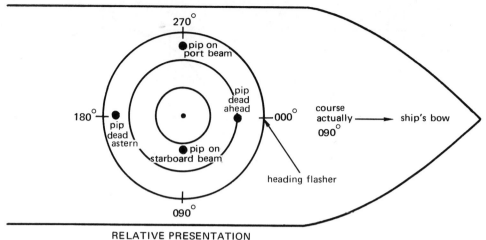

RELATIVE PRESENTATION

Figure 108

   The presentation or display of the radar view varies with the installation. Nowadays the standard picture is a circular plan or down view of the geographical area with the radar antenna at the center. The top of the scope can represent the bow of the radar vessel, and when it does, the presentation is said to be **relative**. In effect the radarscope is then a pelorus or bearing circle. Objects will appear on the scope in relation to the vessel itself. Something dead ahead will appear between the center and the top of the scope . . . it will appear on the heading flasher. An object on the port beam will appear to the left of the center; one to starboard will be on the right; one astern will appear below the center. Ranges indicated will be measurements from the ship at the center; bearings will be relative to the bow of the radar vessel. This is the view of **Figure 108**, and is so common that many accept it as the only view. But there are several others. Since each requires equipment rare on a pleasure vessel, we're only going to give them a passing glance. One is called **true presentation**, shown in **Figure 109**. A gyrocompass is used to stabilize the radar display so that the top of the radarscope is North. Now the picture is really that of a compass rose: North at the top, South at the bottom, East to the right, West to the left. The heading flasher indicating the ship's course will appear in relation to North, just as if it were drawn on the compass rose of a chart. If the course were NE or 045°, the heading flasher would point out from the center 45° to the right of North at the top . . . and so forth. Pips will now show up on the dial by compass bearings, and no longer relative to the ship's bow. A more sophisticated display is **True Motion** radar. By it the radar ship itself is taken out of the center and is presented on the scope as a moving pip. This gives the operator the kind of view he might have if he were in a helicopter hovering over the ocean and observing his ship, other vessels and land masses shifting around on a radarscope. Another interesting variation, photographic display, allows film slides of the radarscope to be taken and then projected on a large screen . . . and, probably, of more practical use, to be preserved as evidence. Enough, though, of this window shopping. Back to the usual we go.

   The **gain control** on radar is much the same as gain or volume on other elec-

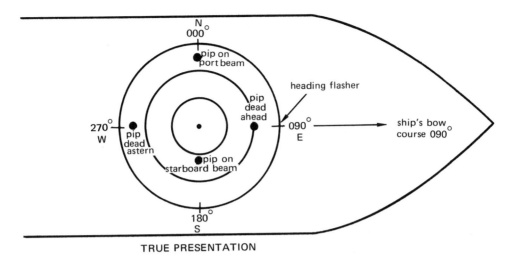

TRUE PRESENTATION

Figure 109

tronic devices. It varies the detectability or sensitivity of the receiving elements. With a high gain setting, the radar receiver "listens harder" to pick up and to display signals more forcefully. And since radar display is to the eye, the variable in display will be brightness. The counterpart in an audible "display" is evident. There the variable is loudness. Turn up the volume on the radio and you will hear the music (and the static) louder. Increasing the gain on radar will cause the pips (both desirable and undesirable) to be brighter. And this brings us to a species of undesirable pips called **sea return** or **clutter**. Water is conductive of electricity and so, material-wise, rates as a good reflector of radar signals. Peak the water into waves and the shape can enhance the rebounds. The result can be a series of small objects, the waves, reflecting pulses back to the antenna. This situation is more pronounced on the windward side, where the waves are peaked towards the vessel. The result is an annoying splash of pips around the center of the radarscope. How far out this clutter of return from the sea prevails will depend on the range scale and on the size of the waves. A six-foot crest at a range of one mile is relatively more objectionable than at a range of ten miles. Sea return, then, is more trouble at close range.

Next to consider is how to minimize this clutter, and the key is time. Radar makes time and distance almost interchangeable. A microsecond is worth 164 yards of range; a mile is worth about 12 microseconds. Let's suppose that the reflections from waves are obscuring the set for a radius of a mile and a half around the vessel. The glare of all those little pips merging into a solid pattern of light makes it very difficult to interpret anything on the radarscope. It would be great if, by decreasing the gain for the first 3000 yards, you could knock out the glare, and then turn the gain up to normal to detect from there on in regular fashion. But 3000 yards out and 3000 yards back is traversed by the radio waves in less than 20 microseconds. Not the fastest draw in the Old West could turn Gain down for 20 millionths of a second and then turn it up to normal for the rest of the scope's range setting. This is a job for an electronic circuit. The name given to that circuit is **STC** (for Sensitivity Time Control). What it does is to reduce the gain for a given period of time and then release its hold so the gain control can go back to normal. For that period of time—in our example, 20 microseconds—the set would not hear well; thereafter it would be its own sensitive self again. But the return from the sea would be suppressed; from which comes another name for the device: **sea suppressor**. And since it is against clutter, it is also sometimes called an **anti-clutter device**. Such controls are almost standard equipment today, and are very important. But here is an equally important caution. The suppression is quite democratic . . . it won't just ignore waves, but will also be insensitive to any small targets in the time-arc of its operation. While it is on, the set is not listening too well to anything. Using STC at all times in choppy weather can be dangerous. You might overlook another vessel in the suppressed sea return. The cure is to release the STC periodically and look around in the sea return glare for a sign of a substantial pip.

We've mentioned already that radar sets are equipped to present several range scales. The accuracy of each is not the same. The error in ranging is said to be a small percentage—an example is 1½%—of the range scale used. For ranges up to 10 miles, this will be no more than 300 yards; but on long range scales it can exceed a half a mile. However, that should be no problem since, on closer approach, a shorter and more accurate range scale can be used. Bearing error, however, is more significant. It depends primarily on the width of the scanner . . . increasing as the scanner narrows. With a four-foot scanner, the error can be about 3°. Worth noting is this. Radar ranging is very nearly accurate in the danger area near the ship. But bearing error can **increase** as the range shortens. Radar is more precise in range than in bearing, and can produce a significant bearing error at close range. The combined result of more energy reflecting from nearby objects and a high gain setting can trigger returns in an abnormally wide arc. The effect at close range can be the same as a wider beam, with its reduced resolution in bearing and less precise definition of direction. We've said enough about the weaknesses to have made the point . . . radar, although the greatest single aid to navigation ever developed for the mariner, has some weaknesses. It is foolhardy not to recognize them. It is foolhardy not only for the radar operator but also for the other vessel. With such recognition, though, both of them can achieve standards of safe passage never in the past possible.

Here, then, is the trip we took with the radar impulse. From the **trans**ceiver we went via the wave guide or coaxial cable to the antenna. From there we rode the focused beam through the atmosphere, being bent down more or less in the process. Then we encountered an object and rode the reflected portion of the beam back to antenna. We went back down the pipeline to the trans**ceiver** to be detected and amplified and then sent along to the indicator for display. And during the trip we got a quick view of what was involved in this truly remarkable process. Sooner or later, radar will probably be in the future of every mariner. But even if he never uses the equipment, he should have this capsule idea of how it works.

Time now to throw the switches to OFF. As the old farmer said, "Stop milking when the pail is full" . . . and our's runneth over. Next time, a look at radar in practice.

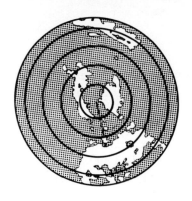

42/Marine Electronics
Radar in practice

The shipboard uses of radar can be placed in three categories, and the job now is to look at each of them. It is invaluable as an anticollision device; it is an important piloting tool; it also gets involved with weather phenomena and weather prediction. Let's warm up to the spirit of things by first investigating radar and the weather.

To speak of weather and radar does not require a special knowledge of meteorology . . . at least the way we're going to do it. Weather observers make great use of radar and put to work special equipment and skills. We benefit, of course, by the greater accuracy of their predictions. But what we want to find out is what the normal observer with a normal shipboard radar should be able to recognize and to interpret. No latter-day Columbuses discovering new lands which are really thunderclouds; no embarrassing position fixes on cold fronts or waterspouts!

What, then, will a normal radar show about weather? First of all, a meteorological echo will differ from a land mass by continuously changing shape, size and intensity. The reflected energy is bounding off water, and the brightness of the display is directly related to the water concentration. In fact, there are several effects when the radar beam encounters weather. One can be deflection or reflection of energy; the other can be absorption of power and so attenuation. Let's look at a few of the common types of weather conditions met.

Showers will have poorly defined edges and be more or less indistinct in character. A **squall line** will be more band-like in appearance. **Thunderstorms** can return strong echoes, with bright central areas grading out to fuzzy boundaries. A **cold front** usually shows a line of strong cloud echoes, suggesting the squall line, heavy clouds and, perhaps, thunderstorms, along its face. A **warm front** is much less well-defined, but will probably cover a larger area.

The appearance of a **tropical cyclone** can be similar to the photographs seen in earlier chapters. When it appears on the scope it's time to flee discreetly with all haste.

Fair weather clouds and very **light rain** will not be displayed. **Moderate** and **heavy rain** can return echoes of varying brightness. **Hail** and **sleet** may be displayed, but **snow** does not return well at all. Neither **fog** nor **smog** should give a pip. But sometimes a very dense fog bank might show as a faint haze. Remember, though, that more dense atmosphere can produce greater attenuation and so materially reduce detection range of any target. What about a **dust storm**? Like heavy fog, it can bring loss of strength and so reduce range.

Generally, a three-centimeter (X-Band) radar set is more sensitive than a 10-centimeter (S-Band) set and so can produce more weather echoes. Still, only a limited amount of weather will show up on either one of them. But all weather phenomena, when they trigger echoes, tend to obscure other objects. So a clutter problem similar to sea return can exist. On some sets there is a special control called **FTC**, (for Fast Time Constant). What it does is cause display of only the leading portion of echoes on the screen. The result is to break up the large masses of weather echoes and allow more concentrated rebounds from vessels and landmarks to appear.

How about **ice**? Smooth field ice gives no reflection. The energy hits and skips on without a rebound. Only crinkled portions where the ice is ridged or jagged can be expected to react. An **iceberg** is a shifty customer. His vertical faces can be good reflectors; sloping surfaces are bad. And the berg is not stationary, so the facet shown to the beam is subject to change. A **growler**, a small broken-off piece, is usually low and well-rounded. It is a poor reflector and a dangerous object.

Tied in with weather echoes is the possible variation in range due to changes in refraction. Frigid weather often produces sub-refraction, and with it, decreased radar range. Unusual weather conditions, such as temperature inversions, can develop atmospheric ducts or channels. A radar signal caught in it can super-refract for even hundreds of miles and return an anomalistic or offbeat echo out of context with the range setting.

What does all this amount to? The necessity, at least, to recognize that weather can return echoes, can vary signal strength, can obscure objects, can produce abnormal ranges. The very appearance of such unusual effects tells an observer something about weather conditions. Should he see a thundercloud on the radarscope, he has warning that the condition to produce a thundercloud is in the area. From that evidence he might predict the advent of a cold front, and with it a drop in temperature, rise in pressure and other accompanying weather changes.

Knowing how to recognize weather phenomena and how to cope with their interference is only learned by experience with the set. And that is beyond our purpose. But knowing that the problems exist is not. Let's be satisfied with having raised the possibilities and move on to the next phase of practical radar.

This brings us to the use of radar to avoid collision. The most outstanding contribution of radar to safety is its all-weather capability. Hardly any need remains to speak much of what it **can** do. Being able to see vessels, rocks, buoys and land masses in thick fog is a dramatic accomplishment. But to stop there and assume that the view is the same as that seen by eye in clear weather would be very ill-advised. So here we go again to pick apart its abilities and identify its shortcomings.

Nearly all radar aboard private vessels shows a view with the vessel fixed in the center of the scope. Whether she is actually going West at 16 knots, North at six knots or is immobile at anchor, she will appear on the radarscope as stopped at the center. So all movement seen on the scope is **relative** to the vessel at the center. Everything is depicted in **relative motion**. For example, suppose a mariner is heading North at 10 knots, and he observes the pip of a lighthouse ahead of him and off his starboard bow. His ship is considered to be at the center of the circular screen . . . and the pip of the lighthouse would appear to move South at 10 knots. The stationary object seems to have a course opposite to that of the observer's ship, and at his speed. Should he encounter another vessel moving South at 10 knots, that pip will travel South at 20 knots . . . opposite to the observer and at their combined speeds. However, should still another ship be heading North at 10 knots (the same course and speed as the observer), her pip would stand still. **Figure 110** sketches the three situations.

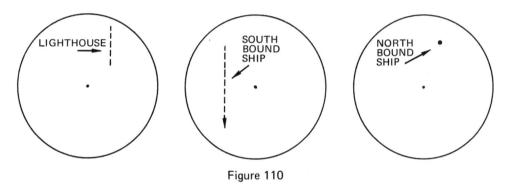

Figure 110

In other words, the pip's speed and its direction are the products of the courses and speeds of two objects: the radar vessel and the other being observed. Just one look at the scope will not reveal the other's true movement.

In **Figure 111** we see on the radarscope a vessel bearing abeam to starboard and seven miles off at 0900; again it is abeam to starboard but six miles off at 0906. And at 0912 it is still abeam to starboard but only five miles off. This other ship is coming towards us; in fact, if things keep up, she's going to hit us. She is approaching at the rate of one mile every six minutes. This figures out to 10 knots. Since at 0912 she is five miles away, she has 30 minutes left before collision. We'll come together at 0942. Radar tells us we are on collision courses and will strike at 0942. What radar doesn't tell us directly is the **true** course and speed of the other vessel.

If we are, in fact, stopped, then the other vessel is truly on the track indicated by the pips. She is traveling due West, or 270°, at 10 knots. But if, in fact, we were bound North, or 000°, at 10 knots, and she were on a course of 315° at 14.1 knots, the radarscope would show the same picture. For it shows the other's motion relative to us presumed fixed at the center. There are quite a few combinations of our course and speed and his course and speed which would produce the very same view. The moral is quite evident. Radar hardly ever depicts the true motion of the other vessel. In fact, it only does so under one set of circumstances: when we are, in fact, stopped. All other combinations of courses and speeds for the two vessels will produce an apparent track resulting from the combinations. In order to learn the other's true motion, it is necessary to solve a radar plotting problem. Now, that's a sticky wicket not within our purpose. Enough, again, to point out the situation. Radar plotting itself is well covered in the **42** pages of *Radar Plotting Manual, HO 257* of the US Navy Oceanographic Office. There are actually **two** kinds of radar plotting. The **speed triangle** method is featured in *HO 257.* The **distance triangle** system, used for years on British ships, and also discussed in *HO 257,* is now finding a place as an alternate on US vessels.

All of this is useful information—even essential—for proper radar navigation by anyone. But having in mind our purpose of introduction and survey, we'll steer around the subject and concentrate on some pointers of observation practical on a small vessel with one person manning the radar, keeping a lookout and otherwise watching the store.

Essential to any judgment on the movement of the other vessel is a series of observations. Watch the movement of each chain of pips. Rotate the cursor to point to an echo. If subsequent pips appear to follow down the cursor towards the center, the object is on a collision bearing. If the pips seem to be following a

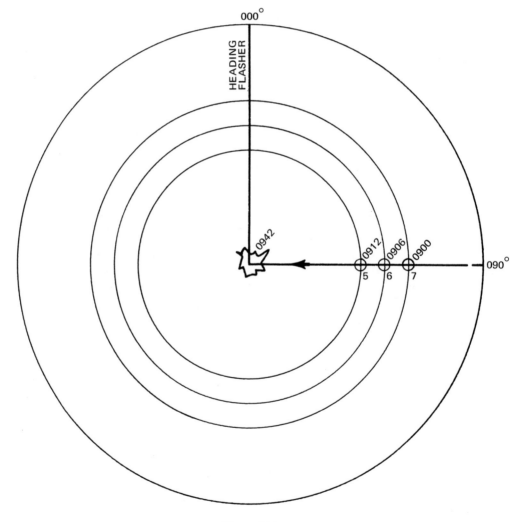

Figure 111

line to pass between the center and your heading flasher, the vessel is passing ahead of you. Should the pips be moving on a line to pass behind the center, the other is passing astern. **Figure 112** shows the idea. In other words, watch how the pips are moving relative to the center. When they are coming towards it, some evasive action will be necessary.

This is easier to do when the pips of only one object are on the scope. In a crowded waterway when the radarscope seems to be speckled with many pips, the problem, of course, gets complicated. Sometimes a grease pencil to mark pips on the glass before they fade out can help. A set equipped with a **reflection plotter** makes this a simple task. Otherwise the curved surface of the glass and the parallax problem of marking directly over the pip on the screen beneath it can be a nuisance.

In any case, a practical approach to a scope with a measles-rash of multiple pips is this. Concentrate first on pips moving towards the center. They are the dan-

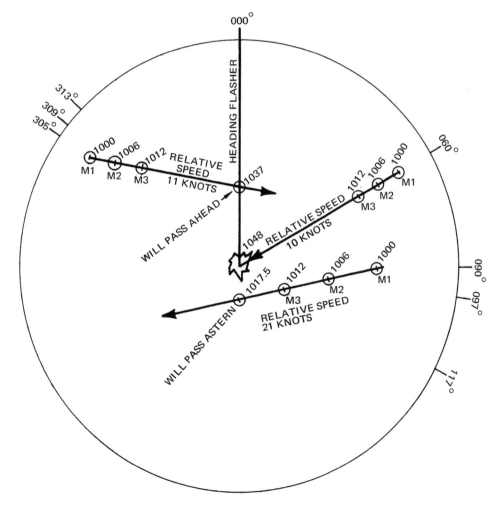

Figure 112

gerous ones. The second priority is to pips that are forward of your beam . . . in the upper half of the scope above the center. They represent objects ahead of you on either bow. And remember, the Rules of the Road pattern of privilege and burden might not apply. When you are in fog, the appearance of pips on your port bow does **not** give you a privilege. In fog no one is privileged; everyone is burdened to navigate with caution. The privilege-and-burden script only has application when vessels are in sight of each other visually.

Figure 113 shows pips moving along a line from broad on the port bow to cross your course and then move down the starboard side. Point **A** indicates the position of the pip when the other ship crosses your bow. The range from the center to there is called the crossing distance. Point **B** is the pip position when the other vessel will be closest to you. This is called **CPA**, (for Closest Point of Approach). It is the perpendicular distance from the pip line to you at the center, and its importance is obvious. Knowing the closest distance to a danger is a classic factor in all navigation. And recall the cautions raised in the last chapter on Radar in Principle. At close range, radar bearing accuracy decreases. What looks like a safe, even though close, CPA might not be so safe at all. Cutting close by radar eyesight can be disastrous.

In Section VII, when speaking of Rules of the Road, we talked about the place of radar. It's probably timely now to suggest that those portions be reread in the light of our present discussion. For radar grants **no** absolution from the rules in fog. We spoke there of predictability. Another way to term the problem is **mutuality**. All maneuvering rules presume mutual awareness of the circumstances. Vessel **A** sees vessel **B** visually, and so presumes **B** sees him. Under such conditions **A** can begin to act on the warranted presumption that **B** is aware of his presence. But not so in fog. There, **A** hears **B**'s fog signal and can presume only that **B** hears **A**'s . . . he must thereafter operate on the theory that **B** has no more knowledge

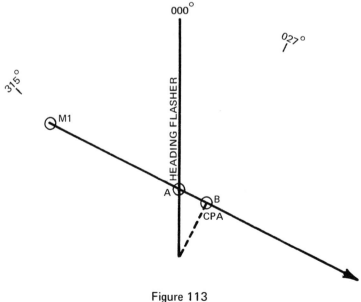

Figure 113

of A's actions than gained from the fog signal. Both know the other is around, but not exactly where or what or proceeding how. And radar doesn't solve this. A electronically sees B. By plotting he might even learn B's true course and speed. But A has no assurance that B is aware of him at all, other than by fog signal. And without that assurance, A cannot maneuver as he would in clear weather. There seems to be no cure in sight by which all the A's on the ocean will have international assurance that all the B's have radar and so "see" the other. Radiotelephone is no cure, for language can be a barrier. And electronic devices to signal radar awareness (like the military IFF "friend/foe" telltales) are not the answer so long as there is no international requirement for radar. So long as vessels can operate legally without radar, there will be "blind" vessels in fog. And just one blindman is enough to upset the whole pattern.

This is all as it should be. Radar is so helpful in fog that whoever can put it aboard should have it. But not everyone from Adak to Zanzibar is going to be **required** to have it for a long, long time.

So, this is the present situation. A vessel equipped with radar can gain data which he must take into account when maneuvering in fog. But because the other vessel might not know what he's doing and might still only know of him by the sound of his fog signal, all must still operate under the standard Rules of the Road.

The situation is spelled out in the **Annex** to the International Rules of the Road. It details eight specific points which are now as much a part of the modern rules as are sections on lights. Here is a reprint of the section. It should be required reading for all mariners.

ANNEX TO THE RULES

RECOMMENDATIONS ON THE USE OF RADAR INFORMATION AS AN AID TO AVOIDING COLLISIONS AT SEA

(1) Assumptions m a d e on scanty i n f o r m a t i o n may be dangerous and should be avoided.

(2) A vessel navigating with the aid of radar in restricted visibility must, in compliance with Rule 16(a), go at a moderate speed. Information o b t a i n e d from the use of radar is one of the circumstances to be taken into account when determining moderate speed. In this regard it must be recognized that small vessels, small icebergs and similar floating objects may not be detected by radar. Radar indications of one or more vessels in the vicinity may mean that "moderate speed" should be slower than a mariner

without radar might consider moderate in the circumstances.

(3) When navigating in restricted visibility the radar range and bearing alone do not constitute ascertainment of the position of the other vessel under Rule 16(b) sufficiently to relieve a vessel of the duty to stop her engines and navigate with caution when a fog signal is heard forward of the beam.

(4) When action has been taken under Rule 16(c) to avoid a close quarters situation, it is essential to make sure that such action is having the desired effect. Alterations of course or speed or both are

matters as to which the mariner must be guided by the circumstances of the case.

(5) Alteration of course alone may be the most effective action to avoid close quarters provided that:—
  (a) There is sufficient sea room.
  (b) It is made in good time.
  (c) It is substantial. A succession of small alterations of course should be avoided.
  (d) It does not result in a close quarters situation with other vessels.

(6) The direction of an alteration of course is a matter in which the mariner must be guided by the circumstances of the case. An alteration to starboard, particularly when vessels are approaching apparently on opposite or nearly opposite courses, is generally preferable to an alteration to port.

(7) An alteration of speed, either alone or in conjunction with an alteration of course, should be substantial. A number of small alterations of speed should be avoided.

(8) If a close quarters situation is imminent, the most prudent action may be to take all way off the vessel.

Notice the admonition in Point No. 2 that the radar vessel because of its superior knowledge might even have to go slower than one not so advised. Point No. 3 says that hearing a fog signal forward of the beam still requires that engines be stopped, regardless of what radar shows. Points No. 5, No. 6 and No. 7 recommend how to change course and speed. The idea is, in general, to make substantial alterations so that the changes will be quickly effective and will be more likely to be noticed on the other ship either by change in bearing of the fog signal or, if the other has radar, by pip movement on his radarscope.

Radar in poor visibility is the very best aid a mariner can have . . . except for common sense. And it only brings grief when the mariner misuses it. Provoking thought is what we've hoped to achieve. Too much is at stake for tolerance of heedless operation.

Now to the third use of radar: as a piloting tool. Most of the time the navigator must combine two instruments in order to determine the bearing and distance to a reference object. Radar does both. By glancing at the range circles, he learns distance; by turning the cursor to point over the pip, he can read the bearing angle off the rim of the radarscope. An observation of one reference point can give him a workable position.

What must be kept in mind, though, is the variation in reflectability of land features, and a possible mix-up in identification of what actually has been observed. Charts should be studied with particular care to recognize the character

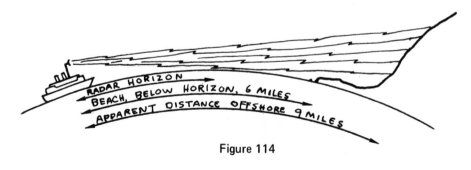

Figure 114

of the area observed, for landmarks used must be identifiable on the radarscope. Features on the beach line might not be suitable for ranging, but prominent inland hills may well be usable. **Figure 114** shows a situation often encountered. There a low shoreline juts out from a row of cliffs several miles inland. A vessel, lying offshore with her radar adjusted to the 10-mile range, sees the coast as nine miles away. Actually, the shoreline is below the radar horizon, but only six miles away. What she sees on radar is the row of cliffs far back from the beach.

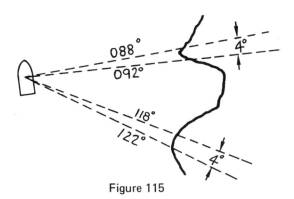

Figure 115

The horizontal beam width bugaboo comes up again in piloting. We've already mentioned that since the beam has an appreciable fan-like spread, bearing inaccuracy can creep into observations. **Figure 115** shows an example. There a ship takes bearing of two headlands. One seems to bear 088° on its left edge and 092° on its right. The other spans from 118° to 122°. This 4° spread is due to beam width error. And if the ship is yawing back and forth across its course while the bearings are being taken, the arc of each headland can widen even further. This is what has happened. When the right edge of the beam sweeps over each headland, reflections start coming back to the scanner. And as the beam passes over, echoes keep coming back until the left edge of the full beam width clears the headland. These echoes are painted on the scope as a wide pip, broader than the headland actually should be. The navigator should then turn the cursor to point right down the middle of the broad pip and take that bearing as the proper direction.

More reliable than a radar range and

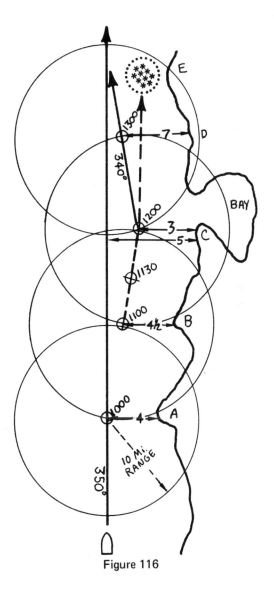

Figure 116

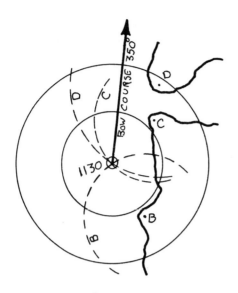

Figure 117

radar bearing combination is the use of a radar range and a visual bearing. Now the perceptible width of the electronic beam is supplanted by the immeasurably small beam width of natural eyesight. Put that together with the great precision of radar range and a good fix is determined.

What about combining radar ranges? **Figure 116** pictures the track of a vessel up a coast on a heading of 350°, with her radar set to the 10-mile range. Let's follow her progress and see how radar ranging made the task easier. Point **A** was abeam at 1000 and four miles off by radar. Point **B** is then just beyond range. But soon it begins to show on the radarscope, and is abeam at 1100. The range to **B** appears then as 4½ miles, and **A** is just moving off the bottom of the scope. The 1100 position off **B** is slightly inshore of the intended track, though not yet enough for any alarm. But at 1200, **C** is abeam at only three miles . . . and it should have been five miles off at this CPA. Sleepy steering or current has brought the ship too far inshore. A course of 350° from the 1200 spot will get the ship tangled up in the rocks up the line off **E**. So a course change to 340° is made to haul clear. At 1300 the distance off a landmark at **D** appears as seven miles. The vessel is working offshore and should clear the rocks safely.

That was a pretty elementary example of radar ranging and navigation. **Figure 117** takes it another step. There several range measurements and a drawing compass team up to give answers. At 1130, the distances to headlands **B**, **C** and **D** are measured. **B** and **C** are just a bit more than five miles off and **D** is found to be at eight miles. First off, the idea is to make positive identification on the chart of the three points observed. Then set the drawing compass to five miles and, with **B** as the center, draw an arc to seaward. Now, keeping the same five-mile measure on the compass, draw another arc with **C** as the center. Finally, reset the compass to eight miles and draw a third arc with **D** as the center. The intersection of the three arcs of range is your position. Of course, most of the time there will be some variation in things and the three arcs will not neatly intersect on the same square foot of ocean. A realist should expect to see a small triangle or "cocked hat." Occasionally navigators have been known to fudge a bit, especially when no one is watching, so that fixes will pinwheel perfectly. Self-delusion is really not a good idea. So with candor in plotting aboard, pick the center of the cocked hat as the position.

Now let's see about combining bearings and ranges. What usually happens is what you might expect would happen: the bearings when plotted give a cocked hat in one location; the range arcs, when plotted, give a cocked hat in another

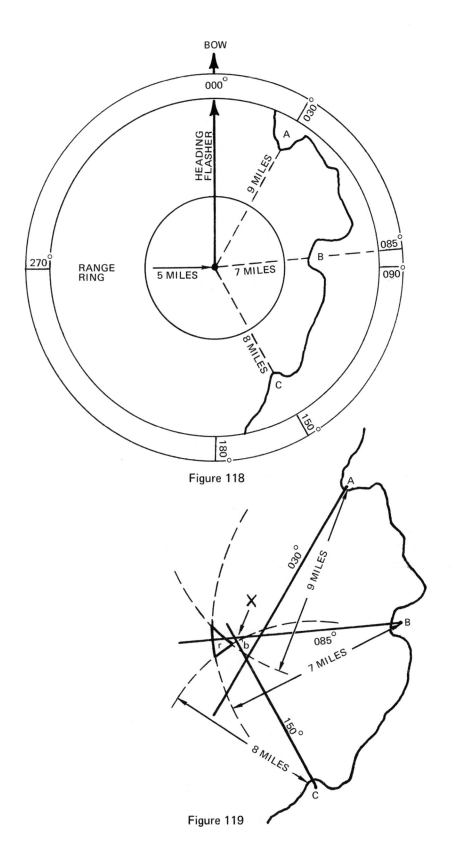

Figure 118

Figure 119

location. **Figure 118** shows the beginning of this dilemma, and **Figure 119** shows the result. First we see the radarscope-view as a vessel is heading North and observes three points of land. **A** is bearing 030° at nine miles; **B** bears 085° at seven miles; **C** bears 150° at eight miles. Then in **Figure 119** we see that the three radar bearings plot to a cocked hat marked **b** and the three range arcs plot to another marked **r**. Actually the navigator should not be surprised . . . the position by bearing and the position by range seldom coincide. The superior fix is the one by range; but the difference between them will usually be very small. And how far apart they might be will vary with the range to the reference marks, the beam width of the set, the certainty of identification of points observed. Of course, the safe thing to do in every case is to consider well the position closest to any dangers. Even if not the most likely position, it should be kept in mind when making any further moves based on the position selected. Accepting that as a standard factor, the navigator here should probably select **x**, a point between the two cocked hats, and label it as the position at the time of the observations.

Not to be overlooked is the mixture of radar information with that obtained by other means. A combination of radar range and visual bearing has already been mentioned. Radar and soundings can be mixed; so can RDF bearings and radar. Radar and Loran are compatible, as are radar and celestial lines of position. They are all tools in the navigator's kit and he should feel no compunctions about shuffling them around into different combinations. Some are better than others; radar is in many respects the best. But flexible thinking and imagination is always good seamanship.

Whenever something new makes its appearance, one of the first steps in presenting it to mankind is to outfit it in a suit of names. Radar has not escaped. The study of techniques for identifying and distinguishing echoes on a radarscope has contracted the label **pipology**. Whether it should be **piposophy** or **piponomy** or maybe even plain old **pipmanship** has little to do with whether the echo seen is that of a helicopter or a hawse pipe. And no discussion of radar in action is adequate without some mention of this "what-do-you-call-it" skill. So we'll lay aside advocacy of **-ship** as more suitable than **-ics** and get back to splashes of light on a screen. What we're now to talk about might well belong to Radar in Principle as much as Practice. But since all the material so far comes into focus, we've saved it for now.

The radar observer has some fundamental clues to use in assessing what he sees on the scope. Confidence in such judgments comes only with experience. Practice comparing a radar display with what your eyes see out the porthole is invaluable. But there are some basics to start with. We've already seen that a radar view is tied to the shape, size, material and texture of the object. Its prime dimensions are height and width . . . radar usually shows no distinction by depth. Whether a cliff face is in front of a flat strip of land ten feet deep or a flat plain ten miles deep makes no difference to the radar image. The cliff face will show, but that's all. And height itself is not so much a distinguishing element. The vertical beam width is tall enough to cover nearly all targets. A high mountain, if of absolutely vertical face, will appear like a lower vertical cliff. A distinction might be brightness, for more energy comes back to the set . . . but not size. Few mountains, though, are

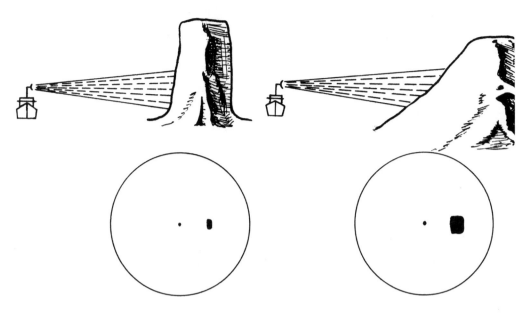

Figure 120

vertical. So there can be a difference here in depth. Echoes return first from a lower section and then progressively from higher portions. So the pip of the high mountain could be thicker. **Figure 120** shows this.

A rough texture creates minifaces from which the energy will deflect in varying ways. Sometimes roughness will diminish reflection from a favorable shape; or it can enhance reflection from an otherwise poor shape. For example, a cylindrical high tension wire which, shape-wise, should yield an unsatisfactory pip, can return a very discernible paint because of weathering, scale and roughness of the surface.

Often topographical features are discerned by the absence of a pip. A valley between two hills can appear as a blank between two echoes. This emphasizes that scope interpretation always involves reference to a chart of the area. Don't expect to see a pictorial representation of the locality. The scope displays prominences which, when studied in conjunction with a chart, give leads to significance in what is not seen. In fact a very important part of pipological proficiency is the ability to interpret a contour map. This phase of radar can really be summarized in that fashion. Compare what radar shows with the contours shown on a chart. Pretty soon patterns will begin to emerge.

Another facet of this subject is the matter of misleading or false echoes and how they come about. A common problem is that of **multiple echoes**. When a large ship is passing nearby and beam-on, the energy from your set is liable to rebound several times between the vessels. This Ping-Pong effect can produce a series of pips with the same bearing but equidistant and increasing ranges. The closest pip is the true one. The others diminish progressively in brightness with increase in range. Reducing the gain will cause them to erase from the outside in until only the true pip remains. **Figure 121** illustrates the problem. And it only exists when the two ships are so placed that the multiple reflections can be collected by your antenna.

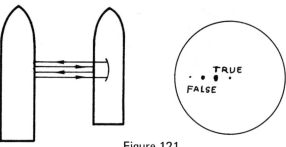

Figure 121

Here's another cause for an odd display . . . **indirect echoes**. A large ship whose scanner is buried in a forest of masts and crosstrees often suffers badly. On smaller vessels, where the antenna is usually clear of shipboard obstructions, the cause is restricted to obstructions not on board. But the problem can still develop. An object can act like a mirror and deflect energy to a second object to be double-reflected back to the scanner. The result is a false picture. **Figure 122** shows the false paint of a second ship which really isn't there. When the scanner is pointed at object **A**, energy not only rebounds from **A** but also deflects to **B** and back to **A** and then on again to the scanner. The scope shows an extra object behind **A**. The false pip usually fades out when one or the other of you moves out of coincidental reflecting position. Chart interpretation, suspicions of nonsense and a bit of applied imagination will usually reveal the hocus pocus. But never summarily disregard an offbeat echo. It might be telling you the truth.

Side lobes can sometimes be troublesome. The scanner projects a main beam or lobe of energy. It is the one described by horizontal beam width; it is the one whose center line is shown by the sweep on the scope. But it might not be the only beam. Weaker side lobes of power, like the petals on a flower, can also be transmitted. They have only short range, so the confusion they create is nearby. But they can bring a problem. **Figure 123** shows a side lobe pattern. Now look at what happens when a nearby object is swept by the scanner. **Figure 124** sketches the build-up of a series of false echoes. In (a) the main lobe is not pointing at the other ship, but side lobe **a** is. Energy reflected then is displayed, not in the

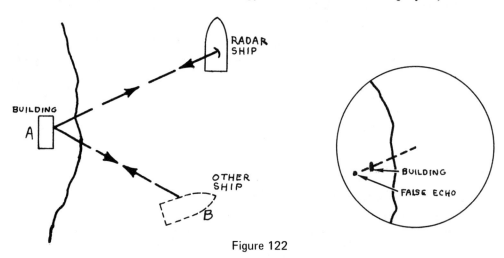

Figure 122

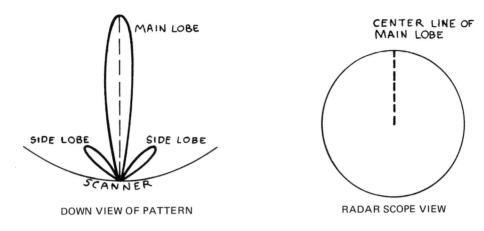

DOWN VIEW OF PATTERN · RADAR SCOPE VIEW

Figure 123

direction of lobe **a**, but down the middle of the main beam. False echo **a** appears. Then the scanner turns and the main lobe covers the other ship. Another echo returns. This is the true one, **t**. Now the scanner moves again and side lobe **b** sweeps the object. Another false echo, **b**, appears in the direction of the main beam. We show only two. The pattern sometimes can show several more. Often the echoes merge into a semicircular smear. Sometimes the smear is carried all around the center. Characteristic is that the true echo is the brightest. Reduced gain will wipe out the false showing and shrink the pip down to truthfulness.

Fortunately, newer scanner design greatly minimizes this troublesome problem. Smaller aerials were very prone to the affliction, and "double-cheese" antennas were notorious. The TPR type has the problem because the wave guide **horn**, which directs the energy into the focal point of the parabolic reflector, tends often to split the beam into segments. **Slotted wave guide** antennas seem to have brought things under control.

How about interference? What bothers a radar transmission is usually another radar. Most other radio signals are far enough away in the radio spectrum not to cause problems. But another radar of the same frequency can show a bothersome display. If both have the same pulse repetition rate (PRR) the display can be a circular pattern of dots on your scope. If the PRR for each is different, the interference should be in spiraling pips or else in light traces converging towards your center. The cure? Be ready for it and then live with it. The STC device can help somewhat. But every cloud has a bit of silver in it. Here, the very evidence of interference is at least revealing the presence of the other radar, and so gives some assurance in thick fog that he will see you. In any case, the unwanted sprinkles of snowflakes are not usually too objectionable.

One type of echo that has perplexed many an observer is that of aircraft. A normal fixed-wing type will be moving so fast to stay in the air that his pip will dart quickly across the scope. He should be easy to distinguish. But this is the age of the helicopter, and a slow-moving or hovering one can sometimes be taken for a strangely maneuvering ship. Hovercraft, hydrofoils and air cushion vehicles are now on the sea. Their faster movement than standard vessels will have to be

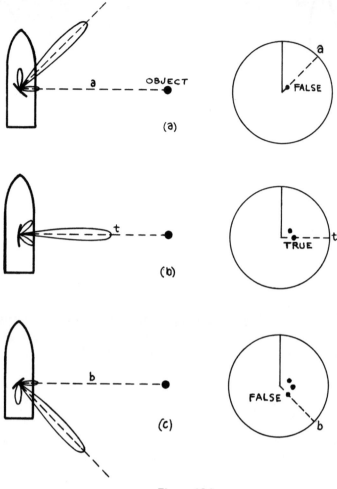

Figure 124

recognized. Unique, probably, is the experience of the very bewildered radar observer who saw an object remorselessly following him however he turned in a low-lying dense fog bank. The explanation: a "blimp" had noticed the ship's mast jutting out of the fog and decided to follow its movements. The vessel's radar displayed a pip unerringly as a prankish echo shadowing its every avoiding maneuver.

These are some of the highlights of pips and their problems. Some are commonly encountered, some are rare. There are many more variations, of course. But they should suggest another part of the overall story of radar.

This completes the survey of practical applications of radar equipment. All through it has run the theme that radar is the most outstanding aid for maneuvering and piloting that has ever been developed; and also throughout has prevailed the tempering suggestion of its shortcomings. Probably the one single fault of radar is that it is so good it sometimes lulls one to accept without question. This chapter has done its job if some defense against such lapses has been built.

Questions

Time for a showdown! Man versus the Magnetron at 10 centimeters. You have 25 chances to quash the invasion. This is not a drill—repeat—this is not a drill.

Marine Electronics—Introduction

1. When a radio frequency is given as 300 kHz the wave length is
   a)   3000 meters.
   b)   30,000 meters.
   c)   1000 meters.
   d)   10,000 meters.
   e)   300 kiloHertz.

2. The speed of sound in air is
   a)   greater than the speed of sound in fresh water.
   b)   greater than the speed of light in air.
   c)   less than the speed of sound in a vacuum.
   d)   all of above.
   e)   none of above.

3. 500 kHz is
   a)   a higher frequency than 2.0 mHz.
   b)   a higher frequency than 1.0 mHz.
   c)   a higher frequency than 600,000 cycles per second.
   d)   the same frequency as 0.5 mHz.
   e)   all of above.

4. Radar signals are transmitted with a (faster) (slower) frequency than are the signals from marine radiobeacons.

5. A radar transmission with a frequency of about 10,000 mHz has a wavelength of
   a)   3 centimeters.
   b)   10 centimeters.

Depth Sounders in Principle

1. The transducer on an echo sounder
   a)   should be painted in drydock with regular hull paint.
   b)   should not be painted in drydock with regular hull paint.

2. The constant for the speed of sound in water used by American depth sounders is
   a)   slower than the standard.
   b)   the same as the standard.
   c)   faster than the standard.

3. Reducing gain will (widen) (narrow) the flash of light on an indicator dial.

4. Aeration can be pronounced when
   a)   going astern.

b) pitching and rolling in choppy seas.
c) both of above.

5. When more than one echo appears on the indicator, the operator should always read as the depth
   a) at the brightest flash.
   b) at the deepest flash.
   c) neither of above.

Depth Sounders in Practice

1. The depth shown by an indicating or recording sounder
   a) is always the depth from the surface or waterline to the bottom.
   b) is the depth as shown on the chart.
   c) must be corrected to account for the stage of the tide and for the depth of the transducer below the surface.

2. An echo sounding has been corrected for the depth of the transducer. When it is compared with a charted depth
   a) they will then always read the same.
   b) the echo sounding will be less when it is taken at Mean High Water.
   c) the charted depth will always be less.
   d) none of above.

3. At Mean Low Water at a US Atlantic Coast position, a depth sounding is taken as 7 fathoms. The transducer is 5 feet below the waterline and has not been allowed for. The chart for the location indicates 8 fathoms. The depth sounder is reading
   a) correctly.
   b) one foot too little.
   c) one foot too much.
   d) one fathom too little.
   e) one fathom too much.

4. A depth sounder indicates 25 feet of water and has been adjusted for transducer depth. The chart shows 27 feet at Mean Low Water. The *Tide Table* indicates the state of the tide at the time of the sounding as (minus) 2 feet. The error of the depth sounder is
   a) no error.
   b) 2 feet under reading.
   c) 4 feet under reading.
   d) 2 feet over reading.
   e) 4 feet over reading.

5. The chart datum used for Long Island Sound is
   a) Mean Low Water.
   b) the same as for Seattle, Washington.
   c) the same as for Honolulu, Hawaii.

    d)   the same as for Anchorage, Alaska.
    e)   all of above.

Radar in Principle

1. One microsecond is
   a) one hundredth of a second.
   b) one thousandth of a second.
   c) one millionth of a second.
   d) the same as one megaHertz.

2. Range accuracy of a radar set is
   a) better than bearing accuracy.
   b) the same as bearing accuracy.
   c) not as good as bearing accuracy.

3. Radar range to the horizon is normally
   a) less than visual.
   b) the same as visual.
   c) greater than visual.

4. Generally speaking, a good electrical conductor
   a) will be a poor reflector of radar energy.
   b) will be a good reflector of radar energy.
   c) will reflect no differently than would a rubber object.

5. Of these the shape least likely to reflect a detectable echo would be
   a) cylindrical.
   b) convex to the beam.
   c) concave to the beam.
   d) spherical.

Radar in Practice

1. Radar will detect a channel buoy
   a) farther if the buoy has a radar reflector.
   b) as far as the maximum range of any marine radar set.
   c) never at more than 1000 yards.

2. Radar range in dense fog will tend to be
   a) greater than in clear weather.
   b) less than in clear weather.

3. The navigator of a radar-equipped vessel in fog observes only one set of pips on the scope. They are forward of his beam and the range is increasing. At the same time he hears a fog signal from forward of his beam. He (must) (need not) stop his engines by International Rules of the Road.

4. A combination of a radar range and a radar bearing is
   a) less accurate than a combination of a radar range and a visual bearing.

b) more accurate than a combination of two radar ranges.

c) less accurate than a combination of a radar bearing and a depth sounding.

5. The FTC device on a radar set is used
   a) to obtain pips in blind sectors.
   b) to break up large echoes, as from thunderclouds.
   c) when crossing the Equator to offset high humidity.
   d) when crossing the International Date Line to readjust the timing circuits.

...and answers

Score 4 for each electron neutralized at the nucleus . . . and here's your wiring diagram:

92 - 100:   Atom Smasher.
84 - 90:   You've Beaten Them Off.
76 - 82:   Next Time Wear Rubber Gloves.
Below 76:   Short Circuit!

Marine Electronics—Introduction

1. (c)   2. (e)   3. (d)   4. faster   5. (a)

Depth Sounders in Principle

1. (b)   2. (a)   3. narrow   4. (c)   5. (c)

Depth Sounders in Practice

1. (c)   2. (d)   3. (b)   4. (a)   5. (a)

Radar in Principle

1. (c)   2. (a)   3. (c)   4. (b)   5. (d)

Radar in Practice

1. (a)   2. (b)   3. must   4. (a)   5. (b)

Note: The solutions to Questions 3 and 4 of **Depth Sounders in Practice** are as follows:

3.   Charted depth = 8 fathoms =   48 feet . . . . 48 feet
      Indicated depth = 7 fathoms =   42 feet
    Transducer depth = ...+55 feet

      Indicated total depth . . . . 47 feet . . . . 47 feet

      Indicator reads . . . . 1 foot too little

4. Charted depth = 27 feet
    tide (minus)   - 2 feet
    ─────────────────
    Actual depth = 25 feet
  Indicated depth = 25 feet
  Indicator error = -0-

section 10
contents

43/Marine Electronics
Radio direction finders

So far our discussion of shipboard electronics has involved equipment whose primary purpose has been detection: finding the bottom by echo sounder, sensing the presence of other objects by radar. We've seen that both are also serviceable in navigation to help determine position. Now we launch into a survey of the electronic devices whose full-time job is to aid the navigator to fix position. The first of these is a bearing instrument . . . to determine direction by radio. In Section VIII's chapter on Aids to Navigation we spoke of radiobeacons and the service they provide. Now we'll consider the shipboard equipment with which radiobeacons work. Here's the general idea. A radio transmitter sends out a signal which is received aboard by a special antenna. The direction from which the signal comes is ferreted out and made known to the observer. He then has a workable bearing from his receiver to the radio station.

About 60 years ago, the first radio direction finding equipment appeared aboard. But it took World War I development to give it everyday practicality. Today its position is as the most common and popular of the mariner's electronic crew members. And there are good reasons. Equipment is minimal, use is worldwide and operation is simple. What's needed is a radio receiver equipped with a special aerial to measure the direction from the ship to the transmitting source of a radio signal. This puts RDF in the **point source** class of devices . . . the source of the radio waves is used to obtain a bearing.

This special aerial aboard points out the source of the incoming radio waves by using either one or two loops. When such a loop aerial is employed, an incoming signal will appear loudest in two parts of a 360° arc and weak-to-non-existent in two others. The single loop aerial (**Figure 125**) turns around in a full circle on a vertical axis, and so is called a **rotating loop**. The points of maximum signal are those in line with the plane of the loop . . . found when the loop is pointing at the station. The points of minimum or **null** are at right angles to the loop . . . found when the hole in the loop, like the hole in a doughnut, is facing towards the station. We are interested in the nulls because it is much easier to pick out the point of no signal than one of maximum strength. So it is the null direction that is used to indicate bearing. On the receiver is an azimuth circle graduated in degrees.

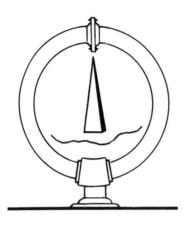

Figure 125

Figure 126

A pointer then indicates on that ring which way the "doughnut hole" is facing, and that is the bearing of the transmitter.

The other type is shown in **Figure 126**. It is the **Bellini-Tossi** or **fixed loop** antenna. In it two loops are crossed on one vertical axis so that the plane of one is fore-and-aft and the other is athwartships. The loops don't rotate at all; but in the receiver is a device called a **radio-goniometer**. It has a rotating coil to search out changes in electrical field received at the loops. The net result is the same as with a single rotating loop: two maximums, two nulls and a bearing circle-pointer affair to indicate direction.

If the device must be manually operated it is called a Radio Direction Finder **(RDF)**. If it can automatically seek out the bearing it is termed an **ADF** (for Automatic Direction Finder). And there are several ways to present the null. The most familiar is by sound . . . you listen for the point of least signal. Another is by readings on an electric meter or by observing the brightness of a neon tube. A late refinement uses a cathode ray tube on which is displayed a lighted sweep or pattern. When the bearing is taken, the pattern is so shaped and aligned that the proper direction is indicated. Another choice is between an instrument fixed in position and one that is portable. Not finished yet! We have still another basis for selection. The idea of the game is to measure a bearing or direction. This can be expressed as an angle from the ship's bow, in which case it is a **relative** bearing and the RDF bearing circle is like a pelorus. It's a simple matter to apply that angle to the ship's compass heading at the moment and get a compass bearing. A more complicated setup has a gyrocompass repeater installed at the RDF. Now the bearings measured are directly read as compass bearings without doing mathematical sums. Less sophisticated sets can come up with the same effect by having a movable ring or rotatable azimuth circle on the RDF. It can be set so the ship's compass course reads at the lubber's line. So long as the ship is on that course when a bearing is taken, the result will directly be the compass bearing of the radiobeacon. But a bit more of this later on.

Now we have to review some things about what the RDF hears. Marine radiobeacons are engineered, installed and maintained for most efficient operation. The selection of frequency and of location is governed by what is most suitable to the job: transmitter at the shoreline and not inland, sending a medium frequency signal best able to present an accurate beam. The marine radiobeacon band is from 190 to 400 kHz. Usually, though, marine RDF's can receive in other bands: entertainment stations in the 530 to 1600 kHz area and voice communications in the general department of 1600 to 4000 kHz. This is to give them multipurpose operation, and not to encourage use of other than marine beacons for radio bearings. Fundamental in radio is that low frequency waves produce more accurate bearings than high frequency waves. So the station to use is the one designed for the job: a marine radiobeacon. We'll be digging into this more as we go along.

Now to an important point: there are **two** nulls, and they are 180° apart. Reading the null yields two possible bearings; for when the "doughnut hole" is open to the North, it is also open to the South. In many cases this ambiguity produces little confusion since the navigator knows generally which direction he is from the transmitter. But at the most inopportune times the choice between a bearing and its reciprocal will become critical. So RDF's can be equipped with an additional aerial, the **sense antenna**. By this device the problem of ambiguity is resolved; it indicates which of the two nulls is the proper direction of the station.

Next comes some common sense applicable to portable units. RDF's have loud speakers so the navigator can hear the signal to identify the station. And usually they have a tuning meter to help find the null when the loop is rotated. Both speaker and meter have permanent magnets as part of their internals. So . . . be sure the unit is not placed too close to the ship's compass.

This intramural interference goes both ways. The rest of the vessel can bother the RDF. Metal masses on the boat, such as wiring, rigging, rails and masts, can

Photo by Benmar Div., Computer Equipment Corp.

Portable 3-band RDF with telescoping sense antenna.

mix up the aerial and cause bearing errors which change as the ship's heading changes. What the instrument detects is variation in strength of electromagnetic fields generated at the loops by incoming radio signals. So any other field near the loop can distort or interfere with accuracy. Many times such influences can be offset. But always they should be recognized and the error they produce recorded. Checking radio bearings against visual bearings to learn of these errors is standard procedure. Again, though, more of that later.

When using a portable unit, the mariner should know that the errors also change with location of the RDF on the vessel. What the rigging will do to the instrument when it is in the cabin might be quite a bit different from what will happen when it is moved to the cockpit. So it is only sensible to select the most convenient spot on the vessel for the portable RDF . . . and then to use it from that location on all occasions.

There are more factors involved, though, than just those aboard. Off the ship the nature of radio waves brings up a few more problems. The major ones are **night effect** and **land effect**.

Radio waves, like light rays, travel in more or less straight lines. If the receiver detects the direct beam it catches the **ground wave**. But there are other waves. The transmitter dispatches radio energy in many directions. Some of it finds its way to the ionosphere, an electrical layer above Earth. From there it bounces back towards the surface as **sky waves**. These rebounds produce inaccurate bearings. The error usually appears between one hour before sunset and one hour after sunrise . . . during the night. Hence the name for the error: **night effect**. But it can show up at other times. On lower frequencies the effect is lessened. That's another reason marine radiobeacons are clustered around the 300 kHz level. And the likelihood of the effect decreases as the distance to the station decreases . . . more reason to use the RDF as a short range instrument.

These sky waves rebound at an angle and so drop back to Earth some distance out from the transmitter. Different people give different minimum distances for sky wave problems. Estimates vary from 25 miles to 75 miles. Whatever the distance, what happens is something like this. Very close in, the sky wave has not

Automatic Direction Finder (ADF) with frequency
bands for marine beacon and broadcast stations.

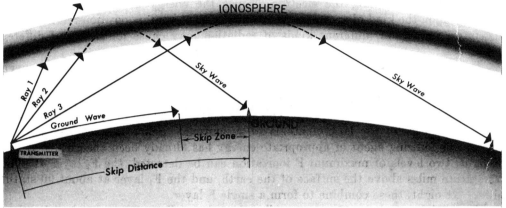

Courtesy of Bowditch/
American Practical Navigator

Figure 127

yet bounced down and so it has no influence. As the vessel's distance from the station increases, it approaches the minimum sky wave range. But even there the ground wave is much the stronger factor. However, someplace beyond 25+ miles the sky wave becomes significant. At first it mixes with the ground wave to cause irregular nulls and fading of the signal. As the distance increases, the sky wave muscles in and takes over, and the bearings become very doubtful. **Figure 127** describes ground wave and sky wave patterns. The cure for the problem should be evident: don't take radio bearings when sky waves are flying. Keeping the range under 50 miles seems to be a good idea.

Another major error is **land effect.** The reflecting and conducting properties of a radio wave over land are not the same as over water. So when it crosses a coastline, the wave can be expected to feel the impact of the difference. When the signal leaves land at an angle to the coastline, its direction will change. In turn, the bearing will be in error. A cure: avoid inland stations if possible. The regular marine radiobeacons are at the water's edge to keep the problem minimal. A caution: recognize the possibility of error in even a bearing of marine radiobeacon if the signal cuts across intervening land or skirts a coastline on its way to you. **Figure 128** sketches the idea.

It is generally found that inland stations behind high hills or mountains can be troublesome on both scores. The chances are you'll not only receive sky waves; and what ground waves do come will probably be bothered by land effect.

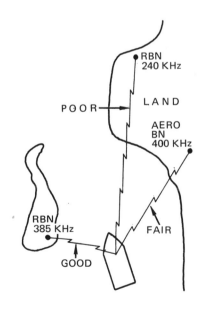

Figure 128

Radio Navigational Aids, HO 117, has this to say on the subject:

> "Night effect may be detected by a broadening of the arc of mini-
> mum signals and by a fluctuation in the strength of signals. It may
> also be indicated by difficulty in obtaining a minimum or by a rapid-
> ly shifting minimum. It is sometimes accompanied by an actual shift
> in the direction of the bearings. If it is essential to obtain a bearing
> when night effect is pronounced, several bearings should be taken
> over a short period of time and an average taken of them."

With reference to bearings on entertainment stations, *HO 117* says this:

> "**Program Broadcasting Stations**:
> "Before taking bearings on a station broadcasting entertainment pro-
> grams, a mariner should consider that its frequency may differ wide-
> ly from the frequency for which his set is calibrated, that published
> location of the station may be that of its studio and not that of its
> transmitting antenna, that if the station is synchronized with other
> stations it may be impossible to tell on which station the bearing was
> taken, and that as the majority of these stations are inland the coast-
> al refraction may be excessive."

These excerpts are very clear and need no further comment.

One more factor probably should be mentioned; but with the preface that it is seldom significant. This is the matter of the **conversion angle.** A radio wave will follow the shortest route over the surface of Earth from transmitter to receiver. And this is a great circle. But in nearly every case such a direction cannot be plotted simply by drawing a straight line on a Mercator chart, the one commonly used for navigation. Precision requires that the great circle bearing be converted to a Mercator bearing by applying a factor called the conversion angle. It can be computed; it can also be found in **Table 1** of *American Practical Navigator, HO 9.* We talk of it here to find out what it is, and also to note that we are seldom concerned with it. For when a vessel is within 50 miles of the transmitter, the conversion angle is seldom significant. The angle increases with distance and with latitude of observer and beacon. But it still remains a minor factor in practical work. Here is some evidence why. For a navigator in the Key West latitude and 50 miles due East or West of a radiobeacon, the correction is 0.2°. When he moves to the level of the St. Lawrence River, it becomes 0.5°. At Seward, Alaska, he would find it to be 0.8°. There are several other influences on RDF precision which outweigh this one. At least, though, the existence of the problem, and the fact of its minor importance for short range bearings should be known.

Now let's start down the line of some practical applications of RDF to piloting. First off, we'd better be sure of the instrument error. This is checked by compar-ing radio bearings with visual bearings taken of the same station at the same time. We've mentioned it already in Section VIII when speaking of the special calibra-tion stations found at some radiobeacon installations. Here's a recap. A simple method to check error is to approach a low power marker beacon . . . from one to four miles away. These beacons are on the air for 13½ seconds out of each 15 seconds and give good short range bearings. Slowly turn in a tight circle, alternately taking a visual bearing by compass and a radio bearing. A good idea would be to do this at 10° intervals. Note the bearings, then use arithmetic to make a deviation card for your RDF. The difference between each compass bearing (corrected for its error) and the radio bearing taken at the same time is the RDF error when on that heading. Let's look at an example sketched in **Figure 129**. There the vessel is on a compass course of due North or 000° and the beacon is seen visually directly over the bow. The RDF bearing is measured as 002°. This means there is a 2° error . . . the RDF over-reads 2° when a bearing is taken over the bow. That error would be marked as 2° plus. Then the vessel is turned to a course of 045°. The corrected compass bearing of the marker beacon is still 000°. But now the RDF bearing is 359°. This is a 1° error. The RDF under-reads 1° when a bearing is taken broad on the port bow; and such an error would be described as **1°-minus**. When the ship's head is 090° the compass bearing of the beacon is still the same

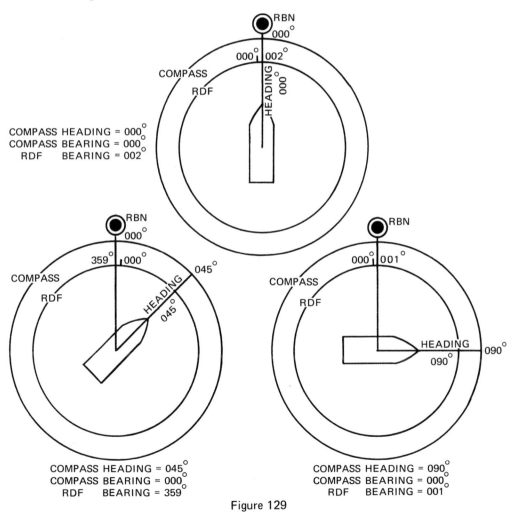

Figure 129

RADIO DIRECTION FINDERS   331

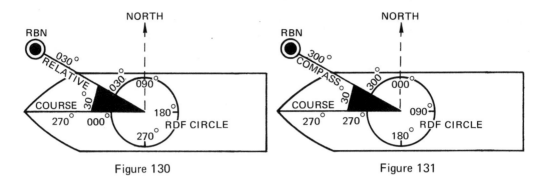

Figure 130   Figure 131

000°, but now the RDF bearing is 001°. It over-reads now by 1° when a bearing is taken on the port beam. Tabulating a schedule of such errors for the complete swing of the vessel is valuable practice. And using that kind of deviation table when taking radio bearings will produce much more satisfactory results.

Before we're up to our goniometers in plotting problems, let's take a quick glance at what's involved in converting a radio bearing measured relative to the ship's bow to one we would call a compass bearing. **Figure 130** shows the relative bearing setup. **Figure 131** shows the compass bearing idea. In the first case the navigator is on a course of 270° and takes a bearing of a radiobeacon as 30° off his starboard bow. He applies this to his compass head of 270° and finds the compass bearing to be 270° + 30° or 300°. The other sketch shows how things would look if his RDF was equipped with a rotatable azimuth ring. He would already have set the ring so that the compass heading of 270° was at the lubber's line of the RDF. Then he'd obtain the null as before and read the compass bearing directly off as 300°. Now let's go to work on some examples of RDF plotting.

The starting point is with the simplest: use of a single line of bearing or line of position. There can hardly be any great mystery here . . . take a radio bearing and apply whatever corrections are appropriate. Then find the radiobeacon on the chart and draw the bearing line. You're on that line somewhere. Often such a line is used for **homing** on a radiobeacon. **Figure 132** shows this one. There a vessel is bound for a harbor and is on course 270°. To start with, he finds that a radio-beacon at the harbor entrance is dead ahead. But as he proceeds he finds that the radio bearings are beginning to move to the right of his bow. Soon the beacon is

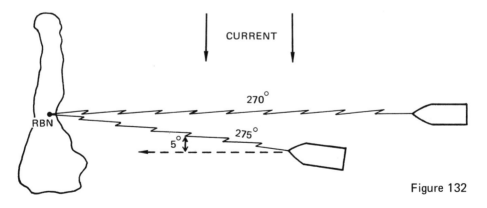

Figure 132

not bearing 270° over his bow, but is bearing 275° or 5° on his starboard bow. To go home to the beacon he changes course to 275° and thereafter keeps the beacon bearing directly over his bow. The opposite of homing is **tracking away**. Its drawback is that accuracy decreases as distance from the station increases. Homing doesn't have that problem, but it has come up with one of its own. Every once in a while a mariner forgets that the beacon he is going towards is on land . . . and he single-mindedly homes right on to the rocks.

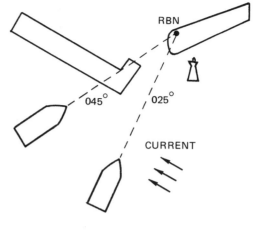

Figure 133

A variation on the homing business is possible when the track between two points is graced with a radiobeacon at **each** end. Keeping the beacon at departure lined up over the stern and the beacon at the destination in line over the bow, is a positive way to stay on the straight-and-narrow.

The use of a single line of bearing involves a few dangers to be recognized. **Figure 133** shows one that is very common. The destination is a harbor entrance with a marker radiobeacon on one breakwater. The navigator wants to arrive at the bell buoy at the entrance and decides to use the marker beacon as a reference for homing. From his DR position he draws a course line passing near the buoy and on to the beacon . . . and notes it to be 025°. It seems to pass clear of other dangers, so he elects it as his course for going in. He decides that an easy way to do things is to home on the radiobeacon. But a current nudges him to the northwest. The radio bearing begins to change and he, with a one-track homing mind, begins to follow it. First he changes course to 030°, then to 035°, then to 045°. By this time, though, the vessel is inside the arm of the other breakwater and is heading for a grounding. There is only one cure for this trap: when the course for homing begins to change materially, a new course should be laid out on the chart to make sure it passes clear of dangers.

Many breakwatered harbors have radiobeacons so placed as to invite calamity. In **Figure 134** the entrance beacon is placed on the end of a groin inside a protective island-breakwater. Boats **A**, **B** and **C** are all homing on the radiobeacon . . . and all are heading for trouble. Here again plotting the compass course steered in homing would spotlight that the breakwater lay across the track.

A combination of radio bearings taken at the same time can produce several lines of position and a position fix. Radiobeacons are not as commonplace as visual landmarks, so the selection of ideal bearings is not always possible. But when there is a choice, stations off course to left and right are better than those over the bow or over the stern. And, in common with all lines of bearings, radio bearings should be spread far enough apart so their intersection will be clean cut.

Figure 135 is a three-beacon problem. There a vessel is homeward bound on a

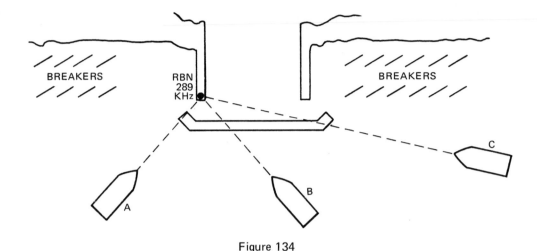

Figure 134

course of 270°. In order to fix position, the navigator takes three radio bearings in quick succession. Beacon **A** bears 30° on the starboard bow, Beacon **B** bears 140° to starboard. The third beacons, C, bears 305° relative, or 55° on the port bow. All this amounts to compass bearings of 300° on A, 050° on B and 215° on C. The three LOP's are drawn on the chart and form a small triangle, the familiar navigator's cocked hat. This is to be expected. There are too many reasons why the radio bearings should not cross exactly: human error in getting the null, atmospheric or terrain influences on the radio waves, movement of the ship is yawing, pitching and rolling . . . and then the added fact that any radio direction finder bearing is seldom better than 2° plus or minus under ideal conditions. In any case, our mariner allows for all this and then picks the center of the triangle as his position. He knows he'll never get to his destination the way he's going, so a course change to 285° is in order.

The convenience of sequenced coastal radiobeacons as described in Section VIII's chapter on Aids to Navigation is apparent here. The navigator tunes the

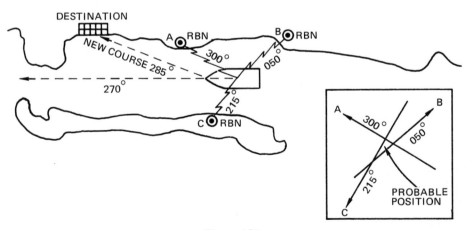

Figure 135

receiver to the common frequency for all the members of the beacon family. Then he measures the bearing of each as the family begins to sound off in sequence a minute apart in their round-robin pattern. Within a few minutes he can get a fix on several beacons. And since the family keeps up the transmission cycle, he can get other fixes as frequently as he wishes.

These uses of the RDF are parallel to procedures suitable to visual bearings: single line of position and intersection of several lines of position. The homing routine is so evident in visual navigation that we might not even recognize it by name. If a lighthouse is at the harbor entrance, then in order to enter the harbor you steer for the lighthouse. Of course, the radio problem with homing doesn't exist in the visual pattern. If you can see the lighthouse you can see the breakwater lying in front of it. Another page out of the visual book which can be applied to RDF is the consecutive bearing procedure. Each of the five special cases discussed far back in Section III's chapter on Piloting is here applicable. Double the radio angle on the bow, combine a 30° bearing with a 60° bearing, use the 45°-90° combination or the 22½°-45° team. How you take the bearing, and on what, is immaterial to the basic mathematics involved.

Here's a variation of a visual method that can be invaluable when using the RDF. **Figure 136** shows your vessel going due North along a rocky coast. She is in fog and wants to use radio bearings of a beacon on an island far ahead. Before you get to the beacon, you are to turn left to a course of 270° in order to enter harbor. How to go about it is the

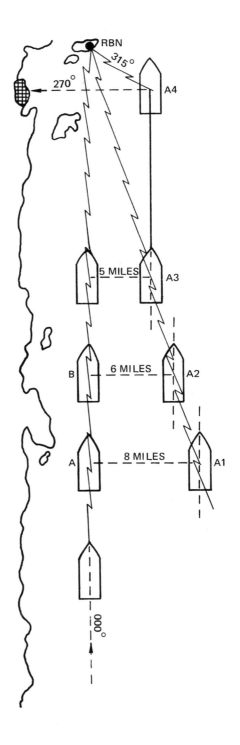

Figure 136

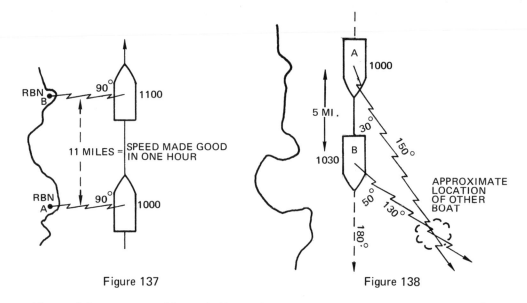

Figure 137   Figure 138

problem of the moment. First of all, a radio bearing is taken, found to be 000° by compass, and then is plotted. This places the radiobeacon dead ahead on your track. Then you make a hard right turn, settle on a new course of 090° and run for a given estimated distance. Let's say the ship turned to 090° when she was at point **A** and then ran on that course for an estimated five miles. At that time she turns hard left and goes back to her original course of 000°. Immediately another radio bearing is taken. It's found to be 345° by compass, and is plotted on the chart. Now you have two lines of position. One was the original radio bearing of 000° taken at **A**, before the course change to the right. The other is the 345° radio bearing just taken. You've got the data before you to make a good estimate of where you are. Set the dividers to the distance estimated as run between the two 000° track lines. Here, it is five miles. Move the dividers along between the two lines of bearing until the difference between them is that five miles. This won't be at A_1 because the LOP's there are eight miles apart. It won't be at A_2 because there the lines are six miles apart. The probable location is at A_3 where the LOP's are five miles apart. Accept that spot as a fair plot of where you are at the time of the second radio bearing. Now draw the 000° course line from there and start following it. Next, though, is to prepare for the course change to 270° to make your destination. Draw a 270° line from your new course line to the harbor entrance. The intersection of your course and that line is the point at which you will change course. How do you know when you get there? Find out what the beacon should bear from that point. Draw a line from there to the radiobeacon and measure the bearing. Our sketch shows it as 315° or 45° on the port bow. When the radio bearing is that much, it is time to come left to the final approach course of 270°. This sort of piloting when done cautiously is the stuff of which safe navigation is made.

A speed check by RDF is a simple routine. Two radiobeacons can often be used as if they were the pylons of a measured mile on the beach. **Figure 137** shows a ship northbound with Beacons **A** and **B** 11 miles apart on the coast to the left. At

1000 **A** is abeam to port. At 1100 Beacon **B** is abeam to port. If the ship has kept a steady course for the hour, she can reasonably say her speed was 11 knots.

What about bearings taken of other vessels? They fall into the category of the least reliable that can be taken because, if the transmission is by radiotelephone, the frequency is too high for precision. But often such bearings are desirable . . . and sometimes they are absolutely imperative. **Figure 138** shows a desirable one. Fisherman **A** by electronic eavesdropping at 1000 learns that Fisherman **B** is working a large school of fish. **A**'s course is 180° and the bearing of **B** by RDF is measured as 30° on the port bow. This puts **B** on a compass bearing of 150°. **A** plots that bearing from his 1000 DR position. He knows **B** is in that direction but doesn't know how far out. So **A** continues on 180° and at 1030 hears **B** again. Quickly a second bearing is taken. This time it is 50° on the port bow, or 130°. **A** draws that bearing in from his 1030 DR. The intersection of the two lines of bearing reveal **B** and the school of fish. This plot for party-crashing will only work if **B** and the fish don't move in the meantime.

Instead of being an interloper, **A** might well be a rescuer. Instead of hearing **B** brag about his catch, what **A** might have heard was his distress call. And in his message **B** might not have given any clue to his position. With much more at stake than a netful of fish, **A** could follow the same routine and gain an idea of **B**'s location. In fact. provision for radio bearings is provided for in the *SOS* call of radiotelegraphy. Large ships will transmit such calls on 500 kHz, a low enough frequency for good radio bearings. And part of the coded message is a special signal, two 10-second dashes, to allow a listening station to take a bearing by RDF.

We're at the end of our survey of the RDF. What it does and generally how it works has been blocked out. When a mariner thinks of putting electronic gear aboard, he should seriously consider the RDF. By even the most critical view it is well worthwhile. It is neither a magic wand nor a divining rod, but is a well-seasoned veteran of decades of operation. Possibly every use to which it can be put has already been tried by someone someplace. To exploit its possibilities requires practice, skill, and understanding its capabilities. Then add the ingredient of imagination and some of its many uses will come to mind. Operated carefully and with good sea sense, it can become one of the most useful aids aboard.

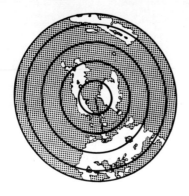

44/Marine Electronics
Consolan

The second layer of a box of candy always seems to be an extra pleasure. We have the same feeling of Christmas coming early whenever we discover an unexpected advantage. In that category for the owner of a radio direction finder would seem to be Consolan.

Essentially it is a long range radio direction finding system. Its principle is distinct from the RDF and its range is far greater. In fact, it takes up where RDF leaves off; for Consolan is unusable within 50 miles of a transmitting station, but will give bearings beyond a range of 1400 miles. What makes Consolan attractive is that no special receiving equipment is needed. Any radio receiver capable of handling low and medium frequency signals and fitted with a Beat Frequency Oscillator (**BFO**) will do. This last item is a device to make unmodulated continuous wave transmissions audible. In short, you need a set to receive the dots and dashes of radiotelegraphy . . . an RDF or an AM receiver equipped with the BFO.

First, to its history. The Germans developed a direction finding system called **Elektra**. In time they modified it to another they called **Sonne**. From it the British evolved **Consol**. And our version of that is **Consolan**. Since these last two are essentially the same, and since there is a Consolan station near San Francisco on the West Coast, we'll concentrate on the Consolan setup. (An East Coast station at Nantucket was decommissioned in 1971.) The story on Consolan is applicable, with very minor changes, to Consol. Aircraft find it useful; in fact, the maintenance of the stations is primarily for their convenience. It is really not a precise method; but then often the aircraft can tolerate less precision than can a surface vessel. A plane traveling at 600 miles per hour can rectify a 20-mile error in two minutes, while a 10-knot surface vessel would need two hours!

At the outset we should understand that the system has shortcomings. Some people even feel the game isn't worth the candle. But the fact is that it is here, a bonus package to the owner of an RDF. So in proportion grows the requirement that we study it closely to see how it works and where it's weak. Then each can accept or reject, use or disregard, as he judges best.

Consolan doesn't work like normal direction finding. You don't find the bearing of a transmitter by listening for the null. Instead, you listen to a sequence of dots and dashes, count their number and then, by table or by special chart, find your bearing from the station.

Technically it comes under the heading of hyperbolic systems. In these, use is made of patterns of radio transmission delineated in hyperbolae. Don't let the terms bother you . . . they aren't at all necessary to efficient use of Consolan. But there's a certain savor to "hyperbolae" not to be cast aside. The very use of it makes one sound expert. In any case, a hyperbola is a curve on which the distance from any point to one focus outside the curve is the same as that from the same point to another focus. Loran uses these curves as lines of position and does not give direction. Consolan used them as lines of bearing.

A Consolan transmission station has several aerials placed in a straight line. From them is sent out a radio signal in all directions. This full circle of radiation is divided into arcs or sectors. In every other one, dots are heard; in the alternate sectors are dashes. And on the line between sectors, the signals merge into a continuous tone called the **equisignal**. This circle of radiation is not stationary; it gradually changes to the right on one side of the line through the aerials and to the left on the other. So a receiver will hear alternately dots and then an equisignal and then dashes as the sectors gradually sweep by.

Figure 139 is reproduced from *HO 117, Radio Navigational Aids,* and shows a sample transmission pattern. There is a total of 26 sectors, averaging about 12° in width. But four of them, at the ends of the line of towers, are unused as ambiguous.

The Southern California coast and the Great Lakes are poor locations Consolan-wise. They are within unused sectors at the end of a line projected through the towers for the stations. Consolan is of questionable value in California, except for the coastline from about Big Sur to Santa Cruz, and then unusable until north

POLAR DIAGRAM OF CONSOLAN PATTERN

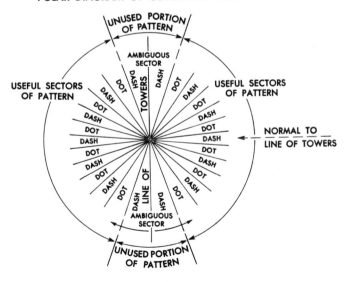

Figure 139

of Eureka. Offshore, though, it is in its element. The usable portion of the full pattern is 140° on each side of the towers. **Plate F** shows a portion of the San Francisco pattern. Note the coastal area falling within the unused sectors. Note also the unusable 50-mile radius from the station. The usable portion of the full pattern is 140° on each side of the towers.

Imagine that the pattern in **Figure 139** is steadily turning so that no point covered by the signals remains in the same sector. If nothing further were added, an observer would hear dots as a dot sector passed over. Then for an instant he would hear the equisignal when the dots and the oncoming dashes merge. Next a new sector would begin to spray dashes over his location. This would continue . . . dot sectors and dashes taking turns covering his area. But something else is added. Periodically, as a child does when he hears "Simon says Stop," the pattern freezes. The dots and dashes and the rotation stop. There are short periods of silence and station identification. Then the pattern starts again where it left off. To use Consolan an observer tunes in and listens for a silent period. Immediately the first signal follows, he begins to count the dots or dashes until he hears an equisignal. Then he counts the dashes or dots after it until the next silent period comes. His count of dots and dashes is his key to special tables or a special chart. From them he learns his bearing from the station.

A complete cycle is 75 seconds long, broken down this way:

> 00.0s to 07.5s . . . . . Call letters of station
> 07.5s to 10.0s . . . . . Silence
> 10.0s to 40.0s . . . . . 60 dots (or dashes)
> and 60 dashes (or dots)
> with an equisignal between
> 40.0s to 42.5s . . . . . Silence
> 42.5s to 72.5s . . . . . Another dot-dash sequence
> and an equisignal
> 72.5s to 75.0s . . . . . Silence

The idea is ingenious and quite simple, once you get the general idea. During the full 75-second cycle there is an identification signal, three silent periods and two dot-dash sequences or "keying cycles." The identification and silent periods are heard at the same time and in the same way by all receivers, regardless of location. The keying cycles will be heard at the same times by all receivers, but they won't be heard in the same way. For example, one observer might start listening when the sweep of a dot sector has almost passed over his position. Counting from a silent period he might hear only three dots before an equisignal and then more than 50 dashes before he meets another silent period. The relation of three dots to 50+ dashes is his factor which will give him a bearing. Another observer in a different location might be under a dash sector at first. His count after the same silent period might be 30 dashes to the equisignal and then 20+ dots between equisignal and the next silent period. His factor is 30 dashes and 20+ dots.

Let's use a "For Instance" and see how it works for the San Francisco station.

Actually, the transmitter isn't in San Francisco . . . it is near Petaluma, about 30 miles north. The call is SFI and it transmits continuously on 192 kHz using the same 75-second cycle we've discussed. *HO 117b* contains its bearing tables. *HO VC-70-4* is an alternative means to convert dot-dash counts to bearings. This is a special Air-Surface Consolan Navigation Chart covering about half the Pacific Ocean . . . and consequently of very small scale. **Plate F** is a reproduction of part of it. Radiating out from the station location are alternate dotted and dashed lines. Each bears a number: 15, 30, 45 or 60. And each identifies a line of bearing when the signal count before an equisignal is 15 dots or dashes, 30 dots or dashes, 45 or 60. By counting and then looking at the chart, a line of bearing can be picked directly. But there is not a line for every count . . . only at 15-signal intervals. So interpolation is necessary to find bearings for intervening combinations of dots and dashes. *HO VC-70-11* was the counterpart chart for the Nantucket station on the US East Coast.

By contrast the tables have bearings for each count from 0 to 60. You will find those for SFI shown at the end of this chapter. In working our example here, we'll use the tables, and not the chart. However, use **Plate F** to gain an idea of its use.

Here, then, is the example. Three ships are simultaneously listening to SFI. The DR position of each is shown on **Plate F**. **Ship A** is 50 miles west of Point Conception, far enough offshore to be clear of the unused sectors. **Ship B** is 50 miles west of Monterey, also in the clear. **Ship C** is 50 miles west of Point Reyes. They each tune to 192 kHz and wait for the call letters to be sent so that identification is certain. Each one hears

... ..⁻. ..

S   F   I

sent slowly enough for non-telegraphers to distinguish. Then comes a silent period and they brace themselves to start counting. At the same instant the silent period is broken for all; but what each thereafter hears is different.

Ship A starts hearing dots. He counts three of them and then hears the continuous equisignal. Next, dashes start, and he counts 51 until the silence period comes. So his count is three dots and 51 dashes.

Ship B first hears dashes, 23 of them. Then comes the equisignal. Next he hears 29 dots before the Silence. His count is 23 dashes followed by 29 dots.

Ship C hears the same sequence as **A**: three dots, then the equisignal, then 51 dashes. His count is three dots and 51 dashes.

The equisignal is not a separate transmission. It is a continuous tone created by the merger of dots and dashes at a sector division. So in making an equisignal, some dots and some dashes are lost. In the above cases, the total of the signals heard (dots and dashes) by **A**—and also by **C**—was 54. Six must have been lost in creating the equisignal, for each should have heard 60 signals during the interval from a Silence through an equisignal to the next Silence. Each now divides the missing signals equally between dots and dashes: he assumes that three of them were dots and three were dashes. In other words, each now corrects his count by adding three dots to his dot count and three dashes to his dash count in order to have a total of 60 signals. The corrected count for **A**, and also for **C**, is six dots (3+3) and 54 dashes (51+3).

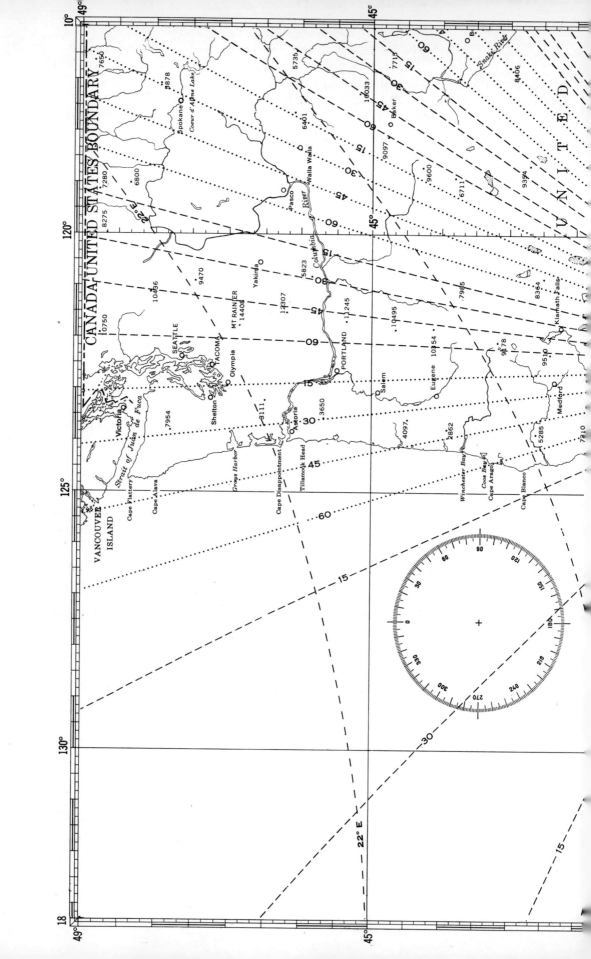

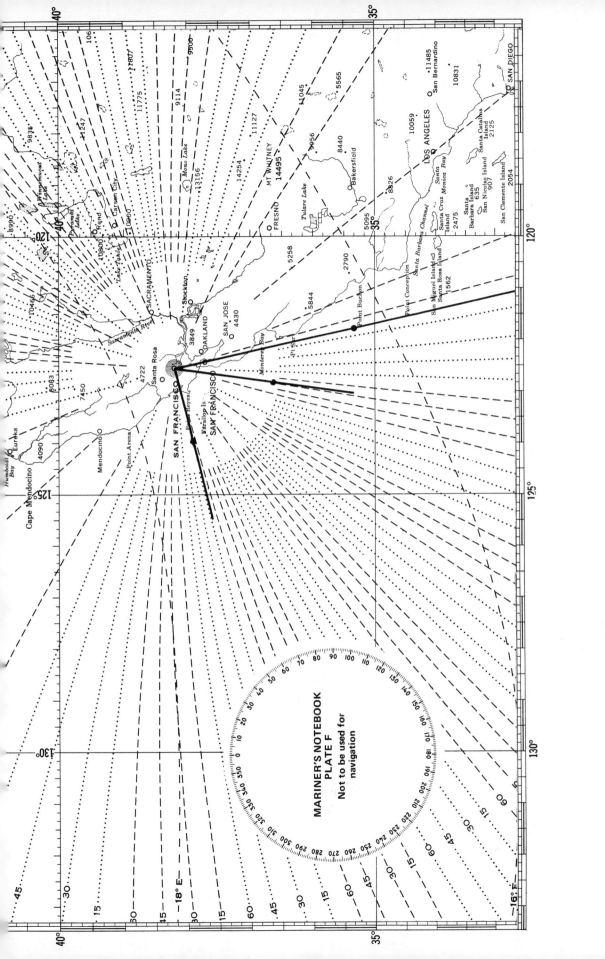

MARINER'S NOTEBOOK
PLATE F
Not to be used for
navigation

Since **B** heard only 52 signals, he missed eight. So four dashes and four dots are added. His count is 27 dashes (23+4) and 33 dots (29+4).

Next step! Each is really only interested in the correct count of what signal he heard first. **A** started off with dots, so his is a dot count of six. The same is true for **C**. **B** first heard dashes, so the count he uses is 27 dashes.

Now each is ready for the tables. Since **A** and **C** have dot counts, they will use the table listing "Count of Dots." **B** uses the "Count of Dashes." **A** enters with six dots and finds a choice of 12 different bearings from the station to him. Consolan won't tell him which is correct . . . it only says he is on one of the 12. But DR will nearly always be close enough to identify which is correct. In this case, it is 166.8°; for any other of the 12 is obviously inapplicable. The only possible alternative is 195.8°, and that would place him far offshore . . . at least 100 miles to the west of his DR.

B enters with 27 dashes. For his DR the only logical bearing is 188.1°. The closest alternative, 210.2°, would show he was about 50 miles more to the west.

C goes in, as did **A**, with six dots. But of course, for his DR, the bearing selected by **A** is inapplicable. **C** would select as the proper bearing, 255.5°. It is to be noted, however, that he has two alternative bearings which would place him in the same neighborhood: 235.7° might have him about 25 miles to the south of his DR; and 279.4° might place him about 25 miles to the north. This should emphasize the importance of a good DR position in Consolan Sailing . . . and also spotlight a drawback.

But one further step is necessary before these bearings can be plotted on a Mercator chart. Radio signals follow the Great Circle, the shortest distance between transmitter and receiver. Before being drawn on a Mercator chart, a radio bearing must be converted to a Mercator bearing. You will also find at the end of this chapter a table for that purpose, made up for the San Francisco Consolan Station. Any radio bearing conversion table, such as **Table 1** of *HO 9 (American Practical Navigator)* can be used.

Let's follow through and see how to use the Consolan Conversion Table. We enter with the DR latitude of the observer and with the difference of longitude (DLo) between him and the station.

A's DR is 34°30'N and 121°30'W. The station is at 38°12'N and 122°34'W. So the DLo between him and the SFI station is about 1°. He enters the conversion table in the column for latitude closest to his (35°) and goes down the left margin to the DLo closest to 1°. He must interpolate. 0° DLo has no correction; 5° DLo has 1.4° correction. So 1° DLo has one-fifth of 1.4°, or 0.3° correction. This is to be added to the true bearing since he is east of the station (see the note at the bottom of the table). He adds 0.3° to the true bearing of 166.8°. The result is the bearing he is to plot on a Mercator chart . . . 167.1°.

B's DR is 36°40'N and 122°50'W. The DLo between him and the station is only 16', or 0.3°. He enters the conversion table for 35°, the column nearest his latitude, and then interpolates between the tabulated values to come up with a correction of about 0.1°. He is west of the station, so he subtracts this from the true bearing of 188.1°. The result is 188°, the bearing to plot.

C has a DR of 37°55'N and 124°05'W. The DLo is 1°31'. He enters the table in

Coast Guard cutter battling rough water.   Photo by NOAA

the 40° latitude column and interpolates to a correction of 0.5°. Again it is subtracted because he is west of the station. From the true bearing of 255.5° he subtracts 0.5° and finds 255°, the bearing to plot.

Now each can take his chart and find the location of the station . . . it is exactly 38°12'13"N and 122°34'08"W. From that point on the chart he lays off the bearing converted as above. He is on that line of bearing. See **Plate F** for the results: **A**'s bearing is 167.1°; **B**'s is 188°; and **C** uses 255°. Note particularly that the Consolan tables give the bearings from the station to the observer, and not the reverse. He draws the line of bearing **from the station**, and not towards it.

That is Consolan . . . and this is a very practical question: is it useful? Probably not for pleasure mariners on the California Coast. In making a Honolulu passage or perhaps an offshore voyage, it might have a purpose. But for inshore work, the mariner should be cautious. Interesting to observe in any consideration of Consolan, is the effectiveness of its parent, Consol. The British *Notice to Mariners,* made this comment in discussing Consol:

> "Although the system is useful for Ocean Navigation, Consol gives bearings which are insufficiently accurate for landfall or coastal navigation, and mariners are warned that these bearings cannot be relied on with safety when closing danger."

And our *HO 117a* has said this about Consol:

> "While Consol bearings are useful in ocean navigation, they are not sufficiently accurate for making landfalls. Bearings should be used with increasing caution as the proximity of possible danger becomes greater."

What goes for Consol would seem equally applicable to Consolan.

Accuracy is best in sectors normal (at right angles) to the baseline through the towers, and is least in the wider sectors towards the ends. But a glance at **Plate F** shows that only a portion of the Pacific Coast falls in the favorable sectors. The balance is either in unused sectors, or in wide questionable ones. Quite apparent is that Consolan SFI was installed for the use of aircraft flying east-west, and not for coastal navigators.

HO 117 says the general accuracy of Consolan bearings is 0.3° average by day and 0.7° by night. The variance comes from the same night effect problem met in RDF, and common to radio systems generally. As we've seen before, short range RDF bearings, particularly at ranges less than 50 miles, are not too bothered by night effect. But Consolan bearings, particularly at ranges of 300 to 700 miles, can have errors of 2½° or more. Recall that in a 60-mile distance, a 1° error creates a one-mile displacement. In 600 miles, a 1° error could put your bearing off 10 miles. So even the Pacific Northwest, in relatively favorable sectors of the SFI pattern, can place only limited confidence in Consolan. For a night effect error of 2½° could place a position 25 miles or more in error. Aircraft might find this tolerable; but in surface navigation it is of no more use than a rough DR position.

Even so, Consolan has its place in your repertoire of navigation arts. For there can be occasions when such a bearing, coupled with another line of position, would be of value. Half the art of any method is recognizing the shortcomings. Know what it can't do as well as what it can. Consolan is not for coastal navigation nor for use close to the station. But at least the price is right. And as a spot-check it might serve a purpose.

38°12'13"N., 122°34'08"W.

7600. San Francisco (SFI).
FREQ.: 192 kc.
CHARACTERISTIC SIGNAL: 7.5 seconds call signal, 2.5 seconds silent, 30 seconds keying cycle (See Fig. 1).
HOURS OF TRANSMISSION: Continuous.

7600.1.   San Francisco Consolan Station—Conversion Table

Difference of longitude	Latitude of Observer																		
	0°	5°	10°	15°	20°	25°	30°	35°	40°	45°	50°	55°	60°	65°	70°	75°	80°	85°	90°
0°	0°.0	0°.0	0°.0	0°.0	0°.0	0°.0	0°.0	0°.0	0°.0	0°.0	0°.0	0°.0	0°.0	0°.0	0°.0	0°.0	0°.0	0°.0	0°.0
5°	1°.1	1°.2	1°.2	1°.3	1°.3	1°.4	1°.4	1°.4	1°.7	1°.7	1°.7	1°.7	1°.7	1°.7	1°.7	1°.7	1°.6	1°.5	0°.0
10°	2°.3	2°.4	2°.5	2°.6	2°.7	2°.7	2°.8	3°.0	3°.2	3°.3	3°.4	3°.4	3°.4	3°.4	3°.4	3°.4	3°.2	3°.0	0°.0
15°	3°.4	3°.6	3°.7	3°.9	4°.0	4°.2	4°.3	4°.5	4°.7	4°.9	5°.0	5°.1	5°.1	5°.1	5°.1	5°.0	4°.9	4°.4	0°.0
20°	4°.6	4°.8	5°.0	5°.2	5°.4	5°.6	5°.8	6°.1	6°.3	6°.5	6°.7	6°.7	6°.8	6°.8	6°.8	6°.7	6°.5	5°.9	0°.0
25°	5°.7	6°.0	6°.3	6°.6	6°.9	7°.1	7°.4	7°.6	7°.9	8°.1	8°.3	8°.4	8°.5	8°.6	8°.5	8°.4	8°.1	7°.4	0°.0
30°	6°.9	7°.3	7°.6	8°.0	8°.3	8°.6	8°.9	9°.2	9°.5	9°.8	10°.0	10°.1	10°.3	10°.3	10°.3	10°.1	9°.7	8°.9	0°.0
35°	8°.2	8°.6	9°.0	9°.4	9°.8	10°.1	10°.5	10°.8	11°.1	11°.4	11°.7	11°.9	12°.0	12°.0	12°.0	11°.8	11°.4	10°.4	0°.0
40°	9°.4	9°.9	10°.4	10°.8	11°.3	11°.7	12°.1	12°.5	12°.8	13°.1	13°.4	13°.6	13°.7	13°.8	13°.8	13°.5	13°.0	11°.9	0°.0
45°	10°.7	11°.3	11°.8	12°.3	12°.8	13°.3	13°.7	14°.1	14°.5	14°.8	15°.1	15°.4	15°.5	15°.6	15°.5	15°.3	14°.7	13°.3	0°.0
50°	12°.0	12°.7	13°.3	13°.8	14°.4	14°.9	15°.4	15°.8	16°.2	16°.6	16°.9	17°.2	17°.3	17°.4	17°.3	17°.0	16°.3	14°.8	0°.0
55°	13°.4	14°.1	14°.8	15°.4	16°.0	16°.5	17°.1	17°.6	18°.0	18°.4	18°.7	19°.0	19°.2	19°.2	19°.1	18°.8	18°.0	16°.3	0°.0
60°	14°.8	15°.6	16°.3	17°.0	17°.6	18°.3	18°.8	19°.3	19°.8	20°.2	20°.6	20°.9	21°.0	21°.1	20°.9	20°.5	19°.7	17°.8	0°.0
65°	16°.3	17°.1	17°.9	18°.7	19°.4	20°.0	20°.6	21°.2	21°.7	22°.1	22°.5	22°.8	22°.9	22°.9	22°.8	22°.3	21°.4	19°.3	0°.0
70°	17°.8	18°.7	19°.6	20°.4	21°.1	21°.8	22°.5	23°.1	23°.6	24°.0	24°.4	24°.7	24°.9	24°.9	24°.6	24°.1	23°.0	20°.8	0°.0
75°	19°.3	20°.4	21°.3	22°.2	23°.0	23°.7	24°.4	25°.0	25°.6	26°.0	26°.4	26°.7	26°.8	26°.8	26°.5	25°.9	24°.7	22°.3	0°.0
80°	21°.0	22°.1	23°.1	24°.0	24°.9	25°.7	26°.4	27°.1	27°.6	28°.1	28°.5	28°.7	28°.8	28°.8	28°.5	27°.8	26°.5	23°.8	0°.0
85°	22°.7	23°.9	25°.0	26°.0	26°.9	27°.7	28°.5	29°.2	29°.7	30°.2	30°.6	30°.8	30°.8	30°.8	30°.4	29°.6	28°.2	25°.3	0°.0
90°	24°.6	25°.8	27°.0	28°.1	29°.0	29°.9	30°.7	31°.3	31°.9	32°.4	32°.8	33°.0	33°.0	32°.8	32°.4	31°.5	29°.9	26°.8	0°.0

Corrections to be *added* to the true bearing to obtain the Mercator bearing when the observer is to the East of the station and *subtracted* when the observer is to the West of the station.

7600.2.   San Francisco Consolan Station–Dot Sectors

Count of Dots	True bearing from station											
0	2. 1	25. 6	45. 3	64. 4	85. 3	115. 1	164. 8	194. 7	215. 6	234. 7	254. 4	277. 9
1	1. 9	25. 5	45. 1	64. 3	85. 1	114. 7	165. 2	194. 9	215. 7	234. 9	254. 6	278. 2
2	1. 7	25. 3	44. 9	64. 1	85. 0	114. 4	165. 5	195. 0	215. 9	235. 1	254. 8	278. 4
3	1. 4	25. 1	44. 8	64. 0	84. 8	114. 1	165. 8	195. 2	216. 1	235. 3	255. 0	278. 7
4	1. 2	24. 9	44. 7	63. 8	84. 6	113. 7	166. 2	195. 4	216. 2	235. 4	255. 2	278. 9
5	0. 9	24. 8	44. 5	63. 7	84. 5	113. 4	166. 5	195. 6	216. 3	235. 6	255. 4	279. 2
6	0. 7	24. 6	44. 4	63. 5	84. 4	113. 1	166. 8	195. 8	216. 5	235. 7	255. 5	279. 4
7	0. 5	24. 4	44. 2	63. 3	84. 2	112. 7	167. 2	196. 0	216. 7	235. 9	255. 7	279. 7
8	0. 3	24. 2	44. 1	63. 2	84. 0	112. 4	167. 5	196. 2	216. 9	236. 1	255. 9	279.9
9	0. 1	24. 0	43.9	63. 0	83. 8	112. 1	167. 8	196. 5	217. 0	236. 2	256. 1	280. 2
10	359.8	23. 8	43.7	62. 8	83. 6	111. 8	168. 2	196. 6	217. 1	236. 4	256. 2	280. 4
11	359.5	23. 7	43. 5	62. 6	83. 4	111. 4	168. 5	196. 8	217. 3	236. 5	256. 4	280. 7
12	359.2	23. 5	43. 3	62. 4	83. 2	111. 1	168. 8	197. 0	217. 5	236. 7	256. 6	280. 9
13	358.9	23. 3	43. 1	62. 2	83. 0	110. 7	169. 2	197. 2	217. 7	236. 9	256. 7	281. 2
14	358.6	23. 1	42. 9	62. 1	82. 8	110. 4	169. 5	197. 4	217. 9	237. 0	256. 9	281. 4
15	358.3	22. 9	42. 7	61. 9	82. 6	110. 1	169. 8	197. 6	218. 0	237. 2	257. 1	281. 7
16	358.0	22. 8	42. 6	61. 7	82. 4	109. 8	170. 2	197. 8	218. 1	237. 3	257. 3	281. 9
17	357. 8	22. 6	42. 4	61. 5	82. 2	109. 4	170. 5	198. 0	218. 3	237. 5	257. 5	282. 2
18	357. 6	22. 4	42. 3	61. 4	82. 0	109. 1	170. 8	198. 2	218. 5	237. 7	257. 6	282. 4
19	357. 3	22. 2	42. 2	61. 2	81. 8	108. 8	171. 2	198. 4	218. 7	237. 8	257. 8	282. 7
20	357. 1	22. 1	42. 1	61. 1	81. 6	108. 6	171. 5	198. 5	218. 9	238. 0	258. 0	283. 0
21	356. 9	21. 9	41. 9	60.19	81. 4	108. 2	171. 8	198. 7	219. 0	238. 1	258. 2	283. 4
22	356. 6	21. 7	41. 7	60. 7	81. 2	107. 9	172. 2	198. 9	219. 1	238. 3	258. 4	283. 6
23	356. 3	21. 5	41. 5	60. 6	81. 0	107. 5	172. 5	199. 1	219. 3	238. 5	258. 5	283. 8
24	356. 1	21. 3	41. 4	60. 4	80. 8	107. 2	172. 8	199. 2	219. 5	238. 7	258. 6	284. 0
25	355. 8	21. 1	41. 2	60. 3	80. 6	106. 9	173. 2	199. 4	219. 7	238. 8	258. 9	284. 3
26	355. 5	20. 9	41. 1	60. 1	80. 4	106. 5	173. 5	199. 6	219. 9	239. 0	259. 1	284. 5
27	355. 3	20. 8	40. 9	59. 9	80. 2	106. 2	173. 8	199. 8	220. 0	239. 1	259. 3	284. 7
28	355. 1	20. 6	40. 8	59. 8	80. 0	106. 0	174. 1	200. 0	220. 2	239. 3	259. 4	285. 0
29	354. 8	20. 4	40. 6	59. 6	79. 8	105. 7	174. 4	200. 2	220. 4	239. 4	259. 6	285. 2
30	354. 6	20. 3	40. 5	59. 5	79. 7	105. 4	174. 6	200. 3	220. 5	239. 5	259. 7	285. 4
31	354. 3	20. 2	40. 4	59. 4	79. 5	105. 1	174. 9	200. 5	220. 6	239. 6	259. 9	285. 8
32	354. 0	20. 0	40. 2	59. 2	79. 3	104. 9	175. 1	200. 6	220. 8	239. 8	260. 1	286. 1
33	353. 7	19. 8	40. 0	59. 1	79. 2	104. 6	175. 4	200. 8	220. 9	239. 9	260.3	286. 5
34	353. 4	19. 6	39. 9	59. 0	79. 1	104. 4	175. 6	201. 0	221. 1	240. 1	260. 5	286. 9
35	353. 1	19. 4	39. 7	58. 8	78. 9	104. 1	175. 9	201.3	221. 3	240. 3	260. 7	287. 2
36	352. 8	19. 2	39. 5	58. 6	78. 7	103. 9	176. 1	201. 4	221. 5	240. 5	260. 9	287. 6
37	352. 5	19. 1	39. 4	58. 5	78. 5	103. 7	176. 4	201. 6	221. 7	240. 7	261. 1	287. 9
38	352. 2	18. 9	39. 2	58. 3	78. 3	103. 5	176. 6	201. 8	221. 9	240. 9	261. 3	288. 3
39	351. 8	18. 7	39. 0	58. 1	78. 2	103. 2	176. 9	202. 0	222. 1	241. 1	261. 5	288.·6
40	351. 5	18. 4	38. 8	57. 9	78. 0	103. 0	177. 1	202. 3	222. 3	241. 2	261. 8	288. 9
41	351. 2	18. 3	38. 7	57. 8	77. 8	102. 7	177. 4	202. 5	222. 5	241. 4	262. 0	289. 3
42	350. 9	18. 2	38. 5	57. 7	77. 6	102. 4	177. 6	202. 7	222. 7	241. 5	262. 2	289. 6
43	350. 6	18. 0	38. 3	57. 5	77. 5	102. 2	177. 9	202. 9	222. 9	241. 7	262. 4	289. 9
44	350. 3	17. 8	38. 2	57. 3	77. 3	101. 9	178. 1	203. 1	223. 1	241. 8	262. 6	290. 2
45	350. 0	17. 6	38. 0	57. 2	77. 1	101. 6	178. 4	203. 2	223. 2	242. 0	262. 8	290. 5
46	349. 7	17. 4	37. 8	57. 0	76. 9	101. 4	178. 6	203. 4	223. 4	242. 1	262. 9	290. 8
47	349. 3	17. 2	37. 7	56. 9	76. 8	101. 1	178. 9	203. 6	223. 5	242. 3	263. 0	291. 1
48	349. 0	17. 0	37. 5	56. 7	76. 6	100. 9	179. 1	203. 7	223. 6	242. 5	263. 2	291. 4
49	348. 6	16. 8	37. 4	56. 6	76. 4	100. 6	179. 4	203. 9	223. 7	242. 7	263. 4	291. 7
50	348. 3	16. 6	37. 2	56. 3	76. 2	100. 5	179. 6	204. 1	223. 9	242. 8	263. 6	292. 1
51	347. 9	16. 4	37. 1	56. 2	76. 0	100. 2	179. 9	204. 3	224. 0	242.9	263. 8	292. 4
52	347. 6	16. 2	37. 0	56. 1	75. 9	100. 0	180. 1	204. 5	224. 2	243. 1	264. 0	292. 7
53	347. 3	16. 0	36. 8	55. 9	75. 7	99. 7	180. 4	204. 6	224. 3	243. 2	264. 1	293. 0
54	347. 0	15. 8	36. 7	55. 7	75. 5	99. 4	180. 6	204. 8	224. 4	243. 4	264. 3	293. 3
55	346. 7	15. 6	36. 5	55. 5	75. 3	99. 1	180. 9	204. 9	224. 5	243. 6	264. 5	293. 6
56	346. 4	15. 4	36. 3	55. 4	75. 1	98. 9	181. 1	205. 0	224. 7	243. 8	264. 6	293. 9
57	346. 0	15. 2	36. 1	55. 2	75. 0	98. 6	181. 4	205. 1	224. 8	243. 9	264. 8	294. 3
58	345. 7	15. 0	36. 0	55. 0	74. 8	98. 4	181. 6	205. 3	225. 0	244. 1	265. 0	294. 6
59	345. 3	14. 9	35. 8	54. 9	74. 6	98. 1	181. 9	205. 5	225. 1	244. 3	265. 1	294. 9
60	344. 9	14. 7	35. 6	54. 7	74. 4	97. 9	182. 1	205. 6	225. 3	244. 4	265. 3	295. 1

7600.3.   San Francisco Consolan Station–Dash Sectors

Count of Dashes	True bearing from station													
0	344.9	14.7	35.6	54.7	74.4	97.9			182.1	205.6	225.3	244.4	265.3	295.1
1	344.5	14.5	35.4	54.6	74.2	97.6			182.4	205.7	225.5	244.6	265.5	295.5
2	344.1	14.3	35.2	54.5	74.1	97.4			182.6	205.9	225.7	244.8	265.7	295.9
3	343.7	14.1	35.0	54.3	73.9	97.2			182.8	206.1	225.8	245.0	265.9	296.3
4	343.3	13.9	34.9	54.1	73.7	97.0			183.1	206.3	226.0	245.1	266.1	296.7
5	342.9	13.7	34.7	54.0	73.5	96.8			183.3	206.4	226.2	245.3	266.3	297.1
6	342.5	13.5	34.5	53.8	73.4	96.6			183.5	206.6	226.4	245.5	266.5	297.5
7	342.1	13.3	34.4	53.7	73.2	96.4			183.7	206.8	226.5	245.6	266.7	297.9
8	341.7	13.1	34.2	53.5	73.0	96.1			184.0	207.0	226.6	245.8	266.9	298.3
9	341.3	12.9	34.0	53.3	72.9	95.9			184.2	207.2	226.8	246.0	267.1	298.7
10	340.9	12.8	33.9	53.2	72.7	95.7			184.5	207.3	227.0	246.1	267.3	299.2
11	340.4	12.5	33.7	53.0	72.6	95.5			184.7	207.5	227.1	246.3	267.5	299.7
12	339.9	12.3	33.5	52.9	72.4	95.4			184.9	207.7	227.3	246.5	267.7	300.3
13	339.4	12.1	33.4	52.7	72.2	95.2			185.2	207.8	227.5	246.6	267.9	300.7
14	338.9	11.9	33.2	52.5	72.0	94.9			185.4	208.0	227.7	246.8	268.1	301.2
15	338.4	11.7	33.0	52.4	71.8	94.7			185.6	208.1	227.8	247.0	268.3	301.8
16	337.8	11.5	32.9	52.2	71.6	94.5			185.8	208.3	228.0	247.1	268.5	302.4
17	337.2	11.3	32.7	52.1	71.5	94.2			186.0	208.5	228.1	247.3	268.7	303.0
18	336.6	11.1	32.5	51.9	71.3	94.0			186.2	208.7	228.2	247.5	268.9	303.6
19	336.0	10.9	32.4	51.8	71.2	93.8			186.4	208.9	228.4	247.7	269.1	304.0
20	335.2	10.7	32.2	51.6	71.0	93.5			186.6	209.0	228.6	247.8	269.3	304.8
21	334.4	10.5	32.0	51.4	70.8	93.2			186.9	209.2	228.7	248.0	269.5	305.6
22	333.6	10.3	31.9	51.3	70.6	93.0			187.1	209.3	228.9	248.1	269.7	306.2
23	332.8	10.1	31.7	51.1	70.4	92.8			187.3	209.5	229.0	248.3	269.9	307.0
24	331.8	9.9	31.5	51.0	70.3	92.5			187.5	209.7	229.2	248.5	270.1	308.2
25	330.8	9.7	31.4	50.8	70.2	92.3			187.7	209.9	229.4	248.6	270.3	309.2
26	329.3	9.5	31.2	50.6	70.0	92.1			187.9	210.0	229.5	248.8	270.5	310.7
27	327.8	9.3	31.0	50.5	69.8	91.9			188.1	210.2	229.7	249.0	270.7	312.2
28	325.8	9.1	30.9	50.3	69.7	91.7			188.3	210.4	229.8	249.1	270.9	314.1
29	323.8	8.9	30.7	50.2	69.5	91.5			188.5	210.5	229.9	249.3	271.1	316.2
30	320.0	8.7	30.6	50.0	69.4	91.3	140.0	140.0	188.7	210.6	230.0	249.4	271.3	320.0
31		8.5	30.4	49.8	69.3	91.1	136.2	143.8	188.9	210.7	230.1	249.6	271.5	
32		8.3	30.2	49.7	69.1	90.9	132.7	147.2	189.1	210.9	230.3	249.8	271.7	
33		8.1	30.0	49.5	69.0	90.7	131.2	148.7	189.3	211.0	230.5	250.0	272.0	
34		7.9	29.9	49.4	68.8	90.5	129.7	150.2	189.5	211.2	230.6	250.1	272.2	
35		7.7	29.7	49.2	68.6	90.3	128.7	151.2	189.7	211.4	230.8	250.3	272.4	
36		7.5	29.5	49.0	68.5	90.1	127.7	152.2	189.9	211.5	231.0	250.5	272.6	
37		7.3	29.3	48.9	68.3	89.9	126.9	153.0	190.1	211.7	231.1	250.7	272.8	
38		7.0	29.1	48.7	68.1	89.7	126.1	153.8	190.3	211.9	231.3	250.8	273.1	
39		6.8	29.0	48.6	68.0	89.5	125.4	154.5	190.5	212.0	231.5	251.0	273.3	
40		6.6	28.8	48.4	67.8	89.3	124.7	155.2	190.7	212.2	231.6	251.2	273.5	
41		6.4	28.7	48.2	67.6	89.1	124.1	155.8	190.9	212.4	231.8	251.3	273.7	
42		6.1	28.5	48.1	67.5	88.9	123.5	156.4	191.1	212.5	231.9	251.5	273.9	
43		5.9	28.3	47.9	67.3	88.7	122.9	157.0	191.3	212.7	232.1	251.7	274.2	
44		5.7	28.1	47.8	67.1	88.5	122.3	157.6	191.5	212.9	232.2	251.9	274.4	
45		5.5	28.0	47.6	66.9	88.3	121.7	158.2	191.7	213.1	232.4	252.0	274.6	
46		5.2	27.8	47.4	66.8	88.1	121.1	158.8	191.9	213.2	232.6	252.2	274.8	
47		5.0	27.6	47.3	66.6	87.9	120.6	159.3	192.1	213.4	232.7	252.4	275.0	
48		4.8	27.5	47.1	66.5	87.7	120.1	159.8	192.3	213.6	232.9	252.5	275.3	
49		4.6	27.3	47.0	66.3	87.5	119.6	160.3	192.5	213.8	233.1	252.7	275.5	
50		4.3	27.1	46.8	66.1	87.3	119.1	160.8	192.7	214.0	233.2	252.9	275.7	
51		4.1	26.9	46.7	65.9	87.1	118.7	161.2	192.9	214.1	233.3	253.1	276.0	
52		3.9	26.8	46.5	65.7	86.9	118.3	161.6	193.1	214.2	233.5	253.2	276.2	
53		3.7	26.6	46.3	65.5	86.7	117.9	162.0	193.3	214.4	233.7	253.4	276.3	
54		3.4	26.4	46.2	65.3	86.5	117.5	162.4	193.5	214.5	233.8	253.6	276.5	
55		3.2	26.3	46.0	65.2	86.3	117.1	162.8	193.7	214.7	234.0	253.7	276.7	
56		3.0	26.1	45.9	65.0	86.1	116.7	163.2	193.9	214.8	234.1	253.9	277.0	
57		2.8	25.9	45.7	64.9	85.9	116.3	163.6	194.1	215.0	234.3	254.1	277.2	
58		2.5	25.8	45.5	64.7	85.7	115.9	164.0	194.3	215.2	234.4	254.2	277.4	
59		2.3	25.7	45.4	64.6	85.5	115.5	164.4	194.5	215.4	234.6	254.3	277.6	
60		2.1	25.6	45.3	64.4	85.3	115.1	164.9	194.7	215.6	234.7	254.4	277.9	

45/Marine Electronics
omni/VOR

Inevitable is a sky-high eyebrow when first encountering the subtitle to this chapter. Mr. Webster relates things omnivorish to less-than-finicky "d'ruthers" when confronted by a menu. Not so here. What we're about to meet is a system of electronic navigation whose dining habits, although not well delineated, can safely be taken as like neither the hog nor the hippopotamus. Having now disposed of a predestined allusion to the unfortunate name for this otherwise respectable device, we can get on with serious study.

For years **omni/VOR** has been the backbone of radio position finding for civil aviation in the United States; but only lately has it been brought to sea. Its name (anything heretofore suggested notwithstanding) is a meld of several things. The **VOR** comes from **V**ery high frequency **O**mnidirectional **R**ange. The source of **omni** is pretty evident. Sometimes it's called **omnirange**; often (but, apparently, not often enough) it is just **VOR**. We'll neither be swayed nor intimidated, however, by connotations; and, ignoring the ignoble, we'll persist in calling it **omni/ VOR**. Certainly it has achieved a measure of omnipresence; there are more than 1000 transmitters in the US, broadcasting on continuous 24-hour schedules. Over 150 of them are located on our continental coastlines.

Like RDF, it is a "point source" system involving bearings related to the origin of a transmitted radio wave. But similarity ceases there. The **V** for very high frequency places it much higher in the radio spectrum than the low and medium frequency signals of RDF and Consolan. Transmission is in the band from 108 to 118 mHz. With this come advantages and a few disadvantages. The basic drawback is that the higher frequency limits it to line-of-sight range. When the transmitter is close to sea level, the usable distance is less than when the station is on a bluff or mountain top. Of course, the height of the receiving antenna can extend the range. That is an advantage uniquely exploited by the aircraft. But a ship can improve things by elevating the cat-whisker antenna to her highest point. Sailing vessels can place it atop the mast without much trouble, for the antenna is only two feet long and weighs about a pound. The result in any case is an effective range, depending on area, from about 10 to as many as 75 miles.

Advantages are that the problem of night effect from sky waves and the shortcoming of refraction by land effect, both of which plague the RDF, don't bother omni/VOR. Nor do the rigging and metal masses aboard produce deviating errors. Add in that bearings given by this system are more accurate than by RDF, and it begins to shape up as a very attractive affair. Let's move in for a closer look.

Located ashore is a special transmitter with a small cluster of aerials from which emerge very high frequency radio signals. Aboard is a special receiver which detects the signals and shows the navigator the magnetic bearing to or from the station. What the transmitter does to create the signals, and how the receiver determines the bearing are really not relevant to our discussion. But the pattern of the signals certainly is. Transmissions from the station are in the form of a spoked wheel, with each of 360 spokes representing a magnetic bearing to or from the station. The receiver defines which spoke you're on. Nautical charts don't yet show the locations of the transmitters, but that is no serious impediment. Manufacturers of omni receivers can be expected to supply lists of the stations, with latitude and longitude, frequency of transmission and identification signal. Aeronautical charts prepared by government agencies are readily available. They show the station at the center of an azimuth circle, and are labeled with call sign and frequency. Station locations can then be transferred to the regular nautical charts for use afloat.

Omni receivers are to a large extent single purpose. They won't receive marine radio communications, broadcast stations or marine radiobeacons. They are intended for one basic job: reception and display of omni/VOR signals. There are voice transmissions, but they are related to aircraft operation. Mariners, though, can make great use of complete and up-to-date local weather information which is broadcast every half hour.

There are two principal types of receivers for use afloat. One is crystal-controlled, like a radiotelephone, to stay on the assigned frequency. With it the operator turns a knob to the desired frequency—say, 113.2 mHz—and the station comes in. The other type requires manual tuning to best reception, the same as conventional RDF.

There are also two ways to display the bearing information. The first has been used by aircraft for years. A rotatable azimuth circle is turned by the navigator until a needle centers on "0." The number then on the azimuth is the station's radial number or bearing. A more recent development is a pointer behind which is a 360° azimuth ring. When the station is tuned in, the pointer will automatically turn to the number on the azimuth which is the station's radial number. This is similar to the read-out on an automatic direction finder (ADF) and saves the navigator one step . . . all he has to do to determine the bearing is to tune in on the station. By either means the operator identifies which spoke of the transmitter's wheel pattern he is on.

Spread around us now are the disconnected pieces of the whole idea. It's time to put them together. **Figure 140** shows an omni/VOR pattern. The navigator on Boat **A** has tuned to 115.3 mHz, the frequency for the station designated as **OCN**. His read-out system on the boat shows 35° . . . that he is on the 035° radial. **To/from** is something that should now get into the act . . . but's let's postpone it for just a few lines more. Over on Boat **B** the operator sees 85° on his dial. He is on the 085° radial. **Omni/VOR** transmissions are oriented to magnetic north at

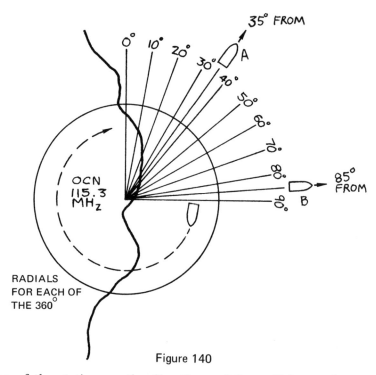

Figure 140

the position of the station, so the directions of the radials are given as magnetic bearings. The receiver need not fuss about the ship's compass heading and relating the radio bearing to it and so forth. Both **A** and **B** could be turning in circles or running steady courses when the bearings are taken. Their headings at the time don't influence the readings. They could be rolling, pitching, heeled over or lurching back and forth across the course line. None of this makes a difference to the omni receiver. **A**'s will show he is on the 035° radial; **B**'s will indicate 085°. In effect, omni/VOR is the reverse of RDF. The older system gives a direction from you to the station . . . as if you are in the center of a circle pointing an aerial out at the stations. Omni/VOR has the station at the center and places you on one of its 360 spokes or lanes.

When we discussed RDF, ambiguity was mentioned. Radio bearings are susceptible to a mix-up . . . they can have difficulty telling whether the transmitter is in one direction or in the exact opposite. RDF handles this by using a sense antenna to point out which is the right way. Omni/VOR radials could also be double-meaning were it not for the **to/from** device on the receiver. What the control amounts to is a sense of ambiguity indicator, and it tells its story in a very simple fashion. On receivers requiring the navigator to turn an azimuth wheel to gain a bearing, a flag signal near the zero needle automatically identifies whether that bearing is **to** the station or **from** it. On the newer receivers we've mentioned—those whose pointer automatically turns to the number on a 360° dial which is the station's radial number—the reading displayed is always heading **to** the station. The **from** reading is at the opposite end of the pointer. Back again to **Figure 140** to put **to/from** to work. If the navigator of **A** had the older type of **to/from**, here's what he would have seen. When he had centered a needle on "0," the instrument dial would show 35° as the radial and the word **from** would be featured. He is being told he is on a radial line bearing 035° magnetic from the transmitter. If he wanted to home-in on the station, he'd turn the azimuth wheel until the flag said **to**. The reading would then be 215°. His radial would then be a magnetic bearing of 215° to the station's location. Over on Boat **B** the navigator is more affluent and has the new equipment. When he tuned to the station frequency, a pointer automatically turned to 265°, the direction **to** the station. If he wanted to track away from the station, he would read the other end of the dial, 085°, as the radial **from** the transmitter.

This really smacks of "dial-a-number-navigation." Before we look at some examples of its marine uses, let's risk one more recap of what we've seen so far. A radio signal is transmitted from a shoreside station in an omnidirectional radial pattern with the transmitting aerials at the center. The signal is in the very high frequency band, is of short range but is not disturbed by night effect, land effect or nearby metal masses. Transmitters are widespread throughout the US and operate 24 hours a day. Each half hour detailed local weather information is also broadcast. Aboard ship is a special receiver which will accept the omnidirectional bearing pattern and also the weather information. The operator tunes the set to the frequency of the transmitter and then by a dial identifies the radial number of the bearing line either to the station or from the station. He locates the station on a chart, draws the line of bearing and so has a line of position on which his vessel is located.

Now it's time to see the system in action. **Figure 141** shows how the navigator of Boat **A** could make excellent use of one or two omni stations to plot his progress. He's on a course of 300° at 10 knots, and at 0900 is somewhere to the

omni/VOR receiver showing on left side the azimuth wheel
for to/from magnetic bearings, and tuning control on right.

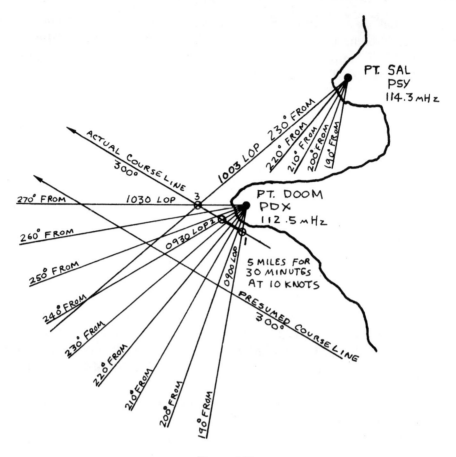

Figure 141

southwest of the omni station **PDX** located at Point Doom. Another omni trans-mitter, **PSY**, is at work on Point Sal up the coast to the north. First off, he tunes his omni receiver to 112.5 mHz for PDX at Point Doom, and finds he is on the 190°-**from** radial. He can't read the Point Sal station because its line-of-sight range is blocked by the terrain at Point Doom. But already he has something to start with. He locates the Point Doom station on his chart and from it draws a bearing in the direction of 190° magnetic. This is his 0900 line of position (LOP). Now he continues on course at his speed and at 0930 takes another reading of PDX. This time he is on the 240°-**from** radial. So he draws that LOP. He estimates that he traveled 30 minutes at 10 knots, or five miles in between the two readings. Everything is at hand for a running fix by LOP's. We talked about that in the Piloting chapter of Section VI. Our omniscient mariner handles it a simple way by setting his dividers to five miles, the distance run, and moving them along the two LOP's until the distance between them in a 300° direction (his course steered) is five miles. He then takes as his 0900 position the spot marked 1, and as his 0930 position, that marked 2. He won't have to wait too long on that course before Point Sal is in the clear and no longer blocked by Point Doom. So now a fix by two radial lines is his for the dialing. At 1003 he takes a reading on both omni stations. PDX on Point Doom reads **270°-from** and PSY on Point Sal reads

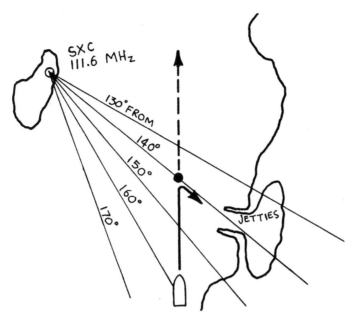

Figure 142

230°-from. Plotting each LOP from its station fixes his position at the intersection of the two lines . . . at **3**.

An omni/VOR transmitter doesn't have to be at a harbor entrance to be useful. Whether the station is on an island or inland makes no difference so long as it gives a clear signal to the ship. **Figure 142** illustrates a situation common along our coastlines, a harbor entrance without a radiobeacon but within range of an omni station. It shows a boat heading up the coast and using omni station SXC on

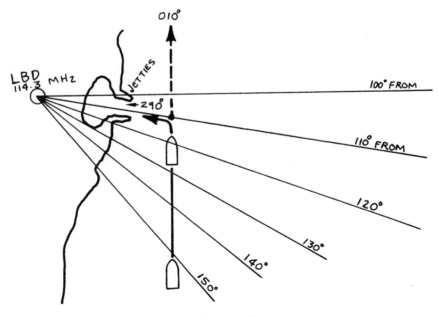

Figure 143

111.5 mHz. By noting the time he crosses the radial, the navigator can keep tabs on his progress. Course, speed and time factor combined into running fixes or routines used in the last example let him rely on a pretty good position as each radial is crossed. In **Figure 142**, this would tell him he was south of the harbor as he passed the **160°-from** and the **150°-from** radials. The **140°-from** radial can become a lane for entering the harbor. He notices that in tracking away from the station on **140°-from**, a vessel would pass right between the jetties. The next step is easy. He delays his turn to the right until he is on the **140°-from** freeway. Then he goes hard right, settles on 140° magnetic and by tracking away on the radial, arrives at the harbor entrance.

Let's look at still another one. In **Figure 143**, omni station LBD is located inland but its radials fan out over the harbor and adjoining coastline. A navigator is heading 010° and expects to turn left to enter harbor. He reads the radials as he goes northward. When the reading is **110°-from**, he turns left to its reciprocal, 290°. This course will lead directly in the entrance. He keeps on the **290°-to** radial and goes home.

Different navigation systems can be married together with little fear of incompatibility. So, an omni/VOR line of position can be combined with one by RDF, or with a sounding or a visual bearing or a radar range . . . or whatever other piece of position data might be at hand. **Figure 144** shows the merger of the old RDF with the younger omni/VOR and nary a generation gap! A boat is on a course of 200° magnetic and wants to fix position by using omni station LGO on 113.5 mHz and a harbor entrance radiobeacon transmitting on 302 kHz. The navigator turns to his omni and learns he is on the **100°-from** radial. Then he uses the RDF

Large motor cruiser underway.   Photo by Burger Boat Company, Inc.

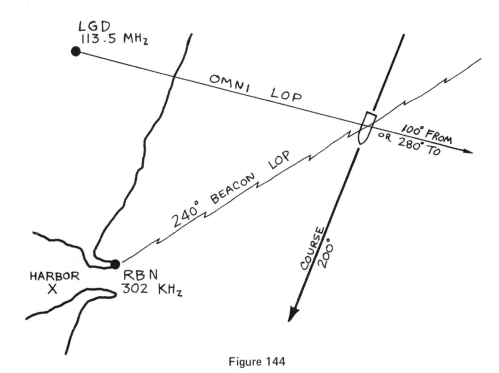

Figure 144

and finds the beacon is bearing 40° on his starboard bow. The omni bearing is 100° magnetic from the station; the **to** bearing is the reciprocal, or 280°. The RDF bearing is 40° relative to the vessel's bow . . . 40° to the right of 200° magnetic, or 240° magnetic. Now he has two magnetic bearings to plot as LOP's and fix his position.

Many a mariner could now ponder, "Where's omni/VOR been all this time?" The answer would be: it's been busy ashore caring for thousands of aviators, and whoever else would take the time to make its acquaintance. Here is another system ready to become a very competent shipmate whenever we can bring him aboard. What's needed for his gangway is the special receiver. Anyone considering electronic aids for coastal navigation should investigate omni/VOR. Check with a marine electronics dealer to learn costs of equipment and usability of omni stations in your area. It might be an inquiry well worthwhile.

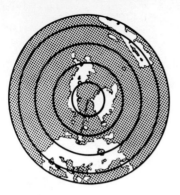

46/Marine Electronics
Omega and Decca

The air around us is alive with busy electrons scurrying about carrying messages ranging from across-town orders for delivery trucks to instructions bound for a distant space craft. We're not here concerned with canceling delivery of an order of chicken legs, and cruising on the Moon's Sea of Copernicus is still an exclusive pursuit. So our emphasis will be on position finding afloat. Lost, though, will be the serenity of far-off Vega as seen in the mirror of a sextant. And we'll miss the feeling of self-reliance that accompanies the bustle of combining Greenwich time with Declination and an hour angle or two to get position. But there is an undeniable security in systems that give instant and accurate answers 24 hours a day, regardless of weather. Add to that the special needs of supersonic aircraft and far-ranging submarines, and the stage is set for featureless electrons to swarm aboard. More and more they are weaving a network of hyperbolic lines to guide the mariner.

The systems available are many; yet they are surprisingly unrelated in pattern. Each of the electronic devices seems to have emerged to fill a particular need or as an improvement on an existing system which itself had been developed to answer a special requirement. The result is somewhat of a "Joseph's coat" of different methods requiring different equipment. There is a move afoot to plan a coordinated pattern best meeting the needs of all. Meanwhile navigators encounter a field peopled with, among many others, three kinds of Loran, Consolan, Decca, RDF, omni/VOR, Omega, satellites, radar, echo sounders, and the age-old self-contained techniques of piloting and celestial navigation.

The private operator frequently falls heir to a workable setup actually devised for aircraft or for military vessels; some others are not in point at all. Not every vessel can sport aerials like the branches of a pine tree and have compartments bulging with displays and consoles. Our aim is to focus on those within the scope of private operation and to see in general what they can do. We've already taken the measure of quite a few: piloting techniques, echo sounders, radar, RDF, Consolan and omni/VOR. Satellite and celestial navigation are outside our present scope, and so not appropriate. In considering a navigation system, the private mariner weighs some basic factors. A paramount one, of course, is cost. Others are accuracy, coverage, speed and ease of use, reliability, maintenance and size. Our purpose is achieved if the available equipment is selectively presented, and the pros and cons of each made evident. Of the other electronic systems not yet discussed, we've chosen three: **Loran** because it is widely used, **Decca** because of its short range capability, and **Omega** because it promises to fulfill its name and become the ultimate in radio systems.

Now we'll start off discussion of **area coverage** radio systems: those by which transmitted patterns of signals are interpreted by special receivers to give position. Here is the general idea. Special single purpose receivers aboard are used to measure the phase or the time differences between synchronized signals received from two or more shore-based transmitters. Used with this information are special charts on which are printed hyperbolic lines of position, each line representing either a phase difference or a time difference. To use the system, the navigator measures a difference in the way the signals are received and then, on the chart, finds its hyperbolic line. He is located on that line. **Omega** and **Decca** measure differences in phase; **Loran** uses differences in time.

First off, let's get to **Omega**. It makes use of very low frequency transmissions: 10.2 kHz, 11.33 kHz and 13.6 kHz, with wave lengths about 16 miles long. This is far down the radio spectrum, well below the marine radiobeacon's 300-ish kHz and millions of cycles removed from omni/VOR in the 110 mHz neighborhood. The reason for the frequency selection is to gain more reliable wave propagation, less problem from static interference and more predictable sky wave effects. But that's not for us to ponder. We're pursuing a **how** or two and skirting the sticky **whys**. The transmissions are synchronized and the phases of radiated radio waves are time-controlled to millionths of a second. One transmitter is located near New York, one is in Hawaii. A third is on the island of Trinidad off the northeast coast of South America, and a fourth is in Northern Norway. Range of the signals is as much as 7,000 miles. Four more stations are to be installed: one in the northwest Pacific, one in the Indian Ocean, one far south in South America and the last in the area of the Tasman Sea. There will be some relocation of stations, probably, as the system gains experience. For example, the New York transmitter is to go to a position in the north central part of the United States. But the outcome is world-wide, 24-hour, all-weather coverage.

The idea is to schedule transmission from the stations on a sequential basis: Station A in Norway followed by B in Trinidad, then by C in Hawaii, D in New York and so on through those in the game. Each station transmits a signal of from 0.9 to 1.2 seconds and repeats each 10 seconds. This allows room for the eight stations to sound off during each 10-second period.

Aboard ship the receiver's job is to measure, count and numerically display the phase difference between the transmissions of pairs of stations, even though they be thousands of miles apart. It works out that, at every half a wavelength, there will be no phase difference between signals. So lanes from eight miles wide and up are created between these regions of zero phase difference. Related to each of these lanes is a hyperbolic line on the Omega chart. Generally, these charts look much like Decca and Loran charts, with sets of lines superimposed on outlines of geographical features. The Omega lines, though, are more nearly straight than the others because of the much greater distance between the transmitters. At departure the operator sets the display to agree with the lane numbering there. As the ship then travels across lanes, a counter device notes the numbers of lanes traversed, and so keeps track of the receiver's location on the hyperbolic pattern. To take a reading, he selects two stations whose hyperbolic lines would most nearly produce LOP's intersecting at right angles. This requires only that he glance at the Omega chart and note his locality. In the Long Island Sound area, for instance, making a suitable pair would be BC (Trinidad and Hawaii). Another would be AC (Norway and Hawaii). In Southern California BC (Trinidad and Hawaii) and BD (Trinidad and New York) work well. A third LOP using CD (Hawaii and New York) could be used to cinch things.

The reading itself is a display of letters and numbers . . . BC 738.21, for example. The letters identify the station pairs and the numbers refer to lane and location within the lane. The full lane number is given to two decimal points, to pinpoint the hyperbolic line to 1/100 of a lane width. The accuracy of plotting is apparent. **Figure 145** pictures an Omega receiver. Indicated is BD 81.92 . . . a line of position involving Trinidad and New York, with lane identification and phase difference shown by the number.

The requirement that the receiver be preset at departure seems to suggest the possibility of some ambiguity in lane identification. That does exist, but second-reading procedures can straighten things out. And more complicated receivers are available, which can take care of any lane ambiguity without the requirement for presetting. **Figure 146** shows an Omega grid pattern for the Southern California area. Trinidad and New York are represented by lanes BD and numbered from 978 through 984. Hawaii and New York team up on the CD's from 894 through 912. Trinidad-Hawaii is shown by the BC pattern from 966 through 987. And the decimal part of the receiver's read-out would be placing the ship on a line within the lanes. The basic Omega system is designed to provide fixes with **least** accuracy averaging one mile . . . and regardless of distance from the station.

Since the system employs sky waves bouncing off the ionosphere, there is a variable—but only one—to be taken into account. The apparent signal speed

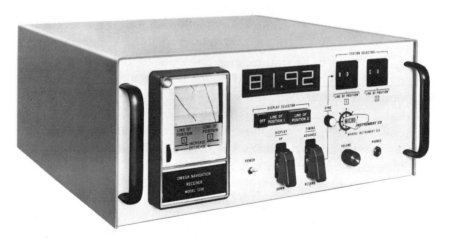

Photo by Micro Instrument Co.

Figure 145

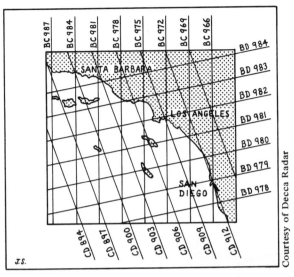

Figure 146

changes during the day with variations in the height of the ionosphere. This produces diurnal phase drift, and requires a sky wave correction dependent on time and location. Tables are prepared to take up this slack. Extraordinary accuracy is obtainable when within 100 miles of a shore-based Omega monitoring station. What is done is that the station observes the sky wave effect on its own receiver which then, by radiotelephone, advises the navigator of the correction to make.

Let's take a quick look at how Omega fares on our list of factors to consider. On accuracy it rates near the top. So far as coverage is concerned, world-wide potential is hard to beat. Speed and ease of use? An LOP a minute by pushing a button, turning a knob, applying a tabular correction and spotting a line. A fix in two or three minutes by going through the routine again. The equipment in **Figure 145** takes up no more space than a suitcase and weighs about 40 pounds. On reliability and maintenance it encounters the same problems met by any sophisticated electronic device. The cost factor is high, but not prohibitive and will reduce with wider use. Where then does Omega fit? Each mariner must judge for himself, of course. But for extended cruising, it certainly is worth inquiry; and everyone should keep a weather eye on it as a likely entry to run off with the Hyperbolic Handicap.

Next in the hyperbolic kit is **Decca**, a short range, extremely accurate British development. It uses low frequency transmissions in the general band from 70 kHz to 130 kHz. Four transmitters set in a special pattern make up a unit called a Decca chain. The key element is a master transmitter sending out signals on one frequency. Located in a triangular pattern, and from 70 to 120 miles away, are three slave stations. They each transmit by direction of the master and at different frequencies. Comparison of the phase differences of the signals forms patterns of hyperbolic lines. These are drawn on special Decca charts and labeled by letters and numbers. The general idea is beginning to sound familiar . . . hyperbolic lines on a chart are labeled with identifying symbols so that the navigator can pick out the ones on which he is located. He does that by use of a special receiver.

There are several types of on-board units. The one pictured in **Figure 147** is about the size of an Omega receiver. It has a digital read-out of lanes and three clock-like indicators called **decometers**. The digital read-out shows lane numbers to 1/10 of a lane width. The decometers give zone identification and narrow down lane numbers to 1/100 of a lane. Decometers are distinguished by color as red, green and purple. This relates each to the zone and lane number shown on Decca charts; for there the hyperbolic lines appear in red, green and purple ink. Normally only two decometers are used. Their job is to compare the phases of the slave signals with that of the master and so indicate the hyperbolic lines involved. Which two of the red, green and purple decometers are selected for reading is related to how the resulting hyperbolic lines might intersect. For with Decca, as with Omega, the aim is to choose lines crossing most nearly at right angles. The model pictured is of a class giving positions with an accuracy measured in yards.

Figure 147

A smaller version, with only a single dial to show lanes and fractions of lanes, is also available. It brings pleasure boat owners an adequate means to put Decca chains to work. During a cycle of ten seconds, the single meter consecutively shows the LOP number for the red, green and purple patterns. Then there is a ten-second break before the cycle starts over again.

Figure 148 is a small section of a Decca chart. It shows a fix based on a reading from the green decometer of 35.80 and from the red decometer of 16.30.

The areas covered by Decca chains include the west coast of Europe from Spain to the northern tip of Norway, the lower coast of South Africa, the Persian Gulf, and parts of Indian, Australian and Japanese waters. In North America the coastal

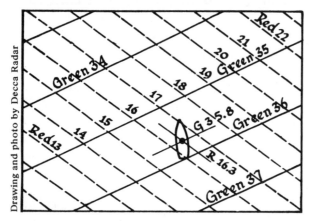

Drawing and photo by Decca Radar

Figure 148. Small section of a typical Decca chart showing fix of boat at intersection of two LOP's.

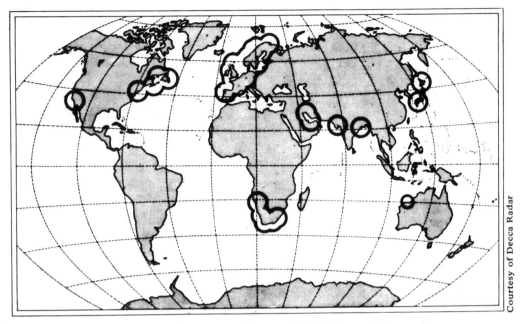

Figure 149. Areas of the world covered with Decca chains, as of 1971; additional chains are planned for future construction.

coverage is from Newfoundland down to New Jersey and, for evaluation purposes, in the Southern California area. Each chain has a usable range of from 250 to 300 miles from the master station. In many regions there is overlap coverage of one chain to the next. **Figure 149** shows the distribution.

The first Decca chain in the United States was installed to serve New York Airways helicopters. Required was a navigation aid that would function at or near ground level as well as at altitude. The conventional radio aids, such as omni/VOR and other VHF systems, would only be of use when line-of-sight between the ground station and the aircraft could be assured at all times. Frequently they gave no assistance when the path for the radio wave to a low-flying helicopter was blocked by intervening structures or terrain. Decca offered a ready solution because its low frequencies are not subject to shadow effects from buildings, hills or islands.

Decca chains in Canada have been in service for some years and cover the waters of New England, Bay of Fundy, Nova Scotia, Gulf of St. Lawrence and Newfoundland. In those areas the use has been primarily for marine navigation. With the New York chain, which provides coverage into Chesapeake Bay, Decca navigation is available to the northern part of the Atlantic Coast.

In 1970 an experimental chain was installed in Southern California. It provides coverage in a radius of about 250 miles from Los Angeles, and the accuracy offered is unequaled. When a vessel is at anchor and swinging on as little as 100 feet of anchor rode, her change in position will be shown on the instrument's read-out dials.

Accuracy of Decca is shown by **Figure 150**, picturing the New York and

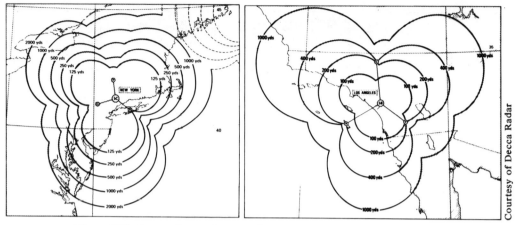

Figure 150. Approximate degrees of accuracy of Decca fixes, during daylight conditions, of the New York and Los Angeles chains

Southern California chains. These are for average conditions during full daylight, when precision is greatest. At dusk and nighttime—particularly winter nighttime—the accuracy is not as great from mid-range to maximum. But as a vessel moves closer to a master station, precision increases. Decca, like Omega, has its sky wave problems. Under conditions of twilight and darkness, sky wave signals will cause varying amounts of error in the read-outs; and the amount of error may change from summer to winter. Decca publishes correction tables for each of the chains. These cover both fixed and variable errors created by terrain over which the radio waves travel as well as other conditions affecting the read-out of the instrument. The special charts themselves are available from Decca and also through National Ocean Survey.

Now to score Decca on our list of factors to consider. By size and weight it compares with Omega. Its accuracy is best of all present hyperbolic systems, but coverage is a problem. There must be a Decca chain in your area, and even then the range is limited. Speed and ease of use are in the Omega league. Reliability and maintenance? It is another sophisticated electronic device, but one that is well-tested. The cost is realistic for anyone ready to consider bringing a hyperbolic system aboard.

This wraps up our discussion of two excellent phase-difference systems. Introductions have been made. Whether close association develops is, of course, an individual affair. But even if you should never become shipmates, knowledge that such crew members are seaworthy is a fit addition to the navigator's file of notes.

47/Marine Electronics
Loran

One more witness is left to call in our hyperbolic hearing, and then we're ready to adjourn this survey of area coverage radio navigation systems. On the stand comes **Loran**, with name derived from **Lo**ng **Ra**nge **N**avigation. Let the record show that there are three members of the Loran family . . . **A**, **C** and **D**. Submitted for identification only is that **Loran-C** is a longer range and more accurate system, but not in wide enough use to have our attention: that **Loran-D** is a short range method developed to fill a special need, primarily military, for mobility of transmitter setup. It is stipulated that, when the term Loran is mentioned, we mean the oldest of the group, **Loran-A**.

Loran states its age as a quarter of a century. Its occupation is as an aid to navigation which supplies hyperbolic lines of position by electronic measurement of the time difference between radio signals from shore-based stations. A demurrer should be sustained to this entire proceedings, for Loran is a veteran system in use for years by overwater aircraft, military and merchant shipping, commercial fishermen and pleasure boat owners. No longer are there grounds to put it on trial. We'll consider a factual brief on its behalf, reciting how it works and where it works, with mention of its strengths and shortcomings.

The general setup as an area coverage system is quite similar to others we've already met. Geometrically located transmitters send out radio waves which are detected by special single purpose receivers. On-board measurements are made of differences in the received signals, and used to select the vessel's line of position from one of a lattice of hyperbolic lines printed on special charts. Loran transmission is in the medium frequency band, where four channels have been reserved for its use. In the Western Hemisphere, those presently employed are **Channel 1** at 1950 kHz and **Channel 2** at 1850 kHz. The other two are **Channel 3** at 1900 kHz and **Channel 4** at 1750 kHz.

Coverage extends the length of the North Atlantic coast from Greenland to the Caribbean and across the Gulf of Mexico. On the Pacific Coast, stations cover from the Aleutian Islands down to Southern California and westward past Hawaii. Patterns also serve European and Asiatic areas. When one adds the long range of the system, the result is a network spanning nearly all the waters of the Northern Hemisphere.

Now to get at how the system works. Synchronized and pulsed signals are sent out by a pair of transmitters. One of these is called the **master** and the other is the **slave.** The master emits a short pulse of about 10 microseconds. It is received not only by shipboard receivers but also by the slave, who, being an obedient servant, then delays for a preset interval before transmitting a 40-microsecond pulse. Next, the ship picks up the slave signal and then measures the time difference in microseconds between receipt of the two signals. **Figure 151** is a sketch of the principle involved.

The receiver on vessel **A** measures 3500 microseconds as the time difference between receiving the master signal and then the slave. **B** is closer to the slave so the time difference there is less . . . 2500 microseconds. Each operator has read his time difference number directly from the panel of his receiver, and with that number has a key to his position. For printed on Loran charts are hyperbolic lines, a set for each pair of stations. Every receiver located on the same line will read the same microsecond difference between detecting the master and then the

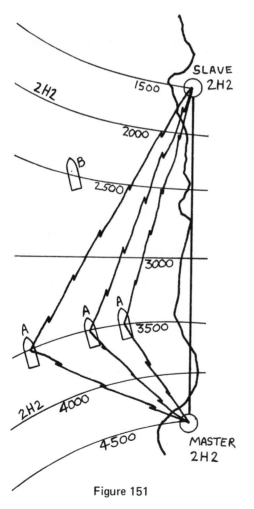

Figure 151

slave. Each line is marked with its difference value, with the identification of its pair, and is also printed in colored ink to distinguish its set from others.

So **A** finds the 3500 line and takes it as his line of position at the time of the reading. **B** places himself on 2500. Since both have used the master/slave pair identified as **2H2,** they will pick their time-difference lines from those labeled and colored for **2H2.** Of course, location on a Loran line is no more definite at this stage than by any other line of position. Either receiver could be a few miles from shore or 500 miles at sea. What the navigator on each vessel can say after reading **2H2** is that he is on the hyperbolic line for his measured time difference. But he can't say where.

The next step is to put another Loran pair to work. Adjoining the 2H2 network is another for 2H3. The two grids of hyperbolic lines overlap on purpose so navigators in the area can fix position by intersecting LOP's. **Figure 152** shows another thing about 2H3 . . . the master in that household is the same as the one in **2H2**. This two-slave affluence is common among masters. Most of the time they are two-voiced transmitters, offering signals on one basis with one slave and then offering different signals with another slave.

Both **A** and **B** are within the service area of such duplex coverage. So each resets his receiver to pick up **2H3** and makes another measurement. **A** finds his time delay for **2H3** is 4500 microseconds; **B** measures the **2H3** difference to be 5000 microseconds. **Figure 152** shows the result. This sketch is neither to scale nor in the detail of Loran charts. For simplicity we see **2H2** lines illustrated as solid and the **2H3** lines as dotted. Nor does the sketch show time difference lines at as frequent intervals as do Loran charts. We see them here at 500 microsecond intervals . . . on "for real" charts they can be as close as 10 microseconds apart. Demonstrated, though, is the end result. **A** finds the intersection of his 3500 line from **2H2** with the 4500 line from **2H3** and has a fix. **B** marks the intersection of the 2500 line from **2H2** with the 5000 line from **2H3** and fixes his position. It's that simple.

What isn't so simple, but quite intriguing, is how Loran pairs keep from interfering with each other. Long range radio waves blanketing nearly half the world from transmitters restricted to only four frequencies can't avoid getting into each other's way without some direction of traffic. How Loran does so is directly connected with the two numbers and the letter which make up the identification symbol for one of its pairs. None of this need disturb the operator, for he can confidently set dials to numbers and letters and go through ritu-

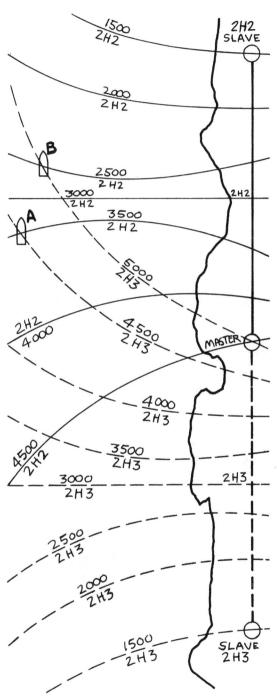

Figure 152

als to take readings and pick hyperbolic lines without having the foggiest notion where the numbers come from or how or why. His involvement with the efficacy of frequency selection can stop at placing his fingers on a knob and setting a dial to "Channel 2." Turning another pointer to "H" can be the apex of his connection with basic pulse recurrence rate. And whether the specific pulse rate alters each second of transmission by adding 3/19 of a pulse or by shortening the interval between pulses by 300 microseconds is made very academic when another dial is set to "3." But let's give an admiring minilook at what this is about. To do more, would initiate extraneous conversation far, far out in left field.

The significance of the Loran pair's rate identification is this:

1, 2, 3 or 4 refers to the channel number.
H, L or S represents the basic pulse recurrence rate.
O, 1, 2, 3, 4, 5, 6, 7 or 8 stands for specific pulse rate.

The channels we've already mentioned, spotlighting that 1 and 2 are those for the Western Hemisphere. The **basic pulse recurrence rate** tells how many pulses or signals a station sends out in a second of time. **H** is for **high** and means 33-3/9 pulses per second. **L** is for **low** and is 25 pulses per second. **S** is **special**, for 20 pulses per second. This last is reserved for future use, so it merits only an over-the-shoulder look.

What about the **specific rate?** In order to open more lanes on this hyperbolic highway, each pulse pattern can be slightly modified by adding a piece of a pulse (and so shortening the interval between pulses) during a second. The numbers **0** through **7** refer to the extent of modification. The result is a theoretical 96

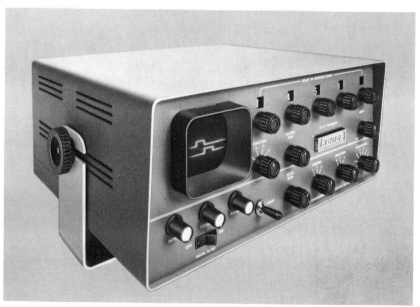

Loran-A receiver with signal pedestals visible on oscilloscope.

Photo by Konel Corporation

different combinations on only four frequencies. For a station could in theory have any of three basic rates on one of the four channels . . . and each basic rate could be modified in one of eight different ways. In practice the population is not so exploded, but the potential is there.

Let's look back, then, at a few Loran designations and see how they are deciphered. The 1 in 1L2 means that master and slave transmit on Channel 1 at 1950 kHz. The **L** says there are basically 25 pulses per second. The 2 defines a pulse modification to add two pieces of a basic pulse in each second and so shorten the interval between pulses. 2H3 unravels this way: 2 for Channel 2, or 1850 kHz; **H** for high basic rate of 33-3/9 pulses per second; and 3 for three fractions of a pulse added. That the pulse fractions added to **H** are in ninths, and that those added to **L** are in sixteenths really shouldn't concern us. Nor should we be exercised that the result in each case is to shorten the interval between pulses by multiples of 100 microseconds. Let's file all this under "G" for "General Idea" and get back to operation.

Of course, there's more to that than just dial-setting. The final step in using a Loran receiver is to measure the time difference between the master pulse and the slave. This is done on a visual display made by an oscilloscope and requires a practiced eye. Master and slave pulses are presented as lines on a viewscope. The idea is to align them one over the other. By a series of magnifications the pulses appear as peaked curves. When the left slopes are matched, a time difference is read from an indicator. This can be shown on the face of tuning dials or on a digital counter like the mileage display in the center of a car's speedometer. But the result in either case is a time measure . . . 3 5 0 0.

Radio signals from the stations follow two paths. Some go directly to the receiver as ground waves; others bounce off the ionosphere as sky waves. And these sky waves can ricochet more than once to become multihop waves. As if that were not enough, they can rebound from either the **E** layer of the ionosphere or from the higher-up **F** layer. So, Loran operators speak of one-hop **E** waves and two-hop **E** waves, one-hop **F** waves and so forth. Coming from each station can be a train of signals made up of combinations of ground waves and various hopping sky waves. The trick is to identify the kind of wave on the display and then to match it with the same kind of signal from the other member of the pair. Within 250 miles of the station, the strong likelihood is that ground waves will be received, and so they are the ones compared. Beyond 700 or so miles, the pulses coming aboard will probably be sky waves, so they are matched. In between, both kinds can be arriving. And in a particular in-between range, confusing displays can appear. This **critical range** usually starts at about 500 miles.

Figure 153 shows a ground wave and two kinds of sky waves. **S-1** is a one-hop E and **S-2** is a two-hop E.

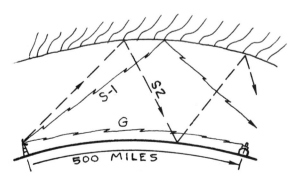

Figure 153

Since it takes longer for a hop to get to the receiver than it does a ground wave, corrections are made to sky wave readings before they are referred to a chart. At intersections of latitude and longitude lines, Loran charts show the number of microseconds to be applied to a sky wave reading to convert it to the time difference values shown by the printed hyperbolic lines. These corrections are computed for one-hop E sky waves, and they normally are received to a maximum distance of 1400 miles. So that sort of describes the workable range of Loran . . . to the maximum limit of one-hop E waves, or about 1400 miles. Loran tables are also available to give locations of the hyperbolic lines, but the simpler procedure is by chart.

There, in substance, is Loran; and again it's time to have it run the gauntlet of our check list. By size and weight, Loran compares with other hyperbolic receivers. Its price, however, is much less than Decca's and Omega's. Accuracy depends on several factors. First of all, there is great importance in the location of the receivers relative to the station pair. On the base line between the transmitters, the accuracy is very high. On the **base line extension** behind either one of them, the accuracy is low. For 80% of the its pattern, though, Loran achieves fix accuracy of from one to five miles. The other factors that can influence the outcome are the waves being used, the time of day, and the skill of the operator. Reliability and maintenance always hinge on the care and feeding of sophisticated electronic equipment. On the score of area coverage, Loran is excellent. Need for display interpretation by the operator makes its use more involved than for some other electronic systems. But it is still not difficult to handle.

As Loran steps down from the witness stand, we complete our investigation of radio location systems. We've heard testimony of prices from low to quite expensive and of equipment from portable and basic to highly sophisticated. Established by weight of evidence has been accuracy and ease of use. Only the unique seagoing factors of unfavorable environment and total isolation tinge the issue of dependability. But, then, nautical standards of reliability are exceedingly high. In fact, most of the time seamen carry separate alternatives. Since everything aboard can suddenly be at risk come midnight on a dark and stormy night, it's a pretty good idea sometimes to wear suspenders as well as a belt. What we've seen here is a cross-section representative of the state of the art. Now it is for the navigator to consider the evidence and to render his individual judgment.

Questions

We've got one more position finding system to hurdle. The name is **Maxe**, **Exam** spelled backwards. Maxe costs nothing, weighs little and is unerring. As for being backwards, he points out where you've been. Happy hyperbolae!

Radio Direction Finders

1. When the plane of the loop of an RDF is pointing towards a transmitting station
   a)   the signal is loudest.
   b)   the signal is weakest.

2. The device used to determine the proper direction at the point of null is
   a)   a fixed loop.
   b)   a goniometer.
   c)   a sense antenna.

3. Marine radiobeacons operate in a frequency band of
   a)   around 300 kHz.
   b)   between 550 kHz and 1500 kHz.
   c)   near 2.0 mHz.

4. Night effect is less bothersome
   a)   when 200 miles from a station than when 20 miles away.
   b)   when using an entertainment broadcast station than when using a marine radiobeacon.
   c)   when 20 miles from a station than when 200 miles away.

5. Three simultaneous bearings by RDF will
   a)   estimate wind velocity and direction.
   b)   always establish an exact position.
   c)   indicate probable position within a triangle of intersecting lines of position.

Consolan

1. Consolan is usable
   a)   with any radio receiver.
   b)   only with special short wave receiving equipment.
   c)   with any set able to receive in the 190-195 kHz range.

2. Consolan is unusable when the observer is
   a)   at right angles to the line through the station towers.
   b)   in sectors near the ends of the line through the towers.

3. Consolan is unusable
   a)   when within 50 miles from the station.
   b)   when beyond 50 miles from the station.

4. A navigator taking a Consolan bearing first hears the equisignal. Then he hears 52 dots. The corrected proper count for use with tables or a chart is
   a)   a dot count consisting of 60 dots and no dashes.
   b)   a dash count consisting of 4 dashes and 56 dots.
   c)   a dot count consisting of 56 dots and 4 dashes.

5. Consolan
   a)   is recommended for coastal piloting.
   b)   is not recommended for coastal piloting.

omni/VOR

1. omni/VOR bearings are
   a)   computed by the navigator.
   b)   adversely affected by masts and rigging.
   c)   transmitted by a land-based station.

2. Bearings indicated by the omni/VOR receiver are
   a)   bearings from True North.
   b)   bearings from Magnetic North.
   c)   bearings measured relative to the bow of the vessel.

3. omni/VOR bearings are transmitted
   a)   only once in a while during fog conditions.
   b)   continuously during daylight hours.
   c)   in the Morse Code only.
   d)   24 hours a day.

4. An omni/VOR bearing of **300° from** means that the direction from the receiver to the station is
   a)   300°.
   b)   120°.
   c)   210°.
   d)   030°.
   e)   190°.

5. omni/VOR transmits on
   a)   very low frequency.
   b)   medium frequency.
   c)   very high frequency.
   d)   the same as Radio Direction Finder.
   e)   (c) and (d) above.

Omega and Decca

1. Omega is
   a)   a point source radio navigation system.
   b)   an area coverage radio navigation system.

2. Omega transmission can be received
   a)   by omni/VOR receivers.
   b)   by Consolan receivers.
   c)   by single purpose Omega receivers.

3. Omega transmits a signal
   a)   of very low frequency.
   b)   of the same frequency as Consolan.
   c)   of very high frequency.
   d)   of the same frequency as Decca.

4. Decca is
   a)   of longer range than Omega.
   b)   of shorter range than Omega.
   c)   of less accuracy than RDF.
   d)   of less accuracy than Consolan.

5. The purpose of the decometer is to indicate
   a)   the bearing of a Decca transmitter for reference to a Decca chart.
   b)   the frequency of a Decca transmitter for identification on a Decca chart.
   c)   the latitude and longitude of the receiver.
   d)   the lane and zone identification of a hyperbolic line on a Decca chart.

Loran

1. Loran transmits
   a)   on a higher frequency than Omega.
   b)   on a higher frequency than omni/VOR.
   c)   from one station only.
   d)   from a cluster of 4 to 6 transmitters located at the center of a circular transmission pattern.

2. The range of Loran
   a)   is less than RDF.
   b)   is less than omni/VOR.
   c)   is less than Decca.
   d)   none of above.

3. The principle on which Loran operates requires
   a)   that the navigator count dots and dashes transmitted.
   b)   that a receiver measure the microseconds of time delay between two signals.

c) that the navigator rotate an aerial to detect the strongest signal.
d) that a receiver measure the phase difference between two signals.

4. Loran charts
   a) have straight lines printed on them starting from the Loran transmitters.
   b) have hyperbolic lines of time delay printed on them.
   c) must be constructed by the navigator from printed tables.

5. Loran signals transmitted from ashore
   a) are on the same frequency as marine radiobeacons.
   b) can be received on the vessel with an omni/VOR receiver.
   c) require a special receiver aboard.

...and answers

Maxe has thrown you 25 curves, so you should allow 4 points for each correct answer. Should you score 100, he self-destructs. Short of that, locate your position as follows:

92 - 100:	Right On!
84 - 90:	Position Probable.
76 - 82:	Position Approximate.
Below 76:	Position Pretty Poor.

Radio Direction Finders

1. (a)   2. (c)   3. (a)   4. (c)   5. (c)

Consolan

1. (c)   2. (b)   3. (a)   4. (b)   5. (b)

omni/VOR

1. (c)   2. (b)   3. (d)   4. (b)   5. (c)

Omega and Decca

1. (b)   2. (c)   3. (a)   4. (b)   5. (d)

Loran

1. (a)   2. (d)   3. (b)   4. (b)   5. (c)

section 11
contents

48/Marine Electronics
Radiotelephones—equipment

No one remains unimpressed by the taming of the electron. Adroit drill has schooled it to measure direction and distance and to wrap Earth in a crisscross of exaggerated curves. So dazzling are these fresh exploits, one might tend to gloss over earlier feats which by now are humdrum routine. The deft manner in which the electron handles marine communications deserves more, and we're going to afford it just consideration. The use of radio waves to carry seagoing messages is as old as the twentieth century . . . and brimful of growing vigor. Far from a quick once-over, our inspection will focus on equipment, procedures and regulations. But first we'll glance astern to review a fact or two bobbing in our wake.

In Section IV, when discussing Signaling, we met the distress call. *Mayday* is the most imperative word spoken afloat, whether heard off Japan, in a Norwegian fiord or when entering the Bay of Naples. It is the heart of marine communications, and ever since the *Titanic* disaster in 1912, there has been no letup in pursuing superior means for ships to call for help. To set our mood, perhaps we can even risk an observation philosophical. Our present world attempts to re-awaken human concern for others on the planet. The fact that *Mayday* gains obedience everywhere, and has been so commanding for years, should impress even the most cynical. Here is undeniable evidence that people voluntarily can become involved. Here, as in International Rules of the Road, is an operational program followed by seafarers regardless of nationality, affluence, belief or pigment. In fact, here is a trust to be used with respectful care and passed along intact to seafarers yet to come. Now we'll nudge the soap box under the bunk and get down to work.

Our focus will be on equipment to carry the **spoken** word from ship to ship and between ship and shore. **Continuous wave (CW)** radiotelegraphy and its dots and dashes from all the ships at sea is not part of our topic. We'll restrict our view to radiotelephones. Three bands of the spectrum are involved: **medium frequency (MF), high frequency (HF)** and **very high frequency (VHF).** Which one is put to work depends on the service required and on the characteristics of the radio waves. In turn, equipment is designed to exploit the weaknesses as well as strengths these waves might have. VHF, for example, has short range because the waves are line-of-sight. So, VHF equipment is made low-power to be easy on the

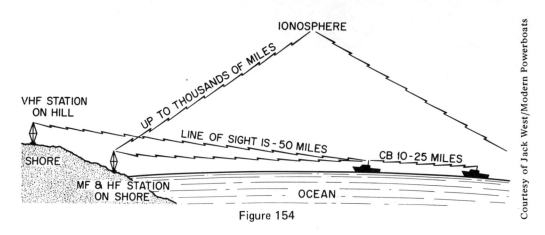

Figure 154

vessel's battery system. Medium and high frequency waves, though, have sky wave characteristics. Their bounces off the ionosphere bring greater range. So the equipment is built to use greater power. Available to the mariner is an assortment of sets, each making best use of what it has to work with. **Figure 154** sketches the range comparisons of the frequencies normally encountered aboard. Here comes another view of the radio spectrum to see where the various radiotelephones fit. **Figure 155** is related to one we've already encountered in Section IX's Introduction to Marine Electronics. But here the focus is on the radiotelephone. The table goes up to 162.55 mHz, the frequency on which continuous weather reports are

Very High Frequency (VHF) (Radiotelephone)	156.0 - 162.55 mHz
Omni/VOR	108.0 - 118.0 mHz
Citizen's Band (CB) (Radiotelephone)	26.9 - 27.3 mHz
High Frequency (HF) (Radiotelephone)	4.0 - 23.0 mHz
Medium Frequency (MF) (Radiotelephone)	1.6 - 3.5 mHz (1600 - 3500 kHz)
Loran-A	1650 - 1950 kHz
Broadcast	530 - 1600 kHz
Consolan and Marine Radiobeacons	190 - 400 kHz
Loran-C	100 kHz
Decca	70 - 130 kHz
Omega	10.2 - 13.6 kHz

Figure 155

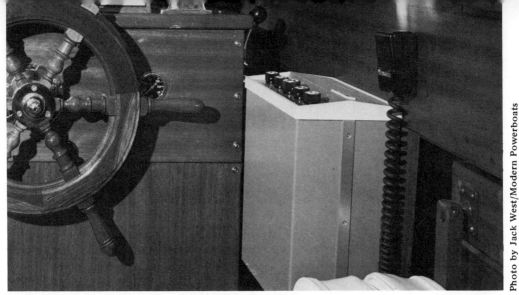

MF radiotelephone mounted vertically near main steering station. It has up to eight channels for ship-to-ship and ship-to-shore use, plus a channel for broadcast band reception.

Photo by Jack West/Modern Powerboats

available in some areas. That is below the ultra high frequencies of television's UHF, which is underneath radar, nestling in the pinnacles of SHF for super high frequency. Marine radiotelephone service shuns that ultra-plus society and consorts with the more conservative MF's, HF's and VHF's.

Most radiotelephones aboard are medium frequency: "2- to 3-mHz" sets. Over 150,000 of them are licensed on US-owned vessels alone. For years little has changed in the way they are put together, other than accommodation of the transistor and its advantages of less power drain and smaller size. For those years the custom has been to rate a set by its wattage, but this calls for a closer look. To say a set is of 30 watts or of 150 watts doesn't really tell much about the power leaving its antenna. The rating refers to the amount of power applied to an element in the transmitter. This, in effect, is **input** power. But what goes in doesn't always come out. The **radiated** power may be 30% to 60% lower. The **talking** power, as we'll see in a bit, is something else again.

Here is a rough rule of thumb to relate power and range of transmission: **for each watt of rated input power, a medium frequency radio will transmit one mile**. So, a 30-watt set may talk 30 miles and a 75-watt radio might reach out 75 miles. But the thumb being used is really pretty gnarled, for many factors can vary the estimate. Two that we've already met are time of day and intervening terrain. As a general rule, range at night is much greater than in daytime. Occasionally a 150-watt set can talk over a thousand miles or even more; yet the same set under adverse conditions might not be able to reach a receiver 25 miles away.

Time now to see what channels are used in the medium frequency band. Every set is required to handle the international distress frequency, 2182 kHz. In addition it must have at least two others. They can be chosen from the ship-to-ship frequencies and from ship-to-shore; they can vary with locality. Common, though, to all US coasts are the ship/ship channel for 2638 kHz, and the Coast Guard working frequency of 2670 kHz. Here is a six-channel pattern often found: 2182 kHz for calling and distress; 2670 kHz for working with the Coast Guard; 2638 kHz and a regional one for ship-to-ship calls; then two more channels for ship-to-shore use.

Additional frequencies have been set aside for Coast Guard Auxiliary use. Authorized boats on official patrols or missions find them convenient and congestion-free for calls within their group and to the Coast Guard.

Being placed before us now is a draught of electronic theory. We don't have to drink too deeply, but a sip or two is unavoidable. From the beginning, marine radiotelephones have used **double-sideband** radio waves. Here's the general idea. When an operator presses a "push-to-talk" button and speaks into the microphone, his message is transmitted on each side of an inaudible carrier wave. But this has not been the most efficient way to handle things. An example shows the shortcomings. Assume that a 150-watt **input** rated set **radiates** 100 watts of power from its antenna. That is a step-down of 1/3 already. But the losses have just begun. The inaudible carrier wave takes about 2/3 of the radiated 100 watts. Now there is only 1/3 of the 100 watts left to be divided between the two sidebands to handle the message. In figures, then, the 150 watts becomes 100 watts; and of the 100 watts, not even 34 get the message. Each sideband has a talking power of only about 17 watts, 1/6 of radiated power. A very high tariff has been charged by the carrier wave. Something had to be done about this inequity.

And in 1967, it was. At the World Administrative Radio Conference held that year in Geneva, a new set of International Radio Regulations was adopted and included was a redressing of the balance. All MF and HF double-sideband equipment aboard and at shore stations was ordered to be phased out and single-sideband substituted.

There are many reasons why this change is in order. Single-sideband is much more efficient. Practically all the radiated power is converted into **talking** power. This brings greater range for the same measure of input power. The other side of that coin is much less power to get equal range. Let's go back to our example of the 150-watt set. For the same range under SSB, the input would be reduced to about 20 watts. Another advantage: SSB uses a narrower channel than does DSB. So the new schedule will allow more channels to handle the inevitable increase in marine radio traffic.

Quite a bit of thought has been given to achieving an easy transition. A five-year period was decreed for most of the changes to be made ... no new DSB licenses issued after January 1, 1972 and only SSB equipment (provided VHF is aboard) licensed after January 1, 1972; but a ruling was also made that vessels with DSB aboard would be allowed to use it until January 1, 1977, so long as ownership of the radio didn't change and the license was renewed prior to expiration.

SSB has been in use for many years by the military, by amateurs and by merchant shipping. So ordering it for the marine radiotelephone field doesn't involve an adventure with untried tools. Of course, that doesn't guarantee trouble-free transition. But in the long run the new setup will bring greater safety and more efficient dispatch of the ship's business.

A **high frequency** radiotelephone is often called a **high seas set.** It has much greater range than medium frequency equipment. In fact, range can be nearly world-wide. A primary use is for communications between ships and shore-based stations such as the marine operator, shipping companies, canneries and the like. There are also channels available for ship-to-ship contacts.

Ten-channel medium and high frequency, single-sideband radiotelephone with frequency range from 1.6 to 13 mHz and peak power output of 100 watts.

The frequency range is from 4000 kHz to 23,000 kHz—or 4.0 mHz to 23.0 mHz—and there are a lot of specific channels in that spread. As usual, range is affected by atmospheric conditions, time of day and season of the year, and normally the higher frequencies are used for longer range. Three US public correspondence stations (marine operators) are maintained for high seas sets . . . in San Francisco, New York and Miami. Because of the long range involved, these three appear to be all that are needed. Finally, high frequency equipment is also being shorn of a sideband and converted to the new SSB arrangement.

Now to **very high frequency** . . . the **VHF** radiotelephones. They are basically line-of-sight transmitters, and so have a range limitation of from 15 to 50 miles. With that come advantages and disadvantages. Here is one of medium frequency's problems. When talking with another vessel only 15 miles away, MF's great range and power might reach out to every vessel within 100 miles. The result can be interference in too wide an area. VHF cures this. Because of its limited range, only sets within the immediate area receive the transmission.

Figure 156 illustrates this. Boats **A** and **B** can talk with each other; Boats **C** and **D** can talk together. Boat **A** can also reach the shore-based marine operator but **C** and **D** will not be bothered by **A** and **B**. By contrast, if all were using medium

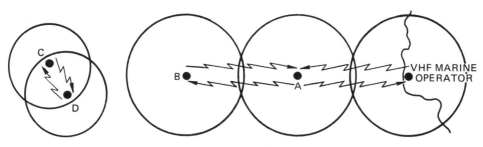

Figure 156

frequency sets, the **C/D** conversation would interfere with the **A/B** exchange, and so forth. So VHF has a definite advantage for ship-to-ship communication at short range. A disadvantage, though, is also evident: both **C** and **D** are too far out to reach the marine operator by VHF. The moral of the story: choice of equipment depends on the task.

VHF channels are available for ship-to-ship talk and for ship to such shore stations as yacht clubs, marine operators, lock tenders, towboat dispatchers and harbor masters. There is also a VHF international distress frequency—156.8 mHz—monitored by the Coast Guard and by shore-based marine operators.

Here is a schedule of the FCC allocation of VHF channels and frequencies. The left-hand numbers in the **Channel Designator** column are the original 18 VHF channels plus Channels 15 and 17. Then by reducing the channel spacing from 50 kHz to 25 kHz, it was possible to add those listed in the right-hand side of that column.

CHANNEL DESIGNATOR	FREQUENCY (MHZ)		POINTS OF COMMUNICATION
	SHIP	COAST	
DISTRESS, SAFETY & CALLING			
16	156.800	156.800	INTERSHIP AND SHIP TO COAST
SAFETY			
06	156.300	156.300	INTERSHIP
PORT OPERATIONS			
65	156.275	156.275	INTERSHIP AND SHIP TO COAST
66	156.325	156.325	INTERSHIP AND SHIP TO COAST
12	156.600	156.600	INTERSHIP AND SHIP TO COAST
73	156.675	156.675	INTERSHIP AND SHIP TO COAST
14	156.700	156.700	INTERSHIP AND SHIP TO COAST
74	156.725	156.725	INTERSHIP AND SHIP TO COAST
20	157.000	161.600	INTERSHIP AND SHIP TO COAST
NAVIGATIONAL			
13	156.650	156.650	INTERSHIP AND SHIP TO COAST
ENVIRONMENTAL			
15	....	156.750	COAST TO SHIP
COMMUNICATIONS WITH US COAST GUARD			
17	156.850	156.850	SHIP TO COAST

CHANNEL DESIGNATOR		FREQUENCY (MHZ)		POINTS OF COMMUNICATION
		SHIP	COAST	
COMMERCIAL				
07		156.350	156.350	INTERSHIP AND SHIP TO COAST
	67	156.375	....	INTERSHIP
08		156.400	....	INTERSHIP
09		156.450	156.450	INTERSHIP AND SHIP TO COAST
10		156.500	156.500	INTERSHIP AND SHIP TO COAST
11		156.550	156.550	INTERSHIP AND SHIP TO COAST
	77	156.875	....	INTERSHIP
18		156.900	156.900	INTERSHIP AND SHIP TO COAST
19		156.950	156.950	INTERSHIP AND SHIP TO COAST
	79	156.975	156.975	INTERSHIP AND SHIP TO COAST
	80	157.025	157.025	INTERSHIP AND SHIP TO COAST
	88	157.425	....	INTERSHIP
NON–COMMERCIAL				
	68	156.425	156.425	INTERSHIP AND SHIP TO COAST
09		156.450	156.450	SHIP TO COAST
	69	156.475	156.475	SHIP TO COAST
	70	156.525	....	INTERSHIP
	71	156.575	156.575	SHIP TO COAST
	72	156.625	....	INTERSHIP
	78	156.925	156.925	SHIP TO COAST
PUBLIC CORRESPONDENCE				
24		157.200	161.800	SHIP TO PUBLIC COAST
	84	157.225	161.825	SHIP TO PUBLIC COAST
25		157.250	161.850	SHIP TO PUBLIC COAST
	85	157.275	161.875	SHIP TO PUBLIC COAST
26		157.300	161.900	SHIP TO PUBLIC COAST
	86	157.325	161.925	SHIP TO PUBLIC COAST
27		157.350	161.950	SHIP TO PUBLIC COAST
	87	157.375	161.975	SHIP TO PUBLIC COAST
28		157.400	162.000	SHIP TO PUBLIC COAST

We've got one more type of radiotelephone to discuss: **Citizen's Band**, or **CB**. These sets are not basically marine units, but are licensed for general radio communications. The others we've seen—MF, HF and VHF—are only for marine service. Even so, CB's are widely used on vessels, and to good advantage.

They are restricted to five watts of input power, and so have a maximum range of five to 20 miles. But that's adequate for within-the-group conversation between a fishing boat and its net tenders, a race committee boat and the clubhouse, a boat owner and his nearby home, or between vessels cruising together.

A CB set can have as many as 23 crystal-controlled channels, but usually handles less. The original idea was for use between a base station and mobile units of the same licensee . . . a trucking company, a taxicab fleet, a towboat company. Under that arrangement, the FCC license was granted for the base station and for any number of additional units, and communication was restricted to those within that system. But in mid-1966, the FCC broadened the concept by permitting one licensee to talk to another on Channels 9 to 14 and on Channel 23.

One of CB's drawbacks is that there are no officially designated channels for ship-to-ship or ship-to-shore messages. You might end up hailing a cab! Well, at least the exclusive feature is not available. Nor is it possible to talk with the Coast Guard or to place a call through a marine operator. However, Channel 9 has been FCC-designated for emergency communications between owners of CB equipment.

In some areas, users of CB have unofficially chosen specific channels for service. So, during a cruise a group could decide on one of the channels between 9 and 14 for enroute talk. But this is purely optional and the channel is not exclusively appropriated.

That's the radiotelephone equipment picture. By this time, the stage might well appear so crowded with channels and sets and sidebands that a summary of the high points would be helpful:

1. Whether service is to be from ship-to-ship or ship-to-shore, and whether range of transmission is usually long or short will influence the selection of the type radiotelephone. Scope of use may make two systems desirable: VHF for short range, and medium or high frequency equipment for use farther at sea.
2. Medium frequency (MF) radios, operating between 2 and 3 mHz, have ranges of 150 miles or more; are the most common equipment aboard.
3. High frequency (HF) radios, operating between 4 and 23 mHz, are mainly for ship-to-shore communication at long range.
4. Both MF and HF are switching to single-sideband emission (SSB) from double-sideband (DSB).
5. VHF equipment, operating in the 156- to 163-mHz area, is limited to a range of 15 to 50 miles. It can be used for exchanges between vessels, or from ship to shore.
6. Citizen's Band radiotelephones are no substitute for marine equipment. Frequencies are not monitored by the Coast Guard or by marine operators; there are no officially designated channels for particular communications. They are useful, though, for short range calls between boats, and from vessels to shoreside units in the immediate area.

Some means of radio communication is obviously desirable. Mercury's winged heels stop at the high water line, and mail buoys are not on the postman's route. The isolation of the sea is too complete to warrant being that out of touch. Every pleasure mariner should seriously consider installing radiotelephone equipment . . . and this chapter might be an adequate guide to his choice.

49/Marine Electronics
Radiotelephones—procedures

Every night of the week, TV presents at least one example of simulated radio-telephone talk. Detective to Headquarters, Spaceman to Ground Control, Secret Agent to his Contact . . . it comes in regularly. From viewing it, we might conclude that the laconic manner and staccato exchanges are exaggerated underplay. Perhaps when an actor fires bursts like "I've got a 325 on a 681 at 514 . . . Roger, Willco, Out," there might be some parting company with reality. But the idea for actual procedure is faithfully there. The radiotelephone is a party line. Official conversations find code and brevity attractive. In private use, the brevity, at least, is to be maintained. But stream-of-consciousness conversation on a private line is so much a part of our lives that we become unaware of the good reasons behind officialdom's impersonal routines. That, however, is no excuse for self-conscious-ness or reluctance in adopting established radiotelephone manners. So, don your earphone-equipped crash helmet, adjust your throat mike and, stoic face rouged with just the right shade of unconcern, read on about how it should be done.

First of all, the Federal Communications Commission (FCC) encourages by rule and example that things be said and done in set patterns. Messages fall into two general categories: those affecting **safety** of life and property, and those concerned with the **ship's business**. The aim is to keep the party lines open for as many users as possible with guarantees that emergency traffic can get through.

The primary use, of course, is safety, and the international distress frequencies of 2182 kHz on MF and 156.8 mHz on VHF are reserved for such calls. The only other time those frequencies are used is when calling up another vessel, and then, both switch to a working frequency for their exchange.

The law of averages says that of all the receivers on Coast Guard units afloat and ashore, on pleasure craft and on commercial vessels, someone is going to hear a distress call. A vessel in trouble is nearly always within range of another station. This is even more likely when the call is on 2182 kHz by medium frequency equipment. Its longer range, coupled with the greater number of MF receivers, almost always assures contact.

In Section IV we discussed the three safety messages: *Mayday* for *distress, Pan* for *urgency* and *Sécurité* for *safety*. But we still have a little more to add about distress. Such a call has the highest priority of all messages, and every vessel must clear the air unless she is in a position to render assistance. Then she reports in and literally plays it by careful ear thereafter. *Mayday* means imminent danger. Merely running out of gas in mid-channel doesn't qualify. Of course, if because of it the vessel is in immediate danger of going on the rocks, that's a different story. Whatever the cause of the peril, here is the procedure to call for assistance. On 2182 kHz or 156.8 mHz, listen for other traffic. You might not be the only one in trouble. When the channel is clear, slowly and clearly transmit the message:

> *MAYDAY, MAYDAY, MAYDAY! This is Bluebird WY 2220, Bluebird WY 2220, Bluebird WY 2220, Position (latitude and longitude, or bearing and distance from an identifiable landmark or reference). Have hit a log and stove hole in bottom; taking on water faster than pumps can handle; six persons aboard; boat is 30 feet long, white hull and green decks. This is Bluebird WY 2220.*

> *Over*

The chances are that Coast Guard personnel will receive the message. Frequently they ask for a repeat of the message to verify their first understanding. They may also ask for a **long count**: the distressed vessel repeats name and call sign and then counts aloud slowly from one to ten and back to one. This gives patrol craft with radio direction finding equipment an opportunity to get a bearing.

Search and rescue may then follow by Coast Guard surface or aircraft. In either case the vessel in distress should stay on 2182 kHz or 156.8 mHz. The search units might have trouble in locating the distressed boat and need another long count for a radio bearing.

Radio Navigational Aids, HO 117, published by the US Navy Oceanographic Office, details in its Chapter 5 the procedures for these emergency messages we've been discussing. It mentions three additional statements that can be used in distress traffic. If the operator on the vessel in trouble hears that his transmissions are meeting interference, he can impose silence by saying clearly (and, one would expect, with firmness), *Seelonce Mayday.* This is the phonetic pronunciation of the French expression, "silence, m'aider." If someone else nearby notes the interference and feels it essential to interpose, he can say *Seelonce, Distress,* followed by his call sign. Of course, those righteously indignant should not become such a large chorus that the details of distress can't be heard through the din. A few outraged "shut ups" in required format should be enough.

Well worth noting is that a distress message may be sent by a station not itself in distress. Here are the three circumstances when this is allowed: (1) when the distressed vessel is not able to transmit a distress message; (2) when the person in charge of the distressed vessel thinks such further help is necessary; and (3) when, although not in a position to render assistance, a vessel hearing a distress message realizes that it has not been acknowledged by anyone. In such cases, though, this other vessel doesn't just say *Mayday.* Listeners might think that he is the one in trouble. He transmits, three times, *Mayday Relay.* Then he says *This is,* and adds his call sign. Then comes the message about the other's trouble.

A welcome part of the distress routine is this. When the distress traffic has ceased, or when silence is no longer necessary, all listeners should be advised that they can get back to normal duties. This is done by a "to all stations" call which starts with *Mayday,* spoken three times. Then comes *This is,* and the identification of the sender. The time of the message is sent next and the name and call sign of the vessel which had been in distress. Then comes *Seelonce Feenee,* phonetics for the French *silence fini.* One could, apparently, be wracked by curiosity over the fate of the distressed boat and glean little from this notice of completion. We'll see later on that the listener to such distress traffic might well never learn any more. His inquisitive streak is not sufficient warrant for a call to find out what happened. There's no point, though, in our pursuing this possibility of torture for gossips. So we'll "seelonce feenee" further mention of safety message routine, and get on to the next piece of business.

And that is the **ship's business** message: one between two vessels or from ship to shore-based marine operator. When ship-to-ship, these messages are called **operational communications.** The FCC defines them as having to do with the navigation, movement or management of the vessel. FCC doesn't have in mind chitchat about cocktail parties, Aunt Susie's health or the size of the fish that fell off the hook.

Navigation messages relate to courses, speed, weather and sea conditions, tides, charts, rendezvous and interception details and the like. **Movement** messages involve destinations, times of departures, estimated times of arrival, harbor conditions and so forth. Management messages speak of fuel and water, stores and supplies, repairs, medical supplies, and such matters.

When a matter of ship's business is to be transmitted to another vessel, the procedure would be this. On 2182 kHz or 156.8 mHz, the caller listens to hear if other traffic is on the air. Not until the channel is clear may he call the other craft. Then he would say:

> *Thunderbird WZ 2100, Thunderbird WZ 2100, Thunderbird WZ 2100. This is Blackbird WB 1000, Blackbird WB 1000, Blackbird WB 1000.*
>
> *Over*

When Thunderbird hears the call, he acknowledges by saying:

> *Blackbird WB 1000, this is Thunderbird WZ 2100. Switching to 2638* (if medium frequency radio is being used) *or, switching to Channel 8* (if VHF is in use).
>
> *Out*

Both would then change to the agreed channel. But, before transmitting, they would listen to hear if it is clear. When it is, Blackbird could start the conversation by saying:

> *Thunderbird WZ 2100, this is Blackbird WB 1000.*
>
> *Over*

And Thunderbird replies:

> *Blackbird WB 1000, this is Thunderbird WZ 2100. Go ahead with your message.*
>
> *Over*

Six-channel VHF radiotelephone.

Notice that in order to minimize time on the air, they no longer make several repetitions of their names. They've already established contact and know who is in the scene. Now Blackbird can get to his message:

> *Thunderbird WZ 2100, this is Blackbird WB 1000. When I reach the harbor I will need 200 gallons of gasoline. Will you advise the station that it may be as late as 1800 hours before I will be at the dock? After fueling we will anchor in the harbor and can then transfer the small boat and sleeping bags to your boat. This is Blackbird WB 1000.*
>
> *Over*

Thunderbird replies:

> *Blackbird WB 1000, this is Thunderbird WZ 2100. I received your message and will comply. This is Thunderbird WZ 2100.*
>
> *Out*

Blackbird need say no more. He has identified himself by name and by call sign at the beginning of his message. That's all FCC requires. To do more would be to clutter the air with unnecessary transmissions. Too often vessels consume another half or full minute by this sort of chatter:

> *Thunderbird WZ 2100, this is Blackbird WB 1000. Thank you very much and we will see you later; take it easy. This is Blackbird WB 1000. Out and clear with Thunderbird.*

Now to distinguish *Over* and *Out*. When one party is at the end of a transmission and wants to indicate to the other that he is finished and that he expects a reply, he says *Over*. When one party wants to show he has had his say and that no further communication is expected, he says *Out*. The two should never be used together . . . *Over and Out* is a contradiction. Either the conversation is completed (*Out*) or it is to be continued (*Over*). It cannot be both.

When talking to a shore-based marine operator, the procedure is much the same as that from ship-to-ship. The radiotelephone frequency control knob would be turned to the marine operator's channel. If there is traffic on that frequency, the calling vessel must wait until it is clear. Then he would place his call to the public correspondence station (marine operator) as follows:

> *San Francisco Marine Operator, San Francisco Marine Operator, San Francisco Marine Operator. This is Blackbird WB 1000, Blackbird WB 1000, Blackbird WB 1000. I would like to place a call.*
>
> > *Over*

The marine operator would reply:

> *Blackbird WB 1000, this is San Francisco Marine Operator. What city and number do you wish?*
>
> > *Over*

Blackbird would then say:

> *San Francisco Marine Operator, this is Blackbird WB 1000. My position is 25 miles northwest of Santa Barbara. I wish to talk with New York City, Area Code 212, phone number PLaza 6-2000.*
>
> > *Over*

When the marine operator has the party on the line, she will call Blackbird and the call can proceed. At the end of the conversation, Blackbird would say:

> *San Francisco Marine Operator, this is Blackbird WB 1000. I am finished.*
>
> > *Out*

When a navigator discovers a menace to navigation, he has an obligation to tell the seagoing world about it. That's what the *Sécurité*, or safety signal, is for . . . to indicate that the station is about to transmit a message concerning the safety of navigation or giving important meteorological warnings. The menace could be an iceberg, a tropical storm, a derelict, wreckage, buoy adrift, and on and on. It is something menacing safe passage. So whom do you call? To an extent, it depends on where you are. When cruising through Melanesia, a call to the Coast Guard might not be too effective; when cruising in Chesapeake Bay, placing a call to the Coast Guard would promise to be most effective. *Sécurité* is the international signal to announce a warning given to shipping in general. A call directed to the Coast Guard is the more or less domestic way to supply data from which a general warning to all can be prepared.

Let's take an example, not of sighting a danger southwest of Fiji, but of noticing one in home waters. A mariner sights what he feels is menacing and wants to report it to the Coast Guard. Before doing so, though, he should take just a few minutes for preparation. Telling the Coast Guard that a telephone pole is floating "out in the middle of Long Island Sound" is really not acting like Mr. Precision. The location and description should be prepared as well as possible.

Latitude and longitude, or bearing and distance from known landmarks, size of the danger, its color and condition . . . these facts will be helpful.

Having done his "homework," the mariner is ready to recite. He tunes to 2182 kHz or 156.8 mHz and listens for other traffic. When the channel is clear, he can start the procedure:

> *Coast Guard Long Beach, Coast Guard Long Beach, Coast Guard Long Beach. This is Blackbird WB 1000. Blackbird WB 1000. Blackbird WB 1000.*
>
> *Over*

The Coast Guard would acknowledge the call, and then Blackbird would say:

> *Coast Guard Long Beach, this is Blackbird WB 1000. My position is five miles bearing 180° magnetic from Long Beach Breakwater Light. I have sighted two logs each about 40 feet long and five feet in diameter. I believe they are menaces to navigation.*
>
> *Over*

Even if the call were not directed to the Coast Guard, the distress frequency would have been used to start the message rolling. Then, though, it could be *Sécurité, Sécurité, Sécurité, This is* . . . and so on. In either case it would probably be a good idea to get off the distress frequency as soon as possible. So, on the *Sécurité*-type call, the operator could announce his call on 2182 kHz or 156.8 mHz, identify himself and then say he was switching to a working frequency to give details. In the Coast Guard-directed call, there might well be an instruction from them to switch to another frequency to talk. However the word is passed, later on a weather broadcast might contain a warning to mariners about the telephone pole. The operator who made the initial report should be ready to shed indifference and feel a real satisfaction. For he has just been a party to a first-class, even though routine, accomplishment: using the radiotelephone for its intended purpose of safety at sea.

He should stand ready to expand that satisfied grin if he is cast in this scene. He sights a cluster of arms waving frantically on a small boat, and goes over to investigate. Their problem is one he can't handle, so he calls the Coast Guard. When a patrol craft or helicopter hurries into view, even the most indifferent person will hear background music and applause. Anyone who has ever been involved in such an incident will recognize the "Well Done" feeling and again be grateful for the miracle of radiotelephony.

Let's put a neat lashing around these procedural points with a recap. The radiotelephone is primarily intended for safety at sea, and should be used with that purpose in mind. Brevity is essential. In every region, tens of thousands of boats may want to exchange information, and some of it may be urgent. Don't block them by unnecessary and long-winded conversation. The FCC has made specific rules about how the equipment is to be used. Not only is standard operating procedure good sense and good manners, it is also what the law demands.

A few more items to mention before ending this chapter on how to call, whom to call, and what you might say and hear. A valuable bonus feature of radiotelephone is the availability of up-to-date weather information. In order to gain full advantage, the mariner should have aboard copies of pertinent *Marine Weather Services Charts*. These are published by the National Weather Service, and are available for about 15 cents each. They are updated regularly . . . and it takes sixteen of them to cover coastal waters of the fifty United States, including the Great Lakes, Puerto Rico and the Virgin Islands.

The information given on them is very impressive. They list the AM and FM broadcast stations transmitting weather information, including call sign and frequency. Also listed are the schedules, calls and frequency of marine forecasts and warnings direct from National Weather Service offices. Information on airways broadcasts, marine radiotelephone station services and special broadcast facilities are also included. Specified is the exact latitude and longitude of the antenna, and indications to what extent it is directional. All this assists in the taking of radio direction finder bearings on these stations. Local offices of the National Weather Service are listed, with telephone numbers. So the mariner not only knows the details of public weather bulletins, but also has at hand the National Weather Service number to call if he feels late information direct from the government source is necessary.

There are still other weather broadcast services to be had. In nearly every cruising area there is at least one low frequency airways beacon station in range. These installations transmit continuous weather information and cover a radius of about 100 miles from the station. They can be received on radio direction finder units.

Another source—one we've already mentioned back in Section X—is the VHF **omni/VOR** airways beacon. The broadcast schedule is usually once each half hour; and, as we've seen, an **omni** receiver is required.

The **marine operator** in the locality schedules two, and sometimes three, daily weather broadcasts on the 2-to-3-mHz radiotelephone band. The Coast Guard puts out the same information. Their broadcasts are first announced on 2182 kHz and then made on 2670 kHz.

The National Weather Service is commissioning VHF stations along coastal and inland waters to broadcast reports and warnings. These are taped reports transmitted continuously for from 16 to 24 hours each day and updated every few hours. A VHF radiotelephone can pick them up on 162.55 mHz; also available are low-cost, flashlight-battery powered receivers.

Prudence suggests that the mariner develop a list of all weather broadcasts in his area and keep it handy. We've given leads to quite a few sources, and there are more. The barometer might appear steady and its pointer might indicate a reassuring "Fair" . . . but storms have a way of popping up at inopportune times to scramble cruising plans. Taking advantage of information prepared by meteorologists after checking data assembled from observers over an entire area requires only that he set a control on the radiotelephone. We've seen here that service is available on RDF, MF, VHF and omni/VOR. What isn't supplied is the service to turn the knob, nor is there any reasonable expectation that this might be made available. So our mariner must, to that extent, be self-sufficient. But he does have a receiver—full of means to extend his weather eye far over the horizon and learn what might be coming his way.

50/Marine Electronics
Radiotelephones—laws, licenses and logs

Cynics are probably more made than born. After a few decades of being jostled about trying to buy a half-time hot dog, or dodging freeway flyers, even the most benevolent of us grows a bit wary. We've already lauded mariners for being surprisingly considerate of their fellows. And that still goes. But even mariners are not immune to shoreside contagion. The FCC takes such a realistic view and has set up strict, teeth-laden rules to encourage mariners to paths of virtue.

The details of applicable regulations are found in Part 83, Volume IV of FCC rules. Titled *Stations on Shipboard in the Maritime Service,* this booklet must be in the possession of the transmitting station's licensee. It is available at low cost from the Government Printing Office, and it explicitly tells what must and must not be done. Moreover, whether he ever reads it or not, the operator of a radiotelephone is held accountable for its contents. Ignorance of law is no more an excuse afloat than it is on shore. Let's take a look at some of its highlights.

Marine radiotelephones are licensed by the FCC for only two uses: safety and the conduct of ship's business. It is as illegal as spiriting money out of a bank vault to talk on a marine phone about last night's yacht club party, or how someone staggered off the gangway and fell into the bay. That is for the pay phone on the dock. When Flossie invites John by marine radio to a cocktail party, don't feel left out of the fun. If the FCC was monitoring the call, the playmates might be over to borrow a few hundred dollars to pay the fine.

Also prohibited is interference with ongoing communications. Before transmitting, the operator must be certain that there is no other traffic on the channel. Should there be, he must wait until it clears. This may mean a long wait, yet it must be done. The only exception, of course, is in case of emergency. That's always a special circumstance. But it must be a true emergency.

The FCC also has seen to it that an operator will not have to wait too long to place his call. There are restrictions on the length of time a communication can continue. First of all, calling up another vessel is limited. The initial "call up" cannot be longer than 30 seconds. If no contact is made, another call to the same station cannot be made until two minutes have elapsed. If still no answer, then another two-minute wait is specified. No more than three "call ups" are permitted within 15 minutes. So, after the third unsuccessful attempt, a wait of 15 minutes is necessary before the next cycle of no more than three tries can be made. Again, of course, under emergency conditions these restrictions don't apply.

After contact is made, the stations switch to a working frequency. But they can't monopolize the air then, even though they are speaking on authorized matters of ship's business. The exchange cannot last more than three minutes. If there is more to say, a breather of 15 minutes is specified before the same two stations can converse again. Either can talk with others in the meantime, but not to each other. So, thinking a bit about the conversation beforehand is a good idea. Too many "I'll think of it in a minute" remarks and your three minutes will be up with nothing accomplished.

Rules are strict and penalties are severe for use of obscene, indecent or profane language, and for transmitting messages of an obscene nature. Every performance on the radiotelephone must have a "G" rating. There's nothing unreasonable about restricting fo'c'sle and locker room talk to its customary forum.

What about secrecy? The radiotelephone is a party line, but that doesn't mean things said on it are public information. It is illegal to repeat to another person information heard over the air . . . except messages having to do with safety. It is also a violation for an operator to use for his own advantage any information he gains by listening in on the conversation of others. You hear two commercial fishermen talking about the location of a school of fish. For them it is a legal exchange of ship's business. Technically, though, you should get Satan behind you and resist the urge to cruise over with your fishing gear. Should that be done, the FBI might not stalk you for your misdeed . . . but it could. It is its job to investigate allegations of obscene, indecent or profane language and of violation of secrecy laws.

Now to licensing. All marine radiotelephones must be licensed by the FCC before they can be used, and the operator must have a permit. The station license requires that the applicant be an American citizen and that the equipment be "type accepted" by the FCC. The license itself is issued in the name of the applicant and the vessel, and is not transferable. When the original licensee sells the boat, the license must be returned to the FCC and the buyer must then apply for a new one. But an owner can replace a radiotelephone on his vessel with another unit without applying again, provided the unit is type accepted and is within the frequency range of the station license. Notification must be given in writing to the FCC of change of owner's address or change of boat name, and a copy of the letter must be attached to the station license. The term of these licenses is five years, and they are renewable. It is also required that the license be kept posted near the radio equipment.

Citizen's Band (CB) equipment involves a slightly different procedure. After application by the owner, the FCC assigns a call sign and issues a license. This is also the licensee's operator permit. The term, though, is the same five years.

For the other radiotelephones, however, the station license is only half the story. It is not enough that a license be issued for the set. What also is needed is that the operator himself have certification. Most pleasure mariners need only a **Restricted Radiotelephone Operator Permit**. It allows the holder to use medium frequency (2 to 3 mHz), high frequency (4 to 23 mHz) and VHF equipment. To secure one, the applicant completes a form declaring, among other things, that he is a US citizen, can understand and speak English, and can keep a written log. No examination is involved, and the permit is for life unless revoked by the FCC.

Another kind is the **Third Class Radiotelephone Operator Permit**. On vessels carrying six or more passengers for hire, one crew member must hold such a permit, even though only MF or VHF equipment is aboard. It has a five-year life and is renewable. An examination on operating regulations and procedures is required before issuance. The FCC has prepared study guide material to help applicants get ready.

Log-keeping is our next topic . . . and a good kick-off point is the distinction between a "voluntary equipped" vessel and one classed as "compulsory equipped." The FCC separates those who carry radiotelephones at their own option from those who are required to do so by law. The pleasure boat is under no mandate to have it aboard; vessels such as those in charter or passenger service must do so. From this comes a difference in watch-standing and logbook.

The volunteer is not required to stand watch on a distress frequency. It's up to the operator whether he wants to turn on the set or not. But if the radio is on and is not being used for communicating with others, it must be tuned to the distress frequency.

On a "compulsory equipped" vessel, the radio must be tuned to its distress frequency at all times underway . . . except when it is being used for communications on a working frequency.

Now to the log. FCC requires that a radio station logbook be kept. On the volunteer vessel, only entries affecting safety communications need be made; but they must be fairly detailed. Even though the station only hears a *Mayday* and does not get involved, the operator must enter the date and time of receipt, and the name and call sign of the distressed vessel. Then he must add an entry stating the gist of the message heard. Should an operator transmit urgent or safety messages, he must log the data on them. But he doesn't have to make those entries unless he does some transmitting.

Each page of the logbook must be numbered and must bear the name of the vessel and its call sign. All entries are to be signed by the person holding the operator permit. When equipment is installed or repaired, an entry is made showing what was done. It must be signed by the technician, with his license number and its date of expiration.

Logs are kept for one year minimum after the date of last entry. Part 83 of the FCC rules states conditions under which logbooks may be subject to inspection for even longer than one year. An example is involvement in a *Mayday* operation. All of this adds up to the importance of taking a good look at Part 83.

Seagoing logbooks of any kind are extremely important documents. They amount to official histories of vessels, with legal significance as course-of-business entries made concurrent with the happenings. Writing up a log three weeks after the fact is not the thing to do. Entries are not so complicated that a set routine of making notations at the time cannot be followed. And erasures don't sit well. If you make a mistake, put a line through the error and then write the correction above it, or alongside. It looks much more straight-forward. What goes for the

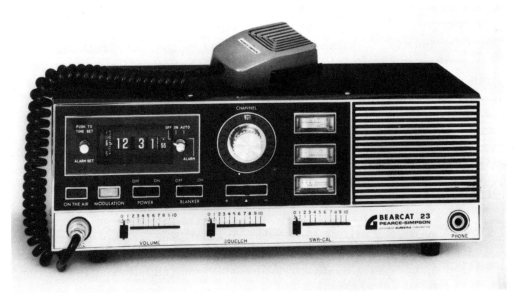

23-channel Citizen's Band (CB) radiotelephone.

radio log also applies to the deck log, and whatever other journals of the voyage may be maintained.

Testing the radiotelephone would seem to be a simple routine, yet it has been a real source of annoyance. The results are both FCC and common sense rules. Before transmitting, listen and be sure you will not interfere with other traffic. When the channel is clear, you are permitted a 10-second test transmission. State the boat's name and call sign, and then repeat *Testing* several times. End the test with the vessel's name, call sign and *Out*. If you are using the distress frequency for the test, another cannot be made until five minutes pass. Should the test be on a working frequency, you'll have to wait one minute.

Of course, so far you haven't talked **with** anyone in this test. Your *testing* word in pear-shaped tones is not always shared only by you and your microphone. You might well have talked **to** someone. At least, if your set has a radiation meter or bulb, you have evidence when it lights up that the carrier wave is on the air and that the transmitter is putting out. But in the electronic world it is often as good to receive as to give. So, the next phase of a test would involve communication, and there's where the annoyance factor cropped up.

Too often operators began acting as if their local Coast Guard station was like a Loran slave, waiting only to respond to every request for radio check directed its way. Coast Guard units have much more to do than to be "warm-up catchers" for mariners. At first gentlemanly requests were made by the score to stop the irritating practice of calling for a radio check. The requests became growls; finally, in 1970, the FCC unveiled its iron hand. Now it is illegal to call the Coast Guard for a radio check. There never was much justification for doing it. It's fairly easy to listen on a calling frequency until another station is heard on the air. Then, when his traffic clears, call and ask him to help you for a few seconds in finishing your test.

Key questions to ask before using a radiotelephone are these: "Is this call really necessary?" and "Does it relate to **safety** or **ship's business**?" Honest answers will screen out most of the calls that clutter the channels and end up being costly to the people involved. Violations of regulations can result in fines, loss of license and even imprisonment. The limit is much too expensive: a possible $10,000 fine, a maximum two-year imprisonment. But even the day-to-day penalties are of a species different to overtime on a parking meter. Fines of $100 for a single violation are not uncommon; $500 fines for groups of them might well be assessed.

Most common in the less-than-capital class of misdeed are:

1. Use of 2182 kHz or 156.8 mHz for other than "call up" transmissions and safety messages.
2. Failure to identify the vessel by name and call letters at the start and end of a communication.
3. Interference with distress messages or with traffic on working channels.
4. Operation of the station without an unexpired station license or operator permit.
5. Failure to answer timely an FCC dun about a violation.
6. Calling the Coast Guard for a radio check.

There's hardly an excuse for any of these; there's seldom the slightest inconvenience suffered by being law-abiding. Here is no Big Brother peering from a picture frame, ready to pounce on trifles. The demands really are no more than the exercise of good manners.

Earlier generations of seafarers knew the three L's as Lead, Log and Lookout. To them, the minimum standards for practical piloting were use of the hand lead for depth, the taffrail log for speed and then the lookout for dangers. We've bent things around a bit to gain our three L's of Laws, Licenses and Logbooks. But if these are respected as much as old-timers favored their ancestors, the modern three L's will keep radiotelephone a practical party line. There's only one way it can possibly work out . . . as a communal service. When users accede gracefully to sensible regulations, few problems arise.

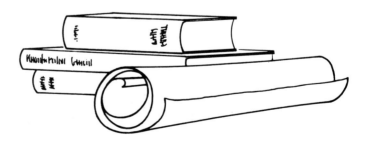

Questions

Coming down the channel on the crest of a carrier wave is a double-sideband crewed by MF's, HF's and VHF's with a CB as a coxswain. Its cargo? That's right, another 25 questions.

Radiotelephone Equipment

1. Medium frequency units
   a) transmit and receive only Morse Code communications.
   b) transmit and receive in the same frequency band as broadcast stations.
   c) have a normal range of several thousand miles.
   d) are called high seas sets.
   e) are the radiotelephones most frequently found on pleasure boats.

2. A rule of thumb for the range in miles of a medium frequency unit is
   a) four times the rated input power.
   b) never more than 20 miles.
   c) roughly as many miles as the rated watts of input power.
   d) the square root of a third of the carrier wave power divided by two.

3. Mandatory channels on a medium frequency unit are
   a) only 2182 kHz.
   b) 2182 kHz and 2670 kHz.
   c) 2182 kHz and two other channels.

4. High frequency radiotelephones
   a) are used only for ship-to-ship communications.
   b) operate in a band from 4 mHz to 23 mHz.
   c) are only good for short distances.
   d) are designed primarily for stations making a large number of calls.

5. Very high frequency radiotelephones
   a) are basically line-of-sight in range.
   b) do not have a channel for distress traffic.
   c) can only be used ship-to-ship.

6. Citizen's Band radiotelephones
   a) can be used to talk with the Coast Guard.
   b) have long range capability.
   c) are limited to 5 watts of input power.

7. Double-sideband equipment
   a) is replacing single-sideband marine radiotelephone units.
   b) is being replaced by single-sideband marine radiotelephone units.

    c)   uses two inaudible carrier waves with the message in the middle.

    d)   because of the frequency bands on each side of the main frequency, has twice the span of channels of single-sideband equipment.

8. Another name for a high seas set is
    a)   high frequency radiotelephone.
    b)   medium frequency radiotelephone.
    c)   very high frequency radiotelephone.
    d)   a soprano set, because of its ability to transmit high pitched sounds without distortion.
    e)   none of above.

Radiotelephone Procedures

1. When in distress, the operator would
    a)   say *Help, Help . . . I'm out of gas* on 2638 kHz.
    b)   use 2182 kHz or 156.8 mHz frequencies.
    c)   precede the distress message with *Sécurité, Sécurité.*

2. When finishing a communication the operator would say
    a)   *Goodby, will talk to you later.*
    b)   *Out.*
    c)   *Off, Over and Out.*
    d)   *Over and Out.*

3. Weather reports and forecasts can be heard on the beacon (low) frequency band
    a)   from Coast Guard radiobeacons.
    b)   from broadcast stations.
    c)   from airways beacons.

4. When an operator has heard a distress call and is asked by the distressed vessel to send out the distress message, he will first say
    a)   *Seelonce Feenee.*
    b)   *Seelonce Mayday.*
    c)   *Mayday.*
    d)   *Mayday Not Me.*
    e)   *Mayday Relay.*

5. Weather broadcasts on an omni/VOR airways beacon
    a)   can be received on a medium frequency radiotelephone.
    b)   can be received on a high seas set.
    c)   are received on the special omni receiver.

6. Weather reports and forecasts are transmitted on medium frequencies
    a)   by the Coast Guard every hour.

b) whenever the navigator requests transmission.

c) usually twice daily by marine operators and also by the Coast Guard.

7. A long count

   a) is a psychological device suggested to help a distressed person ward off panic by having him count slowly from one to 1000 and back again.

   b) is a Coast Guard rescue procedure designed to give a distressed person extra rest, and taking its name from a famous championship prizefight.

   c) is a radiotelephone procedure used in distressed situations to assist rescue craft in taking radio bearings.

8. Messages having to do with navigation, movement or management are termed

   a) operational communications.

   b) urgent communications.

   c) safety communications.

   d) ENEMEM calls.

Laws, Licenses and Logs

1. A medium frequency marine radiotelephone

   a) can be used without an operator permit if for pleasure.

   b) requires a station license and that the operator have at least a Restricted Radiotelephone Operator Permit.

   c) requires a station license and that the operator have a Third Class Radiotelephone Operator Permit.

2. The time limit for a communication is

   a) 15 minutes out of each half hour.

   b) unlimited.

   c) 3 minutes unless an emergency message.

3. Identifying the vessel by name and call sign

   a) is necessary only when first "calling up" another station.

   b) should be done every minute.

   c) must be done at the beginning and at the end of each communication.

4. 2182 kHz and 156.8 mHz frequencies

   a) are used for ship-to-ship communications.

   b) are reserved for distress traffic and for "calling up" other stations.

   c) are MF and VHF channels for public correspondence stations only.

5. A vessel voluntarily equipped with a radiotelephone

   a) need not keep a radio logbook.

   b) must log all traffic heard.

   c) must log all *Mayday* traffic heard.

   d) none of above.

6. The station license
    a) is good for the life of the equipment.
    b) must be posted near the radiotelephone.
    c) is not subject to forfeiture.

7. Radio checks
    a) are to be made only by calling the nearest Coast Guard unit.
    b) are to be made with other private vessels only when the Coast Guard gives express permission to do so.
    c) do not require identifying the vessel by name and call sign.
    d) should be made between boats using proper procedures for "call up" and then transfer to working frequencies.

8. The time limit for a "call up" is
    a) 3 minutes.
    b) 10 seconds.
    c) 3 minutes out of every 15 minutes.
    d) 30 seconds.

9. The number of "call ups" to the same station is
    a) unlimited.
    b) limited to 3 within 15 minutes.
    c) limited to 15 within 3 minutes.
    d) limited to 3 per hour with a minimum of 12 minutes delay between them.

...and answers

Score 4 for each correct response, and use this table to make your log entry:
    92 - 100:   No Communication Gap Here.
    84 - 90:   Adequate Job of Keeping in Touch.
    76 - 82:   Turn Up the Volume a Little.
    Below 76:   Put the Message in a Bottle and Throw it Overboard.

Radiotelephone Equipment

1. (e)   2. (c)   3. (c)   4. (b)   5. (a)   6. (c)   7. (b)   8. (a)

Radiotelephone Procedures

1. (b)   2. (b)   3. (c)   4. (e)   5. (c)   6. (c)   7. (c)   8. (a)

Radiotelephone Laws, Licenses and Logs

1. (b)   2. (c)   3. (c)   4. (b)   5. (c)   6. (b)   7. (d)   8. (d)   9. (b)

ready reference

Ready Reference/Contents

Mathematical Miscellany

Measurements of some kind or another are such nautical fundamentals that a mention of units, values and equivalents is essential.

First of all, a review of some prefixes:

mega-	means one million times a standard unit
myria-	means ten thousand times a standard unit
kilo-	means one thousand times a standard unit
hecto-	means one hundred times a standard unit
deca-	means ten times a standard unit
deci-	means one tenth of a standard unit
centi-	means one hundredth of a standard unit
milli-	means one thousandth of a standard unit
micro-	means one millionth of a standard unit
nano-	means one billionth of a standard unit

In what was called the English system of measurement, such prefixes are seldom encountered. They are decimal in character and so are found throughout the metric system. Now that Britain has decided to forsake feet and inches, perhaps the system we use might be known by its other name of **fps**, for foot-pound-second. This contrasts with Metric's other name of **cgs**, for centimeter-gram-second. In any case, the metric system is now closer to world-wide and comes with increasing regularity into things maritime.

Metric System Highlights

Linear:

kilometer (km)	= 1000 meters	= 3280 feet	= 0.54 naut. mile	= 0.62 stat. mile
hectometer (hm)	= 100 meters			
decameter (dkm)	= 10 meters			
meter (m)	=	3.28 feet	= 39.37 inches	
decimeter (dm)	= 0.1 meter			
centimeter (cm)	= 0.01 meter =	0.39 inch		
millimeter (mm)	= 0.001 meter =	0.004 inch		

Volume:

* cubic decameter (dkm^3) = 10 cubic meters
* cubic meter (m^3)
* cubic decimeter (dm^3) = 0.1 cubic meter
   cubic centimeter (cm^3) = 0.01 cubic meter = 0.061 cubic inch
   cubic millimeter (mm^3) = 0.001 cubic meter = 0.0061 cubic inch

* alternative names: cubic decameter is decastere; cubic meter is stere and cubic decimeter is decistere.

Weight:

metric ton (t)	=	1000 kilograms	=	2204 pounds		=	1.1 short tons
quintal (q)	=	100 kilograms	=	220.46 pounds			
kilogram (kg)	=	1000 grams	=	2.204 pounds			
hectogram (hg)	=	100 grams					
decagram (dkg)	=	10 grams					
gram (g)	=			0.0352 ounce			
decigram (dg)	=	0.1 gram					
centigram (cg)	=	0.01 gram					
milligram (mg)	=	0.001 gram					

Capacity:

kiloliter (kl)	=	1000 liters					
hectoliter (hl)	=	100 liters					
decaliter (dkl)	=	10 liters		= 2.64 US gallons			
liter (l)			= 1.06 quarts	= 0.265 US gallon	= 61.02 cubic inches		
deciliter (dl)	=	0.1 liter	= 0.21 pint				
centiliter (cl)	=	0.01 liter	= 0.34 ounce				
milliliter (ml)	=	0.001 liter					

Some General Values, Formulae and Equivalents

nautical mile	= 6076 feet		kilometer	= 3280 feet
	= 1013 fathoms			= 547 fathoms
	= 2025 yards			= 1093 yards
statute mile	= 5280 feet		cable length	= 600 feet
	= 880 fathoms			= 100 fathoms
	= 1760 yards			

US gallon	= 231 cubic inches		
imperial gallon	= 277.4 cubic inches		
liter	= 61.02 cubic inches		
liter	= 1.06 quarts	= 0.264 US gallon	
US gallon	= 3.785 liters	= 0.87 imperial gallon	
imperial gallon	= 4.545 liters	= 1.2 US gallons	

cubic foot of liquid	=	7.48 US gallons
US gallon fresh water	=	8.34 pounds
US gallon sea water	=	8.56 pounds
US gallon gasoline	=	6.1 pounds (approx.)
US gallon diesel	=	7.2 pounds (approx.)
cubic foot fresh water	=	62.4 pounds
cubic foot sea water	=	64 pounds
cubic foot ice	=	56.0 pounds
cubic foot gasoline	=	46.0 pounds (approx.)
cubic foot diesel	=	54.0 pounds (approx.)

long ton (2240 pounds)	= 35 cubic feet sea water	= 261.4 US gallons sea water
	= 36 cubic feet fresh water	= 269.3 US gallons fresh water
	= 49 cubic feet gasoline	= 364.3 US gallons gasoline
	= 41 cubic feet diesel	= 310.4 US gallons diesel

statute miles   =   1.15 x nautical miles
                   =   0.62 x kilometers

nautical miles   =   0.87 x statute miles
                   =   0.54 x kilometers

kilometers   =   1.61 x statute miles
                   =   1.85 x nautical miles

one knot   =   one nautical mile per hour
            =   101.3 feet per minute   =   32.8 yards per minute

one statute mile per hour   =   88 feet per minute
                                  =   29.3 yards per minute

standard barometric pressure   =   29.92 inches
                                       =   1013.25 millibars (mb)
                                       =   760 millimeters (mm)
                                       =   14.69 pounds per square inch (psi)

Temperature scales:

Fahrenheit: $32°$ =   freezing point of fresh water
                $212°$ =   boiling point of fresh water

Celsius: $0°$ =   freezing point of fresh water
(centigrade) $100°$ =   boiling point of fresh water

                   F   = $1.8C + 32°$
                   C   = $0.55 (F-32°)$

water pressure in pounds per square inch (psi):
      sea water   =   0.444 x depth in feet
      fresh water   =   0.434 x depth in feet

standard speed of sound in air: =   1117 feet per second
                                      =   761.6 statute miles per hour
                                      =   661.8 nautical miles per hour

standard speed of sound in sea water   =   4945 feet per second
                                          =   3371.9 statute miles per hour
                                          =   2930.1 nautical miles per hour

length of ocean waves   = $5.12 \times P^2$

speed of ocean swell   = $3.03 \times P$

(Note: P is period in seconds for one complete wave to pass observer.
          Formula valid when depth of water is more than half a wavelength.)

Magic Circles

Two annoying facets of practical navigation are the recall of a formula and then the tussle with rusty algebra to transpose the equation. Seamen, though, will use a reliable shortcut whenever possible; and a **Magic Circle** is such.

At first, until one gets the hang of it, a Magic Circle is confusing. Certainly for one whose mathematics is still bright and shiny it is unnecessary. But for the rest of us, the device is useful. The next few paragraphs show how it works.

Suppose you know that **A=B/C**. What is the formula to find **C**? When you're rusty in arithmetic, you are apt to rage while tossing the letters around. Magic Circles do the job with the pointing of a finger.

1) Draw a circle and then divide it into these parts:

2) Place the letters in the parts of the circle as shown:

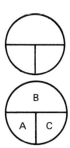

When values are separated by the horizontal line, division is indicated . . . **B/A** and **B/C**.

When values are separated by the vertical line, multiplication, instead, is called for . . . **A x C**.

Now, what is the formula to find **C**? Cover up **C**; what remains visible is the formula:

$$C = \frac{B}{A}$$

To find A:
$$A = \frac{B}{C}$$

To find B:
$$B = A \times C$$

The procedure is a little different when there are four values instead of three:

$$A = \frac{B\,C}{D}$$

$$D = \frac{B\,C}{A}$$

As for **B** or **C** . . . you invert the circle, for the unknown value should be on the bottom . . .

$$B = \frac{A\,D}{C}$$

$$C = \frac{A\,D}{B}$$

The inversion can be done mentally, or actually by capsizing the circle.

Now for some applications to seafaring.

Distance by Sound in Air:

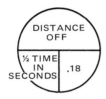

You make the sound and hear the echo.

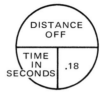

The sound comes from another.

Time, Speed and Distance:

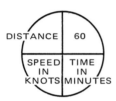

OR

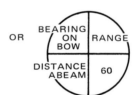

The Rule of 60:

OR

Conversions:

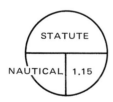

Nautical and statute miles

DEGREES / POINTS / 11.25

Degrees and Compass Points

Millibars and inches

F-32 / 5 / C / 9

Fahrenheit and Celsius (Centigrade)

Ship's Time Systems

The use of four digits to represent hours and minutes from midnight to midnight is standard aboard ship. The two left-hand digits represent the hour; the two right-hand digits are the minutes of the hour:

0000 hr.	=	12:00 midnight	1200	=	12:00 noon
0030	=	12:30 a.m.	1230	=	12:30 p.m.
0800	=	8:00 a.m.	2000	=	8:00 p.m.
1021	=	10:21 a.m.	2221	=	10:21 p.m.
1130	=	11:30 a.m.	2330	=	11:30 p.m.

and 2400 = 12:00 midnight = 0000 hr.

The ship's bell system to strike the time is based on a division of the day into four-hour watches. On each half hour, a bell signal is struck, with eight signals in all during each four-hour cycle. The pattern then repeats in successive four-hour watches throughout the day:

8 bells at 0000 hr. (midnight) 0400 (4:00 a.m.) 0800 (8:00 a.m.) 1200 (noon) 1600 (4:00 p.m.) 2000 (8:00 p.m.) and then at 2400 (midnight)

1 bell at the first half hour of the watch:
0030, 0430, 0830, 1230, 1630, 2030

2 bells at the second half hour of the watch:
0100, 0500, 0900, 1300, 1700, 2100

3 bells at the third half hour of the watch:
0130, 0530, 0930, 1330, 1730, 2130

4 bells at the fourth half hour of the watch:
0200, 0600, 1000, 1400, 1800, 2200

5 bells at the fifth half hour of the watch:
0230, 0630, 1030, 1430, 1830, 2230

6 bells at the sixth half hour of the watch:
0300, 0700, 1100, 1500, 1900, 2300

7 bells at the seventh half hour of the watch:
0330, 0730, 1130, 1530, 1930, 2330

8 bells at the end of the watch and beginning of the next watch:
0400, 0800, 1200, 1600, 2000, 2400 or 0000

Piloting

Five Special Bearing Cases

Name	First ϕ	Second ϕ	Distance Off at Second ϕ	Distance Off Abeam
Bow & Beam	45°	90°	Distance Run	Distance Run
Doubling the Angle	anything	2 x first	Distance Run	. . . .
Seven-Eight Rule	30°	60°	Distance Run	7/8 (0.87) Distance Run
Seven-Tenth Rule	22½°	45°	Distance Run	0.7 x Distance Run
Prediction	26½°	45°	1.4 x Distance run	Distance Run

Relative Bearings

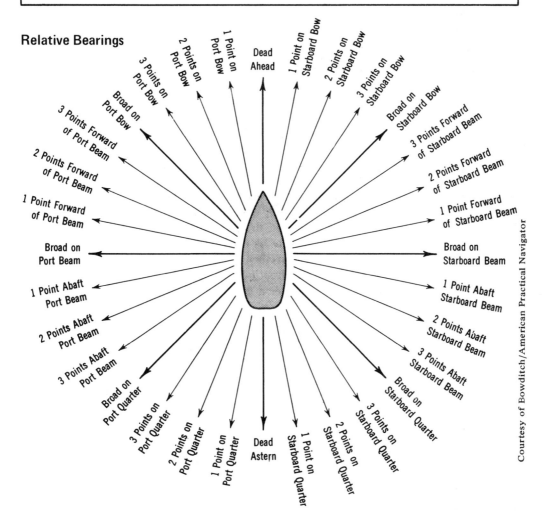

Courtesy of Bowditch/American Practical Navigator

Rule of Sixty

$$\text{Distance Abeam} = \frac{\text{Range x Bearing}}{60}$$

$$\text{Bearing on Bow} = \frac{\text{Distance Abeam x 60}}{\text{Range}}$$

Time, Speed and Distance Scale

Principle: A logarithmic scale of graduations from 0.1 to 60 used with dividers whose legs are named as in sketch. Length on the scale between a given distance and its time interval is the same as the length between corresponding distance in one hour (speed) and "60" mark. Given two of the three values of time, speed and distance, the third can be found on the scale. Here are some examples:

1. At 8.5 knots, how far traveled in 17 minutes?
   a) Right leg to 60, left leg to 8.5, then, keeping that span,
   b) Right leg to 17 and left leg falls on 2.4 miles.

2. If travel 2.4 miles in 17 minutes, what speed?
   a) Left leg to 2.4, right leg to 17, then,
   b) Right leg to 60 and left leg falls on 8.5 knots.

3. How long to travel 0.7 miles at 8.5 knots?
   a) Right leg to 60 and left leg to 8.5, then,
   b) Left leg to 0.7 and right leg falls on five minutes.

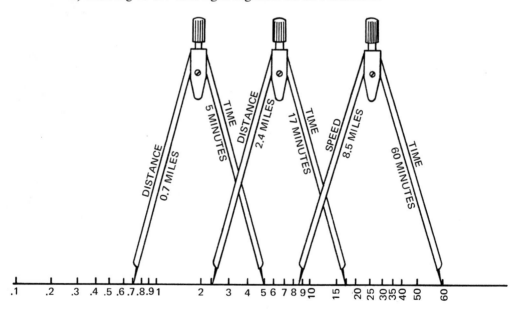

Reprinted on the margin is a logarithmic time, speed and distance scale from *HO 4665-10, Radar Plotting Sheet.* It can be useful aboard ship.

Conversion of Compass Points to Degrees

NORTH TO EAST	Points	Angular measure (° ′ ″)	SOUTH TO WEST	Points	Angular measure (° ′ ″)
North	0	0 00 00	South	16	180 00 00
N¼E	¼	2 48 45	S¼W	16¼	182 48 45
N½E	½	5 37 30	S½W	16½	185 37 30
N¾E	¾	8 26 15	S¾W	16¾	188 26 15
N by E	1	11 15 00	S by W	17	191 15 00
N by E¼E	1¼	14 03 45	S by W¼W	17¼	194 03 45
N by E½E	1½	16 52 30	S by W½W	17½	196 52 30
N by E¾E	1¾	19 41 15	S by W¾W	17¾	199 41 15
NNE	2	22 30 00	SSW	18	202 30 00
NNE¼E	2¼	25 18 45	SSW¼W	18¼	205 18 45
NNE½E	2½	28 07 30	SSW½W	18½	208 07 30
NNE¾E	2¾	30 56 15	SSW¾W	18¾	210 56 15
NE by N	3	33 45 00	SW by S	19	213 45 00
NE¾N	3¼	36 33 45	SW¾S	19¼	216 33 45
NE½N	3½	39 22 30	SW½S	19½	219 22 30
NE¼N	3¾	42 11 15	SW¼S	19¾	222 11 15
NE	4	45 00 00	SW	20	225 00 00
NE¼E	4¼	47 48 45	SW¼W	20¼	227 48 45
NE½E	4½	50 37 30	SW½W	20½	230 37 30
NE¾E	4¾	53 26 15	SW¾W	20¾	233 26 15
NE by E	5	56 15 00	SW by W	21	236 15 00
NE by E¼E	5¼	59 03 45	SW by W¼W	21¼	239 03 45
NE by E½E	5½	61 52 30	SW by W½W	21½	241 52 30
NE by E¾E	5¾	64 41 15	SW by W¾W	21¾	244 41 15
ENE	6	67 30 00	WSW	22	247 30 00
ENE¼E	6¼	70 18 45	WSW¼W	22¼	250 18 45
ENE½E	6½	73 07 30	WSW½W	22½	253 07 30
ENE¾E	6¾	75 56 15	WSW¾W	22¾	255 56 15
E by N	7	78 45 00	W by S	23	258 45 00
E¾N	7¼	81 33 45	W¾S	23¼	261 33 45
E½N	7½	84 22 30	W½S	23½	264 22 30
E¼N	7¾	87 11 15	W¼S	23¾	267 11 15

EAST TO SOUTH	Points	Angular measure (° ′ ″)	WEST TO NORTH	Points	Angular measure (° ′ ″)
East	8	90 00 00	West	24	270 00 00
E¼S	8¼	92 48 45	W¼N	24¼	272 48 45
E½S	8½	95 37 30	W½N	24½	275 37 30
E¾S	8¾	98 26 15	W¾N	24¾	278 26 15
E by S	9	101 15 00	W by N	25	281 15 00
ESE¾E	9¼	104 03 45	WNW¾W	25¼	284 03 45
ESE½E	9½	106 52 30	WNW½W	25½	286 52 30
ESE¼E	9¾	109 41 15	WNW¼W	25¾	289 41 15
ESE	10	112 30 00	WNW	26	292 30 00
SE by E¾E	10¼	115 18 45	NW by W¾W	26¼	295 18 45
SE by E½E	10½	118 07 30	NW by W½W	26½	298 07 30
SE by E¼E	10¾	120 56 15	NW by W¼W	26¾	300 56 15
SE by E	11	123 45 00	NW by W	27	303 45 00
SE¾E	11¼	126 33 45	NW¾W	27¼	306 33 45
SE½E	11½	129 22 30	NW½W	27½	309 22 30
SE¼E	11¾	132 11 15	NW¼W	27¾	312 11 15
SE	12	135 00 00	NW	28	315 00 00
SE¼S	12¼	137 48 45	NW¼N	28¼	317 48 45
SE½S	12½	140 37 30	NW½N	28½	320 37 30
SE¾S	12¾	143 26 15	NW¾N	28¾	323 26 15
SE by S	13	146 15 00	NW by N	29	326 15 00
SSE¾E	13¼	149 03 45	NNW¾W	29¼	329 03 45
SSE½E	13½	151 52 30	NNW½W	29½	331 52 30
SSE¼E	13¾	154 41 15	NNW¼W	29¾	334 41 15
SSE	14	157 30 00	NNW	30	337 30 00
S by E¾E	14¼	160 18 45	N by W¾W	30¼	340 18 45
S by E½E	14½	163 07 30	N by W½W	30½	343 07 30
S by E¼E	14¾	165 56 15	N by W¼W	30¾	345 56 15
S by E	15	168 45 00	N by W	31	348 45 00
S¾E	15¼	171 33 45	N¾W	31¼	351 33 45
S½E	15½	174 22 30	N½W	31½	354 22 30
S¼E	15¾	177 11 15	N¼W	31¾	357 11 15
South	16	180 00 00	North	32	360 00 00

Distance of the Horizon

Height feet	Nautical miles	Statute miles	Height feet	Nautical miles	Statute miles	Height feet	Nautical miles	Statute miles
1	1. 1	1. 3	120	12. 5	14. 4	940	35. 1	40. 4
2	1. 6	1. 9	125	12. 8	14. 7	960	35. 4	40. 8
3	2. 0	2. 3	130	13. 0	15. 0	980	35. 8	41. 2
4	2. 3	2. 6	135	13. 3	15. 3	1, 000	36. 2	41. 6
5	2. 6	2. 9	140	13. 5	15. 6	1, 100	37. 9	43. 7
6	2. 8	3. 2	145	13. 8	15. 9	1, 200	39. 6	45. 6
7	3. 0	3. 5	150	14. 0	16. 1	1, 300	41. 2	47. 5
8	3. 2	3. 7	160	14. 5	16. 7	1, 400	42. 8	49. 3
9	3. 4	4. 0	170	14. 9	17. 2	1, 500	44. 3	51. 0
10	3. 6	4. 2	180	15. 3	17. 7	1, 600	45. 8	52. 7
11	3. 8	4. 4	190	15. 8	18. 2	1, 700	47. 2	54. 3
12	4. 0	4. 6	200	16. 2	18. 6	1, 800	48. 5	55. 9
13	4. 1	4. 7	210	16. 6	19. 1	1, 900	49. 9	57. 4
14	4. 3	4. 9	220	17. 0	19. 5	2, 000	51. 2	58. 9
15	4. 4	5. 1	230	17. 3	20. 0	2, 100	52. 4	60. 4
16	4. 6	5. 3	240	17. 7	20. 4	2, 200	53. 7	61. 8
17	4. 7	5. 4	250	18. 1	20. 8	2, 300	54. 9	63. 2
18	4. 9	5. 6	260	18. 4	21. 2	2, 400	56. 0	64. 5
19	5. 0	5. 7	270	18. 8	21. 6	2, 500	57. 2	65. 8
20	5. 1	5. 9	280	19. 1	22. 0	2, 600	58. 3	67. 2
21	5. 2	6. 0	290	19. 5	22. 4	2, 700	59. 4	68. 4
22	5. 4	6. 2	300	19. 8	22. 8	2, 800	60. 5	69. 7
23	5. 5	6. 3	310	20. 1	23. 2	2, 900	61. 6	70. 9
24	5. 6	6. 5	320	20. 5	23. 6	3, 000	62. 7	72. 1
25	5. 7	6. 6	330	20. 8	23. 9	3, 100	63. 7	73. 3
26	5. 8	6. 7	340	21. 1	24. 3	3, 200	64. 7	74. 5
27	5. 9	6. 8	350	21. 4	24. 6	3, 300	65. 7	75. 7
28	6. 1	7. 0	360	21. 7	25. 0	3, 400	66. 7	76. 8
29	6. 2	7. 1	370	22. 0	25. 3	3, 500	67. 7	77. 9
30	6. 3	7. 2	380	22. 3	25. 7	3, 600	68. 6	79. 0
31	6. 4	7. 3	390	22. 6	26. 0	3, 700	69. 6	80. 1
32	6. 5	7. 5	400	22. 9	26. 3	3, 800	70. 5	81. 2
33	6. 6	7. 6	410	23. 2	26. 7	3, 900	71. 4	82. 2
34	6. 7	7. 7	420	23. 4	27. 0	4, 000	72. 4	83. 3
35	6. 8	7. 8	430	23. 7	27. 3	4, 100	73. 3	84. 3
36	6. 9	7. 9	440	24. 0	27. 6	4, 200	74. 1	85. 4
37	7. 0	8. 0	450	24. 3	27. 9	4, 300	75. 0	86. 4
38	7. 1	8. 1	460	24. 5	28. 2	4, 400	75. 9	87. 4
39	7. 1	8. 2	470	24. 8	28. 6	4, 500	76. 7	88. 3
40	7. 2	8. 3	480	25. 1	28. 9	4, 600	77. 6	89. 3
41	7. 3	8. 4	490	25. 3	29. 2	4, 700	78. 4	90. 3
42	7. 4	8. 5	500	25. 6	29. 4	4, 800	79. 3	91. 2
43	7. 5	8. 6	520	26. 1	30. 0	4, 900	80. 1	92. 2
44	7. 6	8. 7	540	26. 6	30. 6	5, 000	80. 9	93. 1
45	7. 7	8. 8	560	27. 1	31. 2	6, 000	88. 6	102. 0
46	7. 8	8. 9	580	27. 6	31. 7	7, 000	95. 7	110. 2
47	7. 8	9. 0	600	28. 0	32. 3	8, 000	102. 3	117. 8
48	7. 9	9. 1	620	28. 5	32. 8	9, 000	108. 5	124. 9
49	8. 0	9. 2	640	28. 9	33. 3	10, 000	114. 4	131. 7
50	8. 1	9. 3	660	29. 4	33. 8	15, 000	140. 1	161. 3
55	8. 5	9. 8	680	29. 8	34. 3	20, 000	161. 8	186. 3
60	8. 9	10. 2	700	30. 3	34. 8	25, 000	180. 9	208. 2
65	9. 2	10. 6	720	30. 7	35. 3	30, 000	198. 1	228. 1
70	9. 6	11. 0	740	31. 1	35. 8	35, 000	214. 0	246. 4
75	9. 9	11. 4	760	31. 5	36. 3	40, 000	228. 8	263. 4
80	10. 2	11. 8	780	31. 9	36. 8	45, 000	242. 7	279. 4
85	10. 5	12. 1	800	32. 4	37. 3	50, 000	255. 8	294. 5
90	10. 9	12. 5	820	32. 8	37. 7	60, 000	280. 2	322. 6
95	11. 2	12. 8	840	33. 2	38. 2	70, 000	302. 7	348. 4
100	11. 4	13. 2	860	33. 5	38. 6	80, 000	323. 6	372. 5
105	11. 7	13. 5	880	33. 9	39. 1	90, 000	343. 2	395. 1
110	12. 0	13. 8	900	34. 3	39. 5	100, 000	361. 8	416. 5
115	12. 3	14. 1	920	34. 7	39. 9	200, 000	511. 6	589. 0

Conversion Table for Nautical and Statute Miles

1 nautical mile = 6,076.10333 . . . feet   1 statute mile = 5,280 feet

Nautical miles to statute miles				Statute miles to nautical miles			
Nautical miles	Statute miles	Nautical miles	Statute miles	Statute miles	Nautical miles	Statute miles	Nautical miles
1	1. 151	51	58. 690	1	0. 869	51	44. 318
2	2. 302	52	59. 841	2	1. 738	52	45. 187
3	3. 452	53	60. 991	3	2. 607	53	46. 056
4	4. 603	54	62. 142	4	3. 476	54	46. 925
5	5. 754	55	63. 293	5	4. 345	55	47. 794
6	6. 905	56	64. 444	6	5. 214	56	48. 663
7	8. 055	57	65. 594	7	6. 083	57	49. 532
8	9. 206	58	66. 745	8	6. 952	58	50. 401
9	10. 357	59	67. 896	9	7. 821	59	51. 270
10	11. 508	60	69. 047	10	8. 690	60	52. 139
11	12. 659	61	70. 198	11	9. 559	61	53. 008
12	13. 809	62	71. 348	12	10. 428	62	53. 877
13	14. 960	63	72. 499	13	11. 297	63	54. 746
14	16. 111	64	73. 650	14	12. 166	64	55. 614
15	17. 262	65	74. 801	15	13. 035	65	56. 483
16	18. 412	66	75. 951	16	13. 904	66	57. 352
17	19. 563	67	77. 102	17	14. 773	67	58. 221
18	20. 714	68	78. 253	18	15. 642	68	59. 090
19	21. 865	69	79. 404	19	16. 511	69	59. 959
20	23. 016	70	80. 555	20	17. 380	70	60. 828
21	24. 166	71	81. 705	21	18. 249	71	61. 697
22	25. 317	72	82. 856	22	19. 117	72	62. 566
23	26. 468	73	84. 007	23	19. 986	73	63. 435
24	27. 619	74	85. 158	24	20. 855	74	64. 304
25	28. 769	75	86. 308	25	21. 724	75	65. 173
26	29. 920	76	87. 459	26	22. 593	76	66. 042
27	31. 071	77	88. 610	27	23. 462	77	66. 911
28	32. 222	78	89. 761	28	24. 331	78	67. 780
29	33. 373	79	90. 912	29	25. 200	79	68. 649
30	34. 523	80	92. 062	30	26. 069	80	69. 518
31	35. 674	81	93. 213	31	26. 938	81	70. 387
32	36. 825	82	94. 364	32	27. 807	82	71. 256
33	37. 976	83	95. 515	33	28. 676	83	72. 125
34	39. 127	84	96. 665	34	29. 545	84	72. 994
35	40. 277	85	97. 816	35	30. 414	85	73. 863
36	41. 428	86	98. 967	36	31. 283	86	74. 732
37	42. 579	87	100. 118	37	32. 152	87	75. 601
38	43. 730	88	101. 269	38	33. 021	88	76. 470
39	44. 880	89	102. 419	39	33. 890	89	77. 339
40	46. 031	90	103. 570	40	34. 759	90	78. 208
41	47. 182	91	104. 721	41	35. 628	91	79. 077
42	48. 333	92	105. 872	42	36. 497	92	79. 946
43	49. 484	93	107. 022	43	37. 366	93	80. 815
44	50. 634	94	108. 173	44	38. 235	94	81. 684
45	51. 785	95	109. 324	45	39. 104	95	82. 553
46	52. 936	96	110. 475	46	39. 973	96	83. 422
47	54. 087	97	111. 626	47	40. 842	97	84. 291
48	55. 237	98	112. 776	48	41. 711	98	85. 160
49	56. 388	99	113. 927	49	42. 580	99	86. 029
50	57. 539	100	115. 078	50	43. 449	100	86. 898

To determine speed: By stopwatch or clock with sweep-second hand, find the minutes and seconds to cover one nautical mile. Enter table with minutes across top and seconds on left side. Read out speed in knots. So . . . 6 minutes 32 seconds. for the mile is 9.184 knots. To account for wind and current: Make several runs in each direction. Average the times in one direction and find speed. Average times in opposite direction and find speed. Then average the two speeds. Engine RPM and trim must be unchanged on all runs.

Sec.	3 Min.	4 Min.	5 Min.	6 Min.	7 Min.	8 Min.	9 Min.	10 Min.	11 Min.	12 Min.
0	20.000	15.000	12.000	10.009	8.571	7.500	6.667	6.000	5.455	5.000
1	19.890	14.938	11.960	9.972	8.551	7.484	6.654	5.990	5.446	4.993
2	19.780	14.876	11.921	9.945	8.531	7.469	6.642	5.980	5.438	4.986
3	19.672	14.815	11.881	9.917	8.511	7.453	6.630	5.970	5.430	4.979
4	19.565	14.754	11.842	9.890	8.491	7.438	6.618	5.960	5.422	4.972
5	19.459	14.694	11.803	9.863	8.471	7.428	6.606	5.950	5.414	4.965
6	19.355	14.634	11.765	9.836	8.451	7.407	6.593	5.941	5.405	4.959
7	19.251	14.575	11.726	9.809	8.431	7.392	6.581	5.931	5.397	4.952
8	19.149	14.516	11.688	9.783	8.411	7.377	6.569	5.921	5.389	4.945
9	19.048	14.458	11.650	9.756	8.392	7.362	6.557	5.911	5.381	4.938
10	18.947	14.400	11.613	9.730	8.372	7.347	6.545	5.902	5.373	4.931
11	18.848	14.343	11.576	9.704	8.353	7.332	6.534	5.892	5.365	4.925
12	18.750	14.286	11.538	9.677	8.333	7.317	6.522	5.882	5.357	4.918
13	18.653	14.229	11.502	9.651	8.314	7.302	6.510	5.873	5.349	4.911
14	18.557	14.173	11.465	9.626	8.295	7.287	6.498	5.863	5.341	4.905
15	18.461	14.118	11.429	9.600	8.276	7.273	6.486	5.854	5.333	4.898
16	18.367	14.062	11.392	9.574	8.257	7.258	6.475	5.844	5.325	4.891
17	18.274	14.008	11.356	9.549	8.238	7.243	6.463	5.835	5.318	4.885
18	18.182	13.953	11.321	9.524	8.219	7.229	6.452	5.825	5.310	4.878
19	18.090	13.900	11.285	9.499	8.200	7.214	6.440	5.816	5.302	4.871
20	18.000	13.846	11.250	9.474	8.182	7.200	6.429	5.806	5.294	4.865
21	17.910	13.793	11.215	9.449	8.163	7.186	6.417	5.797	5.286	4.858
22	17.822	13.740	11.180	9.424	8.145	7.171	6.406	5.788	5.279	4.852
23	17.734	13.688	11.146	9.399	8.126	7.157	6.394	5.778	5.271	4.845
24	17.647	13.636	11.111	9.375	8.108	7.143	6.383	5.769	5.263	4.839
25	17.561	13.585	11.077	9.351	8.090	7.129	6.372	5.760	5.255	4.832
26	17.476	13.534	11.043	9.326	8.072	7.115	6.360	5.751	5.248	4.826
27	17.391	13.483	11.009	9.302	8.054	7.101	6.349	5.742	5.240	4.819
28	17.308	13.433	10.976	9.278	8.036	7.087	6.338	5.732	5.233	4.813
29	17.225	13.383	10.942	9.254	8.018	7.073	6.327	5.723	5.225	4.806

Sec.	3 Min.	4 Min.	5 Min.	6 Min.	7 Min.	8 Min.	9 Min.	10 Min.	11 Min.	12 Min.
30	17.143	13.333	10.909	9.231	8.000	7.059	6.316	5.714	5.217	4.800
31	17.062	13.284	10.876	9.207	7.982	7.045	6.305	5.705	5.210	4.794
32	16.981	13.235	10.843	9.184	7.965	7.031	6.294	5.696	5.202	4.787
33	16.901	13.187	10.811	9.160	7.947	7.018	6.283	5.687	5.195	4.781
34	16.822	13.139	10.778	9.137	7.930	7.004	6.272	5.678	5.187	4.774
35	16.744	13.091	10.746	9.114˙	7.912	6.990	6.261	5.669	5.180	4.768
36	16.667	13.043	10.714	9.091	7.895	6.977	6.250	5.660	5.172	4.762
37	16.590	12.996	10.682	9.068	7.877	6.963	6.239	5.651	5.165	4.756
38	16.514	12.950	10.651	9.045	7.860	6.950	6.228	5.643	5.158	4.749
39	16.438	12.903	10.619	9.023	7.843	6.936	6.218	5.634	5.150	4.743
40	16.364	12.857	10.588	9.000	7.826	6.923	6.207	5.625	5.143	4.737
41	16.290	12.811	10.557	8.978	7.809	6.910	6.196	5.616	5.136	4.731
42	16.216	12.766	10.526	8.955	7.792	6.894	6.186	5.607	5.128	4.724
43	16.143	12.721	10.496	8.933	7.775	6.883	6.175	5.599	5.121	4.718
44	16.071	12.676	10.465	8.911	7.759	6.870	6.164	5.590	5.114	4.712
45	16.000	12.632	10.435	8.889	7.742	6.857	6.154	5.581	5.106	4.706
46	15.929	12.587	10.405	8.867	7.725	6.844	6.143	5.573	5.099	4.700
47	15.859	12.544	10.375	8.845	7.709	6.831	6.133	5.564	5.092	4.693
48	15.789	12.500	10.345	8.824	7.692	6.818	6.122	5.556	5.085	4.687
49	15.721	12.457	10.315	8.802	7.676	6.805	6.112	5.547	5.078	4.681
50	15.652	12.414	10.286	8.780	7.660	6.792	6.102	5.538	5.070	4.675
51	15.584	12.371	10.256	8.759	7.643	6.780	6.091	5.530	5.063	4.669
52	15.517	12.329	10.227	8.738	7.627	6.767	6.081	5.521	5.056	4.663
53	15.451	12.287	10.198	8.717	7.611	6.754	6.071	5.513	5.049	4.657
54	15.385	12.245	10.169	8.696	7.595	6.742	6.061	5.505	5.042	4.651
55	15.319	12.203	10.141	8.675	7.579	6.729	6.050	5.496	5.035	4.645
56	15.254	12.162	10.112	8.654	7.563	6.716	6.040	5.488	5.028	4.639
57	15.190	12.121	10.084	8.633	7.547	6.704	6.030	5.479	5.021	4.633
58	15.126	12.081	10.056	8.612	7.531	6.691	6.020	5.471	5.014	4.627
59	15.063	12.040	10.028	8.592	7.516	6.679	6.010	5.463	5.007	4.621

Current Help/Hurt Table

The effect of current on speed over-the-bottom of a boat varies with the boat's speed and the velocity of the current, and whether it is flowing in the direction of travel or against. For example: a 10-knot boat requires 6 minutes per mile in "flat water." If a 0.7-knot current is running in the same direction as the boat, the **Help** will be 24 seconds per mile and it will require only 5 minutes 36 seconds per mile. If the current is being bucked, the **Hurt** will be 27 seconds per mile and it will require 6 minutes 27 seconds per mile. The same current—but in relation to a 14-knot boat—**Helps** 12 seconds per mile, and **Hurts** 14 seconds per mile.

SPEED CURRENT	14 KNOTS HELP (seconds)	14 KNOTS HURT	13 KNOTS HELP (seconds)	13 KNOTS HURT	12 KNOTS HELP (seconds)	12 KNOTS HURT
0.1 KN.	2	2	2	2	2	2
0.2 KN.	3	4	4	4	5	5
0.3 KN.	5	6	6	6	7	8
0.4 KN.	7	8	8	9	10	11
0.5 KN.	9	10	10	11	12	13
0.6 KN.	10	12	12	13	14	16
0.7 KN.	12	14	14	16	17	19
0.8 KN.	14	16	16	18	19	21
0.9 KN.	15	18	18	21	21	24
1.0 KN.	17	20	20	23	23	27
1.1 KN.	19	22	22	26	25	30
1.2 KN.	20	24	23	28	27	33
1.3 KN.	22	26	25	31	29	36
1.4 KN.	23	29	27	33	31	40
1.5 KN.	25	31	29	36	33	43

SPEED CURRENT	11 KNOTS HELP (seconds)	11 KNOTS HURT	10 KNOTS HELP (seconds)	10 KNOTS HURT	9 KNOTS HELP (seconds)	9 KNOTS HURT
0.1 KN.	3	3	4	4	4	4
0.2 KN.	6	6	7	7	9	9
0.3 KN.	8	9	10	11	13	14
0.4 KN.	11	13	14	15	17	19
0.5 KN.	14	16	17	19	21	24
0.6 KN.	17	19	20	23	25	29
0.7 KN.	19	23	24	27	29	34
0.8 KN.	22	26	27	31	33	39
0.9 KN.	24	29	30	36	36	44
1.0 KN.	27	33	33	40	40	50
1.1 KN.	29	37	36	44	44	56
1.2 KN.	32	40	49	49	47	62
1.3 KN.	34	44	41	54	50	68
1.4 KN.	37	48	44	59	54	74
1.5 KN.	39	52	47	64	57	80

Conversion Table for Meters, Feet, and Fathoms

Meters	Feet	Fathoms	Meters	Feet	Fathoms	Feet	Meters	Feet	Meters	Fathoms	Meters	Fathoms	Meters
1	3. 28	0. 55	61	200. 13	33. 36	1	0. 30	61	18. 59	1	1. 83	61	111. 56
2	6. 56	1. 09	62	203. 41	33. 90	2	0. 61	62	18. 90	2	3. 66	62	113. 39
3	9. 84	1. 64	63	206. 69	34. 45	3	0. 91	63	19. 20	3	5. 49	63	115. 21
4	13. 12	2. 19	64	209. 97	35. 00	4	1. 22	64	19. 51	4	7. 32	64	117. 04
5	16. 40	2. 73	65	213. 25	35. 54	5	1. 52	65	19. 81	5	9. 14	65	118. 87
6	19. 69	3. 28	66	216. 54	36. 09	6	1. 83	66	20. 12	6	10. 97	66	120. 70
7	22. 97	3. 83	67	219. 82	36. 64	7	2. 13	67	20. 42	7	12. 80	67	122. 53
8	26. 25	4. 37	68	223. 10	37. 18	8	2. 44	68	20. 73	8	14. 63	68	124. 36
9	29. 53	4. 92	69	226. 38	37. 73	9	2. 74	69	21. 03	9	16. 46	69	126. 19
10	32. 81	5. 47	70	229. 66	38. 28	10	3. 05	70	21. 34	10	18. 29	70	128. 02
11	36. 09	6. 01	71	232. 94	38. 82	11	3. 35	71	21. 64	11	20. 12	71	129. 84
12	39. 37	6. 56	72	236. 22	39. 37	12	3. 66	72	21. 95	12	21. 95	72	131. 67
13	42. 65	7. 11	73	239. 50	39. 92	13	3. 96	73	22. 25	13	23. 77	73	133. 50
14	45. 93	7. 66	74	242. 78	40. 46	14	4. 27	74	22. 56	14	25. 60	74	135. 33
15	49. 21	8. 20	75	246. 06	41. 01	15	4. 57	75	22. 86	15	27. 43	75	137. 16
16	52. 49	8. 75	76	249. 34	41. 56	16	4. 88	76	23. 16	16	29. 26	76	138. 99
17	55. 77	9. 30	77	252. 62	42. 10	17	5. 18	77	23. 47	17	31. 09	77	140. 82
18	59. 06	9. 84	78	255. 91	42. 65	18	5. 49	78	23. 77	18	32. 92	78	142. 65
19	62. 34	10. 39	79	259. 19	43. 20	19	5. 79	79	24. 08	19	34. 75	79	144. 48
20	65. 62	10. 94	80	262. 47	43. 74	20	6. 10	80	24. 38	20	36. 58	80	146. 30
21	68. 90	11. 48	81	265. 75	44. 29	21	6. 40	81	24. 69	21	38. 40	81	148. 13
22	72. 18	12. 03	82	269. 03	44. 84	22	6. 71	82	24. 99	22	40. 23	82	149. 96
23	75. 46	12. 58	83	272. 31	45. 38	23	7. 01	83	25. 30	23	42. 06	83	151. 79
24	78. 74	13. 12	84	275. 59	45. 93	24	7. 32	84	25. 60	24	43. 89	84	153. 62
25	82. 02	13. 67	85	278. 87	46. 48	25	7. 62	85	25. 91	25	45. 72	85	155. 45
26	85. 30	14. 22	86	282. 15	47. 03	26	7. 92	86	26. 21	26	47. 55	86	157. 28
27	88. 58	14. 76	87	285. 43	47. 57	27	8. 23	87	26. 52	27	49. 38	87	159. 11
28	91. 86	15. 31	88	288. 71	48. 12	28	8. 53	88	26. 82	28	51. 21	88	160. 93
29	95. 14	15. 86	89	291. 99	48. 67	29	8. 84	89	27. 13	29	53. 04	89	162. 76
30	98. 43	16. 40	90	295. 28	49. 21	30	9. 14	90	27. 43	30	54. 86	90	164. 59
31	101. 71	16. 95	91	298. 56	49. 76	31	9. 45	91	27. 74	31	56. 69	91	166. 42
32	104. 99	17. 50	92	301. 84	50. 31	32	9. 75	92	28. 04	32	58. 52	92	168. 25
33	108. 27	18. 04	93	305. 12	50. 85	33	10. 06	93	28. 35	33	60. 35	93	170. 08
34	111. 55	18. 59	94	308. 40	51. 40	34	10. 36	94	28. 65	34	62. 18	94	171. 91
35	114. 83	19. 14	95	311. 68	51. 95	35	10. 67	95	28. 96	35	64. 01	95	173. 74
36	118. 11	19. 69	96	314. 96	52. 49	36	10. 97	96	29. 26	36	65. 84	96	175. 56
37	121. 39	20. 23	97	318. 24	53. 04	37	11. 28	97	29. 57	37	67. 67	97	177. 39
38	124. 67	20. 78	98	321. 52	53. 59	38	11. 58	98	29. 87	38	69. 49	98	179. 22
39	127. 95	21. 33	99	324. 80	54. 13	39	11. 89	99	30. 18	39	71. 32	99	181. 05
40	131. 23	21. 87	100	328. 08	54. 68	40	12. 19	100	30. 48	40	73. 15	100	182. 88
41	134. 51	22. 42	101	331. 36	55. 23	41	12. 50	101	30. 78	41	74. 98	101	184. 71
42	137. 80	22. 97	102	334. 65	55. 77	42	12. 80	102	31. 09	42	76. 81	102	186. 54
43	141. 08	23. 51	103	337. 93	56. 32	43	13. 11	103	31. 39	43	78. 64	103	188. 37
44	144. 36	24. 06	104	341. 21	56. 87	44	13. 41	104	31. 70	44	80. 47	104	190. 20
45	147. 64	24. 61	105	344. 49	57. 41	45	13. 72	105	32. 00	45	82. 30	105	192. 02
46	150. 92	25. 15	106	347. 77	57. 96	46	14. 02	106	32. 31	46	84. 12	106	193. 85
47	154. 20	25. 70	107	351. 05	58. 51	47	14. 33	107	32. 61	47	85. 95	107	195. 68
48	157. 48	26. 25	108	354. 33	59. 06	48	14. 63	108	32. 92	48	87. 78	108	197. 51
49	160. 76	26. 79	109	357. 61	59. 60	49	14. 94	109	33. 22	49	89. 61	109	199. 34
50	164. 04	27. 34	110	360. 89	60. 15	50	15. 24	110	33. 53	50	91. 44	110	201. 17
51	167. 32	27. 89	111	364. 17	60. 70	51	15. 54	111	33. 83	51	93. 27	111	203. 00
52	170. 60	28. 43	112	367. 45	61. 24	52	15. 85	112	34. 14	52	95. 10	112	204. 83
53	173. 88	28. 98	113	370. 73	61. 79	53	16. 15	113	34. 44	53	96. 93	113	206. 65
54	177. 17	29. 53	114	374. 02	62. 34	54	16. 46	114	34. 75	54	98. 76	114	208. 48
55	180. 45	30. 07	115	377. 30	62. 88	55	16. 76	115	35. 05	55	100. 58	115	210. 31
56	183. 73	30. 62	116	380. 58	63. 43	56	17. 07	116	35. 36	56	102. 41	116	212. 14
57	187. 01	31. 17	117	383. 86	63. 98	57	17. 37	117	35. 66	57	104. 24	117	213. 97
58	190. 29	31. 71	118	387. 14	64. 52	58	17. 68	118	35. 97	58	106. 07	118	215. 80
59	193. 57	32. 26	119	390. 42	65. 07	59	17. 98	119	36. 27	59	107. 90	119	217. 63
60	196. 85	32. 81	120	393. 70	65. 62	60	18. 29	120	36. 58	60	109. 73	120	219. 46

Weather

Here are selected tables from *American Practical Navigator (HO 9)*, all useful in putting weather data to work. The **Beaufort Scale,** with code numbers from 0 to 17 to classify wind speed, has beset seamen for generations by its apparent lack of numerical pattern. Many have wondered what Admiral Sir Francis Beaufort of the Royal Navy had in mind. More than a few suspected his aim was a devilish memory exercise for the iron men in Britain's barques of oak. Lately suggested, however, has been injustice to the shade of Sir Francis. As first devised, his scale related to reactions of a then ship-of-the-line under specific wind influence. It was not intended to rank wind speeds by progressive numbers. However derived, the Beaufort Scale persists today as a recognized basis of wind description.

Correction of Barometer Reading for Height Above Sea Level

All barometers.   All values positive.

Height in feet	Outside temperature in degrees Fahrenheit													Height in feet
	−20°	−10°	0°	10°	20°	30°	40°	50°	60°	70°	80°	90°	100°	
	Inches	Inches	Inches	Inches	Inches	Inches	Inches	Inches	Inches	Inches	Inches	Inches	Inches	
5	0.01	0.01	0.01	0.01	0.01	0.01	0.01	0.01	0.01	0.01	0.01	0.01	0.01	5
10	0.01	0.01	0.01	0.01	0.01	0.01	0.01	0.01	0.01	0.01	0.01	0.01	0.01	10
15	0.02	0.02	0.02	0.02	0.02	0.02	0.02	0.02	0.02	0.02	0.02	0.02	0.02	15
20	0.03	0.02	0.02	0.02	0.02	0.02	0.02	0.02	0.02	0.02	0.02	0.02	0.02	20
25	0.03	0.03	0.03	0.03	0.03	0.03	0.03	0.03	0.03	0.03	0.03	0.03	0.03	25
30	0.04	0.04	0.04	0.04	0.04	0.03	0.03	0.03	0.03	0.03	0.03	0.03	0.03	30
35	0.04	0.04	0.04	0.04	0.04	0.04	0.04	0.04	0.04	0.04	0.04	0.04	0.04	35
40	0.05	0.05	0.05	0.05	0.05	0.05	0.04	0.04	0.04	0.04	0.04	0.04	0.04	40
45	0.06	0.06	0.05	0.05	0.05	0.05	0.05	0.05	0.05	0.05	0.05	0.05	0.05	45
50	0.06	0.06	0.06	0.06	0.06	0.06	0.06	0.06	0.06	0.05	0.05	0.05	0.05	50
55	0.07	0.07	0.07	0.07	0.06	0.06	0.06	0.06	0.06	0.06	0.06	0.06	0.06	55
60	0.08	0.07	0.07	0.07	0.07	0.07	0.07	0.07	0.06	0.06	0.06	0.06	0.06	60
65	0.08	0.08	0.08	0.08	0.08	0.07	0.07	0.07	0.07	0.07	0.07	0.07	0.07	65
70	0.09	0.09	0.09	0.08	0.08	0.08	0.08	0.08	0.08	0.08	0.07	0.07	0.07	70
75	0.10	0.09	0.09	0.09	0.09	0.09	0.08	0.08	0.08	0.08	0.08	0.08	0.08	75
80	0.10	0.10	0.10	0.10	0.09	0.09	0.09	0.09	0.09	0.08	0.08	0.08	0.08	80
85	0.11	0.11	0.10	0.10	0.10	0.10	0.10	0.09	0.09	0.09	0.09	0.09	0.09	85
90	0.11	0.11	0.11	0.11	0.11	0.10	0.10	0.10	0.10	0.10	0.09	0.09	0.09	90
95	0.12	0.12	0.12	0.11	0.11	0.11	0.11	0.10	0.10	0.10	0.10	0.10	0.10	95
100	0.13	0.12	0.12	0.12	0.12	0.11	0.11	0.11	0.11	0.11	0.10	0.10	0.10	100
105	0.13	0.13	0.13	0.13	0.12	0.12	0.12	0.12	0.11	0.11	0.11	0.11	0.11	105
110	0.14	0.14	0.13	0.13	0.13	0.13	0.12	0.12	0.12	0.12	0.11	0.11	0.11	110
115	0.15	0.14	0.14	0.14	0.13	0.13	0.13	0.13	0.12	0.12	0.12	0.12	0.12	115
120	0.15	0.15	0.15	0.14	0.14	0.14	0.13	0.13	0.13	0.13	0.12	0.12	0.12	120
125	0.16	0.16	0.15	0.15	0.15	0.14	0.14	0.14	0.13	0.13	0.13	0.13	0.12	125

Courtesy of Bowditch/American Practical Navigator

Conversion Table for Millibars, Inches of Mercury, and Millimeters of Mercury

Millibars	Inches	Millimeters	Millibars	Inches	Millimeters	Millibars	Inches	Millimeters
900	26. 58	675. 1	960	28. 35	720. 1	1020	30. 12	765. 1
901	26. 61	675. 8	961	28. 38	720. 8	1021	30. 15	765. 8
902	26. 64	676. 6	962	28. 41	721. 6	1022	30. 18	766. 6
903	26. 67	677. 3	963	28. 44	722. 3	1023	30. 21	767. 3
904	26. 70	678. 1	964	28. 47	723. 1	1024	30. 24	768. 1
905	26. 72	678. 8	965	28. 50	723. 8	1025	30. 27	768. 8
906	26. 75	679. 6	966	28. 53	724. 6	1026	30. 30	769. 6
907	26. 78	680. 3	967	28. 56	725. 3	1027	30. 33	770. 3
908	26. 81	681. 1	968	28. 58	726. 1	1028	30. 36	771. 1
909	26. 84	681. 8	969	28. 61	726. 8	1029	30. 39	771. 8
910	26. 87	682. 6	970	28. 64	727. 6	1030	30. 42	772. 6
911	26. 90	683. 3	971	28. 67	728. 3	1031	30. 45	773. 3
912	26. 93	684. 1	972	28. 70	729. 1	1032	30. 47	774. 1
913	26. 96	684. 8	973	28. 73	729. 8	1033	30. 50	774. 8
914	26. 99	685. 6	974	28. 76	730. 6	1034	30. 53	775. 6
915	27. 02	686. 3	975	28. 79	731. 3	1035	30. 56	776. 3
916	27. 05	687. 1	976	28. 82	732. 1	1036	30. 59	777. 1
917	27. 08	687. 8	977	28. 85	732. 8	1037	30. 62	777. 8
918	27. 11	688. 6	978	28. 88	733. 6	1038	30. 65	778. 6
919	27. 14	689. 3	979	28. 91	734. 3	1039	30. 68	779. 3
920	27. 17	690. 1	980	28. 94	735. 1	1040	30. 71	780. 1
921	27. 20	690. 8	981	28. 97	735. 8	1041	30. 74	780. 8
922	27. 23	691. 6	982	29. 00	736. 6	1042	30. 77	781. 6
923	27. 26	692. 3	983	29. 03	737. 3	1043	30. 80	782. 3
924	27. 29	693. 1	984	29. 06	738. 1	1044	30. 83	783. 1
925	27. 32	693. 8	985	29. 09	738. 8	1045	30. 86	783. 8
926	27. 34	694. 6	986	29. 12	739. 6	1046	30. 89	784. 6
927	27. 37	695. 3	987	29. 15	740. 3	1047	30. 92	785. 3
928	27. 40	696. 1	988	29. 18	741. 1	1048	30. 95	786. 1
929	27. 43	696. 8	989	29. 21	741. 8	1049	30. 98	786. 8
930	27. 46	697. 6	990	29. 23	742. 6	1050	31. 01	787. 6
931	27. 49	698. 3	991	29. 26	743. 3	1051	31. 04	788. 3
932	27. 52	699. 1	992	29. 29	744. 1	1052	31. 07	789. 1
933	27. 55	699. 8	993	29. 32	744. 8	1053	31. 10	789. 8
934	27. 58	700. 6	994	29. 35	745. 6	1054	31. 12	790. 6
935	27. 61	701. 3	995	29. 38	746. 3	1055	31. 15	791. 3
936	27. 64	702. 1	996	29. 41	747. 1	1056	31. 18	792. 1
937	27. 67	702. 8	997	29. 44	747. 8	1057	31. 21	792. 8
938	27. 70	703. 6	998	29. 47	748. 6	1058	31. 24	793. 6
939	27. 73	704. 3	999	29. 50	749. 3	1059	31. 27	794. 3
940	27. 76	705. 1	1000	29. 53	750. 1	1060	31. 30	795. 1
941	27. 79	705. 8	1001	29. 56	750. 8	1061	31. 33	795. 8
942	27. 82	706. 6	1002	29. 59	751. 6	1062	31. 36	796. 6
943	27. 85	707. 3	1003	29. 62	752. 3	1063	31. 39	797. 3
944	27. 88	708. 1	1004	29. 65	753. 1	1064	31. 42	798. 1
945	27. 91	708. 8	1005	29. 68	753. 8	1065	31. 45	798. 8
946	27. 94	709. 6	1006	29. 71	754. 6	1066	31. 48	799. 6
947	27. 96	710. 3	1007	29. 74	755. 3	1067	31. 51	800. 3
948	27. 99	711. 1	1008	29. 77	756. 1	1068	31. 54	801. 1
949	28. 02	711. 8	1009	29. 80	756. 8	1069	31. 57	801. 8
950	28. 05	712. 6	1010	29. 83	757. 6	1070	31. 60	802. 6
951	28. 08	713. 3	1011	29. 85	758. 3	1071	31. 63	803. 3
952	28. 11	714. 1	1012	29. 88	759. 1	1072	31. 66	804. 1
953	28. 14	714. 8	1013	29. 91	759. 8	1073	31. 69	804. 8
954	28. 17	715. 6	1014	29. 94	760. 6	1074	31. 72	805. 6
955	28. 20	716. 3	1015	29. 97	761. 3	1075	31. 74	806. 3
956	28. 23	717. 1	1016	30. 00	762. 1	1076	31. 77	807. 1
957	28. 26	717. 8	1017	30. 03	762. 8	1077	31. 80	807. 8
958	28. 29	718. 6	1018	30. 06	763. 6	1078	31. 83	808. 6
959	28. 32	719. 3	1019	30. 09	764. 3	1079	31. 86	809. 3
960	28. 35	720. 1	1020	30. 12	765. 1	1080	31. 89	810. 1

Courtesy of Bowditch/American Practical Navigator

Relative Humidity

Dry-bulb temp. F	Difference between dry-bulb and wet-bulb temperatures														Dry-bulb temp. F
	1°	2°	3°	4°	5°	6°	7°	8°	9°	10°	11°	12°	13°	14°	
°	%	%	%	%	%	%	%	%	%	%	%	%	%	%	°
−20	7														−20
18	14														18
16	21														16
14	27														14
12	32														12
−10	37														−10
8	41	2													8
6	45	9													6
4	49	16													4
−2	52	22													−2
0	56	28													0
+2	59	33	7												+2
4	62	37	14												4
6	64	42	20												6
8	67	46	25	5											8
+10	69	50	30	11											+10
12	71	53	35	17											12
14	73	56	40	23	7										14
16	76	60	44	28	13										16
18	77	62	48	33	19	4									18
+20	79	65	51	37	24	10									+20
22	81	68	55	42	29	16	4								22
24	83	70	58	45	33	21	10								24
26	85	73	61	49	38	26	15	4							26
28	86	75	64	53	42	31	20	10							28
+30	88	77	66	56	45	35	25	15	6						+30
32	89	79	69	59	49	39	30	20	11	2					32
34	90	81	71	62	52	43	34	25	16	8					34
36	91	82	73	64	55	47	38	29	21	13	5				36
38	91	83	74	66	58	50	42	33	25	18	10	2			38
+40	92	84	76	68	60	52	45	37	30	22	15	7			+40
42	92	84	77	69	62	54	47	40	33	26	19	12	5		42
44	92	85	78	70	63	56	49	43	36	29	23	17	10	4	44
46	93	86	79	72	65	58	52	45	39	32	26	20	14	8	46
48	93	86	79	73	66	60	54	47	41	35	29	24	18	12	48
+50	93	87	80	74	68	61	55	49	44	38	32	27	21	16	+50
52	94	87	81	75	69	63	57	51	46	40	35	29	24	19	52
54	94	88	82	76	70	64	59	53	48	42	37	32	27	22	54
56	94	88	82	77	71	65	60	55	50	44	39	35	30	25	56
58	94	88	83	77	72	67	61	56	51	46	42	37	32	28	58
+60	94	89	83	78	73	68	63	58	53	48	43	39	34	30	+60
62	95	89	84	79	74	69	64	59	54	50	45	41	37	32	62
64	95	89	84	79	74	70	65	60	56	51	47	43	38	34	64
66	95	90	85	80	75	71	66	61	57	53	49	44	40	36	66
68	95	90	85	81	76	71	67	63	58	54	50	46	42	38	68
+70	95	90	86	81	77	72	68	64	59	55	51	48	44	40	+70
72	95	91	86	82	77	73	69	65	61	57	53	49	45	42	72
74	95	91	86	82	78	74	69	65	62	58	54	50	47	43	74
76	95	91	87	82	78	74	70	66	63	59	55	51	48	45	76
78	96	91	87	83	79	75	71	67	63	60	56	53	49	46	78
+80	96	91	87	83	79	75	72	68	64	61	57	54	50	47	+80
82	96	92	88	84	80	76	72	69	65	62	58	55	52	48	82
84	96	92	88	84	80	76	73	69	66	62	59	56	53	49	84
86	96	92	88	84	81	77	73	70	67	63	60	57	54	51	86
88	96	92	88	85	81	77	74	71	67	64	61	58	55	52	88
+90	96	92	89	85	81	78	74	71	68	65	61	58	55	52	+90
92	96	92	89	85	82	78	75	72	68	65	62	59	56	53	92
94	96	93	89	85	82	79	75	72	69	66	63	60	57	54	94
96	96	93	89	86	82	79	76	73	70	67	64	61	58	55	96
98	96	93	89	86	83	79	76	73	70	67	64	61	59	56	98
+100	96	93	90	86	83	80	77	74	71	68	65	62	59	57	+100

Conversion Tables for Thermometer Scales

F = Fahrenheit, C = Celsius (centigrade), K = Kelvin

F	C	K	F	C	K	C	F	K	K	F	C
°	°	°	°	°	°	°	°	°	°	°	°
−20	−28.9	244.3	+40	+4.4	277.6	−25	−13.0	248.2	250	−9.7	−23.2
19	28.3	244.8	41	5.0	278.2	24	11.2	249.2	251	7.9	22.2
18	27.8	245.4	42	5.6	278.7	23	9.4	250.2	252	6.1	21.2
17	27.2	245.9	43	6.1	279.3	22	7.6	251.2	253	4.3	20.2
16	26.7	246.5	44	6.7	279.8	21	5.8	252.2	254	2.5	19.2
−15	−26.1	247.0	+45	+7.2	280.4	−20	−4.0	253.2	255	−0.7	−18.2
14	25.6	247.6	46	7.8	280.9	19	2.2	254.2	256	+1.1	17.2
13	25.0	248.2	47	8.3	281.5	18	−0.4	255.2	257	2.9	16.2
12	24.4	248.7	48	8.9	282.0	17	+1.4	256.2	258	4.7	15.2
11	23.9	249.3	49	9.4	282.6	16	3.2	257.2	259	6.5	14.2
−10	−23.3	249.8	+50	+10.0	283.2	−15	+5.0	258.2	260	+8.3	−13.2
9	22.8	250.4	51	10.6	283.7	14	6.8	259.2	261	10.1	12.2
8	22.2	250.9	52	11.1	284.3	13	8.6	260.2	262	11.9	11.2
7	21.7	251.5	53	11.7	284.8	12	10.4	261.2	263	13.7	10.2
6	21.1	252.0	54	12.2	285.4	11	12.2	262.2	264	15.5	9.2
−5	−20.6	252.6	+55	+12.8	285.9	−10	+14.0	263.2	265	+17.3	−8.2
4	20.0	253.2	56	13.3	286.5	9	15.8	264.2	266	19.1	7.2
3	19.4	253.7	57	13.9	287.0	8	17.6	265.2	267	20.9	6.2
2	18.9	254.3	58	14.4	287.6	7	19.4	266.2	268	22.7	5.2
−1	18.3	254.8	59	15.0	288.2	6	21.2	267.2	269	24.5	4.2
0	−17.8	255.4	+60	+15.6	288.7	−5	+23.0	268.2	270	+26.3	−3.2
+1	17.2	255.9	61	16.1	289.3	4	24.8	269.2	271	28.1	2.2
2	16.7	256.5	62	16.7	289.8	3	26.6	270.2	272	29.9	1.2
3	16.1	257.0	63	17.2	290.4	2	28.4	271.2	273	31.7	−0.2
4	15.6	257.6	64	17.8	290.9	−1	30.2	272.2	274	33.5	+0.8
+5	−15.0	258.2	+65	+18.3	291.5	0	+32.0	273.2	275	+35.3	+1.8
6	14.4	258.7	66	18.9	292.0	+1	33.8	274.2	276	37.1	2.8
7	13.9	259.3	67	19.4	292.6	2	35.6	275.2	277	38.9	3.8
8	13.3	259.8	68	20.0	293.2	3	37.4	276.2	278	40.7	4.8
9	12.8	260.4	69	20.6	293.7	4	39.2	277.2	279	42.5	5.8
+10	−12.2	260.9	+70	+21.1	294.3	+5	+41.0	278.2	280	+44.3	+6.8
11	11.7	261.5	71	21.7	294.8	6	42.8	279.2	281	46.1	7.8
12	11.1	262.0	72	22.2	295.4	7	44.6	280.2	282	47.9	8.8
13	10.6	262.6	73	22.8	295.9	8	46.4	281.2	283	49.7	9.8
14	10.0	263.2	74	23.3	296.5	9	48.2	282.2	284	51.5	10.8
+15	−9.4	263.7	+75	+23.9	297.0	+10	+50.0	283.2	285	+53.3	+11.8
16	8.9	264.3	76	24.4	297.6	11	51.8	284.2	286	55.1	12.8
17	8.3	264.8	77	25.0	298.2	12	53.6	285.2	287	56.9	13.8
18	7.8	265.4	78	25.6	298.7	13	55.4	286.2	288	58.7	14.8
19	7.2	265.9	79	26.1	299.3	14	57.2	287.2	289	60.5	15.8
+20	−6.7	266.5	+80	+26.7	299.8	+15	+59.0	288.2	290	+62.3	+16.8
21	6.1	267.0	81	27.2	300.4	16	60.8	289.2	291	64.1	17.8
22	5.6	267.6	82	27.8	300.9	17	62.6	290.2	292	65.9	18.8
23	5.0	268.2	83	28.3	301.5	18	64.4	291.2	293	67.7	19.8
24	4.4	268.7	84	28.9	302.0	19	66.2	292.2	294	69.5	20.8
+25	−3.9	269.3	+85	+29.4	302.6	+20	+68.0	293.2	295	+71.3	+21.8
26	3.3	269.8	86	30.0	303.2	21	69.8	294.2	296	73.1	22.8
27	2.8	270.4	87	30.6	303.7	22	71.6	295.2	297	74.9	23.8
28	2.2	270.9	88	31.1	304.3	23	73.4	296.2	298	76.7	24.8
29	1.7	271.5	89	31.7	304.8	24	75.2	297.2	299	78.5	25.8
+30	−1.1	272.0	+90	+32.2	305.4	+25	+77.0	298.2	300	+80.3	+26.8
31	0.6	272.6	91	32.8	305.9	26	78.8	299.2	301	82.1	27.8
32	0.0	273.2	92	33.3	306.5	27	80.6	300.2	302	83.9	28.8
33	+0.6	273.7	93	33.9	307.0	28	82.4	301.2	303	85.7	29.8
34	1.1	274.3	94	34.4	307.6	29	84.2	302.2	304	87.5	30.8
+35	+1.7	274.8	+95	+35.0	308.2	+30	+86.0	303.2	305	+89.3	+31.8
36	2.2	275.4	96	35.6	308.7	31	87.8	304.2	306	91.1	32.8
37	2.8	275.9	97	36.1	309.3	32	89.6	305.2	307	92.9	33.8
38	3.3	276.5	98	36.7	309.8	33	91.4	306.2	308	94.7	34.8
39	3.9	277.0	99	37.2	310.4	34	93.2	307.2	309	96.5	35.8
+40	+4.4	277.6	+100	+37.8	310.9	+35	+95.0	308.2	310	+98.3	+36.8

Beaufort Scale
with Corresponding Sea State Codes

Beaufort number	Wind speed				Seaman's term	World Meteorological Organization (1964)	Estimating wind speed		Hydrographic Office		World Meteorological Organization	
	knots	mph	meters per second	km per hour			Effects observed at sea	Effects observed on land	Term and height of waves, in feet	Code	Term and height of waves, in feet	Code
0	under 1	under 1	0.0–0.2	under 1	Calm	Calm	Sea like mirror.	Calm; smoke rises vertically.	Calm, 0	0	Calm, glassy, 0	0
1	1–3	1–3	0.3–1.5	1–5	Light air	Light air	Ripples with appearance of scales; no foam crests.	Smoke drift indicates wind direction; vanes do not move.	Smooth, less than 1	1	Calm, rippled, 0–⅓	1
2	4–6	4–7	1.6–3.3	6–11	Light breeze	Light breeze	Small wavelets; crests of glassy appearance, not breaking.	Wind felt on face; leaves rustle; vanes begin to move.	Slight, 1–3	2	Smooth, wavelets, ⅓–1⅔	2
3	7–10	8–12	3.4–5.4	12–19	Gentle breeze	Gentle breeze	Large wavelets; crests begin to break; scattered whitecaps.	Leaves, small twigs in constant motion; light flags extended.	Moderate, 3–5	3	Slight, 2–4	3
4	11–16	13–18	5.5–7.9	20–28	Moderate breeze	Moderate breeze	Small waves, becoming longer; numerous whitecaps.	Dust, leaves, and loose paper raised up; small branches move.			Moderate, 4–8	4
5	17–21	19–24	8.0–10.7	29–38	Fresh breeze	Fresh breeze	Moderate waves, taking longer form; many whitecaps; some spray.	Small trees in leaf begin to sway.	Rough, 5–8	4	Rough, 8–13	5
6	22–27	25–31	10.8–13.8	39–49	Strong breeze	Strong breeze	Larger waves forming; whitecaps everywhere; more spray.	Larger branches of trees in motion; whistling heard in wires.				
7	28–33	32–38	13.9–17.1	50–61	Moderate gale	Near gale	Sea heaps up; white foam from breaking waves begins to be blown in streaks.	Whole trees in motion; resistance felt in walking against wind.				
8	34–40	39–46	17.2–20.7	62–74	Fresh gale	Gale	Moderately high waves of greater length; edges of crests begin to break into spindrift; foam is blown in well-marked streaks.	Twigs and small branches broken off trees; progress generally impeded.	Very rough, 8–12	5	Very rough, 13–20	6
9	41–47	47–54	20.8–24.4	75–88	Strong gale	Strong gale	High waves; sea begins to roll; dense streaks of foam; spray may reduce visibility.	Slight structural damage occurs; slate blown from roofs.	High, 12–20	6	High, 20–30	7
10	48–55	55–63	24.5–28.4	89–102	Whole gale	Storm	Very high waves with overhanging crests; sea takes white appearance as foam is blown in very dense streaks; rolling is heavy and visibility reduced.	Seldom experienced on land; trees broken or uprooted; considerable structural damage occurs.	Very high, 20–40	7	Very high, 30–45	8
11	56–63	64–72	28.5–32.6	103–117	Storm	Violent storm	Exceptionally high waves; sea covered with white foam patches; visibility still more reduced.		Mountainous, 40 and higher	8		
12	64–71	73–82	32.7–36.9	118–133	Hurricane	Hurricane	Air filled with foam; sea completely white with driving spray; visibility greatly reduced.	Very rarely experienced on land; usually accompanied by widespread damage.	Confused	9	Phenomenal, over 45	9
13	72–80	83–92	37.0–41.4	134–149								
14	81–89	93–103	41.5–46.1	150–166								
15	90–99	104–114	46.2–50.9	167–183								
16	100–108	115–125	51.0–56.0	184–201								
17	109–118	126–136	56.1–61.2	202–220								

Note: Since January 1, 1955, weather map symbols have been based upon wind speed in knots, at five-knot intervals, rather than upon Beaufort number.

Courtesy of Bowditch/American Practical Navigator

Safety Afloat

Mariner's Notebook urges you to carry an authoritative First Aid Manual on board at all times, but we caution you that this section of **READY REFERENCE** is not it.

Expect to find here only minimum information at the bare threshold of adequacy. It is far better to be prepared than to grasp at any port in a storm. But if the storm of injury or illness should break on you unexpectedly, then, perhaps, these few pages will serve a purpose.

Normal Values

Body Temperature .... 98.6°F

Pulse Rate .... 72 per minute

Respiration .... 16 to 20 per minute

Notes

Armpit generally 1°F lower than mouth. Rectal generally 1°F higher than mouth.

To Take: place tips of fingers over artery on thumb side of wrist.

To Count: watch rise and fall of chest. One rise and fall is taken as one respiration.

Data Check-list When Calling for Medical Aid

Vessel: Name, position, speed, course, destination.

Patient: Name, sex, age, conscious or unconscious, pulse, respiration, temperature, mental alertness, pallor, manner of speech.

Problem: Cause, pain, location injury, bleeding status, nausea or not, skin cold or hot, skin wet or dry, description of wound, any loss of function or movement, any shape abnormalities, suspected breaks or dislocations, description of steps already taken.

Broken Bone

Fracture: Treat for shock. Do not try to set bone. Apply splints to prevent movement of broken bone. Frequently check extremity beyond splint for signs of impaired circulation. Handle part carefully to avoid further damage to tissues, nerves, blood vessels, muscles, etc.

Compound Fracture: It is a combination fractured bone and open wound extending down to the fracture. Stop severe bleeding. Treat for shock. Wash area carefully with soap and water and remove foreign particles as practicable. Do not try to set bone. Cover wound with sterile gauze compress and splint. Check frequently for impairment of circulation beyond splint.

Shock

In general, shock is an alteration in the normal body functions often following severe injuries. Treatment should be given in all cases of serious injury, and immediately. What to do:

Control any bleeding.

Place in "Shock Position": flat on back or belly, with head and shoulders low.

Wrap in blankets to prevent shivering.

No alcohol.

No liquids if unconscious, or if nauseated or drowsy, or with punctured or crushed abdomen.

Other cases, may give small amount of lukewarm fluids in very small sips.

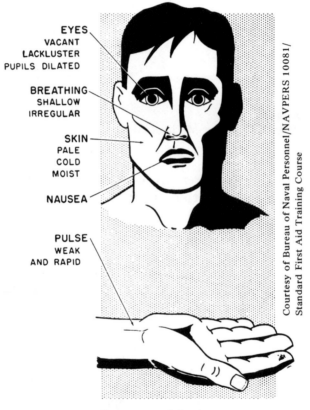

EYES
VACANT
LACKLUSTER
PUPILS DILATED

BREATHING
SHALLOW
IRREGULAR

SKIN
PALE
COLD
MOIST

NAUSEA

PULSE
WEAK
AND RAPID

Courtesy of Bureau of Naval Personnel/NAVPERS 10081/
Standard First Aid Training Course

Symptoms of shock.

Swallowed Poison

A Universal Antidote for use when the specific is not known:

4 tablespoonfuls powdered charcoal (burnt toast).

4 tablespoonfuls tannic acid (strong tea).

2 tablespoonfuls magnesium chloride (milk of magnesia).

Mix 1 tablespoonful compound with 1 pint water and have patient swallow it. Induce vomiting. Repeat as needed.

Minor Puncture Wounds

Treatment:
Carefully remove the object which caused the wound (nail, splinter, fishhook) and let wound bleed freely for a time, without forceful squeezing or "milking." Clean area with soap and water. Touch the wound with a mild antiseptic. Apply sterile gauze compress.

Removing Fishhook:
The barb buried in finger prevents removal without further tissue damage. Push barb on through skin and clip off with pliers. Then withdraw barbless fishhook from finger.

Control of Bleeding

Methods are as follows:
1. Pressure dressing on wound.
2. Finger pressure at "pressure point" on artery supplying blood to a bleeding area.
3. Tourniquet. Fold cloth into strip two inches wide and long enough to circle extremity several times. Wrap snugly at pressure point and tie simple overhand knot, leaving ends free. Then insert pad one inch thick under tourniquet directly over artery. Place six inch stick over knot and secure with square knot. Twist to exert firm but not severe pressure. LOOSEN EVERY 20 MINUTES. Never cover with any clothing or dressings. And if you transfer patient to the care of others while tourniquet still on, tell them of the particulars ... better still, tag him with the fact of his tourniquet, time of application and time of last loosening.

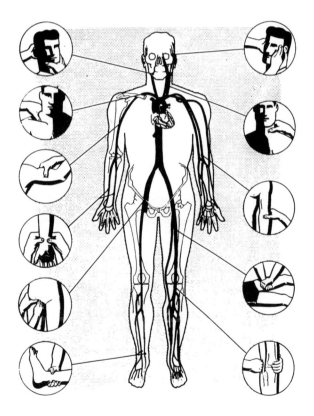

Pressure point for control of bleeding.

Courtesy of Bureau of Naval Personnel/NAVPERS 10081/ Standard First Aid Training Course

Unconsciousness

Until the cause is determined, treatment is based on pallor and pulse.

Red Face, Strong Pulse:	Place on back, head slightly high, clothes loosened. Cold compresses to head. Cover with blanket. Keep him quiet. GIVE NO STIMULANTS.
White Face, Weak Pulse:	Treat for shock if facts suggest. Otherwise, lay him flat or with head slightly low. Clothes loosened. Cover with blanket. Plenty of fresh air. GIVE NOTHING BY MOUTH WHILE UNCONSCIOUS. If no head injuries and no bleeding, pass cloth moistened with aromatic spirits of ammonia under nose.
Blue Face, Weak or Absent Pulse and Respiration:	Begin Artificial Respiration at once.

Below is information on Artifical Respiration, Shock and Asphyxia, reprinted from *CG-175, Manual for Lifeboatmen, Able Seamen, and Qualified Members of Engine Department,* a publication of the United States Coast Guard.

ARTIFICIAL RESPIRATION

ASPHYXIA

When breathing stops for any reason a condition results which is known as asphyxia.

The physiological causes of asphyxia may include lack of stimulation of the respiratory center in the brain, paralysis of the respiratory center, and inability of the blood to absorb oxygen from the lungs or to effect the normal exchange of gases in the body tissues.

When it is due to physical causes, it may be spoken of as suffocation. In asphyxia resulting from physical causes, the lungs are deprived of air because of stoppage of the air passages mechanically. Such causes may include water in the air passages, as in drowning; foreign body in the air passages; tumor in the air passages; swelling of the mucous membrane in the nose and throat, following inhalation of live steam or an irritating gas; constriction around the neck, compressing the windpipe; and the lack of oxygen from any cause. The most frequent causes of stopping of breathing are drowning, electrical shock, and gas poisoning. Asphyxia may be present also in victims of shock or collapse, of extreme exposure to heat or cold, and chemical poisoning. Whatever the cause of asphyxia, death will result unless breathing is started quickly. A few seconds' delay in starting artificial respiration may lead to fatal result.

SYMPTOMS OF ASPHYXIA

The symptoms of which the necessity for artificial respiration may be recognized are: Cyanosis (blueness of the skin and membrane), suspension of breathing, or shallow breathing in some cases of poisoning.

TREATMENT OF ASPHYXIA

The first thing to do in treatment is to remove the cause of the asphyxia or to remove the patient from the cause. Then administer artificial respiration. Later treat as for shock. In some cases artificial respiration can be administered while the patient is being removed from the cause to more suitable surroundings. The treatment for shock can often be started while artificial respiration is being administered.

The patient's mouth should be cleared of any obstruction, such as chewing gum, tobacco, false teeth, or mucous, so that there is no interference with the entrance into and escape of air from the lungs.

Artificial respiration should be started immediately. Every moment of delay is serious. It should be continued at least 4 hours without interruption, until normal breathing is established or until the patient is pronounced dead by a medical doctor.

Not infrequently the patient, after a temporary recovery of respiration, stops breathing again. The patient must be watched and if natural breathing stops, artificial respiration should be resumed at once. Perform artificial respiration gently and at the proper rate. Roughness may injure the patient.

Every precaution must be taken to prevent further injury to the patient. In the application of pressure, injury to the skin, ribs, and internal organs must be avoided.

GENERAL PRINCIPLES OF MANUAL ARTIFICIAL RESPIRATION

Time is of prime importance. Seconds count. Do not take time to move the victim to a more satisfactory place; begin at once. Do not delay resuscitation to loosen clothes, warm the victim, or apply stimulants. These are secondary to the main purpose of getting air into the victim's lungs.

Begin artificial respiration and continue it rhythmically and without interruption until spontaneous breathing starts or the victim is pronounced dead.

As soon as the victim is breathing by himself, or when additional help is available, see that the clothing is loosened (or removed, if wet) and that the patient is kept warm, but do not interrupt the rhythmic artificial respiration to accomplish these measures.

If the victim begins to breathe on his own, adjust your timing to assist him. Do not fight his attempts to breathe. Synchronize your efforts with his.

Remember, it is all-important that artificial respiration, when needed, be started quickly. There should be a slight inclination of the body in such a way that the fluid drains better from the respiratory passages. The head of the subject should be extended, not flexed forward, and the chin should not sag lest obstruction of the respiratory passages occur. A check should be made to ascertain that the tongue or foreign objects are not obstructing the passages. These aspects can be cared for when placing the subject into position or shortly thereafter, between cycles. A smooth rhythm in performing artificial respiration is desirable, but split-second timing is not essential. Shock should receive adequate attention, and the subject should remain recumbent after resuscitation until seen by a physician or until recovery seems assured.

MOUTH TO MOUTH BREATHING

1. Place the unconscious victim on his back, as you must be able to see his face. Move an injured victim carefully.

2. If there is foreign matter visible at the mouth, turn victim's head to the side, force his mouth open and quickly clean the mouth and throat with your fingers or a piece of cloth as shown on page 429.

3. Place the victim's head in the "sniffling position", pulling the head as far back as possible, so that the neck is extended, and hold his lower jaw upward so that it "juts out".

It is important that the jaw be held in this position as shown in illustration on page 429.

After taking a deep breath, blow into the mouthpiece of the airway as shown. Blow forcefully into adults and gently into children. With a baby, blow only small puffs from your cheeks, not from your lungs to prevent damage to the baby's lungs.

It should be considered that after mouth-to-mouth breathing has been performed for a period of time, the victim's stomach may be bulging. This bulging can be caused by air blown into the victim's stomach while blowing air into his lungs.

Air inflation of the stomach is not dangerous, but inflation of the lungs is easier when the stomach is empty. When the rescuer sees the stomach bulging, he should interrupt blowing for a few seconds and press with his hand between the victim's navel and breast bone which causes the air to be "burped". If this causes matter from the victim's stomach to be blown into his breathing passages, the rescuer must be ready to clean the throat at once.

TREATMENT OF SHOCK

When the patient revives, he should be kept under close observation for 48 hours even though he apparently feels all right. He should not be permitted to exert himself in any way.

The fundamental factors in the prevention and treatment of shock are heat, position, and stimulants.

A. Heat.
    1. Preserve body heat.
        a. Protect from exposure to cold.
        b. Remove wet clothing and dry the patient.
        c. Wrap the patient in blankets.
    2. Application of external heat.
        a. Care should be used to avoid burning the patient.
            (1) Test the object used for applying heat by holding against the cheek or elbow for half a minute.
            (2) Wrap in a layer of cloth or paper.
        b. Methods:
            (1) Hot water bottles.
            (2) Chemical heating pads.
            (3) Glass jars and bottles containing hot water.
            (4) Hot bricks.
            (5) Electrical heating pads.
        c. To various regions.
            (1) To the feet.
            (2) Between the thighs.
            (3) Along the sides of the body.
            (4) Over the abdomen if not uncomfortable to the patient.
B. Position.
    1. Place the body in such a position so that gravity will help the blood flow to the brain and heart.
        a. Lay the patient on his back with the head low.
            (1) This can be accomplished by raising the foot of the bed, cot, bench, or litter at least 18 inches higher than the head.
            (2) If on a flat surface and other means are not available, elevate the feet, legs, and thighs.
C. Stimulants.
Do not attempt to make an unconscious person drink. Give in small quantities at a time.
    1. Aromatic spirits of ammonia—a teaspoonful in half a glass of water—is one of the most satisfactory stimulants. This can be repeated every 30 minutes as needed.
    2. Coffee and tea both contain the drug caffeine, which is an excellent stimulant. Give the coffee or tea as hot as can be comfortably taken. A cupful may be given every 30 minutes as needed.
    3. Hot milk, or even hot water, has some stimulating effect, due to the heat.
    4. An inhalation stimulant, such as an ammonia ampule or aromatic spirits of ammonia on a handkerchief, may be placed near the patient's nose in cases in which the patient is not conscious. The one administering the stimulant should always test it on himself first.

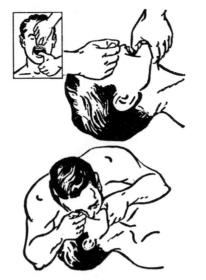

Courtesy of Department of Navigation and Ocean Development

5. Whiskey should not usually be given.

4. Hold the jaw in this position in one hand, approach the victim's head from his left side as shown.

Insert the thumb of your left hand between the victim's teeth and grasp his lower jaw at the midline.

Lift the lower jaw forcefully upward so that the lower teeth are higher than the upper teeth.

Hold the jaw in this position as long as the victim is unconscious.

Close the victim's nose with your right hand.

5. After taking a deep breath, place your mouth over the victim's mouth with airtight contact; his entire mouth must be inside your lips as shown.

Blow into the victim's mouth—forcefully into adults and gently into children.

Watch victim's chest. When it rises, stop blowing and quickly remove your mouth from the victim's.

Let victim exhale passively by the elasticity of his lungs and chest.

When the chest does not rise improve the support of the air passageway and blow more forcefully.

Repeat these inflations 12 to 20 times per minute.

In an adult whose mouth cannot be opened for insertion of thumb, place mouth over victim's mouth, covering the nose with your right cheek.

Do not use the thumb in a child LESS THAN THREE YEARS OLD. Cover both mouth and nose with your mouth. Blow only with small puffs from your cheeks, not from your lungs, TO PREVENT DAMAGE TO THE BABY'S LUNGS.

6. The airway tube may be used for mouth-to-mouth breathing when it is available.

7. To use an airway—approach victim from the top of his head. Force the mouth open with one hand.

Insert the proper end of the airway along the curve of the tongue with the other hand until the flange comes to rest at the victim's lips. Do not push the tongue back into the throat. If the tongue is in the way push its base forward with the finger. If the victim is an adult, insert the long end of the large airway; if he is a small child or a baby, insert the short end of the small airway. The part of the airway which remains outside serves as mouthpiece for the rescuer as shown.

8. Grasp the jaw with both hands firmly and pull upward, extending the neck so that the chin "juts out" and front of neck is stretched.

Close the victim's nostrils by pressing them together with the large part of your thumbs as shown.

9. Close the corners of the victim's mouth by pressing the flange firmly against the victim's lips with your thumbs.

The information in this section has been reprinted and adapted from *CG-175, Manual for Lifeboatmen, Able Seamen and Qualified Members of Engine Department*.

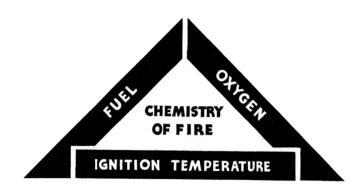

Fires are divided into three classes so that it is possible to decide which type of portable extinguisher is best to use. These classes are as follows:

Class A fires are those in ordinary combustible materials where the quenching and cooling effects of quantities of water, or solutions containing large percentages of water are of first importance.

Class B fires are those in flammable liquids, greases, etc., where a blanketing effect is essential.

Class C fires are those in electrical equipment where the use of a nonconducting extinguishing agent is of first importance.

There are also various types of approved water extinguishers which make use of a pump or CO_2 cartridge to expel water at a blaze.

PORTABLE FIRE EXTINGUISHERS			
TYPE EX-TINGUISHER	CLASS OF FIRE IT IS TO BE USED ON	HOW TO OPERATE	YEARLY MAINTENANCE
Soda and Acid	"A" (Do not use on electrical fires.)	Turn upside down. Direct nozzle at base of fire. Recharge.	Discharge. Clean hose and inside of extinguisher thoroughly. Recharge as directed on name plate.
Foam	"A" and "B" (Do not use on electrical fires.)	Turn upside down. Direct nozzle at base of fire. Recharge.	Discharge. Clean hose and inside of extinguisher thoroughly. Recharge as directed on name plate.
Carbon Dioxide	"B" and "C" CO_2 extinguishers are not permitted in passenger or crew quarters.	Open valve to release snow and gas. Direct discharge at flames in a slow sweeping motion.	Weigh. Recharge if weight is 10 per cent or more under required charge. Check hose and horn.
Dry Chemical	"B" and "C"	Operate release and direct discharge at base of flames in sweeping motion.	Examine pressure cartridge and replace if end is punctured or if cartridge is otherwise determined to have leaked. For pressure type see that pressure gage is in operating range. See that dry chemical is not caked in cartridge type or that there is sufficient quantity of dry chemical in pressure type.

Safe Practices for Seamen

DO NOT

1. wear clothing with loose, dangling parts to catch on machinery or fittings.
2. have pants cuffs on dungarees.
3. put knots in chains.
4. stand in the bight of a line.
5. smoke while lying in your bunk.
6. toss cigarettes or ashes out of portholes.
7. stand close to a radar antenna in operation.
8. walk without a light in dimly lit areas aboard or on dock.

DO

1. use cleaning compounds with care, to avoid injury to eyes or skin. Lye, oxalic acid, caustic soda should be used with care. Some detergents cause rapid rotting of ropes.
2. ventilate compartments being painted. When using a spray painting gear, have face mask, filter, respiratory guard.
3. aloft, over the side, or going on a ladder, remember:
   "One hand for the ship, one for yourself."
4. use a flashlight in dark areas, not a match.
5. ground electric tools before using them.
6. lift with leg and thigh muscles, not your back.

About Electrical Machinery

Treat all electric circuits as though they were "hot" until you are *sure* they are dead.

Before closing a switch be sure you know about the circuit—Don't electrocute a shipmate!!

Never bridge a fuse—fuses are safety devices.

When working on motors or circuits, remove the fuses or, if possible, lock the switch open. Place a tag or sign on the switch to warn others that you are working on the line.

Be sure to ground the frame of portable electric tools before using them.

Stand on a dry rubber mat or board if possible when working on electrical equipment.

Never use emery cloth on commutators of motors and generators.

Do not use portable electric lights or tools with loose connections or frayed cable.

Excessive sparking at the commutator or excessive heat in motors, generators, switches, etc., is a sure sign of trouble and should never be ignored or neglected.

Moisture and mechanical injury are the main causes of insulation failure.

Seamanship

The information in this section has been reprinted and adapted from *CG-175, Manual for Lifeboatmen, Able Seamen and Qualified Members of Engine Department.*

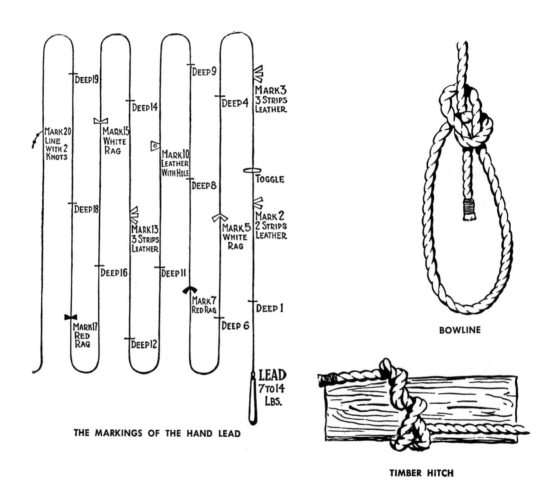

THE MARKINGS OF THE HAND LEAD

BOWLINE

TIMBER HITCH

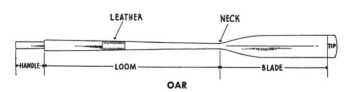

OAR

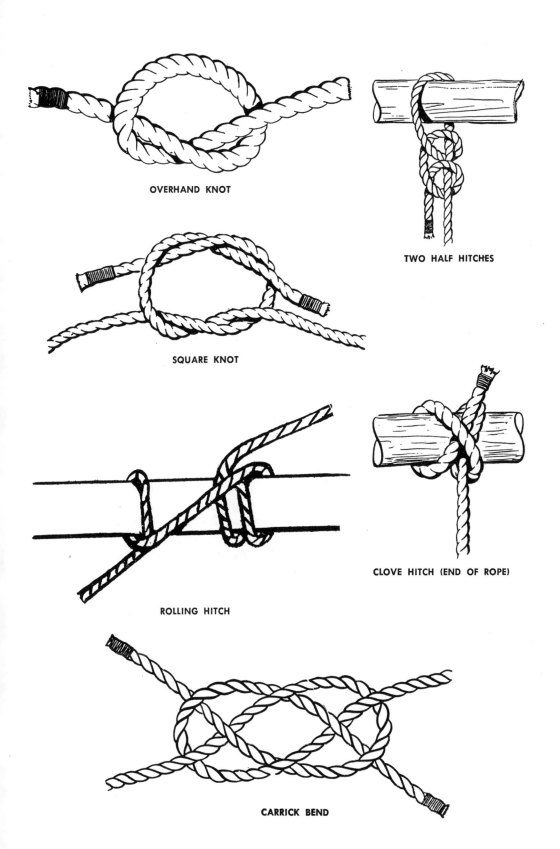

OVERHAND KNOT

TWO HALF HITCHES

SQUARE KNOT

ROLLING HITCH

CLOVE HITCH (END OF ROPE)

CARRICK BEND

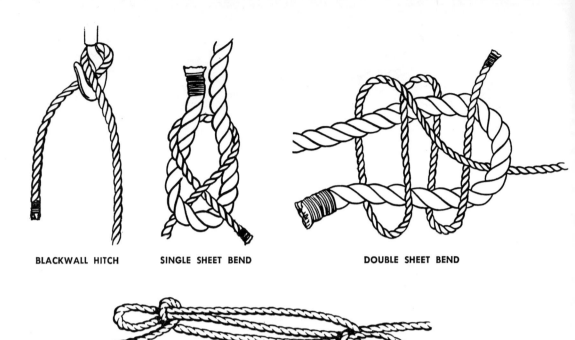

BLACKWALL HITCH   SINGLE SHEET BEND   DOUBLE SHEET BEND

SHEEPSHANK

Seizing a Rope

There's quite a difference between darning a sock and doing needlepoint. Marlinespike seamanship falls into similar categories. The art of intricate rope work is fascinating, and not everyone has the combination of patience and manipulative skill to do it. Of course, that need not make him less a seaman any more than a wife who has never embroidered is less a homemaker.

But there are a few basic skills required. Tying serviceable knots is one of them, and protecting a piece of rope against fraying is another. To fly **Irish Pennants** is not good advertising. Shredded rags and rope yarns not only look untidy, they are sources of danger. Here sketched are two valuable techniques to keep things shipshape. The **seizing** is used to bind two things together; the **whipping** is used on the end of a rope to keep it from becoming unraveled.

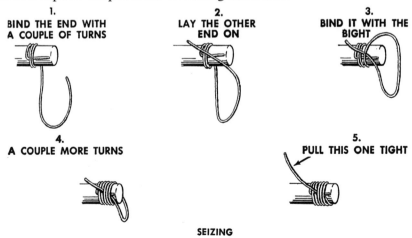

1.
BIND THE END WITH
A COUPLE OF TURNS

2.
LAY THE OTHER
END ON

3.
BIND IT WITH THE
BIGHT

4.
A COUPLE MORE TURNS

5.
PULL THIS ONE TIGHT

SEIZING

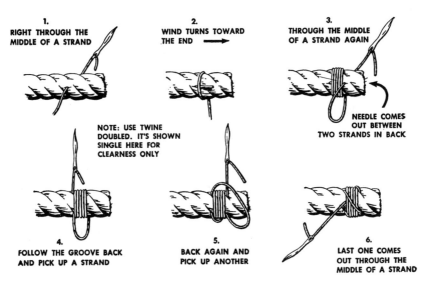

1.
RIGHT THROUGH THE
MIDDLE OF A STRAND

2.
WIND TURNS TOWARD
THE END ➔

3.
THROUGH THE MIDDLE
OF A STRAND AGAIN

NEEDLE COMES
OUT BETWEEN
TWO STRANDS IN BACK

NOTE: USE TWINE
DOUBLED. IT'S SHOWN
SINGLE HERE FOR
CLEARNESS ONLY

4.
FOLLOW THE GROOVE BACK
AND PICK UP A STRAND

5.
BACK AGAIN AND
PICK UP ANOTHER

6.
LAST ONE COMES
OUT THROUGH THE
MIDDLE OF A STRAND

PUTTING A WHIPPING ON A LINE

Steering

That steering is an art has been said for centuries, and it is still as true as ever. Each vessel has its own traits and to reduce it all to a set of instructions is nonsense. The only way to acquire the knack is to practice. Even so, some basic hints are in order.

First of all, the lubber's line marked on the compass bowl is the ship. The marine compass has it forward of the compass card. Aircraft type have it on the after side. In either case, though, it is parallel to the keel and shows the direction

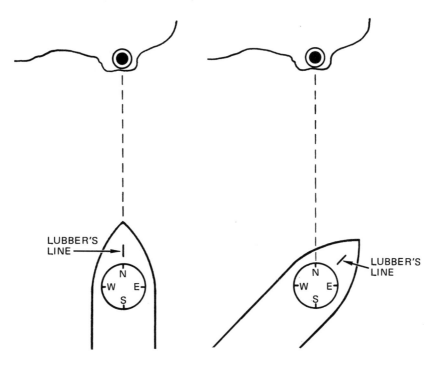

LUBBER'S
LINE

LUBBER'S
LINE

of the ship. It moves around the compass, and not the reverse. The job is to bring the lubber's line to the degrees on the compass card. The sketches show a vessel south of a lighthouse. First she is heading directly towards it. Then she turns to the right. Note that Compass North is still pointing the same way in each sketch. Only the lubber's line has changed direction.

Next, in rough weather the ship may yaw without really getting off course. The mid-point between the compass headings at the ends of the yaw is the course being steered. The idea is not to over-steer and flop back and forth across the course. Most of the time she will swing back on her own, so use as little rudder as possible.

When steering by landmarks, pick those far away. Closer ones open rapidly on the bow as you approach. When steering by stars, remember they change in direction as they move across the sky. So check direction by compass bearing occasionally.

Blocks

A **block** is a shipboard pulley used either to change direction of pull or, with another block, to form a **purchase**. When used to change direction it is a **fair lead** (Sketch a). Blocks in a purchase gain lifting power by **mechanical advantage**. In

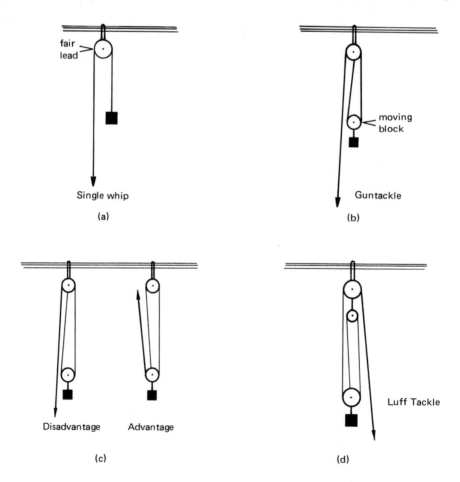

general this equals the number of parts of line moving through and attached to the moving block: the one traveling with the weight (Sketch b).

Attach an end of the line to the moving block and the purchase is **rove to advantage.** Secure it to the fixed block and the purchase is **rove to disadvantage,** for one less part is at the moving block (Sketch c).

Friction occurs when a line leads through a sheave. Although inexact, this rule is used: for friction add 10% of the weight for each sheave in the rig. This errs on the safe side but offsets loss of strength by age, neglect, and so forth.

Here are common names for a few basic purchases: **single whip** (Sketch a); **guntackle** (Sketch b); and **luff tackle** (Sketch d). And here is a formula to compute the force to lift a given weight, or the weight a given force will handle. It is in Magic Circle form and includes friction but not weight of the purchase itself:

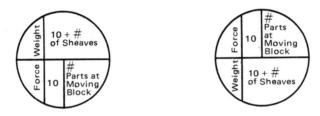

Example: with a guntackle, how much force to lift 100 pounds?

$$\text{Force} = \frac{100 \times 12}{10 \times 2} = \frac{1200}{20} = 60 \text{ pounds}$$

Example: with a luff tackle, what weight will 100 pounds of force lift?

$$\text{Weight} = \frac{100 \times 10 \times 3}{13} = \frac{3000}{13} = 230.77 \text{ pounds}$$

But every advantage is paid for, one way or another. To apply half the effort, you pull on twice as much line . . .

Line Necessary = Distance Weight Lifted x Mechanical Advantage.

So the guntackle requires two feet of pull to lift the weight one foot; the luff tackle requires three.

Anchoring

At the end of a day's cruise and at anchor in a cove, all the care and skill exercised by the navigator in reaching the anchorage can be for naught, unless he does a safe and seamanlike job of anchoring his craft. Just as much thought is needed in anchoring as in plotting courses, taking bearings and steering the boat.

The lives of the crew and safety of the boat can hang on as simple a matter as the ratio of scope paid out, and the care taken in burying the flukes of the anchor.

Types of anchors . . They fall into two broad categories: those that hook themselves to the bottom, and those that bury their flukes in direct ratio to the area of the flukes and amount of pull. Yachtsman's kedge, navy stockless kedge, grapnel and the Northill anchor are of the "hooking" type. The plow and Danforth anchors are of the "burying" type. In comparison with a yachtsman's kedge, which has a holding power of around five times its weight, a Northill will have a holding power of 30 to 40 times its weight, and the Danforth type as much as 300 to 400 times its weight. These are based on a straight pull parallel with the bottom.

Types of rodes . . Before the introduction of synthetic lines, manila rope was most generally used by small craft. It is rapidly giving way to synthetic lines because the latter are stronger for the same diameter, have more stretch or shock absorbing qualities, more resistance to abrasion, and do not rot or deteriorate to the extent that manila does.

Some owners prefer wire for the rode. The main disadvantage of it is its lack of resilience and severe loss of strength when kinked. It also requires a drum on which to coil it, which usually means a motor-driven drum-type windlass.

This table reflects the views of most authorities on the size of anchor, suitable boat lengths, and weights as indicated.

Boat length (feet)	Boat weight (tons)	Navy stockless (pounds)	Kedge anchor (pounds)	Burying anchor (pounds)	Nylon line (inches)	BBB chain (inches)
26	2	50	20	12	3/8	3/16
31	3½	60	25	14	1/2	3/16
36	7	70	40	18	9/16	1/4
38	9½	85	50	20	9/16	1/4
42	12	100	60	23	5/8	5/16
65	30	200	130	45	7/8	7/16

Chain is without doubt the best anchor rode. It will not rot, is far more resistant to abrasion, and its weight will absorb much of the load that is otherwise imposed on the anchor with wire or manila/synthetic rodes. A middle ground is the use of three to six fathoms of chain shackled to the anchor, and synthetic line for the balance of the rode. The length of chain will help keep the anchor's shank lying on the bottom, and avoid part of the risk of the anchor being broken out by a sharp lift on the shank when manila/synthetic rode is shackled directly to it.

Fundamentals of anchoring . . Some people call it an art, whereas in fact it is more nearly a science. Five basic factors are sketched in **Figure 157**. They are:

1. **Type of bottom**: soft mud, or hard sand (which has six times more holding power than mud).
2. **Type of anchor**: one that merely hooks a fluke in the bottom versus one that buries the flukes and possibly the shank.
3. **Type of rode**: all-manila or synthetic rope, all-wire or all-chain, or a combination of chain and rope. An all-rope rode can exert a load on the anchor as much as 100 times greater than an all-chain one, under even moderate conditions of wind and swell.

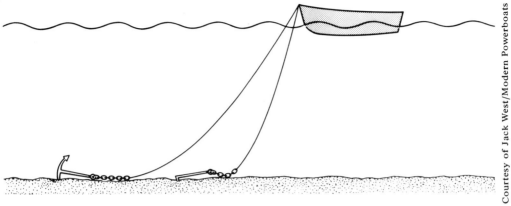

Figure 157

4. **Amount of wind and surge or swell in the anchorage.**
5. **Depth of the water, and ratio of rode length to depth.**

Proper evaluation of each factor gives a very precise answer to the question how best to anchor, and with what type of gear. For instance: with a hard bottom, a lighter-weight burying anchor can be used than a hooking type anchor; manila or synthetic rope with some chain will require a greater scope than if all chain is used; a quiet, shallow anchorage will require less rode length than a deep, windy, surgy one.

Anchoring Techniques . . (1) Never come to a stop with a boat at the desired anchoring place and then toss or throw overboard the anchor and rode. Chances are ten-to-one that the rode will pile on top of the anchor and foul it before it has a chance to get its flukes into the bottom. (2) Head into the wind (or current, if its effect is stronger than the wind) and start backing down slowly; when stern-way is on, start letting the anchor down; when it is on the bottom, continue the sternway to lay out the rode along the bottom; when the rode let out is three to four times the depth, snub it to cause the flukes to dig in, then back down some more until five to eight times the depth is paid out, and back down again to definitely set the anchor. (3) Pick a landmark ashore, or another boat at anchor, when burying the anchor to see that it is holding. Then some of the rode can be brought back aboard to reduce the swinging radius.

Not less scope than 3:1 with all-chain, or 5:1 with manila/synthetic line, should be used in calm or light breeze weather. If it is blowing or there is a surge, pay out more scope to reduce the pull on the anchor. **(See Figure 158.)**

When up-anchoring, use power to move the boat over the anchor. Only the weight of the rode will have to be lifted until the anchor has broken free. If the anchor has been deeply buried and is hard to break loose, secure the rode to a cleat and over-ride it with power.

Bow and stern anchoring is sometimes necessary in small anchorages to keep from swinging into other boats. As long as the wind is mainly on the bow, no special problems exist. But, if the wind swings to abeam, an enormous load can be put on the anchors due to the windage on the side of the boat. The load can reach

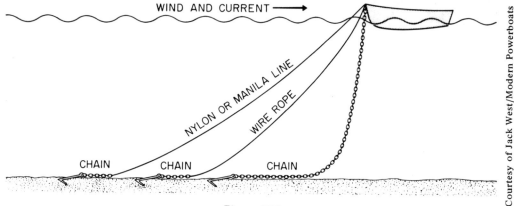

Courtesy of Jack West/Modern Powerboats

WIND AND CURRENT ➜

NYLON OR MANILA LINE

WIRE ROPE

CHAIN   CHAIN   CHAIN

Figure 158

proportions that will break the anchors out of the bottom and the boat will drift onto others or the beach.

Scope can do more to keep anchors holding in a blow or heavy swells than putting out a second anchor. Stretch of manila or synthetic rope absorbs a good part of the load that might otherwise drag an anchor or break it out. With chain, the scope acts like a spring and, before any appreciable load is placed on the anchor, the chain would have to be stretched taut.

Before anchoring in a harbor with other boats, take time to size up the positions of them. Note where their anchor rodes tend to lie; estimate how much they may swing. Lower your anchor when sure that it will not cross the rode of another boat. Remember that the burden is on the latecomer to carry out his maneuver in a way not dangerous to those already at anchor.

Sea Anchors

In heavy weather a serious concern is to keep a floundering vessel from broaching, or ending up with her side to the sea. One remedy is the use of a resistance attached to the end of a strong line secured to the bow or stern and dragged through the water. The name for this is **sea anchor** or **drogue**.

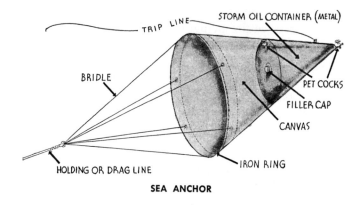

TRIP LINE

STORM OIL CONTAINER (METAL)

BRIDLE

PET COCKS

FILLER CAP

CANVAS

HOLDING OR DRAG LINE

IRON RING

SEA ANCHOR

Figure 159

Courtesy of US Coast Guard/Manual for Lifeboatmen, Able Seamen, and Qualified Members of Engine Department

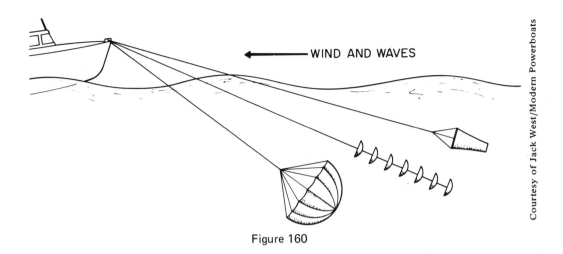

Courtesy of Jack West/Modern Powerboats

A specially made one is depicted in **Figure 159**. It is designed for easy storage on a small boat, and is fitted with a conical can filled with **storm oil** to reduce the peaking tendency of waves. The small size of this sea anchor might not be adequate for many pleasure vessels. Sketched in **Figure 160** are a few alternatives. Found very useful is a surplus parachute. A jury drogue can be fashioned from such items as crossed planks, buckets, stout crates, and so forth. Often the use of some buoying means to keep the sea anchor from sinking is required. Since the strain on the line will be great, care should be taken with the line selected and where it is made fast . . . on a well anchored bitt or even by a round turn around a deck house or mast.

Man Overboard Procedure

When **Man Overboard** is called there's no time left for practice. Any steps in preparation are long over with by then; and there are patterns to be tested beforehand. A vessel's reactions can modify the procedure, but the basic aims are always the same: to keep the person clear of the propeller, and then to find him in the water.

The time element is short. A 30-foot boat moving at eight knots travels her own length in about two seconds. Should someone fall off her bow, he would reach the propeller that fast. Usually best is an immediate turn **towards** the side he fell off, to move the stern the other way.

The next problem is to find him. Darkness and choppy seas, which often cause the mishap, can also hamper the search. Even a nimble vessel moves off her track when she reverses course. How much varies; but on a blustery night when only one try is possible, any amount might be too much. The top of a bobbing head shows less area than the cover of this book.

Every mariner must plan for this emergency, and that means practice. **Figure 161** shows the **Williamson Turn**, a maneuver which, for large vessels, has produced startling results. In one case, a man fell unnoticed from a 15-knot ship and was not missed for over three hours. When alarm was finally given, the ship was 50 miles away. She reversed course by this maneuver and doubled back for the time

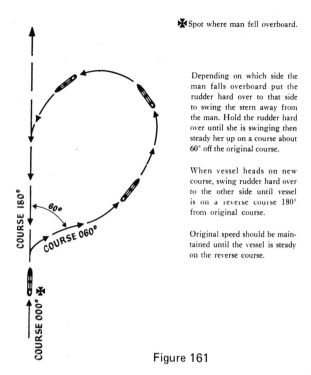

✠ Spot where man fell overboard.

Depending on which side the man falls overboard put the rudder hard over to that side to swing the stern away from the man. Hold the rudder hard over until she is swinging then steady her up on a course about 60° off the original course.

When vessel heads on new course, swing rudder hard over to the other side until vessel is on a reverse course 180° from original course.

Original speed should be maintained until the vessel is steady on the reverse course.

COURSE 180°

60°

COURSE 060°

COURSE 000°

Courtesy of US Coast Guard/Manual for Lifeboatmen, Able Seamen, and Qualified Members of Engine Department

Figure 161

interval between his last noted presence and first known absence. After more than six hours in the water, he was sighted directly ahead. Weather and the Williamson Turn combined to save a lucky crewman. Things might never again work that well. But the odds, at least, will always be shortened. Shaped to the handling habits of any ship, it is a pattern worth trying.

Marine Electronics

The scope of radio frequencies available to navigation is already so wide that a quick reference to the entire spectrum of radiated electromagnetic energy is valuable. And intriguing at least is the basic formula that the speed of propagation (300,000,000 meters per second) equals frequency times wavelength. The pattern ties in neatly in the visible spectrum with our language labels for the colors from red to violet. All have frequencies far above radio transmission and minute wavelengths by contrast. But within themselves the colors rank from long-wave red to short-wave violet. And the general formula of the frequency times the wavelength still works out to the same speed of propagation.

Sections IX, X and XI detail the shipboard use of various radio bands, from **Omega** in the very low frequency (VLF) department to 3-centimeter X-band radar in the super high frequency (SHF) category.

Working up from Omega's VLF place, we'll find **Decca, Loran-C, Consolan** and the bottom of the marine radiobeacon transmissions in LF. In the medium frequency section (MF) come the rest of marine radiobeacons, **Loran-A** and medium frequency radiotelephones. HF holds the high seas radiotelephones and the Citizen's Band equipment. VHF contains omni/VOR and the VHF radiotelephones. At the top of the nautical pile sit 10-centimeter and 3-centimeter radar.

The waves transmitted vary in length from 16-plus miles for Omega to just over an inch for the 3-centimeter radar.

MARINE APPLICATION	BAND & ABBREVIATION	FREQUENCY RANGE
Omega	Very Low Frequency (VLF)	10-15 kHz
Decca and Loran-C	Low Frequency (LF)	70-130 kHz
Consol, Consolan and Marine Radiobeacons	Low Frequency (LF) Medium Frequency (MF)	190-400 kHz
Distress Signal by wireless telegraphy	Medium Frequency (MF)	500 kHz
Loran-A	Medium Frequency (MF)	1750-1950 kHz (or 1.75-1.95 mHz)
Voice communications (radiotelephone)	Medium Frequency (MF) High Frequency (HF) Very High Frequency (VHF)	1.6 mHz - 4.0 mHz 4.0 mHz - 23.0 mHz 156.0 mHz - 158.0 mHz
Omni/VOR	Very High Frequency (VHF)	108.0 mHz - 118.0 mHz
Radar, S-Band (10 centimeters)	Super High Frequency (SHF)	2900 mHz - 3100 mHz
Radar, X-Band (3 centimeters)	Super High Frequency (SHF)	9300 mHz - 9500 mHz

One of the most dangerous conditions of a pleasure vessel in bad visibility develops from its size and construction. Section IX reviews in detail the shortcomings of common building materials—wood, fiberglass, canvas and the like—as reflectors of radar energy. The streamlined form of a modern vessel, designed to reduce vertical surfaces, further diminishes reflection. The answer is to display a special reflector most likely to rebound radar energy. The scanner on large ships can easily overlook a small vessel, particularly at close range. Coast Guard vessels

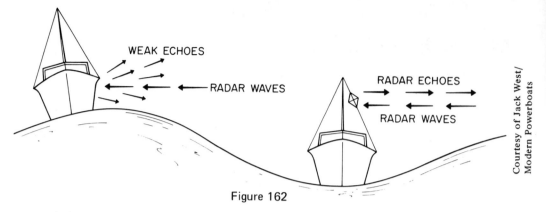

Courtesy of Jack West/
Modern Powerboats

Figure 162

engaged in search and rescue operation have particular difficulty in locating a distressed vessel not fitted with some means to enhance radar reflection.

As shown in **Figure 162**, radar waves bouncing off the side of a boat are not as effective as those returned by a special reflector hung high in the rigging. A vessel so equipped presents more reflecting surfaces, even when it is in the trough of a wave, for the important factors are shape, material and height above the sea.

Specially built radar reflectors can be purchased or can be made up aboard. But even a Jeep-type fuel can, or metal dishpan, or a skillet hung in the rigging is better than nothing. Metal foil taped to the sides of the cabins will help. During World War II, foil strips, called "window," dropped from aircraft swamped ground-based radar. Hanging similar foil strips in the rigging could have the same effect.

Recognition of the problem is most important; the cure can often be improvised. For instance, an effective radar reflector can be concocted aboard by using three panels of aluminum or plywood. (If wood is used, glue metal foil to the panels.) **Figure 163** shows steps to be taken in making a corner reflector:

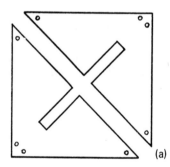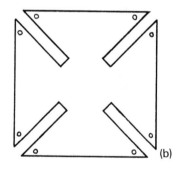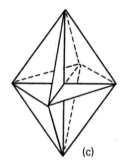

Figure 163

1. Take two of the panels and cut each diagonally in two (Sketch a). Cut slots from the diagonal side, one-half way towards the corners of each; drill holes in the corners.
2. Cut slots in the third panel, one-half way from the four corners, towards the center (Sketch b). Drill holes as shown.
3. Slide the pieces together (Sketch c) and use wire or cord to lash them in place. Hang in the rigging from the center of the top point and attach a downhaul for steadying.

Charts

Presented on a nautical chart is an enormous amount of detailed information. But nearly all of it must appear in symbolic and abbreviated form. A key, then, to this pattern of condensation is essential. Such is *Chart No. 1,* a booklet prepared by the US Oceanographic Office and National Ocean Survey to serve as a catalogue of symbols and abbreviations encountered on US nautical charts, which is reproduced here and on the following 20 pages.

GENERAL REMARKS

Chart No. 1 contains the standard symbols and abbreviations which have been approved for use on nautical charts published by the United States of America.

Symbols and abbreviations shown on Chart No. 1 apply to the regular nautical charts and may differ from those shown on certain reproductions and special charts. **Symbols and abbreviations on certain reproductions and on foreign charts may be interpreted by reference to the Symbol Sheet or Chart No. 1 of the originating country.**

Terms, symbols and abbreviations are numbered in accordance with a standard form approved by a Resolution of the Sixth International Hydrographic Conference, 1952.

Vertical figures indicate those items where the symbol and abbreviation are in accordance with the Resolutions of the International Hydrographic Conferences.

Slanting figures indicate no International Hydrographic Bureau symbol adopted.

Slanting figures underscored indicate U.S.A. and I.H.B. symbols do not agree.

Slanting figures asterisked indicate no U.S.A. symbol adopted.

An up-to-date compilation of symbols and abbreviations approved by resolutions of the International Hydrographic Conference is not currently available. Use of I.H.B. approved symbols and abbreviations by member nations is not mandatory.

Slanting letters in parentheses indicate that the items are in addition to those shown on the approved standard form.

Colors are optional for characterizing various features and areas on the charts.

Lettering styles and capitalization as used on Chart No. 1 are not always rigidly adhered to on the charts.

Longitudes are referred to the Meridian of Greenwich.

Scales are computed on the middle latitude of each chart, or on the middle latitude of a series of charts.

Buildings - A conspicuous feature on a building may be shown by a landmark symbol with descriptive note (See I-n & L-63). Prominent buildings that are of assistance to the mariner are crosshatched (See I-3a, 5, 47 & 66).

Shoreline is the line of Mean High Water, except in marsh or mangrove areas, where the outer edge of vegetation (berm line) is used. A heavy line (A-9) is used to represent a firm shoreline. A light line (A-7) represents a berm line.

Heights of land and conspicuous objects are given in feet above Mean High Water, unless otherwise stated in the title of the chart.

Depth Contours and Soundings may be shown in meters on charts of foreign waters.

Visibility of a light is in nautical miles for an observer's eye 15 feet above water level.

Buoys and Beacons - On entering a channel from seaward, buoys on starboard side are red with even numbers, on port side black with odd numbers. Lights on buoys on starboard side of channel are red or white, on port side white or green. Mid-channel buoys have black-and-white vertical stripes. Junction or obstruction buoys, which may be passed on either side, have red-and-black horizontal bands. This system does not always apply to foreign waters. The dot of the buoy symbol, the small circle of the light vessel and mooring buoy symbols, and the center of the beacon symbol indicate their positions.

Improved channels are shown by limiting dashed lines, the depth, month, and the year of latest examination being placed adjacent to the channel, except when tabulated.

U. S. Coast Pilots, Sailing Directions, Light Lists, Radio Aids, and related publications furnish information required by the navigator that cannot be shown conveniently on the nautical chart.

U. S. Nautical Chart Catalogs and Indexes list nautical charts, auxiliary maps, and related publications, and include general information (marginal notes, etc.) relative to the charts.

A glossary of foreign terms and abbreviations is generally given on the charts on which they are used, as well as in the Sailing Directions.

Charts already on issue will be brought into conformity as soon as opportunity affords.

All changes since the September 1963 edition of this publication are indicated by the symbol † in the margin immediately adjacent to the item affected.

TABLE OF CONTENTS

COLOR LEGEND FOR PAGES 447-461

Blue   Green

Yellow   Red

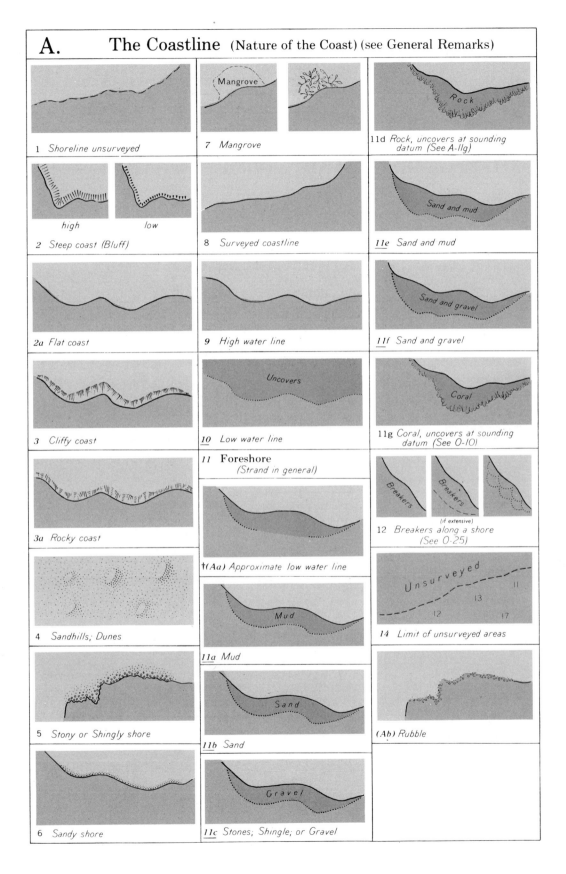

A. The Coastline (Nature of the Coast) (see General Remarks)

1 Shoreline unsurveyed

7 Mangrove

11d Rock, uncovers at sounding datum (See A-11g)

2 Steep coast (Bluff)

high   low

8 Surveyed coastline

11e Sand and mud

2a Flat coast

9 High water line

11f Sand and gravel

3 Cliffy coast

10 Low water line

11g Coral, uncovers at sounding datum (See O-10)

3a Rocky coast

11 Foreshore (Strand in general)

12 Breakers along a shore (See O-25)

(if extensive)

†(Aa) Approximate low water line

14 Limit of unsurveyed areas

4 Sandhills; Dunes

11a Mud

5 Stony or Shingly shore

11b Sand

(Ab) Rubble

6 Sandy shore

11c Stones; Shingle; or Gravel

B. Coast Features		
1	G	Gulf
2	B	Bay
(Ba)	B	Bayou
3	Fd	Fjord
4	L	Loch; Lough; Lake
5	Cr	Creek
5a	C	Cove
6	In	Inlet
7	Str	Strait
8	Sd	Sound
9	Pass	Passage; Pass
	Thoro	Thorofare
10	Chan	Channel
10a		Narrows
11	Entr	Entrance
12	Est	Estuary
12a		Delta
13	Mth	Mouth
14	Rd	Road; Roadstead
15	Anch	Anchorage
16	Hbr	Harbor
16a	Hn	Haven
17	P	Port
(Bb)	P	Pond
18	I	Island
19	It	Islet
20	Arch	Archipelago
21	Pen	Peninsula
22	C	Cape
23	Prom	Promontory
24	Hd	Head; Headland
25	Pt	Point
26	Mt	Mountain; Mount
27	Rge	Range
27a		Valley
28		Summit
29	Pk	Peak
30	Vol	Volcano
31		Hill
32	Bld	Boulder
33	Ldg	Landing
34		Table-land (Plateau)
35	Rk	Rock
36		Isolated rock
(Bc)	Str	Stream
(Bd)	R	River
(Be)	Slu	Slough
(Bf)	Lag	Lagoon
(Bg)	Apprs	Approaches
(Bh)	Rky	Rocky

C. The Land (Natural Features)

1 Contour lines (Contours)

1a Contour lines, approximate (Contours)

2 Hachures

2a Form lines, no definite interval

2b Shading

3 Glacier

4 Saltpans

5 Isolated trees

⊙TREE

5a Deciduous or of unknown or unspecified type

5b Coniferous

5c Palm tree

5d Nipa palm

5e Filao

5f Casuarina

†5g Evergreen tree (other than coniferous)

Cultivated

6 Cultivated fields

Grass

6a Grass fields

Rice

7 Paddy (rice) fields

7a Park; Garden

Bushes

8 Bushes

8a Tree plantation in general

Wooded

†9 Deciduous woodland

Wooded

10 Coniferous woodland

Wooded

†10a Woods in general

2560

11 Tree top elevation (above height datum)

12 Lava flow

13 River; Stream

14 Intermittent stream

15 Lake; Pond

16 Lagoon (Lag)

Marsh

Symbol used in small areas

Swamp

17 Marsh; Swamp

18 Slough (Slu.)

19 Rapids

20 Waterfalls

21 Spring

D. Control Points

1	△		Triangulation point (station)
†1a			Astronomic Station
2	⊙		Fixed point (landmark) (See L-63)
†(Da)	○		Fixed point (landmark, position approx.)
3	· 256		Summit of height (Peak) (when not a landmark)
(Db)	◎256		Peak, accentuated by contours
(Dc)	☀256		Peak, accentuated by hachures
(Dd)	☀		Peak, elevation not determined
(De)	⊙ 256		Peak, when a landmark
4	⊕	Obs Spot	Observation spot
*5		BM	Bench mark
†6	View X		View point
7			Datum point for grid of a plan
8			Graphical triangulation point
9		Astro	Astronomical
10		Tri	Triangulation
(Df)		C of E	Corps of Engineers
12			Great trigonometrical survey station
13			Traverse station
14		Bdy Mon	Boundary monument
(Dg)	◇		International boundary monument

E. Units

1	hr	Hour	†14a			Greenwich
2	m; min	Minute (of time)	15	pub		Publication
3	sec	Second (of time)	16	Ed		Edition
4	m	Meter	17	corr		Correction
4a	dm	Decimeter	18	alt		Altitude
4b	cm	Centimeter	19	ht; elev		Height; Elevation
4c	mm	Millimeter	20	°		Degree
4d	m²	Square meter	21	'		Minute (of arc)
4e	m³	Cubic meter	22	"		Second (of arc)
5	km	Kilometer	23	No		Number
6	in	Inch	(Ea)	St M		Statute mile
7	ft	Foot	(Eb)	msec		Microsecond
8	yd	Yard	†(Ec)	Hz		Hertz (cps)
9	fm	Fathom	†(Ed)	kHz		Kilohertz (kc)
10	cbl	Cable length	†(Ee)	MHz		Megahertz (Mc)
11	M	Nautical mile	†(Ef)	cps		Cycles/second(Hz)
12	kn	Knot	†(Eg)	kc		Kilocycle (kHz)
12a	t	Ton	†(Eh)	Mc		Megacycle (MHz)
12b	cd	Candela (new candle)				
13	lat	Latitude				
14	long	Longitude				

F. Adjectives, Adverbs and other abbreviations

1	gt	Great
2	lit	Little
3	lrg	Large
4	sml	Small
5		Outer
6		Inner
7	mid	Middle
8		Old
9	anc	Ancient
10		New
11	St	Saint
12	conspic	Conspicuous
13		Remarkable
14	D . Destr	Destroyed
15		Projected
16	dist	Distant
17	abt	About
18		See chart
18a		See plan
19		Lighted; Luminous
20	sub	Submarine
21		Eventual
22	AERO	Aeronautical
23		Higher
†23a		Lower
24	exper	Experimental
25	discontd	Discontinued
26	prohib	Prohibited
27	explos	Explosive
28	estab	Established
29	elec	Electric
30	priv	Private, Privately
31	prom	Prominent
32	std	Standard
33	subm	Submerged
34	approx	Approximate
†35		Maritime
†36	maintd	Maintained
†37	aband	Abandoned
†38	temp	Temporary
†39	occas	Occasional
†40	extr	Extreme
†41		Navigable
†42	N M	Notice to Mariners
†(Fa)	L N M	Local Notice to Mariners
†43		Sailing Directions
†44		List of Lights
(Fb)	unverd	Unverified
(Fc)	AUTH	Authorized
(Fd)	CL	Clearance
(Fe)	cor	Corner
(Ff)	concr	Concrete
(Fg)	fl	Flood
(Fh)	mod	Moderate
(Fi)	bet	Between
(Fj)	1st	First
(Fk)	2nd	Second
(Fl)	3rd	Third
(Fm)	4th	Fourth

1		Anch	Anchorage (large vessels)
†2		Anch	Anchorage (small vessels)
3		Hbr	Harbor
4		Hn	Haven
5		P	Port
6		Bkw	Breakwater
6a			Dike
7			Mole
8			Jetty (partly below MHW)
8a			Submerged jetty
(Ga)			Jetty (small scale)
9		Pier	Pier
10			Spit
11			Groin (partly below MHW)
12	ANCHORAGE PROHIBITED	ANCH PROHIB	Anchorage prohibited (See P-25)
†12a			Anchorage reserved
†12b	QUARANTINE ANCHORAGE	QUAR ANCH	Quarantine anchorage
13	Spoil Area		Spoil ground
(Gb)	Dumping Ground		Dumping ground
(Gc)	80 83 85 Disposal Area Depths from survey of JUNE 1968 90 98		Disposal area
14		Fsh stks	Fisheries; Fishing stakes
14a			Fish trap; Fish weirs (actual shape charted)
14b			Duck blind
15			Tunny nets (See G-14a)
15a	Oys	Oys	Oyster bed
16		Ldg	Landing place
17			Watering place
18		Whf	Wharf
19			Quay

20			Berth
20a	14		Anchoring berth
20b	3		Berth number
21		Dol	Dolphin
22			Bollard
23			Mooring ring
24			Crane
25			Landing stage
25a			Landing stairs
26		Quar	Quarantine
27			Lazaret
*28		Harbor Master	Harbor master's office
29		Cus Ho	Customhouse
30			Fishing harbor
31			Winter harbor
32			Refuge harbor
33		B Hbr	Boat harbor
34			Stranding harbor (uncovers at LW)
35			Dock
36			Dry dock (actual shape on large-scale charts)
37			Floating dock (actual shape on large-scale charts)
38			Gridiron; Careening grid
39			Patent slip; Slipway; Marine railway
39a		Ramp	Ramp
†40	Lock		Lock (point upstream) (See H-13)
41			Wet dock
42			Shipyard
43			Lumber yard
44		Health Office	Health officer's office
45		Hk	Hulk (actual shape on lrg. scale charts) (See O-11)
46	PROHIBITED AREA	PROHIB AREA	Prohibited area
†46a	10		Calling-in point for vessel traffic control
47			Anchorage for seaplanes
48			Seaplane landing area
49	Under		Work in progress
50	construction		Under construction
† 51			Work projected
(Gd)	Subm ruins		Submerged ruins

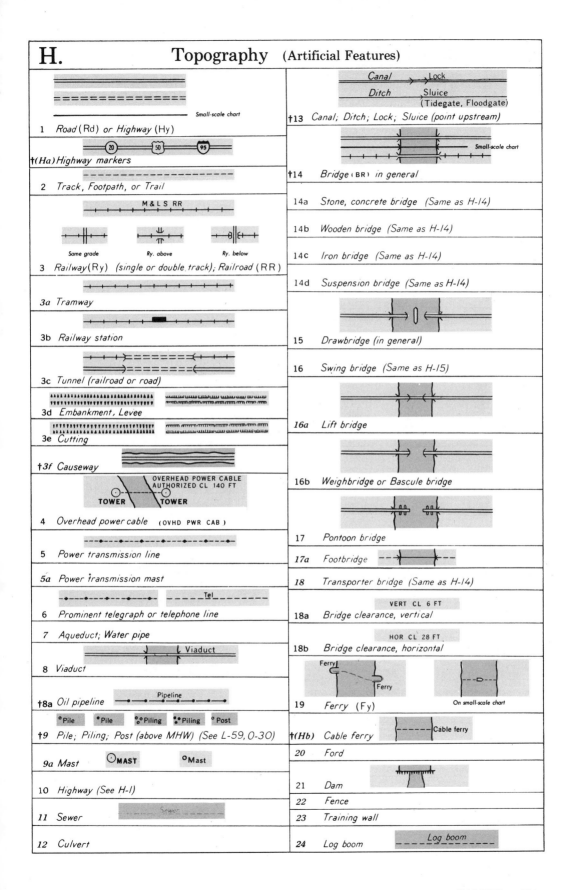

H.   Topography (Artificial Features)

1 Road (Rd) or Highway (Hy)	†13 Canal; Ditch; Lock; Sluice (point upstream)
†(Ha) Highway markers	†14 Bridge (BR) in general
2 Track, Footpath, or Trail	14a Stone, concrete bridge (Same as H-14)
3 Railway (Ry) (single or double track); Railroad (RR)	14b Wooden bridge (Same as H-14)
	14c Iron bridge (Same as H-14)
3a Tramway	14d Suspension bridge (Same as H-14)
3b Railway station	15 Drawbridge (in general)
3c Tunnel (railroad or road)	16 Swing bridge (Same as H-15)
3d Embankment, Levee	16a Lift bridge
3e Cutting	16b Weighbridge or Bascule bridge
†3f Causeway	17 Pontoon bridge
4 Overhead power cable (OVHD PWR CAB)	17a Footbridge
5 Power transmission line	18 Transporter bridge (Same as H-14)
5a Power transmission mast	18a Bridge clearance, vertical
6 Prominent telegraph or telephone line	18b Bridge clearance, horizontal
7 Aqueduct; Water pipe	19 Ferry (Fy)
8 Viaduct	†(Hb) Cable ferry
†8a Oil pipeline	20 Ford
†9 Pile; Piling; Post (above MHW) (See L-59, O-30)	21 Dam
9a Mast	22 Fence
10 Highway (See H-1)	23 Training wall
11 Sewer	24 Log boom
12 Culvert	

I. Buildings and Structures (see General Remarks)

No.	Symbol	Abbr.	Description	No.	Symbol	Abbr.	Description
1			City or Town (large scale)	26a	Locust Ave	Ave	Avenue
(Ia)			City or Town (small scale)	†26b	Grand Blvd	Blvd	Boulevard
2			Suburb	27		Tel	Telegraph
3		Vil	Village	28		Tel Off	Telegraph office
3a			Buildings in general	29		P O	Post office
4		Cas	Castle	30		Govt Ho	Government house
5			House	31			Town hall
6			Villa	32		Hosp	Hospital
7			Farm	33			Slaughterhouse
8		Ch	Church	34		Magz	Magazine
8a		Cath	Cathedral	34a			Warehouse; Storehouse
8b	SPIRE	Spire	Spire; Steeple	35	MON / Mon		Monument
9			Roman Catholic Church	36	CUP / Cup		Cupola
†10			Temple	37	ELEV / Elev		Elevator; Lift
11			Chapel	(Ie)		Elev	Elevation; Elevated
†12			Mosque	38			Shed
†12a			Minaret	39			Zinc roof
(Ib)			Moslem Shrine	40	Ruins / Ru		Ruins
†13			Marabout	41	TR / Tr		Tower
†14		Pag	Pagoda	(If)	ABAND LT HO		Abandoned lighthouse
†15			Buddhist Temple; Joss-House	42	WINDMILL		Windmill
†15a			Shinto Shrine	†43			Watermill
16			Monastery; Convent	43a	WINDMOTOR		Windmotor
17			Calvary; Cross	44	CHY / Chy		Chimney; Stack
17a			Cemetery, Non-Christian	45	S'PIPE / S'pipe		Water tower; Standpipe
18	Cem		Cemetery, Christian	46			Oil tank
18a			Tomb	47		Facty	Factory
19			Fort (actual shape charted)	48			Saw mill
†20			Battery	49			Brick kiln
21			Barracks	50			Mine; Quarry
22			Powder magazine	51	Well		Well
23	Airport		Airplane landing field	52			Cistern
24			Airport, large scale (See P-13)	53	TANK / Tk		Tank
(Ic)			Airport, military (small scale)	54			Noria
†(Id)			Airport, civil (small scale)	55			Fountain
25			Mooring mast				
26	King St	St	Street				

I.   Buildings and Structures (continued)

61		Inst	Institute	72	⊙GAB °Gab		Gable
62			Establishment	73			Wall
63			Bathing establishment	†74			Pyramid
64		Ct Ho	Courthouse	†75			Pillar
65		Sch	School	†76			Oil derrick
(Ig)		H S	High school	(Ii)		Ltd	Limited
(Ih)		Univ	University	(Ij)		Apt	Apartment
66		Bldg	Building	(Ik)		Cap	Capitol
67		Pav	Pavilion	(Il)		Co	Company
68			Hut	(Im)		Corp	Corporation
69			Stadium	(In)	⊙		Landmark (conspicuous object)
70		T	Telephone	(Io)	o		Landmark (position approx.)
71			Gas tank; Gasometer				

J.   Miscellaneous Stations

1		Sta	Any kind of station	13			Tide signal station
2		Sta	Station	14			Stream signal station
3			Coast Guard station (Similar to Lifesaving Sta.)	15			Ice signal station
				16			Time signal station
(Ja)			Coast Guard station (when landmark)	†16a			Manned oceanographic station
				†16b			Unmanned oceanographic station
†4	⊙LOOK TR		Lookout station; Watch tower	17			Time ball
5			Lifeboat station	18			Signal mast
6			Lifesaving station (See J-3)	19	⊙FS ⊙FP °FS °FP		Flagstaff; Flagpole
7		Rkt Sta	Rocket station	†19a	⊙F TR °F Tr		Flag tower
8		⊙PIL STA	Pilot station	20			Signal
9		Sig Sta	Signal station	21		Obsy	Observatory
10		Sem	Semaphore	22		Off	Office
11		S Sig Sta	Storm signal station	(Jc)	°BELL		Bell (on land)
12			Weather signal station	(Jd)	°HECP		Harbor entrance control post
(Jb)	⊙W B SIG STA		Weather Bureau signal station				

†1	● ☆	Position of light	29	F Fl	Fixed and flashing light
2	Lt	Light	30	F Gp Fl	Fixed and group flashing light
†(Ka)		Riprap surrounding light	†30a	Mo	Morse code light
3	Lt Ho	Lighthouse	31	Rot	Revolving or Rotating light
4	● AERO	Aeronautical light (See F-22)			
4a		Marine and air navigation light	41		Period
5	● ● Bn	Light beacon	42		Every
6		Light vessel; Lightship	43		With
8		Lantern	44		Visible (range)
9		Street lamp	(Kb)	M	Nautical mile (See E-11)
10	REF	Reflector	(Kc)	m; min	Minutes (See E-2)
11	Ldg Lt	Leading light	(Kd)	sec	Seconds (See E-3)
12		Sector light	45	Fl	Flash
13		Directional light	46	Occ	Occultation
			46a		Eclipse
14		Harbor light	47	Gp	Group
15		Fishing light	48	Occ	Intermittent light
16		Tidal light	49	SEC	Sector
17	Priv maintd	Private light (maintained by private interests; to be used with caution)	50		Color of sector
21	F	Fixed light	51	Aux	Auxiliary light
22	Occ	Occulting light	52		Varied
23	Fl	Flashing light	61	Vi	Violet
†23a	E Int	Isophase light (equal interval)	62		Purple
24	Qk Fl	Quick flashing (scintillating) light	63	Bu	Blue
25	I Qk Fl / Int Qk Fl	Interrupted quick flashing light	64	G	Green
25a	S Fl	Short flashing light	65	Or	Orange
26	Alt	Alternating light	66	R	Red
27	Gp Occ	Group occulting light	67	W	White
28	Gp Fl	Group flashing light	67a	Am	Amber
28a	S-L Fl	Short-long flashing light	68	OBSC	Obscured light
28b		Group short flashing light	†68a	Fog Det Lt	Fog detector light (See N-Nb)

<table>
<tr><th colspan="3">K.</th><th>Lights</th><th>(continued)</th></tr>
</table>

69			Unwatched light
70	Occas		Occasional light
71	Irreg		Irregular light
72	Prov		Provisional light
73	Temp		Temporary light
(Ke)	D; Destr		Destroyed
74	Exting		Extinguished light
75			Faint light
76			Upper light
77			Lower light
78			Rear light

79			Front light
80	Vert		Vertical lights
81	Hor		Horizontal lights
(Kf)	VB		Vertical beam
(Kg)	RGE		Range
(Kh)	Exper		Experimental light
(Ki)	TRLB		Temporarily replaced by lighted buoy showing the same characteristics
(Kj)	TRUB		Temporarily replaced by unlighted buoy
(Kk)	TLB		Temporary lighted buoy
(Kl)	TUB		Temporary unlighted buoy

L.　Buoys and Beacons　(see General Remarks)

1	Position of buoy
2	Light buoy
3	Bell buoy
3a	Gong buoy
4	Whistle buoy
5	Can or Cylindrical buoy
6	Nun or Conical buoy
7	Spherical buoy
8	Spar buoy
†8a	Pillar or Spindle buoy
9	Buoy with topmark (ball) (see L-70)
10	Barrel or Ton buoy
(La)	Color unknown
(Lb)	Float
12	Lightfloat
13	Outer or Landfall buoy
14	Fairway buoy (BWVS)
14a	Mid-channel buoy (BWVS)
†15	Starboard-hand buoy (entering from seaward)
16	Port-hand buoy (entering from seaward)

17	Bifurcation buoy (RBHB)
18	Junction buoy (RBHB)
19	Isolated danger buoy (RBHB)
20	Wreck buoy (RBHB or G)
20a	Obstruction buoy (RBHB or G)
21	Telegraph-cable buoy
22	Mooring buoy (colors of mooring buoys never carried)
22a	Mooring
22b	Mooring buoy with telegraphic communications
22c	Mooring buoy with telephonic communications
23	Warping buoy
24	Quarantine buoy
†24a	Practice area buoy
25	Explosive anchorage buoy
25a	Aeronautical anchorage buoy
26	Compass adjustment buoy
27	Fish trap (area) buoy (BWHB)
27a	Spoil ground buoy
†28	Anchorage buoy (marks limits)
†29	Private aid to navigation (buoy) (maintained by private interests, use with caution)

30			Temporary buoy (See Ki,j,k,l)
30a			Winter buoy
31		HB	Horizontal stripes or bands
32		VS	Vertical stripes
33		Chec	Checkered
†*33a*		Diag	Diagonal bands
41		W	White
42		B	Black
43		R	Red
44		Y	Yellow
45		G	Green
46		Br	Brown
47		Gy	Gray
48		Bu	Blue
†*48a*		Am	Amber
†*48b*		Or	Orange
51			Floating beacon
52	△RW Bn △W Bn △R Bn		Fixed beacon (unlighted or daybeacon)
	▲ Bn		Black beacon
	△ Bn		Color unknown
†*(Lc)*	⊙MARKER °Marker		Private aid to navigation
53		Bn	Beacon, in general (See L-52)
54			Tower beacon

55		Cardinal marking system
56	△ Deviation Bn	Compass adjustment beacon
57		Topmarks (See L-9, 70)
58		Telegraph-cable (landing) beacon
†*59*	Piles Piles	Piles (See O-30, H-9)
	⊥⊥ Stakes	Stakes
	Stumps	Stumps (See O-30)
	⊥⊥	Perches
61	⊙CAIRN °Cairn	Cairn
62		Painted patches
63	⊙	Landmark (conspicuous object) (See D-2)
(Ld)	°	Landmark (position approximate)
64	REF	Reflector
65	⊙MARKER	Range targets, markers
(Le)	W Or W Or	Special-purpose buoys
†*66*		Oil installation buoy
†*67*		Drilling platform (See O-Ob, O-Oc)
70	Note:	TOPMARKS on buoys and beacons may be shown on charts of foreign waters. The abbreviation for black is not shown adjacent to buoys or beacons.
(Lf)	Ra·Ref	Radar reflector (See M-13)

M.   Radio and Radar Stations

1	°R Sta	Radio telegraph station
2	°R T	Radio telephone station
3	R Bn	Radiobeacon
4	R Bn	Circular radiobeacon
5	R D	Directional radiobeacon; Radio range
6		Rotating loop radiobeacon
7	R D F	Radio direction finding station
(Ma)	TELEM ANT	Telemetry antenna
†(Mb)	R RELAY MAST	Radio relay mast
†(Mc)	MICRO TR	Microwave tower
9	R MAST	Radio mast
	R TR	Radio tower
†9a	TV TR	Television mast; Television tower
10	R TR (WBAL) 1090 Kc	Radio broadcasting station (commercial)
10a	°R Sta	Q.T.G. Radio station
11	Ra	Radar station

12	Racon	Radar responder beacon
13	Ra Ref	Radar reflector (See L-Lf)
14	Ra (conspic)	Radar conspicuous object
14a		Ramark
15	D F S	Distance finding station (synchronized signals)
†16	AERO R Bn 302 ▄▄▄	Aeronautical radiobeacon
†17	°Decca Sta	Decca station
†18	Loran Sta Venice	Loran station (name)
†19	CONSOL Bn 190 Kc MMF ▄▄	Consol (Consolan) station
(Md)	AERO R Rge 342 ▄▄▄	Aeronautical radio range
(Me)	Ra Ref Calibration Bn	Radar calibration beacon
(Mf)	LORAN TR SPRING ISLAND	Loran tower (name)
†(Mg)	R TR F R Lt	Obstruction light

N.   Fog Signals

1	Fog Sig	Fog-signal station
2		Radio fog-signal station
3	GUN	Explosive fog signal
4		Submarine fog signal
5	SUB-BELL	Submarine fog bell (action of waves)
6	SUB-BELL	Submarine fog bell (mechanical)
7	SUB-OSC	Submarine oscillator
8	NAUTO	Nautophone
9	DIA	Diaphone
10	GUN	Fog gun
11	SIREN	Fog siren
12	HORN	Fog trumpet

13	HORN	Fog horn
†13a	HORN	Electric fog horn
14	BELL	Fog bell
15	WHIS	Fog whistle
16	HORN	Reed horn
17	GONG	Fog gong
†18		Submarine sound signal not connected to the shore (See N-5,6,7)
†18a		Submarine sound signal connected to the shore (See N-5,6,7)
(Na)	HORN	Typhon
(Nb)	Fog Det Lt	Fog detector light (See K 68a)

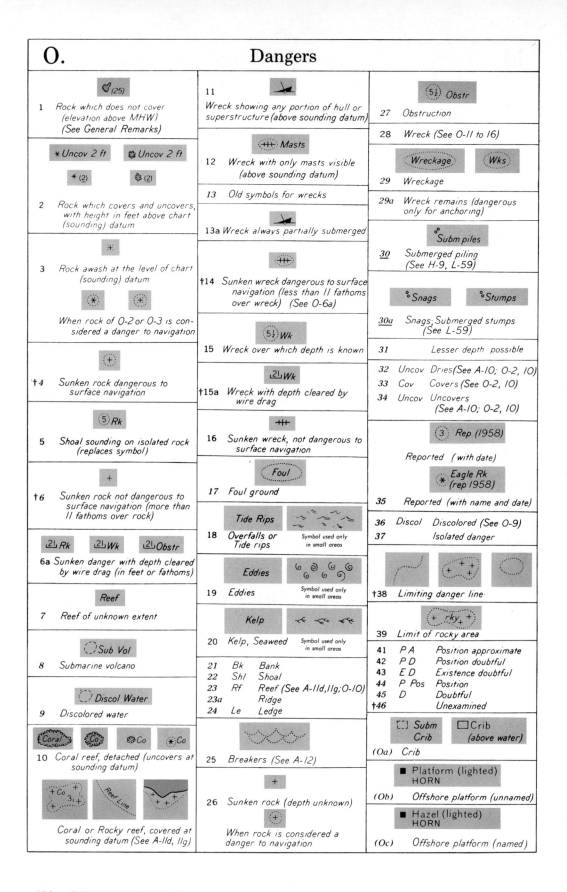

1   Rock which does not cover (elevation above MHW) (See General Remarks)

2   Rock which covers and uncovers, with height in feet above chart (sounding) datum

3   Rock awash at the level of chart (sounding) datum

When rock of O-2 or O-3 is considered a danger to navigation

†4   Sunken rock dangerous to surface navigation

5   Shoal sounding on isolated rock (replaces symbol)

†6   Sunken rock not dangerous to surface navigation (more than 11 fathoms over rock)

6a   Sunken danger with depth cleared by wire drag (in feet or fathoms)

7   Reef of unknown extent

8   Submarine volcano

9   Discolored water

10   Coral reef, detached (uncovers at sounding datum)

Coral or Rocky reef, covered at sounding datum (See A-11d, 11g)

11   Wreck showing any portion of hull or superstructure (above sounding datum)

12   Wreck with only masts visible (above sounding datum)

13   Old symbols for wrecks

13a   Wreck always partially submerged

†14   Sunken wreck dangerous to surface navigation (less than 11 fathoms over wreck) (See O-6a)

15   Wreck over which depth is known

†15a   Wreck with depth cleared by wire drag

16   Sunken wreck, not dangerous to surface navigation

17   Foul ground

18   Overfalls or Tide rips   Symbol used only in small areas

19   Eddies   Symbol used only in small areas

20   Kelp, Seaweed   Symbol used only in small areas

21   Bk   Bank
22   Shl   Shoal
23   Rf   Reef (See A-11d,11g; O-10)
23a   Ridge
24   Le   Ledge

25   Breakers (See A-12)

26   Sunken rock (depth unknown)

When rock is considered a danger to navigation

27   Obstruction

28   Wreck (See O-11 to 16)

29   Wreckage

29a   Wreck remains (dangerous only for anchoring)

30   Submerged piling (See H-9, L-59)

30a   Snags; Submerged stumps (See L-59)

31   Lesser depth possible

32   Uncov   Dries (See A-10; O-2, 10)
33   Cov   Covers (See O-2, 10)
34   Uncov   Uncovers (See A-10; O-2, 10)

Reported (with date)

35   Reported (with name and date)

36   Discol   Discolored (See O-9)
37   Isolated danger

†38   Limiting danger line

39   Limit of rocky area

41   P A   Position approximate
42   P D   Position doubtful
43   E D   Existence doubtful
44   P Pos   Position
45   D   Doubtful
†46   Unexamined

(Oa)   Crib

(Ob)   Offshore platform (unnamed)

(Oc)   Offshore platform (named)

P. Various Limits, etc.

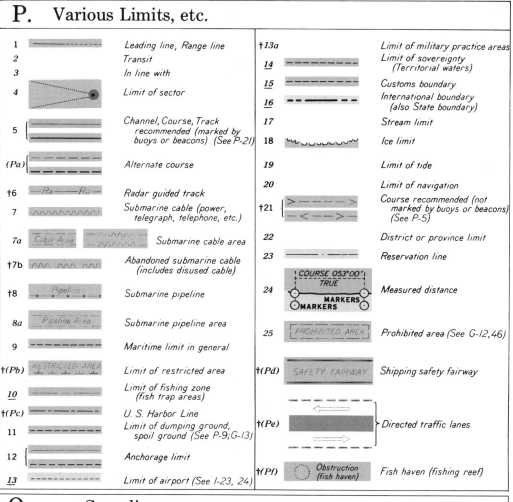

1		Leading line; Range line
2		Transit
3		In line with
4		Limit of sector
5		Channel, Course, Track recommended (marked by buoys or beacons) (See P-21)
(Pa)		Alternate course
†6	Ra ——— Ra	Radar guided track
7		Submarine cable (power, telegraph, telephone, etc.)
7a	Cable Area	Submarine cable area
†7b		Abandoned submarine cable (includes disused cable)
†8	Pipeline	Submarine pipeline
8a	Pipeline Area	Submarine pipeline area
9		Maritime limit in general
†(Pb)	RESTRICTED AREA	Limit of restricted area
10		Limit of fishing zone (fish trap areas)
†(Pc)		U. S. Harbor Line
11		Limit of dumping ground, spoil ground (See P-9; G-13)
12		Anchorage limit
13		Limit of airport (See I-23, 24)

†13a		Limit of military practice areas
14		Limit of sovereignty (Territorial waters)
15		Customs boundary
16		International boundary (also State boundary)
17		Stream limit
18		Ice limit
19		Limit of tide
20		Limit of navigation
†21		Course recommended (not marked by buoys or beacons) (See P-5)
22		District or province limit
23		Reservation line
24	COURSE 053°00' TRUE / MARKERS MARKERS	Measured distance
25	PROHIBITED AREA	Prohibited area (See G-12, 46)
†(Pd)	SAFETY FAIRWAY	Shipping safety fairway
†(Pe)		Directed traffic lanes
†(Pf)	Obstruction (fish haven)	Fish haven (fishing reef)

Q. Soundings

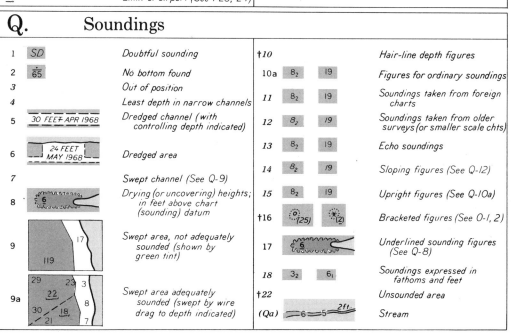

1	SD	Doubtful sounding
2	65	No bottom found
3		Out of position
4		Least depth in narrow channels
5	30 FEET APR 1968	Dredged channel (with controlling depth indicated)
6	24 FEET MAY 1968	Dredged area
7		Swept channel (See Q-9)
8	6	Drying (or uncovering) heights; in feet above chart (sounding) datum
9	17 / 119	Swept area, not adequately sounded (shown by green tint)
9a	29 23 3 / 22 / 30 18 8 / 21 7	Swept area adequately sounded (swept by wire drag to depth indicated)

†10			Hair-line depth figures
10a	8₂	19	Figures for ordinary soundings
11	8₂	19	Soundings taken from foreign charts
12	8₂	19	Soundings taken from older surveys (or smaller scale chts)
13	8₂	19	Echo soundings
14	8₂	19	Sloping figures (See Q-12)
15	8₂	19	Upright figures (See Q-10a)
†16	(25)	(2)	Bracketed figures (See O-1, 2)
17	6		Underlined sounding figures (See Q-8)
18	3₂	6₁	Soundings expressed in fathoms and feet
†22			Unsounded area
(Qa)	6 — 5 2ft		Stream

R. Depth Contours and Tints (see General Remarks)

Feet	Fathoms		Feet	Fathoms	
0	0		300	50	
6	1		600	100	
12	2		1,200	200	
18	3		1,800	300	
24	4		2,400	400	
30	5		3,000	500	
36	6		6,000	1,000	
60	10		12,000	2,000	
120	20		18,000	3,000	
180	30		Or continuous lines, with values		(blue or black) —5— —100—
240	40				

S. Quality of the Bottom

†1	Grd	Ground	24	Oys	Oysters	50	spk	Speckled
2	S	Sand	25	Ms	Mussels	51	gty	Gritty
3	M	Mud; Muddy	26	Spg	Sponge	†52	dec	Decayed
4	Oz	Ooze	†27	K	Kelp	53	fly	Flinty
5	Ml	Marl	28	Wd	Sea-weed	54	glac	Glacial
6	Cl	Clay		Grs	Grass	†55	ten	Tenacious
7	G	Gravel	†29	Stg	Sea-tangle	56	wh	White
8	Sn	Shingle	†31	Spi	Spicules	57	bk	Black
9	P	Pebbles	32	Fr	Foraminifera	58	vi	Violet
10	St	Stones	33	Gl	Globigerina	59	bu	Blue
11	Rk; rky	Rock; Rocky	34	Di	Diatoms	60	gn	Green
11a	Blds	Boulders	35	Rd	Radiolaria	61	yl	Yellow
12	Ck	Chalk	36	Pt	Pteropods	62	or	Orange
12a	Ca	Calcareous	37	Po	Polyzoa	63	rd	Red
13	Qz	Quartz	†38	Cir	Cirripeda	64	br	Brown
†13a	Sch	Schist	†38a	Fu	Fucus	65	ch	Chocolate
14	Co	Coral	†38b	Ma	Mattes	66	gy	Gray
(Sa)	Co Hd	Coral head	39	fne	Fine	67	lt	Light
15	Mds	Madrepores	40	crs	Coarse	68	dk	Dark
16	Vol	Volcanic	41	sft	Soft			
(Sb)	Vol Ash	Volcanic ash	42	hrd	Hard	†70	vard	Varied
17	La	Lava	43	stf	Stiff	†71	unev	Uneven
18	Pm	Pumice	44	sml	Small	†(Sc)	S/M	Surface layer and Under layer
19	T	Tufa	45	lrg	Large			
20	Sc	Scoriae	46	stk	Sticky			
21	Cn	Cinders	47	brk	Broken			
†21a		Ash	47a	grd	Ground (Shells)	76		Fresh water springs in sea-bed
22	Mn	Manganese	†48	rt	Rotten			
23	Sh	Shells	†49	str	Streaky			

T.	**Tides and Currents**	

1	HW	High water
1a	HHW	Higher high water
2	LW	Low water
(Ta)	LWD	Low water datum
2a	LLW	Lower low water
3	MTL	Mean tide level
4	MSL	Mean sea level
4a		Elevation of mean sea level above chart (sounding) datum
5		Chart datum (datum for sounding reduction)
6	Sp	Spring tide
7	Np	Neap tide
†7a	MHW	Mean high water
8	MHWS	Mean high water springs
8a	MHWN	Mean high water neaps
8b	MHHW	Mean higher high water
†8c	MLW	Mean low water
9	MLWS	Mean low water springs
9a	MLWN	Mean low water neaps
9b	MLLW	Mean lower low water
10	ISLW	Indian spring low water
11		High water full and change (vulgar establishment of the port)
12		Low water full and change
13		Mean establishment of the port
13a		Establishment of the port
14		Unit of height
15		Equinoctial
16		Quarter; Quadrature
17	Str	Stream
18		Current, general, with rate
19		Flood stream (current) with rate
20		Ebb stream (current) with rate
21		Tide gauge; Tidepole; Automatic tide gauge
23	vel	Velocity; Rate
24	kn	Knots
25	ht	Height
26		Tide
27		New moon
28		Full moon
29		Ordinary
30		Syzygy
31	fl	Flood
32		Ebb
33		Tidal stream diagram
34		Place for which tabulated tidal stream data are given
35		Range (of tide)
36		Phase lag
(Tb)		Current diagram, with explanatory note

U.	**Compass**	

Compass Rose

The outer circle is in degrees with zero at true north. The inner circles are in points and degrees with the arrow indicating magnetic north.

1	N	North
2	E	East
3	S	South
4	W	West
5	NE	Northeast
6	SE	Southeast
7	SW	Southwest
8	NW	Northwest
9	N	Northern
10	E	Eastern
11	S	Southern
12	W	Western
21	brg	Bearing
†22	T	True
23	mag	Magnetic
24	var	Variation
25		Annual change
25a		Annual change nil
26		Abnormal variation; Magnetic attraction
27	deg	Degrees (See E-20)
28	dev	Deviation

Index of Chart Abbreviations

A

aband.	Abandoned	F 37
ABAND LT HO	Abandoned lighthouse	If
abt.	About	F 17
AERO	Aeronautical	F 22; K 4
AERO R. Bn.	Aeronautical radiobeacon	M 16
AERO R. Rge.	Aeronautical radio range	Md
alt.	Altitude	E 18
Alt	Alternating (light)	K 26
Am	Amber	K 67a; L 48a
anc.	Ancient	F 9
Anch	Anchorage	B 15; G 1,2
Anch prohib	Anchorage prohibited	G 12
approx.	Approximate	F 34
Apprs.	Approaches	Bg
Apt.	Apartment	Ij
Arch.	Archipelago	B 20
Astro.	Astronomical	D 9
AUTH.	Authorized	Fc
Aux	Auxiliary (light)	K 51
Ave.	Avenue	I 26a

B

B	Bay	B 2
B	Bayou	Ba
B	Black	L 42
Bdy. Mon.	Boundary monument	D 14
BELL	Fog Bell	N 14
bet.	Between	Fi
B Hbr	Boat harbor	G 33
Bk	Bank	O 21
bk	Black	S 57
Bkw.	Breakwater	G 6
Bld	Boulder	B 32
Bldg.	Building	I 66
Blds	Boulders	S 11a
Blvd.	Boulevard	I 26b
B.M.	Bench mark	D 5
Bn	Beacon (in general)	L 52,53
BR.	Bridge	H 14
Br	Brown	L 46
br	Brown	S 64
brg.	Bearing	U 21
brk	Broken	S 47
Bu	Blue	K 63; L 48
bu	Blue	S 59
BWHB	Black and white horizontal bands	L 27
BWVS	Black and white vertical stripes	L 14,14a

C

C	Can; Cylindrical (buoy)	L 5
C	Cape	B 22
C	Cove	B 5a
Ca	Calcareous	S 12a
Cap.	Capitol	Ik
Cas.	Castle	I 4
Cath.	Cathedral	I 8a
cbl.	Cable length	E 10
C. G.	Coast Guard	J 3, Ja

ch

ch	Chocolate	S 65
Ch.	Church	I 8
Chan	Channel	B 10
Chec	Checkered (buoy)	L 33
CHY.	Chimney	I 44
Cir	Cirripeda	S 38
Ck	Chalk	S 12
Cl	Clay	S 6
CL.	Clearance	Fd
cm.	Centimeter	E 4b
Cn	Cinders	S 21
Co.	Company	Il
Co	Coral	S 14
Co Hd	Coral head	Sa
concr.	Concrete	Ff
conspic.	Conspicuous	F 12
C. of E.	Corps of Engineers	Df
cor.	Corner	Fe
Corp.	Corporation	Im
Cov	Covers	0 33
corr.	Correction	E 17
cps	Cycles/second	Ef
Cr.	Creek	B 5
crs	Coarse	S 40
Cswy.	Causeway	H 3f
Ct. Ho.	Courthouse	I 64
CUP.	Cupola	I 36
Cus. Ho.	Customhouse	G 29

D

D	Doubtful	0 45
D.; Destr.	Destroyed	F 14; Ke
dec.	Decayed	S 52
deg.	Degrees	U 27
dev.	Deviation	U 28
Diag	Diagonal bands	L 33a
D.F.S.	Distance finding station	M 15
Di	Diatoms	S 34
DIA	Diaphone	N 9
Discol	Discolored	0 36
discontd.	Discontinued	F 25
dist.	Distant	F 16
dk	Dark	S 68
dm.	Decimeter	E 4a
Dol	Dolphin	G 21

E

E.	East, Eastern	U 2,10
Ed.	Edition	E 16
E.D.	Existence doubtful	0 43
elec.	Electric	F 29
elev.	Elevation	E 19
ELEV.	Elevator, Lift	I 37
Elev.	Elevation, Elevated	Ie
Entr	Entrance	B 11
E Int	Isophase lt.(equal interval)	K 23a
Est	Estuary	B 12
estab.	Established	F 28
Exper	Experimental (light)	Kh
exper.	Experimental	F 24
explos.	Explosive	F 27

Explos Anch	Explosive Anchorage (buoy)	L 25
Exting	Extinguished (light)	K 74
extr.	Extreme	F 40

F

F.	Fixed (light)	K 21
Facty.	Factory	I 47
Fd	Fjord	B 3
F Fl	Fixed and flashing (light)	K 29
F Gp Fl	Fixed and group flashing (light)	K 30
Fl	Flash, Flashing (light)	K 23, 45
fl.	Flood	Fg; T 31
fly	Flinty	S 53
fm	Fathom	E 9
fne	Fine	S 39
Fog Det Lt	Fog detector light	K 68a; Nb
Fog Sig.	Fog signal station	N 1
FP.	Flagpole	J 19
Fr	Foraminifera	S 32
FS.	Flagstaff	J 19
Fsh stks	Fishing stakes	G 14
ft.	Foot	E 7
Ft.	Fort	I 19
F. TR.	Flag tower	J 19a
Fu	Fucus	S 38a
Fy.	Ferry	H 19

G

G.	Gulf	B 1
G	Gravel	S 7
G	Green	K 64
G	Green	L 20, 20a, 45
GAB.	Gable	I 72
Gl	Globigerina	S 33
glac	Glacial	S 54
gn	Green	S 60
GONG	Fog gong	N 17
Govt. Ho.	Government House	I 30
Gp	Group	K 47
Gp Fl	Group flashing	K 28
Gp Occ	Group occulting	K 27
Grd, grd	Ground	S 1, 47a
Grs	Grass	S 28
gt.	Great	F 1
gty	Gritty	S 51
GUN	Explosive fog signal	N 3
GUN	Fog gun	N 10
Gy	Gray	L 47
gy	Gray	S 66

H

HB.	Horizontal bands or stripes	L 31
Hbr	Harbor	B 16; G 3
Hd.	Head, Headland	B 24
HECP	Harbor entrance control post	Jd
Hk	Hulk	G 45
HHW	Higher high water	T 1a
Hn	Haven	B 16a; G 4
Hor	Horizontal lights	K 81

HOR. CL.	Horizontal clearance	H 18b
HORN	Fog trumpet; Fog horn; Reed horn; Typhon	N 12, 13, 13a, 16, Na
Hosp.	Hospital	I 32
hr.	Hour	E 1
hrd	Hard	S 42
H. S.	High School	Ig
ht.	Height	E 19; T 25
HW	High water	T 1
Hy.	Highway	H 1
Hz	Hertz	Ec

I

I.	Island	B 18
I Qk; Int Qk	Interrupted quick	K 25
in.	Inch	E 6
In	Inlet	B 6
Inst.	Institute	I 61
Irreg	Irregular	K 71
ISLW	Indian spring low water	T 10
It.	Islet	B 19

K

K	Kelp	S 27
kc	Kilocycle	Eg
kHz	Kilohertz	Ed
km.	Kilometer	E 5
kn	Knots	E 12; T 24

L

L.	Loch, Lough, Lake	B 4
La	Lava	S 17
Lag	Lagoon	Bf; C 16
lat.	Latitude	E 13
Ldg.	Landing; Landing place	B 33; G 16
Ldg. Lt.	Leading light	K 11
Le	Ledge	O 24
LLW	Lower low water	T 2a
L.N.M.	Local Notice to Mariners	Fa
long.	Longitude	E 14
LOOK. TR.	Lookout station; Watch tower	J 4
lrg	Large	F 3; S 45
LS. S.	Lifesaving station	J 6
Lt.	Light	K 2
lt	Light	S 67
Ltd.	Limited	Ii
Lt. Ho.	Lighthouse	K 3
LW	Low water	T 2
LWD	Low water datum	Ta

M

M	Nautical mile	E11; Kb
M	Mud, Muddy	S 3
m.	Meter	E 4, d, e
m. ; min.	Minute (of time)	E2; Kc
Ma	Mattes	S 38b
mag.	Magnetic	U 23
Magz.	Magazine	I 34
maintd.	Maintained	F 36

Mc	Megacycle	Eh
Mds	Madrepores	S 15
MHHW	Mean higher high water	T 8b
MHW	Mean high water	T 7a
MHWN	Mean high water neaps	T 8a
MHWS	Mean high water springs	T 8
MHz	Megahertz	Ee
MICRO. TR.	Microwave tower	Mc
mid.	Middle	F 7
Mkr	Marker	Lc
Ml	Marl	S 5
MLLW	Mean lower low water	T 9b
MLW	Mean low water	T 8c
MLWN	Mean low water neaps	T 9a
MLWS	Mean low water springs	T 9
mm.	Millimeter	E 4c
Mn	Manganese	S 22
Mo.	Morse code light	K 30a
mod.	Moderate	Fh
MON.	Monument	I 35
Ms	Mussels	S 25
M. Sec.	Microsecond	Eb
MSL	Mean sea level	T 4
Mt.	Mountain, Mount	B 26
Mth	Mouth	B 13
MTL	Mean tide level	T 3

N

N.	North; Northern	U 1,9
N	Nun; Conical (buoy)	L 6
NAUTO	Nautophone	N 8
NE.	Northeast	U 5
N.M.	**Notice to Mariners**	F 42
No.	Number	E 23
Np	Neap tide	T 7
NW.	Northwest	U 8

O

OBSC	Obscured (light)	K 68
Obs. Spot	Observation spot	D 4
Obstr.	Obstruction	O 27
Obsy.	Observatory	J 21
Occ	Occulting (light); Occultation	K 22,46
Occ	Intermittent (light)	K 48
Occas	Occasional (light)	F 39; K 70
Off.	Office	J 22
or.	Orange	S 62
Or	Orange	K 65; L48b
OVHD. PWR. CAB.	Overhead power cable	H 4
Oys	Oysters; Oyster bed	S 24; G 15a
Oz	Ooze	S 4

P

P	Pebbles	S 9
P	Pillar (buoy)	L8a
P	Pond	Bb
P.	Port	B 17; G 5
P. A.	Position approximate	O 41

Pag.	Pagoda	I 14
Pass	Passage, Pass	B 9
Pav.	Pavilion	I 67
P. D.	Position doubtful	O 42
Pen.	Peninsula	B 21
PIL. STA.	Pilot station	J 8
Pk.	Peak	B 29
Pm	Pumice	S 18
Po	Polyzoa	S 37
P. O.	Post Office	I 29
P.; Pos.	Position	O 44
priv.	Private, Privately	F 30
Priv. maintd.	Privately maintained	K 17; L 29
Prohib.	Prohibited	F 26
prom.	Prominent	F 31
Prom.	Promontory	B 23
Prov	Provisional (light)	K 72
Pt.	Point	B 25
Pt	Pteropods	S 36
pub.	Publication	E 15
PWI	Potable water intake	

Q

Quar.	Quarantine	G 26
Qk Fl	Quick flashing (light)	K 24
Qz	Quartz	S 13

R

R	Red	K 66; L 15,43
R.	River	Bd
Ra	Radar station	M 11
Racon	Radar responder beacon	M 12
Ra (conspic)	Radar conspicuous object	M 14
Ra Ref	Radar reflector	Lf; M 13
RBHB	Red and black horizontal bands	L 17,18, 19, 20,20a
R Bn	Red beacon	L 52
R. Bn.	Radiobeacon	M 3,4,6
Rd	Radiolaria	S 35
rd	Red	S 63
Rd.	Road	H 1
Rd	Road, Roadstead	B 14
R.D.	Directional Radiobeacon; Radio range	M 5
R. D. F.	Radio direction finding station	M 7
REF	Reflector	K 10; L 64
Rep.	Reported	O 35
Rf	Reef	O 23
Rge.	Range	B 27
RGE	Range	Kg
Rk.	Rock	B 35
Rk, rky	Rock, Rocky	S 11
Rky.	Rocky	Bh
R. MAST	Radio mast	M 9
Rot	Revolving; Rotating (light)	K 31
RR.	Railroad	H 3
R.RELAY MAST	**Radio relay mast**	M b
R. Sta.	Radio telegraph station; Q.T.G. Radio station	M 1, 10a
R. T.	Radio telephone station	M 2
rt	Rotten	S 48

R. TR.	Radio tower	M 9	TB	Temporary buoy	L 30
Ru.	Ruins	I 40	Tel.	Telegraph	I 27; L 22b
RW Bn	Red and white beacon	L 52	Telem Ant	Telemetry antenna	Ma
			Tel. Off.	Telegraph office	I 28
Ry.	Railway	H 3	Temp	Temporary (light)	F 38; K 73
			ten	Tenacious	S 55
			Thoro	Thorofare	B 9
S			Tk.	Tank	I 53
			TR.	Tower	I 41
S	Sand	S 2	TRLB, TRUB, TLB, TUB		Ki, j, k, l
S	South; Southern	U 3, 11	Tri.	Triangulation	D 10
S	Spar (buoy)	L 8	TV TR.	Television tower (mast)	M 9a
Sc	Scoriae	S 20			
Sch.	Schist	S 13a	**U**		
Sch.	School	I 65			
Sd.	Sound	B 8	Uncov	Uncovers	O 2
SD	Sounding doubtful	Q 1	Uncov.	Uncovers; Dries	O 32, 34
SE.	Southeast	U 6	Univ.	University	Ih
sec.	Second (of time)	E 3	unverd.	Unverified	Fb
sec	Seconds	Kd	unev	Uneven	S 71
SEC	Sector	K 49			
Sem.	Semaphore	J 10	**V**		
S Fl	Short flashing (light)	K 25a	var.	Variation	U 24
sft	Soft	S 41	vard	Varied	S 70
Sh	Shells	S 23	VB	Vertical beam	Kf
Shl	Shoal	O 22	vel.	Velocity	T 23
Sig. Sta.	Signal station	J 9	Vert	Vertical (lights)	K 80
SIREN	Fog siren	N 11	VERT. CL.	Vertical clearance	H 18a
S-L Fl	Short-long flashing (light)	K 28a	Vi	Violet	K 61
Slu	Slough	Be; C 18	vi	Violet	S 58
sml	Small	F 4 : S 44	**View X**	**View point**	D 6
Sn	Shingle	S 8	Vil.	Village	I 3
Sp	Spring tide	T 6	Vol.	Volcano	B 30
SP	Spherical (buoy)	L 7	Vol	Volcanic	S 16
Spg	Sponge	S 26	Vol Ash	Volcanic ash	Sb
Spi	Spicules	S 31	VS	Vertical stripes	L 32
S'PIPE	Standpipe	I 45			
spk	Speckled	S 50	**W**		
S. Sig. Sta.	Storm signal station	J 11	W.	West; Western	U 4, 12
St.	Saint	F 11	W	White	K 67; L 41
St.	Street	I 26	wh	White	S 56
St	Stones	S 10	W Bn	White beacon	L 52
Sta.	Station	J 1, 2			
std.	Standard	F 32	W.B. SIG. STA.	Weather Bureau signal station	Jb
stf	Stiff	S 43	Wd	Sea-weed	S 28
Stg	**Sea-tangle**	S 29	Whf.	Wharf	G 18
stk	Sticky	S 46	WHIS	Fog whistle	N 15
St. M.	Statute mile	Ea	Wk	Wreck	O 15, 28
Str	Strait	B 7	Wks	Wreckage	O 29
Str	Stream	Bc; T 17	W Or	White and orange	Le
str	**Streaky**	S 49			
sub	Submarine	F 20	**Y**		
SUB-BELL	Submarine fog bell	N 5,6	Y	Yellow	L 24, 44
subm	Submerged	F 33	yl	Yellow	S 61
Subm	Submerged	Oa, 30	yd.	Yard	E 8
Subm Ruins	Submerged ruins	Gd			
SUB-OSC	Submarine oscillator	N 7	1st	First	Fj
Sub Vol	Submarine volcano	O 8	2nd	Second	Fk
SW.	Southwest	U 7	3rd	Third	Fl
			4th	Fourth	Fm
T					
T.	Telephone	I 70; L 22c	°	Degree	E 20
T	True	U 22	′	Minute (of arc)	E 21
T	Tufa	S 19	″	Second (of arc)	E 22

(This page ends the Chart No. 1 reprint.)

Plotting

Neatness in plotting usually goes with careful navigation in general. Even the most artful work, though, should be readable by others. Standards of labeling have developed and should be followed whenever lines and positions are marked on a chart. Here are highlights of those in common use:

Information with regard to a line should be placed along the line.

Information with regard to a point should be placed at an angle to the line.

C is the abbreviation for course, and is taken to indicate true course.

S is the abbreviation for speed, and is taken to mean speed in knots.

DR is the abbreviation for dead reckoning position . . . that position at which the vessel should be, based on its course, speed and time run from a previous known position.

Fix refers to a position determined by at least two simultaneous observations.

R.Fix describes a position determined by advancing an earlier line of position to join with a later one.

Here are examples of how the labels should appear:

A vessel is on a course of 095° at 12.8 knots:

At 0835, a lighthouse was observed to bear 280° from the vessel:

At 1050, a vessel was observed to be five miles distant from a lighthouse, but her bearing not observed:

A running fix by advancing a line of position of 1125 to intersect another of 1145:

Dead reckoning position indicated for 1150:

Fix indicated at 1150:

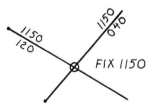

Signaling

INTERNATIONAL FLAGS AND PENNANTS*

*For Official Full Single Letter Signal Meanings as Specified in the *International Code of Signals, HO 102*, see page 470

ALPHABET FLAGS

NUMERAL PENNANTS

Alfa
Diver Down; Keep Clear

Kilo
Wish to Communicate

Uniform
Running Into Danger

1

Bravo
Dangerous Cargo

Lima
Stop Instantly

Victor
Require Assistance

2

Charlie
Yes

Mike
I Am Stopped

Whis-key
Require Medical Assistance

3

Delta
Keep Clear

November
No

Xray
Stop Your Intention

4

Echo
Altering Course to Starboard

Oscar
Man Overboard

Yankee
Am Dragging Anchor

5

Foxtrot
Disabled

Papa
About to Sail
or
Nets Fouled

Zulu
Require a Tug;
or
Am Shooting Nets

6

Golf
Require a Pilot
or
Hauling Nets

Quebec
Request Pratique

SUBSTITUTES

1st Substitute

7

Hotel
Pilot on Board

Romeo
Received (Procedural)

2nd Substitute

8

India
Altering Course to Port

Sierra
Engines Going Astern

3rd Substitute

9

Juliett
On Fire; Keep Clear

Tango
Keep Clear; Am Pair Trawling

CODE
Code and Answering Pennant
(Decimal Point)

0

U.S. Power Squadron

There are scores of official, semiofficial and private flags, pennants, emblems and assorted heraldry devices for display afloat under proper circumstances. Often one of the extra pleasures of boating is the first view of one's own flag designed on a stormy evening when weatherbound. Our aim is not to supply a catalog of

U. S. Power Squadrons' Ensign

Chief Commander

District Commander

Squadron Commander

Aides to Dist. Commander

Vice Commander

Dist. Lieut. Commander

Squad. Lieut. Commander

Flag Lieutenant

Staff Commander

District Secretary

Squad. Elected 1st. Lieut.

Officer in Charge Pennant

PAST OFFICERS' SIGNALS

Aides to the Chief Commander

District Lieutenant

Squadron Lieutenant

Chief Commander

Rear Commander

Dist. Flag Lieut.

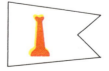

Squad. Flag Lieut.

Vice Commander

and USCGA Flags

every symbol whipping from a jackstaff, nor even a fraction of them. We limit our display to those authorized within boating's two ranking organizations: the US Power Squadrons and the US Coast Guard Auxiliary. Special distinction attaches to members of these units; special recognition of their flags has been well earned.

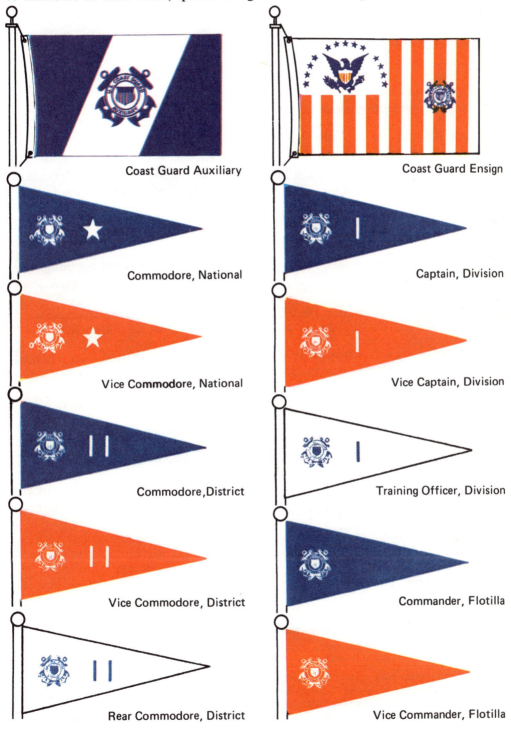

Coast Guard Auxiliary

Coast Guard Ensign

Commodore, National

Captain, Division

Vice Commodore, National

Vice Captain, Division

Commodore, District

Training Officer, Division

Vice Commodore, District

Commander, Flotilla

Rear Commodore, District

Vice Commander, Flotilla

Official Full Single Letter Signal Meanings as Specified in
International Code of Signals, HO 102

(International Flags and Pennants are shown on page 467.)

A I have a diver down; keep well clear at slow speed.

*B I am taking in, or discharging, or carrying dangerous goods.

C Yes (affirmative or: The significance of the previous group should be read in the affirmative).

*D Keep clear of me; I am maneuvering with difficulty.

*E I am altering my course to starboard.

F I am disabled; communicate with me.

G I require a pilot. When made by fishing vessels operating in close proximity on the fishing grounds it means: I am hauling nets.

*H I have a pilot on board.

*I I am altering my course to port.

J I am on fire and have dangerous cargo on board; keep well clear of me.

K I wish to communicate with you.

L You should stop your vessel instantly.

M My vessel is stopped and making no way through the water.

N No (negative).

O Man overboard.

P In harbor: All persons should report on board as the vessel is about to proceed to sea.
At sea: It may be used by fishing vessels to mean: My nets have come fast upon an obstruction.

Q My vessel is 'healthy' and I request free pratique.

R A procedure signal meaning: Received or I have received your last signal.

*S My engines are going astern.

*T Keep clear of me; I am engaged in pair trawling.

U You are running into danger.

V I require assistance.

W I require medical assistance.

X Stop carrying out your intentions and watch for my signals.

Y I am dragging my anchor.

Z I require a tug. When made by fishing vessels operating in close proximity on the fishing grounds it means: I am shooting nets.

*Signal of letter, when made by sound, may only be made in compliance with the requirements of the International Regulations for Preventing Collisions at Sea, Rules 15 and 28. Signals K and S have special meanings as landing signals for small boats with crews or persons in distress. (International Convention for the Safety of Life at Sea, 1960, Chapter V Regulation 16)

STORM WARNING SIGNALS

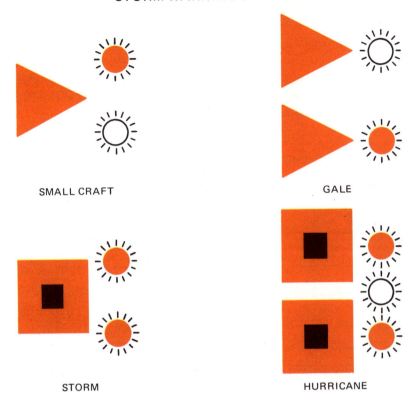

SMALL CRAFT

GALE

STORM

HURRICANE

SMALL CRAFT: one red pennant by day and **one red light over one white light** by night for winds and seas, or sea conditions alone, considered hazardous to small craft. Winds may range -as high as 33 knots (38 mph). 'Small Craft' means small boats, yachts, tugs, barges with little freeboard, and any other low-powered craft.

GALE: two red pennants by day and **one white light over one red light** by night for winds from 34 to 47 knots (39 to 54 mph).

STORM: one single square red flag with a **black center** by day and **two red lights** by night for winds to equal or exceed 48 knots (55 mph).

HURRICANE: two square red flags with black centers by day and **one white light between two red lights** by night for tropical cyclone with winds of 64 knots (73 mph) and above.

A memory aid for the Storm Signal lights ... it relates them to Rules of the Road night signals ...

STORM SIGNAL	RULES OF THE ROAD	COMMENT
Red over White (Small Craft)	Red over White, Fishing at Night.	You could fish while harbor-bound by some dirty weather.
White over Red (Gale)	White over Red, Pilot Ahead.	In a 40-knot wind ... you might need one!
Red over Red (Storm)	Red over Red, Not under Command (International)	When it's blowing up a storm ... who has control?
Red White Red (Hurricane)	Red White Red, Engaged in underwater operations (International)	Glug, Glug.

Beach and Aircraft Signals

Here reprinted from *International Code of Signals (HO 102)* is the pattern of Lifesaving Signals and Aircraft Search and Rescue Signals established by international agreement. Table I refers to directions given from the shore to a boat attempting to land through a surf. Table II covers the dialogue necessary in rigging a breeches buoy or high-line assembly to transfer survivors from a wreck. Table III has the replies to a distress signal. Table IV applies when a surface vessel is to be directed by an aircraft and there is no other means, such as radio, loudhailer or blinker light. The maneuvering aircraft itself then becomes the signal.

TABLE OF LIFESAVING SIGNALS

I Landing signals for the guidance of small boats with crews or persons in distress

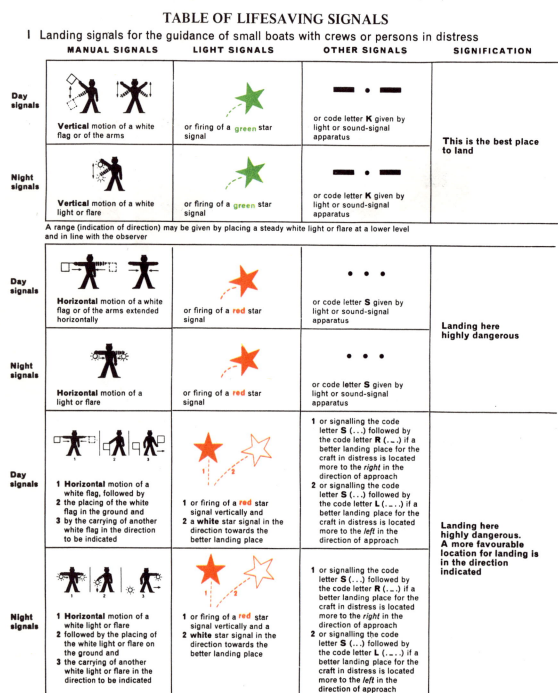

	MANUAL SIGNALS	LIGHT SIGNALS	OTHER SIGNALS	SIGNIFICATION
Day signals	**Vertical** motion of a white flag or of the arms	or firing of a green star signal	or code letter **K** given by light or sound-signal apparatus	**This is the best place to land**
Night signals	**Vertical** motion of a white light or flare	or firing of a green star signal	or code letter **K** given by light or sound-signal apparatus	
	A range (indication of direction) may be given by placing a steady white light or flare at a lower level and in line with the observer			
Day signals	**Horizontal** motion of a white flag or of the arms extended horizontally	or firing of a red star signal	or code letter **S** given by light or sound-signal apparatus	**Landing here highly dangerous**
Night signals	**Horizontal** motion of a light or flare	or firing of a red star signal	or code letter **S** given by light or sound-signal apparatus	
Day signals	1 **Horizontal** motion of a white flag, followed by 2 the placing of the white flag in the ground and 3 by the carrying of another white flag in the direction to be indicated	1 or firing of a red star signal vertically and 2 a white star signal in the direction towards the better landing place	1 or signalling the code letter **S** (...) followed by the code letter **R** (._.) if a better landing place for the craft in distress is located more to the *right* in the direction of approach 2 or signalling the code letter **S** (...) followed by the code letter **L** (._..) if a better landing place for the craft in distress is located more to the *left* in the direction of approach	**Landing here highly dangerous. A more favourable location for landing is in the direction indicated**
Night signals	1 **Horizontal** motion of a white light or flare 2 followed by the placing of the white light or flare on the ground and 3 the carrying of another white light or flare in the direction to be indicated	1 or firing of a red star signal vertically and a 2 white star signal in the direction towards the better landing place	1 or signalling the code letter **S** (...) followed by the code letter **R** (._.) if a better landing place for the craft in distress is located more to the *right* in the direction of approach 2 or signalling the code letter **S** (...) followed by the code letter **L** (._..) if a better landing place for the craft in distress is located more to the *left* in the direction of approach	

TABLE OF LIFESAVING SIGNALS

II Signals to be employed in connection with the use of shore lifesaving apparatus

	MANUAL SIGNALS	LIGHT SIGNALS	OTHER SIGNALS	SIGNIFICATION
Day signals	Vertical motion of a white flag or of the arms	or firing of a green star signal		In general: affirmative Specifically: rocket line is held – tail block is made fast – hawser is made fast – man is in the breeches buoy – haul away
Night signals	Vertical motion of a white light or flare	or firing of a green star signal		
Day signals	Horizontal motion of a white flag or of the arms extended horizontally	or firing of a red star signal		In general: negative Specifically: slack away – avast hauling
Night signals	Horizontal motion of a white light or flare	or firing of a red star signal		

III Replies from lifesaving stations or maritime rescue units to distress signals made by a ship or person

Day signals		Orange smoke signal	or combined *light and sound* signal (thunder-light) consisting of 3 single signals which are fired at intervals of approximately one minute	You are seen – assistance will be given as soon as possible (Repetition of such signal shall have the same meaning)
Night signals		White star rocket consisting of 3 single signals which are fired at intervals of approximately one minute		

If necessary, the day signals may be given at night or the night signals by day

IV Signals used by aircraft engaged on search and rescue operations to direct ships towards an aircraft, ship or person in distress

PROCEDURES PERFORMED IN SEQUENCE BY AN AIRCRAFT			SIGNIFICATION
1 Aircraft circles the surface craft at least once	2 Aircraft crosses the surface craft course close ahead at low altitude opening and closing the throttle or changing the propeller pitch	3 Aircraft heads in the direction in which the surface craft is to be directed	The aircraft is directing a surface craft towards an aircraft or surface craft in distress (Repetition of such signals shall have the same meaning)
	Crossing the surface craft's wake close astern at low altitude opening and closing the throttle or changing the propeller pitch		The assistance of the surface craft is no longer required (Repetition of such signals shall have the same meaning)

Submarine Signals, Morse Code and Radiotelephone Patterns

Radiotelephone distress patterns are recapped here for quick reference. More particular detail is found in Sections IV and XI.

Submarine emergency identification signals are those given by a submerged craft which intends to enter the zone of surface operation. Basically they are like street traffic control lights: **green** for "proceed in safety," **yellow** for "proceed with caution" and **red** for "danger." The signal is made either by release of a colored smoke bomb or by firing a projectile which emerges from the water, ascends to about 300 feet and then releases a colored parachute flare.

The Morse Code, with its pattern of phonetic words, is also shown. Note the ingenuity in selection of key words for numbers. In several languages, one part of the expression keys its number.

Phonetic Alphabet (May be used when transmitting plain language or code)		
Letter	**Word**	**Morse Code**
A	Alfa	· –
B	Bravo	– · · ·
C	Charlie	– · – ·
D	Delta	– · ·
E	Echo	·
F	Foxtrot	· · – ·
G	Golf	– – ·
H	Hotel	· · · ·
I	India	· ·
J	Juliett	· – – –
K	Kilo	– · –
L	Lima	· – · ·
M	Mike	– –
N	November	– ·
O	Oscar	– – –
P	Papa	· – – ·
Q	Quebec	– – · –
R	Romeo	· – ·
S	Sierra	· · ·
T	Tango	–
U	Uniform	· · –
V	Victor	· · · –
W	Whiskey	· – –
X	X-ray	– · · –
Y	Yankee	– · – –
Z	Zulu	– – · ·

Figure Spelling Tables

Number	Phonetic	Pronounced as	Morse Code
0	NADAZERO	NAH-DAH-ZAY-ROH	- - - - -
1	UNAONE	OO-NAH-WUN	· - - - -
2	BISSOTWO	BEES-SOH-TOO	· · - - -
3	TERRATHREE	TAY-RAH-TREE	· · · - -
4	KARTEFOUR	KAR-TAY-FOWER	· · · · -
5	PANTAFIVE	PAN-TAH-FIVE	· · · · ·
6	SOXISIX	SOK-SEE-SIX	- · · · ·
7	SETTESEVEN	SAY-TAY-SEVEN	- - · · ·
8	OKTOEIGHT	OK-TOH-AIT	- - - · ·
9	NOVENINE	NO-VAY-NINER	- - - - ·

Note: Each syllable should be equally emphasized

Radiotelephone Emergency Calls

Distress: Frequency . 2182 kHz.
Call . . . . . *Mayday Mayday Mayday*
Message . . Position; problem; kind help needed; other data pertinent to danger.

Urgency: Frequency . 2182 kHz.
Call . . . . . *Pan Pan Pan*
Message. . . Data regarding predicament of a ship or an aircraft or a person near you.

Safety: Frequency. 2182 kHz.
Call . . . . . *Securité Securité Securité*
Message . . Data regarding a navigational or a weather hazard.

Submarine Signals

Flare fired from submerged US submarine to 300 feet in air to indicate: **Torpedo has been fired.** On special exercises is used to simulate torpedo firing. Can also be **black.**

Flare fired from submerged US submarine to 300 feet in air to indicate: **Submarine about to rise to periscope depth.** Surface craft should clear area and keep propellers turning.

Flare fired from submerged US submarine to 300 feet in air to indicate: **Emergency inside the submarine. Will try to surface immediately. Surface ships clear area and stand by to assist.** If signals repeated or if sub fails to surface in reasonable time, she should be presumed to be disabled.

Distress Signals from Rules of the Road

Here are the distress signals specified by International, Inland and Pilot Rules of the Road. Included under International is an auto-alarm signal to alert a radio operator to receipt of a distress call. Stemming from the *Titanic* disaster, it triggers an alarm when *SOS* or *Mayday* is received. When not in use, the ship's radio receiver should be on and tuned to 500 kHz if a radiotelegraph and to 2182 kHz if a radiotelephone.

INTERNATIONAL RULES

RULE 31   (a) When a vessel or seaplane on the water is in distress and requires assistance from other vessels or from the shore, the following shall be the signals to be used or displayed by her, either together or separately, namely:—

(i) A gun or other explosive signal fired at intervals of about a minute.

(ii) A continuous sounding with any fog-signalling apparatus.

(iii) Rockets or shells, throwing red stars fired one at a time at short intervals.

(iv) A signal made by radio-telegraphy or by any other signalling method consisting of the group ... — — — ... in the Morse Code.

(v) A signal sent by radiotelephony consisting of the spoken word "Mayday".

(vi) The International Code Signal of distress indicated by N.C.

(vii) A signal consisting of a square flag having above or below it a ball or anything resembling a ball.

(viii) Flames on the vessel (as from a burning tar barrel, oil barrel, &c.).

(ix) A rocket parachute flare or a hand flare showing a red light.

(x) A smoke signal giving off a volume of orange-coloured smoke.

(xi) Slowly and repeatedly raising and lowering arms outstretched to each side.

NOTE: Vessels in distress may use the radiotelegraph alarm signal or the radiotelephone alarm signal to secure attention to distress calls and messages. The radiotelegraph alarm signal, which is designed to actuate the radiotelegraph auto alarms of vessels so fitted, consists of a series of twelve dashes, sent in 1 minute, the duration of each dash being 4 seconds, and the duration of the interval between 2 consecutive dashes being 1 second. The radiotelephone alarm signal consists of 2 tones transmitted alternately over periods of from 30 seconds to 1 minute.

(b) The use of any of the foregoing signals, except for the purpose of indicating that a vessel or seaplane is in distress, and the use of any signals which may be confused with any of the above signals, is prohibited.

INLAND RULES

ART. 31. *When a vessel is in distress and requires assistance from other vessels or from the shore the following shall be the signal to be used or displayed by her, either together or separately, namely:*
In the daytime—

A continuous sounding with any fog-signal apparatus, or firing a gun.
At night—
First. Flames on the vessel as from a burning tar barrel, oil barrel, and so forth.
Second. A continuous sounding with any fog-signal apparatus, or firing a gun.

PILOT RULES

80.37 Distress signals.

(a) *Daytime.* (1) Slowly and repeatedly raising and lowering arms outstretched to each side.

Rules of the Road

Day Shapes

Day shapes specified by Rules of the Road are basically to show the limitation or occupation of the vessel. Little emphasis is on direction since to see the signal is to see the vessel beneath it.

Intl abbreviates International Rules; **Inl** is Inland; **Plt** is Pilot. **NM** refers to *Notice to Mariners*, and **IMCO** is Intergovernmental Maritime Consultative Organization of the UN. **Power** means power-driven (Intl) or steam (Inl and Pilot).

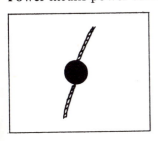

Intl: At anchor.
Inl: Power but under sail only (optional).
Plt: Over 65-feet long at anchor in fairway or channel.

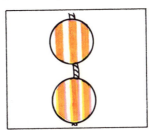

Plt: Coast Guard working on aid to navigation.

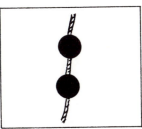

Intl: Not under command.
Plt: Dredge working and underway; or National Ocean Survey vessel at anchor in a fairway or channel and surveying.

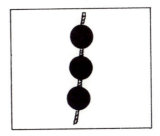

Intl: Vessel aground.

Intl: Minesweeper with danger on side of lower shape. Approach no closer than 3000 feet astern and 1500 feet on danger side.

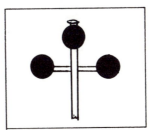

Intl: Minesweeper with danger on both sides. Approach no closer than 3000 feet astern and 1500 feet on sides.

Plt: Moored or anchored and working on cables, pipe, submarine construction, or bank protection.

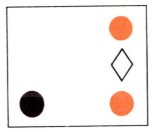

Intl: At anchor working on submarine cable, or navigation mark, or surveying or underwater operation.

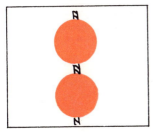

Plt: Dredge held stationary by mooring or spuds.

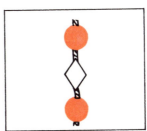

Intl: Underway and working on submarine cable, or navigation mark, or surveying, or underwater operation, or replenishing at sea, or launching or recovering aircraft.

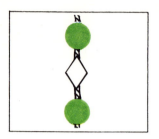

Plt: Hydrographic surveying and underway.

Intl: Fishing and gear more than 500 feet out in direction of the cone.

Intl: Power towing and total tow length over 600 feet; or last vessel in such a tow.
NM: Towing a dracone (flexible oil barge) or float at last dracone in the tow.

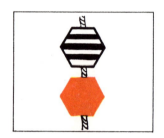

Plt: Towing submerged or partly submerged object.

Intl: Propelled by power and by sail.

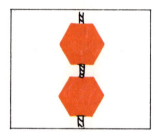

Plt: Secured to or over a wreck.

Intl: Under 65 feet long and fishing.
Plt: Underway and fishing by net, line or trawl.

IMCO: Deep draft Power underway and can only stay inside a narrow channel (optional).

Intl: Under 65 feet long and fishing with gear more than 500 feet out in direction of the cone.

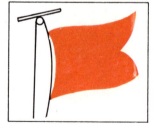

Plt: At dock or anchored and handling hazardous or dangerous cargo.

Intl: Fishing (note . . . fishing with trolling lines is not considered fishing by International Rules).

NM: US Naval surface craft operating with submerged submarine.

Night Signals

Key data on another ship are her direction and inability to maneuver. By day, one glance tells the story. At night, though, the hull is invisible, so Rules of the Road specify light arrays to do the job. Since a central cluster often denotes limitations, those shown here are, when possible, grouped in such fashion. And depiction is realistic . . . only lights without a hull form are shown.

Change in aspect, malfunction or neglect can alter patterns. For example, with the top red light out, a vessel not under command looks like the port side of a sailboat. Usually, though, the required patterns are followed.

As for abbreviations: **Intl** is International; **Inl** is Inland; **Plt** is Pilot; **Mtb** is Motorboat Act; **IMCO** is Intergovernmental Maritime Consultative Organization; **NM** is *Notice to Mariners;* and **Power** is power-driven (Intl), or steam (Inl & Plt).

One white light is no longer **Redcoats by Land,** but mariners wish it were that definite. It can be a light on the beach, an open porthole . . . or among others, these:

Intl: Stern light, or Sail Pilot, or at anchor and under 150 feet, or rowing boat, or masthead of Power at more than two and less than five miles, or seaplane under 150 feet long at anchor.

Inl: Stern light, or at anchor and under 150 feet, or fishing boat at more than two and less than five miles, or Sail Pilot, or rowing boat, or raft.

Plt: Stern view of vessel towing submerged object and using 20-point tow lights.

Intl and **Inl:** Port profile of vessel that is 150 feet, or more, long and at anchor.

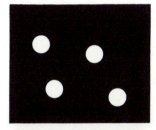

Intl: Seaplane 150 feet, or more, long and with more than 150-foot wingspan, at anchor.

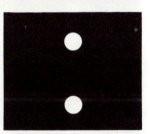

Intl: Masthead and range of Power at more than two and less than five miles, or stern view of Sail Pilot vessel.

Inl: Stern view of tug alongside or pushing ahead, with 32-point towing lights.

Intl: Less than 40 feet long and under oars or sail.

Inl: Fishing boat less than 10 tons underway with no gear in water.

Mtb: Class A or 1 motorboat under sail only.

Plt: Last barge in tow astern or in tandem, or vessel propelled by hand, horsepower or by river current.

Intl, Inl, and **Mtb:** Bow view of Sail underway, or vessel being pushed or towed.

Intl, Inl and **Mtb:** Port profile of Sail underway, or vessel or seaplane being towed.
Plt: At dock handling hazardous cargo.

Intl: Starboard profile of Power under 150 feet and underway.
Intl and **Inl:** Sail Pilot vessel's starboard profile and showing flare on approach.

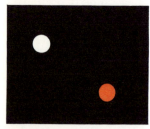

Intl: Port profile of Power under 150 feet and underway, or Sail Pilot showing white flare.
Inl: Port profile of Sail Pilot showing white flare.

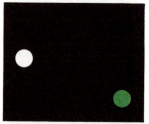

Mtb: Starboard profile Class A or 1 motorboat underway.

Mtb: Port side Class A or 1 motorboat underway.

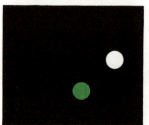

Intl: Starboard profile of Power underway and less than 150 feet long.
Inl: Starboard profile of Power underway.

Intl: Port profile of Power 150 feet, or more, long and underway.
Inl: Port profile of Power underway.
Mtb: Port profile of Class 2 or 3 motorboat underway.

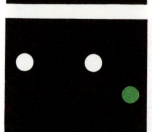

Plt: Starboard profile of double-ended ferry.

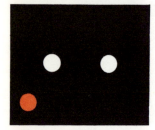

Plt: Port profile of double-ended ferry.

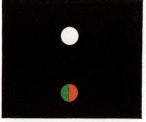

Intl: Bow view Power under 65 feet long and underway.
Mtb: Bow view of Class A or 1 motorboat.

Intl, Inl and **Mtb:** Starboard profile of Sail underway, or vessel or seaplane being towed.

Intl: Bow view Power less than 150 feet long; also Sail Pilot showing white flare.
Inl: Sail Pilot showing white flare.
Plt: Double-ended ferry with central range aligned.

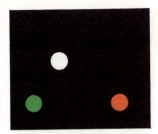

Mtb and **Interpretative Ruling:** Bow view of Class A or 1 motorboat with white light aft offset from the centerline.

Intl: Bow view of Fishing (except trawling or trolling) and underway and making way.

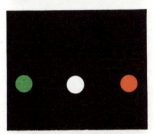

Intl: Bow view seaplane on water underway (the rules do not specify that white light be higher than sidelights).

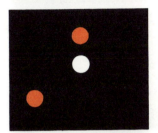

Intl: Port profile of Fishing (except trawling or trolling) and underway and making way through the water.

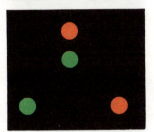

Intl: Bow view of Sail underway and carrying optional foremast lights.

Intl: Starboard profile Fishing (except trawling or trolling) and underway and making way.

Intl: Port profile of Sail underway and carrying optional foremast lights.

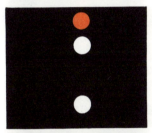

Intl: Stern view of Fishing (except trawling or trolling) and underway and making way, or, same vessel not making way but with gear more than 500 feet out in direction of lower light.

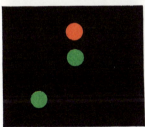

Intl: Starboard profile of Sail underway and carrying optional foremast lights.

Intl: Fishing (except trawling or trolling) and not making way and with gear more than 500 feet out.

Intl: Fishing (except trawling or trolling) and not making way.
Inl: Fishing with any drag nets or lines or trawling or dredging.

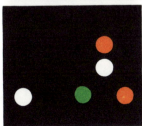

Intl: Bow view of Fishing (except trawling or trolling) and underway and making way with gear more than 500 feet out to starboard.

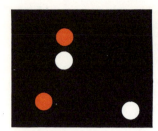

Intl: Port profile of Fishing (except trawling or trolling) and underway and making way, with gear more than 500 feet out in direction of lower white light.

Intl: Stern view of trawler at work underway and making way; also bow view of same trawler not making way and carrying optional white light.

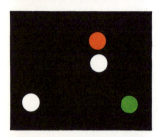

Intl: Starboard profile Fishing (except trawling or trolling) and underway and making way and with gear more than 500 feet out.

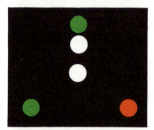

Intl: Bow view of trawler underway and making way and carrying optional white light.

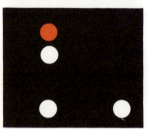

Intl: Stern view of Fishing (except trawling or trolling) and underway and making way and with gear more than 500 feet out to her starboard.

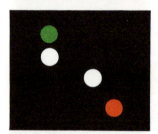

Intl: Port profile of trawler underway and making way and carrying optional white light.

Intl: Trawler at work not making way.

Intl: Starboard profile of trawler underway and making way and carrying optional white light.

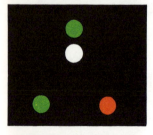

Intl: Bow view of trawler at work and underway and making way.

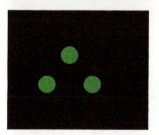

Intl: Minesweeper underway but not making way; dangers on both sides.

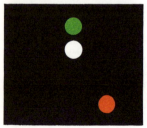

Intl: Port profile of trawler underway and making way.

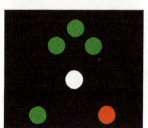

Intl: Bow view Minesweeper underway and making way, with dangers on both her sides.

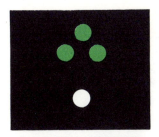

Intl: Bow view of Minesweeper underway but not making way, with danger on both sides; also stern view of same ship making way with danger on both sides.

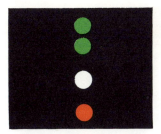

Intl: Port profile Minesweeper underway and making way; danger on either side or on both sides.

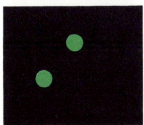

Intl: Minesweeper underway but not making way; danger on side of lower light.

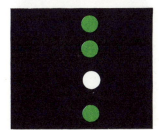

Intl: Starboard profile Minesweeper underway and making way.

Intl: Bow view of Minesweeper underway and making way, with danger on her port side.

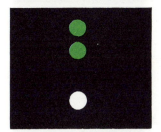

Intl: Port or starboard profile of Minesweeper underway but not making way; danger on either side or both.

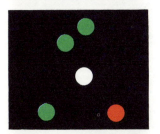

Intl: Bow view of Minesweeper underway and making way, with danger on her starboard side.

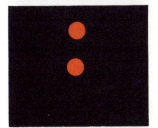

Intl: Not under command and under way but not making way.
Plt: USCG handling aid to navigation, or National Ocean Survey at anchor in channel and surveying.

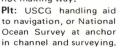

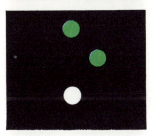

Intl: Bow view of Minesweeper underway but not making way, with danger on her port side; also stern view of same ship making way, with danger on starboard side.

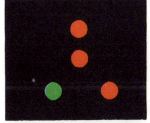

Intl: Bow view not under command and making way through the water.

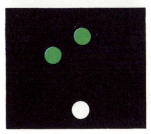

Intl: Bow view of Minesweeper underway but not making way, with danger on her starboard side; also stern view of same ship making way, with danger on her port side.

Intl: Port profile of vessel not under command and making way through the water.

Intl: Starboard profile, not under command and making way through the water.

Plt: Moored or anchored and laying cable or pipe, submarine construction or bank protection work.

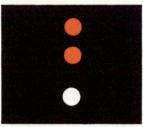

Intl: Stern view, not under command and making way through water.

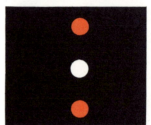

Intl: Vessel working on submarine cable or navigation mark, or surveying, or underwater operation, or replenishing at sea, or handling aircraft . . . and underway but not making way.

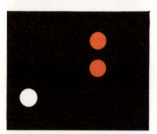

Intl: Port profile of vessel under 150 feet long and aground.

IMCO: Stern view of large deep-draft ship underway and must stay inside narrow channel limits.

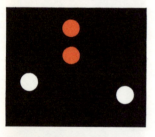

Intl: Port profile of vessel 150 feet, or more, long and aground.

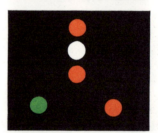

Intl: Bow view vessel working on submarine cable or navigation mark, or surveying, or in underwater operation, or replenishing at sea, or recovery or launching of aircraft . . . and making way.

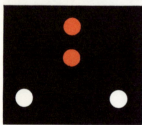

Plt: Alongside or over a wreck.

Intl: Port profile of vessel underway and making way and working on submarine cable or navigation mark, or surveying, or underwater operation, or replenishing at sea, or handling aircraft.

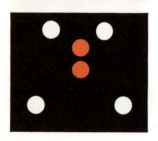

Plt: Dredge held in stationary position by moorings or spuds.

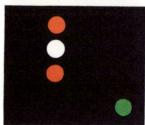

Intl: Starboard profile of vessel working on submarine cable or navigation mark, or surveying, or in underwater operation, or replenishing at sea, or recovery or launching of aircraft . . . and making way.

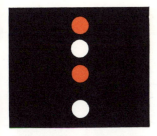

Intl: Stern view of vessel underway and making way and working on submarine cable or navigation mark, or surveying, or underwater operation, or replenishing at sea, or handling aircraft . . . and bow view of same vessel at anchor.

Intl and **Inl:** Port profile of Power Pilot on duty and underway . . . will also show flare-up light at intervals.

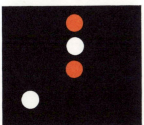

Intl: Port profile of vessel under 150 feet long at anchor and working on submarine cable, or navigation mark, or surveying, or underwater operation, or replenishing at sea, or handling aircraft.

Intl and **Inl:** Starboard profile of Power Pilot on duty and underway.

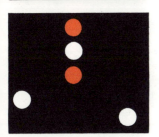

Intl: Port profile of vessel 150 feet, or more, long at anchor and working on submarine cable, or navigation mark, or surveying, or underwater operation, or replenishing at sea, or handling aircraft.

Intl: Stern view of Power Pilot vessel on duty and underway, or bow and stern view of same vessel on duty at anchor.

Intl: Pilot vessel at dock or otherwise not underway or at anchor but on pilotage duty.

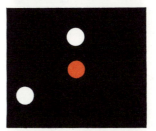

Intl: Port profile of Power Pilot less than 150 feet long on duty and at anchor.

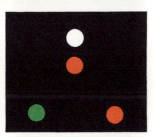

Intl and **Inl:** Bow view of Power Pilot on duty and underway.

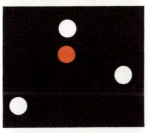

Intl: Starboard profile Power Pilot 150 feet, or more, long on duty at anchor.

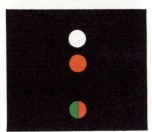

Intl: Bow view of Power Pilot vessel less than 65 feet long.

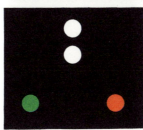

Intl and **Inl:** Bow view of Power underway.
Mtb: Bow view of Class 2 or 3 motorboat.

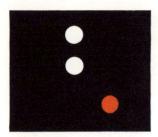

Intl: Port profile of Power towing astern and tow not over 600 feet long, or pushing ahead.

Inl: Port profile of Power towing alongside or pushing ahead and not carrying range light.

Intl, Inl and **Plt:** Bow view of Power pushing a barge ahead.

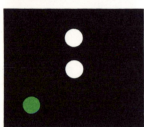

Intl: Starboard profile of Power towing astern not more than 600 feet or tow alongside or pushing ahead.

Inl: Starboard profile of Power towing alongside or pushing ahead and not carrying range light.

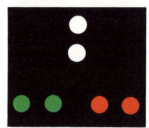

Plt: Bow view of Power with barges on each side, and sidelight on left and right outside barges.

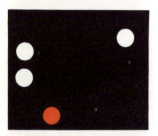

Inl: Port profile of Power towing alongside or pushing ahead and carrying range light.

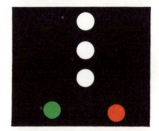

Intl: Bow view of Power towing astern more than 600 feet.

Inl: Bow view of Power towing astern; also when carrying range light, or pushing ahead or tow alongside.

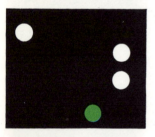

Inl: Starboard profile of Power towing alongside or pushing ahead and using 20-point towing lights and carrying the optional range light.

Inl: Bow view of Power towing astern, using 20-point towing lights and also carrying range light.

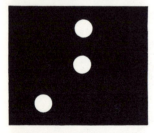

Inl: Stern view of power towing alongside and using 32-point towing lights, and also stern light on tow.

Intl: Port profile of Power towing astern and tow over 600 feet long.

Inl: Port profile of Power towing astern and using 20-point towing lights.

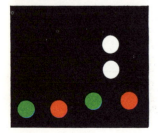

Intl and **Inl:** Bow view of Power with barge on starboard side.

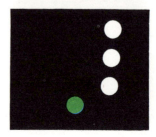

Intl: Starboard profile of Power towing astern more than 600 feet.

Inl: Starboard profile of Power towing astern, using 20-point towing lights.

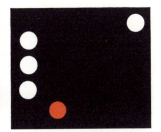

Inl: Port profile of Power towing astern and using 20-point towing lights and carrying the range light.

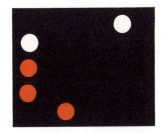

Plt: Port profile of self-propelled dredge underway and engaged in dredging operations.

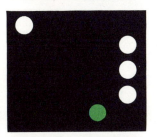

Inl: Starboard profile of Power towing astern, using 20-point towing lights and carrying the optional range light.

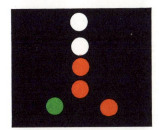

Plt: Bow view of self-propelled dredge underway and dredging.

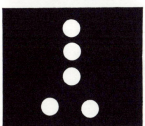

Inl and **Plt:** Stern view of Power towing astern and using 32-point towing lights and also stern lights on tow.

Plt: Bow view (or in sector of a colored sidelight) of a dredge underway and dredging and at more than two but not more than five miles.

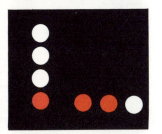

Inl and **Plt:** Port profile of Power towing two barges astern.

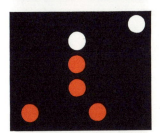

Plt: Port profile of non-self-propelled dredge underway and engaged in dredging and being pushed ahead by a towboat.

Plt: Stern view of a self-propelled dredge underway and engaged in dredging operations.

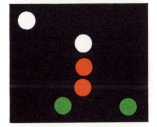

Plt: Starboard profile of non-self-propelled dredge underway and engaged in dredging and being pushed ahead by another vessel.

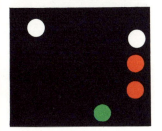

Plt: Starboard profile of self-propelled dredge underway and dredging.

Plt: Stern view of vessel towing submerged object; also bow view of same vessel at distance of more than two but not more than five miles.

Plt: Bow view of vessel towing submerged object and not carrying range light.

Plt: Pipeline either floating or on trestle and attached to a dredge. Red lights mark the shore or the discharge end.

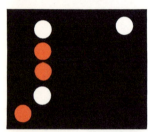

Plt: Port profile of vessel towing submerged object.

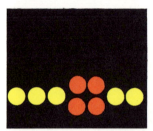

Plt: Pipeline either floating or on trestle and attached to a dredge. Sets of red lights mark opening for ship passage.

Inl and **Plt:** Bow view of vessel towing submerged object and carrying range light.

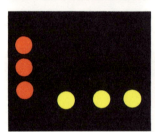

Plt: String of moored barges used in laying cables, submarine construction or bank protection. Red lights mark channel end of stringout.

Inl: Stern view of Power pushing ahead and using 20-point towing lights and also showing the range light.

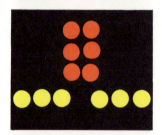

Plt: String of moored barges used in laying cables, submarine construction or bank protection. Sets of red lights mark opening for ship passage.

Inl: Stern view of Power pushing ahead and using 20-point towing lights and not optional range light.

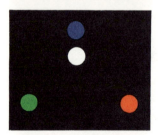

Plt: Bow view of law enforcement vessel with rotating blue identification light. Also: Bow view of double-ended ferry showing designating light of ferry company (in this case a fixed blue light).

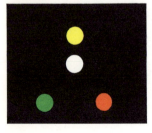

Plt: Bow view of US submarine displaying rotating amber light of 90 flashes per minute.
NM: Hovercraft with rotating amber light of 60 flashes per minute.

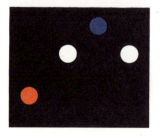

Plt: Port profile of double-ended ferry carrying fixed designation light (in this case, a blue light). It can be of another color or can be white.

NM: Stern view of vessel towing flexible oil barge or dracone. The blue light is on the towing vessel above its stern light. The lower white light is on float at end of last dracone.

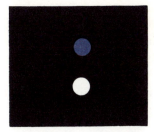

Plt: Stern view of law enforcement vessel with rotating blue identification light. Also: Stern view of double-ended ferry showing designating light of ferry company (in this case a fixed blue light).

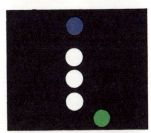

NM: Starboard profile of vessel towing flexible oil barge or dracone.

NM: Port profile of vessel towing flexible oil barge or dracone.

NM: Bow view of vessel towing flexible oil barge or dracone.

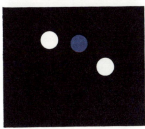

Plt: View on quarter of double-ended ferry carrying fixed designation light (in this case, a blue light). It can be of another color or can be white.

Audible Signals

The Sound Signals depicted here refer to the rules by these abbreviations: **Intl** for International; **Inl** for Inland; and **Plt** for Pilot. They appear in two groups: **In Sight** are those sounded when visible to another vessel; **Restricted Visibility** are those for fog, mist, rain or other condition hampering sight. Since **steam** by Inland and Pilot Rules is **power-driven** by International, the word **Power** describes both. Note that In Sight signals are given only by Power vessels. Under Sail or In Tow make audible signals only in restricted visibility or in distress.

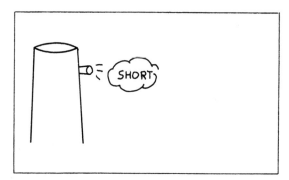

In Sight, Power:
Intl: Altering course to the right.
Inl and
Plt: Intend to turn to right, or holding course and speed.
When meeting: Intend to pass port-to-port.
When overtaking: Intend to pass on starboard side of other.

In Sight, Power:
Intl: Altering course to the left.
Inl and
Plt: Intend to turn to left.
When meeting: Intend to pass starboard-to-starboard.
When overtaking: Intend to pass on port side of other.

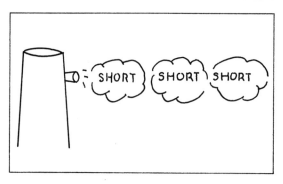

In Sight, Power:
Intl,
Inl and
Plt: Engines going astern, or have sternway.

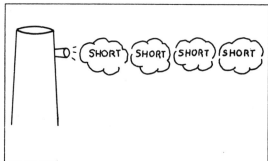

In Sight, Power:
Intl: Pilot vessel identity signal (optional).
Inl and
Plt: Danger signal...Fail to understand intention of other.

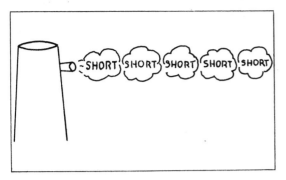

In Sight, Power:

Intl: Doubt signal...When keeping course and speed and doubt whether other's action sufficient to avert collision.
Inl and
Plt: Danger signal... Fail to understand intention of other (can be four or more short blasts).

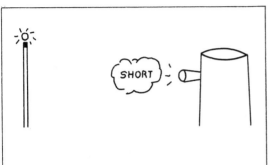

In Sight, Power:

Intl: Synchronized white light in conjunction with the 1-, 2-, 3-blast sound signals or 5-or-more doubt signal.

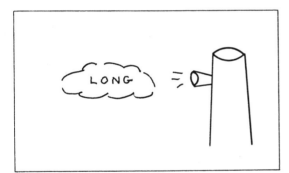

Restricted Visibility, Power:

Inl and
Plt: Nearing a blind bend and cannot see for one-half mile;
or: moving from dock or berth when others are liable to be passing from any direction;
or: any vessel in any visibility within one mile of a dredge or floating plant and intending to pass.

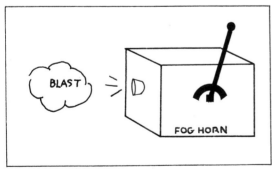

Restricted Visibility, Sail:
Intl and
Inl: Sailing on starboard tack.

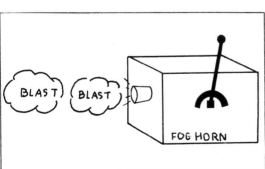

Restricted Visibility, Sail:
Intl and
Inl: Sailing on port tack.

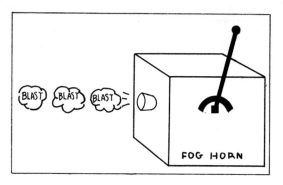

Restricted Visibility, Sail:
Intl and
Inl: Sailing with wind abaft the beam.

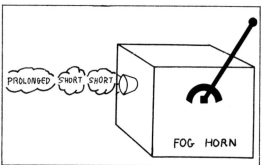

Restricted Visibility, Any Vessel but Power:
Intl: Towing another, or working on submarine cable or navigation mark, or unable to maneuver as required by rules because not under command or other reason (1-minute intervals);
or: engaged in fishing underway or at anchor.
Inl and
Plt: Being towed (1-minute intervals).

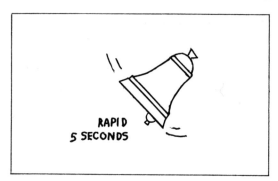

Restricted Visibility, Any Vessel:
Intl: Not more than 350 feet long and at anchor.
Inl and
Plt: At anchor any place;
or: at anchor in a special anchorage and more than 65 feet long or not a barge, canal boat, scow or other non-descript craft.

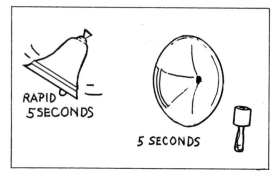

Restricted Visibility, Any Vessel:
Intl: More than 350 feet long and at anchor.

Restricted Visibility, Any Vessel:
Intl: Not more than 350 feet long and aground.

Restricted Visibility, Any Vessel:

Intl: More than 350 feet long and aground.

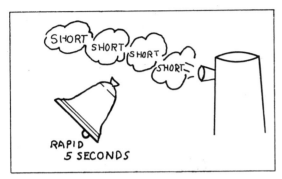

Restricted Visibility, Power:

Intl: Pilot vessel not more than 350 feet long at anchor and on duty.

Restricted Visibility, Power:

Intl: Pilot vessel more than 350 feet long at anchor and on duty.

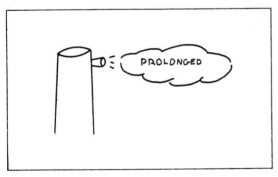

Restricted Visibility, Power:

Intl: Underway and making way through the water (2-minute intervals);
or: in any weather, when within one-half mile of blind channel bend.
Inl: Underway (1-minute intervals).

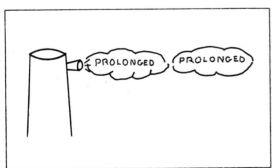

Restricted Visibility, Power:

Intl: Underway but stopped and making no way through the water (2-minute intervals).

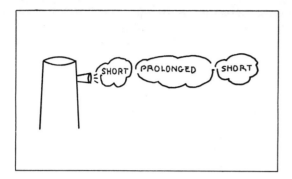

Restricted Visibility, Any Vessel:

Intl: At anchor giving warning of her position and of the possibility of collision.

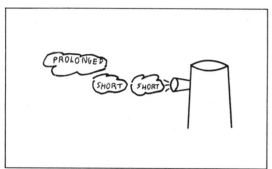

Restricted Visibility, Power:

Intl: Towing another, or working on submarine cable or navigation mark, or unable to maneuver as required by rules because not under command or other reason (1-minute intervals).

Inl and

Plt: Power vessel towing or being towed (1-minute intervals).

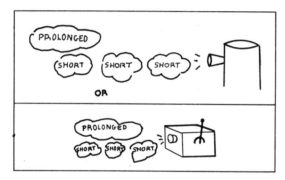

Restricted Visibility, Any Vessel:

Intl: Last vessel being towed, provided she is manned (1-minute intervals).

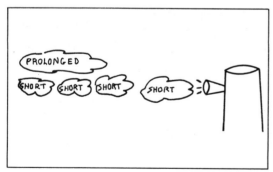

Restricted Visibility, Power:

Intl: Pilot vessel on duty and making way through water.

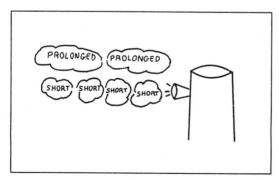

Restricted Visibility, Power:

Intl: Pilot vessel on duty and underway, but stopped and making no way through the water.

Aids to Navigation

AIDS TO NAVIGATION ON NAVIGABLE WATERWAYS
except Western Rivers and Intracoastal Waterway

LATERAL SYSTEM AS SEEN ENTERING FROM SEAWARD

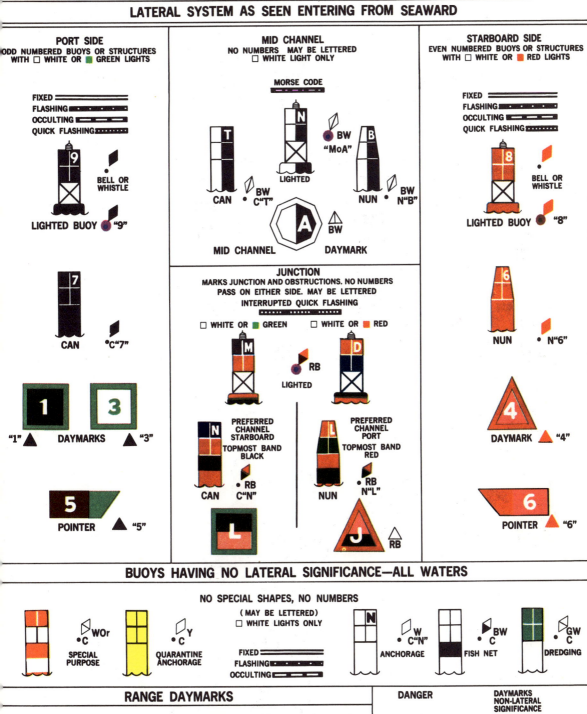

PORT SIDE
ODD NUMBERED BUOYS OR STRUCTURES
WITH ☐ WHITE OR ☐ GREEN LIGHTS

FIXED
FLASHING
OCCULTING
QUICK FLASHING

BELL OR WHISTLE

LIGHTED BUOY "9"

7 CAN • C"7"

DAYMARKS
"1" "3"

POINTER "5"

MID CHANNEL
NO NUMBERS MAY BE LETTERED
☐ WHITE LIGHT ONLY

MORSE CODE

N LIGHTED
BW "MoA"

T CAN • BW C"T"

B NUN • BW N"B"

A MID CHANNEL   BW DAYMARK

JUNCTION
MARKS JUNCTION AND OBSTRUCTIONS. NO NUMBERS
PASS ON EITHER SIDE. MAY BE LETTERED
INTERRUPTED QUICK FLASHING

☐ WHITE OR ☐ GREEN   ☐ WHITE OR ☐ RED

M   RB LIGHTED   D

N CAN • RB C"N"
PREFERRED CHANNEL STARBOARD TOPMOST BAND BLACK

L NUN • RB N"L"
PREFERRED CHANNEL PORT TOPMOST BAND RED

L   J ▲ RB

STARBOARD SIDE
EVEN NUMBERED BUOYS OR STRUCTURES
WITH ☐ WHITE OR ☐ RED LIGHTS

FIXED
FLASHING
OCCULTING
QUICK FLASHING

8 BELL OR WHISTLE

LIGHTED BUOY "8"

6 NUN • N"6"

4 DAYMARK "4"

6 POINTER "6"

BUOYS HAVING NO LATERAL SIGNIFICANCE—ALL WATERS

NO SPECIAL SHAPES, NO NUMBERS
(MAY BE LETTERED)
☐ WHITE LIGHTS ONLY

FIXED
FLASHING
OCCULTING

 • C WOr
SPECIAL PURPOSE

 • C Y
QUARANTINE ANCHORAGE

 N • C"N"
ANCHORAGE

 • C BW
FISH NET

 • C GW
DREDGING

RANGE DAYMARKS

DANGER

SUBMERGED DANGER JETTY

DAYMARKS NON-LATERAL SIGNIFICANCE

AIDS TO NAVIGATION ON THE INTRACOASTAL WATERWAY

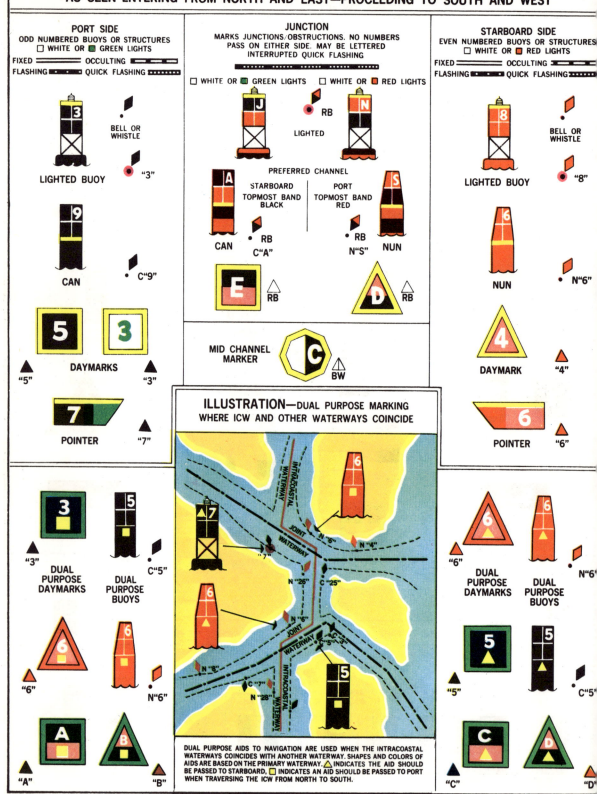

AIDS TO NAVIGATION ON WESTERN RIVERS

AS SEEN PROCEEDING IN THE DIRECTION (DESCENDING) OF RIVER FLOW

LEFT SIDE

☐ WHITE OR ■ RED LIGHTS
GROUP FLASHING (2)

LIGHTED BUOY

NUN

PASSING DAYMARK

CROSSING DAYMARK

123.5

MILE BOARD

JUNCTION

MARKS JUNCTIONS AND OBSTRUCTIONS
PASS ON EITHER SIDE
INTERRUPTED QUICK FLASHING

☐ WHITE OR ■ RED LIGHTS   ☐ WHITE OR ■ GREEN LIGHTS

LIGHTED

NUN   **CAN**

PREFERRED CHANNEL TO THE RIGHT
TOPMOST BAND RED
WHITE OR RED LIGHT

PREFERRED CHANNEL TO THE LEFT
TOPMOST BAND BLACK
WHITE OR GREEN LIGHT

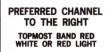

RIGHT SIDE

☐ WHITE OR ■ GREEN LIGHTS
FLASHING

LIGHTED BUOY

CAN

PASSING DAYMARK

CROSSING DAYMARK

176.9

MILE BOARD

BUOYS HAVING NO LATERAL SIGNIFICANCE—ALL WATERS

SPECIAL PURPOSE

QUARANTINE ANCHORAGE

NO SPECIAL SHAPES, NO NUMBERS
(MAY BE LETTERING)
☐ WHITE LIGHTS ONLY

FIXED
FLASHING
OCCULTING

ANCHORAGE

FISH NET

DREDGING

UNIFORM STATE WATERWAY MARKING SYSTEM

USED BY STATES IN STATE WATERS AND SOME NAVIGABLE WATERS

REGULATORY MARKERS (Information)

BOATS KEEP OUT

EXPLANATION MAY BE PLACED OUTSIDE THE CROSSED DIAMOND SHAPE, SUCH AS DAM, RAPIDS, SWIM AREA, ETC.

DANGER

THE NATURE OF DANGER MAY BE INDICATED INSIDE THE DIAMOND SHAPE, SUCH AS ROCK, WRECK, SHOAL, DAM, ETC.

CONTROLLED AREA

TYPE OF CONTROL IS INDICATED IN THE CIRCLE, SUCH AS 5 MPH, NO ANCHORING, ETC.

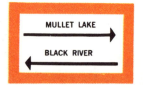

INFORMATION

FOR DISPLAYING INFORMATION SUCH AS DIRECTIONS, DISTANCES, LOCATIONS, ETC.

BUOY USED TO DISPLAY REGULATORY MARKERS

AIDS TO NAVIGATION

(ALL MAY SHOW WHITE REFLECTOR OR LIGHT)

RED-STRIPED WHITE BUOY

INDICATES THAT BOAT SHOULD NOT PASS BETWEEN BUOY AND NEAREST SHORE

MOORING BUOY

WHITE WITH BLUE BAND

BLACK-TOPPED WHITE BUOY

BOAT SHOULD PASS TO NORTH OR EAST OF BUOY

RED-TOPPED WHITE BUOY

BOAT SHOULD PASS TO SOUTH OR WEST OF BUOY

CARDINAL SYSTEM

(MAY SHOW GREEN REFLECTOR OR LIGHT)

(MAY SHOW RED REFLECTOR OR LIGHT)

RED AND BLACK CAN BUOYS

ARE USUALLY FOUND IN PAIRS VESSELS SHOULD PASS BETWEEN THESE BUOYS

LEFT SIDE ——————— (LOOKING UPSTREAM) ——————— RIGHT SIDE

Index

Page numbers preceded by RR are in the Ready Reference Section

notes